[illegible]

Essential Papers on Messianic Movements and Personalities in Jewish History

ESSENTIAL PAPERS ON JEWISH STUDIES
General Editor: Robert M. Seltzer

Essential Papers on Judaism and Christianity in Conflict: From Late Antiquity to the Reformation
Edited by Jeremy Cohen

Essential Papers on Hasidism: Origins to Present
Edited by Gershon David Hundert

Essential Papers on Jewish-Christian Relations: Imagery and Reality
Edited by Naomi W. Cohen

Essential Papers on Israel and the Ancient Near East
Edited by Frederick E. Greenspahn

Essential Papers on Jewish Culture in Renaissance and Baroque Italy
Edited by David B. Ruderman

Essential Papers on Messianic Movements and Personalities in Jewish History
Edited by Marc Saperstein

ESSENTIAL PAPERS ON MESSIANIC MOVEMENTS AND PERSONALITIES IN JEWISH HISTORY

Edited by Marc Saperstein

ST. PHILIP'S COLLEGE LIBRARY

New York University Press
New York and London

Marc Saperstein is Gloria M. Goldstein Professor of Jewish History and Thought at Washington University, St. Louis. He has taught Hebrew literature at Harvard University and Jewish studies at the Harvard Divinity School. He has written books on Jewish intellectual history and Jewish preaching.

NEW YORK UNIVERSITY PRESS
New York and London

Copyright © 1992 by New York University
All rights reserved

Library of Congress Cataloging-in-Publication Data
Essential papers on messianic movements and personalities in Jewish history / edited by Marc Saperstein.
p. cm.—(Essential papers on Jewish studies)
Includes bibliographical references and index.
ISBN 0-8147-7942-5—ISBN 0-8147-7943-3 (pbk.)
1. Jewish messianic movements—History. I. Saperstein, Marc. II. Series.
BM615.E87 1992
296.8—dc 20 92-3350
CIP

New York University Press books are printed on acid-free paper, and their binding materials are chosen for strength and durability.

Manufactured in the United States of America

ST. PHILIP'S COLLEGE LIBRARY

c 10 9 8 7 6 5 4 3 2 1
p 10 9 8 7 6 5 4 3 2 1

In Memory of

my teacher, Samuel Atlas, 1899–1977
and
my colleague, Steven Schwarzschild, 1924–1989.

Neither had much sympathy for messianic movements
but the lives of both were infused by the messianic ideal.

Contents

Preface

A collection of papers originally published over a period of some seventy-five years inevitably raises technical problems. Transcription systems for rendering Hebrew, Aramaic, or Arabic into English letters vary. The same foreign word may be spelled differently in different articles; the same Karaite historian will appear in one paper as al-Ḳirḳisānī and in another as Qirqisani. Hebrew terms and phrases are variously rendered in English, and the untrained reader may not suspect that the terms "Ephraimite Messiah," "Messiah ben Joseph," and "Messiah from the line of Joseph" all refer to the same concept. It is hoped that cross-references in the index will suffice to dispel the potential confusion. Conventions for documentation have changed, and there has been no effort to impose a consistent style on the footnotes; the format of the original authors has generally been left intact.

For technical reasons, Hebrew type could not be included. Where such material appears in the original article, I have transliterated it, translated it, or in some cases eliminated it. A few clearly mechanical errors in the original articles have been corrected, and I have occasionally added bibliographical references to English editions of works cited in other languages or to accessible texts that were unavailable when the study was written. For the most part, however, the papers have been allowed to stand on their own without editorial tinkering.

I am grateful to my colleague Robert Seltzer for inviting me to contribute to what has already become a distinguished series of Judaica publications, and to Niko Pfund, editor at New York University Press, whose guidance through the sometimes labyrinthine process of acquiring the appropriate reprint permission has been a continuing help. My thanks to my former student at Washington University, Dafna Lautman, who prepared preliminary translations for the Hebrew material incorporated, and to Aileen Rabushka, who helped in the mechanics of converting draft into submissible typescript.

I have discussed my ideas for this book with a number of colleagues, including Joseph Davis, James Diamond, David Hadas, and Steven Schwarzschild z"l, all of whom helped me shape its contours, but none of whom bear responsibility for its imperfections. Finally, I would like to express my indebtedness not only to the teachers with whom I once studied the primary texts of Jewish messianism, but also to the students at Washington University who have challenged me in my own further efforts to investigate, comprehend, and present this often perplexing yet invariably fascinating material.

Introduction

Marc Saperstein

The analysis of messianic movements as a category of Jewish historical experience requires some definition of terms. A *movement,* among other things, requires a program leading to significant change and a group of people prepared to act on the basis of that program.[1] Our subject is thus to be distinguished from *the messianic idea,* or *messianic doctrine,* or *messianic speculation.*[2] Jewish thinkers from antiquity to the present have wrestled with various theoretical questions about the Messiah and the messianic age. Is a date for the coming of the Messiah programmed into history, encoded in classical texts? If so, what is that date? Can human actions influence the coming of the Messiah? If so, what actions? Can the signs of imminent advent be detected in historical events? Is suffering and bloodshed an integral part of the messianic scenario? How can the true Messiah be recognized? What effect will the messianic advent have on the Gentile nations of the world? Will history and the natural order be fundamentally different after the Messiah comes? What is the relationship between the messianic age, the resurrection, and the spiritual reward (or punishment) for the soul?[3]

Such questions produced a considerable body of literature. But these speculations, the indulgence of thinkers pondering their books in serenity and solitude, were often devoid of direct, practical social or political or even religious consequences. The answers produced may have been influenced by earlier expressions of messianic activism, and they may in turn have influenced the course of subsequent movements. But unless these doctrines were expounded in connection with a call to act, functioning as the ideology of a movement, they will be beyond the purview of the present book.[4] Thus the voluminous scholarly literature concerning teachings about the Messiah and the messianic age to be found in the Pseudepigrapha, the Dead Sea Scrolls, the Talmud and other works of rabbinic literature; Saadia Gaon, Maimonides, Abravanel, MaHaRaL of Prague and other medieval thinkers; apocalyptic works that interpret historical events as part of some eschatological scenario, literary works that express a longing for the Messiah to put an end to the exile—all of these will figure only indirectly in the present anthology.

In addition to the program for action, a movement requires a response within society, a group of people who attempt to reorient their behavior in accordance with the expected change. When an exotic individual appears making messianic claims or announcing that the Messiah will soon come, we must look for evidence of his impact, evidence of Jews who commit themselves to implement the leader's instructions. The broader the segments of the population that support the program and begin to act on it, the longer the period of time that such a group defines itself by its loyalty to the leaders who enunciate or embody such a program, the stronger will be the case for considering it a true social movement.

It is often difficult to reach a definitive judgment about the response to a messianic claim because of the limited extant sources. The thirteenth-century mystic Abraham Abulafia may be considered a messianic personality. His own writings reveal that he thought of himself in (rather unconventional) messianic terms. But we know little about the possibility of an incipient Abulafian "movement" beyond the concession by a leading contemporary rabbi (Solomon ibn Adret) that Abulafia "seduced some Jews with his lies," making it urgently necessary for the rabbi to act.[5] Another messianic personality, Nahman of Bratslav, has been analyzed in a fascinating study by Arthur Green. Unlike the case of Abulafia, Nahman's circle of devoted followers is well documented; his messianic mission included political dimensions (liberation of the Jews in Russia, return to the land of Israel, conversion of the Gentiles), and concrete tasks were imposed on his Hasidim to prepare for the messianic event. While not a broad social movement, there is considerably more here than mere speculation.

This leads to the second category in our title. The term *messianic* implies, among other things, the expectation of bringing about a fundamental change in the current situation of Jewish life: an end to the dispersion of the Jews and their oppression by foreign powers; an ingathering of the Jews to their ancestral homeland, the land of Israel; a reestablishment of the classical institutions of ancient Judaism (Temple, Sanhedrin, prophecy, sovereignty of the Davidic line); and—perhaps—the reformation of Jewish society in accordance with the highest ideals of social justice, and of international relations in accordance with the dream of universal peace. For a movement to be considered messianic it need not have a program oriented toward the direct attainment of all these goals, but its leaders and adherents must understand its program as necessary to produce the context in which these goals will be fulfilled.[6]

Our sources do not always allow us to determine with confidence whether or not certain expressions of group behavior were understood to be the beginning of this kind of radical transformation of the status quo. A movement of religious reform calling on the people to abandon undesirable patterns of behavior, undertake penitential acts, and return to the way of the Torah may be bound up with the expectation of imminent redemption, but it need not have any explicitly messianic component.[7] A movement of immigration to and settlement in the land of Israel is conceivable on the basis of motivations other than the attempt to bring about the coming of the Messiah.[8] A military uprising by Jews against an oppressive power may be of a purely political nature without claiming any messianic significance.[9] The assumption that any movement challenging the established order must necessarily be messianic is certainly one that needs to be tested. On the other hand, it is certainly likely that the leaders of such movements will be tempted to mobilize the energies bound up with the messianic claim. Even in the absence of direct evidence for such a claim, the hope for redemption may serve as a powerful motivation in both the leaders and those who were led.

An additional element implied by the term *messianic* is, of course, the figure of the Messiah. All of the traditional expectations enumerated above may theoretically be fulfilled through the direct intrusion of divine power, without the appearance of any special human leader. Indeed, many of the Biblical passages most frequently thought of as "messianic," whether prophecies of ingathering and resettlement of the land (Deuteronomy 30: 1–10, Amos 9: 9–15) or of universal peace (Isaiah 2: 2–4), do not mention a messiah-figure at all. They might be considered visions of a messianic age without a Messiah.

ST. PHILIP'S COLLEGE LIBRARY

Perhaps it is preferable to distinguish such eschatological visions by calling them *redemptive* rather than *messianic*.[10] Although less common after the Biblical period, this approach by no means disappeared from Jewish history. The puzzling statement of the third-century Rabbi Hillel, "There is no Messiah for Israel, for they already enjoyed him [lit. ate him] in the days of Hezekiah" (B. Sanh 99a), may be a repudiation of the hope not for redemption but only of *messianic* redemption (by a Messiah) as opposed to redemption directly by God; at least this is how some later commentators understood him.[11] In Lurianic Kabbalah the Messiah plays an almost insignificant role in the cosmic drama of exile and redemption.[12] Contemporary Gush Emunim spearheads a movement energized by the expectation of imminent redemption and its political demands, but no individual is identified as a messianic figure, and little speculation is devoted to questions about the Messiah himself.[13]

A full messianic movement must therefore have some relationship not only to the achievement of redemption but to the active role of the Messiah. Here an additional distinction may be useful in evaluating our material. In some movements, the leader is clearly understood to be the Messiah (or more properly, a Messiah, for much Jewish speculation from the rabbinic period on assumed that there would be two with different roles who would come in sequence).[14] In others, the central figure claims to be playing an introductory role—as prophet or immediate forerunner. We might call the first *Messiah movements*—Sabbatianism would be the paradigm—and the second *messianic*—expecting the imminent arrival of a figure who is not identified with any historic personage. It is often impossible to determine in which category a movement should be classified, because the extant sources usually do not permit an unambiguous understanding of how the central figure understood his own role, what claims he made to his circle of followers and to the world beyond that circle, or how his position was understood while the movement still flourished. The ongoing debate over the messianic claim of Jesus illustrates the difficulties with which we are faced.

There is one kind of terminology, however, that has no place in a proper historical treatment: *false messiah*, or *pseudo-messiah*.[15] To characterize a figure such as Sabbatai Ṣevi as a *false messiah* (or even worse, a *messianic pretender*, implying a conscious deception) is to destroy any possibility of understanding the historical dynamics of the movement that coalesced around him. After all, what kind of people would follow a false messiah? Only by recognizing the importance of the messianic belief in the self-understanding of Jews, the power of the messianic hope in their experience of exile, and the believer's genuine conviction that the time had finally come and the figure at hand was really the fulfillment of the age-old dream, thereby justifying whatever risks a commitment to the cause entailed, can the movement be made intelligible. In the moment when crucial choices must be made, there are no *true* and *false* messiahs, only followers and opponents of an individual who claims a certain role. The *falsity* of the messianic figure, like the falsity of a particular Biblical prophet, can be a historical category only in retrospect and only on the understanding that that category reflects the perspective of a particular tradition.

Messianic movements are not evenly distributed over the chronological and geographical grids of Jewish history. There are periods when considerable messianic activism crystallizing into diverse movements is evident and others when no such turbulence is discernible. Similarly, messianic activism is significantly more prevalent among Jews living in an Islamic environment than among those living under Christian rule—more around the Mediterranean basin than in northern Europe.[16] These empirical realities suggest certain factors that may explain when and where a messianic movement is more likely among Jews.

One important contextual factor is a major upheaval in which the established power arrangement of nations and empires appears to be dramatically changing. Jews who believed that God was the sovereign master of all history found it difficult to concede that such epic events were without any transcendent significance. Convinced that the relationship between the Jewish people and God was the principal drama of history, yet painfully aware that they appeared to be consigned to a minor role far from center stage, these Jews felt a natural tendency to interpret mass movements, major military confrontations, the breakdown of long-established institutions, as part of a messianic scenario in which the Jewish people would be the ultimate beneficiaries.

The rapid defeat of Babylonia by Cyrus and the establishment of a new Persian Empire was viewed by one of the great Biblical prophets as God's redemptive act, with clear implications for Jewish behavior. The Muslim conquest in the seventh century, when a new religious-political force erupted from the Arabian peninsula and quickly mastered the enormous territory that for centuries had been divided between Sassanians and Byzantines, appeared to some contemporary Jews not as the start of a long new era but as the beginning of the end of history as it was known. The Crusades could readily be interpreted as a divinely arranged conflict in which the armed forces of Christendom and Islam would destroy each other so that the Jewish people could return to its proper position of glory. The fall of Constantinople, capital of the eastern Roman Empire, to the Ottoman Turks, followed by the defection of a substantial body of Christians from the Church of Rome, was perceived as portending the collapse of the old order; the expulsion of the great Jewish community from Spain, which occurred between these two events, looked like the beginning of a mass movement of Jews back toward the land of Israel. Such events provide a natural context in which messianic speculation and activism would be expected.[17]

A second factor is the expectation that a particular date was fraught with redemptive significance. Here, too, the underlying assumption is God's sovereign mastery of history, with the corollary that historical events affecting the Jewish people occur in accordance with patterns encoded in the texts of God's revelation. After the catastrophic destruction of the Temple by the Romans in 70 C.E., Jews naturally attempted to make sense of their current plight by appealing to paradigms from the past; the belief that it all fit into a divine scheme was more comforting than the fear that history was lurching out of control. The Biblical span for the exile following the Babylonian destruction of the First Temple was seventy years (Jer. 25:11–12); the seventh decade following the great revolt against Rome saw a new revolt with messianic dimensions.[18]

When this failed different paradigms were sought. The Egyptian affliction was said to be of a four hundred-year duration (Gen. 15:13); as the fourth century after the Roman destruction drew near to an end, expectations of redemption again became more intense, and there are indications of messianic uprisings in Babylonia and Crete.[19] Other pregnant years were derived from interpretations of enigmatic verses in the Book of Daniel, numerical decodings of key words in prophesies of redemption, speculations about the larger patterns of historical chronology, observation of astronomical phenomena or astrological portents.[20] In many cases, there is a correlation between a particular date and an eruption with messianic significance.

A third factor relates to the quality of Jewish life. It seems obvious that conditions of social humiliation, economic oppression, and violent persecution would intensify the forces in Jewish society impelling Jews to abandon the familiar status quo for the risks of a redemptive movement. Conversely conditions of relative prosperity and tranquility should make it less likely that Jews would want to opt for a radical change. Similarly, it seems reasonable that those on the margins of Jewish society, who have the least stake in the established order and the least to lose by transforming it, would be more likely to support a messianic movement than those possessing economic power, political influence, or religious authority.[21]

Related to this is the stability of the political environment in which Jews were living. By its nature a challenge to the Gentile political order, it stands to reason that a messianic movement would be perceived to have a greater chance for success during a period of general upheaval and turbulence, when the central government is weak and already under attack by other revolutionary forces, than during a period in which a strong central government enjoys widespread support and controls powerful resources for keeping the peace. We should therefore expect messianic activism during periods of general political upheaval, which were usually dangerous for Jews as well.[22]

But all these factors, as plausible as they seem, are neither necessary nor sufficient explanations. Not necessary, because the greatest Jewish messianic movement of the past two thousand years—that of Sabbatai Ṣevi in the 1660s—had no such background. It was not a period of distinctive world conflict; the date 1666 had messianic significance for Christians but not for Jews; the movement had considerable appeal among wealthy Jewish merchants as well as among the poor, among lay and rabbinic leaders as well as among the disenfranchised; and the Turkish government at the time was relatively stable and strong.[23] Not sufficient, because any and all of these factors need not entail the conclusion that Jews should do anything other than wait until God sends an unmistakable sign, an unambiguous instruction. They may heighten expectation, increase tension, stimulate speculation, but they do not necessarily produce an actual messianic movement. The relative significance of these factors, therefore, will have to be assessed in relation to each of the movements analyzed in the following pages.

The paradigm for a fully developed messianic movement in Jewish history is Sabbatianism. It is documented in a multitude of contemporary sources from various perspectives; its central figure makes explicit claims to messianic status and its intellectuals articulate a doctrine relating the claims to traditional Jewish tests;[24] it inspires a significant following at all levels of Jewish society and opposition both from Jewish leaders and non-Jewish authorities; it culminates in the shocking ambiguities of unexpected events and ingenious attempts to explain them; its influence continues among "believers" after all the original protagonists have disappeared from the historical stage. No other messianic movement in Jewish history fulfills all these criteria. In many cases the decision about whether to consider a particular historical phenomenon in this category will necessarily involve an element of subjectivity, as becomes obvious in even a superficial chronological review.

Scholars have noted that the actual doctrine of the Messiah did not crystallize in Judaism until after the Biblical period.[25] The Hebrew Bible articulated the idea of redemption—a reestablishment of the proper relationship between God and the Jewish people, situated once again in their land, after a period of disruption. It provided descriptions of an ideal political ruler (some of which may originally have been intended to express the hopes for an actual figure born into the royal line or newly crowned), visions of an ideal age in the future (which may not have been intended to suggest a rupture in history or an eschatological "end of time"), prophecies of divine intervention in history to balance the scales of justice.[26] It furnished characters—especially Moses and David—who could serve as paradigms or types for a redeeming Messiah.[27] And it suggested motifs, such as the "suffering servant," which originally had no messianic significance but could later be mobilized for use in novel ways. These were the threads from which coherent messianic doctrines and eschatological scenarios could be woven in later times.

It is arguable, furthermore, that although the term *messianic* is anachronistic in this context, the first actual messianic movements in Jewish history occurred in Biblical times. Although the Biblical narratives allow us little confidence that we can reconstruct how the Exodus from Egypt was perceived by contemporaries, it certainly contains many of the elements that characterize the *messianic movement:* liberation of the people from oppression through the instrumentality of a human leader who claimed to be working in concert with divine power, significant opposition to the movement not only by the Gentile authorities but within the people themselves, promise of a future life of prosperity ("a land flowing with milk and honey") and a close, secure relationship with

God. Unquestionably, the Exodus served as the central paradigm for the rhetoric and sometimes even the game plan of messianic redemption throughout subsequent Jewish history.[28] The one factor that makes it anomalous is its almost total success.

A second candidate for a Biblical messianic movement is the return from Babylonian Exile following the Persian conquest of Babylonia. Our sketchy knowledge of this movement is essentially limited to the writings of its theorist and propagandist, the prophet whose writings were preserved in the book of Isaiah beginning with chapter 40. Cyrus himself is the messianic figure, God's "anointed" (Isa. 45:1): not the only time in Jewish history when a Gentile ruler would be presented in this role.[29] The prophet's practical message, couched in some of the most glorious rhetoric of Biblical literature, is essentially simple: God has shown by sending this victorious deliverer that the redemption has arrived; it is now time for us to respond by reenacting the Exodus, journeying once again through the wilderness, and returning to our land.[30]

This movement reveals some of the problems characteristic of later Jewish messianism. Many in the Babylonian Jewish community refused to heed the prophet's call to leave their homes and return to Zion.[31] No extant sources were produced by the opponents to the movement, but it is not difficult to imagine their arguments. Jeremiah had urged an accommodation to life outside the holy land, insisting that it was possible to worship the one true God in Babylonia and warning against those who promised an early end to the exile. The time had not yet come; barely two-thirds of the seventy-year period he mentioned had elapsed. This new prophet therefore called upon the people to disregard Jeremiah, whose dire predictions had been proven correct. And he dared to affirm that a pagan king was God's anointed ruler.

As for those who responded to the prophet's call to return, reality must have dampened some of their enthusiasm. Certainly no "way paved in the wilderness" lay before them; after a long and arduous journey they would have found a devastated city, a demoralized people, the Temple still in ruins. The lavish promises of the prophet may well have begun to sound hollow to those confronted with the slow and difficult task of rebuilding. In messianism even more than in ordinary politics the rhetoric of inspiration may easily lead to discouragement and disillusion even if some of the goals are achieved. The Second Commonwealth was thus born in the ambiguities of the messianic claim, a claim that can mobilize tremendous energy but can also become an enormous burden when historical reality falls short of exaggerated hopes.[32]

Like the sixth century B.C.E. the first century of the Christian Era was a period of instability that produced radical challenges to the status quo. The most influential, the movement surrounding Jesus of Nazareth, is one of the very few for which the literature of the movement itself has been preserved; only the Sabbatian movement is more extensively documented. During the life of its central figure and the first generation or two of followers after his death, it was very much a part of Jewish history; its protagonists were Jews, it appealed to Jews, its claims were justified with reference to traditional Jewish sources.

It is now universally recognized that the *Jesus movement* must be understood in the context of Jewish messianic speculation (as evidenced in various works of Pseudepigrapha and the Dead Sea Scrolls), and of political-religious activism.[33] The historian Josephus has provided a series of hostile yet tantalizing glimpses of figures who apparently claimed prophetic inspiration, gathered groups of followers in the wilderness to march across the Jordan river, or ascend the Mount of Olives, in some kind of symbolic expression of independence from the ruling authorities. At least this is the way the Romans perceived these activities, for each was summarily suppressed by Roman military might, its central figure put to death.[34] We know virtually nothing of the internal dynamics of these events, and whether they deserve to be considered either *messianic* or *movements* cannot be clearly established with the limited sources available. But, as the discussion by Richard Horsley demonstrates, they provide a fascinating point of comparison with the *Jesus movement*.

Should the Great Revolt, launched against Rome in 66 C.E. and culminating in the fall of Jerusalem and the destruction of the Temple four years later, be considered a redemptive movement? It is unlikely that leaders of the revolt would have risked so much without believing that their initiative would produce God's intervention to liberate the land of Israel from the pagan rule that forced Jews to compromise their commitment to Torah. Yet no extant literature articulates the leaders' own ideology of revolution, and there is little relevant direct evidence in the hostile accounts of Josephus or the Talmudic sages. The most intriguing is Josephus's statement that Jews were inspired to revolt because of an "ambiguous oracle found also in their sacred writings that 'about that time, one from their country should become governor of the habitable earth.' " The Jews understood this to be a prediction of the Messiah, whereas the oracle really referred to Vespasian, who was named emperor while he was in the land of Israel. Josephus was apparently content to concede the messianic role in his time to Rome.[35]

The revolt of the years 132–135 C.E., led by the man who signed his name Simeon ben Kosiba (better known under the name preserved in Christian sources, Bar Kokhba), has a clearer messianic component. Jewish sources report that Rabbi Akiba, the most respected scholar of his generation, publicly identified ben Kosiba as the Messiah, an assertion so embarrassing after the failure of the revolt that it could not plausibly have been fabricated. Eusebius records what appears to be a messianic claim on the part of the leader himself. And coins and letters from the period, discovered only during the past generation, are dated by a new seemingly messianic calendar: the year "of the redemption of Israel."[36] Subsequent Jewish sources are ambivalent about this military figure who achieved spectacular successes before suffering devastating defeat, and it has been argued that his experience led to the development of a new messianic persona, the Messiah descended from Joseph, who would be killed in battle before the advent of the Messiah from the Davidic line.[37]

The ruthless Roman suppression of the revolt destroyed the taste for open defiance of imperial power; during the Pax Romana, Jewish leaders developed a quietistic messianic ideology, prohibiting all rebellion against the nations.[38] Nevertheless, dramatic external challenges to the established order occasioned sporadic movements. Rabbinic sources are all but silent about the stunning decision by the pagan emperor Julian to permit the Jews to return to Jerusalem and rebuild their Temple, but we can imagine the excitement this must have engendered in Jews who saw clear parallels with Cyrus the Great. The impact of this heady but short-lived reversal is documented as far away as Iran.[39] Other messianic claims surfaced against the background of the barbarian invasions of the fifth century and the Islamic conquest of the seventh. Little is known about the individuals involved, although the seventh-century figure apparently appealed to an element of social discontent, as we are told that he "gathered around him weavers, carpetmakers, and launderers."[40] In both cases, their influence was local and brief.

The turbulent period of the Islamic Umayyad Caliphate (661–750 C.E.), based in Damascus and challenged militarily and ideologically by powerful forces from the east, was the next environment in which Jewish messianic activism flourished. Despite the relatively late provenance of the extant sources, more is known about Abu Isa of Isfahan and his movement than about any other messianic movement between the second century and the twelfth. The provocative study by Israel Friedlaender, still valuable eighty years after publication, shows the profound influence of Islamic doctrines—particularly those of the Shi'a—on the ideology of the Jewish movement. Messianism thus provides an instance of a dialectical relationship between the two traditions: Jewish messianic expectation helped mold the contours of the Shi'ite historical worldview and eschatology, while the movements of Abu Isa and his follower Yudghan are the first major example of Islamic influence within Judaism that would produce the great flourishings of medieval Jewish culture in Baghdad and Muslim Spain. Those who believed in Abu Isa maintained their collective identity and were present as a distinct group in Damascus some two hundred to two hundred and fifty years after his death.[41] They must have developed their own theology, liturgy, legends, and law. Nothing of this has survived.

The establishment of the Abbasid Caliphate in Baghdad stabilized the political environment; strong central Jewish institutions, dependent upon and loyal to the Caliphate, left little space for active messianic challenges. This stability was rocked by the Crusades. A series of twelfth-century messianic personalities and uprisings, from Yemen and Iraq to Morocco and Andalusia, challenged the ingenuity of Jewish leaders such as Moses Maimonides, who worked both to strengthen the hope of ordinary Jews that deliverance from their suffering would come soon and to discredit concrete manifestations of messianic activism and dissuade Jews from the dangers of involvement.[42] One of the most attractive messianic figures was David Alroy, whose intellectual attainments and appealing personality are conceded even in a sarcastically hostile Islamic account. The temporary success of his movement, the opposition by the established Jewish leadership, and the ultimate betrayal leading to his death are recounted with surprising sympathy by the perceptive traveler Benjamin of Tudela.[43]

The upheavals in European and in Jewish history of the late fifteenth and sixteenth centuries produced a dazzling array of activities with messianic significance, though no full-blown movement. Various expressions of prophecy and messianic agitation among groups of *conversos;*

speculation about the eschatological significance of contemporary events; intense expectation focused on particular years; prayer vigils to promote the confession and repentance that would bring the Messiah; even the printing of the Zohar as a vehicle for the dissemination of mystical doctrine—all testify to the urgency of the messianic tension in the generations following the Expulsion from Spain.[44]

Particularly intriguing is the program of the enigmatic eastern Jew David Reubeni. He came to Rome in 1524 claiming to be the emissary of a kingdom of three hundred thousand Jews in northern Arabia and succeeded in getting an audience with Pope Clement VII and in receiving a papal endorsement of his mission to King John III of Portugal. In his memoir Reubeni eschews any messianic claims for his own role. But he apparently promised the Portuguese *conversos* that he would soon return to bring them to the land of Israel, and his secret goal may well have been to initiate an eschatological world war between Christian Europe and the Ottoman Empire.[45]

One of the focal points for messianic speculation and activity was the land of Israel, particularly the city of Safed, which attracted an extraordinary cadre of outstanding personalities. As Jacob Katz has argued, the attempt to renew the traditional ordination of rabbinical judges and thereby establish courts with authority to adjudicate areas of Jewish law that had remained purely theoretical for almost one thousand five hundred years reflects an initiative to prepare the necessary conditions for the messianic advent—and therefore qualifies as a kind of redemptive movement even without a messianic personality at its core.[46] And the new Kabbalistic mythos divulged a generation later by Isaac Luria in Safed, a mythos in which the categories of exile and redemption played a central role, was capable of creating a messianic tension absent in classical Kabbalah.[47] Together with more traditional and popular sources of eschatological ideas, Lurianic Kabbalah would serve as the matrix for the ideology of the Sabbatian movement, helping to explain its paradoxical quirks in familiar terms, as can be seen in Gershom Scholem's magisterial study.

Despite the collective psychological trauma of Sabbatianism, expressions of traditional messianic activity continued into the nineteenth century. Two examples are represented by studies of their social dynamics and ideology: the movement of large-scale resettlement of the land of Israel in preparation for the expected advent of the Messiah in 1840, and the movement surrounding the Yemenite messianic figure Shukr Kuḥayl II. While these were rather marginal phenomena, four major movements of modern Jewish history have a complex and ambiguous relationship to the tradition of Jewish messianism, each raising special conceptual problems.

Scholars continue to debate whether Polish Hasidism should be considered a messianic movement. I have included Benzion Dinur's discussion, which argues the case for the messianic character of Hasidism; his interpretation has been vigorously rejected by Gershom Scholem and other respected historians.[48] But whether the founders intended their movement as a way to bring the Messiah or as a way to neutralize the dangers of messianic activism, it cannot be doubted that a powerful messianic tension has informed certain expressions of Hasidism, including the coterie of Nahman of Bratslav in the early nineteenth century and the Bratslaver and Lubavitcher Hasidim today.[49]

Three nineteenth century movements raise a different problematic. The Reform movement called for fundamental changes in the religious and political structures of traditional Jewish life that would accompany an end to the experience of life in "Exile." It identified its central aspiration as the messianic age envisioned by the prophets, which some of its leaders believed to be imminent. Yet while it claimed to be continuing the genuine messianic tradition of Judaism and often indulged in its rhetoric, Reform severed the connection with much of traditional messianism by abandoning the figure of the personal messiah and by renouncing the national components of the redemption ideal; the ingathering of the exiles in the land of Israel, the restoration of the Davidic kingdom, the rebuilding of the Temple, and the reestablishment of the sacrificial cult.[50] The elements of continuity with earlier expressions of Jewish messianism are outweighed by the decisive changes.

Socialism championed the principle of radical change in the social order that would bring about the fulfillment of the messianic hopes for an end to the oppression of the downtrodden and the beginning of a new age of universal brotherhood. Yet even more than Reform, socialism emptied the messianic ideal of any specifically Jewish content. The socialist ideology required that bonds of solidarity between workers throughout the world take precedence over solidarity between Jews of different economic classes. And unlike Reform, socialism also abandoned the religious dimensions of the messianic hope. Even those Jews who opted for a socialist commitment under specifically Jewish auspices saw their position as a transvaluation of antiquated ideas, as is evident in the following song of the Jewish Socialist Bund:

> The messiah and Judaism are dying, expiring,
> A new messiah is appearing,
> The Jewish worker whom the rich man exploits
> Is raising the banner of rebellion.[51]

Socialism may have roots in the world view that informed the messianic tradition, but it is a mutation that cannot be considered part of that tradition.

Like Reform and socialism, Zionism crystallized as a movement to realize certain traditional messianic goals, in this case the ingathering of dispersed Jews in the land of Israel and the reestablishment of Jewish sovereignty as a means to bring an end to the exile. However, most Zionist thinkers thought of their enterprise as a repudiation of traditional messianism, which they identified with a passive, quietistic reliance upon God and an unwillingness to take any human initiative toward the fulfillment of the desired goals until the Messiah actually arrived. It is therefore problematic to conceive of Zionism as a redemptive movement in the traditional sense; certainly the Zionist ideal of "normalization" of Jewish life would seem to be almost the antithesis of familiar messianic visions that posit divine intervention to reestablish the unique Jewish role in human history.

Yet the relationship between Zionism and messianism remains more dialectical than is the case with the other movements. First, a minority of "proto-Zionist" and Zionist thinkers insisted on seeing their goals as an integral part of the traditional messianic scenario.[52] Second, this conception has been concretized in authoritative liturgical formulations, including the description of the state of Israel as *reshit tsemiḥat ge'ulatenu,* "the beginning of the sprouting of our redemption."[53] Most important, some of the most interesting developments in Zionist thought and practice today—particularly those surrounding the Gush Emunim—have an explicit redemptive character. If it is not accurate to describe Zionism as a messianic movement, it is impossible to avoid confronting the messianic stream within Zionism, and this will be addressed in several of the papers below.

This chronological review of the major expressions of messianic activism against the paradigm of the Sabbatian movement suggests questions to be raised in each specific instance. How do we know about the movement? What is the nature of the source material that provides our information? Is it contemporary with the events? If not, how much later, and how reliable is the author's own knowledge? Were the sources produced inside the movement or outside? If outside, was the author sympathetic, hostile, more or less neutral? The *Jesus movement* would certainly look quite different if all that had been preserved about it were a few lines by a hostile outsider, resembling the sentences in which Josephus describes other first-century challenges by charismatic figures and their followings. Similarly, those movements known only from terse descriptions by Josephus or Maimonides would look quite different if texts from within the movement had been preserved.

What is the role of the messianic figure around whom the movement crystallizes? Can we be certain about the precise nature of his claim: messenger of the Messiah, Ephraimite Messiah, Davidic Messiah? Does he function as a military leader? a charismatic, inspirational preacher of repentance? the bearer of a new teaching? Is he a learned Jew? Are miraculous powers attributed to him? Does he act in a way that violates Jewish traditions or norms? Is the ideology of the movement taught *by* the messianic figure, or *about* him, by others? Is there an identifiable theoretician or propagandist of the movement? If so, what is his relationship with the messianic figure?

To what extent does the ideology of the movement draw from existing doctrine, to what extent does it generate its own doctrine in response to the specific contours of the situation? How much influence from the surrounding Christian or Muslim cultures can be detected in this ideology? Does a revolutionary social doctrine play a significant role? The redistribution of wealth? A different role for women? Are the poor or women particularly discernible among the followers?

One of the underlying regularities of Jewish historical experience is that traditional Jewish leaders oppose messianic movements and Gentile governments suppress them. What are the arguments used by Jewish leaders that enable them both to reassert the fundamental validity of the messianic belief and to repudiate the particular manifestation of it promising the most immediate fulfillment? Did the Gentile authorities pressure the Jewish leadership to act against the messianic claimant? How are we to explain the blatant exception to the rule: the impressive number of rabbis and other Jewish leaders who supported the claims of Sabbatai Ṣevi?

What happens to the movement after the death of the central figure? Where our knowledge comes from external sources the narrative usually ends when the messianic figure dies (usually is killed) and his followers disillusioned. Yet occasionally there is evidence for a group of followers continuing to exist long after the career of the central figure ended without his promises fulfilled. How does a group accommodate itself to shattering disappointment yet manage to maintain its coherence? How is an unusual belief and a potentially dangerous commitment transmitted from those who had personal contact with the charismatic figure to those who did not?

A final set of questions bears upon the role of messianic doctrine within Judaism and of messianic activism within Jewish history. A book such as the present one, focusing on a single theme, inevitably distorts by overemphasizing the importance of its subject, giving the impression that the phenomenon described typifies the normative mode. Did the ordinary Jews living some time between the late first century and the nineteenth feel a sense of acute messianic expectation and urgency? Did praying three times a day for the coming of the Messiah make these Jews predisposed to respond enthusiastically to an individual who claimed to be the awaited redeemer, so that they eagerly anticipated the opportunity to leave their homes and return to the land of Israel?

It is, of course, almost impossible to answer such questions with confidence, for "ordinary Jews" did not leave us much evidence of their *mentalité*. Nevertheless, it should be noted that, with the exception of the Sabbatian movement, messianic uprisings do not appear to have been mass movements. There were many generations, even centuries, when no messianic activism can be documented anywhere in the world. And there are large regions—particularly, as Gerson Cohen has shown, in the northern Europe of Ashkenazic Jewry—where hardly any messianic movements occurred. The accusation made by certain Zionist writers that medieval Jews prayed for the Messiah but, on the whole, were not really eager to leave the Diaspora may be a polemical exaggeration, but it is not without some measure of truth.[54]

Furthermore, we need to make seriously what might be called the peripheralizing of the messianic dimension in respectable understandings of Judaism. Many have noted that the messianic doctrine plays an almost insignificant role in some of the most important texts of the Jewish tradition: the Torah and Hagiographa in the Bible, the Mishnah, Maimonides' *Guide for the Perplexed,* and that masterpiece of medieval German Jewish Pietism, *Sefer Ḥasidim.* Rabbis whose views were recorded in the Talmud were apparently so fearful of the sufferings to come during the turbulent prelude to the messianic advent that they hoped the Messiah would not appear in their time.[55] Medieval Jewish philosophers were convinced that they could achieve the ultimate purpose of human life—cultivation of intellect leading to spiritual immortality—under present conditions of Diaspora life, and some drew the conclusion that the Messiah would not benefit them at all.[56]

There is also the claim that Judaism does not depend upon a messianic doctrine because the basic structure of the commandments, the true foundation of Judaism, could remain intact indefinitely in the Diaspora. Articulated most famously as a defensive ploy in a thirteenth-century polemical context by Moses ben Nahman (Nahmanides), this idea has an intellectual integrity of its own. Jews may reveal devotion to the covenant more powerfully by observing the commandments under the difficult conditions of exile than in the messianic kingdom when obedience will be enforced. Therefore, even if it were certain that the Messiah will never come, that the present (medieval) structure of Jewish life would continue forever, the heart of Judaism would not be affected.[57] This position was reasserted not a few times in the generations following Nahmanides. It was repudiated by those who maintained that the messianic impulse lies at the core of Jewish identity.[58]

Distinct from the question of the importance of messianism in Jewish history and doctrine is an evaluation of the impact of its role. Has messianism, on the whole, been a positive or negative force in Jewish experience? Were the messianic movements described in this book essentially energizing and inspiring or disillusioning and destructive?[59] What kind of "price" does messianism exact of those who give it their commitment? This question is addressed in general terms by some of the scholars in writings below, but it is left to the reader to assess its implications for each specific manifestation of a messianic movement.

The following selection of essays is intended to represent various kinds of diversity: Jewish and Christian scholars, Israelis and Americans, textual and conceptual approaches, older studies that have become classics and recent accounts of new discoveries, idiosyncratic interpretations and statements of consensus, broad surveys and analyses of specific events. A major criterion has been the availability of the material in English. There is an abundant and important scholarly literature on the subject in the Hebrew language; with two exceptions, where special translations have been made, this literature had been bypassed in favor of comparable treatments that did not require translation.

Two comprehensive surveys, ranging from the Biblical period to the present, begin the collection. R. J. Zwi Werblowsky, writing from the perspective of a historian of religion, traces the interaction between beliefs and their manifestation in behavior, raising such central themes as the relationship between the national or social components and the spiritual dimensions of messianic movements, made particularly intense because they are "by definition doomed to failure in the historical sphere." Eliezer Schweid, a historian of Jewish philosophy, identifies some of the fundamental motifs and major points of controversy in traditional Jewish messianic thought and then goes on to illustrate their metamorphosis as expressions of religious and secular messianism in Israel today.

The desire to understand the historical context of the *Jesus movement* has led to extensive investigation of the diversity of messianic conceptions in Jewish literature produced during the generations preceding and following Jesus' public career. More important for our purposes are the actual messianic figures and their followings during that period. Morton Smith argues that a range of possible types, including revolutionary bandits and miraculous healers as well as insightful teachers and charismatic prophets, could all evolve into redemptive heroes in the minds of some contemporaries. And Richard Horsley, moving from literary texts to concrete social phenomena, analyzes a series of popular movements, from the time of Herod to the Bar Kokhba revolt, led by figures who claimed kingship as an expression of the revolutionary political consciousness produced in response to oppressive conditions.

As noted above, Israel Friedlaender's monumental study was a pathbreaking attempt to demonstrate Islamic influences, especially from Shi'ite circles, upon Jewish messianic movements and their ideologies. Because of its length, portions of the article (originally published in three separate volumes of the *Jewish Quarterly Review*) have been eliminated, including an initial account of Shi'ism, material about later Jewish movements (especially Sabbatianism), and technical reviews of outdated scholarly debates. The material presented focuses on the messianic movements during the early Islamic period before the establishment of the Abbasid Caliphate. A more current overview of Jewish messianism in the period of late antiquity and the early Middle Ages is provided by a section from S. W. Baron's magisterial *Social and Religious History of the Jews*.

After decades of study of the documents found in the Cairo Genizah S. D. Goitein published a comprehensive five-volume description of all aspects of medieval Jewish society in a Mediterranean, Islamic context.[60] Part of this world was the messianic speculation and activism engendered by the Crusades. Goitein's article analyzes a newly discovered Genizah text about the excitement that gripped the Jews of Baghdad in 1120, initiated by a Jewish woman's report of having received a redemptive message from Elijah. The events are not remarkable in themselves, but rather illustrative of a common pattern at the time, including the government's decisive reprisal against the Jews. Particularly significant is the role played by the woman, whose perspective is frequently missing from more normative Jewish sources. Here, too, an encompassing review of the messianic manifestations in the twelfth century against the background of the first Crusades is given by S. W. Baron.

Gerson Cohen's seminal essay raises a broader question: why is there so little evidence of messianic activism among the Ashkenazi Jews of northern Europe in comparison with the Jews of Islamic countries and Spain? Cohen outlines a fundamental difference in the way the Rabbinical leadership of the two communities expressed the traditional messianic hope, a difference in "messianic posture" between quiescent reticence and open, active involvement. His explanation of this difference—appealing to the contrast between the more traditional, fundamentalist faith of Ashkenazic Jewry and the rationalist mentality of the Sephardim, and connecting this with different approaches to the challenge of martyrdom—may be supplemented by a recent explanation of the contrast drawing more from sociological analysis.[61]

Quite different from the above material is Abraham Berger's discussion of "The Messianic Self-Consciousness of Abraham Abulafia." At issue here is not a movement but an eccentric personality with an original and powerful mind, who thought of himself in messianic terms and left evidence of this scattered through his largely unpublished writings. A comprehensive analysis of Abulafia's work, thought, and self-conception is in the process of being published by Moshe Idel, but Berger's "tentative evaluation" remains a useful introduction to some of the central issues.

Five years after the Expulsion from Spain, Jews living on Portuguese soil were devastated by a royal decree mandating universal compulsory mass conversion. A small group of Jews was arrested in Lisbon after refusing to convert, and then permitted by the king to leave Portugal for North Africa. The "Genizah Pages," discovered, deciphered, and analyzed by Isaiah Tishby, were written by a leader of this group who believed that he was playing a role crucial to the incipient messianic redemption. While we cannot speak of a crystallized movement here, the text reveals how contemporary events looked to a personality suffused with "acute messianic tension." The section from Tishby's Hebrew book,[62] translated especially for this collection, sets this messianic reading of current history in the context of other expressions of intense anticipation and activism from the late fifteenth and early sixteenth century.

On Sabbatai Ṣevi and the Sabbatian movement, Gershom Scholem's *magnum opus* remains the indispensible starting point, and in many areas the definitive summation. While aspects of his interpretation have been questioned by scholars, in some cases raising substantive methodological questions,[63] there can be no substitute for a full immersion in this masterful work. I have selected the introductory section, in which Scholem reviews some of the standard explanations for the spread of the movement and sets out his own thesis about the role of Lurianic Kabbalah, discussions of the movement's impact on the economic life of the Jews and the manifestation of "mass prophecy" among the enthusiastic followers, and the brilliant and provocative interpretation of the impact of Sabbatai Ṣevi's startling apostasy upon the psychology and theology of the believers. Scholem's analogy with the dynamics of the Christian Apostles' response to the paradox of the crucified Messiah is analyzed by W. D. Davies in a probing exploration of how Scholem's insights illuminate the general phenomenon of messianism and the particular phenomenon of early Christianity.

As indicated above, Benzion Dinur's presentation of Hasidism as a messianic movement has come under attack by leading scholars, including Scholem. In this brief section, translated especially for this volume from a long article on the origins of Hasidism,[64] Dinur argues that the Baal Shem Tov believed that the redemption of the Jewish people depended upon the spread of his doctrine to the masses, and that despite the potential danger of this messianic self-conception and the resulting reluctance to speak about it openly, considerable evidence for it remains in Hasidic sources. The scholarly debate over this issue is a fine example of how the same texts—in particular the authentic letter of the BeSHT to his brother-in-law—can be interpreted in fundamentally different ways. Arthur Green's study of the BeSHT's great-grandson, Nahman of Bratslav, taken from his biography of Nahman, is one of our most penetrating analyses of the dynamics of a messianic personality, riven with aspirations and doubts, soaring hopes and shattering disappointments.

Arie Morgenstern's article summarizes part of a book-length Hebrew study of the immigration from Eastern Europe to the land of Israel in conjunction with the messianic expectations surrounding the date 1840.[65] Here he focuses on the messianic ideology and concomitant actions within circles of the disciples of the Vilna Gaon, archenemy of the early Hasidim. Even more important, this study provides another test case (with the Sabbatian movement) of how believers respond to a potential crisis of faith "when prophecy fails"—in this case when the expected year elapsed with no Messiah in sight. Bat-Zion Eraqi Klorman's study of a nineteenth-century Yemenite messianic figure—perhaps the last such figure to inspire a messianic movement in its classical form—elucidates another aspect of the economics of redemption by analyzing the claim that a new tithe would play a crucial role in the redemptive scenario. Income from the tithe was used both to provide for the poor and to sustain the messianic claimant and his entourage.

Several articles treat the complex, dialectical relationship of traditional messianism, Zionism, and contemporary Israel. Jacob Katz surveys the thought of the leading "proto-Zionist" and Zionist thinkers against the background of the classical messianic posture. He argues that a "messianic determinism" has operated in the Zionist movement, expressing the power of the messianic impulse even in the behavior and thought of individuals who felt or claimed that there was a historical inevitability to their movement, even if they did not recognize the links with the past and, one might add, even if they thought of their program as a conscious repudiation of traditional messianism.

Uriel Tal explores the impact of Jewish redemptive traditions in contemporary Israel, looking at individuals and groups who fit under the category he calls "political messianism." He thereby provides a fascinating description of the conclusions drawn by contemporary thinkers who interpret historical events, beginning with the Six-Day War, not within the context of ordinary geopolitics but as part of the transcendent drama of redemption. Menachem Kellner adds to this picture by demonstrating that the tradition of Jewish messianic thought encompasses divergent views, making it possible for the "religious zionist left" to reach political conclusions dramatically different from those harbored by Gush Emunim. All three articles demonstrate that Israel is the arena in which Jewish messianism is most forcefully active today.

So influential has been the work of Gershom Scholem in defining the parameters of contemporary scholarly understanding of Jewish messianism that it seemed appropriate to conclude the volume with two pieces inspired by his work. David Biale's essay is taken from his assessment of Scholem's entire scholarly ouevre; it summarizes Scholem's positions on the central issues of Jewish messianic expression and raises some critical questions about these positions. Jacob Taubes's brief piece, the title of which is taken from Scholem's own work, succinctly raises significant questions about the overall nature, significance, and value of messianism as an impulse in Jewish history.

NOTES

1. See "Social Movements," in the *International Encyclopedia of Social Sciences,* 17 vols. (New York, 1968), 14:438–52, esp. pp. 438–39. Cf. Bernard Weinryb, *The Jews of Poland* (Philadelphia, 1973), p. 366, no. 1, a corrective statement on this point which pushes it too far, and Moshe Idel's introduction to the new edition of Aaron Zeev Aescoly's *Jewish Messianic Movements* [Heb.] (Jerusalem, 1988), p. 11.
2. Many of the best-known general treatments of Jewish messianism available in English have focused on this dimension; for example, Abba Hillel Silver, *A History of Messianic Speculation in Israel* (New York, 1927), Joseph Sarachek, *The Doctrine of the Messiah in Medieval Jewish Literature* (New York, 1932), Joseph Klausner, *The Messianic Idea in Israel from Its Beginning to the Completion of the Mishnah* (New York, 1955), Gershom Scholem, *The Messianic Idea in Judaism* (New York, 1971). Collections of textual materials in English, such as Raphael Patai, *The Messiah Texts* (New York, 1979), also tend to focus on ideas rather than movements or personalities.
3. Some of these questions are discussed in the article by Eliezer Schweid below.

4. Important discussions of ideas in this context of actual movements include Israel Friedlaender's analysis of Abu Isa of Isfahan, Gershom Scholem's treatment of the Sabbatian movement, and the examinations of Gush Emunim and messianism in contemporary Israel.
5. See the article by Abraham Berger below, and cf. Moshe Idel, *The Mystical Experience in Abraham Abulafia* (New York, 1988), p. 3, and his introduction to Aescoly, p. 12. Unlike Berger, some scholars see in Abulafia's journey to Rome and attempt to meet with the Pope an aspect of his messianic self-conception; see Idel, "Abraham Abulafia and the Pope: An Account of an Abortive Mission," *AJSReview* 7–8 (1982–83) [Hebrew section], pp. 1–17.

   Not long after, there occurred what Yizhak Baer calls "The Messianic Movement of 1295," which "shook the Castilian Jewish communities to their very foundations." But although there was a prophetic figure who apparently announced that the Messiah would appear in 1295, reports of Jewish response to this are limited to an apostate's later, hostile, self-justifying account that is intended to demonstrate the naiveté of the Jews and the pathetic absurdity of their messianic hope. This is a slim foundation for speaking of a *messianic movement*. See Baer, *A History of the Jews in Christian Spain,* 2 vols. (Philadelphia, 1961), 1:277–81.
6. Cf. the discussion of the term at the beginning of R. J. Z. Werblowsky's essay below. Scholars have recently questioned whether the concept of Jewish messianism has been unduly restricted by insisting on the presence of the political historical dimension. See my *Decoding the Rabbis* (Cambridge, MA, 1980), pp. 112–20; Moshe Idel, "Patterns of Redemptive Activity in the Middle Ages," in *Messianism and Eschatology* [Heb.], ed. Zvi Baras (Jerusalem, 1983), pp. 254–63; Judah Liebes, "Sabbatian Messianism" [Heb.], *Pe'amim* 40 (1989), pp. 4–20; Idel, introduction to Aescoly (above, n. 1), pp. 12–14; and Taubes's article below. I have retained the more traditional, restrictive notion in order to keep the focus of the material in this book on history rather than spirituality.
7. For example, none of the evidence about the reforms in Toledo in 1281 indicates a messianic dimension; see Baer, *A History of the Jews in Christian Spain,* 1:257–61.
8. See, for example, Ephraim Kanarfogel, "The '*Aliyah* of 'Three Hundred Rabbis' in 1211: Tosafist Attitudes Toward Settling in the Land of Israel," *JQR* 76 (1986), pp. 191–215, and cf. Gerson D. Cohen on this subject, below. On the messianic motivations and expectation of later movements of *aliyah* see Joseph Hacker, "Links between Spanish Jewry and Palestine, 1391–1492," in *Vision and Conflict in the Holy Land,* ed. Richard I. Cohen (Jerusalem and New York, 1985), pp. 111–39; Benzion Dinur, *Historical Writings* [Heb.] 2 vols. (Jerusalem, 1955, 1975), 1:26–27, 75–78.
9. For example, the best historiographical accounts of the Hasmonean revolt of 168–165 B.C.E. provide no indication of any messianic dimension; see Jonathan A. Goldstein, *I Maccabees* (Garden City, NY, 1976), p. 241.

Werblowsky (below, p. 38), however, points out that the Book of Daniel indicates that at least some contemporaries saw messianic implications in the revolt; cf. Joseph Klausner, "Daniel," in *Messianism in the Talmudic Era,* ed. Leo Landman (New York, 1979), pp. 212–13. See our discussion of the Great Revolt against Rome (above, pp. 10–11).

10. General discussions of this phenomenon often distinguish between *millenarism* (a term derived from Christian eschatology and not appropriate for Jewish material) and *messianism* to express this difference. See Yonina Talmon, "Millenarism," in the *International Encyclopedia of Social Sciences* 10:353: "Millenarism usually involves messianism, but the two do not necessarily coincide. Expectation of a human-divine savior is not always accompanied by expectation of total and final redemption. Conversely, expectation of the millennium does not always involve the mediation of a messiah. Redemption is in certain cases brought about directly by the divine."
11. On the statement by R. Hillel, see Silver, *Messianic Speculation* (above, n. 2), pp. 13–14, and the interesting suggestion by Morton Smith below; cf. the philosophical reinterpretation in my *Decoding the Rabbis* (above, n. 6), pp. 110–11.
12. On the messianic tension in Lurianic Kabbalah see Gershom Scholem, *Sabbatai Ṣevi: The Mystical Messiah* (Princeton, 1973), esp. pp. 46–55, 67. Scholem's view of the inevitable messianic tension accompanying the spread of Lurianic Kabbalah has been recently challenged; see Moshe Idel, *Kabbalah: New Perspectives* (Yale, 1988), pp. 258–59.
13. See the articles by Uriel Tal and Menachem Kellner below.
14. See Joseph Heinemann, "The Messiah of Ephraim and the Premature Exodus of the Tribe of Ephraim," *HTR* 68 (1975), pp. 1–16; David Berger, "Three Typological Themes in Early Jewish Messianiam: Messiah Son of Joseph, Rabbinic Calculations, and the Figure of Armilus," *AJSReview* 10 (1985), pp. 141–64.
15. Note the article by H. G. Friedmann entitled "Pseudo-Messiahs" in *The Jewish Encyclopedia* 10:251–55. By contrast, the *Encyclopaedia Judaica* index volume (p. 703) reads "Pseudo-Messiahs, see Messianic Movements."
16. This phenomenon is demonstrated and explained by Gerson Cohen in his article below.
17. Sometimes such events produced intense speculation among Christians as well as Jews; see David Ruderman, "Hope Against Hope: Jewish and Christian Messianic Expectations in the Late Middle Ages," in *Exile and Diaspora: Studies in the History of the Jewish People Presented to Professor Haim Beinart,* ed. Aharon Mirsky, Avraham Grossman, Yosef Kaplan (Jerusalem, 1991), pp. 190–92.
18. Cf. Silver, *Messianic Speculation,* pp. 18, 19–20 (the view of Elazar ben Azariah, B. Sanh 99a).
19. See R. Hanina's statement in B. AZ 9b. On Crete see the treatment by Baron below; on Babylonia see Jacob Neusner, *A History of the Jews in Babylonia,*

5 vols. (Leiden, 1965–70), 5:65–68. In the latter case the messianic date coincided with severe persecutions by Yazdagird II.

20. See Silver, *Messianic Speculation,* pp. 243–59. To his discussion of astrology, add Ruderman (above, n. 17), pp. 188–90. Striking examples of Biblical exegesis, many based on the numerical equivalents of words *(gematria),* are found in Isaiah Tishby's article below.
21. This is the theory of deprivation, or relative deprivation (the gulf between expectations and the available means for their satisfaction) as a primary factor in messianism. See Talmon, "Millenarism" (above, n. 10), pp. 354–55; Norman Cohn, *The Pursuit of the Millennium,* 3rd ed. (Oxford, 1970), esp. pp. 53–61; Peter Worsley, *The Trumpet Shall Sound,* 2nd ed. (New York, 1968), p. 243; David Aberle, "A Note on Relative Deprivation Theory as Applied to Millenarian and Other Cult Movements," in *Millennial Dreams in Action,* ed. Sylvia Thrupp, (The Hague, 1962), pp. 209–214; Stephen Sharot, *Messianism, Mysticism, and Magic* (Chapel Hill, NC), pp. 241–44.
22. For a clear example of this principle, see Friedlaender's discussion of the Jewish messianic movements in the tumultuous Umayyad period below.
23. See Gershom Scholem, *Sabbatai Ṣevi: The Mystical Messiah* (Princeton, 1973), pp. 1–6 (below, pp. 289–94), 101–2. Cf. Talmon, "Millenarism" (above. n. 10), p. 357: the Sabbatian movement is "clear proof of the inadequacy of a reductionist interpretion."
24. Yehudah Liebes (above, n. 6) has recently argued that the essence of the Sabbatian ideology, as formulated by its leading figures, was not concerned with the traditional political-territorial redemption of the people but rather with the spiritual-mystical redemption of the Jewish faith (see esp. pp. 10–11). However, the appeal of Sabbatianism that made it a mass movement before the apostasy was indeed bound up with traditional Jewish messianic aspirations, as Liebes concedes (although he hesitates to call those Jews who were motivated merely by these elements true "Sabbatians").
25. Cf. Solomon Zeitlin, "The Origin of the Idea of the Messiah," in *Messianism in the Talmudic Era* (above, n. 9), pp. 102–4.
26. For a helpful recent review of these themes see Shemaryahu Talmon, "Biblical Visions of the Future Ideal Age," in *King, Cult and Calendar in Ancient Israel* (Jerusalem, 1986), pp. 140–64.
27. See Joseph Klausner, "The Source and Beginnings of the Messianic Idea," in *Messianism in the Talmudic Era,* pp. 15–18 (Moses), 31–33 (David). Despite the centrality of Moses in early Biblical history and his use as a proptotype of the Messiah ("the last redeemer would be like the first": Num. R. 11:2), it is striking that Jewish messianic speculation did not grant him any role in the eschatological scenario, as it did to Elijah; see Daniel Jeremy Silver, *Images of Moses* (New York, 1982), pp. 152–55.
28. For the power of the Exodus as redemptive paradigm, see Michael Walzer, *Exodus and Revolution* (New York, 1985); note his statement, "Messian-

ism comes late in Jewish history, and it comes, I think, by way of Exodus thinking" (p. 16).

29. For example, there seems to have been considerable speculation in the late fifteenth century that the Ottoman sultan was a messianic figure: see Charles Berlin, "A Sixteenth-Century Hebrew Chronicle of the Ottoman Empire," in *Studies in Jewish Bibliography, History and Literature in Honor of I. Edward Kiev*, ed. Berlin (New York, 1971), pp. 27–28; B. Netanyahu, *Don Isaac Abravanel* (Philadelphia, 1968), p. 323, n. 161); Tishby, below, n. 34. According to a contemporary Christian writer, some Jews viewed the French king Charles VIII, who led a dramatic invasion of Italy in 1494, as an eschatological figure: Amnon Linder, "L'expédition italienne de Charles VIII et les espérances messianiques des Juifs," *REJ* 137 (1978): pp. 179–86; Ruderman, "Hope Against Hope" (above, n. 17), pp. 191–92. Jewish *maskilim* thought of the Austrian emperor Joseph II in messianic terms; see David Biale, below, at n. 5.

30. What makes this atypical of "messianic movements" is that it was a call not to challenge the Gentile ruler but to act on instructions given by the ruler.

31. Later Jewish thinkers referred to this with a mixture of anger and irony; see Josephus, *Antiquities of the Jews,* Book 11, chap. 1, para. 3 ("many of them stayed in Babylon, not willing to leave their possessions"); Judah Halevi, *Kuzari* 2:24 ("the majority and the aristocracy remained in Babylon, preferring dependence and slavery, and unwilling to leave their houses and their affairs"). Their intuition is confirmed by archaeological evidence of Jewish prominence in Babylonian business transactions in the fifth century B.C.E.; see Michael Coogan, "Life in the Diaspora: Jews at Nippur in the Fifth Century B.C.," *Biblical Archaeologist* 37 (1974), pp. 6–12; John Hayes and J. M. Miller, eds., *Israelite and Judean History* (London, 1977), pp. 482–84.

32. The uprising of 522 B.C.E. against Persian rule in Judea may also be considered a messianic movement. Situated at a time of severe problems for the central authorities (rebellions all over the Persian empire), the "messianic" hope for a genuine restoration of Davidic sovereignty, focused on the figure of Zerubbabel, was articulated by the prophets Haggai and Zechariah. The results remain a mystery, except that nothing more is heard about Zerubbabel or any of his descendants from the Davidic line throughout the Persian period. The Persians probably suppressed this movement ruthlessly, a paradigm for the reaction of Gentile rulers to Jewish messianism. See John Bright, *A History of Israel* (Philadelphia, 1959), pp. 351–55; Hayes and Miller, *Israelite and Judean History,* p. 521.

33. For a fine collection of recent essays on this subject, see Jacob Neusner et al., eds., *Judaisms and Their Messiahs at the Turn of the Christian Era* (Cambridge, Eng., 1987).

34. Josephus, *Antiquities of the Jews,* Book 18, chap. 1, para. 1, Book 20, chap. 5, paras. 1–2 and chap. 8, para. 6; *The Jewish War,* Book 2, chap. 13, paras. 4–6. These are discussed in the essay by Richard Horsley, below, and

in John Hanson and Horsley, *Bandits, Prophets, and Messiahs: Popular Movements at the Time of Jesus* (Minneapolis/Chicago/New York, 1985).

35. *The Jewish War,* Book 6, chap. 5, para. 4. This passage has received considerable attention in the scholarly literature: see Louis Feldman, "Selective Critical Bibliography," in *Josephus, The Bible and History,* ed. Feldman and Cohei Hatu (Detroit, 1989), pp. 410–11, and Tessa Rajak, *Josephus: The Historian and His Society* (Philadelphia, 1984), pp. 192–93. On possible messianic elements accompanying the Great Revolt see Richard Horsley below; cf. Yisrael Levin, "Messianic Tendencies at the End of the Second Commonwealth" [Heb.], in *Messianism and Eschatology* (above, n. 6), pp. 138–39, 147–52, arguing that there is no evidence for any significant messianic component.
36. The literary sources are accessibly translated in Yigael Yadin's *Bar Kokhba* (New York, 1971), pp. 255–59: Yadin's book also presents the dramatic numismatic and epistolary discoveries. For a general review of the scholarly literature, see Benjamin Isaac and Aharon Oppenheimer, "The Revolt of Bar Kokhba: Ideology and Modern Scholarship," *Journal of Jewish Studies* 36 (1985), pp. 33–60; on the messianic dimension, see Oppenheimer, "The Messianism of Bar Kokhba" [Heb.], in *Messianism and Eschatology* (above, n. 6), pp. 153–65.
37. See the article by Joseph Heinemann in n. 14 above. The polyvalent attitudes toward Bar Kokhba in later Jewish writings have been treated by Richard Marks, "The Image of Bar Kokhba in Jewish Literature up to the Seventeenth Century: False Messiah and National Hero," Ph.D. Dissertation, UCLA, 1980.
38. See Nahum Glatzer, "The Attitude Toward Rome in Third-Century Judaism," in *Politische Ordnung und Menschliche Existenz,* ed. Alain Dempf (Munich, 1962), pp. 243–57.
39. Geo Widengren, "The Status of the Jews in the Sassanian Empire," *Iranica Antiqua* 1 (1961), p. 133, text cited in n. 2, and the discussion by Neusner, *A History of the Jews in Babylonia,* 4:32–34. On Julian's Jewish policy and possible Jewish responses, see Baron, *A Social and Religious History of the Jews,* 18 vols. (Philadelphia and New York, 1952–83), 2:160–61, 392; G. W. Bowersock, *Julian the Apostate* (London, 1978) pp. 88–90, 120–22; Jacob Neusner, *Midrash in Context* (Philadelphia, 1983), pp. 113–17 (and frequently elsewhere in his writings); Michael Avi-Yonah, *The Jews Under Roman and Byzantine Rule* (Jerusalem, 1984), pp. 185–207, esp. 193–98 on the Jewish reaction).
40. See the discussion by Baron in his first selection below.
41. This is reported by the Karaite historian Jacob al-Kirkisani; see Leon Nemoy, *Karaite Anthology* (New Haven, 1952), p. 51.
42. This is one of the purposes of Maimonides' *Epistle to Yemen;* see Abraham Halkin and David Hartman, *Crisis and Leadership* (Philadelphia, 1985), pp. 96 and 123–26. This text provides an important review of messianic movements in the twelfth century (pp. 127–30 and appertaining notes).

43. See Baron, second selection, below. In addition to the account by Benjamin (see *The Itinerary of Benjamin of Tudela* [New York, 1983], pp. 111–13), the other major source is by a hostile and contemptuous Jewish convert to Islam; see Jacob Marcus, *The Jew in the Medieval World* (New York, 1965), document 50, pp. 247–50.
44. See the recent discussion by Isaiah Tishby below. For other expressions of messianism in this period, see Netanyahu, *Don Isaac Abravanel* (above, n. 29), pp. 195–247; Yosef Yerushalmi, "Messianic Impulses in Joseph ha-Kohen," in *Jewish Thought in the Sixteenth Century,* ed. Bernard Cooperman (Cambridge, MA, 1983), pp. 460–87; Ira Robinson, "Messianic Prayer Vigils in Jerusalem in the Early Sixteenth Century," *JQR* n.s. 72 (1981–82), pp. 32–42; Isaiah Tishby, "The Controversy over the Zohar in Sixteenth-Century Italy" in *Studies in Kabbalah and its Branches* [Heb], (Jerusalem, 1982), pp. 102–6.
45. I know of no adequate monographic study in English of the events surrounding David Reubeni. Baron's discussion is, as always, a fine starting point (*A Social and Religious History of the Jews* 13:109–15). Reubeni's "Diary," actually a memoir written after the events, is accessible in English in Elkan Adler, *Jewish Travellers* (New York, 1931), pp. 251–328; the full text was published by A. Z. Aescoly, *The Story of David Reubeni* [Heb.] (Jerusalem, 1940), and see the fuller collection of sources in Aescoly, *Messianic Movements,* pp. 335–408. There is considerable material in Hebrew on the subject; see the bibliographical review in Azriel Shochat, "On The Matter of David Reubeni" [Heb], *Zion* 35 (1970), p. 96, n. 1.
46. Jacob Katz, "The Dispute between Jacob Berab and Levi ben Habib over Renewing Ordination" [Heb.], *Zion* 16 (1951), pp. 28–45; reprinted in Katz, *Halakhah and Kabbalah* [Heb.] (Jerusalem, 1985), pp. 213–37. An adapted version is available in English in *Binah,* vol. 1: "Studies in Jewish History," ed. Joseph Dan (New York, 1988), pp. 119–41, esp. 132–35.
47. See above, n. 12.
48. See Gershom Scholem, "The Neutralization of the Messianic Element in Early Hasidism," in *The Messianic Idea in Judaism,* pp. 176–202. Crucial to the dispute is the proper interpretation of the letter by the Baal Shem Tov to his brother-in-law Gershon of Kuty, cited extensively by Dinur; cf. Scholem, pp. 182–84. On this issue cf. also Isaiah Tishby, "The Messianic Idea and Messianic Trends in the Growth of Hasidism" [Heb.], *Zion* 32 (1967), pp. 1–45; Rivka Schatz Uffenheimer, *Quietistic Elements in Eighteenth Century Hasidic Thought* [Heb.] (Jerusalem, 1980), pp. 168–77.
49. On messianic activism among the Bratslaver Hasidim during the past generation, see Mendel Piekarz, "The Transition in the History of the Messianism of Bratslaver Hasidism" [Heb.], in *Messianism and Eschatology* (above, n. 6), pp. 325–42. I have not found an academic analysis of the messianic trends in contemporary Lubavitcher Hasidism, including the rumors that the current rebbe is conceived as a messianic figure.

50. On the attitudes toward messianic doctrine in the early Reform movement see David Philipson, *The Reform Movement in Judaism* (New York, 1931), pp. 173–80; W. Gunther Plaut, *The Rise of Reform Judaism* (New York, 1963), pp. 133–45; Steven Schwarzschild, "The Personal Messiah—Toward the Restoration of a Discarded Doctrine," *Judaism* 5 (1956), pp. 123–35; Michael Meyer, *Response to Modernity: A History of the Reform Movement in Judaism* (New York and Oxford, 1988), pp. 122, 137–38.
51. Sharot, *Messianism, Mysticism, and Magic,* p. 217, part of a chapter discussing "The Secularization of Millenarianism." Sharot questions the interpretation that Jewish socialists, including Marx, were motivated by a secularized form of traditional Jewish messianism (pp. 214–15). Cf. Irving Howe's formulation: the messianic fervor "would flame in the immigrant world, a blazing secular passion appearing first as socialism. . . . The Messiah would be replaced by the messianic principle, the grandiose solitary figure by a collective upheaval." *World of our Fathers* (New York and London, 1976), p. 223. And cf. Shlomo Na'aman, "Socialist Thought in the Tension between Emancipation and Messianism," in *Messianism and Eschatology* (above, n. 6), pp. 365–79.
52. See Jacob Katz's essay "Israel and the Messiah," below, and the sources in *The Zionist Idea,* ed. Arthur Hertzberg (New York, 1975), pp. 105–7, 111–14, 403–5.
53. This is the formulation of the prayer for the State of Israel incorporated into the liturgy of most orthodox congregations in Israel. It is also used in the most recent prayerbook of the American Conservative movement, *Sim Shalom.* On the authorship of this prayer see the beginning of Katz's article, and Barry L. Schwartz, "Praying for Israel: The Liturgical Imbroglio," *CCAR Journal* 38:3 (Summer 1991), pp. 43–45.
54. Joseph Brenner, "Self-Criticism," in *The Zionist Idea,* p. 310; Hayyim Hazaz, "The Sermon," in *Modern Hebrew Literature,* ed. Robert Alter, pp. 278–81. This charge of insincerity in the traditional messianic prayers was also a theme raised by spokesmen of the Reform Movement (though with a very different purpose); see Jacob Petuchowski, *Prayerbook Reform in Europe* (New York, 1968), p. 278; Paul Mendes-Flohr and Jehuda Reinharz, *The Jew in the Modern World* (New York and Oxford, 1980), p. 164. And note the trenchant comments of the Haskalah poet Judah Leib Gordon (*Iggerot* 1:172–74, cited Dan Miron, *Hayyim Hazaz* [Heb.] (Merhavia, 1959), pp. 195–96, and Michael Stanislawski, *For Whom Do I Toil: Judah Leib Gordon and the Crisis of Russian Jewry* (New York and Oxford, 1988), pp. 100–1. Actually, the accusation that many Jews did not really want to leave their homes for the eschatological ingathering in the land of Israel was made in traditional ethical literature; see, for example, Ephraim Luntschitz's attack on those Jews who live prosperously in the lands of the Gentiles and "never sincerely beseech God to bring them to their own land": *Keli Yaqar* on *Va-Yeḥi.* And cf. David Reubeni's report of an Italian Jew who tells him, "I have no desire in Jerusalem, but only in Siena" (*Jewish*

Travellers [above, n. 46], p. 281; and the popular contentment with diaspora life attributed to contemporary Jews by Abner of Burgos, cited by Yitzhak Baer (above, n. 5), 1:352.

55. B. Sanh 98b.
56. See, e.g., the idea expressed by Isaac ben Yedaiah in the thirteenth century that the intellectual elite among the Jews will not be benefited by the Messiah at all: Saperstein, *Decoding the Rabbis* (above, n. 6), pp. 109–11.
57. Moses ben Nahman (Nahmanides), *Writings and Discourses,* ed. Charles Chavel, 2 vols. (New York, 1978), 1:606–7, 672–73.
58. Subsequent statements of the view that Judaism can stand as an integral whole without the hope for the coming of the messiah were made by Isaac Polgar, *'Ezer ha-Dat,* chap. 6 (Jerusalem, 1984), p. 57, and Saul Levi Morteira in his manuscript sermons (material that I hope to discuss in a separate publication). Writers such as Nahmanides, Polgar, and Morteira certainly did not question the coming of the Messiah, but were contrasting the function of the messianic doctrine in Judaism and in Christianity. This provides a background for the position of Lazarus Bendavid cited by Jacob Katz in "Israel and the Messiah," below, which was not quite as much of an innovation as Katz implies. There is also evidence of Jews who doubted the future coming of the Messiah yet remained Jews. See the view of Ḥayyim Galipappa discussed by Joseph Albo, *Sefer ha-Iqqarim,* ed. Isaac Husik (Philadelphia, 1946), Book 4, chapter 42 (vol. 4, pt. 2, p. 418).
59. For a recent provocative yet overly extreme and polemical assessment of messianism as a negative, idolatrous force in Jewish history, see Lionel Kochan, *Jews, Idols and Messiahs* (Oxford, Eng. and Cambridge, MA, 1990), pp. 160–91.
60. S. D. Goitein, *A Mediterranean Society,* 5 vols. (Berkeley/Los Angeles/London, 1967–1988).
61. See Steven Sharot, *Messianism, Mysticism, and Magic: A Sociological Analysis of Jewish Religious Movements* (Chapel Hill, 1982), pp. 73–75.
62. Isaiah Tishby, *Meshiḥiyut be-Dor Gerushei Sefarad u-Portugal* (Jerusalem, 1985).
63. For some examples in English, see Yosef Hayim Yerushalmi, *From Spanish Court to Italian Ghetto* (New York and London, 1971), chap. 7 and esp. pp. 340–41; Bernard Weinryb, *The Jews of Poland* (Philadelphia, 1973), chap. 10 and esp. pp. 225–28; Moshe Idel, *Kabbalah: New Perspectives* (New Haven and London, 1988), pp. 257–59; and see the essay by David Biale included below.
64. Much of Dinur's article was translated for inclusion in *Essential Papers on Hasidism,* ed. Gershon Hundert (New York, 1991), pp. 86–208. The present selection complements that offering.
65. Arie Morgenstern, *Meshiḥiyut ve-Yishuv Erets Yisrael* (Jerusalem, 1985).

I

OVERVIEWS

1

Messianism In Jewish History

R. J. Zwi Werblowsky

The least that can reasonably be asked of a writer on messianic ideas and messianic movements in Jewish history is to provide an adequate definition of the term "messianism" whose history is to be described. Alas, it is easier to give an account of the historical developments than to define the term itself, which seems to mean all things to all men—or at least, to all theologians. In fact, messianism is often said to be an essential and characteristic feature of Judaism from which it was then transmitted also to other religions and civilizations.

No doubt the word derives etymologically from Hebrew and semantically from Jewish tradition, and the term indicates that in the course of Jewish history there arose a complex of ideas and expectations and an attitude to the time-process and to the future which borrowed their name from the politico-religious and cultic-national vocabulary of Israelite Kingship. The Hebrew noun *mashiaḥ* (messiahs), from the verb *mashaḥ* "to anoint", means "the anointed one" in general and (in later Judaism) "the anointed one" in particular, i.e. the ultimate redeemer, the expected king of the Davidic line who would deliver Israel from foreign bondage and restore the glories of its Golden Age. In Biblical Hebrew the adjective or noun *mashiaḥ* is used of material objects as well as of consecrated persons, such as High Priests and Kings. The latter would also be described as "the Lord's anointed", the title expressing the charismatic character and divine sanction of their office as well as the inviolability of their status. In exilic and post-exilic usage, the term

Reprinted by permission of UNESCO from *Journal of World History* 11 (1968).

"anointed" could denote anyone with a special mission from God—prophets, patriarchs, and even a gentile king like Cyrus the Mede (Isaiah 45:1). The Old Testament does not speak of an eschatological messiah and we look in vain for even traces of messianism in many books of the Bible, including the Pentateuch. Even the "messianic" passages containing prophecies of a future Golden Age under an ideal king do not use this word as a technical term.

Nevertheless, beliefs and ideas that could later be subsumed under the heading "messianism" were gradually taking shape under the stresses and disillusionments of Israelite history. No doubt the tribes that crossed the Jordan with Joshua and conquered the Land of Canaan had neither cause nor use for messianic beliefs. They were, after all, the generation not to whom a promise was given but in whom the promise to the Patriarchs was being fulfilled. This fulfillment reached its apogee in the King of Victory, David, and the King of Peace, Solomon, and in retrospect this double reign appeared surrounded by a halo of divine blessing and invested with the significance of a "normative" and ideal paradigm of history consummated. It is difficult to imagine the champion of pure theocracy and author of the violently anti-monarchic diatribe found in I Samuel 8 waxing enthusiastic over the idea of a messianic king. Evidently the growth of the messianic idea presupposes the establishment of an Israelite kingship ideology, and the expectation of a divinely operated tide in the affairs of Israel did not grow out of nothing. It seems to have crystallized round certain ideas drawn from the ancient Near-Eastern mythologies. Reading the biblical books and particularly the Book of Psalms, we cannot fail to detect mythological overtones, echoing archaic notions of creation as a victorious divine battle against the forces and monsters of chaos, and of the cyclical renewal of nature as a re-enactment or reaffirmation of this archetypal event. This old mythology contains an element of genuine universalism, since it is concerned with creation, i.e. with the world as such, but it was transformed in the context of the Israelite theology of covenant and election. Even as God had smitten the heads of Leviathan on the waters, so also will he (represented by the tokens of his presence: the Ark of the Convenant, and his anointed King, the present and "pre-eschatological" Messiah) smite the historical representatives of evil, death and destruction. But whereas the pattern of nature is cyclical and that of early Israelite history, as told in Joshua and Judges, was repetitive (idolatry-tribulation-repentance-relief), later history became oppressively monotonous and unrhythmical. The present was unmitigated oppression and rule of wickedness. Slowly but thoroughly the significant features of the cyclical pattern were transferred to the linear, once-for-all dimension of history. There had been one cosmic victory in the beginning. What mattered now was not the annual repetition of this event but the day of the Lord, that is, the final victory at the end of history. The establishment of the Israelite kingship ideology and its interpretation as part of God's eternal convenant with His people are reflected in the accounts given in the historical and prophetic books of the Old Testament and in the Psalms. As actual reality and the careers of the historical kings proved more and more disappointing, the messianic kingship ideology was projected on the future. With the declining national fortunes of Israel, the notion developed of an eschatological change for the better. The greater the contrast between the unsatisfactory present and the imagined future, the more thoroughly utopian the quality of this future. Whilst much of the early Biblical eschatology (and especially that drawing on the historical books with their idealized view of the reigns of David and Solomon) is restorative, looking forward to better times, that is, to a restoration of the good old times in a relatively near, or at least historically accessible future, other trends—partly influenced by the more radical and universalist style of prophetic hyperbole—were more utopian in outlook (e.g. Isaiah 2). The expected future was not merely better; it was totally and absolutely different. It not only restored an original happy state but was to bring about something that was completely and fundamentally new. In some forms of apocalyptic eschatology the expected change was not an event *in* history, but something *outside* history.

But whether in history or outside it, fully developed messianism represents a decisive transformation of the notion of time. For time and the time process are now held to be directed to a final event or consummation. This *eschaton* is not necessarily the fulfillment and achievement of the forces and dynamisms at work *in* the process of history (as e.g. according to the messianic version of the modern evolutionist view that history is progress); it may also be conceived as the final victory *over* history, a victory that abolishes a history which is essentially negative. But either way, there is a directedness in the time process and a peculiar tension which is expected to find its discharge in the decisive consummating event. Hence the adjective "messianic" has been applied, with greater or lesser justification, to various types of nativistic, utopian, millenarian (chiliast) and apocalyptic ideologies and movements. Marxism, too, as is well known, has frequently been described as "messianic" because of the eschatological structure of its doctrine.

For the student of Jewish history the problem of messianic movements is historical rather than purely phenomenonological, i.e. the question is not so much one of deciding whether or not a certain movement deserves the epithet "messianic", but rather one of describing the continuity of messianic belief and expectation as it manifested itself in the events and crises of Jewish history.

Whilst the Old Testament period laid the foundations of Jewish messianism, the last two centuries of the Second Temple Period bear witness to a variety of established or emerging messianic beliefs and to an active messianic ferment. The developments that brought this about are, in part, still obscure. We do not know enough about the extent, nature and impact of the disillusionment that followed the very partial and inadequate fulfillment of the high-pitched hopes focussed on the return to Zion of the Babylonian exiles (see Deutero-Isaiah). A similar contrast and tension between sanguine expectation and sobering reality must have characterized the period following upon the successful Maccabean revolt, 165 B.C. The analysis of modern "messianic" movements (nativistic, millenarian, revitalization, cargo cults, etc.) in primitive societies suggests that these are to a large extent connected with the stresses and tensions of an acculturative situation. Perhaps Jewish history at the end of the Second Temple Period has not been sufficiently studied from the point of view of the acculturative crisis as a decisive factor in the wider situation of foreign (i.e. Roman) domination. At any rate, there is evidence of the proliferation of both messianic beliefs and messianic movements, as well as of an increasingly "messianic" character of the various national risings, though as regards the latter our sources are not clear and explicit enough. It is easier to describe the history of messianic ideas as they evolve in the several sects and circles whose theological literature has by chance been preserved, than to gauge the messianic character of e.g. an uprising or a revolt of which we only know the date or the name of its leader, or a few other incidental details. Thus, the Maccabean insurrection against the Seleucid policy of enforced Hellenization seems, on the evidence of the Book of Daniel, to have had messianic overtones, though it can hardly be described as a fully messianic movement. Messianic ideologies and acutely eschatological movements proliferated after the Hasmonean period, and several main types emerged. At times, alternative or even mutually exclusive ideas and beliefs existed side by side, without anyone apparently bothering to arrange them in a logical and coherent system. This was attempted only later by the medieval theologians desirous of harmonizing all ancient, and hence venerable and authoritative, texts and traditions with some degree of consistency. Ideas and hopes were current about a glorious national restoration under a victorious military leader, or through a miraculous intervention from above. The ideal redeemer would be a king—the Lord's anointed—from the line of David, or a Heavenly Being referred to as "Son of Man". Redemption could thus mean a better and more peaceful world, or the utter end and annihilation of "this age" and the ushering in, amid catastrophe and judgement, of a new era, and of "a new Heaven and a new Earth." As a matter of fact, this catastrophic element remained an essential feature of the dialectic of messianic utopia: ultimate salvation was accompanied, or preceded by destruction and by the terrors of the "birth pangs" of the messianic age. In fact, this catastrophic aspect became so much part and parcel of the messianic complex that in later periods, the occurrence of particularly cruel persecution and suffering was frequently regarded as heralding the messianic redemption. This was not merely wishful thinking, a defence mechanism to make suffering bearable, but an application to concrete historical situations of one of the traditional dialectical patterns of messianic belief. The terrors of these pre-eschatological birth pangs were taken so seriously that more than one Talmudic rabbi would affirm his traditional hope in the advent of the Messiah with the qualifying rider: "Let Him come, but I do not want to witness it."

The chaotic welter of these ideas is visible not only in the apocryphal books of the Bible but also in the New Testament writings, and particularly in their accounts of the diverse attitudes towards Jesus adopted by his disciples and by the various groups in Jerusalem. The ministry of Jesus has to be seen in the context of a messianic complex that included such ideas as the coming of Elijah, the Son of David, the Son of Man, deliverance from the yoke of the Gentiles, and the ushering in of a new age. It was a period that saw the activity of many messianic leaders, as we learn from Josephus and from Acts 5:35–37. The original biblical tradition of thinking about the future in social, collective and historical terms was now further complicated by the emergence (or absorption) of new patterns of thought. The increasing preoccupation with the destiny of the individual together with the demand for a satisfactory account of the ways of divine justice in meting out reward and punishment produced the notion of the resurrection of the dead. (This Pharisaic doctrine was also affirmed by Jesus as against the Sadducees who rejected it). There also was the notion of an immortal soul that would go to its heavenly reward (or alternatively eternal punishment), after its departure from the body. The tension between these incompatible traditions, and more particularly between the spirituality of the doctrine of immortality and the materiality of the doctrine of resurrection, is well expressed by the compromise solution, also found in Paul, according to which the soul ultimately returned to a spiritual or "glorified" body. These ideas are relevant here because it is important to emphasize that the doctrine of immortality (as many mystery-cults and religions of salvation attest) lifts individual eschatology out of the historical messianic context. The course of history as such becomes irrelevant to the fate and destiny of the individual. In the later development of Judaism the tension between the two tendencies remains discernible and it seems that historic sense and messianic fervour are related in inverse ratio to the strength of the philosophical or mystical preoccupation with the fate and progress of the spiritual soul.

We have thus at least three strands making up the thread of eschatology: the "messianic" era of national restoration, and possibly of universal peace; the new *aion* of God's kingdom, including the resurrection of the dead; and the celestial hereafter in which the soul eternally enjoys the blessed vision. But even the first two varieties leave scope for further varieties and subdivisions. It goes without saying that the eschatology of the new *aion* is more radically utopian than the expectation of a future that knows no new heaven and new earth but rather a peaceful dwelling, on this earth, of every man under his vine and under his fig tree (Micah 4:4). Also the nature and function of the messianic personality that is at the centre of the decisive changes is conceived differently in the different trends. The messiah may be the presiding figure in what is essentially a messianic situation without being its main cause or agent. This would seem to be the Pharisaic and Rabbinic view of the matter, and one which is clearly indebted to at least one major strand in Biblical literature: a

Davidic king rules over the House of Israel, and his rule is the tangible symbol of the restoration of the Golden Age. There is nothing to indicate that he, or his actions, military or otherwise, would bring about the desired new dispensation. Even for Jeremiah the glorious future is simply a matter of Israel's faithfulness to God's Law for "if ye do this thing indeed, then shall there enter in by the gates of this town, Kings sitting upon the throne of David, riding in chariots and on horses, he and his servants and his people" (Jeremiah 22:4). On the other hand, the personality of the messiah may be more central, its character and function more clearly outlined and—consequently—a stronger personal bond to it on the part of the believers may be deemed to be essential. The small Jewish messianic sect composed of the disciples and followers of Jesus of Nazareth is a case in point. Considerable light has been thrown on the kaleidoscopic variety of Jewish messianic beliefs during the end of the Second Temple Period by the discovery in the Judaean Desert of the library of the congregation of the New Covenant (also known as the "Dead Sea Sect"). The sect is remarkable among other things for envisaging a future presided over by two anointed heads: a Davidic king and (superior to him) a messianic High Priest of the House of Aaron. It seems obvious that here the messianic pair functions as a sign and symbol of the perfect social order—as envisaged already in the prophecy of Zechariah concerning Zerubbabel and the High Priest Joshua—rather than as bringing about this order by their messianic ministry.

The reference to the Qumran Covenanters may serve to turn our attention to yet another point of interest for the sociology of messianic sects. Biblical eschatology was a collective, ethnic-national affair, since the nation (or its faithful remnant) was the bearer of the religious calling and promise. Membership in the messianic community is ascriptive: "and Thy people shall all be righteous: they shall inherit the land for ever, the branch of My planting, the work of My hand, that I may be glorified" (Isaiah 60:21)). On the other hand, membership in the congregation of the New Convenant of the Qumran Sect is elective rather than ascriptive or, to be more exact, elective-charismatic in an ascriptive framework: the chosen ones are the Children of Light from the House of Israel. This elective conception completely ousted the ascriptive one in the development of the Christian church.

The messianic beliefs affirmed and cultivated by Pharisaic and later Rabbinic Judaism (or "normative" Judaism, as it is frequently called) thus emphasized the more restorative ethnic-national and historical elements. Evidently, after the destruction of the Temple, the Ingathering of the Exiles and the rebuilding of the Temple were added to the messianic programme of an ideal future. Nevertheless, a strong apocalyptic current continued to flow and to crystallize in eschatological legends and prophecies describing the sufferings preceding the messianic advent, the War of Gog and Magog, the wreaking of vengeance on the gentiles, and the building of the New Jerusalem. Many of the Jewish patriots who participated in the great revolt against Rome in A.D. 66–70 surely believed themselves to be fighting in the eschatological battle that would be followed by the reign of the messiah. Both the revolt of 115–117 and the uprising led by Bar Kokhba, 132–135, were probably influenced by messianic hopes and speculations. Whether Bar Kokhba himself entertained any messianic pretensions is doubtful, though Rabbi Akiba, one of the leading rabbinic masters of the age, considered him as such and applied to him the prophecy (Numbers 24:17): "There shall come a star out of Jacob and a sceptre shall rise out of Israel". The messianic character of the revolt seems, however, to be confirmed by an interesting development in Jewish eschatology that took place after the death of Bar Kokhba. There arose the concept of a second messianic figure, the Warrior Messiah of the House of Joseph (or Ephraim), who would precede the triumphant Messiah of the House of David but would fall in the battle against Gog and Magog. It should be noted that this Messiah of the House of Joseph is not a suffering messiah; he is a warrior-martyr. To the extent that a ministry of suffering is mentioned in Jewish apocalyptic texts or legends, it is ascribed to the Messiah of the House of David during his hidden period, i.e. before he manifests himself in triumphant glory. Referring to the aforementioned two sides of Jewish apocalypse—catastrophe and messianic triumph—the Messiah of the House of Joseph may perhaps be said to represent the catastrophic aspect of the expected redemption. In many apocalyptic texts, which later became part and parcel of the popular messianic belief among the Jewish masses and even among the learned, this catastrophic stage included wars, plagues, famine and other social and cosmic upheavals, such as licence, heresy, a general defection from God's law, earthquakes, hailstorms, etc. The important point about most of these mythological notions is that they assume a radical discontinuity between our present age and the messianic reign. There is no smooth transition from the one to the other but rather a violent break marked by violent upheavals and catastrophes, after which, behold, all things shall be made new, or at least very different.

As the above brief sketch has indicated, by the time the Jewish people embarked on its long and gruelling history as a people in exile, dispersed, humiliated, despised and often physically threatened and persecuted, it was already equipped with messianic beliefs and hopes that were too axiomatic to be questioned. No matter what the details of the historic genesis of the messianic idea might be, and no matter what emphasis would be placed by different thinkers at different periods on the various aspects of this idea (physical-political or more spiritualized; popular-mythological or philosophical-rationalist; restorative or utopian; national or more universalist; catastrophic or more gradual; focussed upon a personal messiah or upon a messianic era, etc.) the messianic dimension was a permanent and ever-present feature, at times latent, at times manifest, of Jewish history. Whilst the messianic quality of certain movements and insurrections in the Second Temple Period and immediately afterwards may still leave room for discussion and for correction in matters of detail, subsequent history is much more unequivocal in this respect. The messianic idea had been firmly established both on the popular, and on the more theological level. The unending experience of oppression and humiliation, persecution and bondage, far from leading to disintegration and despair, kept the messianic orientation alive and gave to eschatological hope as well as to actual movements of liberation, revolt, social protest and religious revival, a fixed, dogmatic point of reference. There is thus a close connection between the generally accepted and practically axiomatic messianic belief on the one hand and messianic movements on the other. No doubt the existence of the former by itself was not sufficient to precipitate social movements, but it certainly provided a permanent potential and a latent structure within which historic dynamisms, revivals and responses to particular situations could take shape and articulate themselves. In their turn many of these messianic revivals had significant repercussions on messianic ideology, often by way of stimulating a restatement of belief that would safeguard orthodoxy and the institutions of society against the inevitable disillusionment and consequent despair, as well as against the heretical and antinomian dangers inherent in any messianic explosion. At other times the relationship would be less apologetic, and in the course of the development of a messianic movement the concomitant theology would change and adjust to the facts and pressures of the historical situation. Among the dangers of potential heresy that were felt to be inherent in actual messianism, there is one that in a Jewish context is particularly significant. Antinomianism is a feature that is well known in many movements of redemption and salvation, but in an historical tradition based on obedience and fidelity to a divine law conceived as a supreme expression and vehicle of the relationship of the people to its God, its critical significance is even greater. Certain ancient Rabbinic utterances (e.g. the statement that in the messianic era all ritual prohibitions would be suspended, or references to the "Halakhah [the law] of the messianic age") seemed to harbour explosive charges and to invite dangerous speculations. There was an inner logic to these antinomian potentialities. After all, the "yoke" of the law, whilst beloved, light and sweet on the conscious level, undoubtedly represented on the unconscious level the symbol of a life circumscribed and limited on all sides. It thus functioned as the internal counterpart (both from the point of view of individual experience, and in the social life and organization of the Jewish communities) of the outer limitations and restrictions imposed by life in exile and by subjection to a hostile, gentile environment. If the messianic advent meant freedom, shaking off the yoke, and the making of all things new and different, then it is not surprising that the possibility of untramelled, antinomian freedom should also manifest itself now and then.

One other point deserves to be mentioned at this juncture. Jewish messianism, for the greater part of its history, retained its national, social and historical basis whatever the universalist, cosmic, or inner and spiritual meanings accompanying it. One may, perhaps, speak of a spiritual deepening of the messianic idea in the history of Jewish religious thought, but these allegedly more "spiritual" elements never replaced the concrete, historical messianism; they were merely added to it. Jewish apologists tended to view Christian accusations of a "carnal" understanding of messianic deliverance as a compliment. To them it seemed that a certain type of spirituality was merely an escape into a realm where one was safe from the challenges of historical reality whose tests one evaded. "Humankind cannot bear very much reality", and hence it tries to evade the crucial tests. If messianic redemption has a spiritual dimension, then according to the Jewish theologians and mystics it must be the inner side of a process that manifests itself essentially in the outer sphere of historical facts.

The corollaries of this are obvious. Messianic movements are by definition doomed to failure in the historical sphere. If they wish to remain messianic, they either have to relinquish the historical sphere or to spiritualize themselves, or else to admit failure and to postpone the hope for consummation to a more successful future. The vitality and reality of the messianic idea among the Jews is attested by the fact that messianic outbreaks, revivals and movements were an almost permanent feature of their history. Most of these movements were limited in time and space; very few of them embraced the whole Jewish people or left a prolonged and noticeable aftermath. As a rule what happened was this: somewhere a prophet, a precursor, or a messianic pretender would raise, proclaim that the end of days or the redemption of Israel was at hand, and launch a movement limited to a smaller or larger area. In the usual course of things, none, or few of the initial promises could be fulfilled. Reports at first eagerly believed turned out to be untrue, the messiah disappeared or was killed, and the movement petered out. But for an occasional temporary chronicler or letter-writer, not even an echo of many of these movements would have reached us, and it is more than probable that there were many such movements which left no trace at all and are unknown to the modern historian. There is no need here to give a catalogue of messianic movements, or of the names of messianic pretenders and prophets, or of the many messianic revivals in Jewish history that testify to acute or latent millenarian expectations and longing. Many of these movements did not result in actual eschatological outbreaks though they bear eloquent witnesses of the existence of a messianic ferment. Lists of these names and movements can be found in any Jewish encyclopaedia or work on Jewish history. Nevertheless, a word seems to be in order here on the significance of these "pseudo-messianic" movements, for they are the tragic and moving witnesses of the powerful sway of messianic hope and belief over the Jewish people throughout their historic existence. As the philosopher Franz Rosenzweig once put it: belief in the advent of the messiah would be no more than an empty phrase if false messiahs did not constantly arise in whom this belief might assume reality and shape. The false messiah exists as long as does the genuine hope in the true messiah, and he divides every generation in which he appears into two camps: those who have the power of faith to believe and hence to err, and those who have the power of hope not to err but rather continue to endure until the advent of the true redeemer. The former were perhaps the better Jews, the latter were the stronger Jews. Of course, messianic movements are not to be accounted for solely in terms of messianic doctrines, eschatological beliefs and traditional hopes. Whilst facts require ideas and social symbolism before they can assume cultural shape and historical reality, it is no less true that beliefs and doctrines require a specific constellation of facts in order to pass from potentiality to actuality. The historian, faced with the aforementioned catalogue of messianic movements, will therefore always ask what factors precipitated a messianic outbreak at a certain place and at a certain time. He will want to know in what circles the movement originated, in what groups it spread, and who were its spokesmen and propagators as well as opponents. He may, to give just one random example, wonder why several pseudo-messiahs appeared in the 11th and 12th centuries in Western Europe, and particularly in Spain, or why Persia proved during a certain period such a fertile hotbed of messianic sectarianism—from Abu Issa al-Isfahani and his disciple Yudghan in the 8th century, to David Alroy in the 12th. Abu Issa, who proclaimed himself the Messiah of the House of Joseph, duly fell in a futile battle against the Abassid forces against which he marched with his ten thousand followers, while David Alroy—known to many from Disraeli's fanciful novel—staged a revolt against the sultan. Sabbetai Ṣevi (see below), on the other hand, fought only with the mystical-magical weapons of the Kabbalah. Social tensions, class distinctions, the common fate of all Jews as a despised and persecuted minority in a hostile environment, sharing the same culture, all these played their role and would have to be examined for each messianic movement individually.

To do justice, however, to the strength of messianic dynamism in Jewish history one has to take into account not only the acute messianic outbreaks centered on the figure of a messianic prophet, pretender or precursor, but—as has been hinted above—also the many movements that were less obviously and blatantly millenarian but whose inspiration and strength derived from messianic sources. Thus, the phenomenon of smaller or larger groups of Jews leaving their countries of origin in the Diaspora to settle in the Holy Land was not infrequent. Of course, one can settle in the Holy Land in order to live, to pray and to die there, without any messianic overtones. But in point of fact many of these movements were inspired by messianic motives, though not necessarily by the belief that the messiah had appeared and was calling his followers to leave the lands of exile and move to the Promised Land. Very often the motivation was "pre-eschatological" and seemed to assume that a life of prayer and ascetic sanctification in the Holy Land would hasten the advent of the messiah. This notion of actively hastening the advent of the messiah is of considerable interest and seems to point to a curious tension in the Jewish soul as it reacted to the experience of exile. An ancient Rabbinic source comments on the Song of Songs 2:7: "I charge you, O ye daughters of Jerusalem, by the roes and by the hinds of the field, that ye stir not up nor awake my love till it please", by saying: "Four charges are contained in this verse: Israel should not revolt against the kingdoms of this world; they should not force the end; they should not divulge their mystery to the nations of the world; and they should not go up [to Eretz Israel] in a great mass". Whatever the historical experience that led to this unequivocal rejection of all messianic activism, the temptation was evidently there and had to be guarded against. The only activism that was admitted was of a spiritual kind. In the words of the Talmud, if Israel would do penitence for one day only, they would immediately be redeemed, as it is written (Psalms 95:7): "Today if ye will hear His voice". Spiritual activism, when all realistic and practical outlets are closed, easily turns into magical activism, and Jewish legend knows of kabbalist masters who decided to force the messianic advent by means of extreme mortifications, special meditations and kabbalistic incantations. These legends, the best known of which is that concerning Rabbi Joseph della Reyna, usually end with the kabbalist adept falling a prey to the daemonic powers which he had meant to vanquish.

The appearance of such legends in the late mediaeval kabbalist context is no accident, for kabbalism is an essentially activist, viz. "theurgic" type of mysticism. In the form that it assumed in Galilee in the 16th century under the influence of the kabbalist Rabbi Isaac Luria, it interpreted exile and redemption in terms of a cosmic—or rather divine—drama, in which God himself was involved. According to this strangely "gnostic" myth, a primordial catastrophe or "fall" occurred as the divine light-essence externalized itself with a view to creating the world, and divine sparks fell into chaos. These sparks of divine life, imprisoned and "exiled" in chaos, sustain the life of the daemonic realm. Israel's exile and suffering merely reflect on the external, historical and material level, the more fundamental mystery of God's exile and suffering. Redemption means the liberation of the divine sparks from the defiling embrace of the daemonic powers, no less than the liberation of Israel from its subjection to the gentiles. Indeed, the latter process would follow as a natural consequence from the former, which it was Israel's true and mystical calling to bring about by a life of piety and holiness. This is spiritual activism at its most extreme, for here God has become a real *salvator salvandus*. But to the Jew, Israel's exile became meaningful because it was seen as a participation in the profounder exile of God, and God Himself required Israel's active participation in the redemption of Himself and His people. It is not surprising that in this kabbalistic system the personality of the messiah played a relatively minor role. He was not so much a redeemer as a sign and symbol that the redemptive process had been achieved. In fact, the messianic doctrine of Lurianic Kabbalah comes close to the structure of an evolutionist scheme.

This kabbalistic system provides the background of one of the most remarkable messianic episodes in the course of Jewish history. In spite of its uniqueness it is, however, sufficiently representative of the various forces at work in Jewish history and of the interaction of external and internal factors to deserve a brief account here. I am referring, of course, to the messianic movement that grew up around the person of Sabbetai Ṣevi of Smyrna.

With the expulsion of the Jews towards the end of the 15th century first from Spain and then from Portugal, a new phase had begun in Jewish history. The magnitude of the sufferings seemed to indicate the birth pangs of the messianic age as foretold by tradition. False messiahs arose and disappeared but still salvation tarried, and new and greater sufferings followed instead, reaching their climax in the Chmelnitski massacres. Tens of thousands of Jews perished in these massacres between 1648 and 1658 in Poland and Lithuania, which represented a peak of Jewish suffering unparalleled until the 20th century. But now at least every single Jew knew without any doubt that the messiah was coming, for he had to come. The Kabbalah flourished at this period and within a short time gained complete control of Jewish thought and piety mainly because of its strongly eschatological orientation. The kabbalists focussed all their religious fervour and asceticism, their power of prayer and meditation, on the imminent redemption. It was, indeed, from the circle of kabbalists that the messiah did come. The beautiful and fascinating youth from Smyrna soon succeeded in bewitching a group of friends and (after some initial difficulties and even, like Mohammed, flight from home) finding rich adherents. Soon he also had his prophets. It was not long before Sabbetai was venerated as "our Lord and King", and homage was paid to him from Cairo to Hamburg, from Salonika to Amsterdam. With very few exceptions, the sceptics kept their doubts to themselves and no longer dared to speak out. When things seemed to the Sultan to be going somewhat too far he had Sabbetai imprisoned, yet the belief in the messiah went on growing. After all, everyone knew that the Messiah must suffer for a time before revealing himself with miracles in all his power and glory. Sabbetai lived like a king in captivity, receiving embassies and assigning the provinces of his future kingdom to his relatives and friends, until the Sultan summoned him and gave him the choice between death and Islam. From the Palace, a short time afterwards, there emerged no longer the Rabbi Sabbetai Ṣevi but Mehemet Effendi. Later, as he continued to make trouble, Sabbetai was exiled to Albania where he died alone in 1676.

Now only did the well-nigh incredible happen: betrayed and disillusioned, Jews had once more to choose. Many of them who had believed, and indeed believed not only with an easy faith without works, but selling or flinging aside their property and chattels to go and meet the messiah, now recognized with a heavy heart that history had once more given its verdict. There was no change in the world and no salvation; they had to go on waiting. But not all were prepared to submit themselves to the verdict of history. They had experienced salvation themselves; they had felt the thrill of renewal and change within their hearts. The inward experience was too powerful, it could not be annulled or invalidated even by history. In this way there arose a Sabbatian heresy and a Sabbatian theology which finally led out of Judaism and vanished, at least as far as the Jewish people is concerned. It would lead us too far to pursue further the extremely complex and psychologically fascinating development of the Sabbatian sect. Of more immediate interest to our present analysis of messianism is the analogy in certain respects with Christianity. Since history proved a disappointment there grew up a theology and a paradoxical mystical belief which turned the rational stumbling block into its very corner stone. Both Christianity and Sabbatian theology owe part of their emotional appeal to their very paradoxicality. Because the messiah had abdicated so unexpectedly there arose the belief in his resurrection and return and—in later Sabbatianism—also in his reincarnation. Since salvation was not manifest to those who saw with eyes of flesh, a distinction was made between an unvisible redemption, accessible only to the eye of faith, and the final consummation, in which all things would become manifest and the redemption, wrought by the messiah, would clearly be visible to all. Because the messiah had ended his earthly career in disgrace, a theology evolved which explained how this disgrace actually represented the climax of his messianic ministry. One of the main differences between the Christian and Sabbatian theologies is the nature of the messianic paradox. In the case of Jesus of Nazareth it takes on a form that might be called metaphysical. Jesus accepts the disgrace of death for the sake of redemption. For Sabbatianism the paradox is of a more moral kind. Sabbetai accepts worse than death, namely the disgrace of sin, and of the worst sin at that, apostacy. Sabbatians believed that the process of salvation had begun in the inner, spiritual layers of the cosmos, but that our visible, tangible and material world would finally be caught up, too, in this process. Then salvation would be visibly manifest and complete. This theology was the way, perhaps the heroic way, of escape for those who maintained the overriding validity of their inward experience over and against what seemed to be the judgement of external history. But Israel as a whole reacted in the old and well-tried way. The world was not changed and hence Sabbetai Ṣevi was an imposter like all his predecessors. Since then, "auto-messianism", as Martin Buber has called it, declined steadily. A few more minor convulsions in the wake of the Sabbatian movement and personal messianism ceased to be a real possibility and thus a real danger. The spiritual revival movement in 18th-century Polish and Ukrainian Jewry, known as Hassidism, seems to have brought about, at least to some extent, a neutralization of the explosive possibilities of utopian and apocalyptic messianism by teaching a way of redemption through mystical inwardness. Whilst Hassidism may therefore be said to have provided an answer to the challenge of the Sabbatian aftermath in traditional religious terms, other and more modern versions were slowly coming to be enunciated by a European Jewry that was seeking and gradually finding its way to religious liberal reform and civil emancipation. It is not difficult to show that these modern ideologies, even if they were not messianic movements in the strict sense, had certain messianic overtones or, at least, consciously made use of traditional messianic terminology. No doubt these progressive liberals, or later socialists, did not think in terms of Armageddon, or a heavenly Jerusalem descending from above, or the Son of David riding on a donkey, but civil liberties, equality before the law, increased human welfare, universal peace and all-round ethical and human progress, appeared to them transformed with a biblical halo and as the true essence of the traditional messianic hopes. The messianic dimension, in many cases unconscious, of the Jewish national revival which began in the 19th century in Europe, developed into the Zionist Movement and culminated in the establishment of the State of Israel in 1948, is even more obvious. Of course, Jews rarely ask the literalist questions so congenial to Christian fundamentalist minds. They do not as a rule, inquire, whether this or that historical event is the "fulfillment" of this or that Biblical prophecy, even though some religious circles nowadays speak of "the beginning of the sprouting of our redemption". But although there is no question of fundamentalist messianism or apocalyptic eschatology, there can be no doubt of the presence of messianic undertones. The end of the Exile, the return to the Promised Land, the re-establishment of Israel as a Jewish commonwealth, the experience of "completeness" connected with the return to the ancestral soil and with the somewhat Tolstoyan ideal of manual labour and the socialist ideal of justice and equality (as attempted by the kibbutz movement)—all these, whilst not strictly "biblical", nevertheless could not but strike responsive chords in the Jewish soul.

In fact, even the most secularized Jew realized that the certainties enunciated in the Scriptures and the reality of his own experience somehow coincided. Both operated, as it were, on the same experiential wavelength. The fact that the birth of the State of Israel took place in the aftermath of a tragedy which even in Jewish history is unparalleled, the cold-blooded murder by the Nazis and their accomplices of six million Jews, and amid toil, sweat and heroic struggle for survival, seemed to make actual modern history conform to the almost archetypal notion mentioned above of a double-faced messianism composed of catastrophe on the one hand and redemption on the other. Contemporary history is notoriously more difficult to study than that of past generations. Consequently, the history of the religious, apocalyptic and mystical messianism of ancient, mediaeval and early modern Jewish history has been written more or less satisfactorily, whilst a thorough and authoritative analysis of the messianic elements in the religious thought and the national and social movements of late modern and contemporary Judaism is still outstanding. Yet it is a significant fact that Jewish messianism seems to be passing through something like a crisis. For close on two thousand and five hundred years the Jewish people have waited for a better king or for better times, for a glorious restoration or for a new heaven and a new earth. Their theologians and mystics expanded this notion of redemption from exile, suffering and persecution to include redemption from sin and from all evil. The Return to Zion and the Ingathering of the Exiles would be a redemptive consummation because it seemed beyond the range of natural possibilities and hence in no way less miraculous and supernatural than the conquest of sin and evil and the realization of complete communion with God. In fact, both would come together. By the middle of the 20th century a largely secularized Jewish people found itself in an unprecedented situation within a secularized world. That which many generations had prayed and hoped for, or rather believed in with that stubborn faith that springs less from fanaticism than from a profound inner certainty, had come to pass, and yet nobody would be bold enough to speak of a messianic consummation, even though some might speak of a messianic beginning. There is as yet no peace on the borders, and both individual man and society as a whole know that they are still far removed from that wholeness and completeness which traditional utopianism had associated with the messianic age, notwithstanding the more rational and antiapocalyptic statement of one ancient Rabbi, to the effect that the only difference between exile and the messianic age would be Israel's freedom from gentile domination. It seems that precisely because the Zionist Movement has realized so many—though not all—of its aims, and fulfilled so much of the dynamism of Jewish history, that its immense achievement renders the absence of a messianic consummation even more glaring. It has posed the question of messianism anew, for realization is the strongest enemy of hope, even as the life of hope is the most eloquent witness to the truth that realization is still outstanding. But if the past holds any clue to the future, it would seem to suggest that the present crisis of messianism will lead to a new reinterpretation rather that to the total abandonment of a complex symbol that for millennia has served as the expression of the Jew's unshakeable conviction of his national identity, religious destiny, inalienable promise and absolute certainty of a future for himself bound to that of mankind.

2

Jewish Messianism: Metamorphoses of an Idea

Eliezer Schweid

Messianism plays a unique role in the polarized controversy which marks the Israeli political scene today. At one end of the ideological spectrum it is a battle cry; at the other, an object of scorn. It lies at the center of current ideological conflicts in the political arena, and endows the controversy with a broad cultural and historical resonance. An understanding of the significance of messianism is necessary in forming a clear picture of the spiritual ambience of Israeli society today.

Before embarking upon a description of messianism and its history, it is worth examining how the current political controversy came to revolve around a philosophical-theological concept of this sort. A look at the recent past will help us to understand this spiritual phenomenon which at the outset appears so alien and peculiar to non-religious Israelis.

In the pre-state period, most of the political controversies that raged between the different Jewish parties in *Eretz Israel* and worldwide had their roots in solidified ideologies, each based upon a comprehensive world-view. Ideology, in those days, played a central role in education, in formulating the social issues with which any given party was concerned, in gathering broader public support for the party and in shaping its strategies. The preponderance of ideology in the society made it widely accepted to view messianism, at least in a metaphorical sense, as

Reprinted by permission from *The Jerusalem Quarterly* 36 (Summer 1985). The essay was first published in Hebrew in *Seqirah Hodshit* 122 (December 1984).

an exalted sentiment useful in arousing enthusiastic support for the platforms of the parties. Each party, of course, had its own interpretation of the concept, and the debate between them was fierce indeed. There was general agreement, however, about the importance and desirability of messianic aspirations.

The fact that a movement is ideologically based clearly has some bearing on its espousal of a messianic view. Nor is it difficult to understand this connection. In order to bring about a revolution and establish a new order, movements must try to convince the public that the existing order is rotten to the core and must be overthrown in favor of a more desirable order. That is the task of ideology, which is intrinsically messianic, seeking as it does the total rectification of all the perversities of the present and the realization of all the good it so eagerly desires.

In the pre-state period most Jewish movements sought links in messianism and its past manifestations. Their primary motivation lay in the desire for the perfect redemption of the Jewish people. Once the state was established, however, an opposing trend set in, one in which ideology receded before a more 'pragmatic' approach. In an ideologically-based movement even such a transformation may take on an ideological character with messianic overtones—and the ideology of statehood which in *Eretz Israel* swept the Labor Party, headed by David Ben-Gurion, into leadership and guided the nation's steps after the establishment of the state is an excellent example of this. Ben-Gurion saw the establishment of the State of Israel as a messianic event. To him the vision had been realized, and it was precisely this fervent declaration that justified his political pragmatism. There was no longer the need to seek the overthrow of the existing order or the building of a new one. What was needed, rather, was to preserve and consolidate what had been achieved, and the best way to do this was to make the most efficient use of the existing implements of state. Defined in this way, the new situation demanded a non-ideological pragmatism. Can there be an ideology of liberation from ideology? If so, this may well be an example. It resulted, at any rate, in the fairly quick 'neutralization' of the ideological element, especially in the ruling parties.

However, the fierce controversy buffeting Israeli society has precipitated the climax of a transformation which began with the trauma of the Yom Kippur War in 1973. The aftermath of that conflict led to profound self-criticism, to the upset of the nation's social and political balance and to cultural tensions verging on violence, and all of these combined to shake the pragmatic complacency which had set in after the 1967 Six-Day War. The controversy splitting the country once more became ideological. To be sure, this transformation does not embrace the whole society. In the large parties, or more precisely in their governing bodies, pragmatism is still considered the only ideology suitable for guiding a firm administration. At either end of the political spectrum, however, radical ideological movements have appeared, and these are having a progressively wider effect upon the supporters of the large parties. At a time when the institutionalized pragmatism of the large parties seems unable to cope with the weighty problems facing the nation, the ideological movements point to hard and fast solutions, and their influence is growing. In their attitude towards messianism, however, a curious equation is taking shape as a result of this whole process. At one end of the spectrum there has appeared an ideological movement whose very 'soul' is messianism; its understanding of the concept, however, is decidedly different from that accepted in the pre-state *yishuv,* with regard both to the vision and to its realization. At the other end, meanwhile, has appeared a protest movement whose opposition is directed against messianism as well. It decries the messianism of its antagonists, offering instead an ideology bent on justifying the pragmatic approach which sees in the present, in the attainment achievable right now, its sought-after ideal—an ideal it pursues with such passion that its devotion to it at times, ironically, takes on a messianic character.

THE MESSIAH KING—REDEEMER OF THE PEOPLE

Like many other concepts in Jewish thought, messianism has borne a wealth of meanings in the course of Jewish history. The need for constant reinterpretation under changing historical and cultural circumstances made the meanings attached to it expand and split into different streams, giving rise to fierce controversies. The best way to gain an understanding of the phenomenon, with all its variations and internal contradictions, will thus be to follow the principal historical developments that have taken place within it from its scriptural origins up to the present day.

Even in the Bible itself, several stages are discernible in the development of the concept. The earliest finds expression in the term 'God's anointed' *(meshiah Elohim)*,[1] by which the legal king of the people of Israel (as recognized by the prophets) was identified. Saul was anointed king of Israel by Samuel, at God's command. After his fall from grace, the kingdom was taken from him—and Samuel anointed David. The kings who descended from him were considered God's anointed—it was they, in other words, who were considered the legitimate kings of Israel by the will of God. David, the founder of the dynasty, was viewed as the people's model king even in the biblical literature, and this evaluation left its abiding mark upon the further development of the messianic idea, even after the kingdom was destroyed. Nor was this influence confined to Judaism alone—Christianity awarded Jesus the title of God's anointed, and traced his lineage to the House of David. When the idea of the re-establishment of the royal line was transformed into a vision of the future, it was accepted by the people that the one destined to renew it, too, would be 'a shoot out of the stock of Jesse'. But this idealization of David and his dynasty gave the concept of the 'anointed king'—the 'Messiah king'—an additional significance as well.

As we may gather from the preceding description, the prophet's anointment of the king with holy oil was a ceremony by which legitimate authority was conferred upon him by God. Two assumptions underlie this rite. The first is that the monarchy needs legal confirmation of both the identity of the king and his methods of governing. True sovereignty does not derive merely from the arbitrary wielding of power by a man who has gathered sufficient strength to seize the government. The government is a legal framework which requires justification from an ethical, social and religious point of view, and whoever stands at its head must also justify his status within it. Secondly, the sole source for conferring legal authority on the king is not human but Divine, and that is because sovereignty in its original and essential sense belongs to God. God is the creator of the world; it is He who determines the laws of nature and the laws which guide man. The world and its creatures belong to Him, and it is to Him that men owe their obedience, for their own good. The prophet or priest who anoints the king thus acts in the name of God, entrusting the king with an authority that is limited and defined. God does not forego His sovereignty, and the king merely acts in His name; he is 'God's chosen'. Needless to say, then, the king must govern according to the will of God—that is, according to the Torah and the word of God to His prophets. As Scripture puts it, the king must do 'that which is good in the eyes of God'. When the anointed king is faithful to his task, then, the people gain all of the bounty, both ethical and material, with which God promised to endow them upon His land.

There is a strong connection between this understanding of the sovereign's appointed role and the idea of redemption. In the original, biblical sense of the word, a 'redeemer' is a person of social and legal standing who on this account has the ability, and thus also the obligation, to extend his protection to his kin and dependents within his family, tribe or people. This role devolves upon the patriarch of the family, the elder of the tribe and so forth. The redeemer must ensure his dependents the status appropriate to them in consequence of their place and prestige within the society, and if they should fall from this status by reason of some disaster or injury, it is incumbent upon him to make every effort to restore them to their original position. The act of redemption, then, consists of restoring one who has fallen to his original status. In accordance with this view of society, the Torah obliges leaders of the people, judges and representatives of the public to take up the redeemer's role towards those whom misfortune has denied 'kin and redeemers': the orphan, the widow and the proselyte. The same view obliges every able individual in society to see to the needs of the poor. It was in accordance with this view that Boaz took upon himself the role of redeemer towards Ruth the Moabitess and her family. And so God, too, bears the task of redeeming His people. The Exodus from Egypt was an act of redemption in this sense. The people had fallen from the original status which it deserved, and God—its father—redeemed it by bringing it out of slavery and back to Him, to shelter under His wings. It is easy to see how this line of thought was thence extended to the king chosen by God. The anointed king, too, takes upon himself the role of redeemer of the people. David—acting as redeemer—fortified the people's hold upon the land and kept its enemies at bay, while Solomon brought it peace and prosperity. Their deeds completed the act of redemption which had begun with the Exodus. It was on this account that David was considered a model king who had fulfilled his appointed role. On this account, too, it would be one of his descendants who brought the people ultimate redemption.

This vital connection between the task of the appointed king and that of the redeemer became the source of the unique significance acquired by the concept of messianism in the course of its future evolution.

THE MESSIANIC VISION: THE RIGHTEOUS JUDGE

The subsequent development of the messianic idea, beyond the conception described above of the role of the anointed king, was a consequence of the ever-present and increasingly wide gap between the expectations which the people, the prophets and the Sages had of the kings who ruled them and the actual deeds and achievements of the latter, particularly with regard to the requirement that they establish a reign of justice and righteousness. The rulers of the kingdom of Israel, which had broken away from the kingdom established by David, were never considered legitimate by the prophets. But even the kings of the Davidic dynasty, who had been legally anointed, did not live up to expectations. As seen through the eyes of the prophets, they were unfaithful to the covenant they were expected to fulfill and failed to serve God as they ought; they did not do His command and did not judge the people righteously. That, in the opinion of the prophets, was why the condition of the Israelites continued to deteriorate, both in their internal and in their external affairs. The deterioration described in the biblical narrative thus continued until the Temple lay in ruins, the kingdom was destroyed and the people exiled. Even as the race towards destruction was in progress, however, the prophets continued to nurse their hope that the Davidic dynasty would yet produce a sovereign worthy of his role who would redeem the people and restore it to its original status, as in the days of David and Solomon. It was from this hope that the messianic vision described in the works of the later prophets sprang. The true 'Messiah king', as opposed to these unworthy kings, would judge the people righteously and ensure them peace and prosperity:

> And there shall come forth a shoot out of the stock of Jesse, and a twig shall grow forth out of his roots. And the spirit of the Lord shall rest upon him, the spirit of wisdom and understanding, the spirit of counsel and might, the spirit of knowledge and of the fear of the Lord. And his delight shall be in the fear of the Lord; and he shall not judge after the sight of his eyes, neither decide after the hearing of his ears; but with righteousness shall he judge the poor, and decide with equity for the meek of the land . . . They shall not hurt nor destroy in all My holy mountain; for the earth shall be full of the knowledge of the Lord, as the waters cover the sea. And it shall come to pass in that day, that the root of Jesse, that standeth for an ensign of the peoples, unto him shall the nations seek; and his resting-place shall be glorious (Isaiah 11:1–4, 9–10).

These verses from the prophecy of Isaiah provide a concise, eloquent summation of the messianic idea as it took shape in the thinking of the later prophets, and they are also a source for the much more complex conception found in the prophets after Isaiah and in the post-biblical literature. The true king who will surely, but at some undefined time, accede to the throne of David will of course be a legitimate heir, a 'shoot' out of the stock of Jesse and a 'twig' out of his roots. In contrast to most of the kings who ruled in the past, however, this one will fulfill the expectations of the prophet, in the name of God and of the people. He will display all of the spiritual qualities required of one who is God's anointed. He will judge the people with righteousness, and his rule will bring the people ethical and material prosperity and peace. Nor is it only the people of Israel that will be redeemed by this king; all the peoples of the world will accept his justice and be redeemed. The hope of redemption in this vision acquires a universal and perhaps even cosmic dimension.

THE LITERATURE OF MESSIANIC VISION

Isaiah's vision contains an element which was to be of growing importance in the development of the messianic idea, both in the prophets who succeeded Isaiah and in the post-biblical literature. We have already noted that the time of the appointed king's appearance is undefined, though it is expected with absolute certainty. The king's historical identity is also not explicit. What king did the prophet have in mind? There are commentators who believe that he was referring to a particular candidate and a particular time very close at hand. The prophecy itself, however, leaves this a mystery. Moreover, it does not describe the circumstances in which this king is to appear—the actual historical moment, that is, remains undisclosed—and the vision itself is shot through with fabulous idealization. This is more than the rectification of the defects and perversions of an evil reign. The contrast between the darkness of the present and the perfection of the future is absolute, representing a revolutionary transformation in the nature of the human race, the peoples of the world and perhaps even the universe. The prophet's conception would seem vastly to exceed the restoration of the good order and prosperity which had prevailed in the days of David and Solomon. The king he describes is far superior to any of his predecessors, and has qualities not given to ordinary men. Moreover, his power is exclusively spiritual, and yet all respond to it. This kind of response, too, is uncharacteristic of the human race as we know it; ultimately we find that he expects even beasts of prey to undergo a transformation in their behavior. Is this merely a flight of poetic imagery, or does he really have in mind an essential transformation in the order of nature and in the natural qualities of man? The commentators are divided in their opinions on this point. There is no doubt, however, that in the later prophets, and even more so in the post-biblical apocalyptic literature, the description of the redemption took on a consistently supra-historical, miraculous character.

The anticipated events embrace the whole world, far exceeding those described in the biblical story of the Exodus. We must emphasize, to be sure, that this development did not entirely supplant the earlier biblical tradition of a redemption which was to take place within history, subject to the regular laws of nature, in which a king descended from the Davidic dynasty would rise to gather in the exiles, re-establish the kingdom, rebuild the Temple and guide the nation in accordance with the laws of the Torah. But the visions of the messianic, apocalyptic literature (that which set about revealing the hitherto unknown wondrous events which were to take place at the 'end of days', when the course of history would transcend the natural order) had the upper hand. This was especially true of the period which began with the failure of the Bar-Kokhba rebellion. The Jewish people gradually lost its majority in the land of Israel; the remnants of its independence vanished; the dispersion of the people increased, and with it their distance from the land of Israel; and the hope that the nation would one day be able to restore its sovereignty by political and military means faded almost completely. It could only hope now for a miracle, for direct intervention from on high, for a transformation in the order of nature. A rich literature of messianic visions thus came into being, authored by men possessed of esoteric wisdom or prophetic inspiration.

The literature in question was written over a long period, lasting several centuries. In each work one senses its unique historical, spiritual and religious background and the unique personalities of the thinkers or seers who created it. They cannot, therefore, be taken together as a single movement, for they are necessarily separated by great differences, antitheses and even contradictions. It is possible, however, to trace some schematic outlines which define the phenomenon in a broad sense, and since we cannot here go into a detailed analysis of several examples, we shall briefly note these outlines:

1. a radically critical portrayal of the present human condition: evil, arrogance, unrestrained tyranny, persecution of the righteous and their cruel suffering. The people of Israel are persecuted and oppressed on account of their loyalty to the Torah, and idolatry dominates. Even the order of nature is crumbling because of the depravity that mars mankind;
2. a belief that the present bleak state of affairs cannot last much longer. It does not accord with the will of God, who created His world, and man within it, for a good purpose. The human race, to be sure, has sinned and corrupted Creation, but God has not abandoned His world. He directs it according to a particular, predetermined plan, in which the suffering of the present is a necessary stage on the road to redemption;
3. ordinary men cannot understand why this reign of evil is not stopped, or how the world will reach its predestined goal. However, there is an esoteric wisdom, originating in inspiration from on high, whose practitioners can decipher the course of events and foresee the future by means of signs existing in the present. These visionaries usually see their own time as the climax of the period of crisis and anticipate the End of Days very shortly thereafter. This understanding gives them strength to bear the suffering and do whatever can be done to hasten that End, or at least ensure that it will occur at its appointed time;
4. when the time comes, the 'Messiah king', the son of David, will appear and extend his sovereignty over Israel, and perhaps over the world as a whole. Then will come the redemption. The descriptions of this redemption are not consistent in all their details, but they typically speak of justice and a terrible vengeance to be exacted upon the evil-doers, the destruction of idolatry, the return of the exiles to Zion, the re-establishment of the kingdom and of the Temple service, an abundance of crops which will spring forth by supernatural means, the establishment of legal ties and just and peaceful relations between Israel and the other nations, the exaltation of existence and the resurrection of the dead. Eventually a time will come when all pain, sickness and evil will pass from the world, and even death will be no more.

As we have said, this is a schematic outline covering a vast and fascinating wealth of visions. We must again emphasize, moreover, that despite the expectation of a supernatural and supra-historical redemption which characterizes most of the messianic literature created after the Bar-Kokhba rebellion there also remained a more earthbound popular version, according to which 'the only difference between this world and the time of the Messiah lies in the ingathering of the exiles'. This version carefully distinguishes between the national redemption to take place in messianic times and the redemption of individual souls in the 'world to come'. We shall return to this distinction further on.

CAN THE COMING OF THE MESSIAH BE HASTENED?

Before we discuss the modern metamorphosis of the messianic idea into secular-political, social and national movements, it will be helpful to examine several points of controversy among the messianic conceptions which evolved within Judaism up to the beginning of the modern era (which in Jewish history begins with the Emancipation).

The first such point of controversy is one we have already mentioned above, the question of whether the messianic redemption was to have a historical or a supra-historical character. In the Middle Ages, the historical view was buttressed by the vigorous, influential and authoritative support of Maimonides. The future Maimonides describes is, to be sure, ideal, and as such it can be defined as 'utopian'. He continually emphasizes, however, that the events of redemption will take place in a natural way, as they did at the time of the restoration led by Ezra and Nehemiah. This aspect of Maimonides' thinking was to be of great importance to the religious Zionists of the modern era.

Maimonides will also help us to understand the link between the first and second points of messianic controversy. Maimonides, even as he rejected the miraculous dimensions of the people's national redemption, clung to its spiritual, supernatural dimension. He, too, saw man's destiny as involving a degree of spiritual perfection that would overcome all the ills of earthly reality: pain, suffering, sickness, evil and death. He distinguished, however, between the messianic redemption, which would take place on a national level and redemption in the spiritual, absolute sense. In his view, 'the days of the Messiah' and 'the world to come'—two commonly used expressions which had been handed down from rabbinic times—referred to two different things. 'The days of the Messiah' denoted the period of national redemption, to be characterized by the ingathering of the exiles, the establishment of a sovereign realm governed by the laws of the Torah, and the re-establishment of the Temple service. When this came about, of course, the people would be released from all their sufferings, and made free to spend their time studying the Torah and keeping the commandments so as to earn their part in the world to come. In itself, however, this 'part in the world to come' did not depend upon the advent of the messianic era. It referred to individual spiritual perfection, which could be achieved by every individual, as a member of the people of Israel, through study of the Torah and keeping the commandments, each according to his ability. Study of the Torah enabled man to elevate and perfect his soul, and this perfection was eternal, untouchable by death. The 'world to come', then, referred to the eternal existence of the soul after death, and this spiritual level could be attained at any time—under Jewish sovereignty or in exile—through purely motivated devotion to the study of the Torah.

As we have noted, Maimonides also described the 'days of the Messiah' as a means by which every individual Jew would move closer to achieving his part in the world to come. Clearly, though, the possibility of achieving personal, spiritual redemption in the most exalted sense even in exile lessened the tension with which the advent of the Messiah was anticipated. Maimonides was not the only one to make this distinction, but he also had some vigorous opponents. As a number of scholars have argued, the approach taken by the proponents of the school represented by Maimonides' ideas sought, in effect, to 'neutralize' the messianic idea; that of their opponents, on the other hand, intensified the urgency with which the Messiah was expected and sought ways of hastening the end.

A third point of controversy centered around the question of whether the messianic vision depended for its fulfillment upon some deliberate human acts. This question had three parts: First of all, was the advent of the Messiah at all dependent upon the deeds of man, or would it simply occur at some predetermined time? Secondly, was it possible—and if so, advisable—to attempt to 'hasten the end'? And finally, if it was indeed possible to try to hasten the Messiah's coming, then by what deeds? The first of these questions had two radically opposing answers. The first assumes a divine plan, predetermined down to the last detail, which man has no power whatever to influence. The second, on the other hand, holds that the time of the Messiah's advent is not preordained, but redemption will come about when the Jews are worthy of it. A third approach was also possible, according to which there is a fixed time for the Messiah's coming, regardless of man's deeds, but the people of Israel can hasten the redemption through righteous acts. This last, intermediate view seems to have been the majority view.

According to the second and third views, then, the Jewish people can hasten the advent of the Messiah by their deeds. But by what deeds? We will find a number of different and opposing views on this issue as well. Up to the time of the Bar-Kokhba rebellion, the numerous large-scale uprisings against foreign domination which arose from Hasmonean times onward expressed a view that the Jews can—and must—take political and military initiatives in order to hasten the redemption. In the wake of the grim consequences of Bar-Kokhba's failure, however, most of the leaders were won over to the belief that active rebellion—'mounting the ramparts'—was forbidden. The people had been sentenced to exile, and only intervention from on high could restore it to its land. There were several attempts to found movements of return, but these were always doomed to early failure, and the general rule did not change until the first stirrings of the Hibbat Zion movement in modern times. But such efforts did not exhaust the means available to the people for attempting to hasten the end. The first, most accepted and conservative of these means was that of repentance. The Jews must make themselves worthy of redemption before their Father in Heaven through wholehearted study of the Torah and observance of the commandments. Special efforts to hasten the redemption by those who took this view expressed themselves in greater emphasis upon mourning over the destruction of the Temple and the nation's exile, and occasionally in the undertaking of pilgrimages to the Holy Land for the sake of bewailing its desolation and praying in the holy places for redemption.

A second, move vigorous means for hastening the end was that at times attempted by practitioners of esoteric wisdom, who, after sanctifying themselves in order to attain a spiritual elevation which would enable them to act upon the supernal realms, endowed their prayers with special *kavvanot* (meanings, purposes) directed towards this aim. Such spiritual activity was, of course, the province of a few select individuals. Given the people's great distress, however, a number of such individuals, sensing themselves agents for the rest, were able at various times to arouse tremendous excitement, tense anticipation and preparations for proximate messianic events. The dashed hopes which always followed these awakenings unsettled the people's faith and were often accompanied by despair and conversions. The majority of the rabbinic leaders, traumatized by these experiences, consistently opposed such attempts, but they could not prevent their latent embers flaring up again strongly in times of crisis.

FROM RELIGIOUS TO SECULAR MESSIANISM

Messianism, as it was described above, is essentially a religious and spiritual phenomenon. Faith in divine providence—that is, in the idea that history follows a divine plan—is its essential ingredient. Nevertheless, the modern era has seen the rise of great secular messianic movements among both the Jews and the peoples of Europe, who inherited the messianic tradition in the form of Christianity. The profound social and cultural crisis through which nations have passed, which involved, among other things, a transition from religious to secular world-views and ways of life, can explain this transformation of messianism, though it may seem strange at the outset for such enormous religious energies to have been expended in a secular struggle to rectify the ethical perversions and material distress of humanity, and redeem it, moreover, even from the distortions, lies and oppression which had their source—in the view of the secular leadership—in religion itself and the institutions associated with it. Religious elements and ways of thinking were part and parcel even of the war against religion, with messianism the most outstanding religious motif to undergo this kind of dialectical transformation from the 'old' to the 'new'.

This revolutionary shaking off of the 'outmoded' aspects of religious messianism was to express itself in the vigorous, aggressive and scornful rejection of the anticipation of redemption by a miraculous event or by divine intervention. This, according to secular prophets of redemption, was merely a myth designed to keep the simple masses enslaved, to blind them to their own enormous strength and their ability to take their dismal fate into their own hands, and so to stave off the revolution. A secular movement, on the other hand, based itself on what was natural and down to earth. It stood for an independent social and political initiative powered by the intrinsic resources of mankind. This demanded on the one hand scientific investigation into the laws governing nature, society and the natural development of history, so as to discover what could and must be done in order for human society to progress, and on the other hand effective organization for action. But the structure of the ideas guiding these scientific investigations, organizational activities and plans of action remained remarkably similar to that of messianic thought, with the belief that history develops according to its own immanent, hidden laws taking the place of the concept of divine providence.

Let us again note the structural characteristics shared by many secular messianic ideologies, however much they may differ from one another:

1. a critical analysis of the current state of the nation or of society, from an economic, socio-ethical and political point of view. The existing situation is intolerably perverted in all of these respects;
2. the existing situation is intolerable and untenable. Historical processes have their own inner laws of development, like the laws of nature, and an understanding of them reveals the current situation to be one of transition to a higher stage in which history will reach its goal and the paradoxes and perversions of the present will disappear;
3. the superficial observer does not understand the internal logic and direction of the process of historical development; those equipped with the tools of scientific study and dialectical analysis, however, are able to identify precisely the significance of historical events—and to guide the masses towards the revolution that will redeem them from all the sufferings of the present;
4. a general description of the goal towards which history is progressing, which will put an end to social conflicts, exploitation, servitude, alienation and injustice, and to wars between peoples. All this will happen, of course, in the wake of a great revolutionary upheaval which will enable the oppressed to overcome their oppressors and lay down a just and harmonious new order. After that mankind will be able to draw far more efficiently upon nature's resources and use them to find solutions to all suffering, whose source lies in want and in human arrogance.

As we have said, the movements involved differed vastly from one another in their vision, their interpretation of the course of history and the ways and means they adopted. They included the European movements of national liberation, the movements which brought about the rise of liberal-democratic and social-democratic regimes in Europe and the United States, and the socialist movements, some of which went in the direction of Democratic Socialism and others in the direction of Communism. These latter evolved—in a further stage of development—into the radical movements which were to have such a decisive influence upon the fate of western culture and of mankind as a whole in the first half of the twentieth century—Communism on the one hand and Fascism and Nazism on the other.

SECULAR AND RELIGIOUS MESSIANISM IN ISRAEL

All of the movements mentioned above affected the fate of the Jewish people in modern times—and not only as external factors. They made their way into the people itself and there found fertile ground for the growth of secular Jewish messianic movements. The influence of the democratic and liberal nationalist movements led on the one hand to the development of those movements which saw the realization of the messianic redemption in the emancipation of the Jews and their integration into western culture, and on the other to the development of the Zionist movement, which sought to redeem the people of Israel in its own land, by means, however, of the implements of modern secular nationalism. Next came the turn of the socialist movements, which led to the mapping of paths to redemption which called either for the integration of the Jews into the world revolution which would unite all of mankind into one society, undivided by distinctions of nationality, religion or race, or for the addition of a Socialist dimension to the nationalist, Zionist vision. Both of these broad trends split into a number of differing paths and visions, all of them marked by a belief that the rectification of the fate of the Jewish people would come about within the framework of an overall rectification of the fate of all mankind.

The appearance of these secular messianic movements did not spell the end of religious messianism within Judaism. On the contrary: the struggle against secularism proved a powerful factor in the arousal of an opposing messianic response, and the appearance of secular messianism also had the effect of provoking a dialectic reaction on the religious side. Two especially striking messianic responses were that which produced the religious Habbat Zion movement in answer to nationalist movements in Europe and, later, that which brought forth religious Zionism in response to the type of secular Zionism espoused by Pinsker, Lilienblum, Ahad HaAm and Herzl. The religious-messianic reaction to secular Zionism reached its climax in the doctrines of Rabbi Kook and his followers. It must be noted, on the other hand, that there was a messianic awakening in this period even within the anti-Zionist community of the ultra-Orthodox, who saw in the appearance of the secular heresy the culmination of the 'birth-pangs of the Messiah'. After this, they felt, redemption had to come.

It is easy enough to see that religious messianism, in responding to secularism, also caught some of its influence. The most outstanding expression of this was the revival of the idea that the people ought to take an independent, national, historical initiative of its own, by returning to Zion, settling it and establishing a state. These were steps to be taken in order to greet the miraculous redemption which would come in response to this awakening. This change in the prescribed means of hastening the redemption would seem, moreover, to presuppose a transformation in the description of the messianic vision. This now included a dream of the complete revival of the national culture, so defined as to incorporate many of the social and cultural elements of secular Zionism.

We have briefly surveyed a wide variety of modern messianic movements which vied with one another over the image of western culture and of the Jewish people in modern times. We must emphasize, however, that while the affinity between these movements' ideological-messianic thought structure do constitute a common denominator and even a cultural and historical meeting-ground, this still does not justify lumping them all together for good or ill simply because they are messianic in character. The phenomenon of messianism can be positive or negative, constructive or destructive, depending upon the nature of its vision, the means it uses and the paths it takes in order to realize that vision. Each of these movements must be evaluated singly with regard both to its content and to its achievements.

MARVELOUS ACHIEVEMENTS, DISASTROUS ERRORS

The tendency to prejudge a movement simply on the basis of its messianic nature is characteristic of our generation, which has seen several great messianic movements end in failure or in terrible disillusionment. This generation would seem to have been left with the task of evaluating the enterprises of the great messianic movements of the first half of the century and formulating a sober response to them. Its own enterprises, after all, are grounded on the one hand in the impressive achievements of liberal democratic nationalism and of socialism, and on the other in the disappointments and failures that have issued from these same movements and in the disastrous consequences of Fascism, Nazism and Leninist-Stalinist Communism. The same is true of the messianic movements active within the Jewish people, whose marvelous achievements were countered by disastrous errors and terrible disappointments. The current situation does not encourage secular messianism, at least not in its classical pattern. A sober secular view would no longer describe as redemption a possible improvement in the existing state of affairs or an alleviation of particular woes, while the numerous disappointments yielded up by messianic ideology, together with the new and unexpected kinds of distress that have appeared in the alienated mass society of our time, obscure the great achievements of the messianic movements in the last generation. However, there are nevertheless those who cannot accept the existing situation, and their response to it generally takes one of two opposing directions. The first is that of pragmatic anti-messianism, which rules out all messianism as a dangerous, arbitrary, fanatical, visionary and tyrannical sentiment capable of much harm and very little good; the second, that of corrective messianism, seeks to learn lessons from the disappointments and failures of the past in order to launch a renewed effort to realize its vision.

Each of the messianic movements described above gave rise to a corrective messianic movement in its wake. A typical example of this, in response to secular Zionism, is to be found in the historical, nationalist and social ideas of Martin Buber. Buber rejected the deterministic understanding of history so characteristic of secular messianism in the nineteenth century and the first half of the twentieth, and together with it he rejected what he saw as the pretentious view that absolute ideals can ever be realized. His version of corrective messianism involved a willingness to devote oneself to the realization of an ethical ideal within the defined circumstances of a particular time and place, in the hope of drawing closer—however partially—to that ideal and simultaneously, in so doing, endowing the present with purpose and meaning and charting a positive direction for the future. The religious Zionism of our day, by contrast, has produced its version of corrective messianism in the ideas of the students of Rabbi Kook. They seek a return to religious

Zionism's original messianic vision, from which, they claim, the historical movement has backed away, compromising for pragmatic reasons. It is such compromise and retreat, in this view, which have led to the disappointingly incomplete achievements of Zionism. What is required, then, is a return to the sources and pursuit of the total, radical realization of the original vision. These two ways, Buber's and that of Rav Kook's students, thus represent opposing efforts at the conscious formulation of a corrective messianism. It would seem, however, that even opposition to messianism can turn into a kind of corrective messianism, when it consolidates itself into an ideology and takes on the urgency of an effort to stave off disaster. An anti-messianic ideology of this kind points to what can be achieved now, immediately, if only there is a general consent to relinquish absolute ideals as the greatest good—it points, that is, to an ideal whose achievement spells redemption from the disasters lurking in the wake of a radical messianism.

And this last note brings us directly back to the thick of the controversy currently playing itself out in our society with such intensity.

NOTE

1. Hence the origin of the Hebrew term Messiah.

II

THE LATE SECOND COMMONWEALTH PERIOD

3

Messiahs: Robbers, Jurists, Prophets, and Magicians

Morton Smith

Some years ago I discussed the various uses of the term *mashiah* and its equivalents in the Greco-Roman period[1] and tried to show that it did not invariably have eschatological connotations, that there were both messiahs without ends of the world and ends of the world without messiahs, that even those messiahs who were connected with some end had different roles in the different programs for the end which were being circulated, and that these different programs, while evidently of considerable importance in the thought of the time (to judge from the number of works about them and the stories of messianic disturbances) were not matters of credal authority but rather of free speculation: many mutually contradictory programs might be collected in the literature of a single group, or even in a single document like the Book of Enoch. Hence it seemed unlikely that adherence to any program, or even to any particular messianic figure, was the cause for the separation and distinction of any sect of the time, nor should the rituals of any sect be seen as the acting out of a particular eschatological myth. The causes of sectarian splits seemed rather such differences about questions of halakah as might lead to irreconcilable differences of practice. Questions of theory, especially those belonging to the realm of haggadah, are not known to have led to the formation of separate sects.

This position I supported in a number of other papers, examining the

Reprinted by permission of the American Academy for Jewish Research from *Proceedings of the American Academy for Jewish Research* 44 (1977).

alleged reasons for the formation of several sects,[2] and particularly for the separation and persecution of Christianity. These latter seem to have resulted, in the main, not from the preaching that Jesus was "*the* Messiah," still less from any theory of messianism, but rather from Jesus' claim to set some of his followers free from the Law, from the consequent (though often sub rosa) neglect of the Law by many of his followers, and from their claim to offer the same freedom to their converts.[3]

So far, so good. The theory was coherent, supported by many passages in the primary sources, and consistent with the general characteristics of Greco-Roman Judaism. But how could one explain the libertine element in Jesus' teaching? Whence and how did his notion of freedom from the Law arise? For this question the evidence led to types of thought quite different from halakah and also from messianic and eschatological speculations. Miracles and their magical parallels, the miraculous and magical contexts in which the term "Son of God" is commonly used in the Synoptics,[4] the magical parallels to the union with Jesus promised in baptism and the eucharist, and the salvation and release from the Law effected by that union (this theme is the heart of Paul's preaching)—all these now came to the fore as essential elements of the picture and were so presented in my books on the secret gospel of Mark.[5]

This was a somewhat disconcerting result. The argument had set out from the evidence that messianic beliefs were not uniform even within sects that held them; it had therefore sought in halakic differences the universal basis for sectarian differentiation. But now the halakic—or, anti-halakic—peculiarity of Christianity led back to peculiar beliefs about the role of a figure believed to be a messiah. But there was a complication. While the figure was identified as "the Messiah," those elements of the role that were essential to freedom from the law were not typically messianic. Nobody before had ever been baptized into a messiah,[6] let alone eaten one. (I know that Rabbi Hillel said "There is no Messiah for Israel because they ate him up in the days of Hezekiah,"[7] but R. Hillel probably spoke in the fourth century,[8] and his metaphor is so strange that I think it may involve a mocking reference to the eucharist: If Jesus had given his flesh and blood to his disciples, he, too, would by that time have been wholly consumed.)

So in Jesus' case the messianic image contains elements hitherto unparalleled. I do not want, here, to review the evidence that may serve to identify those elements—that is cited in my books and anyone interested can find it there.[9] Instead I want to approach the general problem of first-century messianic and related figures from the other side—that of the practically possible types of figures, and the steps by which different men might come to be thought messianic.

We have here a problem arising from the continuous interplay between behaviour and vocabulary. Society presents the vocabulary, the types which a child is encouraged to imitate or avoid ("What do you want to be when you grow up?" or "You don't want to be like that when you grow up.") Individuals produce a constant supply of new behaviour which both constitutes the social types and, so far as it differs from the previous norms, changes the types. The society constantly struggles to describe and categorize these changes, using old words in new senses, making up new terms to fit new behaviour, and so producing a new vocabulary, a new set of types which a new generation will, in its turn, begin to imitate, reject, and alter.

In terms of the problem before us, these generalizations mean that the Jews of first-century Palestine had inherited many fantastic accounts of the world, both present and future. In these accounts there were many different figures called messiahs, and these figures could serve both as models to men who wanted to be thought messiahs, and as categories used by other men who were trying to identify the various and surprising figures that the world presented. Both processes, imitation and identification, were necessarily somewhat slipshod. A man who wanted to be thought a messiah usually could not do everything with which his model was credited, he would imitate only such traits as he could. Similarly, when trying to decide whether or not a man was a messiah, his contemporaries would find that he matched their favorite picture in some points, but not in others. Insofar as the messianic pretender won followers, or those determined to be followers found a figure they could identify as a messiah, the meaning of the term "messiah" was changed to accommodate these new phenomena. While every instance of such identification was, of course, peculiar, yet it seems possible to pick out, mainly from the material in Josephus and the New Testament, a number of typical careers that might lead to messiafication. Let me sketch four of these as examples.

The most likely way to become a messiah was to begin as a robber. If an industrious and affluent robber decides to move his business out of the city, finds himself a stronghold in the countryside, attracts a gang of followers and preys on wealthy travellers and the country estates of the rich, he becomes a bandit. It's a recognized social position and normally terminal; he may remain a bandit for years without any higher pretensions. But if his band is drawn largely from the surrounding villages and consequently has many friends and supporters there, if he builds up a following among the poor, if the country is governed by an alien power to which, and to its agents, the people are generally hostile, and if this power is losing its grip, so that bandits are not put down promptly, our man can develop into a local political leader. He will then gather more forces: if the situation deteriorates further he may venture to attack government garrisons, or even defeat a force sent to capture him. He thus becomes a revolutionary; his band will grow yet larger; he may win the allegiance of some other bandit chiefs, dream of making himself king, and claim in advance to be the destined king, the Lord's Messiah. After all, David had made it.

Another such pattern is that leading from teacher of the Law to messiah. If a persuasive teacher, helped by the prestige of his position, extends his teaching from his classes to sermons in the synagogue and public lectures, if he forms around himself a study group of devoted disciples, and advances an interpretation of the kingship of God so extreme as to prohibit ordinary acts of obedience to civil authorities, he will soon find himself the leader of a potentially revolutionary circle. If he then incites his followers to open defiance of the authorities and organizes a campaign of civil disobedience, if he develops a casuistic justification of violence for the sake of "the cause," and first excuses, and then encourages his followers' acts of violence, he will head a criminal revolutionary secret society. The members of this society will need encouragement and will probably derive it from the pervasive eschatological thought of the time: God will surely intervene to destroy the wicked (i.e. their enemies), reward the righteous (i.e. themselves), and establish a new kingdom of which the destined king, the Lord's Messiah, will surely be their revered teacher (or his legitimate successor —in such a closed group the messiahship can become hereditary).

Another possible pattern began with mental derangement. Of course, the village halfwit was a familiar figure for whom nobody felt any reverence. If he had violent fits and was dangerous he might be thought possessed by some demon, and his words and actions might then have ominous importance as demonic utterances. But if he was harmless while possessed and merely "spoke with tongues" (i.e. poured forth inarticulate sounds), or uttered more or less comprehensible tirades like the obscure passages of the Biblical prophets, and if he had the extraordinary drive and intuition that sometimes characterizes such persons in their lucid intervals,[10] then he might be thought a prophet. The expectation of prophets was alive in the land. He might encourage this interpretation by acting the part, dressing himself like Elijah in a camel's hair cloak and a leather girdle, and affecting extraordinary ascetic practices.[11] Even with such added attractions he would be lucky if he got much following;[12] but if he did, mobs would follow him into the desert, or march on Jerusalem, or climb the holy mount of Gerizim and expect him to produce the hidden vessels of the tabernacle.[13] His followers would surely identify him as the prophet like Moses, promised in Dt. 18.18;[14] but they might also believe that he had been anointed by God as Elisha should have been by Elijah,[15] and they could, therefore, even after his death, revere him as the Lord's anointed, the Messiah.[16]

Yet another pattern began not with insanity but with its cure. As the connection between mental derangement and psychiatric ability is proverbially close in our own time, so it was in antiquity. The Greek expression, "He has a demon," is ambiguous—it leaves uncertain which of the two is in command. No doubt the uncertainty was often justified. But if the man emerged triumphant from the struggle with what we should call his subconscious (what the gospels called Satan), then he might well believe himself and be believed by others to be able to command not only his own demon, but the rest of the demonic powers. Such belief, with his own experience, might enable him to quiet lunatics (in ancient terms, to cast out demons) and to produce apparently miraculous cures of blindness, deafness, aphasia, paralysis, and the like, cures which are now explained as the sudden cessation of hysterical symptoms.

Such cures and exorcisms, in ancient Palestine, were often thought to be effected by magic. Josephus boasts that the Jews were famous for their skill in this branch of the magic arts, and tells of a demonstration given by an exorcist in the presence of Vespasian.[17] This exorcist was a professional who worked with an inscribed ring, the root of some plant prescribed by Solomon, and spells from a Solomonic manual. But magical manuals preserved on papyri teach that magical operations can be effected without any such paraphenalia by one who has command of a powerful spirit.[18] Again, Josephus' man, though an exorcist of repute, was apparently not involved in politics. But we can easily imagine that a man with remarkable gifts of this sort, if he made his powers available freely, would soon be the center of crowds of persons come in search of cures and anxious to believe. In such crowds, some cures and exorcisms would certainly occur, and each would intensify the expectations and exaggerate the rumors and elicit new speculations: Who do you think he is? What is the source of his power? Is he a prophet? Is he the Messiah? Is he the son of a god?

We should ask rather, What would he think of himself? That would doubtless depend on the history of his case. If he had had experiences of the sort commonly described as "illuminations" he might easily conclude that he had become some supernatural being, above the laws of ordinary life. It would be understandable that he should try to communicate his powers and privileges to his closest disciples, and should use both religious and magical ceremonies, like baptism and a communion meal, for this purpose. It would be expectable that he should interpret his experiences in terms of the mythology current in Jewish Palestine—stories of ascents into the heavens, speculations about the coming of a messiah, and so on. Of the possible identifications this mythology offered him, he might easily opt for a messiahship, and if he did, it might easily cost him his life. Roman provincial governors were not *au courant* in questions of messianic typology; anybody who got to be known as a messiah was likely to end on a cross.

I submit that these four ultimately messianic careers—the robber's, the teacher's, the prophet's, the magician's—are all of them credible within the society of first-century Palestine. If so, this fact would resolve the apparent contradiction set forth at the beginning of this paper: The variety of the meanings of the term "messiah" remains clear, and the basis for the distinction of Christianity as a peculiar sect remains, not messianic beliefs as such, but the libertine consequences drawn by many members of the sect from the teachings and practices of its particular messiah. These teachings and practices, and the consequences drawn from them, were not, as such, messianic. Jesus might have decided to reject the title "messiah" and to claim some other—"the prophet"[19] or "Elijah,"[20] or "Jeremiah,"[21] or "John the Baptist,"[22] or "the Son of Man,"[23] or "the Son of God,"[24] or, as his competitor in Samaria was called, "the Great Power of God."[25] The first half dozen of these titles are said to have been attributed to him, and several were not wholly rejected. His choice of "messiah" turned out to be a fatal mistake, but would the choice of any other have saved him? An idle question, but it serves to emphasize the extent to which the "messianism" of early Christianity is secondary and superficial.

So, too, would be the "messianism" of the other careers and the movements that might arise from them. For the robber the essential facts would be the gradual growth of his military and hence his political power, and his decision to take advantage of the weakness of Rome with the hope, no doubt, of winning some favorable settlement. His messianic claims would be a political device adopted late in his career with the hope of winning additional support. For the teacher of the Law, or his descendants, the messianic claim was surely not their original point of departure; it must have emerged as a late corollary of the working out of a line of legal interpretation that led to the creation of a terrorist revolutionary party whose members ultimately saw that they had to dominate the revolution or be destroyed by it. For the prophet the basic things were his prophetic experiences. For those prophets who gained any considerable following, these experiences must have issued in some sort of message or messages. While it is not impossible that some of these immediately identified the speaker as a messiah,[26] it is likely that the main concern was usually something more tangible, "Put off your sins by baptism," "Follow me into the wilderness to be purged of your sins," "Follow me to Jerusalem" (or "to Gerizim") "to see the Lord's salvation," or something of the sort. What would happen when the Lord's salvation arrived, and just what role the prophet would have in the new order, were questions that doubtless received answers at least as various as those preserved in apocalyptic literature. Accordingly, while some prophets may have emerged as messiahs, it is likely that more had messianic dignity thrust upon them. As we know even from Tacitus[27] and Suetonius,[28] messianic speculation was wide-spread, and the identification of one or another individual as the messiah could have important consequences. Even Vespasian was not above taking advantage of such claims.[29] But for most of the claimants, as for Vespasian, the claim was probably an afterthought. The atmosphere of speculation was not produced by the would-be beneficiaries, nor did it, usually, produce them. They rose to prominence for more practical reasons—power politics, or legal teaching and sectarian leadership, or personal psychology —and then took advantage of existent messianic expectations, some of them, no doubt, with complete cynicism, others, probably, with complete sincerity, finding in these fantastic prophecies and symbolic figures the terms they needed to explain themselves to themselves.

NOTES

1. "What is Implied by the Variety of Messianic Figures?" *JBL* 78 (1959), 66–72.
2. "The Dead Sea Sect in Relation to Ancient Judaism," *NTS* 7 (1960–61), 347–360; "Zealots and Sicarii, Their Origins and Relation," *HTR* 64 (1971), 1–19.
3. "The Reason for the Persecution of Paul and the Obscurity of Acts," in *Studies in Mysticism and Religion presented to G. Scholem,* Jerusalem, 1967, 261–268; "Jesus' Attitude Towards the Law," in *Papers of the Fourth World Congress of Jewish Studies,* Jerusalem, 1967, vol. I, pp. 241–244.
4. Mk. 3.11, exorcism; 5.7 and parallels, exorcism; 15.39, after the *prodigia* accompanying his death; Mt. 4.3, 6 and parallels, the devil demands miracles; 14.33, the disciples' inference from the stilling of the storm; 16.16, the revelation given through Peter (cf. 17); 27.40, 43, the mocking of his inability to perform a miracle; Lk, 1.35, the angel's prediction of his birth; 4.41, exorcism; Mk. 1.11 and parallels, the voice from heaven after the baptism *(ho huios mou);* 9.7 and parallels, the voice at the transfiguration *(ho huios mou);* Mt. 11.27 and parallel, none knows the Son save the Father, nor the Father save the Son. Against all these in clearly magical or esoteric contexts can be set only Mk. 14.61 and parallels, the use as the critical question in the trial before the Sanhedrin (but this is a demand for esoteric information! Mk. makes the High Priest say *ho huios tou eulogetou,* but Mt. and Lk. have *tou theou*); and Mk. 1.1, the book's title. In three passages persons other than Jesus are promised that they will eventually be called sons of God: peacemakers in Mt. 5.9; those who love their enemies, do good, and lend without hope of repayment in Lk. 6.35 ("sons of the Highest"); and those thought worthy of the other aeon and the resurrection from the dead, in Lk. 20.36. These evidently belong to a wholly different tradition than the sayings about Jesus. So does the parable of the wicked tenants in Mk. 12.1–12 and parallels, where the owner of the vineyard, i.e. God, decides to send his "beloved son" (Mk. and Lk., Mt. only "son") to collect the rent. This is the only instance in the Synoptics in which anything like "Son of God" is used in an eschatological prophecy; all other such passages use "Son of Man" or "Son of David." The difference is hardly accidental. "Son of God" is connected with "Christ" or "Messiah" only in the title of Mk., the trial before the Sanhedrin, and by Mt.'s addition of it to the confession of Peter and the mocking on the cross. Elsewhere "Mes-

siah"/"Christ", like eschatology, always goes with "Son of Man" or "Son of David." This distribution of the material strongly suggests that "Son of God" in the Synoptics was not primarily an eschatological or messianic title.

5. *Clement of Alexandria and a Secret Gospel of Mark,* Cambridge, Mass., 1973; *The Secret Gospel,* N.Y., 1973. For the magical parallels to baptism and eucharist, see *Clement,* pp. 217 ff., 221, 232. For release from the law by union with Jesus, and the role of this concept in Paul's thought, see *ibid.,* pp. 213–217; 231 f.; 248–265.
6. *Pace* St. Paul, I. Cor. 10.2, on which see my *Clement,* p. 215, n. 6. Paul's argument indicates the existence of a belief that people could be baptized into the Messiah, but is not good evidence for any actual baptisms; cf. J. Weiss, *Der erste Korintherbrief,* 9 ed., Göttingen, 1910, repr. 1970, *ad loc.* (p. 250).
7. Sanhedrin 98b, 99a.
8. W. Bacher, *Die Agada der palästinensischen Amoräer,* Strassburg, 1892–99, vol. III, p. 703.
9. *Clement,* ch. IV, pp. 195–266.
10. Notably Paul, who boasted that he more often "spoke with tongues" than did any of his Corinthian converts, I Cor. 14.18.
11. The asceticism (Mk. 1.6 and parallels; Mt. 11.18; Lk. 7.33) is an interesting trait. It is not clearly characteristic of Biblical prophets and probably comes from Cynicism. The Baptist evidently took it for granted that a prophet of Yahweh must be a "holy man" by current Greco-Roman standards and set out to satisfy the demands of both traditions. Jesus refused to go to the trouble, and his reputation suffered in consequence, Mt. 11.19; Lk. 7.34. The hellenized Palestinian Jewish population expected asceticism of holy men. Lk. 1.15 biblicized the tradition by making the Baptist a Nazirite.
12. Prophets seem to have been in oversupply, Mk. 13.5 f., 22 and parallels, and many similar passages. Consequently the tacit competition for followers was probably pretty sharp and we may suppose that only the exceptional figure achieved enough significance to secure notice in our sources. The same situation prevails at present.
13. Desert and Jerusalem, Josephus, *War* 2. 258–263; *Ant.* 20. 167–172; Gerizim and tabernacle, *Ant.* 18.85.
14. Jn. 1.21 and the studies by H. Teeple, *The Mosaic Eschatological Prophet,* Philadelphia, 1957 (*JBL. Monograph Series,* X), and W. Meeks, *The Prophet-King,* Leiden, 1967 (*Supplements to Novum Testamentum,* XIV). A forthcoming study of Dositheus, by S. Isser, to be published in *Studies in Judaism in Late Antiquity,* will present evidence indicating that the messiahship of Dositheus was also of this type.
15. I Kings 19.16.
16. As John's disciples reportedly did, *Clementine Recognitions* I. 54.8; Ephraem Syrus, *Commentaire de l'Évangile concordant,* tr. L. Leloir, Louvain, 1954 (*CSCO* 145, *Armeniaci* 2), Appendix de sectatoribus, 1, p. 249.
17. *Antiquities* 8.46.

18. *Papyri Graecae Magicae,* ed. K. Preisendanz, 2 ed., ed. A. Henrichs, Stuttgart, 1973, Papyrus I, lines 181 ff.; etc.
19. Jn. 1.21.
20. Jn. 1.21; Mk. 8.28 and parallels.
21. Mt. 16.14.
22. Mk. 8.28 and parallels.
23. Mt. 16.13; etc.
24. Mt. 16.16; etc.
25. Acts 8.10.
26. Cf. the use of Is. 61.1f. for Jesus in Lk. 4.18.
27. *Histories* 5.13.
28. *Life of Vespasian* 4.5.
29. Josephus, *War* 3.399–407; 6.313. This propaganda was paid for by the emperors, *Vita* 361ff., 423; *Apion* 1.50ff.

4

Popular Messianic Movements around the Time of Jesus

Richard A. Horsley

Recent investigations of such terms as "messiah" and "son of David" in texts contemporary with Jesus and the NT writings have shown that they are remarkably infrequent prior to the end of the first century A.D. There seems to be a consensus emerging that there was no consistent concept of "the anointed one" at the time of Jesus.[1] Recent analyses have thus demonstrated that contemporary Jewish messianology is a rather weak foundation from which to explain early Christian christology. The focus of such investigations on ideas and expectations, however, has given only limited consideration to evidence of concrete social phenomena that may well be relevant to Jesus and the NT. Indeed, to judge from certain events recounted in Josephus' histories, Pontius Pilate was neither the first nor the last Roman official to be faced with a popular Jewish leader who was viewed as *rex iudaeorum*.

Indeed, although the sources are meager—primarily several brief and hostile reports by Josephus—social phenomena among the Jewish peasantry would appear to provide more concrete and relevant evidence for messianic activity at the time of Jesus than the literary texts usually adduced. That is, while the two principal groups which left literary remains, the Pharisees and the Qumran community, looked to idealized "anointed" figures with either scribal features or primarily ceremonial functions, the Jewish peasantry at the time of Jesus produced *several*

Reprinted by permission of the Catholic Biblical Association of American and the author from *Catholic Biblical Quarterly* 46 (1984).

concrete movements led by figures recognized as *kings,* movements and leaders who actually ruled certain areas of the country for a time.

The purpose of the analysis below is to determine as precisely as possible the distinctive social form taken by movements led by popular "kings." The presentation is also a sketch of one part of a broader typology of social movements and leaders at the time of Jesus[2] needed to fill the historical vacuum left by the demise of the concept of "the Zealots," which has become a principal foil for interpretation of Jesus and the Gospels. Now that "the Zealots" have been shown to be a modern scholarly construct—no group known as "the Zealots" ever existed prior to the second year of the great Jewish Revolt of 66–70[3]—it makes no sense to shift to the even more vague concept of "the resistance movement" and to continue to lump together groups and leaders that our principal sources clearly distinguish.[4] Thus, for example, Josephus clearly separated the Sicarii who arose in the 50s from the ordinary brigands who regularly appeared in Jewish society throughout the early Roman period.[5] Moreover, it is abundantly clear that the movements led by certain popular prophets were different in form from those led by "kings." In only one case was a "king" associated with any of these other distinctive groups: Menahem, who posed as king briefly in A.D. 66, was a leader of the Sicarii. If we are to construct a typology of popular movements and leaders at the time of Jesus, the distinctive character of each type of movement must be grasped partly by comparison with other types.

Sociology and social history may be a welcome complement to the "history of ideas" approach which has previously dominated biblical studies.[6] It will be important, however, to move toward greater precision in the application to biblical and related historical materials of concepts and analyses borrowed from other disciplines. For example, M. Weber saw clearly that the peasantry could become a "carrier of (genuinely ethical) religion" when threatened with domestic oppression or foreign enslavement. With a considerably more confined focus than that taken by Weber, with his broad comparative interests, we can discern with greater precision more than one distinctive type of leadership (and movement) in the expressions of "the ancient religion of the Palestinian peasantry."[7]

In reconstructing the distinctive popular movements led by "kings," attention will be given to what makes them different from other popular movements of the time such as banditry and prophetic movements. The investigation, therefore, includes both an anaylsis of the socio-historical situation of the participants in the popular "messianic" movements and an examination of the particular background or traditions out of which they responded to that situation. Indeed, because these kings and their movements appear to stand in, or to be a revival of, an ancient Israelite tradition of popularly elected or "anointed" kings, it is appropriate to describe the particular social form taken by these groups as "messianic movements." (Whereas the term messiah/messianic has come to be used rather broadly by some—in the sense of "eschatological" or even "political"[8]—the attempt will be made below to confine the term to agents of redemption who were anointed and/or recognized as kings.)[9]

THE ISRAELITE-JEWISH TRADITION OF POPULAR "ANOINTED" KINGSHIP

The distinctive forms of popular social movements have been obscured by the sources upon which we depend. Not all those called *hapiru* in the Amarna archives, for example, were really outlaws or fugitives or mercenaries.[10] Like the Amarna age officials before him, Josephus also scorns rebellious elements as "banditry." He called the Sicarii "another species of bandits." And, in summarizing his account of some of the popular uprisings upon the death of Herod, he begins: "And so Judea was filled with brigandage" (*Ant.* 17.10,8 §225 [following the Marcus translation in the LCL]). It may well have been just this passage that had led scholars such as M. Hengel to lump the leaders of the popular messianic movements together indiscriminately under the general concept of "the Zealots"—as "messianic pretenders in the Jewish freedom-movement."[11]

Now, although there is no basis whatever for linking the popular messianic movements indiscriminately with the hypothetical "Zealots," there is a basis for confusion between these movements and Jewish social banditry. Banditry was a regular feature of Jewish society at the time of Jesus. Numerous brigand groups were active in the rebellions of the period, especially in the revolt of A.D. 66–70. Nor were banditry and other movements mutually exclusive. According to Josephus, for example, there were brigands among the followers of two of the "kings" he mentions, Simon the former Herodian servant in 4 B.C. and Simon bar Giora in A.D. 68. Moreover, many of the socio-economic conditions conducive to widespread banditry have been the same historically as those in which the movements around the time of Jesus are rooted.[12]

Josephus, however, besides his scornful summarizing epithet of "banditry," pointedly explains that the two Simons (just mentioned) and other leaders such as Athronges, Judas son of Ezekias (both 4 B.C., and Menahem (A.D. 66) "claimed the kingship," "were acclaimed as king," or "set the diadem on their heads" (*J.W.* 2.4,1–3 §55–61; *Ant.* 17.10,5–7 §272–279; cf. Tacitus, *Hist.* 5.9). Why is it that Josephus mentions "kingship" in these particular cases, and that we claim to discern here a distinctive form of popular Jewish social movements. Indeed, perhaps there would have been no distinctive form of "messianic movement," no form of popular resistance other than social banditry, had there not been a tradition of popular kingship and historical prototypes of a popular "anointed one" among the Jews.

Although ancient Israel had known the phenomenon of banditry since earliest times, Israel also clearly distinguished banditry from more legitimate or politically organized forms, such as that of kingship or judgeship. Israel, however, resisted even popular kingship until the Philistine crisis, toward the end of the eleventh century. The distinctive form of popular messianic movement emerged first in the recognition of Saul and then especially of David as chieftains or kings of the coalition of Israelite peasant tribes. The rise of David, in particular, shows that although a king might begin as a bandit-chief, popular kingship was a distinctive socio-political form. David shrewdly maneuvered himself into recognition first as the king of the tribe of Judah, then as king over all the tribes.[13] David and his movement thus provided the principal precedent and the historical prototype for subsequent popular messianic movements, something qualitatively very different from mere banditry. It seems unnecessary as well as impossible to go into detailed analysis of the complex problems of terms (and sources) at this point.[14] Whether known as "chief" or "king"—both terms could possibly have been used, as in the case of the Midianite rulers (Num 31:8 and Josh 13:21)—the first, popular kings of Israel, like the "chieftains" of clans or tribes, were seen as regularized, as well as centralized, political leadership.[15]

During the reign of Solomon, of course, an official ideology of the unconditional establishment of the Davidic dynasty developed, with heavy borrowings of mythic motifs from Canaanite culture.[16] Much of the scholarly discussion of the origin and development of ideas about "the messiah" has focused on this official royal ideology. This is with good reason, for many of the scriptural texts that figure prominently in NT christology originate in this ideology (e.g., Psalms 2 and 110). Yet, however dominant the official ideology of the Davidic monarchy may have been in the subsequent history of biblical literature, the institutionalization of unconditional kingship never succeeded in completely suppressing or replacing the popular tradition of kingship in which David himself had begun.[17]

It would be naive to imagine that this popular tradition comes directly to expression in the heavily edited historical narratives of the OT which, in turn, may often have used "court histories" as their sources. Yet evidence for the characteristics—and the survival—of popular kingship can still be discerned among the strands and layers of the biblical narratives insofar as this tradition is reflected in the literature and presupposed in the events described. F. M. Cross has shown how such literature and events can be adduced as evidence for an ideology of the conditional and covenantal character of kingship which survived in the northern kingdom of Israel.[18] It is clear from both narratives and events that the principal social location of this ideology was not in official courtly circles—although a figure such as Absalom was capable of exploiting it. Ideas of conditional and covenantal kingship operated primarily among the people, the army, and popular prophetic circles (Elijah, Elisha, etc.). Such ideas operated primarily as a popular memory and expectation capable of reappearance and concrete expression in social movements at later points in Judean history.[19]

In positing this tradition, one might appeal for procedural legitimation to the distinction commonly made by anthropologists between the "great tradition" and the "little tradition."[20] In a society such as monarchic Israel and postexilic Judea the consciously cultivated ideas of professional scribes and priests will have been more reflective and systematized than the very basic memories, tales, and ideals of the unlettered peasantry. The two traditions, however, will have been interdependent. The fact that the ruling elite sponsors literature does not mean that they originate all cultural traditions. Nor is the literature produced by the cultural specialists the only means of transmission of particular cultural traditions. For example, a particular epic might originate among the tribal ancestors or common folk, then be given literary form by the literate classes, which in turn may influence the ongoing narrative form of the epic among the common people. The "great" and "little traditions" may evolve different twists and interpretations of given cultural materials, but there will be continuing interaction between them. This makes it possible to draw at least certain minimal inferences from literary sources to what may have been present among the populace at large.

Judging from its occasional appearance in biblical narratives and events, the popular Israelite tradition of kingship can be summarized according to three principal characteristics: Kingship was constituted *by popular* election or *anointing;* it was *conditional* on the king's maintenance of a certain social policy; and the anointing of a new king was generally a *revolutionary* action.

Physical prowess and force of arms may have been a prerequisite for recognition as chieftain/king (1 Sam 10:23; 16:18; cf. Judg 6:12, 8:22). But one was made king by popular election, either by all the people or by the assembly of the peasant militia or by the representative assembly of elders.[21] In the case of David, first "the men of Judah" and then "all the elders of Israel" "anointed David king" over Judah/Israel (2 Sam 2:4; 5:3; cf. 1 Sam 11:15 on the popular election of Saul). What is more, popular recognition could be withdrawn and another elected. Apparently a large proportion, perhaps the majority of Israel had at one point abandoned David in favor of his son Absalom, whom they had anointed to be (king) over them (2 Sam 15:19; esp. 15:10–12; 19:10). When it became clear that Rehoboam was planning to continue his father Solomon's oppressive practices, Israel called Jeroboam "to the assembly and made him king" (1 Kgs 12:20; cf. 2 Kgs 23:30). The accounts of Yahweh's anointing of the king through the hand of a prophet such as Samuel, Ahijah, or Elisha is a confirmation, not a contradiction, of the reality of popular election, another or parallel way of stating the same thing. That is, Yahweh's anointing anticipated popular action and the people's action fufills the will of Yahweh (see 1 Kgs 11:26–40 and 12:1–20; 1 Kgs 19:15–17 and 2 Kgs 9:1–2 and 9:13).

Second, the independent-minded peasantry of ancient Israel was committed to egalitarian social-economic ideals expressed in the Mosaic covenant. They were profoundly suspicious of kingship in its Canaanite form, which had been so oppressive in their own experience. Hence in a situation of political crisis, when they experimented with a new political form, they made kingship conditional, subject to certain covenantal stipulations. According to subsequent historical narratives, the duties and responsibilities of kingship were "written up in a book and laid up before Yahweh" (1 Sam 10:25). The conditions of kingship were transmitted in convenantal traditions (Deut 17:14–20) and even found liturgical expression in the "great tradition" as well (Ps 132:12). Yet another reflection of this same popular attitude toward kingship as conditional is the prophecy of Jeremiah against Davidic kings (Jer. 22:1–9,13–19).[22]

Finally, the anointing of a king by people or prophet was clearly a revolutionary act, as evident in cases from Saul and David in the eleventh century to the case of Jehoahaz at the end of the seventh century. In its very origins Israelite popular kingship was a means of marshalling centralized political-military power against foreign domination. Most of Israel, including apparently the tribe of Judah, rebelled against David by anointing Absalom over them. Like Ahijah's and the people's designation of Jeroboam, Elisha's and the army's anointing of Jehu meant a revolutionary overthrow of an established regime that had become intolerably oppressive, hence illegitimate. The popular anointing of Jehoahaz in 609 following the defeat and death of his father Josiah by the Egyptians involved both resistance to foreign domination and an internal struggle against the reactionary aristocratic (or court) party (2 Kgs 23:30).

This last example also shows how resilient the popular tradition was, especially considering the apparently complete domination of Judah by the established Davidic monarchy and its absolutist royal ideology. It is perhaps another indication of this resilience that in the oracles of the (peasant) prophet Micah no mention whatever is made of the official Davidic royal theology. Instead, the one "messianic" prophecy in (or, added to) the collection of Micah's oracles has the future ruler born, not in the royal court in Jerusalem, but in Bethelehem Ephrathah, "the least of the clans of Judah," i.e., whence the shepherd David originated (Mic 5:2). That is, regardless of whether this oracle stems from Micah himself or later, it provides an important window on the survival of hopes for a return of popular kingship among the Judean peasantry at a point when the northern kingdom of Israel (and periodic events of revolutionary "anointings") had ceased to exist.

Not long after the initial return from the Babylonian exile there was a brief resurgence of the royal ideology of the Davidic dynasty in connection with Zerubbabel, grandson of Jehoiachin, the last king of Judah. But whatever messianic excitement was generated around Zerubbabel must have faded rapidly. Although the succession of Davidids continued until the time of Nehemiah (mid-fifth century), the messianic themes of Haggai, Zechariah, and the earlier narratives of the Chronicler disappeared.[23] We also have virtually no evidence for what happened to the popular tradition of kingship during the Persian and Hellenistic periods. Indeed, as J. Bright pointed out some years ago, there is simply no evidence as to whether or not the eschatological hopes of Judeans focused strongly, let alone primarily, on an anointed or royal agent of God during the periods of Persian and Hellenistic domination.[24]

Yet there are fragmentary hints that the popular tradition was still alive. One of the prophecies appended to the Book of Zechariah would appear to borrow from the popular tradition, even if it is not a direct expression of it. Juxtaposed, in synthetic parallelism, with the coming king who is "triumphal and victorious" is his character as "humble and riding on a donkey" (Zech 9:9), evoking the image of the leader of tribal Israel prior to the time of a professional army with the advanced military technology of horses and chariots.

In terms of the dual level of traditions, the absence of new expressions of messianic expectations in the great tradition does not mean that the popular idea of kingship was extinct. The absence of any new cultivation of the official Davidic royal ideology and of any reflection of more popular expectations in the great tradition may merely be a function of our paucity of texts from the Persian and Hellenistic periods. But there are also understandable reasons why messianic ideas would be absent from the great tradition in postexilic times. Judea was now subject to the Persian and, later, Hellenistic kings. In order to remain loyal subjects, the postexilic Judean elite would have obediently suppressed any Judean royal or "messianic" pretensions. Moreover, the Judean people (no longer a state) was now headed by the high priesthood, which shaped religio-cultural life, including the official tradition. It would hardly have been in its interest to cultivate ideas about kings with whom it would have to share power.

Later in the Hellenistic period, however, there emerged a "bridge" that enables us to project the survival or reemergence of the popular tradition of kingship on the basis of the appearance of messianic ideas among literate strata. From early in the second century B.C. on there were groups of Hasidim and then Pharisees who attempted to make the "great tradition" relevant and applicable among the people as a whole.[25] Insofar as the great tradition by this time apparently included the "Prophets" as well as the "Torah," it contained materials originally derived from the ancient Israelite "little tradition," such as the popular anointing of kings. And we know from texts such as the Dead Sea Scrolls and the *Psalms of Solomon* that the self-appointed guardians of the great tradition knew and used messianic ideas. Now there are two possible ways in which this revival of messianic ideas may have developed: either the Hasidim and their successors revived the ideas from scriptural traditions on their own initiative, or they were responding to popular memories and hopes. Either way, with their purposeful and regular contacts with the peasantry, they constitute a "bridge," i.e., between the literate strata and the peasantry, and hence a basis for positing the presence of popular ideas of kingship in the late Second Temple period. Hence it would be justified to conclude not that the tradition of popular kingship was extinct, but that it had simply been dormant. The principal question that remains, then, is what the circumstances were that provoked the resurgence of the tradition of kingship among the people, either directly or indirectly, as mediated through the Pharisees.

THE SOCIO-HISTORICAL CONTEXT OF THE POPULAR MESSIANIC MOVEMENTS

The kings and their movements mentioned by Josephus occurred at two particular points during the early period of Roman domination: during the massive popular uprising following the death of Herod, and during the first great Revolt against Rome, A.D. 66–70. The particular social-political circumstances prevailing in the late Second Temple times provide the occasion for the revival of the popular tradition of kingship. And the concrete messianic movements can be at least partly explained as a reaction to these circumstances.

While unusually glorious by Hellenistic-Roman standards, Herod's reign was especially oppressive for the Jewish peasantry, economically and politically.[26] Herod's extensive building projects in Palestine and the munificence he lavished on imperial figures and Hellenistic cities served only to intensify the onerous burden on his taxpaying subjects. By the end of his long reign he had virtually bled the country dry (Josephus,

Ant. 17.11,2 §307–8). Yet his security forces were extensive and the measures they took extremely tight so that there was absolutely no opportunity for any serious resistance to gain a foothold among the people. With no outlet whatever, popular resentment could only build up an increasingly explosive pressure toward the end of his reign. When Herod finally died, the explosion came—in every district of his realm.

Rome reimposed order ruthlessly and reestablished Herodians and the Jewish sacerdotal aristocracy in power (Josephus, *J.W.* 2.5,1–6,2 §66–100; *Ant.* 17.10,9–17,11,4 §286–320). Not surprisingly, the same difficult conditions continued for the Jewish peasantry. They were taxed, doubly and heavily. Besides the elaborate Jewish Temple apparatus and the Roman tribute, taxation of the people supported lavish new building projects and diplomatic gifts. Then the prolonged drought and serious famine in the late 40s brought desperate conditions for much of the peasantry (*Ant.* 20.5,2 §101). Increasing numbers were apparently forced off their land and into the ranks of the hired laborers. The periodic insensitivity of the Roman governors and the irresponsible greed of the high priestly cliques provoked the people into sporadic outbursts of protest. A dramatic indicator of the desperation of the common people was the banditry that increased steadily throughout the 50s and 60s. Widespread popular revolt finally erupted in A.D. 66.

Such conditions may well have led to the outbreak of widespread popular uprisings. But are there any indicators of a revival of the tradition of popular kingship which would help explain why these uprisings took the particular form of messianic movements? There is some evidence for such a revival, although most of it is indirect, involving extrapolation from the reappearance of messianic expectations among the literate strata of Jewish society.

Unless it is due simply to our lack of sources for the early Hellenistic period, there was a dramatic reappearance of messianic expectations among the literate groups at the very end of the Hellenistic period, shortly after these groups themselves had emerged. It is interesting that there is little evidence for revival of royal imagery or messianic hopes during the Maccabean revolt and in Hasmonean literature.[27] Judean society had been focused on the Temple and the high priesthood since the fifth century. Under Antiochene persecution, however, both people and leaders, whether Hasidim or Hasmoneans, must have been sorely disillusioned with the Hellenizing high priests. What is more, since the

Hasmoneans were not a Zadokite family, Jonathan and Simon could not legitimately assume the high priesthood. Yet instead of reviving royal expectations and titles, the Hasmonean leaders assumed the high priestly office—thereby attesting the strength and centrality of the latter and the apparent dormancy of the former in Maccabean times.

It has been suggested that the Roman conquest (and the demise of the Hasmoneans) occasioned the revival of hopes for an anointed king.[28] But the revival may have begun even earlier, as a reaction by the literate groups, Pharisees and Essenes, to the assumption of the royal title first by Aristobulus I and then also by the arrogant Alexander Jannai (Josephus, *J.W.* 1.3,1 §70; *Ant.* 13.11,1 §301; 13.12,1 §320; cf. the cautious allusions in 1 Macc 14.41–43). Jannai also forcibly reduced the Pharisees' political-religious power and then defeated and even crucified and exiled Pharisees and others in brutal civil war (*J.W.* 1.4,3–6 §88–98; *Ant.* 13.14,2 §379–83; 13.15,5 §401). It is at least suggestive that the same *Psalm of Solomon* 17, in which occurs the only elaborate appeal for the eschatological king, "the son of David," "the anointed of the Lord," also harks back to the promise to David and then laments that sinners have taken by violence what was not promised to them and have arrogantly set up an illegitimate monarchy (17:5–8). The Roman conquest must then have served to intensify the feeling among Pharisees and others already suffering under the Hasmonean usurpers that they needed not only legitimate but righteous royal leadership—i.e., the new David, anointed by God and empowered to liberate the Jews and to rule the nations (*Ps. Sol.* 17:23–51).

If illegitimate Hasmonean kingship and Roman conquest had stimulated longing for an eschatological "anointed" king among the Pharisees (and Essenes?), the even more illegitimate and repressive Herodian kingship (and later direct Roman domination) must have stimulated an eagerness among the common people for their own genuine king to lead them in liberation. Generally speaking, peasants tend to take their kings seriously and trustingly. For example, they tend to believe that if only the king were not being manipulated by his deceitful advisers he would surely rectify the injustices they are suffering at the hands of the gentry and royal officials.[29] And the legitimacy of the royal power is all-important. But Herod was an illegitimate king in every sense. Not only was he a "half-Jew," but he was the very opposite of a leader of the people. A puppet of Rome, he had found it necessary to conquer the people he now ruled with the help of Roman legions. He maintained control by using alien mercenaries as a security force, and the whole Hellenistic style of his court and bureaucracy was alien to the people.[30]

It would only have exacerbated the alienation of his subjects when Herod, attempting to overcome or obscure his illegitimacy, created his own royal ideology. A speech placed into his mouth by Josephus probably reflects Herod's propaganda of peace and prosperity as the benefits of a divinely blessed reign and his posturing as the new Solomon, the son of David, who was now rebuilding the Temple of God (*Ant.* 15.11,1 §380–87).[31] Such propaganda would only have served to deepen the sense of contradiction between Jewish expectations and the realities of Herod's rule. If the popular legendary material behind the Matthean infancy narrative is any indication, Herod appeared to the people as the epitome of a tyrant, the very opposite of the anointed one (Matt 2:16).

Another story reported by Josephus indicates how intense the longing was for the true, divinely designated king toward the end of Herod's reign. Although the story centers around court intrigue and the misunderstandings of discontented members of the royal family, it may provide a window on the general mood at other levels of the society as well. Not only is there eager reception of "God's decrees," announced by the Pharisees in this case, that Herod's throne would be taken from him and his descendants; but there is the fantasy of a certain eunuch Bagoas that the one who would be set over the people as king would give him a wife and the ability to beget children of his own (*Ant.* 17.2,4 §41–45). The story also shows that Herod's brutal repression was more intense than ever. Suffering thus under an illegitimate and oppressive king installed by an alien power, the Jewish people must have been eager for an "anointed" king from their own ranks, like David of old.

The foregoing sketch is somewhat tentative because of the dearth of sources for popular expectations at the time (or at any time!). It is offered as a possible explanation of the occasion, broadly speaking, for the reemergence of the tradition of popular kingship which informed the messianic movements that sprang up at the death of Herod.[32]

By the time of the great Revolt of 66–70, of course, popular hopes for an anointed king must have been widespread and intense. Josephus explains straightforwardly that what more than anything else inspired the people to rebellion was "an ambiguous oracle, (likewise) found in their sacred scripture, to the effect that one from their country would become ruler of the world" (*J.W.* 6.5,4 §312). As Tacitus says independently, the common people interpreted this "mysterious prophecy" "in their own favor, and could not be turned to the truth even by adversity" (*Hist.* 5.13).

POPULAR MESSIANIC MOVEMENTS FOLLOWING THE DEATH OF HEROD

The popular kings at the time of Jesus appear to have been different from the spiritualized or formalized "anointed ones" expected in Pharisaic or Essene literature, whose *modus operandi* was to be pedagogical or ceremonial. The popularly recognized kings, by contrast, led their followers directly to the business of liberating themselves from foreign and tyrannical rule and of reestablishing more egalitarian social relations by putting an end to socio-economic privilege.

Josephus apparently avoids any suggestion of the distinctive Jewish tradition of an anointed king in his accounts of Judas, Simon, and Athronges.[33] Serious note should be taken of Josephus' Hellenistic terminology, however, especially that of "donning the diadem" and related terms. J. Hanson has recently demonstrated that Josephus, precisely with the language of diadem, the standard symbolism for designating royal office, is focusing attention on the political authority seriously claimed by these leaders of popular revolts.[34] It would seem reasonable that when Josephus writes that these figures "donned the diadem," or "claimed the kingship," or "were proclaimed king" by their followers, we can surmise on the basis of other sources for Palestinian-Jewish socio-religious forms that these figures were messianic pretenders, to be understood against the background of the longstanding Jewish tradition of popular anointed kingship. Furthermore, the information we can glean from Josephus on other aspects and actions of these movements fits well with their interpretation as informed by the popular tradition of kingship.

The popular kings' great physical stature and prowess mentioned by Josephus (in cases of Simon and Athronges as well as Simon bar Giora later, *Ant.* 17.10,6–7 §273, 278) is very likely a reflection of the tradition that the king elected by God or the people was to be a mighty man or warrior. It is unnecessary in this case, as well as virtually impossible, to separate historical data about the actual physical characteristics from the literary accounts. For the point is that, whether at the level of Josephus' accounts or at the level of the more popularly influenced reports which Josephus used, the image of the popular king was informed by the great heroes or kings of popular memory, David being the principal prototype (1 Sam 16:18).[35]

In the movements that sprang up following the death of Herod the leaders were all men of humble origins. It is inherently unlikely that the peasants would have looked to the gentry for leadership, since most of the latter owed their position to Herod or were otherwise implicated in collaboration with the Herodian-Roman system. Simon had been a royal servant; Athronges was a "mere shepherd" (as David had been, according to the tradition; *J.W.* 2.4,2–3 §57, 60; *Ant.* 17.10,6–7 §273, 278). In Galilee the royal pretender was the son of a brigand chief: i.e., Judas led the revolt at the death of the tyrant who had murdered his father Hezekiah nearly four decades earlier. Apparently under the influence of the modern scholarly construct of "the Zealots," some scholars have mistakenly identified Judas son of Hezekiah with Judas of Galilee who founded the "Fourth Philosophy" ten years later.[36] But Josephus writes nothing that would suggest such an identification. Chronologically, moreover, the identification is virtually an impossibility, for it would make "Judas" well over fifty years old at the beginnings of the Fourth Philosophy, when he sired Menahem, a leader of the Sicarii who was supposedly his son—who correspondingly would than have been sixty or over when he in turn became royal pretender in 66. On the contrary, Josephus says rather clearly that Judas of Galilee was a teacher, a sage (*sophistēs, J.W.* 2.8.1 §118), like the revered teachers who inspired their pupils to pull down the Roman eagle over the Temple gate (*J.W.* 1.33,2–4 §648–55; *Ant.* 17.6,2–4 §149–68). The Judas who claimed the kingship in 4 B.C., however, was probably a peasant, although as the son of a famous brigand-chief perhaps already recognized as a popular leader.[37]

The followers of Judas, Simon, and Athronges were also largely from the peasantry. All three movements were based in the countryside. Josephus clearly distinguishes other rebel groups active at the same time, whether the resistance in the metropolis of Jerusalem or the separate revolt by a group of Herod's veteran troops. A large number of the people involved in the messianic movements may have been "desperate men" (*Ant.* 17.10,5 §271) because of tightening economic circumstances for the peasantry in which many were losing their land. In

Simon's movement "the brigands he collected" may be simply Josephus' pejorative term for the rebels or, more likely—once we recognize the reality of Jewish social banditry throughout the period and, in this case, the mountainous territory of Trans-Jordan which could have provided them a base of operations—peasants who had been driven into banditry before joining Simon (*J.W.* 2.4,2 §57).

In the comment that the Pereans proclaimed Simon king in their "madness" (or enthusiasm) and that they fought with "more recklessness than science," Josephus reveals that such movements were motivated by a special spirit or inspiration (*Ant.* 17.10,6 §274–76). They also appear to have been at least somewhat organized, at least into "companies" for military purposes. Athronges used his brothers as heads of subdivisions of his large force. This Judean shepherd-king also apparently held councils to deliberate on policies or courses of action (*Ant.* 17.10,7 §280–81).

The goals of the messianic movements were twofold, generally speaking: to achieve liberation from Herodian-Roman domination, and to reestablish the traditional ideals of a more egalitarian social structure. Josephus indicates explicitly that they stormed the royal palaces at Sepphoris and Jericho not simply as symbols of the hated Herodian tyranny, and not merely to obtain weapons, but also in order to retrieve the property that had been seized by Herodian officials and stored there (*Ant.* 17.10,6 §274; *J.W.* 2.4,2 §57). Understandably enough, they attacked their oppressors, both Romans and royalists. But they also raided the estates of the gentry along with the royal residences. Their long-frustrated resentment at prolonged social-economic inequity and exploitation was now released into the concrete social form of an egalitarian anarchism typical among peasant uprisings.[38]

Once we have a clearer sense of Josephus' (and Tacitus') reports that leaders such as Judas, Simon, and Athronges presumed to claim the kingship (or were acclaimed king—and not simply "aspired to" the kingship), it becomes evident that these movements were far more serious than extended riots or marauding bands of raiders. Indeed there were movements which took effective control of certain areas within their respective districts of Galilee, Perea, or Judea. Perhaps the size of the military force which Varus, Legate of Syria, believed necessary to reconquer Jewish Palestine helps us gauge the size and scope of the messianic movements. To reinforce the Roman legion already in Judea he brought the two remaining legions in the Province of Syria, four regiments of cavalry and all the auxiliary troops supplied by the client rulers and Hellenistic cities in the region. The Romans found, however, that it was not a simple matter to reestablish their control of the areas now dominated by the popular messianic movements. In Judea especially the movement led by Athronges continued on for some time before the Roman or Herodian forces could eventually subdue the various companies of Athronges' peasant followers. Archelaus finally persuaded the last remaining brother (Athronges himself?) to surrender—"but this happened later" (*Ant.* 17.10,7 §281–84).

It would be nothing but pure speculation to draw any connection between these three messianic movements which began in 4 B.C. and the movement focused on Jesus of Nazareth somewhat more than a generation later. Yet anyone familiar with the significant geographical locations of the Christian gospel narratives must be struck by the geographical locations in which these messianic movements were active—and the towns or villages that bore the brunt of the fierce vengeance wrought by the Romans when they reconquered the country—especially considering that these events were taking place within a few years of Jesus' birth. Here were mass movements comprised of Jewish peasants from villages round such towns as Bethlehem, Emmaus, and Sepphoris, people taking common action under the leadership of a popular figure they recognized as king of the Jews. Perhaps it is worth noting (as a reminder that we are dealing with concrete movements and concrete places) that in 4 B.C., just a few miles north of the village of Nazareth, the town of Sepphoris was burned and its inhabitants sold into slavery.

MESSIANIC MOVEMENTS DURING THE JEWISH REVOLT, A.D. 66–70

Perhaps due partly to the general paucity of sources we have no evidence of any particular messianic movements between those in 4 B.C. and the outbreak of the great revolt in A.D. 66—unless one were to include the movement focused on Jesus of Nazareth. There was, of course, a great deal of social-political-religious turmoil throughout the period, including the famous tax-revolt of A.D. 6, popular prophetic movements led by such figures as Theudas and an "Egyptian"-Jewish prophet, and widespread social banditry that escalated dramatically following the serious famine of the late 40s. Moreover, during the great revolt itself, a messianic movement was by no means the only social form taken by the widespread uprising. At the outbreak of the rebellion in A.D. 66, for example, the large and numerous bands of brigands provided leadership for the peasantry, especially in Galilee. Two of the groups prominent during the great revolt, however, appear to have taken the form of a messianic movement: the relatively small group of Sicarii led by Menahem, and the extremely large force following Simon bar Giora.

It would be more accurate to describe the first of these, toward the beginning of the rebellion, as a messianic incident or episode (because it was ended so quickly) in the longer history of activity by the group of terrorists called the Sicarii. Because the fact has not been widely recognized, it bears repeating that the Sicarii and the Zealots were quite different groups. Hence it would only obscure the distinctive historical realities to perpetuate a falsely synthetic concept such as "Zealot Messianism."[39] Although a more detailed examination of this surprising messianic episode among the Sicarii cannot be done in this context, it is important here to note at least its popular orientation.[40]

Since the mid-50s the Sicarii had carried out a series of terrorist actions against members of the Jewish ruling class who were collaborating with Roman rule. Once the widespread revolt erupted they were quick to join the insurgents in Jerusalem. In one of the more dramatic actions taken by Sicarii, Menahem armed his colleagues from Herod's old arsenal at Masada, returned to Jerusalem "as king" and became a leader of the insurrection (*J.W.* 2.17,9 §425–34). It is clear precisely through Josephus' contemptuous language (*J.W.* 2.17,9 §443–45) that Menahem was posturing as the divinely elected king, being recognized as such by his "fanatical" followers. Not only did he presume to take sole political control of affairs in Jerusalem, but he and his followers were giving ceremonial expression to his office in the Temple, "whither he had gone up in state to pay his devotions, arrayed in royal robes and attended by his suite of armed fanatics" (§443). However much Menahem and company constituted a threat to the Jerusalem *dēmos,* which favored the leadership of Eleazar, the Temple captain, the "dagger men" and their messiah sided with the common people.[41] Most significantly, they participated in the burning of the public archives "to destroy the money-lenders' bonds and to prevent the recovery of debts . . . in order to cause a rising of the poor against the rich," as the wealthy priestly aristocrat Josephus saw quite clearly (*J.W.* 2.17,6 §427).

Far more serious and important than the Menahem episode was the messianic movement focused on Simon bar Giora, who eventually became the principal political-military commander in the besieged holy city and whom the Romans recognized as the enemy general or chief of state. For Simon's career Josephus provides much more information than for any of the other popular kings. Since there are also two fine scholarly treatments of Simon that complement each other,[42] we can concentrate on key features of his movement as a distinctive social form.

Simon's very name, "son of the proselyte," indicates that he was not from a notable or "respectable" family. From the very beginning of the revolt he was leader of a fairly substantial fighting force and was apparently one of the real heroes of the audacious victory over the Roman army advancing on Jerusalem in October 66 (*J.W.* 2.19,2 §521). But he was then passed over for a command by the provisional government. Undoubtedly the last thing the aristocratic junta wanted was such a popular leader at the head of a peasant army. Nevertheless, because of his charismatic (messianic?) qualities of "physical strength and courage" he continued as a popularly recognized leader of the social revolution in the toparchy of Acrabatene (*J.W.* 4.9,3 §503–4; 2.22,2 §652–53). He bided his time, and even stayed for a time with the Sicarii at Masada, when the governing group in Jerusalem took serious steps to suppress his activities in Acrabatene.

When Simon heard of the death of the High Priest Ananus, however, he began systematially to build his movement. A number of "Davidic" features are discernible in the rise of Simon, despite Josephus' special hostility to this "despot" who had imprisoned his parents in Jerusalem during the Roman siege. His very rise from a leader of a local fighting force (guerrilla band)—who posed a threat to the provisional government—to one followed as king by thousands of people, as well as by a sizeable army, parallels the rise of David himself. As with the great messianic prototype, the initial ones to join his band were the "worthless" and discontented (*J.W.* 4.9,3–4 §507–13). Eventually, however, with the people as a whole groping for effective leadership against foreign domination, large numbers of people, including some of the notables, came to recognize him "as a king." Also, with O. Michel, one must question whether it was only for strategic reasons that Simon solidified his control of as much of southern Judea and Idumea as possible, and especially the town of Hebron, before pressing on to Jerusalem. Was he not rather "liberating"—and establishing righteous government in—the original territory of Judah, including Hebron, which was surely remembered as the place where David was first anointed prince of Judah, and from which, recognized as king of all Israel, he went to take Jerusalem and to liberate the whole country? One is tempted to speculate in precisely this direction because it is just at this point in his narrative that Josephus diverts the reader's attention to the great antiquity of Hebrew and its association with Abraham (*J.W.* 4.9,7 §529–34).

Like the messianic movements seventy years earlier, Simon and his followers seem to have been strongly motivated by resentment at their previous oppression by the wealthy. One of the principal goals of the movement, its social program, was the restoration of social and economic justice. One might even detect an apocalyptic overtone in the proclamation of "liberty for slaves and rewards for the free." Was Simon here announcing eschatological liberty and blessings? Whether eschatological or not, equity for the meek and justice for the poor were central to the program of the future anointed king, the righteous branch of David, at least according to prophecies such as Isaiah 11 and Jer 23:5 (cf. Jer 34:8–9).

Another part of the program of Simon and his movement that is very striking—assuming that we can trust Josephus' account in this respect—is the military organization and discipline they achieved, including forethought and preparation of the support system necessary for a prolonged war of liberation. However much they may have been caught up in fantasies of God's eschatological holy war (like the Qumran community?), this movement was by no means simply a spontaneous horde of peasants wildly plundering the mansions of the gentry or naively storming the barricades of the holy city.

As surmised by O. Michel,[43] Simon's entry into Jerusalem to take the reins of government may have involved his formal recognition as king (by whatever title) by the "citizen body" of Jerusalem and chief priests. It may not have involved any dramatic demonstration or posturing, like those of Menahem and the Sicarii, but Simon was henceforth the ruler of the city. Michel also sorts through the bitter condemnation of Simon's execution of deserters by Josephus (that most successful of deserters!) to find there the social-political discipline necessary to maintain order among the people under prolonged siege.[44] One is tempted to go one step further. This could well have been understood in a manner somewhat similar to phrases in *Psalm of Solomon* 17. In the (final) "war" against and victory over the oppressive foreign nations the king would "thrust out sinners from (the) inheritance" and "not suffer unrighteousness to lodge anymore in their midst, thus purging Jerusalem, making it holy as of old" (17:26,29,33,36).

That Simon bar Giora had assumed the role of the king of the Jews, finally, is manifest in two highly symbolic and ceremonial events: his dramatic surrender to the Romans after the destruction of Jerusalem and the Temple, and his ritual execution in Rome as the enemy general or head of state. Michel believes that the account of Simon's surrender rests on solid historical tradition.[45] After attempting to escape through the tunnels and secret passages under the city of Jerusalem, Simon apparently decided on a ceremonious and symbolic surrender: "Simon . . . dressed himself in white tunics and buckling over them a purple mantle arose out of the ground at the very spot whereon the Temple formerly stood" (*J.W.* 7.2,2 §29).

The significance of the apparel is unmistakable.[46] It is that of the king —in this case of the king of the Jews. The symbolism would have been clear to all. It had long since been used in mockery—both Agrippa I and Jesus were mocked by means of such apparel (Philo, *In Flaccum* 36–39; Mark 15:16–20)—as well as on formal state occasions, such as the funeral of Herod the Great (Josephus, *War* 1.33,9 §671; *Ant.* 17.8,3 §197). Precisely what Simon was attempting to accomplish with his self-surrender is not clear from Josephus' account. He may have been attempting either to bring about the divine apocalyptic intervention or, more likely, to lighten the punishment that would befall his people through the self-sacrifice of the leader to the enemy. In any case, he surrendered—and was taken by the Romans—as the king of the Jews.

The ritual execution of Simon formed part of the triumphal procession and celebration of the great Roman victory over the rebellious Jewish nation—portrayed by Josephus with the proper sense of the pomp and circumstance (*J.W.* 7.5,6 §153–55). It could not be clearer that the Romans recognized Simon as the leader of the Jewish nation. His rival for leadership during the prolonged Roman siege of Jerusalem, John of Gischala, the Romans simply imprisoned. Simon, on the other hand, was ceremonially paraded (one would assume appropriately robed, on the basis of *J.W.* 7.5,5 §138),[47] scourged, and executed as the leader, perhaps explicitly as "king" of the Jews in one of the principal events of the triumphal celebration in Rome. Taken together with the manner of his surrender, clad in the symbolic robes of the king of the Jews, the ceremonial event in Rome provides a significant manifestation of the way in which Simon bar Giora had assumed the role of the anointed king of his people, the recognized leader of a messianic movement that had begun among the Judean peasantry in the midst of their assertion of independence from Roman rule.

THE BAR KOCHBA REVOLT

The Bar Kochba Revolt, the final revolt of Jewish antiquity, has been the most clearly recognized in the scholarly literature as a messianic movement.[48] In reconquering Galilee and Judea during the War of A.D. 66–70, the Roman legions had devastated numerous villages and towns and had either killed or sold into slavery much of the population of Jewish Palestine. The spirit of resistance, however, remained very much alive among the Judean people. Rome may have suppressed the messianic movement led by Simon bar Giora, but it could not suppress the people's yearning for liberation, which now more than ever focused on an anointed royal agent.

Apparently Johanan ben Zakkai and most of the other Rabbis, sobered by the defeat and devastation of the country at the hands of the Romans, had little interest in further eschatological revelations. Nevertheless, a few scholars must have continued the apocalyptic tradition of the Hasidim, the Essenes, and the Pharisees. Toward the end of the first century A.D., some Jewish scholarly visionaries, in literature such as the apocalypses of 2 *Baruch* and 4 *Ezra,* produced more vivid and highly developed expectations of "the Messiah" than those expressed in earlier literature.[49]

We have no solid evidence for the degree to which the Jewish peasantry may have shared the more fantastic features of the literary apocalyptic expectations. The fourteenth and fifteenth of the *Eighteen Benedictions,* however, provide evidence that expectations focused on a Messiah or a "shoot of David" were very much alive among the common people at this time. Because the *Šĕmônēh ʿEśrēh* did not reach its final form until after the fall of Jerusalem in A.D. 70,[50] one can only speculate on the degree to which such popular prayers represent Palestinian Jewish piety prior to the first great revolt. For the period just prior to the Bar

Kochba Revolt, however, the *Eighteen Benedictions* do provide reliable evidence that the people's hopes for liberation were focused on a new David, an anointed one.

Thus it should come as no surprise that the revolt that erupted about sixty years after the end of the first great revolt took the form of a messianic movement. The revered elderly Rabbi Akiba, who had not forgotten his peasant roots, proclaimed that Simon bar Kosibah, the leader of the renewed rebellion, was the expected anointed king, in particular as the fulfillment of the Oracle of Balaam (Num 24:17): "a star shall go forth from Jacob" (*j. Taan.* 4,68d—hence the name bar Kochba, "son of the star"). Other Rabbis, probably the majority, were hardly convinced. Rabbi Johanan ben Torta answered him: "Akiba, grass will grow out of your cheek-bones and the Son of David will still not have come." The royal pretender himself, moreover, is denigrated in later rabbinic traditions, which refer to him with a pun on his name, i.e., bar Koziba = "Son of the Lie," or "Liar." For Akiba and the followers of Simon bar Kosibah, however, the leader of the revolt was clearly understood as the Anointed One. Akiba's application of the star prophecy is unambiguously royal-messianic, in contrast to the Qumran literature, in which the star of Num 24.17 was interpreted with some variation (e.g., CD 7:9–21; 1QM 11:4–7). Coins from the first year of the revolt and letters from Murabbaʿat and Ḥever now provide corroborating evidence that Simon bar Kosibah was regarded as the elected ruler, the "Prince *(Nāsîʾ)* of Israel." Although there was also apparently a priestly leader, "Eleazar the Priest," Simon clearly took precedence.[51]

Undeterred by the rabbinic rejection of its messianic pretensions, large numbers of the Judean peasantry must have joined the movement. Simon and his followers established their own government in extensive areas of Judea while defending themselves against Roman attempts at reconquest. Their coins, inscribed "Year I of the Liberation of Israel," or "Year II of the Freedom of Israel," indicated that they believed a new era had begun with their assertion of independence from Roman rule. The recently found Murabbaʿat and Ḥever documents reveal, moreover, that Simon exercised rigorous military and administrative discipline, and that he and other leaders placed great emphasis on strict observance of traditional religious stipulations.[52] Some members of Bar Kosibah's movement must even have occupied the ruins of Jerusalem for a time. When the Romans sent massive military forces to reconquer the Jews,

Simon and his men forced them into a prolonged war of attrition through skillful guerrilla operations based in caves and mountain strongholds. Only after extended campaigns and costly individual battles could the Romans finally "annihilate, exterminate, and eradicate" them from the land (Dio Cassius 59.13,3).

CONCLUSION

In the last few decades we have become aware that the word "anointed" and closely related terms were used infrequently in Jewish literature before the time of Jesus. That is, an "anointed" royal (or other) agent of God was not necessarily central or essential in the future expectations of the Palestinian Jewish groups that left literary remains. Among the Palestinian Jewish peasantry, however, there were actual movements led by kings. A few decades before and after the ministry of Jesus several extensive popular movements took this form. Recognizing one of their number as king, large numbers of Jewish peasants periodically proceeded to liberate themselves from Roman rule and domination by the Jewish aristocracy and to restore more egalitarian social relations, in accordance with (their traditional understanding of) the will of God.

It is important to recognize the characteristic form as well as the concrete reality of these messianic movements because this was not the only possible form that popular social movements could have taken. In the same period of time, in the same general circumstances, there were also other distinctive forms of popular discontent: social banditry, prophetic movements, more general peasant uprisings (i.e., without distinctive "kings" or "prophets" as leaders), and rather amorphous spontaneous urban demonstrations and riots. For a popular movement or revolt to have taken the particular form of a messianic movement instead of banditry or a riot, there had to have been a certain critical level of religio-political consciousness. A popular messianic movement involved a particular historical memory among large numbers of peasants and some leaders who could appeal to, and constructively mold, that memory toward common action in dealing with their life situation.

Thus, like social banditry, the messianic movements were reactions to socio-economic conditions which had gradually or suddenly become unacceptable to the peasants in a certain area. Banditry, however, appears to have lacked a particular political consciousness of what was wrong with the situation and program of how to go about alleviating or rectifying it. The messianic movements, on the other hand, presupposed such a political consciousness and carried out a particular program of action. Informed by the popular memory of messianic movements among their distant ancestors led by David or other anointed figures, groups of Jewish peasants were now attempting to assert their independence of outside control and to reestablish just social relations in their society under the leadership of a new king whom they (and God) had acclaimed. The popular prophetic movement of this period may have had similar goals to establish anew the independence of the people and to restore utopian social-economic relations. But the prophetic movements looked to the divine initiative in signs and wonders like those of the exodus from Egypt or the battle of Jericho of old, whereas the messianic movements took direct political and military action.

The fact that the popular kings and their movements governed only a limited area and were able to maintain their popular sovereignty and independence for only a short time—from a few years (Simon bar Giora, bar Kochba, Athronges?) to a few weeks (Judas son of Hezekiah)—does not lessen their significance. The occurrence of these concrete movements indicates that the Jewish peasantry, working out of their particular memory of previous liberation and popular sovereignty, were capable of producing their own leadership and of taking collective action in a politically conscious way. Perhaps this should not be surprising from a society a principal part of whose "great tradition," as well "little tradition," consisted of essentially revolutionary actions by the peasantry in "anointing" one of their number to lead them in liberating action.

NOTES

1. See especially M. de Jonge, "The Use of the Word 'Anointed' in the Time of Jesus," *NovT* 8 (1966) 132–48; D. C. Duling, "The Promises to David and Their Entance into Christianity—Nailing Down a Likely Hypothesis," *NTS* 20 (1973–74) 68; "The Therapeutic Son of David: An Element in Matthew's Christological Apologetic," *NTS* 24 (1977–78) 407–8; E. Rivkin, "Messiah, Jewish," *IDBSup*. 588–91; M. Smith, "What Is Implied by the Variety of Messianic Figures?" *JBL* 78 (1959) 66–72.
2. Briefly sketched in R. A. Horsley, "Ancient Jewish Banditry and the Revolt Against Rome, A.D. 66–70," *CBQ* 43 (1981) 422–24.
3. S. Zeitlin, "Zealots and Sicarii," *JBL* 81 (1962) 395–98; M. Smith, "Zeal-

ots and Sicarii: Their Origins and Relations," *HTR* 64 (1971) 1–19; R. A. Horsley, "Josephus and the Bandits," *JSJ* 10 (1979) 37–63.

4. *Vs.* G. Theissen, *Sociology of Early Palestinian Christianity* (Philadelphia: Fortress, 1978), e.g., 34–35, 61; E. M. Smallwood, *The Jews Under Roman Rule* (Leiden: Brill, 1976) 153–55.
5. R. A. Horsley, "The Sicarii: Ancient Jewish Terrorists," *JR* 59 (1979) 435–58. For Josephus texts I have used the LCL; in quotations I have adapted the LCL translations by Thackeray or Marcus.
6. Good examples of how this can be done are: V. Tcherikover, *Hellenistic Civilization and the Jews* (New York: Atheneum, 1970; orig. 1959); J. Gager, *Kingdom and Community: The Social World of Early Christianity* (Englewood Cliffs, NJ: Prentice-Hall, 1975); N. Gottwald, *The Tribes of Yahweh* (Maryknoll: Orbis, 1979); W. A. Meeks, *The First Urban Christians: The Social World of the Apostle Paul* (New Haven: Yale, 1983).
7. *Sociology of Religion* (Boston: Beacon, 1964; orig. German, 1922) 80–81.
8. E.g., cf. the label "messianic prophet," in R. Meyer, "Προφητης," *TDNT* 6.826; still being perpetuated in D. Hill, "Jesus and Josephus' 'Messianic Prophets,'" in *Text and Interpretation: Studies in the New Testament Presented to Matthew Black* (ed. E. Best and R. McL. Wilson; Cambridge: University Press, 1979) 143–54.
9. The recent practice of similarly confining usage of the term messiah/messianic is exemplified in R. E. Brown, "The Teacher of Righteousness and the Messiah(s)," *The Scrolls and Christianity* (TC 11; London: SPCK, 1969) 41; and J. A. Fitzmyer, *The Gospel According to Luke I–IX* (AB 28; Garden City, NY: Doubleday, 1981), esp. 197–98.
10. E. F. Campbell, Jr., "The Amarna Letters and the Amarna Period," *BA* 23 (1960) 14 (-*BAR* 3 [1970] 66); for the broader social-historical context, see now N. Gottwald, *Tribes,* esp. chs. 35–36.
11. M. Hengel, *Die Zeloten* (rev. ed.; Leiden: Brill, 1976) 296–303.
12. E. J. Hobsbawm, *Bandits* (rev. ed.; New York: Pantheon, 1981) 19–24; R. A. Horsley, "Ancient Jewish Banditry," 416–20.
13. On the rise of David, see J. Bright, *A History of Israel* (2d ed.: Philadelphia: Westminster, 1972) 186–97.
14. See esp. F. M. Cross, *Canaanite Myth and Hebrew Epic* (Cambridge, MA: Harvard University, 1973), esp. pp. 220–21, 230 n. 45; J. R. Bartlett, "The Use of the Word *rosh* as a Title in the Old Testament," *VT* 19 (1969) 1–10; E. A. Speiser, "Background and Function of the Biblical NASI'," *CBQ* 25 (1967) 111–17.
15. E. A. Speiser, ibid., 115–17.
16. See the careful treatment of the official "Judean royal theology" by F. M. Cross, *Canaanite Myth,* 241–64. Cf. the brief recent survey of the development of messianic ideas in J. Becker, *Messianic Expectations in the Old Testament* (Edinburgh: Clark, 1980).
17. Z. Weisman ("Anointing as a Motif in the Making of the Charismatic King," *Bib* 57 [1976] 378–83) comes right to the edge of making his

distinction between a popular kingship and the official royal ideology (and its elaborate cultic ritual), but does not pose the requisite sociological questions in his motif-study.

18. F. M. Cross, *Canaanite Myth,* 222–37.
19. E.g., Hayim Tadmor, "The People and the Kingship in Ancient Israel: The Role of Political Institutions in the Biblical Period," *Cahiers d'histoire mondiale (Journal of World History)* 11 (1968) 60.
20. R. Redfield, *Peasant Society and Culture* (Chicago: University of Chicago, 1969; orig. 1956) 70–72; E. R. Wolf, *Anthropology* (New York: Norton, 1974) 73–74; applied to the rise of David's monarchy by J. W. Flanagan, "The Relocation of the Davidic Capital," *JAAR* 47 (1979) 225–27.
21. C. U. Wolf, "Traces of Primitive Democracy in Ancient Israel," *JNES* 6 (1947) 105–7; Z. Weisman, "Anointing as a Motif," 382; H. Tadmore, "The People of the Kingship," 46–68; cf. E. A. Speiser, "Background of Biblical NASI'," esp. p. 115.
22. See further F. M. Cross, *Canaanite Myth,* 221, 224, 233 n. 62.
23. F. M. Cross, "A Reconstruction of the Judean Restoration," *Int* 29 (1975) 199.
24. J. Bright, *A History of Israel,* 439–43; see also J. A. Fitzmyer, "The Son of David Tradition and Matthew 22,41–46 and Parallels," in *The Dynamics of Biblical Tradition* (Concilium 20; New York: Paulist Press, 1967) 80.
25. On the origins of the Hasidim and Pharisees, see J. Neusner, *From Politics to Piety* (Englewood Cliffs, NJ: Prentice-Hall, 1973) esp. pp. 50–52; E. Bickerman, *From Ezra to the Last of the Maccabees* (New York: Scribner's, 1966) 160–77; V. Tcherikover, *Hellenistic Civilization and the Jews,* 124–26, 196–98, 254–65.
26. A. Schalit, *König Herodes: Der Mann und sein Werke* (Berlin: de Gruyter, 1969) 256–98.
27. 1 Macc 3:3–4 alludes to the Blessing of Jacob on Judah, Gen 49:9, i.e., possibly a royal messianic reference. But the "anointed one, a prince" in Dan 9:25 probably refers to the first high priest after the exile, Joshua ben Jozadak (cf. Dan 11:22 for "prince" as a high priest); see L. F. Hartman and A. A. Di Lella, *The Book of Daniel* (AB 23; Garden City, NY: Doubleday, 1978) 251.
28. E. Schürer, *The History of the Jewish People in the Age of Jesus Christ* (new ed. by G. Vermes and F. Millar; Edinburgh: Clark, 1973—), 1. 503.
29. E. J. Hobsbawm, *Bandits,* 51–55; *Primitive Rebels* (New York: Norton, 1965) 186–87.
30. On Herod's security, alien mercenaries, Hellenistic court, and bureaucracy, see A. Schalit, *König Herodes*. S. Freyne (*Galilee: From Alexander the Great to Hadrian* [Wilmington: Glazier, 1980] 215) uses the term "legitimacy" in a sense very different from the concept presupposed in this essay.
31. Schalit, *König Herodes,* 473–79.
32. Cf. S. Freyne, *Galilee,* 213–16. Apparently presupposing that the peasantry had no messianic ideas of their own and that they were incapable of produc-

ing their own leadership, Freyne argues that "in realistic terms Judas son of Hezekiah would have had to represent himself as carrying forward some recognizable tradition of kingship—Hasmonean or Herodian" (p. 215). To appreciate the difficulties of such an approach, one need only consider the irony of that particular argument: the original Hasmonean leaders in the 160s to the 140s B.C. would have been highly "illegitimate" in Freyne's terms, due to the utter impossibility of their "carrying forward some recognizable traditon" of high priesthood.

33. M. Hengel, *Zeloten,* 333–36.
34. J. Hanson, "Diadem and Popular Messiahs in Josephus," unpublished paper.
35. O. Michel, "Studien zu Josephus," *NTS* 14 (1967–68) 403.
36. M. Hengel, *Zeloten,* 298–99; M. Black, "Judas of Galilee and Josephus's 'Fourth Philosophy,' " in *Josephus-Studien* (ed. O. Betz, K. Haacker, M. Hengel; Göttingen: Vandehoeck & Ruprecht, 1974) 45–54. Against Hengel, the essay by J. S. Kennard ("Judas of Galilee and his Clan," *JQR* 36 [1945–46] 281–286) hardly seems "ausführlich."
37. R. A. Horsley, "Josephus and the Bandits," 39–40 & n. 8.
38. E. R. Wolf, "Peasant Rebellion and Revolution," in *National Liberation: Revolution in the Third World* (ed. N. Miller and R. Aya; New York: Free Press, 1971) 60–62.
39. See M. Smith, "Zealots and Sicarii," and the earlier article Smith cites by Kirsopp Lake, "Appendix A: The Zealots," in K. Lake and F. J. Foakes-Jackson (eds.), *The Beginnings of Christianity* (5 vols.; London/New York: Macmillan, 1920–33), 1. 421–25; *vs.* M. Hengel, *Zeloten,* 296–307.
40. The following discussion builds on R. A. Horsley, "The Sicarii" (see n. 5 above). A further critique of the misnomer "Zealot Messianism" and a more detailed analysis of the Menahem episode among the Sicarii will be the subject of a separate paper.
41. "The Sicarii," 453–55.
42. O. Michel, "Studien zu Josephus;" and C. Roth, "Simon bar Giora, Ancient Jewish Hero," *Commentary* 29 (1960) 52–58. Roth provides a good sketch of Simon's heroic career, although with little analysis of "messianic" or any other social forms, while Michel critically and imaginatively probes Josephus' account for important symbolism with sensitivity to the social forms and social rationale of Simon's actions. D. M. Rhoads (*Israel in Revolution, 6–74 C.E.* [Philadelphia: Fortress, 1976] 140–48) adds little. M. Hengel (*Zeloten,* 303) devotes only a page to the messianic pretender about whom we know the most, but then it would be virtually impossible anyhow to claim the rival of the actual Zealots as a "Zealot" messiah!
43. O. Michel, "Studien zu Josephus," 404.
44. Ibid., 406.
45. Ibid.
46. R. Delbrueck, "Antiquarisches zu den Verspottungen Jesu," *ZNW* 41 (1942) 124–45. See also Diodorus of Sicily, 36.2,4 for the wearing of the

purple cloak along with the *diadem* by the *king* of one of the slave rebellions.

47. O. Michel, "Studien," 407.
48. See the analysis of the recently discovered evidence and critical reconstruction in a definitive treatment by J. A. Fitzmyer, "The Bar Cochba Period," *Essays on the Semitic Background of the New Testament* (Missoula: Scholars Press, 1974; orig. 1962) 305–54; see also H. Mantel, "The Causes of the Bar Kokba Revolt," *JQR* 58 (1968) 225–42, 274–96, esp. pp. 275–85; P. Prigent, *La fin de Jérusalem* (Neuchâtel: Delachaux et Nietslé, 1969) 102–18, esp. pp. 104–5.
49. E. Schürer, *The History of the Jewish People* (see n. 28 above), 2. 510–12; M. de Jonge, "Χρίω Χριστός" (TDNT, 9. 515–16; H. Mantel, "Causes of the Bar Kokba Revolt," 175–76. On 2 *Baruch* and 4 *Ezra,* see G. W. E. Nickelsburg, *Jewish Literature between the Bible and the Mishnah* (Philadelphia: Fortress, 1981) 281–94.
50. See, e.g., E. Lohse, "Der König aus Davids Geschlecht: Bemerkungen zur messianischen Erwartung der Synagoge," in *Abraham Unser Vater: Festschrift für Otto Michel* (ed. O. Betz et al.; Leiden: Brill, 1963) 337–45, esp. p. 342; D. C. Duling, "The Promises to David," 63–64 (and the literature cited there).
51. See J. A. Fitzmyer, "The Bar Cochba Period," 312–16, on the name and title; on the coins, see also Y. Yadin, "The Expedition into the Judean Desert, 1960: Expedition D," *IEJ* 11 (1961) 51; and G. F. Hills, *Catalogue of Greek Coins of Palestine* (London: Oxford, 1914) 288, 302; on messiah(s) at Qumran, see R. E. Brown, "The Teacher of Righteousness and the Messiah(s)" (n. 9 above) 37–44, esp. p. 42; and his earlier article, "The Messianism of Qumran," *CBQ* 19 (1957) 53–80.
52. See J. A. Fitzmyer, "The Bar Cochba Period," 333; G. F. Hill, *Catalogue of Greek Coins,* 284–300; Y. Yadin, *Bar-Kokhba* (New York: Random House, 1971) 175–83; further on Murabbaʿat, etc., see Y. Yadin, "The Expedition into the Judean Desert, 1961: Expedition D," *IEJ* 12 (1962) 235–257; M. Lehmann, "Studies in the Murabbaʿat and Nahal Ḥever Documents," *RevQ* 4 (1963) 53–81; E. Koffmahn, *Die Doppelurkunden aus der Wüste Juda* (STDJ 5; Leiden: Brill, 1968). The most important texts are now easily accessible in J. A. Fitzmyer and D. J. Harrington, *A Manual of Palestinian Aramaic Texts* (Rome: Biblical Institute, 1978).

III

The Early Islamic Period

5

Shiitic Influences in Jewish Sectarianism

Israel Friedlaender

It has long since been recognized[1] that the rise of Jewish sectarianism under the dominion of Islam was in a large measure the reflection of a corresponding phenomenon in the Muhammedan world. "In the second half of the seventh century and in the whole of the eighth," says the veteran investigator of Jewish sectarianism,[2] "as a result of the tremendous intellectual commotion produced throughout the Orient by the swift conquests of the Arabs and the collision of victorious Islam with the older religions and cultures of the world, there arose a large number of religious sects, especially in Persia, Babylonia ('Irāḳ), and Syria. Judaism did not escape the general fermentation; the weak remnants of early schism—the Sadducees and Essenes—picked up new life and flickered once more before their final extinction. But new sects also arose in Judaism, the most important of which were the 'Īsawites (called after their founder Abū 'Īsa), the Yūdġānites and the Shādġānites (followers of Yūdġān and Shādġān)." This correspondence between Jewish and Muhammedan heterodoxy is, indeed, not to be wondered at. Considering the close contact between Judaism and Islam from the very birth of the latter, it is but natural that their reciprocal influence should not be confined to their main currents, but extend as well to their tributaries and branches. The recognition of this inter-relation, however, has remained an abstract generality and has not been pursued in detail. In view of the great strides which our knowledge of the inner development

Reprinted by permission of Dropsie University from *The Jewish Quarterly Review* n.s. 1 (1910–11); 2 (1911–12); 3 (1912–13) (with omissions).

of Islam has made in recent years, this task becomes more pressing and at the same time more promising in results. A careful study of the points of contact between the Jewish heterodoxy of that period and the corresponding process in Islam will enable us to grasp in its full significance the make-up of these Jewish sects which is otherwise incomprehensible. Of course, in confronting Jewish sectarianism with its Islamic predecessor one must guard against exaggerations and not drive analogies to the extreme. The influence of Islam over Judaism has never been of so disintegrating a nature as to suppress all genuine elements of Judaism even in its farthest ramifications. Karaism proper, except for the general condition of religious unrest characteristic of that age, scarcely shows any effect of heterodox Islam. And even the more radical sects, as the ʿĪsawites, Yūdġānites and the like, are largely swayed by halakic interests which are purely Jewish. Yet, with all these restrictions, the influence of Muhammedan heterodoxy on Jewish sectarianism cannot be doubted and presents a phenomenon which is of interest not only for the Jewish scholar but also for the student of comparative religion.

In speaking of Jewish sectarianism, a word must be said about our sources of information. The latter are, indeed, scanty and often fragmentary. Our main source is Ḳirḳisānī (wrote in 937), who in the introductory chapters of his *Kitāb al-anwār*[3] gives a description of Jewish sects. Ḳirḳisānī's material is mainly drawn from Dāwud b. Merwān al-Muḳammiṣ (IX. century),[4] as is also the almost identical account of Hadassi (XII. century).[5] Valuable material bearing on these early and on some later Jewish movements is contained in the Arabic original of Maimonides' *Iggeret Tēmān* in the paragraphs dealing with the Pseudo-Messiahs which in the Hebrew translations have been reduced to a few meager sentences.[6] To these Jewish sources must be added the detailed account of Shahrastānī (died 1153)[7] who undoubtedly followed old sources, in this case perhaps Abū ʿĪsa al-Warrāḳ, who is also quoted by Bīrūnī as his authority in Jewish matters.[8] Scattered references by Bīrūnī (about 1000),[9] Ibn Ḥazm (d. 1064), Maḳrīzī (d. 1442), and other Muhammedan writers[10] occasionally contain valuable data. The information derived from these sources, however, is not always reliable and is sometimes even contradictory,[11] an observation by no means surprising to the student of Muhammedan heterodoxy and no doubt applicable to every religious sect which is only known from the description of its opponents. It will therefore be necessary to proceed with caution and discretion and to keep a steady eye on the general conditions and influences which dominate these sects. . . .

As far as Muhammedan heterodoxy is concerned, I propose to deal on this occasion with the sects of Shiism, because out of the numerous factions of Islam it is the Shiitic heresy, with its peculiar mixture of doctrinal and political elements, which has more than any other profoundly affected the destinies of Islam and has succeeded in getting a strong and permanent hold over large sections of the Muhammedan community. . . .

It is certainly not accidental that the rise of Jewish sectarianism under Islam belongs to the same period which forms a turning point in the history of Islam and Shiism, marked by the struggle between the Omayyad government and the forces opposed to it. The earliest[12] representatives of Jewish sectarianism were Abū 'Īsa of Ispahan—his first name is not certain[13]—and his followers the 'Īsawiyya, or Iṣfahāniyya.[14] The date of Abū 'Īsa's appearance is differently transmitted by Ḳirḳisānī and Shahrastānī. According to the former, "his appearance took place in the days of 'Abdalmelik, the son of Merwān,"[15] who reigned 685–705. Shahrastānī, however, circumstantially relates that "he lived in the time of Manṣūr (754–775), but his propaganda began in the time of the last king of the Omayyads, Merwān b. Muhammed al-Ḥimār (744–750)"[16] and then narrates,[17] how he and his army were killed by Manṣūr at Rai (near Teheran). Grätz,[18] who did not know Ḳirḳisānī, follows Shahrastānī. Harkavy[19] unhesitatingly accepts Ḳirḳisānī's statement and bases on the earlier appearance of Abū 'Īsa the conjecture that he influenced the rise of Karaism. It is, however, impossible to follow Ḳirḳisānī. The historical conditions decidedly speak against it. The systematic outbreaks of Shiitic sectarianism in 'Irāḳ and the other Persian provinces did not, owing to the causes indicated above, take place before the reign of Hishām (724–743 = 105–125 Hijra), the son of 'Abdalmelik.[20] And even then the uprisings were of small dimensions;[21] they were quickly put down by the Omayyad governors and they scarcely affected the Caliphate to such a degree as to make it possible for a Jew to gather any army and resist the government. Particularly the reign of 'Abdalmelik, despite frequent skirmishes with the Khārijites in the East, which, however, were local,[22] was characterized by strength and discipline. On the other hand, the date given by Shahrastānī agrees most perfectly with the historical circumstances. Under the last Omayyad Muhammed b. Merwān the 'Alidic propaganda which had till then been undermining the Empire, especially in the East, broke out openly. With the moment when Abū Muslim, the chief of the propagandist forces, unfurled the black standard of the 'Abbasids in a village near Merv (June 9, 747), Persia became a seething caldron of anarchy and revolution. It was, as Wellhausen[23] puts it, "a time of adventurers and men of pluck," and Abū Muslim was often compelled to fight the latter, as he did the forces of the Omayyad government. One of these adventurers was Bīhāfarīd,[24] who rose in Nīsābūr preaching ancient Persian doctrines and was put to death by Abū Muslim. Another sectarian, who is of immediate interest to us, was 'Abdallah b. Mu'āwiya[25] who rebelled in Kufa *against the last Omayyad,* combining political claims with extravagant doctrines. He was forced to retreat into the East, where he formed an independent empire and even struck his own coins, and settled temporarily in Ispahan. He was put to death by Abū Muslim in 129^{H} (=747 C.E). But centuries later there were still people who believed that 'Abdallah was concealed in the mountains of Ispahan and would return thence to fill the earth with justice. Abū Muslim himself was not merely a political agitator but also the representative, at least the object, of certain extravagant doctrines. There was a sect named after him the Muslimiyya[26] which believed in his Divine nature and expected his "return" as the Messiah. When Abū Muslim had been treacherously murdered by Mạnṣūr (February 12, 755), fresh revolts, headed by Sinbāḏ, Ustaḏsīs, Muḳanna', and others, broke out to avenge his death, and they were encountered and put down by Manṣūr. In the chaotic condition of the empire caused by the resurrection of Abū Muslim, perhaps during the short-lived glory of 'Abdallah b. Mu'āwiya it was quite possible for a Jew of a courageous temperament and Messianic aspirations to gather in Ispahan, which was a strong Jewish center,[27] a Jewish army.[28] Abū 'Īsa was probably able to keep up an attitude of independence during the uncertain reign of the first 'Abbasid as-Saffāḥ (750–754) and was put down, with many other sectarians, by the energetic Manṣūr.[29]

The rôle of Persia as the home of Jewish sectarianism is also easily accounted for by historical conditions. The sects of Shiism first rise in 'Irāḳ, expecially in Kufa, and gradually move to the eastern Persian provinces. When we examine the long list of Jewish sectarians contained in Ḳirḳisānī's account,[30] we find, as was long ago observed by Harkavy,[31] that their *gentilicia,* with very few exceptions, point to inner

Persia. We encounter such designations as Iṣfahānī, ʻOkbarī (twice), Nahāwendī, Zaʻfarānī, Tiflīsī, Damaġānī, or Ḳūmisī, to which may also be added names like Yūdġān, Shāḏakān or Shārakān,[32] and Mūshkān,[33] of undeniably Persian origin.[34] The Shiitic movement in ʻIrāk did not affect the Jewish population of that province. Babylonian Jewry was too strongly imbued with the Talmudic spirit and too firmly ruled by the authority of the Exilarch and the Geonim to submit to new-fangled doctrines of extravagant non-Jewish sectarians. This was different in Persia. The Jews of Persia were nominally under the jurisdiction of the Geonim[35] but they certainly did not possess the same power of resistance as their brethren in Babylonia. They were exceedingly ignorant,[36] more ignorant, in fact, according to a well-informed author,[37] than any other Jews, and especially the followers of Abū ʻĪsa are described as "barbarian and ill-bred people, destitute of intellect and knowledge."[38] This lack of a strong Jewish influence made the Persian Jews a ready victim to all possible heresies which were set afloat by ambitious sectarians and, because rooted in ancient Persian tradition, were eagerly grasped by the Persian population.[39]

The character of Jewish sectarianism is sufficiently determined by the above expositions: it is exotic and in the main the reflection of Muhammedan, more correctly Shiitic, heterodoxy, as manifested in Persia, and presenting a combination of doctrinal and political, or Messianic, tendencies. . . .

The acceptance of a later date for the appearance of Abū Īsa and his disciple Yūdġān[40] makes it highly improbable that the founder of Karaism who rose very soon afterwards should have been influenced by them to any appreciable extent. It is altogether difficult to assume that a man of the deep learning and the high social standing of Anan should have succumbed to the influence of these sectarians who were very ignorant and occupied a very low social position.[41] The character of this type of Jewish sectarianism and the Karaitic schism are indeed entirely different. Karaism is *anti*-Talmudic. It is based on a definite system of interpretation and presupposes a community of scholars and a highly developed Talmudic culture. The heterodoxy of Abū ʻĪsa and others like him is not directed against the Talmud. If we are to believe Ḳirḳisānī,[42] Abū ʻĪsa placed the Rabbinical sages on almost the same level with the prophets.[43] This heterodoxy affects likewise Biblical and Talmudical ordinances and has, besides, a strong Messianic character. As its bearers we have to picture to ourselves a community of simple-minded uneducated Jews, removed from the center of Talmudic learning and unable to grasp the intricacies of the Halakah, an easy prey to Messianic adventurers and the influences of the non-Jewish surroundings. The Karaitic secession therefore is an inner-Jewish movement. It owes the outside world nothing except the general spirit of the age which, as a result of the mixture of cultures, was characterized by scepticism and a marked tendency to schism. Jewish sectarianism of the type of Abū ʿĪsa, while retaining the main elements of Judaism, is deeply influenced by the non-Jewish environment and is indebted to it for many of its characteristics.

We will now proceed to examine these characteristics and to illustrate by some striking examples the rôle of Shiitic elements in Jewish sectarianism.

1. THE RAJʿA DOCTRINE

Rajʿa or "Return" is defined by the Arabic lexicographers as "the returning to the present state of existence after death, *before the Day of Resurrection.*"[44] It is the belief in the returning to life of certain individuals and is sharply distinguished from resurrection which involves the returning to life of mankind in general. Originally the date set for the "return" of these individuals was forty days after their death.[45] Gradually the time limit was extended and was vaguely fixed in the vast expanse between the moment of death and the day of resurrection. Without entering into the genesis and long-winded development of this remarkable doctrine,[46] we may state that it appears very early in connection with various heterodox teachings clustering around the person of Christ. The Rajʿa belief is, above all, closely connected with the ancient and widespread doctrine of Docetism which taught that the sufferings and death of Jesus did not take place in reality but were a mere ophthalmic delusion. Accordingly, Jesus' death is not to be looked upon as the close of his earthly career but as a mere interruption of it, as a temporary disappearance. His condition after this fictitious martyrdom is not that of death, but a state of concealment, of occultation, or, to use the Arabic term, a mere *ġaiba,* an absence.[47] His appearance on earth to take up his interrupted mission and to carry it to triumph is, in consequence, a *re*-appearance, a "return."

The influence of this set of conceptions, transmitted through the medium of some obscure heterodox Christian sect,[48] manifests itself already in the beginnings of Islam. The dogma of Docetism, as applied to Jesus, is taught wth great emphasis in the Koran[49] and there is reason to believe that the Raj'a doctrine in its larger application was known to Mohammed and probably constituted the original form of the Messianic hope in Islam.[50] In orthodox Islam, however, owing partly to political circumstances, partly to the influence of post-biblical Judaism, the Messianic speculations, which were gradually detached from the person of Jesus, assumed more and more an abstract and impersonal character and the Raj'a doctrine was pushed to the background.

The richer was the soil and the ampler the scope which this dogma found in Shiism. For in Shiism, whose very basis is Messianic, the Messianic hopes were not a mere dogmatic abstraction but an intense and immediate reality. They were not connected, as in orthodox Islam, with some ideal mysterious individuals, who in reality were rather types than individuals, but with definite and living personages of flesh and bone, with 'Alī or his descendants.[51] These 'Alidic Mahdīs or Messiahs, with scarcely an exception, failed of their purpose and they were ruthlessly persecuted and in most cases cruelly murdered by the governing powers. Here the doctrine of Raj'a and Docetism stepped in as the salvation of Shiism. Transferred from Jesus to the Shiitic Messiahs, it made their death ineffectual by denying its reality and saved the Shiites from disappointment and despair by teaching them to wait and to work for the speedy return of their living though hidden Mahdīs. The Raj'a doctrine became of incalculable importance in that it detached the Messianic movements within Shiism which sprang from permanent sources and often involved large and vital issues, from the short-lived 'Alidic figure-heads and rendered the progress of the cause independent of the fate of the fragile Messiahs. The death of the Mahdī which would otherwise have been identical with the death of the movement became a mere incident. Instead of being the close of the Messiah's career, it became a stepping stone to his future glory and an auspicious indication that the Mahdī, having temporarily withdrawn, would soon appear, or re-appear, for his final triumph.

The force of this doctrine is seen very early in the history of Shiism. Its introduction into Islam is ascribed by the Arabic historians and theologians to a certain 'Abdallah b. Sabā who, peculiarily enough, was a Jew of Southern Arabia.[52] If we are right in combining the different and not wholly harmonious reports about this curious Jewish-Mohammedan heresiarch, he originally applied his doctrine to Mohammed whom he apparently believe to be the Messiah and later transferred it in a more elaborate form to ʿAlī of whom he preached that his violent death was but a delusion and that he would return from his hiding place to fill the earth with justice.[53]

This belief was subsequently applied to every Shiitic pretender. The cases of its application which extend over the whole history of Islam down to the present day are too numerous to be specified in detail.[54] The Rajʿa belief became the mainstay and the motive power in every Shiitic movement. It also became the *principium divisionis* in the formation of Shiitic factions. For after the death of a Messianic candidate his followers invariably split into two camps, into those who believed in the reality of his death and therefore, having recognized the falsity of his Messianic claim to fill the earth with justice, looked out for another Messiah, and into those who thought that his death was a mere delusion and therefore, expecting his own return in person, appointed but a temporary viceregent. These two factions which often appear as correlative in the history of Shiism are usually designated as the *Ḳiṭṭīʿiyya,* "the assertive ones," those who assert the reality of the Messiah's death, and the *Wāḳifiyya* "the doubtful ones," those who are doubtful about his death and are inclined to regard its as fictitious.[55]

Before turning to our Jewish evidence to show the general application of this dogma within Jewish sectarianism, it may be advisable to illustrate by one particular detail the curious manner in which some of these Shiitic heterodoxies were reproduced in Judaism.

Once the death of the Messiah or Mahdī is denied in its reality and looked upon as a mere disappearance or concealment, it is natural that religious speculation should be called upon to answer the question as to the *place* in which the Messiah was concealed. Accordingly, the Messiah, during his period of occultation, is placed either in heaven or on earth. The former conception is represented in Islam by the belief, equally attributed to ʿAbdallah b. Sabā, that ʿAlī was riding in the clouds, whence he would gloriously "return," a belief which was so deep-seated that, as we are told on reliable authority, faithful Shiites would send up their greetings to the clouds in the thought of thereby addressing themselves to ʿAlī.[56] More frequently however, the messiah is located in some mysterious spot on earth. Thus the twelfth Imām of the Shiʿa, the

Messiah of the present day Shiitic High Church, is believed to be hidden in a cave flooded with sun-light[57] or in the holy of holies in the mosque of his native town or in the legendary cities of Jābalḳā or Jābarṣā.[58] The 'Abbasid general Abū Muslim, who after his death was regarded by some of his enthusiastic Persian adherents as the Messiah, was similarly thought to be concealed in a mysterious Copper Castle.[59]

But seclusion and inaccessibility being the primary requirements of a Messianic retreat, it is natural that the hiding place of the Messiah, in preference to any other spot, is located in mountains, more especially in mountain clefts or ridges. This characteristic detail, which has numerous analogies in the folk lore of other nations,[60] looms with particular prominence in the legends surrounding the various Shiitic Messiahs. Thus the celebrated Shiitic Mahdī Mohammed Ibn al-Ḥanafiyya, a son of 'Alī by a woman of the Ḥanīfa tribe,—hence his designation as "the son of the Ḥanafite woman,"—who was the object of worship of the once powerful Keisāniyya sect[61] and whose name was the war-cry of a far-reaching and powerful revolutionary movement against the young Caliphate[62] was believed to have disappeared and to reside secretly in one of the ridges of the Raḍwā mountains in the region of Medinah.[63] Innumerable legends hovered around this Messianic retreat and found literary expression in the poems of the great Keisānitic bards of the seventh century Kuthayyir and as-Sayyid al-Ḥimyari. In glowing colors do these highly gifted poets picture the Mahdī as dwelling in a glen of the Radwā mountains, surrounded by beasts of prey on which eternal peace has descended, holding intercourse with angels and sustained from overflowing fountains of milk and honey,[64] and with genuine religious fervor do they call on him to emerge from his retreat and, preceded by noble steeds and flying banners, return to his believers in order to inaugurate the Messianic age of justice and peace.[65] The vitality of this belief may be inferred from the fact that as late as the time of al-Bīrūni (died 1038), three centuries after Mohammed Ibn al-Ḥanafiyya, his "return" was still awaited by numerous Mohammedans.[66] Similarly a later Messianic pretender Mohammed b. 'Abdallah, a great-great-grandson of 'Alī, who rose in Medinah against the Caliph Manṣūr and was killed by him in 762, was believed by many of his followers to be hidden in Ḥājir, likewise a spot in the Raḍwā mountains.[67] In like fashion the Messianic rebel 'Abdallah b. Mu'āwiya (d. 747) was thought after his ephemeral triumph and his execution at the hands of Abū Muslim to have concealed himself in the mountains of Ispahan.[68] Abū Muslim himself, having been treacherously murdered by his ungrateful master, the Caliph Manṣūr, was believed to have escaped death and to be hidden in the mountains of Rayy,[69] where in true Messianic style he was miraculously fed.[70] It is true, the mountainous character of the Messianic hiding-place is not an inseparable feature of it. Yet, the frequency and the emphasis with which it is pointed out convincingly demonstrates that this particular detail of the Raj'a doctrine was not a fleeting fancy but a deep-seated belief among Shiitic Mohammedans and sufficiently widespread to penetrate eventually beyond the boundaries of Islam.

In the light of these facts we learn to understand the full import of a statement, otherwise unintelligible, relating to the earliest Jewish sectarian of this period, Abū 'Isa al-Iṣfahānī. Abū 'Isa, profiting by a favorable political constellation, rose, in true Mahdistic fashion, against the governing powers to free his people from the yoke of Islam and to usher in the Golden Age. He was killed by the army of the mighty Caliph Manṣūr.[71] Yet, as the Karaite Ḳirḳisānī, without being aware of the bearing of his words, informs us, "*among his adherents there were people who maintained that he had not been killed, but had merely entered a ridge in the mountains,* so that nothing further was heard of him."[72]

If Abū 'Isa had had the fortune of finding a Homer as did his fellow-Messiah, Ibn al-Ḥanafiyya, we should probably be fully acquainted with the character and location of the secret abode of this first Jewish Mahdī.

In view of the extreme paucity of our sources, it is not at all surprising that this particular detail, accidentally preserved by Ḳirḳisānī, which so strikingly illustrates the force of Shiitic influence, stands entirely isolated. Yet the general effect of the Raj'a doctrine can be substantiated by other examples.

Abū 'Isa was succeeded by Yūdġān who, profiting by the bitter experience of his predecessor, kept his peace and died a natural death. Yet, to quote Ḳirḳisānī again, "*his adherents maintained that he was the Messiah and that he had not died, and they still hope for his return.*"[73]

In the second half of the twelfth century, more exactly in 1160, there arose among the Jews in Northern Persia, who were very ignorant and stood in intimate relations to the ultra-Shiitic sect of the Assassins,[74] the celebrated David, or Menahem,[75] ar-Rūhī, or Alroy.[76] He proclaimed himself, or was proclaimed, the Messiah and, followed by many thousands of Jews, tried to overthrow the Mohammedan power and to lead the Jews to Palestine. He found an ignominious death at the hands of a treacherous relative. "In spite of it," to quote a contemporary witness,[77] "the matter was not unraveled to them (i. e. to the Jews), although it must have become evident to every man of intelligence, so that down to this day, they, I mean the Jews of Amadia, still esteem him more highly than many of their prophets, nay, some of them belive him to be the Messiah, the Expected One.[78] I have seen scores of Persian Jews in Khoy, Silmās, Tabrīz, and Marāġa who make his name the object of their most solemn oath. In the same province (Amadia) a large number of them profess a religion which they refer to Menahem,[79] the above-mentioned impostor."

It is clear from the foregoing expositions that the Persian Jews refused to believe in the reality of Alroy's death and continued to wait for his "return." How natural such a belief seemed in that environment may be inferred from the tragicomic sequel which is described by the same writer.[80] When the rumor of Alroy's death reached Bagdad, two swindlers took advantage of the superstitious credulity of their fellow-Jews to cheat them out of their money. They sent in the name of the dead Messiah, who was believed to be alive and temporarily concealed, letters to the Jews of Bagdad in which they proclaimed his speedy return and announced the exact day on which he would appear to lead them to Palestine. . . .[81]

In connection with the above facts which clearly demonstrate the influence of the Shiitic Raj'a doctrine, attention may be called to a few points of contact between heterodox Islam and heterodox Judaism. I mention them with a great deal of hesitation, for I fully realize the slippery nature of their similitude which, I expressly admit, may be accidental. Yet, the possibilty of cause and effect is by no means precluded, and with the increase in our data which are at present so scanty this possibility may grow into probability or even certainty.

As in Judaism, so in Islam the returning Messiah is pictured either as a supernatural being who dispenses with human weapons and smiteth the wicked with the rod of his mouth or as a human conqueror who acts in the way of men.[82] It is not accidental that, in accordance with the latter conception which is predominant in Shiism,[83] the Shiitic Mahdī invariably appears *riding*, not like the meek and unassuming figure of the post-exilic Messiah on an ignoble ass, but, after the manner of warriors, on a noble horse.[84] Thus, in contrast to 'Alī, whose return is pictured in supernatural colors,[85] his son Mohammed Ibn al-Ḥanafiyya is heralded on his return by prancing steeds and flying banners.[86] Ibn al-Ḥanafiyya's champion, the Keisanitic poet Kuthayyir (died 723), who seems himself to have posed as a Messianic personage,[87] announced before his death that after forty days[88] he expected to return on a full-blooded horse.[89] Similarly, the Persian Shiitic Messiah Bihāfarīḏ who appeared in the eighth century[90] but in the tenth century was still believed to be alive[91] was thought to have ascended to heaven on a dark-brown horse and was expected to return in the same manner to take vengeance on his enemies.[92] The famous Shiitic pseudo-Messiah Muḳanna‘ (died 780)[93] made his followers believe "that his spirit would pass into the form of a grizzle-headed man riding on a grey horse and that he would return unto them after so many years and cause them to possess the earth."[94] Nowhere, however, does this particular feature loom so prominently as in the beliefs clustering around the Mahdī of official present day Shiism, Mohammed b. al-Ḥasan. This particular conception is so intimately bound up with the belief in the return of this Mahdī that at the court of the Ṣafawid Shahs in Ispahan, who became masters of Persia in 1501 and declared Shiism the state religion of the land, two gorgeously mounted horses were always kept ready, the one for Mohammed b. al-Ḥasan, the other for his lieutenant Jesus.[95]

There can be no doubt that the origin of this conception is to be sought in the ancient Judæo-Christian Messianic speculations and it is not imposssible that a trace of their influence is to be found in Arabia prior to Mohammed.[96] But if the instances to be quoted presently from late Jewish sectarianism be more than meaningless coincidences, the connecting link will have to be looked for in Shiism whose influence on Judaism is evident from many other particulars and in which the above Messianic feature has received such great prominence.

Turning to Jewish evidence we find that when Abū ‘Isa al-Iṣfahānī, who, as we have repeatedly seen, exhibits the features of a Shiitic Mahdī, was attacked by the army of the Caliph, he left the magic line drawn by him as a protection around his followers and, *riding on a horse,* engaged single-handedly in a battle with the Mohammedans.[97]. . .

Finally attention may be called to a curious feature in these Messianic speculations which can be traced both in Judaism and in Islam and offers at all events a striking point of comparison, while the causal connection between them can in the present condition of our sources be nothing but a matter of conjecture. Whether in consequence of the Messiah's association with the heavenly regions or for some other reason, the accomplishment of *flying* is found in Islam in connection with Messianic manifestations. 'Alī, like his ancient prototype in the apocryphal writings,[98] is believed to be flying through the clouds,[99] and the same accomplishment is attributed to other Messianic and semi-Messianic personages.[100] A curious illustration of this peculiar conception is afforded by a remarkable incident in the history of Islam. The sect of the Rāwandiyya from Rāwend in Khorāsān which regarded the Caliph Manṣūr as a divine incarnation and believed him to be the Mahdī[101] appeared in large numbers in the year 758 before his palace in Hāshimiyya and began to call on him to manifest himself. They believed that they were able to fly and, ascending the roof of the palace, precipitated themselves from it.[102] It is not improbable that similar scenes were to be witnessed simultaneously in other cities. At least the local historian of Aleppo[103] not only speaks of the appearance of the Rāwandiyya in the year 141 H. (=758) both in Aleppo and in Ḥarrān, but also informs us that "they maintained that they were in the position of angels.[104] They ascended, as people narrate, a hill in Aleppo and, having dressed themselves in silken garments,[105] flew from it, so that they broke their bones and perished."

Similar notions are found in connection with Jewish sectarian movements.

The early pseudo-Messiah Serene who arose in the beginning of the eighth century among the Jews of Syria[106] announced, according to the testimony of a contemporary witness, that he would lead the Jews *flying* to the Land of Promise.[107]

The two imposters, who made their appearance in Bagdad after the death of Alroy, forged letters in the name of the dead Messiah, who was believed to be temporarily hidden, promising to lead the Jews on a certain night *flying* to Jerusalem.[108] A contemporary witness gives an elaborate and striking description of that tragicomical scene.[109] On the appointed night the Jews of Bagdad, having formerly deposited their money with the two swindlers, dressed themselves in green garments[110] and gathered themselves together on the roofs, expecting to fly to the Holy Temple on the wings of angels.[111] The confusion and the noise, particularly among the women who had their infants with them, was indescribable. "They did not cease to make attempts at flying until the morning unraveled their shame and their credulity. The two impostors, however, escaped with what they had obtained of the property of the Jews to whom the manner of swindle and the excessive viciousness[112] exhibited by them[113] thus became evident." The year in which this incident took place became known as the "Year of Flying," *'ām aṭ-ṭayarān,* and the Jews of Bagdad reckoned a new year from that memorable event.[114]. . .

2. THE ONE TRUE PROPHET

The doctrine which will now engage our attention has been of tremendous importance in the development of the religious thought of the East. It would widely exceed the scope of our present enquiry, were we to treat of this far-reaching as well as fascinating doctrine with any amount of detail. We must perforce limit ourselves to those aspects of it which afford points of contact with similar teachings within Judaism. . . .

A striking formulation of this dogma which deserves our special attention is found in the teachings of Manichæism. Giving a nationalistic coloring to this essentially universalistic doctrine, Mānī declares: "Wisdom and deeds have always from time to time been brought to mankind by the messenger of God called Buddha to India, in another by Zoroaster in Persia, in another by Jesus in the West. Thereafter this revelation has come down, this prophecy in this last age, through me Mānī, the messenger of the God of Truth to Babylonia."[115]

It was probably through the medium of Manichæism that this profound conception gained access into Mohammedanism. It has fundamentally affected the prophetology of orthodox Islam in which the belief in a series of dispensations,[116] the recognition of their transitory value,[117] and the admission at the same time of the prophetic, hence God-inspired, character of their representatives clearly point to this source. But it became of infinitely greater significance in heterodox Islam which is not only more generous in the recognition of the relative truth of the dispensations preceding Mohammed,[118] but, denying the fundamental Islamic dogma of the finality of his message, consistently admits of an endless chain of prophetic manifestations after him.[119] In this form the conception of the One True Prophet has been in constant operation in Mohammedan sectarianism and has found expression in innumerable movements and doctrines.

Looked at in this light, a fundamental doctrine of the Jewish sectarian Abū ʿĪsa stands out in its full meaning and assumes wide historic significance.

Abū ʿĪsa manifested himself in an age and in a land which were marked by the wide currency of the belief characterized above. He addressed himself exclusively to the Jews, whom he endeavored to free from political oppression, and he retained all the fundamental tenets of Judaism. Yet, actuated by the conception which recognizes the relative truth of the various, yet identical, manifestations of the Divine, Abū ʿĪsa, in a manner which vividly reminds us of the formulation of Mānī, "*acknowledged the prophecy of Jesus, the son of Mary, and the prophecy of the Master of the Muhammedans, contending that each of these two was sent to his own people. He advocated the study of the Gospels and of the Koran as well as the knowledge of their interpretation, and he maintained that the Muhammedans and Christians were both guided in their faith by what they possessed, just as the Jews were guided in their faith by what they possessed.*"[120]

This doctrine of Abū 'Īsa, recorded by Ḳirḳisānī, is fully confirmed by Ibn Ḥazm (d. 1064), who regards this theory of Abū ʿĪsa as the corner stone of his teachings,[121] and is often referred to by other Mohammedan theologians who take great pains to refute this attempt of the ʿĪsawiyya to limit the validity of Mohammed's message to the Arabic race.[122] If we are to believe Ibn Ḥazm,[123] Abū ʿĪsa gave expression to his reverence for the founders of Christianity and Islam by calling himself Mohammed, the son of Jesus,[124] and went so far as to believe in the immaculate conception of Christ.[125] Ḳirḳisānī is inclined to ascribe the recognition of Christianity and Islam on the part of Abū ʿĪsa to a selfish motive. For by acknowledging these two prophets outside of the canonical range of Jewish prophecy, he had, in the opinion of this author, greater chances of finding credence for his own prophetic pretensions.[126] But Ḳirḳisānī can scarcely have taken his own explanation seriously. For his thorough and elaborate refutation of this view of Abū ʿĪsa, to which he devotes two separate chapters in his work,[127] distinctly shows that this opinion was not the freakish fad of an irresponsible sectarian, but the settled conception of the age.[128] As a matter of fact, this view which admits the relative truth of Christianity and Islam is found not only among the sects closely related to the Isawiyya, such as the Raʿyāniyya,[129] the Shārakāniyya (or Shādakāniyya)[130] and the Mushkāniyya[131] as well as the

Karaitic faction of the Dusturians,[132] but it also attributed to Anan,[133] and we have positive evidence that it was shared by representative and otherwise irreproachably orthodox Jews.[134] . . .

3. SUCCESSIVE INCARNATION

The theory of the One True Prophet is logically inseparable from the doctrine of Successive Incarnation. At the bottom of both lies the fundamental Gnostic or rather Neo-Platonic conception that God, "the unoriginated, inconceivable Father," who is without material substance, is entirely unknowable and therefore can make himself known to man only by incarnation, by embodying himself in human form, i. e. in the prophets.[135] Thus the prophet or the Messiah, the "Christ," becomes the manifestation, and the only manifestation, of God on earth, a view which logically leads and has in the course of history actually led to the deification of the prophet. In conjunction with the theory of the One True Prophet, the doctrine of Incarnation is widened to that of *Successive Incarnation,* which teaches the *periodic* manifestation, or incarnation, of God in various ages in different human personalities who, embodying, as they do, the same Divine substance, are, in reality, one: the One True Prophet. As to the number and identity of the persons, in whom the Divine has thus been successively incarnated, a great deal of uncertainty seems to have prevailed from the very beginning. Thus in the Pseudo-Clementines the persons in whom the One True Prophet has revealed himself are specified in one place as Adam, Enoch, Noah, Abraham, Isaac, Jacob, and Moses, in another as Adam, Enoch, Noah, Abraham, Isaac, Jacob, and Christ, in both the number seven seems to be intended.[136] Later applications of this dogma show numerous variations, in accordance with local and historic requirements.

The theory of Successive Incarnation has had far-reaching consequences for the dogmatic development of Islam. It succeeded in forcing its way into orthodox Islam whose prophetology is profoundly affected by it,[137] but here it was checked in its course by the emphasis laid on the final character of Mohammed's prophetic message.[138] In heterodox Islam, however, in which this barrier was partly or completely removed,[139] the doctrine of Successive Incarnation has found an almost unlimited field of operation.

We can observe the march of this conception from the early development of Shiism down to the present day. The attempt has been made to find in the theory of Successive Incarnation the very germ of Shiism, by identifying it with the *Raj'a* doctrine enunciated by the founder of Shiism, 'Abdallah b. Saba.[140] This view can scarcely be upheld, for *Raj'a* in its original meaning excludes incarnation.[141] But the doctrine of Successive Incarnation begins to appear in full-fledged size among the numerous Shiitic factions which sprang up in 'Irāḳ in the second century after Mohammed. Without making the slightest attempt at completeness, we may single out a few representatives of this doctrine within heretodox Islam. The sectarian Muġīra b. Sa'īd (d. 737) of Kufa, whose teachings betray throughout the profound influence of Gnostic ideas, taught "that the prophets never differed in anything concerning the laws."[142] His contemporary and townsman Abū Manṣūr al-'Ijlī held similarly the belief in the uninterrupted succession of apostles,[143] or, as another report puts it, "that the apostles would never cease and the apostleship would never cease."[144] 'Abdallah b. Mu'āwiya, the contemporary of Abū 'Īsa al-'Īṣfahānī, maintained that he was God and that the Divine Spirit manifested itself in Adam, then in Seth, then it circled through the prophets and finally revealed itself in him.[145] The famous rebel and Pseudo-Messiah Muḳanna' (d. 780) asserted in exactly the same manner that he was a Divine incarnation and that the Divine Spirit, after having manifested itself in Adam, Noah, Abraham, Mohammed, 'Alī, and others, finally settled in him.[146] It is the same doctrine for which in a later century the celebrated mystic Ḥusein b. Manṣūr al-Ḥallāj, whose influence survived long after his death and penetrated beyond the boundaries of Islam,[147] suffered martyrdom at the hands of the 'Abbasid government.[148]

The same theory of prophetic cycles, with a complicated and systematic elaboration of the various manifestations and their mode of succession, forms the basis of the Ismā'iliyya doctrine which, after tremendous upheavals, led to the establishment of the Fatimid dynasty and became the acknowledged religion of that powerful empire.[149]

It lies at the bottom of the doctrine of the Ḳurūfī sect whose founder Faḍlallāh of Astarabād in Persia maintained that God manifested himself in him, "after having revealed himself in the person of Adam, Moses, Jesus, and Muhammed," and suffered martyrdom for his belief at the hands of Mīrānshāh, the son of Timur, in 1393.[150]. . .

I belive it is not too far-fetched to find a reflection of this widespread idea in the abrupt notice of Shahrastānī[151] that "Abū 'Īsa al-Iṣfahānī maintained that he was a prophet and that he was the messenger of the Messiah the Expected One. He also maintained that the Messiah had five messengers who appeared before him one after the other," and "that the Messiah is the most excellent of all the children of Adam and higher in station than the preceding prophets."[152] The fragmentary character of our material unfortunately does not enable us to judge whether the adoption by Abū 'Īsa of the theory of Successive Incarnation involved the consequence of the deification of the Messiah, drawn by radical Shiism.

The effect of this heterodox Mohammedan dogma may perhaps extend to a specific detail. In spite of the fact that the number of Divine manifestations is unlimited and endless, the sum of the Divine incarnations is frequently fixed at seven, the old sacred figure. This number is already discernible in the Pseudo-Clementines[153] and is possibly applicable to Mohammed.[154] It occurs with astonishing frequency in the history of Shiitic sectarianism[155] and forms the basis of the complicated dogmatic system of the Ismā'īliyya who are for this reason called *Sab'iyya* or Seveners.[156]

Perhaps it is also applicable to the belief of Abū 'Īsa, recorded by Shahrastānī and vividly reminiscent of the five ante-Mohammedan dispensations assumed in Islam,[157] that the Messiah was preceded by five apostles. For in as much as, according to the same author, Abū 'Īsa considered himself the forerunner of the Messiah[158] the sum of all the manifestations would amount to seven.

4. PROPHET AND MESSIAH

The Gnostic doctrine of the successive incarnation of God in the One True Prophet had originally a purely theological character. It assumed a political tendency through the identification of the "Prophet" with the Messiah (the "Christ," the Mahdī, or the Imām) who is expected not only to represent in flesh the spiritual and incomprehensible Divine Being but also to fill the earth with justice and to bring back worldly power to those who have lost it. The Prophet *par excellence,* who represents the periodic manifestations of Divinity, is thus distinguished from and raised above the prophets commonly so-called, who, too, are inspired by God but who are neither charged with a political mission, nor do they as fully and immediately participate in the Divine essence as the Prophet-Messiah.

This is probably the background of Abū 'Īsa's doctrine that the Messiah is superior to all prophets, while, with the lower rating of the prophets, he was able to place the Rabbis on the level of prophecy.[159]

But more specifically the Hebrew term *nābī'* assumes the meaning of a forerunner or herald of the Messiah, who, probably under the influence of the rôle assigned to the prophet Elijah in Jewish and Christian Messianism,[160] predicts and prepares his return. In this restricted sense of a lower grade of divinity and a subordinate political function the term *nābī'*, as contrasted with the title *Mashī*^a*ḥ,* is occasionally found in the accounts of Jewish sectarians. . . .

Instead of *nābī'*, we find in the same connection the expression *rasūl* "messenger, apostle," not in the sense of *rasūl allāh,* as Mohammed is commonly styled, but rather signifying the *rasūl of the Messiah.*[161] In this particular meaning of the term we must understand the notice of Shahrastānī[162] that "Abū 'Īsa maintained *that he was a prophet* and that he was the *messenger (rasūl)* of the Messiah the Expected One.[163] He also maintained that the Messiah had five *messengers* who appeared before him, one after the other."[164] In a similar sense must be interpreted the "prophecy," claimed by Yūdġān, the successor of Abū 'Īsa,[165] and so must also be taken the words of Bīrūnī[166] who informs us that the Jews expected the Messiah to appear in the year 1023, "so that many pseudo-prophets among their sects, such as ar-Rā'ī,[167] Abū 'Īsa and others like them, pretended that they were his (i.e. the Messiah's) messengers (in Arabic *rusul*) to them (i.e. their sects)."

5. THE DĀ'Ī

The complicated character of the Messianic idea and the variety of Messianic forerunners, such as the prophet Elijah, the Ephraimitic Messiah, the Antichrist, gave the Messianic imposters, as long as they were content with the subordinate position of a forerunner and did not aspire to the supreme post of the Messiah or Mahdī, a choice of rôles. But a peculiar coloring was given to the idea of the Messianic forerunner through the identification of the latter with the characteristically Persian figure of the Dā'ī, or propagandist, a figure which plays so tremendous a rôle in all the Mahdistic movements of Islam. No one who has studied the history of early Islam can, to quote but one example, withhold his admiration from the wonderful spirit of organization and discipline which characterizes the *da'wa* (propaganda) of the 'Abbasids and from the many *Dā'īs* representing it who often suffered death and torture in executing their mission.

For our present purpose it is necessary to call special attention to the *political* significance of the Dā'ī which was exceedingly great. The head of the 'Abbasid propaganda Abū Muslim wielded such tremendous influence that it excited the jealousy of his sovereign and resulted in his assassination. Abū Muslim's influence became even more evident after his death when he was regarded as a divine incarnation by his adherents and when the desire to revenge him led to dangerous insurrections against the Caliphate. In the Karmatian propaganda the Chief Dā'īs, though ostensibly working in the interest of some Mahdī, were little less than the Mahdī himself and the title *Manṣūr* borne by them[168] had a distinct Messianic connotation.[169] Some of the *Dā'īs* were even looked upon as Divine incarnations.[170] No wonder then if so many who began as *Dā'īs* soon realized their superiority over the Mahdīs for whom they worked and often set themselves up as such.

Perhaps these peculiar notions and conditions are reflected in the report of Shahrastānī about Abū 'Īsa and Yūdġān. Both made their appearance in a land and in an age in which the Dā'ī was a familiar and at the same time a prominent figure wielding great political power. If we are to believe Shahrastānī,[171] Abū 'Īsa, realizing his mission, went to the distant Banū Mūsa behind the "sand river"[172] to preach to them after the manner of the Persian Dā'īs the word of the Lord. He regarded himself, at least in the beginning, merely as a forerunner of the Messiah, but he thought none the less highly of the dignity of his station. "And he maintained that the Messiah is the most excellent of the children of Adam and that he is superior in station to all the prophets that have gone by, and that he (himself) as his messenger was also the most excellent of all. He demanded faith in the Messiah *and he magnified the propaganda of the Dā'ī, maintaining that the Dā'ī, too, is the Messiah.*"[173]

In a similar manner Shahrastāni[174] relates of Yūdġān, who in all probability looked upon himself merely as the Dā'ī of Abū 'Īsa,[175] in as much as the latter was believed to be alive,[176] and was expected to return as the Messiah, that "among the things which are reported of him was the fact that he magnified the office of the Dā'ī."[177]

Shahrastānī's remarks are none too lucid and perhaps they ought not to be pressed too strongly. But if they are to convey any meaning, they can only be understood in the light of the Persian Shiitic propaganda.

6. SUCCESSION

In the course of the above expositions mention has already been made of the contrast, based upon the conception of Raj'a and Docetism, between the Wāḳifiyya and Ḳiṭṭī'iyya, a contrast which invariably reveals itself after the death of a Mahdī. Two examples will suffice to illustrate the practical issue involved in this contrast. When Mūsa, the son of the sixth Shiitic Imām Ja'far as-Sādiḳ, died (about 800), there were many who doubted or denied that he was dead and who expected his return as the Mahdī. They were called *Wāḳifiyya* "the doubtful ones." Others, however, termed *Kiṭṭī'iyya* "the assertive ones," among them some of his intimate associates, transferred the dignity of Imām and Mahdī to his son 'Alī b. Mūsa.[178] Again after the death of the eleventh Shiitic Imām al-Ḥasan al-'Askarī (d. 873), there were people, termed Wāḳifiyya, who doubted or denied the reality of his death and awaited his return as the Expected Mahdī.[179] Others, however, styled Kiṭṭī'iyya, asserted that he was actually dead and accordingly transferred the Messianic claim to his baby son Mohammed b. al-Ḥasan, the twelfth and last Imām and the acknowledged Expected One of present day Shiites, who are for this reason, in addition to their appellations as *Ithnā'ashariyya* (Twelvers) and Imāmiyya, also designated as *Kiṭṭī'iyya.*[180]

It is clear that the Wāḳifiyya, those who deny the Messiah's death and believe in his concealment and return, cannot consistently appoint a permanent successor to one who is but temporarily absent. They do however need and are consequently forced to appoint a temporary leader to take charge of the affairs of the faithful, pending the Messiah's appearance, in other words, a vice-gerent, a *Khalīfa.*[181] Thus when the famous Messiah of the Keisāniyya sect Mohammed b. al-Ḥanafiyya disappeared, his political agent Mukhtār, whose insurrection shook the young Caliphate in its foundation, proclaimed himself his *Khalīfa.*[182] The notorious Shiitic sectarian Abū 'l-Khaṭṭāb denied the death of the Imām Ja'far aṣ-Sādik and, pending his return, assumed the title and the functions of a *Khalīfa.*[183]. . .

Such or similar speculations will probably have to be drawn upon to explain the succession of the Messianic claim from Abū 'Īsa to Yūdġān, although the paucity of our material can justify nothing beyond vague conjectures. Abū 'Īsa, in this the sources unanimously agree, considered himself merely the precursor, or the Dā'ī, of the Messiah, which fact however did not prevent his followers from regarding him as the Messiah himself. When he died, a split was inevitable. There were those who, like the Wāḳifiyya, denied the reality of his death and, believing him to be hidden, expected his return. They were called the 'Īsawiyya.[184] Among them was his disciple Yūdġān who, assuming temporary charge over the faithful, declared to be his "prophet" or *Khalīfa.* There were others, however, who, like the Kiṭṭī'iyya, insisted that Abū 'Īsa was dead. They therefore regarded Yūdġān as the Messiah and, when he died, they expected his own return. They were called the Yūdġāniyya.[185] Curiously enough, a migration and a geographical separation appears to have taken place. For it seems that the 'Īsawiyya,[186] those who continued to expect Abū 'Īsa's return, left Ispahan and migrated to Damascus, where Ḳirḳisānī, two centuries later, still found remnants of them to the number of twenty or thirty souls, while the Yūdġāniyya seem to have remained in their old home.[187]. . .

7. ANOINTMENT

It would be a futile task to attempt to penetrate into the dark recesses of the pseudo-Messianic consciousness which rather belongs to the domain of psychology or pathology. On the whole it will be found that the Messianic pretenders are more modest in their claim than their followers, and while the leader is satisfied to be the forerunner of the Messiah, the believers insist that he is the Messiah himself. Often, indeed, the pretender himself is in doubt as to the exact nature of his claim, which will be found to increase with the increase of his influence. It will hardly be possible to throw light into this dark domain and I have touched on the subject merely to show that this uncertainty of Messianic pretensions has colored the reports about our much quoted sectarian Abū 'Īsa.

The few existing data clearly suggest that he claimed to be a precursor or a messenger of the Messiah. At the same time, as Shahrastānī[188] informs us, he maintained, or was said to maintain, that "God had spoken to him and had charged him to deliver the children of Israel from the ungodly nations and wicked rulers," and, as a result of this charge, he headed an armed uprising, a fact which is attested both by Ḳirḳisānī and Shahrastānī.[189] It is not farfetched to assume with Graetz[190] that, not being of Davidic stock,—a condition indispensable for a Messianic candidacy,—he contented himself with the rôle of the Ephraimitic Messiah,[191] while his Jewish opponents, if we are to trust Maḳrīzī, looked upon him after his defeat as the Antichrist, whose manifestation would take place in Ispahan.[192] Be this as it may, the following notice preserved by Maḳrīzī seems to point to some such Messianic conception. "The Iṣbahāniyya," says Maḳrīzi[193] "are the adherents of Abū 'Īsa al-Iṣbahānī. He laid claim to prophecy and (he maintained) that he was lifted up to heaven, *fa-masaḥa arrabb 'alā ra'sihi* and that the Lord patted him on his head, also that he beheld Muhammed and believed in him. The Jews of Ispahan maintain that he is the Dajjāl (the Antichrist) and that he will come forth from their region."

Curiously enough the identical story of a heavenly visit is reported of the Pseudo-Messiah Abū Manṣūr of Kufa, a younger contemporary of Abū 'Īsa.[194] Abū Manṣūr, who originally considered himself the "prophet" of the fifth Shiitic Imām Mohammed al-Bāḳir (d. 735), but after his death advanced his own candidacy as the Mahdī,[195] maintained that "he was lifted up to heaven and beheld the object of his worship (i. e. God) who patted his head with his hand[196] and said to him, 'My child, descend and bring a message from Me.' "[197]

Of course, both in the case of Abū 'Īsa and Abū Manṣūr the story was suggested by the *mi'rāj*, the "heavenly journey" of Mohammed, alluded to in the Koran.[198] But apart from the desire of using Mohammed as a pattern, another tendency was undoubtedly in operation. In the case of Abū Manṣūr the motive seems clear: the story is to convey Abū Manṣūr's familiarity with the Almighty who, according to one source, even condescended to address our heresiarch in Persian, his native idiom.[199] I have, however, the feeling that in the case of Abū 'Īsa some more solid claim is involved. *Masaḥa* in Arabic means generally "to touch, to rub, to pat,"[200] but it also signifies "to anoint" and the national lexicographers explain properly the term *al-masīḥ* "Messiah" as *mamsūḥ bi'd-duhn* "annointed with oil."[201] In the history of the Jewish Pseudo-Messiahs we often find that they insist on having been miraculously anointed and in this way fitted for their Messianic task.[202] It is therefore to be assumed that the words *fa-masaḥa 'alā ra'sihi* originally[203] meant to convey that God had poured holy oil on his head and by consecrating him as the *Mashīªḥ,* "the Anointed one," empowered him to become the redeemer of Israel.[204]

8. INSPIRATION

Prophecy, in accordance with the Gnostic theory, is the incarnation of the Divine essence in man. Hence the knowledge possessed by the prophet must be supernatural and free from human admixture. The Shiites have drawn the full consequences of this conception. The Imāms, as the incarnation of Divinity, are credited with the knowledge of "what is within the borders of the seven earths below and what is in the seven heavens above and what is on land and on sea,"[205] and this knowledge is immediately derived from a Divine source, not conveyed by any human means of information or instruction. A Shiitic theologian gives the following explanation of the omniscience of the Imāms: "Their source is either a tradition which every one of them has received from his father, the latter from his own father and so on up to the Prophet, or it is Revelation and Inspiration. For this reason it has never been recorded of any of them that he has ever gone to a teacher, or studied under a master, or asked any questions."[206]

It is in consequence of this conception which regards inspiration as the only true source of knowledge and is therefore bound to mistrust all knowledge transmitted through a human medium that Mohammed proudly designates himself as *nabī ummī* "an illiterate prophet"[207] and otherwise boasts of his ignorance. Whether Mohammed was able to read and write is a mooted point often discussed by scholars,[208] though it is a well-established dogma of Islam. But that he was sorely ignorant is admitted by all and this ignorance, instead of proving a drawback, was of effective assistance in establishing his claim as a prophet. . . .

Mohammed's claim of illiteracy has no other purpose than that of enhancing the uniqueness of his literary achievement. The Koran is the only miracle of which Mohammed professes to be capable. Every Koran verse is an *āya,* a sign or a miracle, and the inimitability of the Koran, not only as regards its contents but also as regards its Arabic diction, is constantly appealed to by Mohammed, and so it is by the Mohammedans down to the present day, as the principal argument for its divine origin.[209] . . .

We are now sufficiently prepared to comprehend the full significance of the statement of Ḳirḳisānī regarding Abū ʿĪsa: "His miracle of legitimation in the eyes of his adherents consisted in the fact that, although, as they assert, he was by profession a tailor and, according to their assertion, *was ummī, illiterate, and not able to write or to read, he brought forth books and writings, without anyone having instructed him.*"[210] The same statement Ḳirḳisānī repeats in a later passage:[211] "We have already related in what has preceded that Abū ʿĪsa claimed prophecy and that his miracle of legitimation in the eyes of his adherents consisted in the fact that he was *ummī,* illiterate, without being able to write or to read and then brought forth books and writings and that this was only possible by means of prophecy." In the special chapter which the same author[212] devotes to the refutation of Abū ʿĪsa's doctrine he reverts to the same claim which he cleverly endeavors to invalidate. "As to the miracle which they claim in that he had been *ummī,* illiterate, and then brought forth books and writings,—even if the matter had been as they mention, even then it might be possible that he (Abū ʿĪsa) had applied himself to it from the beginning of his cause and its very start and that he had (merely) simulated ignorance and illiteracy, in order to facilitate what he had in his mind."

The same claim of ignorance meets us in later times in heterodox Jewish circles. . . .

9. SOCIAL POSITION

As in all revolutionary upheavals, so in sectarian movements the first to respond are usually the lower classes, those that have nothing to lose and much to gain from the overthrow of the existing order of things. Shiism, being Messianic, was revolutionary in character. When transferred to Persia, it became the organized protest of the Persian nation not only against the political dominion of the Arabic conquerors but also against the religion represented by them.[213] While, however, the higher Persian classes, in the expectation of political and financial benefits, hastened to make their peace with the new masters,[214] the adherents of Shiism mainly recruited themselves from the lower classes which expected their salvation from the political and social revolution preached and prepared by Shiism.

This social contrast manifested itself very early in the great Shiitic uprising of Mukhtār who pretended to act on behalf of the expected

Mahdī Ibn al-Ḥanafiyya. Mukhtār's main support came from the *Mawāli,* the emancipated slaves of Persian origin in Kufa. Their social position may be gauged from the fact that, not being able to afford regular arms, they had to content themselves with clubs and were for this reason nicknamed *Khashabiyya* "men of wood."[215]

This condition becomes even more evident when we call to our mind the professions of some of the Shiitic sectarians which, in accordance with oriental usage, are often indicated in their names. Thus we find among the Shiitic Pseudo-Messiahs Bazīġ the weaver,[216] the most despised profession in the East,[217] and it is worthy of mention that one of the authors who record the existence of this sectarian[218] sneeringly implies that the recognition of prophets of such low social standing is typical of Shiism.[219] The 'Abbasid *Dā'ī* and "prophet" Khidāsh who was executed by the Omayyads in 736, was a potter.[220] The famous general and sectarian Abū Muslim was a saddler.[221] The celebrated Pseudo-Messiah Muḳanna' was a fuller.[222] The great rebel and heresiarch Bābak was as shepherd.[223] The famous Shiitic mystic Ḥallāj was, as his name indicates, a wool-carder.[224] The Keisanitic champion and poet as-Sayyid al-Ḥimyarī was the object of ridicule, because his associate in doctrine was a cobbler.[225] . . .

When we turn to Jewish sectarianism, we find substantially the same state of affairs. From the account of Ḳirḳisānī we gain distinctly the impression, and occasionally we are expressly informed, that the Jewish sectarians were people of low standing both socially and intellectually.[226] We are, in consequence, not surprised to hear that the most important Jewish heresiarch of that period, Abū 'Īsa al-Iṣfahānī, was not only illiterate but by profession a tailor.[227] On the same ground we are justified in assuming that, if his disciple and successor is designated as ar-Rā'ī,[228] he was purely and simply a shepherd. His designation by Hadassi,[229] in the clumsy manner characteristic of that author, as *ro'eh gemalekha,* which was unjustifiably taken to be sarcastic,[230] would characterize him more exactly, if it be not a mere paraphrase of the Arabic word, as a camel-herd. The name *Ra'yāniyya* which is found in connection with this sect[231] would lead us to assume that Yūdġān's by-name ar-Rā'ī was also pronounced Ra'yā or Ra'yān.[232] Perhaps the further conjecture may be ventured that this designation, pointing to a low social occupation, was annoying to his adherents and was therefore interpreted by them, in accordance with the biblical usage, which is occasionally found in Arabic,[233] in a metaphorical meaning as "the shepherd of the nation."[234]

The above derivation of the name of Yūdġān does not in any way militate against the assumption that he was at the same time a Dā'ī of Abu 'Īsa and, like his master, held that office in high esteem. The attempt to explain Dā'ī as a scribal error for Rā'i[235] is not convincing, for the importance accorded to the Dā'ī by Abū 'Īsa and Yūdġān is in perfect agreement with the conceptions of their age and environment.

10. JIHĀD

Jihād or the fight against unbelievers is one of the fundamental precepts of Islam. But apart from the duty of fighting unbelief outside the Mohammedan community, the faithful Muslim, in obedience to the Koran which frequently emphasizes "the command to do right and the prohibition to do wrong,"[236] is called upon to fight wrong and injustice wherever they meet him. As to the mode in which this fight ought to be carried on, the view shared by a variety of sections within orthodox Islam or bordering on it is that it is not sufficient to fight with the heart and the tongue (i.e. by conviction and persuasion), "but that appeal must be made to arms."[237] The Shiites, however, are of the opinion that the use of arms is prohibited. "All the Rawāfiḍ,[238] so the dogmatist Ibn Ḥazm[239] informs us, hold to it, though they be killed . . . But they believe in it (in the prohibition of arms) only so long as the speaking Imām (= the Mahdī) does not come forth. When he does come forth, then the drawing of swords becomes obligatory." Peculiarly enough this view is quoted in an old source[240] as one of the analogies between Shiism and Judaism. "The Jews say, There shall be no fighting for the sake of God, until the Messiah, the Expected One, goes forth[241] and a herald from heaven proclaims (his arrival). The Rāfiḍa[242] say, There is no fighting for the sake of Allah until the Mahdī goes forth and a herald[243] descends from heaven."

This theory which restricts all fighting to Mahdistic movements places every Mahdistic candidate in the necessity to rise in arms against the powers that be, without any regard to possible consequences, for his neglect to fight would immediately disqualify him as a Messianic candidate. From this logical but extremely dangerous conclusion the Shiites were saved by the adoption of the principle of *taḳiyya* "fear, precaution."[244] This principle which acknowledges the claim of practical expediency became of utmost importance to Shiism which has always been in opposition to the existing order of things and has constantly knocked up against reality.[245] It also offered a convenient solution to the perplexing question which must trouble the conscience of every faithful Shiite why the Mahdī who must be cognizant of all the wrong and injustice rampant in this world yet remains hidden and does not come forth to fill the earth with justice.[246]

While the saner elements within the Shī'a thus made peace with reality, there were radical sections which repudiated this pact with convenience and considered it their duty to fight, without any regard to their strength or their fate. *Fiat iustitia, pereat mundus* became their watchword. This view is in all likelihood the source of the terroristic Shiitic movements which played a considerable part in the eighth century in 'Irāḳ.[247] One of these terrorists was Muġīra b. Sa'īd of Kufa.[248] He regarded Ja'far as-Ṣādiḳ, the sixth 'Alidic Imām, as the Mahdī.[249] When the decisive moment arrived, he rose in arms, accompanied by a small band of *mawālis* (emancipated slaves), against the governor of Kufa. They were, as was to be expected, exterminated (in 737). Muġīra's "army" consisted altogether of twenty men.[250] According to Ṭabarī,[251] they were no more than seven men.

Perhaps some such notions may have prevailed among the Jewish sectarians who arose about the same time and in similar surroundings. Abū 'Īsa considered it his duty to fight the Mohammedan power and met his fate. His successor Yūdġān who otherwise upheld his views thought it wiser to keep his peace. One of the followers of Yūdġān was a certain Mushkā or Mushkān. He adhered, as Shahrastānī[252] informs us, "to the doctrine of Yūdġān, with the exception that *he considered it obligatory to rise against his adversaries and to wage war against them.* He rose, *accompanied by nineteen men,* and was killed in the neighborhood of Ḳumm." . . .

11. PROHIBITION OF MEAT

When after the destruction of the Second Temple certain ascetically inclined people proposed to forbid the use of meat and wine, because they had been offered on the altar which now lay in ruins, they were checked by the judicious R. Joshua ben Hananiah who pointed out to them that by the same analogy they would have to renounce many other eatables indispensable for life.[253] This tendency, which was thus suppressed in talmudic Judaism, asserted itself, like many other austerities of the law disposed of by the Rabbis, in Jewish sectarianism,[254] notably in Karaism. Already Anan forbade the eating of meat in the exile[255] and he was followed in this prohibition by later Karaite authorities, even by those who, like Ismāʿīl al-ʿOkbari, otherwise violently opposed him.[256] This restriction, together with the prohibition of wine,[257] became particularly characteristic of the Karaite ascetics who settled in the Holy Land and formed the community of the so-called "Abele Zion."[258] In the time of Ḳirkisānī, as we learn from his own words,[259] the bulk of Karaites refrained from eating meat, and the wide currency of this restriction may perhaps be best inferred from the exceptions quoted by the same author who circumstantially relates that one of the Karaitic sectarians had composed several pamphlets to prove that meat was permissible[260] and that there were Karaites who "considered permissible the eating of the flesh of sheep and cattle in the exile."[261]

It would lead us too far afield to inquire into the motives underlying this restriction. . . . Be the motive whatever it may, the prohibition of meat was, as its formulation clearly indicates, confined to the state of the Jews in the dispersion. Nor was it prompted by any vegetarian or humanitarian considerations. For the prohibition of meat by the Karaites was by no means absolute. Anan allowed the flesh of the deer[262] and that of the pigeon and turtle-dove among the birds,[263] while the later Karaites distinctly confine the prohibition to the flesh of sheep and cattle.[264]

The same prohibition of meat and wine is reported of the Jewish sectarians Abū ʿĪsa and Yūdġān.[265] This spirit of self-abnegation which was regarded as the only attitude befitting the unfortunate condition of the Jews in the exile found a particularly favorable soil in these sectarian circles which believed in the approaching Messianic redemption and partly endeavored to bring it about by the force of arms. The Yūdġāniyya particularly were characterized by ascetic tendencies and were given, as both Ḳirḳisānī and Shahrastānī inform us, to much praying and fasting.[266] The same disparaging attitude towards the exile reveals itself in another doctrine, preached by Yūdġān and shared by some Karaites, "that the sabbaths and festivals are no more valid in this age and are (to be observed) merely as a recollection."[267]

While the prohibition of meat by these sectarians is thus fully in accord with widely current Jewish tendencies, there is something in the formulation of this prohibition, as reproduced by Shahrastānī, which cannot possibly be ascribed to these influences. For, according to this author, Abū 'Īsa "prohibited in his book[268] all slaughtered animals and he forbade the eating of any creature endowed with a living spirit *unconditionally, be it a bird or an animal.*"[269] The contrast to the Karaite practices discussed above is palpable. The complete prohibition of birds differs essentially from the Karaitic custom and the motive underlying this prohibition seems essentially different as well: it is neither asceticism nor the exile, but the objection to the destruction of life. I am therefore inclined to assume that, in addition to Jewish influences, Abū 'Īsa was swayed in his prohibition by foreign non-Jewish conceptions.

I believe that the source of Abū 'Īsā's prohibition is to be found in the doctrines and practices of Manichæism and the sects emanating from it, whose influence on Jewish sectarianism has already been proved by other instances. The prohibition of meat and wine is a characteristic feature of Manichæism. Already before the birth of Mānī his father Futtak was repeatedly warned by a heavenly voice to refrain from meat and wine[270] and the same restriction is one of the essential conditions for admission into the Manichcæan community.[271] The Manichæans, as Ibn Ḥazm tersely remarks, "do not believe in (the use of) slaughtered animals."[272] The motive is supplied by Bīrūnī who relates that Mānī "forbade to slaughter living creatures or to cause them pain."[273] Mazdak, who is dogmatically a lineal descendant of Mānī, was prompted by the same motive when he forbade the slaughtering of animals until they died a natural death.[274] The heresiarch Bihāfarīd, a contemporary of Abū 'Īsa, who seems to have been largely influenced by Manichæism and Mazdakism, prohibited, in contradistinction to Mazdak, the flesh of dead animals, but that he was none the less actuated by the same tendency is shown by the fact that he allowed the slaughtering of small cattle when they were enfeebled,[275] apparently believing that to kill them in this state involved no cruelty to them but charity.[276]

It is in doctrines like these which were undoubtedly in vogue in the age and in the environment of Abū 'Īsa that we have to look for an explanation of his sweeping prohibition of the destruction of life which is both in its extent and motive different from similar practices current in Jewish sectarian circles.

Perhaps this may also throw some light on the remark of Ḳirḳisānī: "He (Abū 'Īsa) prohibited meat and wine, not on the basis of Scripture but because he maintained that God had commanded him to do this *through prophecy*."[277] Anan, who is designated by Ḳirḳisānī as the first who forbade the eating of meat, tried to deduce this prohibition from the Bible.[278] Abū 'Īsa, however, was conscious of the fact that this prohibition was an innovation of his own and had no source in the similar practices current in certain Jewish circles hitherto.[279]

12. NUMBER OF PRAYERS

According to Shahrastānī,[280] Abū 'Īsa instituted *ten* daily prayers and he also specified the time at which they should be recited. Ḳirḳisānī, however, reports that he instituted *seven* daily prayers, in accordance with the Psalm verse (119, 164): "Seven times a day do I praise Thee because of thy righteous judgments."[281] It is to be assumed *a priori* that the smaller number is the correct one. Now while it may be possible that Abū 'Īsa justified the new number of prayers by the Psalm verse, it is little likely that he derived it from it, particularly when we remember that, as Ḳirḳisānī further informs us, he also retained the regular prayers of the Jews.[282] We have already had repeated occasion to point to the extraordinary prominence accorded to the number seven in heterodox Mohammedan circles whose influence on Abū 'Īsa has been traced above. It is no wonder therefore that it should also have influenced the number of prayers. Thus Mānī is said to have instituted seven prayers.[283] Of still greater importance is the fact that the contemporary of Abū 'Īsa, the Persian Bihāfarīd, who also in this instance proves himself a follower of Manichæism and Mazdakism—in the latter the seven, together with the twelve, looms most prominently as a sacred number—,[284] established *seven* prayers, the character of which is thus specified by Bīrūnī:[285] "one in praise of the one God, one relating to death, one relating to the Resurrection and Last Judgment, one relating to those in heaven and hell and what is prepared for them, and one in praise of the people of Paradise." It needs no great stretch of imagination to assume that the example of this or a similar sectarian is responsible for the new number of prayers instituted by Abū 'Īsa. In the character of the prayers established by Bihāfarīd there is nothing which a professing Jew could not with a clear conscience adopt. They were, to judge by the description of Bīrūnī, more in the nature of supplications or praises than a collection of liturgies, as in the case of the Jewish or Mohammedan ritual, and their content is in striking harmony with the Psalm word by which Abū ʿĪsa *a posteriori* justified them. The character of these prayers as short individual eulogies also makes us understand why they did not replace the regular *Shmaʿ* and *Shmōne ʿEsrē* which, as Ḳirḳisānī tells us, he was commanded by God to retain, "according to the order of the Rabbanites.'[286] In the light of these facts, we are also able to explain the discrepant statement of Shahrastānī who speaks of *ten* prayers. The ten prayers of Abū ʿĪsā consisted of the seven special prayers suggested to him by heterodox Islam and the three regular prayers retained from the Jewish liturgy.

NOTES

The works regularly or frequently referred to in this article are quoted under the following abbreviations: *Shiites I* and *II* = my treatise *The Heterodoxies of the Shiites according to Ibn Ḥazm,* New Haven 1909, reprint from the *Journal of the American Oriental Society,* 28 and 29.—*AbS I* and *II* = my article " ʾAbdallah b. Sabā, der Begründer der Šīʿa, und sein jüdischer Ursprung" in *Zeitschrift für Assyriologie,* 23 and 24 (1909–1910).—*Browne, Persia* = Edward G. Browne, *A Literary History of Persia,* vol. I, New York 1902.—*Browne, Tarikh* = B., The *Ta'rīkh-i-jadid,* or New History of Mīrzā Ḥuseyn of Hamadān. Cambridge 1893.—*Darmesteter* = D., *Le Mahdi,* Paris 1885.—*Goldziher, Religion des Islams* in *Orientalische Religionen,* Berlin and Leipzig 1906 (*Die Kultur der Gegenwart,* Teil I, Abteilung III, 1).—*Goldziher, Vorlesungen* = G., *Vorlesungen über der Islam,* Heidelberg 1910.—*Grätz* = G., *Geschichte der Juden,* third edition; vol. V, fourth edition.—*van Vloten* = v. V., *Recherches sur la domination arabe, le chiitisme et les croyances messianiques sous le khalifat des Omayades,* Amsterdam 1894.—ARABIC AUTHORS: *Baġdādī* = B., *Kitāb al- farḳ beina'l-firaḳ* (see *Shiites,* I, 26), edited by Muḥammad Badr, Cairo 1910.—Birūnī = B., *Al- ātār al-bāḳiya,* ed. Sachau; Sachau's translation, London 1879.—*Ibn Ḥazm* = I. H., *Milal wa'n-niḥal,* Cairo 1317–1321.—*Ḳirḳ.* = Ḳirḳisānī, *Kitāb al-anwār,* ed. Harkavy, in *Zapiski,* St. Petersburg 1895.—*Shahr.* = Shahrastānī, ed. Cureton.—*Ṭabarī* = T., *Annales,* ed. de Goeje.—PERIODICALS and DICTIONARIES are quoted under the current abbreviations: *JQR.,* = *Jewish Quarterly Review; JRAS.,* = *Journal of the Royal Asiatic Society; MGWJ.* = *Monatsschrift für die Geschichte und Wissenschaft des Judenthums; PRE*³ = *Protestantische Realencyklopädie,* third edition; *WZKM.,* = *Wiener Zeitschrift für die Kunde des Morgenlandes; ZA.,* = *Zeitschrift für Assyriologie; ZDMG.,* = *Zeitschrift der deutsch-morgenl. Gesellschaft; ZfhB.,* = *Zeitschrift für hebräische Bibliographie.* [For technical reasons, most quotations in the original languages have been eliminated from the notes—Ed.].

1. Already by Pinsker, *Likkute Kadmoniyot,* pp. 11, 13, and even earlier by Rappoport in *Kerem Ḥemed* V (1841) p. 204.
2. Harkavy in *Jew. Enc.* I 553[b], article "Anan."
3. Published by Harkavy with a Russian introduction Petersburg 1894 (reprinted from the Memoirs of the Oriental Department of the Imperial Russian Archæological Society volume VIII). See also Bacher in *JQR* (o.s.) 7:687 ff.
4. I may incidentally remark that the famous Spanish-Arabic theologian Ibn Ḥazm (died 1064) makes mention of al-Muḳammiṣ in his *Milal wa' n-Niḥal III, 171.*
5. *Eshkol ha-kofer* Goslov 1836 fol. 41[c].
6. I refer to a manuscript, apparently a *unicum,* recently purchased from Mr. Ephraim Deinard and presented to the Library of the Jewish Theological Seminary by Judge Mayer Sulzberger.
7. Ed. Cureton I 168 f. I collated Cureton's text with four MSS. of the British Museum (Add. 7205; 7251; 23349; 23350). They differ only in details.
8. Shahrastānī quotes al-Warrāḳ I 141, 143 on Shiitic doctrines, and p. 189, 192 on Manichæan and Mazdakæan heresies. According to p. 189, he was originally a Magian.
9. Cf. Bīrūni's *Chronology of Ancient Nations* translated by Sachau pp. 270, 33; 278, 22 and 279, 13, where al-Warrāḳ's *Kitāb al-Maḳālāt* "Book of Heresies" is quoted. See also p. 431. I have not been able to ascertain the date of al-Warrāḳ.
10. Cf. Poznański in *JQR* (o.s.) 16: 770.
11. See later. Already Pinsker, *l. c.* p. 5 *top* refers to this circumstance.
12. The movement of Serene in Syria stands entirely apart.
13. According to Ḳirḳisānī (in several places) and Hadassi his Jewish name was Obadiah. Ibn Ḥazm, *Milal wa'n-Niḥal* I 99 l. 11 says: "it has reached me that his name was Muhammad b. 'Īsa." This combination of the names of Jesus and Muhammed is most probably an afterthought, cf. Poznański in *JQR* (o.s.) 16: 770. Shahrastānī calls him Isḥāḳ b. Ya'ḳūb and adds: "but *it is said* that his name was *'Ufid Alūhīm.*" The latter is undoubtedly ʿObed Elohīm and identical with Obadiah. The form of the name is very strange. I am inclined to think that the Jews of Ispahan or those who are responsible for Shahrastāni's data refrained from pronouncing YHWH and used instead Elohim.
14. The first form is the most frequent and is used by all Arabic writers. Ḳirḳisānī prefers the second form, cf. p. 284, 11 (where a variant reads 'Isawiyya) and in the Manuscript of the British Museum Or. 2524 fol. 33[b]. Similarly Hadassi: ha-ʿIsunīm. Iṣfahāniyya or, more correctly, Iṣbaāniyya is found in Maḳrīzī, *Khiṭaṭ* (ed. Cairo)) IV 372 l. 18 and in Su'udi (wrote 1535), *Disputatio pro religione Mohammedanorum contra Christianos* Leiden 1890 p. 189.
15. Ḳirḳisānī 284, 6. This statement is left out by Hadassi. Did David al-Muḳammiṣ have it?

16. Shahrastānī I 168.
17. Prefacing it by *wa-ḳīla* "and it is said".
18. *Geschichte* V³ 404.
19. In his introduction to Ḳirḳisānī p. 277, also in his notes to Grätz-Rabinowitz III 502.
20. Cf. the movements of Khidāsh (on him and similar rebels see Wellhausen, *Das arabische Reich* p. 315 ff.), Muġīra, Bayān, Abū Manṣūr, Abū 'l-Khaṭṭāb, and the numerous factions of the Khattābiyya (see on all these *Shiites* Index), nearly all contemporaneous, in the first half of the second Muhammedan century. The rebellion of Mukhtār (died 67=687) nearly half a century earlier (Wellhausen, *Die religiös-politischen Oppositionsparteien* p. 74 ff.) was of a different character. Moreover, it did not affect Persia proper.
21. See, e. g., *Shiites* II 79 l. 36. This is the impression one gets throughout from the accounts on the sects of this period.
22. Cf. August Müller, *Der Islam im Morgen- und Abendland* I 389.
23. *Das arabische Reich* p. 231.
24. Browne, *Persia,* l. l. p. 308 ff.
25. *Shiites* II 44 ff. Wellhausen, *Das arabische Reich* p. 239 f.; 311.
26. See *Shiites* Index s. v. *Abū Muslim.*
27. It was supposed to have been founded by Jews. The older city was called *Yahūdiyya.* Cf. *Jew. Enc.* VI 659[b] f. s. v. Ispahan.
28. Shahrastānī I 168: "a large crowd of Jews followed him." According to Maimonides (*Iggeret Tēmān,* Lichtenberg *Kobez,* II p. 7[b]), Abū 'Īsa was followed by 10,000 Jews. Ḳirḳisānī says (284, 7): "and people followed him, so that there was an army with him and he was encountered in battle and killed." This does not contradict the statement of the same Ḳirḳisānī in his refutation of Abū Īsa (MS. British Museum Or. 2524 fol. 34[c]) that "in the beginning of his career only a few persons followed him in affirming his prophecy." Shahrastānī, too, speaks of his *da'wa* (propaganda) and it is quite possible that many joined his army who did not believe in his prophetic character.
29. This does not contradict Maimonides' words *(ibidem) bi-teḥilat malkhut Yishma'el 'amad ish* which Harkavy (introduction to Ḳirḳisānī p. 227) quotes in support of an earlier date. Maimonides who lived in the sixth century of the Hijra could very well speak of an event which took place about 130 H. as in the "beginning" of the Muhammedan dominion. I may remark here that although,—because of the mention of Ispahan,—one is reluctant to detach Maimonides' words from Abū 'Īsa's appearance, there are difficulties in the way of this identification.
30. p. 284–285.
31. *REJ.* 5: 208.
32. The Muhammedan theologian Baġdādī (died 1038) in his *Kitāb al-farḳ* (MS. Berlin No. 2800, cf. *Shiites* I 26 f.) mentions, alongside of the 'Īsawiyya, the Shārakāniyya (sic), supposedly (cf. note 3) named after their founder Shār-

akān (fol. 4[a]; this passage was discussed and published by Schreiner in *REJ*. 24: 206 ff.). In another passage (fol. 92[b]), however, not mentioned by Schreiner, the same sect is spelt Shāḏakāniyya. Schreiner (*ibidem* p. 207) rightly supposes that this sect is identical with the Shādagāniyya mentioned by Yefet b. ʻAlī (in Pinsker's *Likkute* p. 26. The Arabic *kāf* in these names is the Persian *gāf*.

33. Shahrastānī I 169. The name of the sect and its supposed (see following note) founder varies in the manuscripts (cf. *supra* note 7).
34. I have a strong suspicion that the last two names are not names of persons, as assumed by the Arabic writers who derive such names mechanically, but names of places. At least *Shādakān* is mentioned as a place in Khūzistān (Yāḳūt III 228) and *Mūshkān* as the name of localities in the province of Hamadan and one in Fāris (Yāḳūt IV 543).
35. According to R. Nathan ha-Babli (Neubauer, *Mediaeval Jewish Chronicles* II 78; *JQR* (o.s.) 17: 753), "the jurisdiction of Khorasān had in olden times belonged to Pumbadita, whence the *dayyānim* used to be sent thither, and all the tax on her revenues used to go to Pumbadita." This was the cause of the quarrel between Kohen Zedek and ʻUḳba. The ignorance of the Persian Jews may be inferred from the fact that they were unable to raise religious magistrates from their own midst. The same fact is reported by R. Pethahiah of Regensburg (*Sibbub* ed. Grünhut p. 10).
36. Cf. Kirḳisānī's (p. 285 l. 18) remark about the sect founded by Meswi al-ʻOkbarī: "there has never been seen among them a learned man or a thinker."
37. Samuel ibn ʻAbbās (in *Emek habacha* ed. Wiener p. 22).
38. Ḳirḳisānī (MS. British Museum Or. 2524 fol. 34[a]).
39. Ḳirḳisānī (316, 2) expressly states that "the heresies were numerous among the (Jewish) inhabitants of Jibāl, i. e. Media." Interesting in this connection is the list of heresies enumerated by Yefet b. ʻAlī in Pinsker's *Likkute* p. 26. More about it later.
40. Yūdġān is placed by Grätz (V^3 190, cf. 447) at 800. This is certainly too late. Yūdġān who was Abū ʻĪsa's disciple must have succeeded his master immediately.
41. See later.
42. p. 311, 25.
43. This is meant by Hadassi when he clumsily says (p. 41[c]) *meʻat dibre bene be rab maḥazikim hem ki-nebu'ah*. On the conception underlying this excesive veneration see later.
44. *Shiites*, II, 23.
45. *Ib*., 23, 27; 24, 9. 17.
46. See on Raj'a *Shiites*, II, 23–26; Goldziher, *Vorlesungen*, 227 ff.
47. *Shiites*, II, 28; *AbS*., I, 327.
48. *AbS*., II, 2, n. 2.
49. Sura III, 47–50; IV, 155–156. Comp. *AbS*., II, 2.
50. Snouck-Hurgronje, *Der Mahdi*, p. 8.

51. The same tendency originally prevailed in Judaism, the Messiah being identified with David (Hosea 3, 5; Ezek, 34, 23 f., comp. p. Berakot 2, 4), with Elijah (comp. Friedmann, *Seder Eliyahu Rabbah,* Introduction, 26) or with Hezekiah (see Klausner, *Die Messianischen Vorstellungen des jüdischen Volkes im Zeitalter der Tannaiten,* Berlin 1904, 69 ff.). A similar tendency is observable in the attempts to assign a definite name to the Messiah; Klausner, *l. c.,* 64 ff.
52. *AbS.,* II, 21 ff.
53. *Ib.,* 14 f.
54. Comp. *Shiites,* Index, *s. v.* "Return."
55. *Ib.,* II, 50 f.
56. *Ib.,* II, 42 f.; *AbS.,* I, 325, n. 3.; Goldziher, *Vorlesungen,* 256.
57. Darmesteter, 48.
58. Browne, *Tarikh,* 287, n. 1; *idem, Persia,* 246, n. 1, and in Hastings' *Encyclopedia of Religion and Ethics,* II, 300*a.* Both cities figure prominently in the Alexander legend.
59. Darmesteter, 43. This castle or, more correctly, citadel of copper (in Persian *ruyin diz*) probably stands for the famous City of Copper (*madīnat annuḥās,* or *madīnat aṣ-ṣufr,* see Yāḳūt, *s. v.*) known from the Alexander legend.
60. Darmesteter, 32 f.
61. On the Keisāniyya see Index to *Shiites, s. v.,* particularly II, 33 f.
62. On the uprising of Mukhtār, the agent of Ibn Al-Ḥanafiyya (killed in 687), see Wellhausen, *Die religiös-politischen Oppositionsparteien im alten Islam,* 74 ff.
63. *Shiites,* II, 36.
64. *Ibid.,* 35, 37–39. The fountains of milk and honey from which the Mahdī is miraculously fed do not necessarily go back to biblical conceptions, as was conjectured *Shiites,* II, 39, but rather reflect pseudepigraphic ideas, comp. *AbS.,* II, 37, n. 1. On milk (or cream) and honey in the Babylonian religion see Winckler and Zimmern, *Die Keilinschriften und das Alte Testament,* 3rd edition, p. 526.
65. *Abs.,* II, 18.
66. Bīrūnī, 212, 10.
67. *Shiites,* II, 87, 17.
68. *Shiites,* II, 44, 16.
69. *Ibid.,* II, 119, 15.
70. *Ibid.,* l. 12 and 38, 13. The expression *ḥayyun yurzaḳu* occurs frequently in connection with Messianic personages.
71. Ḳirḳ., 284, and Shahr., 158.
72. Ḳirḳ., 284, 7.
73. Ḳirḳ., 312, 16. This sect still existed in the time of Ḳirḳisānī, see later in the course of this article.
74. Grätz, VI, 244.
75. Both names suggest a Messianic character, comp. Grätz, *ib.,* 387.

76. See *ibid.* 244 ff.
77. The apostate Samuel Ibn 'Abbās (died 1174; Grätz, *ib.*, 387) in *Emek habacha,* translated by Wiener, Appendix, p. 23.
78. *Ib.*, l. 15: *al-masiḥ al-muntaẓar. Al-muntaẓar* (the Expected One), which is a standing title of the Shiitic Mahdīs, is applied in Jewish literature to the Messiah; comp. Goldziher, *Kitāb ma'ānī al-nafs,* p. 38*. In the same way the title *al-ḳā'im* (he who rises, the Rising One), which is a constant epithet of the Shiitic Mahdī, is used of the Messiah; Goldziher, *ibid.*, p. 39*. For other examples see *Emek habacha,* translated by Wiener, Appendix, p. 22 ult., 23, l. 4 and my *Selections from the Arabic Writings of Maimonides,* p. 22, l. 8. In the Arabic original of his *Iggeret Tēmān* Maimonides introduces his account of the French pseudo-Messiah with the words: "A *Ḳā'im* (i. e. Messiah) arose in the interior of France."—*Al-ḳa'im al-muntaẓar* as a combined title of the Messiah is found in a Genizah fragment in Oxford (*Catalogue of Hebrew MSS.* II, No. 2745, 24).
79. The Arabic phrase might mean that they regarded Menahem as the originator of the religion they professed or that their religion was designated as "Menahemite." Grätz, VI, 247, follows the latter explanation: "Nannten sich Menahemisten und schwuren bei seinem Namen."
80. Samuel b. 'Abbās, *ibid.*, p. 23 f.
81. Grätz (VI, 246) has missed the point of the whole story by placing it in the life-time of Alroy. See also later.
82. Comp. *AbS.*, II, 2 ff. and 18 f.
83. This is largely due to the fact that in Shiism the Messiah is identified with historic personages.
84. Occasionally also on a mule. In biblical times also, prior to the introduction of the horse, the mule appears as a noble animal used on state occasions and even in war, comp. II Samuel 8, 4, 9; 18, 9; I Kings 1, 33; comp. also Isa. 66, 20.
85. *AbS.*, II, 4 ff.
86. *Ib.*, p. 18, note 5.
87. He claimed to be the prophet Jonah (*Shiites,* II 26, 28) which in all probability means that he considered himself the forerunner of the Messiah Ibn al-Ḥanafiyya. Jonah, according to an old Jewish conception, is identical with the Ephraimitic Messiah, the forerunner of the Davidic Messiah. Comp. *Seder Eliyahu Rabbah,* ed. Friedmann, p. 97 f. and the editor's remarks in the introduction p. 11 f. and p. 98, note 57. As early an authority as Jerome (Preface to Jonah) records the tradition of the identity of Jonah with the son of the woman of Sarepta.
88. See above, note 45.
89. *Shiites,* 24, 10.
90. On Bihāfarīd see Bīrūnī, 210 f.; Shahr., 187, Browne, *Persia,* 308 ff.; Houtsma in *WZKM.*, 1889, p. 30 ff.
91. Browne, *Persia,* p. 309, n. 4; Houtsma, *l. c.*, 30 and 37.
92. Bīrūnī, 211, similarly Shahr., 187 penult.

93. On Muḳanna see *Shiites,* II, 120 f., and the literature enumerated there, to which are to be added Bīrūnī, 211, and Browne, *Persia,* 318 ff.
94. Browne, *l. c.,* 323.
95. Darmesteter, 50. Another example *ib.,* note 39.
96. When Ḏū-Nuwās, the Jewish ruler of Yemen, was routed in battle by the invading Abyssinians in 525, "he directed his horse towards the sea, then, spurring it on, rode through shallow water till he reached the depth and finally threw himself *with his horse* into it; *this is the last that was known of him*" (Tabari, I, 927 f.; similarly 930, 13). This description, which no doubt represents, as was observed by Nöldeke, *Geschichte der Perser und Araber zur Zeit der Sasaniden,* p. 191, n. 2, the attempt to glorify the end of the last national ruler of Yemen, may possibly reflect old Messianic expectations. The Southern Arabs believed in a Messiah of Ḥimyaritic-Sabæan stock "who will bring back the royal power to the Ḥimyarites in justice" (comp. *AbS.,* II, 16, n. 8; *ibid.,* p. 5, n. 6) and the last national king was certainly not unworthy of that honor. Already Beer (*ZDMG.,* 9 (1855): 793) suggests that the Jews of Arabia looked upon Ḏū-Nuwās as a Messianic personage. His name Pinehas points in the same direction, comp. Goldziher, "Pineḥas-Manṣūr," in *ZDMG.,* 56: 411 f.—According to a slightly different variant of our legend, Ḏū-Nuwās precipitated himself with his horse into the sea from the height of a rock (Grätz, V, 90). Both variants are careful to mention the horse.
97. Shahr., 168.
98. See *AbS.,* II, 6.
99. On 'Alī in the clouds see *Shiites,* II, 42 f.; *AbS.,* I. 325, n. 3. Comp. also Goldziher, *Vorlesungen,* 256.
100. Thus the prophets Khadhir and Elijah are represented as flying to protect the wall erected by Alexander the Great against Gog and Magog. They are both brought in connection with the Mahdī. See the reference in my book *"Die Chadhirlegende und der Alexanderroman,"* (Leipzig: B. G. Teubner, 1913).
101. *Shiites,* I, 70, 13 and the literature quoted II, 121, to ff. Comp. also Browne, *Persia,* p. 316.
102. Tabari, III, 418. See van Vloten 48, who also quotes a Byzantine source.
103. *Selecta ex historia Halebi,* ed. Freytag, Paris 1819, Arabic text, p. 15.
104. This reminds one of the claim of the Shiitic sect of the Khaṭṭābiyya "that they would not die, but would be lifted up to heaven," *Shiites,* I, 69, 10. See also *ibid.,* II, 24, n. 1; 72, 30, and 118, n. 4.
105. See later note 110.
106. Grätz, V, 169 ff.; 457 ff.
107. Isidor Pacensis quoted by Grätz, *ib.,* 458. "Messiamque se praedicans, illos ad terram repromissionis *volari* enuntiat." Perhaps it is not too far-fetched to assume that this conception was suggested or supported by a literal interpretation of Isa. 60, 8: "who are these (returning to Zion) that *fly* as a cloud and as the doves to their windows?"

108. Samuel ibn 'Abbās in *Emek habacha,* translated by Wiener, Appendix, p. 23 penult.

109. *Ibid.*, pp. 23–24.

110. P. 24, 4. The Rāwandiyya in Aleppo dressed themselves on a similar occasion in silken garments (above note 105). The most natural assumption would be that both the Persian sectarians and the Jews of Bagdad put on festive attire to receive the Messiah in a befitting manner. As for the color, one ought to think of the fact that green as the color of the turban or dress is considered a sign of distinction (comp. Lane, *Manners and Customs of the Modern Egyptians,* London, p. 28). There are however, several considerations which suggest a deeper meaning. Thus the pseudo-Messiah Muḳanna' (above note 93) was called by this name ("the veiled one"), because he used to veil himself in *green silk* (Browne, *Persia,* 318). The Persian heresiarch Bihāfarīḏ (above note 92) claimed that God had dressed him in a *green* shift before he sent him down on earth to take up his prophetic mission (*ibid.*, 308). Another author (quoted by Houtsma in *WZKM*., 1889, 30 ff.) narrates with even greater emphasis that Bihāfarīḏ had in his possession a shirt and a mantle of *green silk* to which he referred as "Paradise garments" and in which he solemnly attired himself before he manifested himself as a God-sent prophet.

111. I believe that the original meaning of this statement is that the Jews expected to be endowed with wings of angels and to be able to fly *themselves* to Jerusalem. This would agree with the rest of the account, according to which the Jews themselves made attempts at flying, and would also form an exact analogy to the belief of the Rāwandiyya (above, note 104).

112. P. 24, l. 12 read *ġulwāṇ* instead of *ġalayān.*

113. I. e.. by the two imposters.

114. *Ibid.*, p. 24; comp. Grätz, VI, 246. Samuel ibn 'Abbās' account is quoted by Abulfeda, see de Sacy's *Chrestomathie Arabe,* I, 363 f.

115. Birūnī, 207; Sachau's translation, 190. See also p. 192. The Babylonian particularism of the Manichæans is also evident from the fact that the head of the sect was obliged to reside in Babylonia, Flügel, *Mani,* 97 and 105.

116. The five prophets who are believed to have appeared as founders of new religions before Mohammed are Adam, Noah, Abraham, Moses, and Jesus. These, with Mohammed and the Mahdī who is to appear in fulness of time, make seven, see later.

117. This is involved in the *naskh* doctrine, according to which the previous revelations have been abrogated and superseded by the Koran. Comp. Goldziher in *Orientalische Religionen,* 98.

118. This applies particularly to Zoroaster. According to Ibn Ḥazm (d. 1064), many otherwise orthodox Mohammedans believed in the prophecy of Zoroaster (*Milal wa'n-niḥal,* I, 113, 6).

119. Perhaps the most striking formulation of this doctrine of infinite manifestations is the one given by the Bāb in one of his epistles (Browne, *JRAS.*,

1892, 473): "In the time of Noah, I was Noah, in the time of Abraham Abraham, in the time of Moses Moses, in the time of Jesus Jesus, in the time of Muhammed Muhammed, in the time of 'Alī Muhammed (the name of the Bāb) 'Alī Muhammed (this is undoubtedly the meaning of *'Alī-ḳabla-nabīl, nabīl* being the numerical equivalent of *Muhammed*). In the time of "the Greater One to Come" I shall surely be "the Greater One to Come," in the time of "the Greater One to Come Later" "the Greater One to Come Later," in the time of "the Greater One to Come still Later" "the Greater One to Come still Later" (etc.) until the end of Him who has no end, just as in the beginning of Him who has no beginning I was in every manifestation the proof of God towards his creatures."

120. Kirk. 312, 5.

121. Ibn Ḥazm's report about Abū 'Īsa (*Milal wa'n-Niḥal,* I, 99) contains little else beyond a statement of the view mentioned in the text. Shahrastānī, on the other hand, who gives an elaborate *historical* account of Abū 'Īsa, leaves this particular doctrine unmentioned and attributes it to one of the subdivisions of the 'Īsawiyya (see later n. 131). Ibn Ḥazm's account has been reproduced in text and German translation by Poznański in *JQR.,* (o.s.) 16: 765 ff. The 'Īsawiyya, according to the Ibn Ḥazm, advanced the argument that Mohammed as the prophet of the Arabs occupied the same position and deserved the same recognition as Job, Balaam, and the other non-Israelitish prophets mentioned in the Bible, who were sent to their respective races. Ibn Ḥazm winds up his account by making the following interesting statement: "I have met many distinguished men among the Jews who hold the same doctrine."—Abū 'Īsa and the 'Īsawiyya are referred to incidentally in other passages of his *Milal.* Thus in one passage (I, 112, *penult,* ff.) Abū 'Īsa is mentioned among Shiitic and non-Mohammedan pseudo-prophets of whom miracles are reported, which miracles, however, are worthless, "since miracles can only be relied upon when transmitted by multitudes." He refutes the 'Īsawiyya with the same arguments as Ḳirḳisānī (in the polemical chapters mentioned below, n. 127), pointing out their inconsistency in accepting Mohammed as prophet and yet refusing to accept his claim that he was sent to the whole world (I, 114 f.). As one of the Jewish sects the 'Īsawiyya are briefly referred to I, 117, 16 and V, 122, 8.

122. See Poznański, *JQR.,* (o.s.) 16:770 f. According to Baġdādī and Ibn Ḳayyim al-Jauziyya (Poznański, *ibidem*), Mohammed was believed to have been sent to the whole world, *except to the Jews and such nations as possess revealed writings.* See also later, note 131.

123. *Milal,* I, 99.

124. Comp. Poznański, *l. c.,* 770. I may mention in passing that the passage in Hirschfeld's *Arabic Chrestomathy,* objected to by Poznański, *ib.,* note 3, is confirmed by the MS. and that Jesus, and not Abū 'Īsa, is meant there.

125. *Milal,* II, 12: *"The 'Īsawiyya from among the Jews* agree with us, and so

do the Aryūsiyya (Arians), the Bulḳāniyya (Paulicians), and the Maḳdūniyya (Macedonians) from among the Christians, that he (Jesus) was a human being created by God in the womb of Mary without a male."

126. Ḳirḳ. 312, 9 ff. Elsewhere (Hirschfeld, *Arabic Chrestomathy*, 117, 1 ff.), Ḳirḳisānī makes the same charge against Mohammed who pretended to believe in Jesus, so that his own claims as a prophet might not be denied, "in the same manner as mentioned by us of Abū 'Īsa al-Iṣfahānī."

127. Chapter 13 and 14, MS. British Museum Or. 2524, fol. *33b–39b*. The refutation of Islam and Christianity which follows immediately is only a part of his polemics against Abū 'Īsa who acknowledged Jesus and Mohammed.

128. This may also account for the answer of Jacob ben Ephraim (Ḳirḳ., 312, 2 ff.) which so greatly shocked our author. To the Rabbanites of that period the Karaites who renewed the ancient vexatious contentions about the festivals seemed less sympathetic than the 'Īsūniyya, in spite of the fact that the latter "ascribed prophecy to those who did not possess it."

129. Baġdādī (ed. Mohammed Badr, p. 263, 13): "The 'Īsawiyya and the Ra'yāniyya . . . admit the prophecy of Muhammed." The Ra'yāniyya are probably identical with the Yūdġāniyya, see later.

130. Baġdādī 9, 14; comp. Schreiner in *REJ*., 29: 211, and above, n. 32.

131. Shahr., 169: "It is mentioned of a number among the Mushkāniyya that they firmly believe in the prophecy of the Chosen One (= Muhammed) for the Arabs and the rest of mankind, with the exception of the Jews, the latter being a people (forming) a religious community and (possessing) a revealed book" (MS. British Museum Add. 7250 omits *wa-kitābin*). See above, note 122.

132. Ḳirḳisānī MS. British Museum Or. 2524, fol. 35[b]: "Among the Dusturians there are people from among our adherents (i. e. Karaites) who agree with him (with Abū 'Īsa) in this opinion to a certain extent."

133. Grätz, V, 188, comp. Ḳirḳ., 305, 2. Poznański, *REJ*., 60: 308 f. doubts this generally accepted opinion. In view, however, of the statements of Ḳirḳisānī as well as of Arabic authors, his doubts seem scarcely justifiable. Anan may have been a politician, but, considering the facts adduced above, it would be unfair to seek political reasons (Harkavy, *Studien und Mitteilungen,* VIII, 102, n. 39), or even more objectionable motives (Pinsker, *Liḳḳute,* p. 20; Weiss, *Dor dor we-dorshow,* IV, 51) for his advocating a conception, which was in his age widespread in the East. It was scarcely of immediate benefit in a Mohammedan state to recognize Jesus as prophet. Steinschneider's harsh judgment (*Polemische und apologetische Literatur,* 343 f.) is certainly not justified.

134. Ibn Ḥazm, above note 121. In another passage, which seems to be missing in the printed edition, I. Ḥ. insinuates that the leading Jews were convinced of the truth of Mohammed's claim, but refused to admit it (Goldziher, Kobak's *Jeshurun,* 8: 78). Ibn Ḳajjim al-Jauziyya (d. 1350) reports the same view of a distinguished Egyptian Jew, Goldziher, *l. c.,* 9:22 f.

135. Comp. Uhlhorn in *PRE.*,[3] IV, 171; comp. also *Shiites,* II, 86, 4 ff.
136. *Shiites,* II, 85 f.
137. See Goldziher's article "Neuplatonische und gnostiche Elemente im Ḥadīt" in *ZA.*, 22: 324 ff.
138. The title of "Seal of the Prophets" assumed by Mohammed (Koran 33, 40) is interpreted in this sense and is emphasized by the canonical ḥadīth which makes Mohammed declare "there is no prophet after me," comp. *Shiites,* I, 47, and II, 48. According to Bīrūnī, 207, already Mānī believed that he was "the Seal of the Prophets." According to Shahrastānī (I, 192), Mānī predicted that "the Seal of the Prophets" (i. e. Mohammed) would come *to the Arabs*. The latter is no doubt a clumsy Mohammedan fabrication.
139. On this fundamental distinction between orthodox and heterodox Islam see Goldziher, *Vorlesungen,* 249 f.
140. See *AbS.*, II, 11.
141. *Ibidem.* In the same manner *Raj'a* is to be distinguished from the Transmigration of Souls.
142. *Shiites,* I, 60, 1.
143. *L. c.,* I, 62, 13.
144. *L. c.,* II, 92, 5 ff.
145. *L. c.,* II, 45, n. 8.
146. *L. c.,* II, 120 30 ff., Goldziher in *ZA.*, 22: 337 ff. The number of manifestations specified by Muḳanna' (*ibidem,* 338, n. 4) amounts to seven.
147. Comp. *JQR.* (o.s.) 19: 92, n. 1 and *Shiites,* II, 115, n. 2.
148. *Shiites,* II, 114 f. and Browne, *Persia,* 428 ff. Ḥallāj is addressed as "the eternal and luminous Creator who assumes human form in every age and period and in our own time has assumed the form of al-Ḥusein b. Manṣūr (=Ḥallāj)," Bīrūnī, 212, 1.
149. See the eleborate presentation of the Ismā'iliyya doctrine by Browne, *l. c.,* 405 ff., and Goldziher, *Vorlesungen,* 247 ff. For further literature see *Shiites,* II, 19, 27 ff. On the influence of these originally Neo-Platonic ideas on Judaism see Goldziher, *Kitāb ma'ānī al-nafs,* p. 41 ff. On their effect on Judah Halevi see the same in *REJ.*, 50: 32 ff. The doctrine quoted by Goldziher in *ZA.*, 22: 329, n. 1, according to which the "Luminous Substance" was transferred from the forehead of Adam to that of Seth, then Enoch, etc., and through Ishmael to the ancestors of Mohammed, strikingly resembles even in its details Judah Halevi's theory of *segulah*.
150. *Textes Persans relatifs à la secte des Ḥouroufis* (E. J. W. Gibb Memorial Series, Vol. IX), p. xiii, xvii. See also *ibidem,* 30 ff.
151. I, 168, 10 ff. Instead of *'Īsa* read *Abū 'Īsa.*
152. Shahr., *ibidem.*—The conception of Abū 'Isa as the One True Prophet probably underlies the curious distinction which Abū'l-Fadl as-Su'ūdī (ca. 1535), *Disputatio pro religione Mohammedanorum contra Christianos,* Leyden 1890, p. 189, draws between the 'Īsawiyya and the Iṣbahāniyya. The former are "the adherents of Abū 'Īsa al-Iṣbahānī who maintain that Jesus and Muhammed were prophets sent to their respective races only." The latter are "the adherents of Abū 'Īsa al-Iṣbahānī who maintain that

Abū ʿĪsa was a prophet sent *prior to Moses,*" a view which, as Su'ūdī polemically points out, is at variance with the general Jewish belief that "there was no prophet prior to Moses, the latter being in their opinion the key of prophecy and the first-born of apostleship," and also contradicts the Torah "which expressly declares that God's commands were given to men prior to Abū ʿĪsa." It would be interesting to know whether this distinction is an invention of Su'ūdī or whether it was, as seems more natural, derived from an older source.

153. *Shiites,* II, 85 f.
154. Above, n. 116. Perhaps the same applies to Mohammed's contemporary Omayya b. Abi Ṣalt who was anxious to assume a prophetic rôle, *Shiites,* II, 28 n. 1.
155. Comp. *Shiites,* II, 89 f., 127.
156. See, e. g., Browne, *Persia,* 408 ff. On the same number in the doctrine of Bihāfarīd, comp. *ib.,* 310, and among the Ḥurūfis *Textes persans relatifs à la secte des Ḥouroufis, p.* xviii.
157. Above, note 116.
158. See later.
159. Ḳirḳ., 311, 25: "He exalted the station of the Rabbis and respected them highly, so that he placed them on a level similar to that of the prophets."
160. Comp. Ginzberg, *Jewish Encyclopedia,* V, 126 f.; Friedmann, *Tanna de-be Eliyahu,* introduction, p. 21 ff.
161. The Pseudo-Messiah of Yemen is called by Maimonides (Kobez, ed. Lichtenberg, II, 26, 4 where the British Museum MSS. differ somewhat) *sheluḥo shel mashiaḥ*. The same expression *l. c., 7a,* second column, l. 6 from below.
162. I, 168.
163. *wa-zaʿama* [*Abū*] *ʿIsa annahu nabiyyun wa-annahu rasūl al-masiḥ al-muntaẓar.* That Abū ʿIsa claimed no more than prophecy is repeatedly asserted by Ḳirḳisānī (ed. Harkavy), 284, 6, 311, 20; see note 165.
164. *wa-zaʿama anna li'l-masīḥ ḥamsatan min ar-rusul ya'tūna ḳablahu wāḥidan baʿda wāḥidin.*
165. Ḳirḳ., 284, 14; 312, 16. In another passage, *ZfhB.,* 3:176 Ḳirḳisanī says: "and others like Abū ʿIsa al-Iṣbahānī who claimed prophecy, and just as Yūdġān claimed *that he was the Messiah.*" Similarly (Hirschfeld, Arabic Chrestomathy, 121, 24): "Yūdġān the Dāʿī and his claim that he is the Messiah." The latter statement contradicts his own words, ed. Harkavy, 312, 16. See later, note 175.
166. 15, 11.
167. Undoubtedly the title of Yūdġān.
168. *Shiites,* II, 109, 27.
169. *Ibidem,* note 2. Compare also *AbS.,* II, 30, n. 4.
170. *Shiites,* I, 68 and footnotes. "Every human being, after having succeeded in reaching the degree of a Missionary, is able to raise himself to the rank of the Preexistent (the Mahdī) and to substitute him," Blochet, *l. c.,* 60.
171. I, 168.

172. The "sand river" is the Sambation, compare my remarks in *JQR*, New Series, 1:256. The liberation of the Lost Tribes was considered an integral part of the Messianic redemption and the Messianic candidates had to live up to it. For this reason the Pseudo-Messiahs are often brought in connection with the Lost Tribes, particularly with the *Benē Mōshe* and the Sambation. The Messianic enthusiast Abraham Abulafia (d. ca. 1291) claimed, like Abū 'Īsa, to have penetrated to the Sambation (Grätz, VII, 192). David Reubeni's pretensions hinge on his connection with the Lost Tribes and the Benē Mōshe (Grätz, IX, 229). Among those who denied that Sabbathai Ṣevi was dead, there were many who maintained that he was hidden among the Benē Mōshe. He was generally expected to proceed to the Benē Mōshe living on the Sambation and to marry the daughter of Moses.
173. *wa-za'ama anna'd-dā'iya aiḍan huwa'l-masīḥu* (Shahr., I, 168, 13 ff., comp. also line 10). MS. British Museum Add. 7250 puts more correctly *aiḍan* after *wa-za'ama,* so that the meaning is: "he *also* maintained that the Dā'ī was the Messiah."
174. 168, *ult.*
175. That he did not consider himself the Messiah is clear from Ḳirḳisānī's words (284, 13): "It is said that he (Yūdġān) was a disciple of Abū 'Īsa Obadiah and also claimed prophecy. *His pupils* (variant: adherents), *however, maintain that he was the Messiah.*" The same is repeated 312, 16. The contradictory statement (above, note 165) can scarcely be correct.
176. Above, note 72.
177. Shahr. *wa-fīmā nuḳila 'anhu ta'ẓīm amr ad-dā'ī.* Yūdġān is designated by Ḳirḳisānī as Dā'ī, above, note 165.
178. Comp. *Shiites,* II, 51.
179. *Ib.,* 52.
180. *Shiites,* II, 52, 15 ff.
181. In a measure this idea is implied in the title *Khalīfa* (Caliph), the vicegerent of Mohammed, comp. Wellhausen, *Das arabische Reich,* 22 f.
182. *Ab.,* II, 15.
183. *Ibidem.* Similarly the Shiitic pseudo-prophet Abū Manṣūr (see note 195) claimed to be the *Khalīfa* of Mohammed al-Bāḳir, the father of Ja'far aṣ-Ṣadiḳ, Baġdādi, 234, 12. The successors of Faḍlallāh al-Ḥurūfi, who was believed to be hidden, are also designated as *Khalīfas, JRAS.,* 1907, 536, 540.
184. Or Īsūniyya (Ibn Ḥazm and Ḳirḳisānī), also Iṣfahaniyya, comp. above, n. 14.
185. Ḳirḳ., 312, 16.
186. Ḳirḳ., 284, 11: "In Damascus there are a number of his (Abū 'Īsa's) adherents, known as the 'Īsūniyya (var.: 'Īsawiyya)"; 317, 5 "As for the adherents of Abū 'Īsa al-Iṣfahānī, those who have remained in Damascus alone are about twenty souls"; MS. British Museum Or. 2524, fol. 34*a*:

"so that no one was left of them, except about twenty or thirty souls in Damascus. Perhaps a few of them can also be found in Ispahan." The latter statement in all probability refers to the Yūdġāniyya as a subdivision of the 'Īsawiyya (see next note). It is natural to assume that, when Abū 'Īsa had been defeated and killed, his adherents, at least some of them, fled to Syria. That there were relations between Syria and Persia is shown by such names of Persian-Jewish sectarians as Ba'lbekki and Ramlī.

187. Ḳirḳ., 317, 6: "As for the Yūdġāniyya, a few persons of them are still to be found in Ispahan." This is probably the reason why the 'Īsawiyya are not designated as Iṣfahāniyya by Ḳirḳisānī. The 'Īsawiyya evidently expected the manifestation of their prophet to take place in Damascus.
188. I, 168, 12.
189. To these Maimonides might be added, above, n. 28. See, however, note 191.
190. V, 462.
191. Speaking of the Pseudo-Messiah of Ispahan, Maimonides maintains that he considered himself the Messiah (*Iggeret Teman,* in Kobez, II, 7a, second column, l. 1). In the Arabic original Maimonides still more clearly emphasizes the fact that he was of Davidic origin. It can, however, be shown that Maimonides in this part of his account confused Abū 'Īsa with David Alroy, a confusion which has been taken over from Maimonides by Grätz.
192. That the Dajjāl (Antichrist) would proceed from Ispahan was also believed by Mohammedans, Bīrūnī, 211, Ibn Faḳīh, ed. de Goeje, 299, Muḳaddasī, 399. Schreiner (*ZDMG.,* 42: 596) suggests that this belief arose from the fact that Ispahan was supposed to have been founded by Jews. From Muḳaddasī, *l. c.,* it would seem, however, that Ispahan was connected with the Antichrist because of its violent opposition to 'Alī. Another widespread conception locates the Antichrist at Lydda, Bīrūnī, *ibidem,* and many others.
193. *Khiṭaṭ,* ed. Cairo, IV, 372.
194. See *Shiites,* I, 62 and the sources quoted *ib.,* II, 89, 14 f.
195. *Ib.,* II, 95, 32. Comp. above, note 183.
196. Ibn Ḥazm, *Milal,* IV, 185 (= *Shiites,* I, 62, 7) *masaḥa ra'sahu biyadihi,* Shahr. 136 *fa-masaḥa bi-yadihi ra'sahu,* Baġdādī 215, 1 and 234, 13 *masaḥa yadahu* (or *bi-yadihi*) *'alā ra'sihi.*
197. Alluding to Koran 5, 71.
198. Sura 17, 1. According to Blochet in *Revue de l'histoire des religions,* 40 (1899), p. 19 ff., the legend is of Persian origin. Mānī as well as Bihāfarīd claimed to have similarly ascended to heaven, Bīrūnī, 209 and 211.
199. *Shiites,* II, 90, 22.
200. In the sense "to touch" the Hebrew *mashaḥ* is used by Ḥisdai Crescas in his *Or Adonai* (ed. Vienna), p. 48*b*. It is undoubtedly an Arabism.
201. *Lisān al-'arab. s. v.*
202. Already Justin Martyr (second century) in his *Dialogus cum Tryphone* (ch. VIII) reports it as generally accepted that "Christ . . . has no power, until

Elias come to anoint him," comp. Klausner, *Die messianischen Vorstellungen,* 62, n. 2. From the later history of Jewish Messianism the following examples, which no doubt can be considerably multiplied, present themselves. The Messianic enthusiast Abraham Abulafia (d. ca. 1291) pretended that, when in ecstasy, "he felt as if his whole body from head to foot had been anointed with anointing oil" (Bernfeld, *Da'at Elohim,* p. 381). The Pseudo-Messiah Moses Botarel (about 1409) claimed that the prophet Elijah anointed him with holy oil, Grätz, VIII, 98, and *MGWJ.,* 1879, p. 80. Joseph Caro claims that Solomon Molcho "was anointed with a great and supernal anointing" (Grätz, IX, 545). See also the curious picture representing the anointment of Sabbathai Ṣevi, *Jew. Enc.,* XI, 222.

203. Although subsequently *masaḥa* may have been taken by the Arabic authors, who reproduce Abū 'Īsa's story, in its ordinary meaning "to touch" or "to pat." This meets the objection of Baron Rosen, Ḳirḳisānī (ed. Harkavy), Introduction, p. 265, n. 3.
204. Already suggested by Harkavy, *ibidem,* and *Le-Ḳorot ha-Kittot be-Yisra'el,* p. 10.
205. *Shiites,* II, 105.
206. *L. c.,* 55.
207. Koran 7, 156; comp. also 29, 47. *Ummī* (from *umma* "nation") shows exactly the same development in meaning as the Hebrew word *goy.*
208. See the material collected by Pautz in his *Muhammeds Lehre von der Offenbarung,* Leipzig 1898, p. 257 f.
209. Comp. Schreiner in *ZDMG.,* 42: 663 ff.
210. Ḳirḳ., 284, 9. This was misunderstood by Grätz, V, 173 f., who represents Abū 'Īsa as being well-versed in Bible and Talmud and gifted with literary ability. Nor has Eppenstein, *ibidem,* 173, n. 3, who points out Grätz's mistake, grasped the underlying conception of Ḳirḳisānī's notice.
211. *Ib.,* 311, 20 ff.
212. MS. British Museum Or. 2524, fol. 34*a.*
213. Comp. *Shiites,* Introduction, I, 2.
214. Comp. van Vloten, 20.
215. *Shiites,* II, 93 ff., particularly 94, 15 ff.
213. Comp. *Shiites,* Introduction, I, 2.
214. Comp. van Vloten, 20.
215. *Shiites,* II, 93 ff., particularly 94, 15 ff.
216. *Ib.,* I, 64, 6; II, 96, 9 ff.
217. *Ib.,* II, 96, 15 ff. On the odium attaching to the weaver trade see, in addition to the references given *l. c.,* Wellhausen, *Das arabische Reich,* 146, n. 1, Barhebraeus, *Laughable Stories,* ed. Budge, No. 470 ff. and already Josephus, *Ant.,* XVIII, 9, 1 (the last two references were indicated to me by Professor Joseph Horovitz and Professor Louis Ginzberg).
218. Ibn Ḥazm (d. 1064), *Shiites,* I, 64, 7–8.
219. Very characteristic is the story told by Barhebraeus (*l. c.,* No. 471) of a weaver who wanted to become a prophet. "The people told him: 'Never has there been seen a prophet who was a weaver.' He, however, replied to

them: 'Shepherds with all their simplicity have been employed as prophets, why should not weavers be fit for it?' " (Budge's translation misses the point).

220. *Shiites,* I, 64; II, 98; van Vloten, 49.
221. He was called Abū Muslim *as-Sarrāj*. The latter is correctly explained by Darmsteter, 40, and Browne, *Persia,* 236, as saddler. This is to be added to *Shiites,* II, 118, 9.
222. *Shiites,* II, 120, 9.
223. Browne, *Persia,* 325.
224. *Ibidem,* 433.
225. *Shiites,* I, 78, 2; II, 134, 31. As further examples may be quoted the ultra-Shiitic propagandists Abū Zakariyya al-*Khayyāṭ* (the tailor) and 'Alī an-Najjār (the carpenter), *Shiites,* II, 17, 9. From Shahr., 187, 12, it would seem that the famous heresiarch Bihāfarīd was a *khawwāf* (shoemaker). But the correct reading is Khawāf, the name of a district in Nīsabūr (comp. Houtsma, *WZKM.,* 1889, p. 30). Cureton's edition and Haarbrücker's translation, I, 283, *penult.,* are to be corrected accordingly.
226. Of the followers of the sectarian Meswi (or Mēshūye) of 'Okbara (near Bagdad) Ḳirḳisānī makes the rather uncomplimentary remark that "there has never been seen among them a scholar or a thinker" (Ḳirḳ., 285, 18).
227. Above, note 210.
228. Bīrūnī, 15, 11, comp. above, n. 167. A Pseudo-Messiah by the name ar-Rā'ī who in all likelihood was a Jew is mentioned by a Mohammedan author (*ZDMG.,* 20: 490) as having appeared in Tiberias. He is certainly not identical with ar-Rā'ī mentioned by Bīrūnī (as suggested by Sachau in his translation, p. 373), but he affords a good example of another shepherd who laid claim to prophecy.
229. *Eshkol ha-Kofer,* alphabet 97.
230. Harkavy in Grätz, V, 483; *Le-Ḳorot ha-Kittot be-Yisra'el,* p. 19.
231. Baġdādī *"al-'Īsawiyya wa'r-Ra'yāniyya"* (above, note 129). Goldziher's objections to this reading (*ZDMG.,* 65: 361) which he regards as an error for "Yūdġāniyya" are not justified. Comp. also next note.
232. Just as we find *Mūshkā* and *Mūshkā'iyya,* alongside of *Mūshkān* and *Mūshkāniyya,* above, n. 33. Ra'yān looks like a Persian adaptation of Rā'ī, while Rā'yā looks Aramaic.
233. Thus the Caliph Yazīd, son of Mu'āwiya, is designated as "the *rā'ī* (shepherd) of all religious people," van Vloten, 36.
234. Kirk., 284, 12: "After Abū 'Īsa came Yūdġān, the same who is called by his adherents Rā'ī (shepherd, var. Ra'yā? see note 232), i. e. the Shepherd of the Nation."
235. Harkavy is his introduction to Ḳirḳisānī, p. 206, n. 1, in Grätz, V, 477, *Le-Ḳoret ha-Kittot,* 19.
236. *al-amru bi'l-ma'rūf wa'n-nahyu 'ani'l-munkar,* Koran 3, 100, 106, 110, *et passim.*
237. *Shiites,* II, 93, 15.
238. Nickname for Shiites.

239. *Shiites,* II, 92, 33 ff.
240. In the anthology of the Spaniard Ibn 'Abdi Rabbihi (d. 940), comp. *Shiites,* II, 95.
241. This is probably a reference to the wars with Gog and Magog and the Antichrist which play so prominent a part in the later Messianic speculations of Judaism.
242. i. e., the Shiites.
243. *sabab,* comp. *Shiites,* II, 95, n. 1.
244. Corresponding in substance to the Talmudic *ʾones.* Compare on *taḳiyya* Goldziher, "Das Prinzip der taḳiyya im Islam," in *ZDMG.*, 60: 213 ff., particularly p. 217 ff., *idem, Vorlesungen,* 215, and on the application of the *taḳiyya* among modern Babis, *ib.*, 303.
245. One is vividly reminded of this Shiitic principle when one reads how some of the Sabbathians justified the apostasy of their Pseudo-Messiah. "Moses, too, who lived at first with Pharaoh, used to change (i. e. to simulate) his action, so also did Sabbathai change his actions" (Grätz, X, 457). A clear reflection of the *taḳiyya* principle is the 16th rule of the modern Sabbathians (the so-called Dönmeh) in Salonika which enjoins upon them "to observe carefully the customs of the Turks, whose eyes would be blinded in this way" and particularly to practice "everything which is visible to the eye" (Danon, in *Sefer ha-Shanah,* I, 169).
246. Goldziher, *Vorlesungen,* 218 f.
247. *Shiites,* I, 35, 12; 62 f.; II, 92 f. (= Jāḥiz, *Kitāb al-ḥayawān,* ed. Cairo, II, 97), 153.
248. *Shiites,* II, 79, 22 ff.
249. *Ib.*, II, 107. *Ib.*, I, 60, 10 probably not Muġīra himself, but his successors are meant, comp. II, 87, 12 ff.
250. *Ib.*, II, 79, 36.
251. *Ib.*, line 37.
252. I, 169, 3 ff.
253. Tosefta Soṭah, end; b. Baba batra 60*b.*
254. Already the Dositheans refrained from the use of meat, Krauss in *Jew. Enc.*, IV, 643*b.* Benjamin of Tudela (Itinerary, ed. Adler, *JQR.* (o.s.) 17: 763) mentions "mourners of Zion" among the Jews of Arabia (to be distinguished from the "Abele Zion" known from Karaitic literature, comp. Marx in *ZfhB.*, 14: 138) who refrained from meat and wine.
255. "The first to forbid meat in exile was the Exilarch Anan, and he was followed in this by Benjamin (an-Nahāwandī), Ismā'īl al-'Okbarī and Daniel al-Ḳūmisī as well as by a large section of Karaites of this generation" (Ḳirḳisānī, quoted from a MS. by Harkavy in the Russian-Jewish monthly *Woshkod,* February 1898, p. 9, n. 3). On the prohibition of meat by Anan see also Harkavy, *Studien und Mitteilungen,* VIII, 4, 141, 148, and 193.
256. Comp. Ḳirḳ., 284, 27; 315, 12.
257. Anan also forbade the drinking of wine in the exile, Harkavy, *Studien,* 4, 21.
258. Grätz, V, 269; 507 f.

259. Above, note 255.
260. Ḳirḳ., 315, 22.
261. *Ib.*, 318, 18.
262. Harkavy in *Jew. Enc.* (article "Anan"), I, 555*a*. Harkavy does not indicate his source. See also next note.
263. Harkavy, *Studien*, 67; 155, comp. 188. On the meat of the cock, *ib.*, 145, n. 5, 154, 156, n. 5. Elsewhere (Grätz, V, 477) Harkavy formulates Anan's prohibition with a slight difference: "Vom Fleische gestattete er bloss Geflügel, mit Ausnahme der Hühner, und den Hirsch."
264. Ḳirḳ., 318, 18, and the passages enumerated in note 255.
265. Ḳirḳ., 311, 24; 312, 17. Shahr., I, 168, *ult.* only of Yūdġān.
266. Ḳirḳ., *ib.;* Shahr., *ib.*
267. Ḳirḳ., 312, 18. The Shadġāniyya, a sect closely related to the Yūdġāniyya, held the same opinion, Pinsker, *Liḳḳute*, 26.
268. This is apparently one of the revealed books which he produced, after the manner of Mohammedan sectarians, in spite of his ignorance (comp. above, note 210).
269. Shahr., I, 168.
270. Flügel, *Mani*, 83. According to the old Persian conception which is still voiced by Firdausī in the tenth century, it was the Devil who beguiled the people "from the primitive and innocent vegetarianism supposed to have hitherto prevailed into the eating of animal food" (Browne, *Persia*, 115).
271. Flügel, *l. c.*, 95, 1.
272. *Milal wa'n-niḥal*, I, 36, 14: *wa-hum lā yarauna 'ḏ-ḏabā'iḥa*, the same expression as used by Shahrastānī (above, note 269) of Abū 'Īsa.
273. 207, 21.
274. Bīrūnī, 209, 16. This motive would meet the difficulty pointed out by Nöldeke, *Geschichte der Araber und Perser*, 460.
275. Bīrūnī, 211; Shahr., 187.
276. In addition Bihāfarīd, just like Mānī, forbade the drinking of wine, *ibidem*.
277. 311, 24. According to Hadassi (Alphabet 97), he adopted the prohibition of meat and wine from the Rechabites, but this would only apply to meat.
278. See Harkavy, *Studien und Mitteilungen*, VIII, 193 f. The same applies to his prohibition of wine. For the later Karaites comp. Grätz, V, 508.
279. Whether Abū 'Īsa's prohibition of wine which is characteristic of Mānī and Bihāfarīd is to be ascribed to these influences or to the general tendency observable among Karaites is difficult to determine. It certainly was not suggested by the precept of orthodox Islam which in Persia more than elsewhere was and still is very frequently violated.
280. I, 168, 16.
281. 311, 23. Similarly Hadassi.
282. 311, 26.
283. Flügel, *Mani*, 41.
284. Comp. Shahr. 193.
285. P. 210. Sachau's translation 193.
286. 311, 26.

6

Messianic and Sectarian Movements

Salo Wittmayer Baron

Speculations [about the Messiah] did not remain limited to scholarly circles which, in periods of great crisis, for the most part merely responded to popular pressures. We have seen how popular folklore, nurtured by yearnings of the masses and preachments by a host of anonymous homilists, forced the hands of even the rationalist thinkers and colored their messianic theories. On the other hand, once a scholar of distinction suggested, however timidly, a possible date for the advent of the Messiah, his computation sometimes evoked an immediate mass reaction going far beyond his wildest dreams.

One such widespread computation, reinforced by the sociopolitical upheavals of the age, led to a major tragedy of Cretan Jewry in the second half of the fifth century. Neither the precise date nor the detailed circumstances of that messianic movement are known. The Palestinian rabbinate had long been silenced, while that of Babylonia had likewise lost much of its articulateness. Even in earlier periods, moreover, they rarely reported events outside these two great centers of Jewry. Our information is limited, therefore, to a hostile description by the Byzantine chronicler Socrates. It appears that the combined impact of the Roman Empire's progressive dissolution, the waves of barbarian migrations which the excited fantasy of persecuted Jews readily magnified into wars of Gog and Magog, and the decline of both the Palestinian and Babylonian Jewish communities, had generated a mass hysteria condu-

Reprinted by permission of Columbia University Press from *A Social and Religious History of the Jews,* by S. W. Baron, vol. 5.

cive to the appearance of a messianic pretender. The belief in the approaching redemption was deepened by such computations as that the Exile could not last longer than the Egyptian bondage or a maximum of four hundred years. Hence the liberation could confidently be expected not later than in 468 C.E. That approximate date received further support from a talmudic legend which, harking back to the ancient chronologies of the book of Jubilees, had attributed to the prophet Elijah (appearing to one R. Judah, brother of R. Salla the Pious) the annunciation that the world would endure eighty-five jubilees, and that the son of David would arrive during the concluding fifty-year cycle. With their general penchant for *gemaṭrias,* some homilists found confirmation of that forecast in the Lord's assertion to Job, "Hitherto [*'ad po,* the last two letters have the numerical equivalent of 85] shalt thou come, but no further" (38:11), in which they saw a clear hint that the Exile would not outlast the eighty-fifth jubilee. The redemption was thus due sometime during the years 4200–4250 A.M. (440–490 C.E.). In the non-Jewish world too, rumors had spread that Rome was destined to last altogether 1,200 years and that, hence, the end of the world would come in 447 C.E.[1]

It is small wonder, then, that a visionary appearing at that time in Crete found an immediate response among Jews. According to Socrates, this messianic pretender assumed the name of Moses, claiming that the Redeemer would be none other than Moses redivivus, and in the course of a year traversed the island from one end to the other. So effective was his preachment that the Jews neglected their daily affairs, allowed their possessions to be dissipated, and concentrated on preparations for their miraculous journey to the Holy Land. On the appointed day, they all assembled at the seashore and, at a given sign, many plunged into the Mediterranean, expecting to witness a repetition of the miracle of the Red Sea. But the waters did not separate for them, and many drowned, though many others were saved by local fishermen and sailors. "Moses" himself vanished from the scene, creating a legend that he was a demon bent on the destruction of Jews.[2]

Messianic currents spread with particular intensity to the Arabian Peninsula, where Jewish tribes, living in relative isolation, had assimilated many ingredients from the local Arabian folklore as well as all sorts of heterodox admixtures germinating in their own and in the neighboring Christian communities. H. Z. Hirschberg has marshaled an impressive array of sources and arguments to prove how deeply influenced Mohammed and the subsequent *ḥadith* were not only by general Jewish religious concepts, but specifically by the visions of the final redemption to be initiated by Elijah and fulfilled by a prophet-messiah. Some Jews actually recognized these pretensions of the new Messenger, while others insisted on the Messiah's indispensable Davidic descent. In accordance with older Jewish traditions, one of these Jewish followers of Mohammed, 'Abdallah ibn Saba, began preaching that the Messenger would reappear before very long to usher in the end of days, and that in the meantime, his son-in-law 'Ali, ought to occupy his place. 'Abdallah's preachment thus paved the way for the Shi'ite schism long before it materialized as a result of the political breakup. Without altogether discounting the Christian factors in this evolution, we may readily admit that this overcharged messianic atmosphere among the Arabian Jews helped to create that intellectual and religious ferment out of which emerged the new faith.[3]

At the same time these trends, for which we possess largely later, insufficient, and partially dubious attestation, already adumbrated that mixture of messianic yearnings with heterodox beliefs and practices which was to characterize the Jewish sectarian movements under early Islam. In fact, it is difficult to speak of Islam as an entity in that period. Under the Caliphate there existed so many subsidiary religious currents that only Islam's great elasticity enabled it to maintain a semblance of unity until the more pacific period of consolidation. The sectarian habits of the western Asiatic and North African peoples; their inveterate differences in outlook and attitudes; the dissenting trends within Christianity and Zoroastrianism before the rise of the new religion; the rapid growth in population; the ever sharpening political conflicts—all contributed to the spread of great divergences in belief and action. Like Judaism, Islam paid less attention to the purely dogmatic than to the actional sides of religion, and hence the distinctions in theological fundamentals appeared less important than those in actual life. This fact, in connection with the far-reaching principle of *idjma'* (universal consent), by which the customs and beliefs of local majorities were declared to be authoritative interpretations of the law, helped keep the Muslim world together. Some sects, however, developed into serious schisms, with disastrous effects in the religious, as well as in the political field.

Such sectarian movements, reciprocally, affected Judaism, where the people's rapid growth and geographic expansion prepared the ground for increasing nonconformity. It had been much easier to maintain the unity of a persecuted minority in Palestine and Babylonia, under Rome or Persia, than that of relatively prosperous masses in a Jewish world extending over thousands of miles. The experiences of the Second Commonwealth were repeated now, although neither scope nor intensity of the sectarian clashes could rival those of the ancient period before the thorough and comprehensive reformulation of orthodox Judaism by the talmudic sages.

According to Qirqisani, only two more or less significant sects emerged under Islam before 'Anan [ben David, the founder of Karaism] and four after 'Anan (not including the intra-Karaite schools of Benjamin Nahawendi and Daniel al-Qumisi). The first to found a sect which long survived him was Abu 'Isa al-Isfahani, known in Hebrew as Obadiah. He started a rebellion in the turbulent days of Caliph 'Abd al-Malik (685–705). Although defeated, he was followed by an alleged disciple, Yudghan (Yehudah), surnamed the Shepherd, who likewise claimed to possess the gift of prophecy. (From other sources we learn also of Yudghan's disciple, Mushkha, who headed a group of his own.) Qirqisani still knew of 'Isawites in Damascus some two and a half centuries after the death of their founder. After 'Anan there appeared Isma'il al-'Ukbari (under Mu'tasim, 833–42), Musa al-Za'frani, also known as Abu 'Imran at-Tiflisi (said to have been Isma'il's pupil), Malik ar-Ramli, and Mishawayh al-'Ukbari. Followers of all these ninth-century sectarians, known as 'Ukbarites, Tiflisites, Ramlites (or Malikians), and Mishawayhites, still adhered to their schismatic beliefs in Qirqisani's days. There is no way of telling how many more such splinter groups operated for years or even decades without being mentioned by him. He makes no reference, for instance, to the pseudo-Messiah Severus (about 720), probably because the latter's heterodox teachings did not long survive their exponent. In all, the total number of Jewish heterodoxies under Islam probably exceeded the twenty-four sects which, according to an ancient homilist, had existed during the declining Second Commonwealth and were responsible for its downfall. Shahrastani's figure, however, of seventy-one Jewish sects is obviously exaggerated; even more so than that of seventy-three Muslim sects, quoted from an old tradition by Goldziher, or that of three hundred such heterodoxies given by Maqrizi.[4]

The Iranian Plateau, in particular, was a fertile soil for all sorts of movements, social, political, religious, and philosophical. This is true of Islam as well as of Judaism. Although Persia apparently offered less military and religious resistance to the invading Arabs than did most other Asiatic and African countries, the accumulated forces of millennia persisted beneath the surface. Persia, in fact, was the only country which, after about three centuries of linguistic assimilation, underwent a national reaction and returned to the old Persian tongue.

Zoroastrian survivals, whether overt or underground, the more readily influenced Jewish schismatics, too, as many of them doubtless believed that Zoroaster himself had been a native of Palestine, a descendant of the Hebrew patriarch Isaac, and a pupil of Baruch, Jeremiah's associate. It is no mere accident that, as indicated by such names as Nahawendi and Kumisi, the most important Karaite leaders also came from Persia. Nahawend, especially, with its large Jewish population, which, although situated in the midst of "sick" Media was largely of pure Jewish descent—even the rabbis of the Talmud had to admit it—gave birth to more than one protagonist of the Karaite schism. As pointed out by Israel Friedlaender, not only such geographic designations as Isfahani, 'Ukbari, Za'frani, Tiflisi, and Damaghani, but also the names of some heresiarchs like Yudghan, Shadakan or Sharakan, and Mushkhan are all "of undeniably Persian origin." Even 'Anan is said to have spent many years of his life in the Persian provinces before he came West to take up the struggle for succession. He is also said to have brought from there a more authentic manuscript of the Pentateuch than the one in use in Babylonia and Palestine. The leaders of the other Jewish sects, from the days of Abu 'Isa, were generally Persians. Similarly, the Shi'a, the largest sect in Islam, resembling the Karaite sect in its origin from a strife over the legitimacy of a dynastic succession, its denunciation of the prevalent traditions and customs, and its emphasis upon an authoritative rather than popular religion, soon found its most numerous followers in the Iranian districts.[5]

NATIONAL UPSURGE

In many of the Jewish movements, messianism played a prominent part. Mohammed's success induced many individuals to feign or really to believe that they too had a call to prophesy. Sudden political transformations likewise stimulated the millennial hope. The main principle of Islam, the Muslim state, exercised a universal appeal, and even Jewish messianism was now interpreted more and more in political terms. The Messiah was to be the redeemer of the scattered people of Israel, who had to reestablish the Jewish state in Palestine. No sooner did the Arab invaders occupy the rapidly disintegrating Sassanian empire, when (in the days of the Nestorian Patriarch Mar Emmeh, 643–47), according to a Syrian chronicler,

> some Jew, native of Bet Aramaye, got up in a town named Pallughta [Pumbedita?] at the point where the waters of the Euphrates separate for the irrigation of the soil, and asserted that the Messiah had come. He gathered around him weavers, carpetmakers [?] and launderers, some four hundred men. They burned down three [Christian] sanctuaries and killed the chief of that locality. A military force, however, sent from the city of Aqula, intervened, slew them with their wives and children, and crucified their leader in his own village.

Similarly when the Visigothic regime in Spain crumbled away under the blows of a small Moorish expeditionary force, the sudden release from a century-old state of utter insecurity induced, as we shall see, a great many Spanish Jews to listen to the blandishments of a Syrian adventurer, Severus, who promised to make them miraculously "fly to the Promised Land."[6]

Few if any of these visionaries seem to have claimed Davidic descent, one of the rare constants in the multicolored story of Jewish messianic movements. Even the few extant records, stemming all from hostile quarters, indicate that they often merely announced the coming of the redeemer, pretended to be his "messengers" or, at the most, ascribed to themselves the functions of the messiah of the house of Joseph who, through his military victories, would pave the way for the advent of the final Redeemer. Their unsophisticated followers drew no such fine distinctions. Abu 'Isa, for example, seems to have claimed only to be the last of five "messengers," forerunners of the Davidic Messiah. As such he felt superior to all his prophetic predecessors, including the four "messengers" (probably Abraham, Moses, Jesus, and Mohammed). His adherents nevertheless invested him with supernatural qualities, especially since they believed, as did some of Mohammed's contemporaries, that their leader had been wholly illiterate and yet, under divine inspiration, had succeeded in writing unaided a memorable book. Harking back to an old aggadic concept of the reiterated concealment and reappearance of the messiah—this idea was doubtless interrelated with the Christian belief in the second coming of Christ and, together with it, greatly influenced the manifold Muslim sectarian teachings of the concealed and ever reappearing *Mahdi*—some " 'Isawites" still believed two centuries later that their leader had not been killed but had "entered a hole in a mountain" and, before long, would reappear to lead them to the Holy Land. Abu 'Isa's pupil, Yudghan, too, only "pretended to be a prophet; [but] his followers assert that he was the Messiah and that he did not die; they expect him to return (any moment)."[7]

Concomitant with these messianic currents there was an intensified longing for the Holy Land. Never absent from the innermost yearnings of Diaspora Jewry, love for Palestine was constantly reactivated in periods of great stress or epochal transformations. The rise of Islam, too, gave new impetus to pilgrimages and permanent settlement there by pious and learned Jews. Living a life of self-abnegation and politically rather impassive, this ever growing group of "Mourners for Zion" formed an important segment of Jerusalem's population. After the disasters which sooner or later overtook the more strictly messianic movements, the ranks of these "mourners" were swelled from both the Rabbanite and the sectarian camps. The Karaite Bible commentator, Daniel al-Qumisi, actually exhorted his brethren to return *en masse* to the Holy City. "But if you do not come," he added, "for you are engrossed in and running after your trades, send five men from each city and provide them with a livelihood. In this manner we shall become a united people, dedicated to constant prayers to our Lord on the mountains of Jerusalem." Clearly, this call to organized action remained unheeded. Nonetheless, urgent appeals of this kind, reiterated also by Qumisi's successor, Sahl ben Maṣliaḥ, attracted many Karaites to the Holy City. Rabbanites, too, flocked to Palestine in large numbers even from distant Spain. Joseph ibn Megas of eleventh-century Lucena discussed the case of a Jew who had vowed to abstain from both meat and wine until he reached the Holy Land. The streets of Jerusalem reverberated with sectarian disputations, which merely accentuated the internal cleavages natural to a community recruited from all corners of the dispersion.[8]

Nationalist revival could well go together with greater religious tolerance, on the one hand, and with ethnic exclusivism, on the other hand. Abu 'Isa, for instance, readily acknowledged both Jesus and Mohammed as the prophets for their peoples. According to Ibn Ḥazm, he even assumed that Jesus had been sent only to the children of Israel, while Mohammed served as a messenger to the children of Ishmael, just as Job had prophesied to the children of Esau, and Balaam to the children of Moab. "I have encountered," Ibn Ḥazm added, "many distinguished Jews who professed that doctrine." 'Anan, too, although claiming no prophetic gifts for himself, was ready to admit that Mohammed was sent to the Arabs by God, whereas the ordinary Rabbanite Jew, to quote Sherira Gaon and Maimonides, regarded the Arab "Messenger" as nothing but a "madman." This was not a mere political gesture on the part of these rebels, for the government, as well as the orthodox Muslim public, doubtless condemned all these opinions as subversive and running counter to Mohammed's assertion that he was "the Seal of the Prophets" (Qur'an 33:40). This objection to Abu 'Isa's attempted harmonization was, indeed, to be raised by both Qirqisani and Baqillani. Only such Muslim sectarians as the Kharidjites were prepared to accept as equals Jews and Christians subscribing to the credo *(shahada)* that "Mohammed is a messenger of Allah to the Arabs but not to us." There are indeed many subtle threads, ideological as well as political, linking the 'Isawites to the Kharidjite movement.[9]

At the same time, however, 'Anan rigidly forbade the Jews to live in the same quarter with the Gentiles, a measure rarely and always timidly suggested by a rabbi, either as a precautionary measure or for the sanctification of the Sabbath. Later, Daniel al-Qumisi and Sahl ben Maṣliaḥ bitterly censured the intimate social contacts of the Rabbanites with the Gentiles, which, the latter asserted, often went so far that Jews partook of Gentile food. In other words, Judaism became for these sectarians a purely national religion, frankly renouncing all claims to universalism.

These new national-religious emphases would have created a state of mind conducive to a revival of Sadducean teachings, even if there had been no direct vestiges of ancient Sadducean writings and oral traditions. The controversy over the existence of such literary remains in the early Muslim age has been raging for many years. It cannot be completely resolved until such time when a lucky find in a medieval *genizah* might bring forth some authentic text stemming from this sectarian group. However, the rare unanimity among the earlier medieval writers, both Rabbanite and Karaite, that the movement initiated by 'Anan was a direct offshoot of these ancient schismatics, although not conclusive proof, creates a strong presumption in favor of some such historical connection.

Nor have any valid reasons been advanced to cast serious doubt on Qirqisani's familiarity with "Zadok's" books in which the ancient heresiarch allegedly "did not adduce any proofs for anything he said, but limited himself to mere statements, excepting one thing. . . ." Another tenth-century Karaite (Ḥasan ben Mashiaḥ, or Sahl ben Maṣliaḥ) was even more explicit and in his commentary on Exodus argued against the Rabbanites by referring to "the writings of Sadducees [which] are generally known." We need not be too much concerned about the simon-pure authenticity of these letters. Most likely they contained a great many interpolations and alterations which would have made them unreliable witnesses of the ancient sectarian tradition as such. But they doubtless preserved many fundamental Sadducean and related teachings, just as many Philonic doctrines and a large variety of concepts borrowed from the pre-Christian apocalyptic literature had come down the centuries. The presence in the Cairo Genizah of copies of the "Zadokite" fragment of the ancient New Covenanter and of the Hebrew text, however altered, of Sirach; the attested withdrawal by Jews of some documents from a cave (about 800 C.E.); and the uninterrupted use of such caves as that recently found at Murabba'at in the Dead Sea wilderness, from the days of Bar Kocheba to the Muslim age—all strongly confirm the impression of the underground persistence of many unorthodox teachings throughout the first millennium. Together these remnants of ancient thought helped fructify the religious thinking of the newly receptive and religiously creative generations after the rise of Islam. Residua of outside heterodoxies, carried down through the ages by the Judeo-Christian fringe movements, must have reinforced these inner Jewish reminiscences.[10]

Many of these discussions, moreover, are vitiated by their exclusively "literary" approach. Important as it may be to ascertain the existence per se of such ancient literary remains in the earlier Middle Ages, this quest has relatively little bearing on the genesis and evolution of the medieval religious movements. Where these were influenced by heterodox traditions, the latter must have been oral and folkloristic much more than literary and canonical. We need not imagine that even the relatively few learned men among the sectarian leaders derived their inspiration or appealed to their followers by citing chapter and verse from some such older writings. Of course, they made whatever use they could of the revealed biblical sources with the aid of their own hermeneutics. But they hardly invoked other sources, unless they wished specifically to controvert certain rabbinic sayings. They and their followers must have received their main direct stimuli from heterodox teachings transmitted orally from generation to generation, from widespread and constantly intermingling folkloristic tales and superstitions, and from many unorthodox practices which they could readily observe in their respective communities.

Just as talmudic lore could be handed down orally for centuries by faithful recorders, so did the suppressed, but far from extinct, minorities doubtless find some loyal adherents to perpetuate their views through an equally unwritten chain of tradition. Suffice it for us to imagine, by way of illustration, that some overwhelming catastrophe had engulfed Palestinian Jewry before 200 C.E., or both Palestinian and Babylonian Jewry before 400 C.E., when practically none of the tannaitic or amoraic teachings had been committed to writing. Would it not have been preposterous for us to deny, on this score, the very existence of a great and ramified rabbinic Oral Law? Except for the questionable *Sefer Gezerata* mentioned in the "Scroll of Fasts," we know nothing of any ancient Sadducean *literature,* and yet we feel confident that the Sadducees possessed a rich oral tradition which remained alive for untold generations. Why should it, or similar oral traditions of lesser sects, not have been carried on for several more centuries by overt or clandestine devotees? General historic experience certainly makes it highly unlikely that such tremendous energies as had been released by the sectarian movements before 70 C.E. should have completely vanished during the period of talmudic consolidation. Many of their teachings, and even those of many Judeo-Christian sectarians, must have percolated by word of mouth into the Jewish masses, particularly in those outlying regions where the steamroller of the Palestino-Babylonian academies had not yet succeeded in leveling all overt expressions of dissent.[11]

Sooner or later all these sectarian movements, whatever their outward manifestations and sociopolitical objectives may have been, developed legal deviations from the orthodox *halakhah.* If, true to its peculiar Hellenistic Jewish origins and early evolution, Christianity always channelized its sectarian diversities into some ultimate *dogmatic* divergences, if in Islam the primarily *political* conflicts over the legitimacy of succession to the Caliphate overshadowed all other issues, Jewish sectarianism became truly meaningful only when it seriously infringed upon the domain of *law*. Here again a sharp line of demarcation was drawn between overzealous extension of existing prohibitions or even their violation, however otherwise serious, which did not lead to the disruption of overall Jewish unity, and those heterodoxies which threatened to undermine the people's ethnic foundations.

Official opinion frowned upon the former and at times adopted stringent measure to suppress them. But it never excluded such deviationists from the community of Israel. Asked about the treatment to be accorded the followers of the false messiah Severus, Naṭronai I replied:

> It seems to us that those evildoers, although they have strayed into bad ways, denied the words of the sages, profaned holidays, violated [other] commandments and polluted themselves with dead carcasses and forbidden meats, ought nevertheless to be attracted, rather than repelled. As to their transgressions, such as their consumption of dead carcasses and forbidden meats or their despoiling of their marriage contracts [by disregarding the required rabbinic forms], you shall flog them before the courts, impose fines upon them—each according to his evil deeds—punish them and make them stand up in the synagogues and promise never to return to their aberrations, but you shall accept and not repulse them.

When, however, an opposing faction began tampering with the laws governing the calendar in a way entailing the celebration of holidays on other than the accepted days, such deviation could readily lead to irremediable separation. That is why when Qirqisani asked Jacob ben Ephraim the Syrian (hardly identical with Saadiah's pupil, Jacob ben Samuel) why the Rabbanites allowed intermarriage with 'Isawites but not with Karaites, the latter answered bluntly, "Because they [the 'Isawites] do not differ from us in the observance of holidays." Jacob could also have pointed to the Karaite deviations in family laws which, by threatening chaos in all Jewish family relations, even more directly menaced the ethnic consistency of the people. Orthodox Judaism, rightly observed L. M. Epstein, could afford to be relatively lenient toward other deflections from the established law. But "the moment a group subscribed to a doctrine which taught a fundamental deviation from the accepted law of marriage, it was doomed to the status of a 'sect' and was gradually eliminated from Jewish group life."[12]

Needless to say, not all legal digressions led to sectarian groupings.

Even most of the Jewish "sects" listed as such by medieval students of religion, and through them also by modern historians, hardly deserve to be thus dignified. The propensity to find seventy-three sects in Islam, in order to justify a saying attributed to Mohammed by a faulty linguistic interpretation, led to many artificial distinctions between otherwise kindred movements. This tendency communicated itself also to medieval students of Jewish heterodoxies, both Muslim and Jewish. Shahrastani, as we recall, actually claimed that there existed seventy-one Jewish sects of which he described only the four best known and most widespread.[13]

MILITARY AND IDEOLOGICAL COMMOTIONS

We need not repeat here in any detail the thrice-told tale of the medieval sectarian movements. The earliest and in some respects the most important of them, apart from the Karaites, namely the interrelated movements of 'Isawites, Yudghanites or Shadghanites, and Mushkhanites, did not seriously depart from the main teachings or practices of orthodox Judaism, but merely tried to sharpen the existing provisions so as to live an even holier and more ascetic life. In fact, Abu 'Isa himself (his real name seems to have been Isaac ben Jacob but, with reference to his messianic role, he was surnamed Obadiah or servant of the Lord), held the talmudic sages in high esteem and likened them to the prophets. On the other hand, he seems to have rated the ordinary prophets far below the "messengers" or the Messiah. To be sure, to quote Qirqisani, "he prohibited divorce as do the Sadducees and the Christians. He prescribed seven daily prayers, inferring this from the saying of David [Ps. 119:164] 'Seven times a day do I praise Thee.' He also prohibited meat and intoxicating drinks, not on the authority of the Scripture, but asserting that God commanded him to do so by direct revelation." But any Rabbanite Jew could refrain from divorcing his wife, abstain from any kind of food and add as many prayers as he wished. Nor did this allegedly ignorant tailor cite any Sadducean, Christian, or other heterodox writings in support of his measures, but merely enacted them on his own authority. The Yudghanites, too, "Forbade the consumption of wine and meat and increased greatly the fasts and prayers."[14]

More serious would have been Abu 'Isa's insistence, doubtless inaccurately reported by Yehudah Hadassi, on the observance of holidays in accordance with the solar year. All he may have meant to say was that, unlike the strictly lunar calendar of the Muslims with their movable holidays, the Jews observed their holidays according to the solar seasons of the year. This seems to be, indeed, the meaning of Hadassi's own admission that the 'Isawite computation agreed with that of the Rabbanites *(ke-dibrehem)*. Abu 'Isa may also have theorized about the calendar in the same vein as Yudghan, namely that holidays in the dispersion were merely memorial days, rather than legally binding. But evidently neither master nor pupil ever shifted the actual days of their observance. 'Isawite conformity in this matter was indeed advanced, as we recall, by Jacob ben Ephraim as the main reason for their preferential treatment on the part of Rabbanite leadership.[15]

The messianic claims of Abu 'Isa, Yudghan, and Mushkha could be treated by the communal leaders with far greater condescension. The various miracle tales told by their followers for generations thereafter could be viewed as fairly innocuous fantasies. Abu 'Isa's alleged drawing of a circle around his camp which the attacking Muslim army was unable to penetrate, his single-handed victorious sorties, his visit, beyond the desert, to the legendary *Bene Moshe* (descendants of Moses) "to announce to them God's word," and his final withdrawal to a mountain "hole" (perhaps in some connection with the then still remembered ancient sect of *Maghariya* [Cave Men], reminiscent of the depositors of our Dead Sea scrolls)[16] from where he was to stage a comeback in a later generation—all lay in that obscure domain of uncontrollable popular beliefs and superstitions which most rabbis were prepared to dismiss with a shrug. Even his (and some Mushkhanites') acceptance of the prophetic qualities of Jesus and Mohammed, on a par with such Gentile prophets as Balaam, seemed rather harmless so long as it was not accompanied by any direct syncretistic action and did not involve any recognition of the latter's prophetic authority with respect to Jews.

All these were aberrations, to be sure, not to be indulged in by the truly orthodox. But they were not serious enough to call forth concerted action on the part of the central leadership in Babylonia. Exilarchs and geonim doubtless viewed all such movements as but ephemeral excesses of the popular mind in a period of epochal transformations, and probably expected their quick suppression by Muslim arms. In fact, all three leaders fell in battle; Abu 'Isa allegedly at the head of "hundreds of thousand" men, after reaching the vicinity of Baghdad, while Mushkha's die-hard followers at the battle of Qumm (an Arab garrison city and early Shi'ite center) had already dwindled to nineteen individuals. True, the 'Isawite sect survived these military defeats, and with remarkable tenacity persisted particularly in Damascus, that ancient home of Jewish heterodoxy. In 937, Qirqisani still found twenty 'Isawites in that Syrian city. A "small number" of Yudghanites had also survived in Isfahan. But evidently these sectarians neither separated themselves voluntarily from the Jewish people, nor were they considered a sufficient threat to general Jewish conformity to call forth their drastic excision from the main body of Jewry by the leaders of the majority.[17]

No more serious were the legal divergences introduced by Severus the Syrian a generation after Abu 'Isa (about 720). This Christian convert to Judaism seems to have been an outright adventurer. Whether or not we believe the yarn of the early Syriac chronicler Pseudo-Dionysius about Severus seducing a Jewish girl in Samaria, his chastisement by the enraged Jewish populace, and his ensuing vow of vengeance, it appears that this skilled *jongleur* presented himself to the Jews from Mesopotamia to Spain as their redeemer. His timing was excellent. The messianic expectations of the people had surged higher and higher when the Muslim conquests in Spain and southern France seemed to carry the flag of the Caliphate to the ends of the known world and the siege of Constantinople in 717–18 promised to eliminate the last bastion of resistance in the West.

Severus played his game carefully. According to a well-informed Christian chronicler of the thirteenth century, contemporaries were not sure whether he had pretended to be the Messiah in person, or only a "messenger" and forerunner of the real Redeemer. Out of ignorance or design, he introduced a number of ritualistic alleviations. His followers at least, to quote an inquiry submitted to Naṭronai I, "do not pray, do not abstain from forbidden meats or guard their wine from turning into wine of oblation [by contact with Gentiles], work on second holidays, and do not write marriage contracts in the form prescribed by our sages." All these acts, however serious, were contrary to talmudic rather than biblical law. Nor were they antinomian in principle, although antinomianism of both the messianic and the rationalist variety was not totally absent from the Jewish community of the time. In fact, the same gaon subsequently answered an inquiry concerning such a schismatic group which was "different from all other heretics in the world" inasmuch as they did not repudiate merely talmudic law, but also "denied the very core of the Torah." In this case Naṭronai decided to refuse their members readmission to the Jewish community even after due repentance, lest their children, "bastardized" because of their defiance of the biblical laws of marriage and divorce, contaminate the purity of the Jewish families. That is why, after a few years of successful financial exploitation of his credulous adherents—he himself was supposed to have admitted to the caliph that he had "made fun of the Jews"—Severus was unmasked and executed, and left behind neither a military nor a sectarian heritage. We do not hear of any armed uprisings or of permanent sectarian deviations of the kind engendered by Abu 'Isa, Yudghan, or Mushkha. Almost all of Severus' followers seem to have returned meekly to the fold, without even attempting to preserve for posterity the name of their leader.[18]

By the middle of the eighth century, with the stabilization of imperial power, the military phase of the Jewish separatist movements drew to an end. It was not to be revived until the conditions became again more propitious after the collapse of the Great Caliphate and the invasions of the Seldjuks and Crusaders. This self-imposed military restraint not only deprived Mushkha's successors of the glamor of a "holy war," but also ran counter to the deep-rooted tradition of the Messiah's warlike exploits. An old Muslim source, already cited by the tenth-century Spanish writer, Ibn 'Abd Rabbihi, ascribes to the Jews a saying, "There shall be no fighting for the sake of God, until the Messiah, the Expected One, goes forth and a herald from heaven proclaims [his arrival]." This reconciliation of actual Jewish powerlessness with high national aspirations for the future, understandably enough, appealed also (as that Muslim author suggests) to similarly disarmed Muslim sectarians. That is why, Shahrastani carefully notes, Mushkha "considered it his duty to rise against his enemies and to wage war against them," although he and his nineteen followers apparently were fully aware of the suicidal nature of their undertaking. His ninth-century successors were far more careful, and they toned down the messianic element in their preachment. Even Isma'il al-'Ukbari who, according to Qirqisani, dared coin "many sayings that are harmful, shameful, and absurd to the utmost degree," only ordered that his tomb be inscribed, "The chariot of Israel and the horsemen thereof" (II Kings 2:12)—an obvious allusion to Elijah who had long been viewed in the Aggadah as the forerunner of the Messiah.[19] Deprived of their essential messianic appeal, the leaders of the later deviationist movements had to stress exclusively legal and ritualistic disparities.

NOTES

1. 'A. Z. 9b (with Ḥananel's, Rashi's, and the Tosafists' comments); Sanhedrin 97b; Ibn Shemuel's intro. to his *Midreshe ge'ulah,* pp. 44 ff. As here pointed out, there were also computations based upon the duration of the First and Second Temples of 410 and 420 years respectively, according to the accepted chronology of *Seder 'olam rabbah.* Assuming that the Exile could not last longer than either era of freedom, some Jews expected the Messiah to arrive on or before 478 or 488. All these dates fell within the 85th jubilee cycle. We recall that the then regnant Christian chronology, too, by setting the birth of Jesus at approximately 5,500 A.M., postulated the end of the world at the end of the sixth millennium, that is about 500 C.E. See Hippolytus' *Commentary* on Daniel, Fragments IV–VI, in *PG,* X, 645 ff.
2. Socrates Scholasticus, *Historia ecclesiastica,* VII.38, ed. with a Latin trans. by R. Hussey, II, 822 ff. (taken over verbatim into the *Historia ecclesiastica tripartita,* compiled from Socrates, Sozomenus, and Theodoret by Cassiodorus or Epiphanius, XII.9, ed. by W. Jacob and revised by R. Hanslik, pp. 677 f.). Understandably, the Christian chronicler seized this opportunity to heap ridicule on Jewish gullibility, and he claimed that all survivors accepted baptism. Hence, some verification from an independent and more impartial source would be doubly welcome.
3. H. Z. Hirschberg's "Messianic Vestiges in Arabia during the Fifth and Sixth Centuries after the Fall of Jerusalem" (Hebrew), *Vienna Mem. Vol.,* pp. 112–24; and his *Yisrael ba-'Arab,* pp. 175 ff. These messianic expectations were, of course, but part of the much-debated impact upon the rise of Islam of Judaism, Christianity, and the various syncretistic Judeo-Christian trends. Despite the availability of considerable monographic literature, a careful reexamination of the similarities of and the divergences between the Jewish, Christian, and Muslim messianic teachings, as reflected not only in the recognized theological works but also in the more obscure domains of folklore still is likely to prove rewarding. According to Ta'labi, for instance, a Muslim legend, current in the eleventh century or earlier, attributed to a young Jew, Baluqiya, a role resembling that of Moses and Mohammed. He was supposed to traverse the world's seven lands and seven seas in search of the miraculous spring which had allegedly enabled Alexander (Du'l Qarnayim) to survive to the days of Mohammed. Baluqiya thus hoped to await the ultimate day when all men would worship the true God. See M. Asín Palacios's data in *La Escatología musulmana en la Divina Comedia,* pp. 315 f.

4. Qirqisani's *K. al-Anwar,* 1.2.12 ff., ed. by Nemoy, I, 12 ff. (in his English trans., *HUCA,* VII, 328 ff.). Cf. J. Rosenthal's convenient Hebrew summary "On the History of Heterodoxy in the Period of Saadiah," *Horeb,* IX, 21–37, which discusses, however, mainly the contemporary gnostic and dualistic trends. We may note that Al-Baqillani, writing about half a century later, still took the 'Isawites with sufficient seriousness to count them among the four principal Jewish sects, together with Rabbanites, 'Ananites, and Samaritans, and to combat some of their arguments. Cf. his *K. aṭ-Ṭamhid,* p. 131; and R. Brunschvig's comments thereon in *Homenaje a Millás,* pp. 226 f. Minor bits of information about these Jewish sects have also been preserved later by Shahrastani. Cf. his *K. al-Milal,* I, 163 ff. (in Haarbrücker's German trans., I, 247 ff.). On the seventy-one sects see *infra,* n. 13. Equally important as these stray items is the general knowledge of the sectarian controversies raging within the Muslim majority which may be derived from these and other Arab students of comparative religion. Cf. H. Ritter's brief survey of the "Muhammedanische Haeresiographien," *Der Islam,* XVIII, 35–55. Of course, the number of Muslim sects and the intensity of their struggles far exceeded anything known in Judaism. According to a Shi'ite tradition, a long list of Muslim sects had already been prepared by the police for Caliph Mahdi (775–87) for guidance in the administration's repressive legislation. These political aspects played a far lesser role in Jewish sectarianism. Nevertheless students of the latter may yet learn a great deal from these internal controversies under both Islam and Christendom.

On the other hand, Jewish influences were often a significant factor in the rise and development of both Muslim and Christian heresies. The early converts K'ab al-Aḥbar and 'Abdallah ibn Salam seem to have been particularly impressive teachers. Wahb ibn Munabbih (died about 732), himself classified as a forbidden historian by the fifteenth-century historian of history, As-Sahawi, claimed that they were "the most learned men of their times, and that he collected what they knew." Cf. F. Rosenthal's trans. in *A History of Muslim Historiography,* p. 265. This is true even if we discount the exaggerations inherent in the epithet "Jew" freely attached to religious opponents. Of the vast modern literature, see esp. W. Thomson's study of "The Character of Early Islamic Sects," *Goldziher Mem. Vol.,* I, 89–116; B. Lewis's "Some Observations on the Significance of Heresy in the History of Islam," *Studia Islamica,* I, 43–63; F. Frade Merino's more comprehensive study of *Sectas y movimientos de reforma en el Islam;* as well as, mainly on the Western evolution, S. Luciano's bibliographic survey of "Studi recenti sulle eresie medievali (1939–1952)," *Rivista storica italiana,* LXIV, 237–68; and the symposium on "Movimenti religiosi popolari ed eresie nel medioevo" by R. R. Betts *et al.* at the Tenth International Congress of Historical Sciences in 1955, summarized in its *Relazioni,* III, 305–541. As Lewis pointed out, Arabic had no term for heresy until modern writers borrowed it from the West. Hence the legal concept, too, was equivocal and full of often arbitrary nuances. The same holds true for Jewish terminology, where the term *kofer* (older than the Arabic *kafir*) likewise had many shades of meaning. Even "La Concezione di eretico nelle fonti giustiniane," as analyzed by A. Berger in the *Rendiconti* of the Accademia Nazionale dei Lincei, 8th ser., X, 353–68, though more sharply defined, still oscillates between the narrower range given it in the earlier sources, which is limited to Christian dissenters, and the broader scope employed in the codification of Justinian, which embraces also Jews and Samaritans.

5. Friedlaender in *JQR*, I, 207 f. [reference is to the preceding article in the present collection—Ed.] The former conception that the Shi'a was exclusively the reaction of the Iranian spirit against Islam was greatly modified when J. Wellhausen, I. Goldziher, and others proved that the 'Alite movement had genuinely Arabian origins. However, it cannot be denied that soon thereafter Persia, together with Babylonia, became the classic territory of the great sect. Cf. also M. G. S. Hodgson's "How Did the Early Shī'a Become Sectarian?" *JAOS*, LXXV, 1–13. In the case of the Jewish sects, the battle certainly had to be carried on in Babylonia and Palestine, the centers of Jewish life, but the antirabbanite opposition even in those countries was steadily reinforced by the numerous immigrants and travelers from the Iranian Plateau. Persia's influence on the Jewish sectarian movements was first suggested by Harkavy and elaborated by Poznanski, Friedlaender, and others. Little effort, however, has thus far been made to relate these movements to Parsee teachings, whether orthodox or sectarian, except in so far as these had already been assimilated by Muslims. The direct Judeo-Parsee interrelations, reaching back to the Achaemenid empire, must have been greatly intensified during the last two centuries of Sassanian rule, when the counterpoise of Babylonian Jewry's effective control over the provincial communities had been greatly weakened. The priority of some such Jewish adaptations of Parsee concepts and their influence on similar early Muslim synthesizing efforts is, therefore, wholly within the realm of probability.

6. Anonymous chronicle, ed. and trans. into Latin by I. Guidi in "Un Nuovo testo siriaco sulla storia degli ultimi Sassanidi," *Actes du VIIIe Congrès international des Orientalistes*, Section Semitique, pp. 1–36; and in *CSCO*, Scriptores Syri, 3d ser., IV, 33 (text), 27 f. (trans.); with T. Nöldeke's comments thereon in *SB* Vienna, CXXVIII, Part 9, p. 36 (the chronicle seems to have been written by a Nestorian author about 670–80). On the identification of Pallughta with Pumbedita, see J. Obermeyer's observations in *Die Landschaft Babylonien*, pp. 219 ff. The latter's effort, however, to connect this commotion with the upheaval under Mar Zuṭra II is very questionable. The pseudo-messiah Severus will be more fully discussed *infra*, n. 18.

7. Qirqisani's *K. al-Anwar*, 1.2 (12–13), 11, 12, ed. by L. Nemoy, I, 12 f., 51 ff. (English trans. in *HUCA*, VII, 328, 382 f.); Shahrastani's *K. al-Milal*, I, 168 ff. (in Haarbrücker's trans., I, 254 ff.). Shahrastani does not mention the names of the previous four messengers. But in view of Abu 'Isa's relative recognition of Jesus and Mohammed (see *infra*, n. 9), their inclusion to-

gether with Abraham and Moses appears most likely. The doctrine of the "return of the messiah," mentioned in Cant. r. II.9 and other aggadic sources, and its importance to Muslim and Jewish sects, is discussed by Friedlaender in *JQR*, II, 481 ff. [see the preceding article, section 1—Ed.]; and in his "Messianic Idea in Islam" in *Past and Present*, pp. 139 ff. On Maimonides' apparent assumption that Abu 'Isa had claimed Davidic descent, the equally erroneous contention of some later "Iṣbahaniyya," reported by a Muslim apologist of the sixteenth century, As-Su'udi, that Abu 'Isa "was a prophet sent prior to Moses," and Friedlaender's own rather forced connection between Abu 'Isa's *five* messengers, and the number *seven* prominent in both Jewish and Muslim soteriology, see the latter's observations in *JQR*, III, 246 ff., 251 n. 237, 272 n. 348 [in the preceding article, nn. 152, 191—Ed.].

8. Daniel al-Qumisi, ed. by J. Mann in "A Tract by an Early Karaite Settler in Jerusalem," *JQR*, XII, 285; and *Texts and Studies*, II, 5 ff.; Sahl ben Maṣliaḥ, *Iggeret mokhaḥat* (Epistle of Admonition) to Jacob ben Samuel in Pinsker's *Lickute kadmoniot*, II, 31; Joseph ibn Megas' *Resp.*, No. 186. Cf. also S. Assaf's data on Spanish Jews in Palestine of that period in his *Meqorot u-meḥqarim*, pp. 103 ff. "Mourners for Zion," a term going back to Isaiah (61:3), are recorded under various designations in many countries and periods. A particularly interesting messianic sermon on Isa. 61:9 alluding to them was preserved by an early medieval homilist in the ninth-century compilation, *Pesiqta rabbati*, XXXIV, ed. by M. Friedmann, fols. 128 f. This particular sermon probably stems from an earlier period. Cf. H. Albeck's note on L. Zunz's *Ha-Derashot be-Yisrael*, pp. 119 ff., 389 nn. 65–66; Mann, *Jews in Egypt*, I, 47 f. While sometimes ridiculed as excessively idealistic and pietistic, these Mourners' ascetic self-abnegation so long as the Temple lay in ruins greatly impressed the masses. Even in far-off eleventh-century Germany, a liturgical poet, Meir bar Isaac of Worms, was generally known under the honorable designation, "representative of the people [synagogue leader] from among the Mourners for Zion." Among that author's numerous poems the Aramaic *Aqdamut millin* (Introduction to the Recitation of the Targum) is still read in many synagogues on the first day of the Festival of Weeks. Cf. the literature listed in I. Davidson *Oṣar*, I, 332 No. 7314; the numerous other poems by that author listed *ibid.*, IV, 432; and I. Elbogen's data in *Der jüdische Gottesdienst*, pp. 334 f. A number of like-minded ascetics were said to have been encountered in Germany a century later by Benjamin of Tudela who definitely found a large group of "Mourners for Zion" also in the Yemen. *Massa'ot*, ed. by Adler, pp. 47, 72 (Hebrew), 48, 80 (English). The latter passage, probably interpolated, may date from an even earlier age. Cf. especially, S. Schechter's "Jewish Saints in Mediaeval Germany" in his *Studies in Judaism*, 3d ser., pp. 6 ff.

Benjamin's description of the life and external appearance of the Yemenite Mourners probably applied also to other Diaspora communities. But their main center remained in Jerusalem, where they lived a saintly life, supported by benefactors from various lands. For example, Aḥimaaz, ancestor and namesake of the chronicler, made three pilgrimages to the Holy City and each time donated 100 gold pieces (dinars) for the support of "those who were engaged in the study of His law, and those who mourned the ruined house of His glory." Aḥimaaz' example was followed by Palṭiel and his son Samuel. Cf. the *Chronicle of Ahimaaz,* ed. by Salzman, pp. 4, 19, 21 (Hebrew), 65, 95, 97 (English); ed. by Klar, pp. 15 f., 44, 47. Extolling the beauties of Palestine and expatiating on the people's yearning for restoration thereto served also as a constant refrain in the liturgical poetry of the period. See, for one example, M. Zulay's "Palestine and Holiday Pilgrimages in the Liturgical Poetry of R. Phinehas" (Hebrew), *Yerushalayim,* I, 51–81. We also recall the legal fiction adopted by the geonim for commercial transactions, whereby each Jew could theoretically transfer his inalienable share of four ells in the Holy Land.

9. Qirqisani's *K. al-Anwar,* 1.11, ed. by Nemoy, I, 51 f. (English trans. in *HUCA,* VII, 382 f.); Ibn Ḥazim's *K. al-Fiṣal,* 1.14, pp. 99, 112, 114 (in Asin Palacios's trans., II, 211 f., 231, 234); Baqillani's *K. aṭ-Ṭamhid,* pp. 147 f.; and R. Brunschvig's comments thereon in *Homenaje a Millás,* pp. 226 f. On the Karaite mixture of theological broadmindedness with ethnic exclusivity, see the next chapter. Qirqisani doubtless exaggerated the opportunistic motivations of Abu 'Isa's almost "henotheistic" attitude which culminated in his injunction to his followers to study carefully both the Gospels and the Qur'an with their commentaries. The Kharidjites themselves, as well as many other Muslim sectarians, looked forward to the advent of a Redeemer who would then become the real "seal of prophecy." On their negative attitude toward the state, which revealed many similarities to, and probably influences from, the predominantly apolitical contemporary Judaism, and their general acceptance of a *dhimmi's* qualified recognition of Mohammed as a messenger sent only to the Arabs, see G. Levi della Vida's "Kharidjites," *EI,* II, 1907; and M. Guidi's "Sui Hārigiti," *RSO,* XXI, 1–14.

10. The medieval testimonies in favor of the historic continuity from the ancient Sadducees to the Karaites are well assembled in Harkavy's supplementary note on Graetz's *Geschichte,* 4th ed., pp. 472 ff.; and, with minor additions, in Z. Cahn's *Rise of the Karaite Sect,* pp. 13 ff. Cf. especially Qirqisani, 1.2.7, p. 11 (*HUCA,* VII, 326); and the Karaite commentary on Exodus as well as a comment by Ben Mashiaḥ, cited by S. Poznanski in his "Anan et ses écrits," *REJ,* XLIV, 176 f. That the author of the former commentary was Ḥasan ben Mashiaḥ, or Sahl ben Maṣliaḥ, was timidly suggested by Harkavy and accepted by Poznanski, *ibid.,* and in *The Karaite Literary Opponents of Saadiah Gaon,* pp. 16, 32 f. Both stress the fact that "the Sadducean writings are known to all." True enough, no Sadducean or even pro-Sadducean medieval documents have as yet come to light. Schechter's original attempt to identify as such his *Fragments of a Zadokite Work* has rightly been rejected by later scholars on both ideological and chronological

grounds. See *SRHJ,* Vol. II, pp. 52 ff., 348 ff. In the heat of their victorious battles against the Sadducean character of these fragments, however, these scholars, especially L. Ginzberg, went too far in altogether denying any historic connection between the ancient Sadducee doctrines and the medieval heresies. Somewhat inconsistently, Ginzberg himself was prepared to admit on occasions the survival of ancient apocalyptic teachings, even when he could not document them from any older source other than the Gospel of John. Cf. his *Ginze Schechter,* I, 310, 547; II, 470, 478. The very survival of some Sadducee literary remnants, asserted by the two Karaite authors, appears the more probable as we seem to possess evidence for the existence as late as the ninth and tenth centuries of some Philo manuscripts, possibly in Syriac translation. Cf. S. Poznanski's "Philon dans l'ancienne littérature judéo-arabe," *REJ,* L, 10–31

The likelihood that some ancient sectarian letters were rediscovered in the early Muslim age has been greatly enhanced by a report of the Nestorian patriarch Timothy I of Baghdad (780–823) that in his day ("ten years ago"), Palestinian Jews had discovered precisely such a hoard of ancient writings in one of the Judaean caves. See O. Braun's ed. of "Ein Brief des Katholikos Timotheos I," *Oriens christianus,* I, 301–11. The attention of the scholarly world to this important report was first drawn by O. Eissfeld in "Der gegenwärtige Stand der Erforschung der in Palästina neu gefundenen hebräischen Handschriften," *Theologische Literaturzeitung,* LXXIV, 595–600; followed by Guy de Vaux in "À propos des manuscrits de la Mer Morte," *RB,* LVII, 420 ff. (connecting this story with Qirqisani's description of the Magharians); H. Grégoire in "Les Gens de la caverne, le Qaraïtes et les Khazars," *Le Flambeau,* XXXV, 477–85; and others. An historical reminiscence that ancient writings had been hidden in caves after the destruction of the Temple was preserved in Spain and became part of the inquiry addressed by Ḥisdai ibn Shapruṭ to the king of the Khazars. Because of that hiding place for their books, the Jewish statesman explained, the ancient refugees had "taught their children to pray in the cave on mornings and evenings, until after the passage of time their descendants forgot the reason for that ancient custom." Cf. Ḥisdai's letter in Kokovtsov's *Perepiska,* p. 17; and S. Segert's comments thereon in "Ein alter Bericht über den Fund hebräischer Handschriften in einer Höhle," *Archiv orientalni,* XXI, 263–69. This query must have struck a familiar chord in Khazar circles, since worship in caves had a long and venerable tradition in the Crimea and neighboring lands. Regrettably, these stray tidbits do not yet allow for any far-reaching hypotheses concerning the underground links, if any, between the ancient Magharians or Qumran sectarians and their medieval successors. Cf. also *infra,* n. 16.

11. The main argument to the contrary, namely the prolonged absence of any reference to Sadducean teachings before the tenth century, is inconclusive because of the general paucity of extant Jewish sources in the preceding half millennium. Even if we were to assume that some of these ancient letters

had reemerged not long before Qirqisani by a lucky find in one of the Palestinian caves (see *infra,* n. 16), we could not rule out the underground survival of Sadducean and other sectarian teachings in oral transmission.

12. Naṭronai's responsum in *Sha'are ṣedeq,* VI.10, fol. 24b (on its date, see *infra,* n. 18); Qirqisani, I.11, p. 52 (*HUCA,* VII, 382); L. M. Epstein's *Marriage Laws,* p. vii. Poznanski's identification of Jacob ben Ephraim with Jacob ben Samuel was rejected by Mann in *Texts and Studies,* II, 26.

13. Shahrastani's *K. al-Milal,* I.171 (in Haarbrücker's German trans., I, 259). Cf. I. Goldziher's "Dénombrement des sectes mohamétanes," *RHR,* XXVI, 129–37; and I. Friedlaender's data on *The Heterodoxies of the Shi'ites according to Ibn Ḥazm,* p. 6.

14. Qirqisani, I.2 (11–13), 11–12, ed. by Nemoy, I, 12 f., 51 ff. (*HUCA,* VII, 328 f., 382 f.); Shahrastani, I.168 f. (Haarbrücker, I, 254 ff.); Yehudah Hadassi's *Eshkol ha-kofer,* No. 97, fol. 41c. The identity of Yudghan with the author Yehudah the Persian, mentioned by Abraham ibn Ezra and Elijah Bashyatchi, appears dubious. So does the equation of his followers with the Shadghanites, mentioned by Jephet ben 'Ali in his Commentary on Deut. 30:2 (Pinsker's *Lickute,* pp. 25 f.). Cf. Graetz's *Geschichte,* V, 212 f. (Hebrew trans., III, 217 f.). Yudghan's surname, "the Shepherd," bitingly paraphrased by Hadassi as "herder of thy camels," is explained by Qirqisani and all his successors as having had the semimessianic connotation of "shepherd of the people." However, it would seem strange that these sectarians should have selected this particular epitheton from among all possible messianic designations, without some direct provocation. The people at large had certainly not forgotten the Talmud's reiterated disparagement of the shepherd's calling. On the other hand, it would not have been at all incongruous for Yudghan, a native of the Persian highlands around Hamadan, to have started life as a shepherd and for his followers to rationalize this occupation as a symbol of his divine mission. L. Nemoy is quite right in ascribing the rise of some of these heterodoxies, though not necessarily as he assumes of the Karaite schism, to the "uncouth pioneers" from the Iranian Plateau. See his "Early Karaism (The Need for a New Approach)," *JQR,* XL, 307–15. Cf. also the Muslim parallels cited by Friedlaender in *JQR,* III, 282 ff.; and on the prohibition of meat and wine, as well as on Abu 'Isa's additional prayers, *ibid.,* pp. 293 ff., 298 ff. [the preceding article, sections 9, 11 and 12—Ed.]. Graetz's description of the medieval sects, particularly in his Notes XIV–XVIII, together with Harkavy's comments thereon, as well as the latter's excursus "On the History of Jewish Sects" in the Hebrew edition of Graetz, III, 493–511, still are the best general summaries based on full documentation. S. A. Poznanski's careful survey of "Founders of Jewish Sects in the Geonic Period" (Hebrew), *Reshumot,* I, 207–16, was unfortunately never completed.

15. Only one writer, Jephet ben 'Ali (in Pinsker, *Lickute kadmoniot,* pp. 25 f.), claims that the Yudghanites believed that all commandments had lost their binding force in the dispersion. For this reason they "relaxed many com-

mandments and permitted the Jews Gentile food and the consumption of abominable things." If true, this report would merely indicate that some later Yudghanites more liberally interpreted the practical implications of their founder's theories.

16. Both Qirqisani, I.2(8).7, pp. 11 f., 41 f. (*HUCA*, VII, 326 f., 363 f.); and Shahrastani, I, 169 f. (Arabic), 257 (German), offer brief descriptions of the Magharians, which have long intrigued scholars. Since they are placed by Qirqisani before Jesus, and since Shahrastani reports a tradition that Arius (died 336 C.E.) had borrowed his doctrine of the Messiah as the Lord's angel from these sectarians "who had lived 400 years before Arius and had laid great stress on continence and a simple mode of life," Harkavy's hypothesis that we deal here with an offshoot of the Essenes or Therapeutae found wide acceptance. Harkavy's explanation, however, that their name of Cave Men was derived from the Essenes' predilection to live in deserted regions is not only controverted by the ancient records about the dispersed, in part even urban, Essenian communities, but also by Qirqisani's etymology that "they were called so because their (sacred) books were found in a cave." Clearly this description fits far better the New Covenanters and their spiritual kinsmen of Qumran.

Even with these new materials we are still unable safely to identify the Magharian writings mentioned by Qirqisani. "One of them," writes this Karaite historian, "is the Alexandrian whose book is famous and (widely) known; it is the most important of the books of the Magharians. Next to it (in importance) is a small booklet entitled 'The Book of Yaddua',' also a fine work. As for the rest of the Magharian books, most of them are of no value and resemble mere tales." Poznanski's alluring hypothesis (following Harkavy) that Qirqisani referred to some works by Philo the Alexandrian, whether or not he assumed that the latter's Hebrew name was Yaddua' (*REJ*, L, 23 ff., 28), encounters the almost insuperable barrier of the lack of evidence for the survival of any Philonic writings considered "famous and widely known" in the tenth century. The description here also gives the impression that Qirqisani referred to Hebrew, or possibly Arabic, works, whereas no such medieval translations of Philo are mentioned anywhere else. At best there may have been extant some Syriac translations. Neither does the mere fact that the Magharians believed in an intermediary angel who created the world necessarily link them directly to the Philonic *logos*. The doctrine of a *demiurge* had been much alive in the Christian, as well as Jewish, gnosis long before it was turned into a vehicle of anti-Jewish propaganda by Marcion of Pontus. It is barely possible that Qirqisani referred here to some Hebrew, Aramaic, or Arabic version of the pseudo-Philonic *Liber Antiquitatum Biblicarum* which, in its Latin garb, was soon to make such a strange career in the West.

17. The figure of hundreds of thousands combatants under Abu 'Isa is mentioned only in the Sulzberger MS of the relatively late *Epistle to Yemen* by Maimonides, ed. by Halkin, pp. 98 ff. (Arabic and Hebrew), xviii f. (En-

glish). This number evidently is a gross exaggeration; it is reduced to 10,000 in other MSS and old versions. Although the sage of Fusṭaṭ had at his disposal many since forgotten sources, and his general description of the messianic movements is distinguished by both lucidity and general reliability, he himself expressed doubts about the veracity of the traditions concerning Abu 'Isa, whom he failed to mention by name. His emphasis, too, that "they reached, according to the information I received, the vicinity of Baghdad. This happened in the beginning of the reign of the 'Umayyads," is pointless in so far as Baghdad was not to become the imperial capital until more than half a century after Abu 'Isa's downfall. Maimonides himself drew the distinction between this episode which he had "learned from oral reports" and the following incident which "we have verified and know to be true." Cf. also J. Mann's "Messianic Movements in the Period of the First Crusades," *Hatekufah,* XXIV, 355.

18. Naṭronai's resp. in *Sha'are ṣedeq,* VI.7 and 10, fol. 24ab; and the sources listed *supra,* n. 46. These sources for the story of the pseudo-messiah Severus (Serene, Zonaria), in themselves confused and contradictory, have given rise to endless hypotheses. They have been subjected to renewed careful and judicious scrutiny by J. Starr in "Le Mouvement messianique au début du VIIIe siècle," *REJ,* CII, 81–92. Here the name Severus seems definitely established, whereas Serene, mentioned in Naṭronai's responsum, should be read, according to Friedlaender's suggestion, *Suryani* (the Syrian). "Zonaria" is merely a corruption of the latter. Starr goes too far, however, in denying the spread of that movement to Spain and Gaul. The pertinent passage in the chronicle of Pseudo-Isidorus Pacensis (cf. the version cited by T. Mommsen in his ed. of the *Continuatio Byzantia-Arabica* to St. Isidore's *Historia Gothorum,* in *MGH,* Auct. ant., XI, 359 n. 1) may indeed be a later interpolation. Yet the interpolator's substitution of the name of an oriental Arab governor by the western Emir Anbasa, without some backing by an older authority, would require a far more cogent explanation that has hitherto been offered. The term *volari* (fly), rather than the purely conjectural *nolari* (transport in ships), is likewise genuine. Cf. Friedlaender's comments in *JQR,* II, 503 ff.

Some of the chronological difficulties may be eliminated if we assume that Severus' agitation continued for a number of years. It probably started about 721–22 (according to our relatively oldest source, Theophanes) and continued into the reign of Hisham (724–43). In the meantime Severus may have been apprehended by Maslama, brother and active collaborator of Caliph Yazid ibn 'Abd al-Malik (720–24), but he seems to have been released after Maslama had "confiscated all his property." Cf. the anonymous chronicler's report, ed. by J. B. Chabot, in *CSCO,* 3d ser., XIV, Part 1, p. 308. This outcome of the prosecution hardly discouraged Severus from resuming his lucrative undertaking, or his excited followers from continuing to believe in his divine mission. Only when, to put an end to the disturbance, Hisham executed the messianic pretender, did most, or all, of the latter's adherents repent their delusion and apply for readmission to the regular community. Their acceptance was sanctioned by Naṭronai I (bar Nehemiah) whose regime, according to Sherira's Epistle (p. 102), began in 719 and lasted until some time before 739. The repeated efforts since E. H. Weiss to ascribe the crucial responsum to Naṭronai II (bar Hilai) after 853 have not met with success. The principal argument for the ninth-century date advanced, for instance, by L. Ginzberg (in his *Geonica,* I, 50 n. 1), that in the second responsum by that gaon (No. 7), "a plain reference is made to the Karaites" founded by 'Anan some three decades after Naṭronai I's death, is but the result of the unawareness of the strong protokaraite trends before 'Anan and the usual exaggerations concerning the impact of Karaism on the contemporary community. This assumption is controverted by the entire tenor of the responsum, which refers to opponents of the written, as well as the oral, Law. In fact, the language of the informed questioners, even more than that of the gaon, tends to indicate that these sectarians lived in sexual promiscuity *(peruṣin ba-'arayot),* a term which would hardly have been used for any Karaite misinterpretation of the legal impediments to marriage. We probably have here some early Jewish counterpart to the Qarmatian schism and later the followers of Ibn ar-Rawandi among the Muslims, which took over some of the Mazdakite teachings concerning the community of women and property. Cf. Friedlaender's *Heterodoxies,* p. 37. To what extent Platonic teachings in their neo-Platonic garb contributed to the theoretical justification of these doctrines is yet to be examined. Certainly neo-Platonism had started to exert a growing influence on the Arabic-speaking intelligentsia, through literary media, as well as through the Mazdakite heritage. Cf., for the time being, F. Altheim and R. Stiehl's "Mazdak and Porphyrios," *Nouvelle Clio,* V, 356–76. Certainly, such sectarian extremism fits much better into the turbulent Muslim and Jewish community life of the eighth century than into the somewhat better organized communal structure of the ninth century. The attribution of both these responsa to Naṭronai II would also encounter the insuperable barrier of Qirqisani's and the other heresiologues' total silence about the movement initiated by Severus. An ephemeral commotion led by a self-seeking adventurer could easily be ignored. But a sectarian group which lasted for more than a hundred and thirty years, almost to the lifetime of David Al-Muqammiṣ, would certainly have been recorded by him and, through him, by Qirqisani and Hadassi. Our harmonization of the existing records may not quite suit the tastes of supercritical scholars, but it seems to offer the most acceptable reconstruction of the actual events.

19. Ibn 'Abd Rabbihi's *K. al-Iqd al-Farid* (Collar of Unique Pearls); Shahrastani, *supra,* n. 16; and the sources cited by Friedlaender in *JQR,* III, 286 ff. [the preceding article, section 10—Ed.]. Friedlaender raises the intriguing question as to whether the number nineteen had any of the mystic connotations it possessed among some Zoroastrians and Muslims.

IV

THE PERIOD OF THE CRUSADES

7

A Report on Messianic Troubles in Baghdad in 1120–21

S. D. Goitein

The great intensification of religious feeling in Christian and Muslim countries during the 11th and 12th centuries, as well as the cataclysmic events of the Crusades, gave rise to an almost universal Messianic movement among the Jewish communities of Europe and Asia. In his Hebrew paper, "Messianic movements during the first three Crusades," *Ha-Tekufah,* vols. XXIII–XXIV, Jacob Mann enumerates no less than eight cases in point from Germany, France, Spain, North Africa, Palestine, Yemen and Kurdistan.[1] To these a ninth case, a very typical event which took place in Baghdad in 1120–21, may now be added.

A bundle of seven sheets from the Cairo Genizah, preserved at Oxford (Heb. ms. f. 56, vol. 2821), proved, after closer examination, to contain a report of Messianic troubles in the Jewish community of Baghdad, in many respects a most interesting account in spite of the fragmentary preservation.

Although comparatively short, the report introduces a fairly large number of personalities. On the Muslim side there appear the Sultan and the Caliph,[2] the Chief Qadi, a "wicked man" called Ibn Abū Shujā' (to be identified below), and the "viziers" and "marshals of the nobles," the counsellors of the Caliph. On the Jewish side, the heroine is a pious woman, known as "the daughter of Joseph, the son of the physician," and other figures are "our lord, R. Daniel, the son of our master, the

Reprinted by permission of Dropsie University from *The Jewish Quarterly Review* n.s. 43 (1952–53).

President of the Seder," Abu Sahl, a scion of the famous Ibn Kammūna family, while, owing to the incompleteness of the manuscript, we do not know what was said of the *resh galutha,* the Exilarch, though he is referred to also.

The part beginning the story is missing, but it would appear that not much has been lost. We are told (fol. 13b) of Jews being persecuted, and being set free after having suffered for a number of years; we learn that they had to pay 1,000 dinars because they were unwilling to let their womenfolk wear the distinctive badges of non-Muslims, a manner of discrimination which later on was virtually confined to persons of higher rank.

Such was the situation, when on the 25th of Elul 1120, the pious "daughter of Joseph the physician," who had led an ascetic life and had married during that year only under special pressure exerted by the above-mentioned R. Daniel, appeared in public declaring that she had seen the prophet Elijah in a dream and had been told by him that the redemption of Israel was at hand (fols. 13b–14a).

A page or so is unfortunately missing in this connection. When the tale is taken up again, we learn that the Seljuq Sultan, who had been angry with the Jews because some illegal taxes he had imposed on them had to be discontinued, and who had sought an opportunity to injure them, was pleased to hear of the commotion caused by the Messianic expectations raised by the pious woman. He declared that the Jews would not condone the existence of a single independent realm after the establishment of their own kingdom, whereupon the Caliph ordered the immediate imprisonment of all Jews in the imperial mint. He then asked the Chief Qadi whether he was entitled to deal them a final blow, as "their time was up," unless a new prophet appeared among them or they embraced the Muslim faith. The Chief Qadi, however, who was a man of very high authority, warned the Caliph that no person who had ever done evil to the Jewish people remained unpunished, and added that the Jewish people would endure forever. The rest of the Qadi's answer and the account of subsequent events have not been preserved except a mention of some matter that had occurred at the house of the exilarch (16b–17a).

Matters must have come to a very serious juncture, for we find, on fol. 17b, the community, including its leader, still imprisoned, fasting and praying for its deliverance. Then a Jew, obviously Abu Sahl b.

Kammūna, who is mentioned on fol. 18a, appeared in full freedom at the prison gate, thus giving them hope that they, too, would soon be released. Ibn Kammūna's liberation was attributed to Elijah's appearance to the pious woman, who is also referred to by Abu Sahl in an audience granted to him by the Caliph. The latter ridiculed the story, and said that the Jews were obviously of very low intelligence if they believed such a tale by a woman; he gave orders that she be burned the next day, and that the Jews be outlawed. The same night, however, Elijah appeared to the Caliph himself, who was struck with awe (fol. 18a).

Here again the manuscript presents a gap. The remainder of the preserved report refers mainly to the taxes from which the Jews had been exempted. They had evidently been released, under the double impact of the Qadi's letter and the mysterious appearance of Elijah. By bribing the viziers and marshals of the nobles, they succeeded in having their exemption from certain taxes kept secret: had it been made public, the Jews would have been assaulted by the mob, for the payment of taxes by the Jews was regarded as a benefit and a sort of protection for themselves (fol. 19a).

In order to be able to understand and evaluate the document summarized, its character must first be defined. As its closing formula "we-shalom" ("and so, peace") indicates, it is a *letter*. It cannot, however, be the original, for it is written on the verso and partly also on the free spaces of various documents bound together into a booklet. One of these documents, fol. 14b, is dated "Fostat, 1440 Sel.," i.e. 1129, or eight years later than the events, which, we are told, occurred "in this year that has just passed, 1431 Sel.," or 1120. As the document written in 1129 is a valid deed signed by a number of respectable persons, it could not have been used as scrap paper before a number of years had elapsed; hence the letter, which was sent in 1121 from Baghdad to Egypt, must have made a considerable impression, since it was regarded as being valuable enough to be copied so many years later. It is not impossible that in the introduction to the letter, the recipient was asked to make its contents widely known because of the miraculous appearance of Elijah which it reports, and it may also have been an answer to a request made when the rumors of the strange event that had taken place in the capital of 'Iraq reached Egypt.

Despite the repeated references to the appearance of the prophet

Elijah, a detail which, in a medieval account, must be regarded as a fact, and despite the legendary character (to be demonstrated later) of other material included in the report, the letter generally gives the impression of a matter-of-fact eye-witness account. It was obviously meant for someone familiar with local affairs, probably one of the *peqīdē ha-yeshīvā,* the representatives in Egypt of the Babylonian houses of learning (cf. Mann, *Texts,* vol. I, p. 205). The historical value of the document is enhanced by the fact that Muslim historical sources clearly refer to the events it describes. During a brief sojourn at Istanbul in September 1951, I was able to consult various relevant manuscripts, especially the bulky history of the elder Ibn al-Jawzī, (d. 1200), called *al-Muntaẓam* (ms. Ayasofya 3092–8) in which the following statement appears (vol. VII, p. 475):

"In that year (i.e. 515 A. H., or 1121) the non-Muslims were asked to wear their distinctive signs; the affair ended in their paying 4,000 dinars to the Caliph and 20,000 dinars to the Sultan; the Jālūt[3] (i.e. Ra's al-Jālūt, the Exilarch or head of the Jewish community) was brought into the imperial presence, guaranteed the above-mentioned sums, and collected them."

This statement of Ibn al-Jawzī was copied by the famous historian Ibn al-Athīr in his world history, ed. Thornberg, vol. X, p. 420, but without the passage referring to the Jewish exilarch.[4] Muslim historians often speak of Ahl adh-Dhimma, the Protected People, i.e. the non-Muslims, in general, when they really mean a specific community. Here, the mention of the resh galutha clearly shows that the Jews are being referred to, while the details concerning distinctive signs to be worn by them, the long negotiations with and the payment to the authorities, indicate that Ibn al-Jawzī alludes to the events described in our document, to the historical evaluation of which we now turn.

In 1120, there reigned in Baghdad the 'Abbasid Caliph al-Mustarshid (1118–1135), who tenaciously tried to show a more independent attitude toward the Turkish Seljuq rulers (Maḥmūd, Sultan of 'Iraq, 1118–1131, and his overlord, the Great Sultan Sanjar), a fact which is reflected in our document.[5] The endless wars of the Seljuqs among themselves, as well as those of the Seljuqs and the Caliphs against various rebels, and the senseless luxury indulged in by the reigning monarchs and their high dignitaries, forced them to be looking constantly for new ways of extracting money from their subjects. Thus Ibn adh-Dhahabī relates in his

Ta'rīkh al-Islām (ms. Ayasofya, 3005, vol. XV, fol. 14b): "In this year (i.e. 515 A. H., or 1121) the illegal imposts were again introduced, and the merchants were forced to pay the Sultan one-third of their net profit . . . ; after some time it was announced to the merchants that the new taxes had been abolished, and that they were to pay to the Sultan a sum of 5,000 dinars as a sign of gratitude for this action." It is related that the Sultan's palace containing a million dinars' worth of treasure burned down that year which was regarded as being a punishment sent from heaven, as even the nobility and the religious scholars and judges had been forced to do the meanest manual labor towards its construction (Ibn al-Athīr, *loc. cit.*).

At such a time of oppression and extortion, it was only natural that the Jews should not be spared. A very common and popular device for extracting special contributions from them consisted in enforcing the old provisions which imposed a distinctive dress upon the non-Muslims.[6] Again and again these provisions, which the Muslims had adopted from the Byzantines, had to be enforced anew, which only shows that during most of the time they were observed but imperfectly. Already the Caliph al-Muqtadī, Mustarshid's grandfather and second predecessor (1075–1094) had ordered that the Jews should wear yellow caps and the Christians black gowns (Strauss, *Hirschler Memorial Volume*, p. 79) and, as our document shows, for disobedience of this decree, the Jews had had to suffer imprisonment and other punishment "a number of years before" (1120), i.e. under al-Mustaẓhir, Mustarshid's father and immediate predecessor. This is in conformity with the statement made elsewhere in the letter indicating that a rascal named Ibn Abū Shujā' was the source of all these troubles. The name of Abū Shujā' was rather common in those times,[7] but it appears fairly certain that the reference is to ar-Rabīb Abū Manṣūr, the son of Abū Shujā', the vizier of the Seljuq Sultan, who had been appointed, upon his father's request, as vizier to the Caliph, first under al-Mustaẓhir (in 1114, cf. Ibn al-Athīr, vol. X, p. 349, l. 7) and, after having been dismissed for misconduct, again under al-Mustarshid (ibid., vol. X, p. 376).

As is shown by the wording of the letter ("they pulled off the distinctive signs of the women," fol. 13b, l. 7), Jewish women had been ordered, as was the case later in Egypt, to wear badges, most probably of the same color as the turbans of the men of their community, i. e. yellow.[8] The passage from the *Muntaẓam* of Ibn al-Jawzī the elder quoted above, as well as our letter, clearly indicates that at this time, too, restrictions were not rigorously enforced.[9] The only strange detail in this connection is the assertion made in the letter that Jewish persons of higher rank, both local and foreign, were to wear the distinctive badge; as a rule, these were the very persons, especially government officials and physicians, who succeeded in being *exempted* from this onerous discrimination (cf. Strauss, *Hirschler Mem. Vol.*, p. 91; and Khazrejiy, *The Pearl Strings*, ed. Redhouse, vol. I, p. 106, anno 1240; etc.). It is, however, natural that in a more fanatical age special emphasis was placed on discrimination against the higher class non-Muslims, who had more opportunity to mix with Muslim society and to exercise authority over sections of it. The persons imprisoned and fined pursuant to the prohibition of appearing in public without the distinctive badge (fol. 13b, II. 1 and 6) obviously belonged to the Jewish upper class.

The comparative stability reached by the Jews of Baghdad at the beginning of Mustarshid's reign was shaken in the fall of 1120 by the Messianic excitement stirred up by "the pious daughter of Joseph, the son of the physician." Reference was made, at the beginning of this article, to the many Messianic movements that had arisen all over the Jewish world; to this should be added the fact that inside Islam the situation was no different. For in the very year 515 A. H., or 1121, Ibn al-Athīr reports that a man of the family of 'Alī, who had formerly been a professor at the Niẓāmīya madrasa in Baghdad, appeared in Mecca preaching repentance (amar bi-l-ma'rūf), and, after having won a great following, tried to have himself proclaimed Caliph. Other instances could easily be cited.[10] In both Islam and Judaism, such movements had an essentially religious root, but their goal was political power. When the Seljuq Sultan proclaimed that the Jews, after the establishment of their kingdom, would not leave a single other realm in existence, he certainly was not quoting any actual utterance of a Jewish leader; but the true Messianic idea was, of course, that every knee should bow before God and His representative on earth.

That a woman should be at the source of the movement is nothing unusual. The same thing occurred, for instance, in Sicily, during the events described in the interesting document published by J. Mann, *Texts* I, pp. 34–44. Neither is it surprising that this woman intended to lead an unmarried life. Though Judaism, like Islam, is firmly opposed to celibacy as a form of asceticism,[11] there have always been people who believed that marriage was a great impediment to spiritual life (Shim'ōn b. 'Azzai in Israel, Ṭabarī in Islam[12] are famous examples). Women saints in particular shunned marriage, as for instance the famous Rābi'a al-Adawīya.[13] That this trend became stronger in an intensely religious age is also natural, and it is testified to by a famous passage of Abraham Maimonides' *Highways of Perfection,* ed. Samuel Rosenblatt, vol. I, p. 147, l. 1 (cf. N. Wieder, *Melilah,* Manchester, vol. II, pp. 68–69). It is, however, characteristic, that our heroine was induced to wed through the efforts of R. Daniel, the son of the president of the Academy, obviously a community leader of that time.

Our knowledge of the Baghdad community in the first quarter of the 12th century is so scanty that the few details given in our document are not without historical value. For chronological reasons, our Daniel could not be identical with the Daniel b. Yesha'yah Rosh ha-Seder mentioned in the document quoted by Mann, *Jews,* vol. II, p. 270, l. 8, p. 319, ms. fol. 2, recto, l. 12, but, as it often happened that the same names and titles have occurred in the same pedigree,[14] our Daniel may be a representative of the Baghdad branch of that family, other members of which, like Abu Sa'id b. Dosa, whom Yehuda Halevi praised in a poem, were at the same time prominent in Egypt.[15] While there had previously been several *rashe sedarim,*[16] the important office held by them, second only to that of the Gaon himself,[17] seems to have been confined to one person, or at least to have its official appellation reserved for one of its occupants only. The statement that the exilarch was accompanied by his students (fol. 17a, l. 2) makes it clear that he was a learned man, and not merely the secular head of the community. This tallies with the well-known remark of Benjamin of Tudela that the pseudo-Messiah David Alroy, who was active about a quarter of a century after the events described here, studied under an exilarch.

In connection with the third leader mentioned, Abū Sahl b. Kammūna, it is interesting that a member of this family should have already been prominent in 1120. Another one, Abū Ghālib, obviously a high official, died in the underground prison *(maṭmūra)* of Wasit in 601 A. H., or 1204/5 (Ibn as-Sā'i, ed. 1934, p. 165); a third, Abū al-Ma'ālī, was famous for his philanthropy in 1207 (Asaf, *Letters of Samuel b. 'Eli,* p. 109); and a fourth was the famous philosopher 'Izz ad-Dawla, one of the most interesting Jewish personalities of the entire Middle Ages.[18] The latter had to be rescued from a fanatical Baghdad mob in

683, or 1284/5, and carried in a coffin to al-Hilla, where his son, the fifth member of the family known to me, held the position of a *Kātib* (government official).[19]

Owing to the gap between fols. 14a and 15b, which deprives us of one or several pages, we are unfortunately left in the dark as to how the Baghdad Jewish community reacted to the pious woman's statement that Elijah had announced to her the imminent redemption of Israel. Appearances of Elijah, the Great Messenger, were a standing feature in the Messianic stories of the period, so that in Saloniki, for instance, even Gentiles reported that they had seen him in full daylight.[20] At any rate, the excitement of the Babylonian Jews must have been extraordinary, for their behavior was followed by considerable repercussions. The Caliph imprisoned them all[21] in the imperial mint, perhaps because a number of Jews lived there, since they were employed in this most favored branch of government service.[22] They were threatened with death, a fate which was averted through the efforts of the chief justice ad-Damghānī, whom the Caliph had to consult before proceeding against the People of the Book, since all dealings with them were subject to the religious law of Islam.

It is not easy to identify this Damghānī. The Damghānīs were a well-known family of Hanafi qadis; one of their number, who had held the office of chief qadi for over twenty-four years, 'Alī b. Muḥammad, died in Muḥarram 513, i.e. April 1119.[23] The latter's father, too, had been chief justice for many years (*Jawāhir,* ib., vol. II, p. 96); his brother, 'Abdallah, who was still alive in 1120 (he died in 518 or 1124) was not in office during that year, and served as judge of *naẓar fi l-maẓālim,*—the Caliph's secular court,—and not as a religious judge (*Jawāhir,* ib., vol. II, p. 287). However, although the chief justice of the religious court in 1120/21 was not a Damghānī, it is quite natural that the Jews should have called him so, after the office had been occupied by men of this name for at least two generations. A parallel practice is found in the fact that the Muslims of Ṣan'ā, at the end of the last century, called the chief rabbi "al-Gāreh," because two members of a family bearing this name, Joseph and Solomon, had successively occupied the post of chief rabbi for about eighty years.

The author of the document here discussed could not, of course, know the contents of the correspondence which passed between the Caliph and the Chief Qadi, and all his reports of it must be regarded as essentially legendary. The Caliph gave the Jews the choice between extermination and conversion to the ruling religion, unless "a prophet appeared among them"; this is not so much an allusion to the widespread belief that the gift of prophecy would return to Israel as a preparatory step to the Messianic age,[24] as it is an indication that, as often occurred during Messianic excitement, the Gentiles at the beginning bided their time, not completely denying the possibility of such an event. In any case, it may be safely concluded that "Damghānī" objected to the Caliph's plan to destroy the Jews, most probably not out of any sympathy with them, but out of respect for the law, a respect characteristic of the better Muslim legal scholars.

Owing to its bad state of preservation, the end of the report can only imperfectly be related to its main parts. We no longer hear of the Messianic excitement or of the wearing of distinctive dress, but of Jews' exemption from certain taxes. The word *kharāj* used here had at that time the most general meaning of "tax."[25] The non-payment of taxes is a characteristic feature of Messianic upheavals,[26] but clearly here an officially recognized exemption is alluded to (fol. 19a, l. 7), and as the tax concerned is called *jizya,* the most rigorously collected poll-tax, we must here again be in the realm of legend. Various sections of the non-Muslim community tried, by producing fabricated documents, to be exempted from this tax, which was regarded more as a social discrimination than a financial burden. There are repeated references in Muslim literature to Jews allegedly from Khaybar, who produced such documents, sometimes with success.[27] The payment by the Jews of a large sum to the Caliph's counsellors reported here is, no doubt, a historical fact. The reason given for it, namely that they should keep secret the fact that the Jews were exempt from the poll-tax, is an obvious invention destined to enhance the prestige of the Jewish community of Baghdad in the eyes of their coreligionists.

It may be asked why the passage from Ibn al-Jawzī's *Muntaẓam* carries no reference to the Messianic excitement reported in the letter here discussed. Anyone conversant with later Muslim historical literature will, however, find this quite natural: these writers were interested only in details affecting the Muslim community directly. Furthermore, it is clear that Ibn al-Jawzī abridged an older source, just as Ibn al-Athīr further abridged his work by leaving out his remark on the Jewish exilarch (cf. above). However, as the Muslim historical literature of the

12th century is far from being fully known, more may eventually be learned concerning the details described above. In addition, as our letter is incomplete, there is still some prospect that the original or parts of this or other copies may be found elsewhere.

NOTES

1. Cf. also B. Dinaburg, *Yisrael ba-Golah,* II, 231 sq. Baer, *MGWJ,* LXX (1926) 113 sq. Nearest in time to the events discussed in this paper is the appearance of the Karaite Messiah Shelomo Hakohen, whom the Norman proselyte Ovadya met in Banias (Northern Palestine) in 1121, cf. J. Mann, *Texts and Studies* I, p. 42.
2. I.e. the Seljuk Sultan and the Abbasid Caliph, who mostly had to surrender his temporal power to the former.
3. Such strange abridgments are common to the language of that period. In our very document, fol. 14a, l. 7, the president of the Academy, *rosh ha-seder,* is simply referred to as *"ha-seder."* The President of the rabbinical court, *āv bēt dīn,* is called *bēt dīn* in the document Bodl. 2805, l. 15, pub. by Asaf, *Tarbiz,* vol. 9, p. 218, l. 3; similarly in the letter Bodl. 2873, no. 37, anno 1092, pub. by Wertheimer, *Ginze Yerushalayim,* vol. III; cf. Baer, *Zion,* 1951, p. 21; in the letter quoted by Mann, *Jews in Egypt,* II, p. 203 and 232; and I recall having come across it a fourth time, while studying Genizah fragments at Oxford and Cambridge in the summer of 1951. As I have already pointed out in *Commentary,* July 1951, p. 28, this usage is still fully alive among the Yemenite Jews; a *bēt dīn* is, among them, a *man* authorized to make a religiously valid legal decision, so that even in a small place three to four *"bēt dīn,"* literally "courts", are to be found. The formula *yorunu bēt dīn ṣedeq maḥaziqē kol bedeq* is used by the Yemenite Jews as an official opening in inquiries addressed to a *single* rabbi to this very day.
4. The very valuable Istanbul manuscript of Ibn al-Athīr, *Carullah,* 1593, vol. II, p. 171, contains here no more than the printed edition.
5. The Sultan most probably had to discontinue his illegal impositions on the Jews under the pressure of the Caliph, who had to watch over the welfare of the 'protected peoples' and who, by such measures, stressed his religious authority over the Sultan.

   The fact that our document never mentions the rulers by their names is in full accord with the usage of the time; they are always merely referred to as "the Caliph" or "the Sultan." Cf. e.g. Mir'āt az-Zamān of Sibṭ, the younger Ibn al-Jawzī (d. 1257), vol. VIII, p. 96: "In this year (515 A. H., or 1121), the Sultan intended to leave Baghdad, whereupon the Caliph sent word to him, saying . . ."

6. Christian travellers of the Middle Ages, as well as modern scholars, have paid much attention to this feature of Islamic civilization. Since von Hammer's paper in *Journal Asiatique*, 1855, "Les ordonnances égyptiennes sur les costumes des Chrétiens et des Juifs," much has been written about it; for the latest comprehensive treatment, cf. E. Strauss, "The Social Isolation of the Ahl adh-Dhimma," *P. Hirschler Memorial Volume*, Budapest, 1949, pp. 75–82, and the same author's work, *The Jews in Egypt and Syria under the Mamluks* (in Hebrew), vol. II, p. 210–214.
7. I had at first thought to have identified this person as Shujā' b. Abū Shujā' Fāris b. Ḥusayn, a famous preacher who died in 1113/4 (Ibn al-Athīr, vol. X, p. 350, l. 6). The popular preachers in Baghdad were, in those days, the source of endless trouble; they stirred up hatred among the various Muslim groups and sects, as well as between Muslims and 'unbelievers'. Nevertheless, the writer of the letter would have expressed himself otherwise had he been referring to a person who had been dead for seven years.
8. Al-Muqtadī, Mustarshid's grandfather, had, however, ordered them to wear honey-colored *girdles* and *shoes of different colors*, one black and one white (al-Fuwaṭī, p. 68, ll. 1–2 from bottom).
9. The same seems to have been the case in Baghdad in later times. For when the fanatical Shafi'ite chief justice Ibn Faḍlān (d. 631 A. H., or 1233), in a letter to the Caliph,—which remained unanswered—stressed that in *Aleppo* every non-Muslim wore the distinctive dress (al-Fuwaṭī, p. 69, l. 9), it may be safely concluded that a more lenient practice was in vogue in Baghdad. When Ibn al-Fuwaṭī reports, under the year 627, (1229) that the same Ibn Faḍlān insisted that the leaders of the non-Muslim communities appear before him in person, under most humiliating circumstances, for the payment of the poll-tax (cf. W. J. Fischel, *MGWJ*, LXXIX, (1935), pp. 309–310) we may similarly assume that the historian would not have registered this as a noteworthy event, had it not been exceptional. It seems, in general, the picture presented by the sources as to how non-Muslims lived in Muslim countries is somewhat distorted by the fact that it was mostly the fanatically religious scholars who dealt with these matters in their works.
10. The characteristic end of the Yemenite Messiah of that century, who let his head be cut off because he firmly believed no sword could harm him (cf. Maimonides' account in his *Iggeret Teman*) has a striking parallel in the death of the Sūfi fanatic Abū al-Karam of Bukhara and Samarqand. This mystic led 60,000 of his followers, completely unarmed, against the Mongols (1239); the Mongol chief, astonished by the manifestation of such faith, cautiously left his army behind and encountered Abū al-Karam alone. After having easily killed him, he let all his followers be cut down by his soldiers (Ibn al-Fuwaṭī, pp. 127–128).
11. Although Islam, as usual, was more exposed to foreign influence. For literature on the question, see Goldziher, *Vorlesungen*, chapt. 4, sect. 2, n. 11; for further details, see George Vajda, *La théologie ascétique de Baḥya ibn Paquda*, 1947, pp. 108–109, and notes.

12. Yāqūt, *Mu'jam al-Udabā*, vol. XVIII, p. 55.
13. Cf. M. Smith, *Rabi'a the Mystic and her Fellow Saints*, Cambridge, 1928.
14. Numerous examples in Mann, *Jews*, vol. II, pp. 270–271.
15. The name Daniel was so common at that time that any attempt at identification with unspecified other persons of that name would be mere guesswork. "Our great pupil, the alluf Daniel" was the representative of the Gaonate in 1152, cf. Asaf, *Letters of Samuel b. 'Eli*, pp. 81–2; Mann, *Texts*, vol. I, pp. 212–33; he *could* be identical with our Daniel, who appears in our document as yet the *son* of his father. On the other hand, an alluf Daniel appears also in 1191 or later, cf. Asaf, *ibid.*, p. 74; Mann, *Texts*, vol. I, pp. 221, n. 45a.
16. Cf. e.g. Samuel B. Hofni's *Letter to the Fez Community*, quoted by Poznanski, *Rivista Israelitica*, vol. V, 1908, p. 134, and Mann, *Texts*, vol. I, p. 150, note 1.
17. Cf. Samuel's letter just quoted. Our letter fully confirms the thesis expounded by Poznanski in *Rivista Israelitica*, namely that the *rosh ha-seder* was not merely a title but an office, that of president of the academy, held as early as talmudic times by such Babylonian scholars as Rav, Shela, and Rav Huna. The *rosh ha-seder* at the time of Benjamin of Tudela's visit (1170) was also the head of the fifth (out of ten) *yeshivot*. Cf. also Asaf, *Letters of Samuel b. 'Eli*, p. 11, n. 7, Mann, *Texts*, vol. I, pp. 386 and 407, and S. Abramson, *Kirjath Sefer*, vol. XXVI, p. 72 sq.
18. He also was, in all likelihood, a high government official; cf. the most illuminating analysis of his thought by D. H. Baneth in *MGWJ*, vol. LXIX (1925), pp. 295–311.
19. Cf. W. J. Fischel, *ibid.*, vol. LXXIX (1935), pp. 302–322.
20. Neubauer, *JQR*, O. S., vol. IX (1897), p. 97, and Dinaburg, *Yisrael ba-Golah*, vol. II, p. 238. Cf. also A. Heschel, *Alexander Marx Jubilee Volume*, II, p. 198. For Elijah's appearance to an earlier Caliph see A. Harkavy, *Berliner Jubilee Volume*, p. 41. (The Neṭira-story, confirmed by al-Masūdī, vol. VIII, pp. 181–2).
21. At the time of Benjamin of Tudela, only 1,000 families lived in Baghdad, if the text is correct.
22. Cf. the data collected by W. J. Fischel concerning the Jewish inspectors of the imperial mint of Baghdad, *Tarbiz*, vol. VIII, p. 236.
23. 'Abd al-Qādir b. 'Abd al-Wafā, *Al-Jawāhir al-Maḍīya fī Tabaqāt al-Ḥanafīya*, Hyderabad, 1332, vol. I, p. 374.
24. As is well known, Maimonides, in his *Iggeret Teman*, fixes the date for this event at 1216 (or 1210, according to the Arabic text, cf. Halkin's new edition, p. 82, note 110), or 40 years after the composition of this letter.
25. Cf. the philosopher Ibn Kammūna's usage in his "Treatise on the Three Religions," *MGWJ*, vol. LXIX, p. 305.
26. *JQR*, O. S., vol. IX (1897), p. 28.
27. That many such deeds were in vogue among the Jews is attested to by a marginal note to Balādhurī, *Futūḥ al-Buldān*, ed. de Goeje, p. 60. Hilāl as-

Ṣābī, in his *Ta'rīkh al-Wuzarā*, p. 67, reports a case of exemption from *jizya* brought up by a Jew before the famous vizier Abū Ḥasan Ibn al-Furāt (908–924) in Baghdad. Yāqūt, *Irshād*, ed. Margoliouth, vol. I, p. 247, cites a similar case from the middle of the 11th century. Such deeds have been found in the Genizah and were much in vogue among the Yemenites. Cf. my paper "Kitāb Dhimmat an-Nabī" in *Kiryat-Sefer*, vol. IX, pp. 507–521 and the subsequent publication of another Yemenite copy in the *David Yellin Jubilee Volume* by J. J. Rivlin

The view that the payment of the poll-tax served as a means of protection to the non-Muslims was expressed by the famous Neṭīra, when the Caliph al-Mu'taḍid (892–902) allegedly offered to exempt the Jews from this tax. Cf. A. Harkavy, *Berliner Jubilee Volume*, p. 36; Hebrew translation, ib., p. 39.

8

Messianic Postures of Ashkenazim and Sephardim

Gerson D. Cohen

Although the subject of my paper is temporally—and to some extent even spatially—far removed from the themes usually discussed under the auspices of this Institute, it will, I trust, not be devoid of interest to students of modern Jewish history and particularly to the broader concerns of the Leo Baeck Institute. As heirs to a long tradition, Jews of our own day consciously and unconsciously give expression to ideas, and reflect patterns of behavior, the roots of which are enmeshed in the depths of the remote past. No better or more obvious example is afforded than by modern Zionism, which through its political, social, and cultural achievements has set Jewish history on an entirely new course. Yet Zionism drew much of its substance and momentum from the traditional Jewish messianic faith, a faith which has been transmitted through the ages.

In examining some of the roots of pre-modern messianism, we must inevitably touch on a second subject, which also is not without interest to us: that is, the Jewish response to pressure and persecution, to alternatives of life through compromise, or of death through steadfastness and martyrdom. For messianism provided the energy and ideological substance for Jewish resistance in a world in which the Jews were always outnumbered and in which they frequently had to contend with unbridled animosity. In scrutinizing some of the forms and circumstances in

Reprinted by permission of Naomi W. Cohen and the Jewish Publication Society from *Studies in the Variety of Rabbinic Cultures*, by Gerson D. Cohen, 1991.

which Jewish ultimate hope was persistently maintained, we offer some humble tribute to the name of the man who for our age was the symbol *par excellence* of Jewish faith in vindication and of steadfast hope while in the very bowels of darkness. To Leo Baeck the *Essence of Judaism* and *This People Israel* meant eternity and ultimate redemption; and to countless of his people Israel, Leo Baeck spelled a hold on faith, hope, justification.

While the Jewish hope for "our Messiah that is yet to come"[1] is so well known as to be a virtual commonplace, close examination of the way this hope was expressed will reveal considerable differences among various Jewish groups. Like any other cultural phenomenon, this religious national dream underwent a certain amount of development and took on many different forms not only in ancient times but throughout the medieval period as well.

To make but brief reference to the earliest messianic movements of the Middle Ages, Near Eastern Jewish messianism found expression in three distinct, and frequently mutually exclusive, types of behavior. The first may be categorized as an elitist-rabbinic-quietist millenarism, which was expressed in the Hebrew apocalyptic tracts that were compiled in Palestine in the first two centuries of the Muslim conquest.[2] Although quite violent in *tone,* these documents paradoxically became vehicles of emotional release for a Jewish ruling class whose interests and program of life led them to renounce all millenarist activity which might upset the smooth and steady functioning of their community. Rabbinism in the Near East realistically channeled messianism into commemorative ritual and into visionary fantasy.[3] At best, the rabbis tolerated the yen of some Jews to settle in the Holy Land, but the extremely restricted extent of such settlement betrays the true nature of the elitist-rabbinic messianic posture. Israel was to hope and to be ready for the end, but it was not to anticipate it. We shall see that while later rabbinic authorities of Europe played several variations on this theme, their policy and programs were basically identical with that of the elitist elements of Palestine and Babylonia.

The second type of messianic expression in the Near East consisted of popular uprisings under leaders, who, on occasion, combined aggressive military action with extreme pietism or sectarian innovation.[4] While the military programs of each of these visionaries were nipped in the bud, the leaders of these uprisings were able to begin their movements by generating local popular sentiment to white heat, thereby inducing many to follow them into battle, flee to the desert, dispose of their possessions and subsequently, even after defeat, to organize themselves into loyal fellowships that became known as distinct sects. What is revealing about their respective fates is not that they encountered the quick and determined opposition of the Muslim government, but that the gentile overlords found willing allies in the rabbinic authorities themselves, who helped eliminate these dissidents as active threats to the peace and well-being of the Jewish community.

The third type of messianic expression can be conveniently subsumed under the rubric of mature Karaism. While the extent of the messianic orientation of Ananism and early Karaism is a matter of considerable scholarly dispute, the Palestinocentricism of later Qumisian Karaism is not subject to question.[5] Indeed, it has been recently, and I believe plausibly, argued that the renowned mourners of Zion, far from having been one of the elements which Karaism drew upon, were actually an outgrowth of the new schism, which incorporated settlement in the Holy Land, and/or extreme mourning for its desolation and subjection, into its ideology as one of the pivots of its anti-Rabbanite orientation.[6] Be that as it may, the messianic posture of Karaism is best understood not as pure messianic activism but as a compromise between the extreme quietism of the Rabbanite elite and the explosive activism of fringe groups in the Iraquian and Persian Jewish community. Daniel al-Qumisi's brand of messianism—settling in Palestine and hastening the end of time by wailing and weeping over the destruction and the Dispersion—was a new form of nomian quietism, a carefully harnessed pre-millenarism, which gratified and yet controlled the hopes of restive and disaffected masses.

These salient types of messianic posture in the Near East afford us considerable insight into the variety of forms of Jewish messianism on the Continent of Europe. As is well known, the two branches of medieval Jewish culture—namely the Andalusian-Spanish, or Sephardic, and the Franco-German, or Ashkenazic—trace their cultural parentage to Babylonia and Palestine, the early Sephardic drawing almost exclusively on Babylonian books and teachings, the Ashkenazic deriving much of its heritage from Palestine. What was true of *halakah*, philosophy, liturgy, poetry and Hebrew style had its counterpart in messianic posture and expression as well.

If we survey the history of messianic activity and speculation in Europe, we are immediately confronted with several striking differences in the manifestation of this faith between Andalusian and Spanish Jewry, on the one hand, and Franco-German or Ashkenazic Jewry on the other. In the first place, we must note the remarkable phenomenon that while between c. 1065–1492 there were close to a dozen messianic pretenders —and I include under that category men who claimed only to herald the Messiah—in Andalus, Christian Spain, and North Africa, there is not a single unequivocal instance of such activity among Franco-German Jewry.[7] The only apparent exception was a messianic movement, which Maimonides reported to have taken place c. 1065 in the city of Linon in Ifranja, or the land of the Franks.[8] While most scholars have identified this place as Lyons, France, I believe there are cogent reasons to locate the incident in Leon of Christian Spain, which Arab geographers also called the Land of the Franks, and with which the Jews of Andalus did have relatively easy and indeed direct contact.

It may not be inappropriate to mention here that just shortly before this messianic incident, the descendants of the Babylonian exilarch, Hezekiah, had moved from Andalus to Christian Spain, while one of them, the renowned Hiyya al-Daudi, was buried in the land of Leon c. 1150.[9] Whether there was any connection between the appearance of these Davidides in the north and the messianic incident reported by Maimonides, we, of course, have no way of knowing. But the fact that all of our information on this family comes from Andalusian sources strengthens our feeling that the Linon mentioned in Maimonides' *Epistle* to *Yemen* is to be identified with the Leon of Spain. While from the point of view of an Andalusian like Maimonides, the Jews living there were dwelling among Franks, the contiguity of the northern Spanish community to Andalusian culture makes it highly likely that the incident was fomented by a Jew or Jews very much under the influence of Judeo-Arabic culture. The incident is probably a case of Sephardic messianism, not French.

The location of other instances of messianic activity in Spain is far less equivocal.[10] Some forty years after the incident in Linon-Leon (i.e., c. 1105), a certain Ibn Aryeh in Cordova was designated as the Messiah after astrological signs were interpreted to point to the year, the place, and the man. Some fifteen to twenty years after that, a Moroccan Jew, who had been educated in Lucena under Rabbi Joseph ibn Megash, stirred up a messianic affair in Fez. The incident had repercussions in Spain, of which Morocco was culturally a branch, for the father of

Maimonides tried desperately to stop people from following his lead. Why there should have been three such incidents in relatively rapid succession, I shall try to explain later on.

The rabbinic authorities of Spain rebuffed Abraham Abulafia, a prophet of Avila, a pretender of Ayllon, and perhaps one or two other would-be messiahs in the latter part of the thirteenth century. Whatever the extent of their adherents, these messiahs and their followers were all Spaniards.

Throughout this period, no segment of Ashkenazic Jewry is known to have risen in messianic revolt. Indeed, we may go even further and say that there is not a single case of a messianic movement or of a pseudo-messiah known from Ashkenazic Jewry until the beginning of the sixteenth century, and even that one instance, namely the call of Asher Laemmlein, is an obscure and short-lived affair, which shows traces of Sephardic influence on the mind of an Ashkenazic Jew.[11]

On the other hand, again, the great messianic ferment after the expulsion from Spain, which was expressed in a variety of ways—in Abravanel's tracts, in the great attempts of David Reubeni and Solomon Molko, in the millenarian activity of the kabbalists of Safed, and finally in the first real *mass* messianic movement that swept all strata of the Jewish population off their feet, that of Sabbatai Ṣevi—emanated from and found greatest support in the Sephardic elements of Jewry.[12] To be sure, even the Sephardic messianic attempts were few and far removed from each other, but surely it is a matter of no mean interest that whatever messianic activity occurred in Western Europe almost entirely emanated from one corner of occidental Jewry.

I trust that my remarks will not be misconstrued to mean that there were never any messianic movements elsewhere. The surprises held in store for us moderns in the arcana of the Cairo Geniza have been too rich and revolutionary in their revelations to deny that new instances will not yet turn up. Indeed, from the Geniza, we have learned of two messianic incidents in Byzantium, c. 1096, and in Sicily, at a time which has not yet been definitely determined.[13] But in the first place, each of these two communities had cultural affinities with the East and Spain respectively. Moreover, they seem to have been isolated incidents of hysteria that left no impression in Jewish literature. The basic classification we have laid down, that messianic activity in Europe was essentially of Babylonian-Spanish vintage, still holds true.

In this connection we must repeat the findings of sober scholarly analysis that another seeming exception to our generalization is reflected by the migration of several hundred rabbis from France and Germany to the Holy Land in 1210 and 1211. That event, however, does not constitute an exception at all, for the migrants betrayed little, if any, messianic activity. Certainly they made no move to carry masses of Jews along with them. The migration, which probably did not number the hundreds of whom later chroniclers wrote, seems to have been motivated by general considerations of piety rather than by millenarist anticipations.[14]

This is as we should expect, for messianic acts in Europe no less than in Asia were usually undertaken without rabbinic sanction. Those rabbis of Spain from whom we do have opinions, like the Geonim before them, in their charitable moments looked on messiahs as sadly deluded men, or more probably, downright impostors. There is no reason to believe that in this regard at least, the rabbis of France and Germany were any different from those of Babylonia, Spain, and North Africa. In other words, messianic activity in Europe was, as it had been in the East, a manifestation of popular revolt against what the millenarists considered "the establishment."[15]

Although, as far as we can determine, the attitudes of the Sephardic and Ashkenazic rabbinates to popular messianic uprisings were basically identical, there were some notable differences in the way the two Jewish elites gave expression to the traditional messianic hope. Among the many differences in the type of literary productivity which emanated from Sephardic and Ashkenazic circles, and these embrace differences in approach to, and expression of, the Hebrew language, exegesis, halakic codification, writing in the vernacular, belles-lettres, science, and philosophy, we must also include the genre of messianic speculation. While in Spain messianism appears constantly to have been on the agenda of scholarly exchange and to have evoked a whole string of messianic tracts, such discussion was extremely limited in medieval France and Germany and has left only the faintest traces in literature.

By way of documentation, perhaps it is best to begin this aspect of our survey with Ashkenaz, which until the sixteenth century produced no original messianic literature whatever. This startling phenomenon stands out in much bolder relief if we examine closely the nature of those literary traces of early messianic speculation in France and Germany that have come down to us. Actually, they amount in sum total to three fragmentary statements and one exegetical work. The first consists of a late tenth-century (906) query from the sages of the Rhineland to the academy of the Holy Land concerning the expected date of the messianic redemption. The inquiry, Professor Marx has suggested, was evoked not by any spontaneous messianic ferment but by the text of the "Apocalypse of Zerubbabel" which had by that time gained a quasi-official status and which seemed to point to a date close at hand.[16] In other words, the logic of a text, not the independent research of a learned group, stimulated curiosity. No less significant is the fact that the inquiry seems to have been a brief one and was appended to a second question concerning the criteria for disqualifying ritually slaughtered meat. The text gives not the faintest trace of any real messianic awakening.

The second Ashkenazic literary manifestation of any overt interest in messianism is Rashi's commentaries to the Book of Daniel and the Talmud, in which he indicated that the Messiah was to be expected in 1352 or in 1478.[17] However, Rashi's conclusions, far from betraying an avid expectation of the messianic redemption, actually lend support to our contention. Rashi's dates were nothing more than an exegete's elucidation of texts, which he interpreted with no greater emphasis than he had the rest of the vast corpus of Scripture and the Talmud. He could not very well have skipped over these particular passages in Daniel and the Talmud. But there is a far more revealing point about Rashi's interpretations, which excludes them from the genre of genuine messianic speculation. If there is one characteristic that underlies two thousand years of messianic literature from the Book of Danial in the second century B.C.E. to the commentary of Rabbi Meir Leibush Malbim in the nineteenth century C.E., it is the relative imminence of the messianic denouement. The function of messianic tracts is to alert and console the audience in the context of contemporary events, not by postponing comfort to the remote future, which the author's audience could not have the faintest hope of living to see and enjoy. Far from being messianically oriented, Rashi's commentary, by postponing the end some three or four centuries, was the very antithesis of millenarist excitation.

How quiescent Franco-German Jewry really was may be seen from the reports of several authors that the Messiah was expected to come sometime between Tishri of 1084 and Tishri of 1103, or in the 256th cycle of creation. The date was derived from a word in Jeremiah 31:6: "For thus saith the Lord: Sing [*ronnu*] with gladness for Jacob and shout at the head of the nations; announce ye, praise ye, and say: 'O Lord, save thy people, the remnant of Israel.' " However, this calculation did not make its way into Ashkenazic *literature* until considerably after it had failed to materialize. What is more, even this messianic symbol seems to have come to Ashkenazic circles from the outside, for the Jews of France and Germany apparently first became aware of it through the *Leqaḥ Tob,* in which Rabbi Tobiah ben Eliezer of Castoria had recorded this date as his own discovery.[18] Now, Rabbi Tobiah was a Byzantine, not an Ashkenazi. Moreover, as we have already indicated, the messianic ferment in Salonica and its environs at the time of the First Crusade, with which this messianic date was connected, was a local and ephemeral affair which was confined to visions and miraculous manifestations that had no repercussions, and the stimulus for which is to be sought outside the Jewish community itself. But whatever the case, the event betrays no sign of having been connected with a general messianic ferment in the Jewish communities of the world or of having been inspired by other Jewish messianic incidents.

A rash of messianic predictions did begin to crop up, almost dramatically, in France and Germany in the twelfth and thirteenth centuries in the circles of the Tosafists and German mystical pietists. However, what is revealing about this wave of speculation is the nature of the predictions and the extent to which they were communicated. Interestingly enough, much of the Tosafistic-pietistic messianic speculation is communicated to us second-hand, that is to say not by the speculators themselves but by reporters who heard of their statements. Thus, Rabbi Joseph Bekhor Shor cites the Spaniard Abraham bar Ḥiyya for his computation, while Rabbi Isaac ben Judah ha-Levi invokes the authority of Rabbi Joseph and of the biblical commentary known as *Sefer ha-Gan.*[19] The derivative character of the messianic communications of the pietists is even more apparent in a little messianic excursus inserted into a thirteenth-century commentary on the *Ethics of the Fathers* by an as yet not fully identified member of the German pietist school.[20] What this little parenthesis affords us is a report of messianic computations made by the author's father, a certain Rabbi Solomon, and the latter's teachers and colleagues. Most prominent among them are the renowned Rabbi Judah of Paris, Rabbi Samuel he-Ḥasid and his son Rabbi Judah he-Ḥasid, Rabbi Isaac of Dampierre, Rabbi Ezra the prophet of Montcontour, and Rabbi Troestlin the prophet. Mention is also made of a certain book of visions or visionaries, *Sefer ha-Ḥozim,* from which the astrological signs associated with the advent of the messianic era are cited.[21] Apart from these few instances, and they are decidedly not evidence of a messianic literature of the kind we encounter from Spain, there has come down no real messianic literary genre from France and Germany. To the contrary, the few fragments that have survived from Ashkenaz testify to speculation that was conducted esoterically, in the confines of a very restricted circle. Most important, we have no evidence of any communal reverberations of messianic speculation in France or Germany. The only trace of some wider echo of these computations is from a letter written in Arabic, in other words from an oriental or Andalusian area, to the community of Alexandria. This letter tells us of reports arriving from Marseille and from France generally to Qabes in Tunis of the arrival of Elijah, expected sometime after 1225/6, and of the coming to the Messiah in 1232/33. Among those reported to have verified the prophecies, which the late Professor Assaf conjectured were uttered by Rabbi Ezra of Montcontour, was the renowned Rabbi Eleazar Rokeaḥ.[22] At best, then, we have in this letter the echo of an isolated incident. Nevertheless, careful analysis of some of the circumstances surrounding these prophecies of the Franco-German pietists will once again serve to place the nature of the far different Spanish messianic activity in bolder relief.

The most salient characteristic of the messianic predictions of the Franco-German rabbis is the prophetic character of the informants and of their information. Thus, two of the pietists mentioned in the little German appendix, Rabbi Ezra and Rabbi Troestlin, are specifically called prophets.[23] Rabbi Ezra of Montcontour was reported to have ascended to Heaven and determined the date of the end by consulting with Haggai, Zechariah, and Malachi. Rabbi Samuel and Rabbi Judah, the pietists, and Rabbi Meir ben Baruk of Rothenberg ascertained the date of the end through information imparted in dreams.[24] It hardly needs belaboring that such messianic calculation as well as the title of prophet were distinctly alien to the Sephardic rabbinic temper. Indeed, the only upper-class Spaniard who was openly recognized as a prophet, Rabbi Sheshet Benveniste of Barcelona, was a product of the French academy of Narbonne.[25] One need but recall the reception that Abraham Abulafia reports he received and Rabbi Solomon Ibn Adret's fulminations against would-be prophets to appreciate the vast difference between the Sephardic and Ashkenazic ways of eschatological speculation.

To be sure, there are points in common in the detailed explanation of messianic dates of the Sephardim and Ashkenazim. Both groups, for example, worked with *gematriaot* (cryptographs) and with symmetrical periodizations of Jewish history. However, here again there is a thin, but quite palpable, line that divides them. Whereas in Sephardic calculations the *gematriaot* play an ancillary role, and are usually invoked as vital only for points in the remote past, in Franco-German calculations the *gematriaot* are central to the calculation and as often as not point to the future, to the denouement of history. For example, the Sephardim frequently cited Talmudic mnemonics, but these were always invoked as classically attested dates or hints, and only as *part* of a much wider exposition on messianic calculation.[26]

In the case of the Ashkenazic computations, the *gematriaot* are often quite novel and point to the exact date of the end of the present stage of history: for example, "Sing *[ronnu]* with gladness for Jacob" (Jeremiah 31:6), as pointing to the 256th cycle of creation (1084–1103); or "My beloved is white and ruddy" (Song of Songs 5:10), as referring to the year 1238 C.E.; or "I will keep . . . hidden" *[haster astir]* (Deuteronomy 31:18), as being equal to 1335 years in Daniel 12:12; and so on.[27]

Now the modern student, to whom *gematria*-style thinking is so basically alien, may easily be tempted to lump Spanish and Franco-German *gematriaot* into one medieval bag. But in reality, there is a chasm dividing them. As traditional Jews, the Spaniards invoked *gematriaot* that had been formulated by their rabbinic forebears. However, the German mystics took the ancient *gematriaot* as a hint that all of classical Jewish literature—the Bible as well as the liturgy—was worded in accordance with the principles of *gematria.* Accordingly, they were forever coming up with new *gematriaot,* thus extending to messianic calculation the methods they employed in their liturgical devotions.

To a certain extent, it is true, the new tendencies in Ashkenazic messianic calculation may also be discerned in thirteenth-century Spanish kabbalistic circles, notably in the writings of Nahmanides and especially in the works of Abraham Abulafia and the Zohar. These Spanish circles are notorious for the new techniques of substitutions of letters and words of equal numerical values which they employed for mystical theosophy and messianic calculation.[28] However, it is hardly an accident that the first Sephardim to employ these characteristically Ashkenazic techniques were those dwelling in Christian Spain at the very time when the influence of Ashkenazic literature and orientations had made significant inroads into Spain. The men of Spain who indulged in these typically Franco-German interpretations of texts were people who had been subjected to much influence from areas beyond the Pyrenees and who attempted to integrate the wisdom of Ashkenaz with the legacy of Andalus. These were the very times and the very same areas in which the controversy over the works of Maimonides was inflaming Jewish passions as a consequence of the Ashkenazic challenge from Provence and France. Ashkenazic fundamentalism had gained ground in many respectable areas in Spain, and even some fine Sephardim had more or less absorbed the northern temper.

But the new cross-influences were by no means unilateral, for the men, academies, and literature of Spain had a deep impact on Ashkenazic leadership. Whatever the source of Provençal and Franco-German mysticism, it is significant that this speculation north of the Pyrenees was undertaken largely by man who had either studied in Spain or had access to Sephardic literature and especially to the works of Saadiah and Maimonides. I am not suggesting that Franco-German pietism drew its inspiration from Spain; what I do contend is that these circles did have access to Andalusian literature and reflected the effects of some of its seminal ideas. And among the Sephardic preoccupations which could easily have excited the pietists of Ashkenaz and stimulated them to further speculation was the authentically Jewish concern with the date of the messianic redemption. In other words, even the brief messianic ferment among the pietists of Ashkenaz probably drew much of its inspiration from Sepharad. How crucial the influence of the Andalusian Maimonides was on the messianic computations of the Ashkenazim may be seen from the way the French pietists cited legends about Maimonides and Arabs in support of their calculations.[29] Maimonides' *Epistle to Yemen* came to Provence no later than 1215, and though the work was not translated into Hebrew until at least a decade later,[30] it may well be that its messianic calculation had made its way northward even before Ibn Tibbon released a Hebrew version. In short, France and Germany had little by way of an indigenous tradition of messianic speculation, and this tradition, to the extent that it did exist, had few literary or public reverberations.

By way of contrast, Andalus had a long, continuous, and, what is most important, public tradition of messianic calculation. Beginning with Abraham bar Ḥiyya's *Megillat ha-Megalleh* down to Isaac Abravanel's *Mashmi'a Yeshu'ah, Ma'ayenay ha-Yeshu'ah,* and *Yeshu'at Meshiḥo,* the date of the Messiah was forever being discussed publicly and with an originality of approach in each new work that puts this whole body of literature on an entirely different plane from the fragments deriving from Franco-German circles. Circa 1125, Abraham bar Ḥiyya calculated the advent of the messianic age from several points of view: from the account of creation in Genesis, from the Torah as a whole, from astrological signs, and from an exegetical analysis of Daniel. In other words, he used what a medieval man recognized as strictly empirical data. Now, although Abraham bar Ḥiyya's tract is the first full-scale discussion is Spain of the date of the Messiah, there is ample evidence that his was not the first public conjecture on the messianic end in the rabbinic circles of Andalus. Abraham ibn Ezra reports that Solomon ibn Gabirol early in the eleventh century had also invoked astrological data to predict the end, while not much earlier Samuel ibn Nagrela had infuriated the Muslim Ibn Ḥazm by contending that he was himself a fulfillment of the messianic promise "until Shiloh come." If we recall that not much earlier (c. 950) Ḥisdai ibn Shaprut was said to have written to Joseph, King of the Khazars, and to have inquired, among other things, whether the Khazar monarch had any trustworthy information on the date of the messianic end, we begin to realize that Abraham bar Ḥiyya's work was perhaps the first systematic treatise and the climax of several generations of speculation, but by no means the inauguration of a totally new genre.

Indeed, five of Abraham bar Ḥiyya's contemporaries, some of them far removed from one another, testify to the extent of the elitist but open discussion in Andalus of the probable date of the fulfillment of the messianic promise. Judah ben Barzillay of Barcelona, though he was opposed to astrological calculation, reaffirmed the tenability of other methods of calculation based on older rabbinic schemes of discerning the fulfillment of history.[31] At approximately the same time Judah ha-Levi expressed in poetry the general grief that the Messiah had not come at the date popularly believed to be the time of the end (1069), and then proceeded to recount his own vision of the imminent fulfillment of another classically attested rabbinic promise.[32] A Jewish prophecy of the age, predicting on astrological grounds the beginning of the messianic era for 1186–87, made its way into Christian circles and has been preserved in Latin.[33] At about the same time, Maimon the Dayyan imparted to his children a tradition which he had received from his father—that the messianic age would be initiated with the reinstitution of prophecy around 1210 or 1216. Although his son Moses Maimonides, in his renowned *Epistle to Yemen,* protested vigorously against public speculation on the date of the end and obliquely criticized others for doing so, he himself proceeded in good Andalusian fashion to report and explain the tradition he had received from his father.[34] Shortly after Maimonides had written his *Epistle,* Abraham ibn Daud of Toledo wrote a series of works in each of which he vigorously reaffirmed the traditional messianic faith. My own investigation into Ibn Daud's work has led me to the conclusion that his historiography was in reality a thinly disguised trilogy, the real purpose of which was to reassure the learned classes that the messianic age would soon be inaugurated by great upheavals in Spain in 1188–89. In other words, far from being objective historiography, Ibn Daud's works deserve to be reckoned among the Sephardic works dealing at least in part with eschatology.[35]

Before going any further with examples of Spanish literature in this vein, it would be well to pause and recapitulate some of the features of this learned Sephardic messianology. Apart from the fact that this speculation was conducted quite out in the open with little practical regard for the rabbinic injunction against messianic speculation, the conjectured dates are reported to us at first hand—that is, by the speculators themselves. What is more, without indulging in apocalyptic fantasy, the Sephardim created or revived eschatology as a Jewish literary genre. Far more important, Spanish calculations were derived not by mystical techniques but by means of rationalist exegesis either of Scripture or of rabbinic traditions. This point must be underscored, for just as Franco-German speculation constituted an extension of the literary canons of German pietism to messianology, so, too, the Spanish calculations were made in consonance with the general *weltanschauung* of the Andalusian elite.

It is noteworthy that every one of the names I have mentioned in connection with Sephardic messianic calculation is known to us as a protagonist of the distinctly Andalusian Jewish way of life, and is associated with the golden age of Spanish Jewish creativity. Rationalism, science, philosophy, and Hebrew classicism were the hallmarks of this group. Superstition and non-rational exegesis were anathema to them all. Indeed, much of their intellectual energy was expended in reinterpreting into rational categories what they regarded as the embarrassing legacy of miracles, anthropomorphisms, and trivial stories of their classical literature. Hence, they would have little truck with apocalyptic fantasy. Accordingly, it is not surprising to discern in their writings an effort to calculate the end by the movements of the stars or by rhythmic periodizations of history. Having been trained in philosophy, they regarded the universe and human history as mechanisms or organisms, the functioning of which had been committed by the Creator to immutable laws. Built into these mechanisms as part of the law of their operation they postulated laws of time which would—in the fullness of time—catapult the elect segment of the cosmos—indeed, the world at large—into a happier and more harmonious course. Since it was all a question of a particular manifestation of the laws of nature, fixed by God, to be sure, but capable of rational analysis nonetheless, if one could but permeate the complex secrets of the essential part of the machine or organism, one could determine when its course would change.

Accordingly, in the view of the Sephardim, the key to the secret of the destiny of Israel lay not in ecstatic ascents to Heaven for revelations by angelic powers, who would inform men whether the Almighty had decided that the Jews had had enough; rather, it lay in a study and proper understanding of God's books of laws—the Bible and the Talmud—and of their prerequisites, logic, mathematics, physics, astronomy, metaphysics, and history. Sephardic messianology was harmoniously blended with philosophy and a rationalist approach to life.

While eschatology obviously bespeaks an intense yearning for national redemption and rebirth—and the predominance of this longing in Andalusian Hebrew poetry is too well known to be belabored here—the two, the prayer for redemption and messianic speculation, were by no means synonymous. Jews have prayed for the sound of the horn of redemption since ancient times, but relatively few gave way to the temptation to permeate the heavenly veil concealing the secret of the time appointed for the end. Indeed, there were strong religious injunctions inhibiting the Jews against giving vent to their impatience or against revealing what they believed to be the appointed time. The open speculation of the philosophers of Spain, however well intentioned and however well precedented by earlier generations, was not likely to appeal to meticulous adherents of classical rabbinic teachings. Even Maimonides had qualms about divulging the tradition he had inherited on this score.

And if a philosopher felt squeamish about such speculation, how much more so would a penitent like Judah ha-Levi have felt about men who enter areas strictly forbidden to them![36]

Viewed from this perspective, Judah ha-Levi's apparently messianic act of leaving Spain for Palestine was not a logical conclusion of Andalusian messianism but a total rejection of it. His decision, it will be recalled, was taken only after the rationalist system in which he had been reared had, in his estimation, broken down. The rabbi in ha-Levi's *Kuzari* and Judah ha-Levi in his later poems rejected, bag and baggage, the whole mechanistic view of the universe which had become the regnant view of life in the circles of the Spanish-Jewish upper classes. It is no coincidence that the very work of medieval Jewish philosophy that reaffirmed in unequivocal terms the traditional forms of Jewish faith—the superiority of Israel, the uniqueness of the Holy Land, the mystery of prophecy—offered no solace in the form of a messianic prediction. The *Kuzari* suggested no date for the Messiah, for such speculation had become alien to a man who had reappropriated Talmudic faith in God's Providence. The Almighty would act in His good time; man's task was but to try to earn His mercy. Judah ha-Levi's departure for Palestine was an act in that direction and nothing more. Far from attempting to anticipate the Messiah, ha-Levi's move was a rejection of the Sephardic culture of his day; it was a Franco-German-type act of piety that committed all into the hands of a free and inscrutable God.

One of the factors that doubtless helped ha-Levi rationalize his latter-day negative evaluation of Andalusian Jewish culture was the wide currency which a second type of Sephardic messianic speculation, totally at variance with the predominant Sephardic eschatological schools, had gained in his environment. Grounding its views in a scientific study of Scripture, this school of exegesis denied whole blocs of biblical messianic lore as valid sources of hope or prediction for the future. The three names associated with this type of exegesis are Moses ha-Kohen ibn Gikatilla and Judah ibn Bala'am, of the eleventh century, and Ḥayyim Galipapa of the fourteenth. From Nahmanides' and Abravanel's reports, it would seem that a fourth name is to be added to this list, namely that of Abraham ibn Ezra of the twelfth century. In reality, they were by no means the only skeptics of Spain.

The view shared by all these exegetes was that the messianic prophecies in the Bible could not be interpreted eschatologically. Rather, these visions were to be understood as exhortations and predictions that the prophets had intended for immediate fulfillment. Indeed, study of history convinced these rationalists that these prophecies had been fulfilled in the days of Hezekiah and especially in the early days of the Second Temple. Whether the prophecies were *ad hoc* predictions or merely sermons *ex eventu,* they could not serve as sources of hope to the Jews of the Middle Ages, for their capital had run out long since. These men, it should be emphasized, did not deny the validity of the messianic dogma; they affirmed it as a rabbinic tradition only, not as a legacy of Scripture. However, there can be little doubt that many in Spain regarded the messianic reaffirmation of these exegetes as mere lip service, as formal concessions to the requirements of official piety. With the undermining of the Scriptural foundations for faith in the messianic redemption, to many a thinking person the messianic dogma seemed to rest on thin air.

To Judah ha-Levi the skepticism engendered by this school of thought was only one or two steps removed from the rationalism that saw in Scripture the clues to the mathematics of the Divine economy. Nor was he wrong, for, in its own way, the more tradition-oriented rationalism had also conceded its embarrassment with some of the graphic promises of miraculous upheaval and had thereby added fuel to the fire of doubt and even despair. The outstanding literary expression to the watered-down traditionalist view, the writings of Moses Maimonides, appeared long after ha-Levi's death, but the views Maimonides expressed on the subject were well known in Spain much earlier. Far from innovating in this respect, Maimonides' attenuation of certain traditional messianic hopes betrays how widespread the skepticism had become, had indeed permeated even the highest rabbinic circles.[37] Thus, whether Maimonides had really meant originally to eliminate the doctrine of the resurrection—one of the cardinal promises vouchsafed for the messianic era—from his creed of Judaism, and substitute for it the more philosophically fashionable doctrine of immortality, is a matter on which latter-day Maimunists and anti-Maimunists are still divided. What is beyond question is that Maimonides and many of his disciples considered the promises of resurrection and even of the messianic deliverance far less important than the more rationally acceptable assurance of immortality. Moreover, in his *Guide of the Perplexed,* Maimonides made it very clear that he considered many of the miraculous portents foretold by the prophets for the messianic age mere figures of speech that had not been meant literally. From this last position he never retreated, and even in his legal magnum opus, he indicated that he was not committed to belief in their literal fulfillment.[38]

Maimonides, of course, was in the first instance the great spokesman of an intelligentsia that was bent on restructuring all of Jewish education and indeed even community life on rationalist principles. While the Maimunist controversy in the thirteenth century was soon focused on the question of allegorical interpretations of the ritual commandments and the study of philosophy as the source of all evil within the Jewish community, it should not be forgotten that the first signs of protest against the *Guide* were evinced by Arabically cultured Jews who were astounded at the flippancy with which Maimonides had treated the promise of resurrection.[39] And the promise of resurrection, be it not overlooked, is the central rabbinic motif in its representation of the messianic promise. These protesters sensed, quite rightly, that an authoritative rabbinic license to gloss over the resurrection struck at the root and the heart of the Jewish messianic faith.

While Maimonides' orthodoxy was vindicated, the continued extreme skepticism in the camp of the Andalusian intelligentsia on the meaning of messianic doctrines gave renewed stimulus to the traditionalists to add to the corpus of Spanish eschatological literature. In the thirteenth century, Moses Nahmanides defended the integrity of the traditional messianic faith not only in his commentary on the Pentateuch, but in a special treatise on the messianic redemption, as well as in his Hebrew summary of the disputation of Barcelona in 1263. While recapitulating many of the older arguments, Nahmanides' treatise on redemption reflects the newer emphasis of the rabbinic circles of which he was a member on *gematriaot,* thereby providing a bridge between the Franco-German computations and the indigenously Andalusian literary genre. In the middle of the fourteenth century, when Abner of Burgos shook the Jewish community of Spain by his apostasy, and then proceeded to rationalize his defection by eschatological arguments, his Porphyrian-like exegesis of Daniel evoked a vigorous denunciation coupled with a defense of traditional messianism on exegetical grounds by Rabbi Joseph Shalom.[40] That the eschatological debate, provoked by continued skepticism in upper-class circles, remained alive may be seen in the vigorous reaffirmation of Hasdai Crescas, the equivocal acceptance of Joseph

Albo, and the compendious recapitulations of the whole question by Don Isaac Abravanel. Thus, a second source of Spanish eschatology was a widespread skepticism over messianic articles of faith, of which we have no evidence from Ashkenazic circles, and which prompted Sephardic traditionalists to speculate on the end of history in much the same way that rationalist Andalusians had done much earlier.

Having seen that underneath the consistent rabbinic opposition to messianic movements there was a vast difference between the rabbis of the Sephardim and of the Ashkenazim in their treatment of the traditional messianic dogma, the question that commands our attention is whether there is any discernible relationship between elitist expression and the behavior of the laity. Given the rabbinic renunciation of any precipitous messianic behavior, is it nevertheless possible to correlate Spanish intellectual expression with the messianic behavior of occasionally rebellious Spanish laity and the French rabbinic posture with the behavior of French-Jewish masses?

It will be noted that in posing the question this way, we have quite deliberately sought to account for particular messianic postures in the psyche of the Jews themselves rather than in any external or objective set of circumstances. For, if there is any one conclusion that the data force upon us, it is that, contrary to the popular impression, there is no discernible connection between persecution and messianic movements. Jewish messianic movements were not "the religion of the oppressed."[41] The Crusades, the Almohade invasion, the expulsions from England and France, the blood libels, the Pastoureaux onslaughts, and the persecutions at the time of the Black Death, indeed, even the expulsion from Spain and the Chmelnitzki massacres did not generate a single messianic movement. Conversely, all the messianic efforts made in Iraq and Persia, and above all in Spain and North Africa, were undertaken in areas and periods of relative stability. Active messianism or quiescence must have derived from sources other than political or economic. If Franco-German Jewry produced neither a messianic pretender nor a messianic literature, it must be because quiescence and passivity had somehow so permeated the whole mentality of that community as virtually to eliminate such aggressive behavior. Doubtless fear of failure and reprisal played a major role; but hysteria is often strong enough to overcome realistic considerations and we must, accordingly, seek other explanations.

Perhaps the explanations I shall suggest will be a bit more cogent if we revert to the contrast afforded by the data from Spain. Intellectual activism in the form of open speculation on the date of the end by the intellectual elite was paralleled by occasional unbridled eruptions of Jews who could not wait. Activism of two kinds, literary and physical, seems to have permeated Spain much more than France and Germany. But it was a peculiar form of activism, quite unlike the military-sectarian ventures known from Babylonia. In Spain this activism consisted in reading the signs of the times independently of rabbinic authorities and then proceeding to announce miraculous portents and the advent of the redemption. It was, paradoxically enough, Spanish traditionalist rationalism carried to its logical end by the acting out of what Spanish rabbis had merely contemplated. Put differently, it was the translation of the theory of the elite into acts of popular piety. The announcement of a miracle or portent could induce credulous groups of ingenuous believers to divest themselves of their wealth and assemble in readiness for the great deliverance. Conversely, the intellectual quietism of the rabbis of Ashkenaz, motivated in the first instance by religious injunctions against calculating the date of the Messiah, doubtless percolated outward and downward to the laity and lower strata of society and inhibited them from attempting to alter their destiny.

However, in reality, this explanation only pushes the problem back a step. The fact is that the rabbis of Spain, no less than those of France and Germany, advocated political quietism, and both groups of leaders grounded their stance in very much the same classical rabbinic sources. Given the basic uniformity of the classical rabbinic tradition in Spain and France and Germany, what in Jewish culture oriented the one group to intellectual or physical activism and the other to a basic passivity? In the first instance, it seems to me, we must go back to the particular cultural roots of each of the two branches. Ever since the downfall of Bar Kokhba, Palestinian Jewry had politically been fairly quiescent. Its leadership released deep emotions of hostility and hope in prayer, poetry, and apocalyptic literature. But as custodians of the *Pax Romana* in Palestine, the patriarchate and the rabbinate taught submissiveness and acceptance of the Divine decree until the Almighty should intervene in history and restore His people. This basic attitude of submission permeated even the ostensibly explosive literature of Palestinian mysticism and apocalypticism. As in the case of Daniel of old, so, too, in later apocalyptic literature, while the visionary is reassured of Divine vengeance against the Gentiles, he is no less emphatically enjoined to wait for the deliverance of God. In the meantime, he may take comfort in violent and bloody fantasies that will one day become a reality. In other words, far from inciting to riot, apocalyptic literature actually tranquilized and served as a release, a channel by means of which excess emotions were syphoned off. So it was in the case of the Dead Sea sect and the early Christians; so it was in Roman and medieval Palestine.

This attitude and posture were doubtless conveyed to all parts of the Diaspora over which the academies of the Holy Land exercised influence. It is not surprising, therefore, that when in 960 the elders of the Rhineland sent their two inquiries to the Holy Land—on the date of the Messiah and the laws of *terefot*—they were roundly rebuffed on the first question: "You are unworthy of a reply concerning the advent of the Messiah. Do you not trust the words of the sages and the signs which they provided? These have not yet been fulfilled." The mere question was an affront, a violation of religious propriety.

How much the Franco-German spirit owed to its Palestinian progenitor is also reflected in some of the forms surrounding Ashkenazic messianic speculation. Like its Palestinian apocalyptic models, which circulated in France and Germany as early as the tenth century, Ashkenazic calculation depended largely on information gleaned in the course of mystical ascents to the heavens, where a prophet or angel disclosed the secret.

The quietism of the Palestinian-Ashkenazic branch was given its endorsement by the tenth-century Italian paraphrase of Josephus in Hebrew, *Sefer Yosifon*. The major burden of the work was to demonstrate that the Zealots, the lawless ones of Israel who had tried to defy the Divine decree which had installed the fourth empire as mistress of the world, had brought incalculable misery and suffering on their people. Conversely, the righteous of old willingly accepted their fate of martyrdom, confident in the fulfillment of the promises of the great illumination and the resurrection which were vouchsafed for them. What Josephus had failed to convey to his people in Aramaic and Greek, a pseudepigrapher now avidly embraced in Hebrew, and his authority as an authentic interpreter of Jewish history was widely acknowledged.[42]

Spain, on the other hand, modeled itself largely on Babylonian paradigms. From Baghdad it had received not only Gaonic responsa, a translation of and commentaries on the Bible in Arabic and legal codes, but also the guidelines for a Jewish philosophy, and to a large extent the foundations of their own *weltanschauung* and *paideia*. Like the Babylonians in Babylonia, the Sephardim in Andalus became extremely nativist, proud of their genealogy, sensitive to the challenges of Arabic poetry, science, and philosophy, and speculative on the secrets of the universe and of Jewish history. And as in Babylonia, the Jews of Spain witnessed two types of political posture: elitist cooperation with the government, and dissident revolt on the part of disaffected groups. Hence, even though Abraham ibn Daud gave his full approbation to the political stance of *Yosifon*, his endorsement could not dissipate the basic restlessness in the Sephardic temper. Indeed, the very same Ibn Daud had preached quietism out of one side of his mouth and theorized on the end of history out of the other.

However, there were other factors as well. To a certain extent, the political successes of Jews in Spain must have whetted the appetites of the elite for even further conquests. The rise of Jews to heights of power unknown since ancient times was accompanied by a neo-classicism that revived biblical Hebrew and biblical imagery in "secular" as well as religious poetry. It was a Jewish vizier of Granada who defiantly proclaimed: "I am the David of my generation."[43] To a potential David, relative deprivation is much more irritating than absolute deprivation. To a would-be king, as the same Ibn Nagrela confessed, nothing short of conquest of the heavens and the heights of the moon would satisfy. The elite of Spain were restive and eager, and lesser pretenders caught the bug and from time to time announced their messiahship.

Moreover, political success underscored the new confidence in the powers of human understanding that was born of the scientific and philosophic studies cultivated in Spain. While the elite would forever be prudent and judicious, the more deprived and the less stable would lose their inhibitions and jump to messianic action.

But in the final analysis the two different messianic postures of medieval European Jewry betray two different approaches to the same religious faith. Quiescence, passive resistance, is symptomatic of absolute faith in the total transcendence of God, in His unbounded liberty and power, and of perfect certainty that the Divine promise will be fulfilled. It was no coincidence that Ashkenazic Jewry was always basically fundamentalist, unabashed by anthropomorphism or outlandish legends. Who was man to sit in judgment on God or His word?

Activism of the Andalusian type, on the other hand, emanated from a society which, although formally proclaiming its faith in the classical God of Israel, had in reality appropriated much of the Hellenic scientific spirit; it was largely fatalist-predestinarian and committed to a belief in the inexorable law of nature and, we may add, of history. When the time came for the end to unfold, if indeed it ever would, nothing could stop it.

This difference in underlying faith, of which the form of messianism is but one significant symptom, is far more important than what appears on the surface, for I believe that it provides a clue to understanding the Jewish posture in the face of pressure and dire persecution. While, as I have already affirmed, there is no demonstrable connection in Jewish history between periods of extreme persecution and messianic uprisings, the record of history does entitle us to establish a close connection between a particular type of faith generally, and of messianic faith in particular, and the Jewish response to the challenging alternative of conversion or death. That is because messianism is the substance on which all Jewish tenacity was predicated. God's elect would be vindicated, and on the basis of that promise alone Jews would endure not only persecution but interminable alienation and humiliation. It is a reasonable assumption, then, that the form of a Jew's ideology of resistance will be reflected in the nature of his response to physical threats.

During the Middle Ages, there were four instances of which we have some rather full accounts in which scores of Jewish communities and thousands of Jews were confronted by the alternative of apostasy or death, two of them affecting Ashkenazic Jewry and two of them Sephardic. I make reference, of course, to the First Crusade of 1096, to the Almohade persecutions in North Africa and Spain beginning in 1147, to the riots of 1391 in Spain and the persecutions that followed, and to the Cossack uprisings in Poland and Russia in 1648 and after. Now in each of these instances, many Jews were killed outright; some fought back; some preferred martyrdom to apostasy; some converted as a means of saving their lives. Of the latter, some attempted to return to Judaism; others had found the final solution to their Jewish problem and remained Christians or Muslims. However, if no one description will suffice to describe the behavior of all the Jews involved in any one of these upheavals, it is nevertheless fair to say that in each of these instances there was a dominant behavioral pattern, one that was so pronounced as to make an indelible impression on eye-witnesses and chroniclers.

In each of the two cases involving Ashkenazic Jewry, those of 1096 and 1648 and after, the outstanding feature of the Jewish response was *kiddush ha-shem*—martyrdom. In both of the persecutions endured by Sephardim, although *kiddush ha-shem* was by no means lacking, the dominant behavioral pattern, the one that left the greatest impression on witnesses and future generations, was apostasy and marranism.

There were, of course, basic differences between each of the two experiences affecting Ashkenazic Jewry, even with respect to the martyrdom accepted by the Jews involved. In the later Chmelnitzki onslaught, it would seem that far fewer Jews had any choice in the matter than in the other three cases. The Cossacks often seemed to have been bent on outright murder, rapine, and pillage. But even in those cases where Jews were in a position to choose between alternatives, they elected to die fighting or to die *passively at the hands of their attackers*.[44] That had not been quite the case in 1096. Then, while many Jews died fighting or even passively, many of them took an active hand in their martyrdom by committing a kind of ritual suicide. The ritual slaughter-knife was used, a blessing was pronounced, and blood of the human sacrifice was even smeared on the pillar of the ark in the synagogue.[45] Martyrdom was not mere sanctification of the Name through faith; it was an atonement sacrifice, an *aqedah*. That is important to bear in mind, for the commemorative chronicles, dirges, and penitential prayers that subsequently emerged from Ashkenaz frequently construed martyrdom as an *aqedah* sacrifice, as the highest act of worship, the martyr being referred to as *ha-Qadosh,* the saint.[46] Hence, despite the different circumstances surrounding the voluntary death of thousands of Jews in the two great massacres of Ashkenazic Jewry, the ideal of service to God through martyrdom, in whatever form, had become for Ashkenazic Jewry the only legitimate choice in terms of persecution. This is not to say that Ashkenazim did not sympathize with those who could not stand up to the ultimate test. What it does mean is that, under such circumstances, death on behalf of God was the only admissible solution in theory. Consequently, every martyr, willing or unwilling, would attain the rank of the saint, of the one who had willingly, indeed gladly, offered up his life as a sacrifice.

Now the obvious feature of voluntary martyrdom is its stance of profound trust, its unflagging certainty of vindication and ultimate triumph. In Jewish literature, the souls of the righteous were described as stored under the Throne of Glory, accepted into the great light vouchsafed for the world to come, and held in readiness for the resurrection and redemption.[47] Quiescence, passivity, resignation were possible for thousands of Ashkenazic Jews, for to them the age of the Messiah was not merely a concept, a vision of bliss, or primarily an age when the Holy Spirit would be restored to Israel. The day of messianic redemption was the one when "eye to eye they would see the Lord restoring Zion" (Isaiah 52:8), that is, themselves, their loved ones, their people, their Temple, their king, their home. Quiescence and martyrdom sprang from a classical faith untroubled by rationalist doubts or scholastic distinctions between the intentions of the heart and the utterances of the lips.

That this was the case may be seen by a closer examination of the circumstances under which Ashkenazim preferred to undergo martyrdom. At the time of the First Crusade, many of the leadership and learned preferred suicide to death at the hands of their tormentors, despite the formal prohibition in Judaism against suicide; for they construed the Talmudic injunctions against suicide in the context of Talmudic literature as a whole. Now, while rabbinic law formally prohibits suicide, there are a considerable number of cases in the Talmud recording suicide as a religiously praiseworthy act not only to avoid apostasy or forced immorality, but even as a form of voluntary atonement. The penitent, in popular views, could justifiably impose the death penalty on himself as a form of expiation.[48] To many, the willingness of Isaac to be sacrificed by his father Abraham, in proof of which there was an amplitude of rabbinic legend, was construed as a form of voluntary religious martyrdom.[49]

Please do not misunderstand me as arguing the halakic rectitude of their acts. That is a matter for jurists to decide, though I may add that I have support for my understanding of their behavior in the juridic defenses of these acts by outstanding halakists of the Middle Ages.[50] What I am trying to do is to understand their religious temper. The Ashkenazim were not at all *emotionally* passive in their martyrdom. To the extent that their religious sentiments would allow the chroniclers and poets to admit, many of the martyrs and their contemporaries expressed great resentment over the fate that God had meted out to them. While some piously rehashed the ancient platitudes of Job's friends that it was because of their sins that they were suffering, others protested that it was not because of their shortcomings that they were dying but because of their perfection. As a generation unmatched in piety since the days of Rabbi Akiba and the ten martyrs, they had been elected to serve as the sacrifice of atonement for all others.[51]

It may well be that the Christian environment had stimulated them to think along these particular rabbinic lines rather than along others, which I will suggest influenced many Sephardim. But the crucifixion motif as a vicarious atonement had ample parallels in authentically Jewish sources to allow them to construe their choice as a totally Jewish one.[52] In a word, they treated *aggadah* and *halakah* as a unit and behaved accordingly.

In the case of the dominant Sephardic responses to persecution through marranism and even unqualified apostasy, the situation is far more complex. Many doubtless elected to live out of sheer instinct. But why assume that Ashkenazic instincts are weaker than Sephardic ones? Obviously other factors came into play, and it is these that interest us in the present context.

In his famed *Treatise on the Sanctification of the Name,* Maimonides informs us that some Jews, although they had the opportunity to escape to safer pastures, elected to remain under Almohade rule as marranos, for they were sure the Messiah would soon be at hand in any case.[53] This is a most revealing statement, for the same messianic faith that prompted Ashkenazim to elect death at their own hands prompted some Sephardim—of whom the North Africans were a part—to try to have their cake and eat it too. What better evidence do we need of the messianic predestinarianism that had circulated in Sephardic circles? Nor can this be dismissed as the quirk of a few Jewish crackpots, for Maimonides regarded the notion as sufficiently serious to treat it as a problem. The fact of the matter is that this point of view became one of the dominant characteristics of marranist thinking in the second great period of persecution confronting Sephardic Jewry, that is, in the persecutions of 1391 and after. What Professor Baer has regarded as evidence of a messianic movement on the part of many marranos shortly before the expulsion from Spain, will, upon more dispassionate examination, be seen to be not so much a movement as expressions of hysterical guilt, of hope and of reaffirmation of faith in the *inevitability* of the imminent messianic deliverance.[54] In other words, whereas Ashkenazic political quiescence could generate mass emotional religious activism in the form of martyrdom, the open speculation and even occasional active outbursts of the Sephardic milieu would, in times of severe stress, produce extreme religious passivity.

In the case of the marranos of the Almohade period, we are beset by a lack of copious source materials. There are only two circumstances that do appear worthy of mention in the present context. While Maimonides unequivocally recognized the martyrs of the Almohade persecutions as sacrifices in sanctification of the Name, he nevertheless urged Jews to avoid martyrdom if they could. He, of course, justified his directive on strictly halakic grounds. But I wonder if it is not more than a coincidence that a representative of those circles of Judaism that had reservations at least on the primacy of the resurrection in the messianic fulfillment should be more reluctant to put his stamp of approval on wholesale martyrdom? As is widely known, even after all the apparent halakic differences on martyrdom between Maimonides and the Franco-German codifiers have been leveled and harmonized, there exists a hard core of dispute between them which cannot be resolved and of which many Jewish jurists have taken note. That is the question of the option open to a person to undergo martyrdom in certain situations when the law does not prescribe it. Maimonides in his *Mishneh Torah* absolutely forbade it, while the Franco-Germans proclaimed almost to a man that it is a matter for the individual himself to decide.[55] Although what was formally at issue was the interpretation of classical texts, I cannot help but feel that in borderline cases the spokesman of each branch of Judaism read the texts in accordance with the overall pattern of his thinking. The hesitancy that attended such reservations on the ultimate reward and on the right of a man to decide his own destiny through martyrdom doubtless percolated down to the laity and influenced their behavior. Add to this the widespread skepticism of the extreme type that we discussed earlier and you have the seedbed on which marranism could sprout and ultimately become a phenomenon of major proportions.

If that is a matter of conjecture in the case of the Almohade persecutions, in the case of the riots of 1391, and the environment of the fifteenth century, the pattern is much clearer. Indeed, a whole complex of Jewish factors was available to rationalize sympathy for the "forced converts." Whatever rationalizations were invoked after the fact, Baer has argued convincingly that the deep religious skepticism that had spread in the economically higher classes of Sephardic Jewish society was one of the chief factors in bringing about wholesale Spanish apostasy. Christian polemicists and missionaries made capital of the widespread doubts in the messianic fulfillment that had become part of many a Jewish man's spiritual baggage. Despair of the messianic promise to Israel was doubtless a major factor in swaying many to make the decision they did between 1391 and 1492.[56]

Coupled with skepticism there was yet another product of the Andalusian golden age that colored the Spanish temper. That was the posture of the Arab-type philosopher, the conclusion that true salvation was being held in store for the worthy individual rather than for the group as a whole. Secondly, what counted ultimately was not what one did so much as what one believed. If one's heart remained steadfast, then formal defection was of secondary importance. Add to this the ever-growing conviction in respectable Jewish circles that Christianity was not really an idolatry[57] and you have fertile soil for the rationalization of those marranos who remained secretly loyal, and above all for the indubitable and widespread rabbinic sympathy for them. They knew that the Messiah must come and soon, and they were sure that those who could justify their inner-most intentions would also be redeemed. Spanish activism coupled with Spanish sophistication and skepticism helped to produce the characteristic Sephardic response to the Messiah and His challengers.

To sum up, two traditions, two distinct medieval approaches to the Messiah gained strong footholds in medieval society. Although the times and circumstances that generated them changed radically, the traces of these two approaches, and variations on them, have remained down to modern times.

NOTES

1. Christopher Marlowe, *The Jew of Malta,* Act II, ed. by R. W. Van Fossen (Lincoln, Neb., 1964) pp. 52, l. 305.
2. These have been collected, edited, and annotated by J. Even-Shmuel in *Midreshay Geulah* (2nd ed., Jerusalem, 1954).
3. Cf. further A. S. Halkin, ed., *Zion in Jewish Literature* (New York, 1961), pp. 38 ff., 65 ff., 83 ff.

4. For a convenient collection of the relevant texts, see A. Z. Aescoly, *Jewish Messianic Movements* [in Hebrew] (Jerusalem, 1956), pp. 117 ff. Cf. further S. W. Baron, *A Social and Religious History of the Jews,* V (2nd ed. Philadelphia, 1952–65), 182, 191 ff. [in the sixth paper of the present collection—Ed.].
5. For the latest discussions of the stages in the development of Karaism, cf. M. Zucker, *Rav Saadya Gaon's Translation of the Torah* [in Hebrew] (New York, 1959), pp. 145 ff.; Baron, *op. cit.,* V, chap. XXVI.
6. M. Zucker, "Tegubot li-Tenuʻat Abaylay Zion ha-Qarraiyyim ba-Sifrut ha-Rabbanit," *Sefer ha-Yobel le-R. Ḥanokh Albeck* (Jerusalem, 1963), pp. 378 ff.
7. For surveys of medieval Jewish messianic efforts, see Aescoly, *op. cit.,* chaps. IV–VI; A. H. Silver, *A History of Messianic Speculation in Israel* (Boston, 1959), chaps. III–V.
8. Moses Maimonides, *Epistle to Yemen,* ed. by A. S. Halkin (New York, 1952), pp. 102–103; Eng. trans. *ibid.* (by B. Cohen), p. xx.
9. Abraham ibn Daud, *Sefer ha-Qabbalah,* ed. and trans. by G. D. Cohen (Philadelphia, 1967), Hebrew text, p. 45 l. 148 and variants; Eng. trans., VI. 217; *idem* in *Medieval Jewish Chronicles,* I, (ed. by A. Neubauer), 67.
10. On the following incidents see Moses Maimonides, *op. cit.,* pp. 100–101 ff.; Eng. trans., pp. xix ff.; Aescoly, *op. cit.,* pp. 194 ff.; Silver, *op. cit.,* pp. 87 ff.
11. Cf. Silver, *op. cit.,* pp. 143 ff. For reasons which will be fully spelled out elsewhere, I have not reckoned either reports about Jewish messianic movements that are not attested by Jews, or obscure incidents that cannot as yet be dated with certainty.
12. To be sure, a number of Jews of Ashkenazic descent were prominent in the messianic "ferment" in the century and a half following the Spanish expulsion, but the dominant Jewish temper in the Ottoman Empire, where this speculation took place, was clearly Sephardic.
13. Aescoly, *op. cit.,* pp. 154 ff., 286 ff.
14. J. Prawer, "The Jews in the Latin Kingdom of Jerusalem" [in Hebrew], *Zion,* XI (1945–46), 50 ff.; *idem, A History of the Latin Kingdom of Jerusalem,* II [in Hebrew] (2 vols., Jerusalem, 1963), 387 ff.; *idem,* "Ḥobebay Zion bi-May ha-Baynayyim," *Maʻarabo shel Galil we-Ḥof ha-Galil* (Jerusalem, 1965), pp. 129 ff. Certainly the considerations of piety motivating settlement of the Holy Land were messianically oriented, but they were "pre-millenarist" in character, very similar to those motivating the move of Judah ha-Levi; cf. below. On Ashkenazic realism and coolness to migration to Palestine at that time, cf. E. E. Urbach, *The Tosaphists* [in Hebrew] (Jerusalem, 1955), pp. 108 ff., 231.
15. On Maimonides' views, cf. Halkin's introduction to *Epistle to Yemen,* pp. xxvi ff. On Abulafia's conflict with traditionalists, cf. Aescoly, *op. cit.,* pp. 198 ff.; G. Scholem, *Major Trends in Jewish Mysticism* (3rd ed., New York, 1961), pp. 128 ff. On the anti-"establishmentarian" character of messian-

ism, cf. *idem, Sabbatai Ṣevi* (Princeton, 1973), pp. 10–12, 93–101 [the first passage is included in paper 12 below—Ed.].

16. For the text and bibliography, see *Sefer ha-Yishub,* II, ed. by S. Assaf and L. A. Mayer (Jerusalem, 1944), pp. 22 no. 30, 113 no. 20; Aescoly, *op. cit.,* pp. 133 ff. Aescoly recounts all the scholarly conjectures on the fragment with the exception of the one which, it seems to me, best explains the motivation of the query, namely that of A. Marx, "Studies in Gaonic History and Literature," *JQS,* NS, I (1910–11), 75 ff. Aescoly's efforts to connect the question of the rabbis of the Rhineland with the "mourners of Zion," described in a gloss to Benjamin of Tudela's *Itinerary,* is unconvincing. Whatever the historical value of that gloss, it does not reflect messianic activity or ferment, but only messianic faith, which all Jews shared and which some expressed a bit more conspicuously than others; cf. Aescoly, pp. 152 ff.

17. J. Sarachek, *The Doctrine of the Messiah in Medieval Jewish Literature* (New York, 1932), p. 59; Silver, *op. cit.,* p. 66.

18. *Ibid.,* pp. 58 ff.; A. M. Habermann, ed., *Sefer Gezerot Ashkenaz we-Ṣarfat* (Jerusalem, 1945), pp. 24, 83; Tobiah ben Eliezer, *Leqaḥ Tob,* ed. by S. Buber (Vilna, 1880), part 2, p. 20.

19. Rabbi Joseph Bekhor Shor, *Payrush 'al ha-Torah,* III (Jerusalem, 5719), p. 65; Silver, *op. cit.,* pp. 85 ff.

20. A. Marx, "Ma'amar 'al Shenat ha-Geulah," *Hazofeh le-Ḥokmat Israel,* V (1921), 194 ff.

21. On the eschatological interests of that circle, cf. Scholem, *Major Trends,* pp. 88 ff.

22. Aescoly, *op. cit.,* p. 188; S. Assaf, *Meqorot u-Meḥqarim* (Jerusalem, 1946), pp. 146 ff.

23. A. J. Heschel, " 'Al Ruaḥ ha-Qodesh bi-May ha-Baynayyim," *Alexander Marx Jubilee Volume* (New York, 1950), Hebrew vol., p. 184; and cf. Scholem, *Major Trends,* p. 85.

24. Marx, *op. cit.,* pp. 195 ff.; Heschel, *op. cit.,* p. 184; and cf. L. Zunz, *Gesammelte Schriften,* III (3 vols., Berlin, 1875–76), 227. On knowledge acquired in dreams in Ashkenazic rabbinic circles, cf. Heschel. *op. cit.,* pp. 195 ff.; R. J. Z. Werblowsky, *Joseph Karo* (Oxford, 1962), pp. 42 ff. On an inquiry on the date of the Messiah in a dream, cf. *ibid.,* p. 43, n. 1.

25. Heschel, *op. cit.,* pp. 185 ff. Significantly, Sephardim occasionally used the term "prophet" to designate a poet; cf. D. Yellin, *Torat ha-Shirah ha-Sefaradit* (Jerusalem, 1940), p. 3, n. 1.

26. Cf. Abraham b. Ḥiyya, *Megillat ha-Megalleh,* ed. by A. Poznanski (Berlin, 1924), pp. 36 ff.; Maimonides, *Epistle to Yemen,* pp. 82/83; and cf. G. D. Cohen, "The Story of the Four Captives," *Proceedings of the American Academy for Jewish Research,* XXIX (1960–61), 102 n. 146, 104 nn. 148, 150. For an Andalusian view of *gematriaot,* cf. Abraham ibn Ezra to Gen. 14: 14. That Ibn Ezra's skepticism was not peculiar to him may be seen from Nahmanides' impassioned defense of *gematriaot* in his treatise on

redemption; *Kitbay Ramban,* I, ed. by D. Chavel (2 vols., Jerusalem, 1963), 262. The freest use of *gematria* by a Sephardic Jew known to me is in the third chapter of Abraham b. Ḥiyya's *op. cit.;* cf. pp. 67, 79 ff. However, even he uses *gematriaot* only as supporting evidence and not as the sources of his findings. Moreover, as a Jew of Barcelona, Abraham b. Ḥiyya may well have been inspired in this regard by northern scholars, who were closer to the Ashkenazic spheres of influence and to the emphasis on the power of letters propounded in *Sefer Yeṣira,* which strongly influenced Ashkenazic circles.

27. Cf. Silver, *op. cit.*, pp. 59 ff., 85 ff. On the importance attached to *gematriaot* in Ashkenazic circles, cf. [the German] *Encyclopaedia Judaica,* VII, 178; Scholem, *Major Trends,* p. 100.
28. Cf. *ibid.*, pp. 127, 135; Aescoly, *op. cit.*, pp. 196 ff. Cf. also n. 26.
29. Marx, *op. cit.*, p. 195.
30. Halkin's introduction to *Epistle to Yemen,* p. xxxii.
31. Judah ben Barzillay, *Commentar zum Sepher Jezira,* ed. by J. Halberstamm (Berlin, 1885), pp. 237 ff.
32. Silver, *op. cit.*, pp. 67 ff.; Cohen, *op. cit.*, p. 104, n. 150.
33. Y. Baer, "Eine jüdische Messiasprophetie auf das Jahr 1186 und der dritte Kreuzzug," *MGWJ,* LXX (1926), 113 ff.; *idem, A History of the Jews in Christian Spain* (2 vols., Philadelphia, 1961–66) I, 66.
34. Moses Maimonides, *Epistle to Yemen,* pp. 58 ff., 80 ff.
35. Cf. the Analysis in my ed. of *Sefer ha-Qabbalah,* chaps. III–V, where this interpretation is documented in detail.
36. Judah ha-Levi's famous suggestion of a date for the fall of the Muslim Empire, which ha-Levi credited to a dream, could easily be dismissed by his contemporaries as poetic fancy; cf. Judah ha-Levi, *Diwan* (ed. Brody), II, 302.
37. In support of his views Maimonides refers to Ibn Bala'am and Ibn Gikatilla approvingly; cf. "Maimonides' Treatise on Resurrection," ed. by J. Finkel, *PAAJR,* IX (1938–39), Hebrew section, p. 21, par. 31.
38. Cf. Maimonides, *Guide of the Perplexed,* II, 29, trans. by S. Pines (Chicago, 1963), 337 ff.; *idem, Mishneh Torah,* Melakhim, 12.1 ff.; cf. also J. Levinger, *Maimonides' Techniques of Codification* [in Hebrew] (Jerusalem, 1965), p. 163. On the curious silence of Joseph ibn Aqnin on messianic dogmas, see A. S. Halkin, "Li-Demuto shel R. Joseph b. Judah ibn Aqnin," *Harry Austryn Wolfson Jubilee Volume* (Jerusalem, 1965), Hebrew vol., p. 111.
39. Cf. "Maimonides' Treatise on Resurrection," pp. 10 ff.; Meir ben Todros ha-Levi Abulafia, *Kitab al-Rasail,* ed. by J. Brill (Paris, 1871), p. 1.
40. J. Rosenthal, "From 'Sefer Alfonso' " [in Hebrew], *Studies and Essays in Honor of Abraham A. Neuman* (Leiden, 1963), pp. 621 ff.
41. See the observations of G. Scholem, *Sabbatai Ṣevi,* p. 1 ff.
42. Baer, "Sefer Yosifon ha-'Ibri," *Sefer Dinaburg* (Jerusalem, 1949), pp. 178 ff.
43. Samuel ibn Nagrela, *Diwan,* ed. by D. S. Sassoon (Oxford, 1934), p. 41, line 38 (=ed. A. M. Habermann and S. Abramson, I, part 1, p. 37);

J. Schirmann, *Ha-Shirah ha-'Ibrit bi-Sefarad u-bi-Provence,* I, 111. For the ascent to the heights of the moon, cf. *ibid.,* p. 83 (ed. Habermann, I, part 3, p. 5).

44. While there were, of course, instances of suicide even in the Chmelnitzki onslaughts, the contrast with the widespread and organized suicides of 1096 is quite evident. For sources on the events of 1648, see *Gezeros Taḥ* [in Yiddish] (Vilna, 1938); M. Hendel, *Gezerot Taḥ-Tat* (Jerusalem, 1950); S. Bernfeld, *Sefer ha-Dema'ot,* III, 109 ff.; H. J. Gurland, *Le-Qorot ha-Gezerot 'al Israel* (Odessa, 1892).
45. See the account of Solomon ben Simeon in Habermann, *Sefer Gezerot Ashkenaz we-Ṣarfat,* pp. 24 ff. For the sprinkling of the ark, cf. p. 37.
46. See the classic study of S. Spiegel, "The Legend of Isaac's Slaying and Resurrection" [in Hebrew] *Alexander Marx Jubilee Volume,* Hebrew vol., pp. 471 ff. and especially pp. 477 ff., 534 ff., where the connection of the *aqedah* with sacrifice and resurrection is documented; cf. also *idem,* "Payrur me-Aggadot ha-Aqedah," *The Abraham Weiss Jubilee Volume* (New York, 1964), pp. 553 ff.; H. J. Zimmels, *Ashkenazim and Sephardim* (London, 1958), pp. 263 ff.
47. On the rewards vouchsafed the martyrs, cf., in addition to the works listed in n. 46, Y. Baer's paper referred to in n. 42; *idem,* "Geserot Tatnaw," *Sefer Assaf* (Jerusalem, 1953), pp. 126 ff. For the sources of these expressions cf. V. Aptowitzer, "Bet ha-Miqdash shel ma'alah 'al Pi ha-Aggadah," *Tarbiz,* II (1930–31), 264, n. 8; S. Lieberman, "The Martyrs of Caesarea," *Annuaire de l'Institut de Philologie et d'Histoire Orientales et Slaves,* VII (1939–44), 443 ff.
48. On the meritoriousness of martyr-suicide in earlier literature, cf. *Mishnah of R. Eliezer* (ed. Enelow), p. 169; H. Fischel, "Martyr and Prophet," JQR, NS, XXVII (1946–47), 275; Cohen, *The Story of the Four Captives,* pp. 59, 74. On meritorious suicides of remorse and repentance, cf. *Bereshit Rabba* 65:22 (ed. Theodor-Albeck), pp. 742 ff.; B. A. Z. 18a (the latter is told of a Gentile executioner). I hope to deal with the subject at greater length in another paper. On the sentiment in Ashkenaz, cf. J. Katz, *Exclusiveness and Tolerance* (Oxford, 1961), pp. 90 ff.; N. Guedemann, *Geschichte des Erziehungswesens und der Cultur der Juden,* I (Vienna, 1880), 150, n. 5. The sacrificial and expiatory quality of physical suffering, especially of death, although quite evident in rabbinic literature, is given renewed emphasis by the German pietists; cf. Eleazar of Worms, *Rokeah* (Jerusalem, 1960), p. 3.
49. Cf. n. 46.
50. Menahem ben Solomon ha-Meiri, *Magen Abot* (Jerusalem and New York, 1958), p. 89; cf. also Zimmels, *op. cit.,* p. 263, n. 4; cf. also n. 55.
51. Cf. Solomon ben Simeon, *op. cit.* (ed. Habermann), *passim* and especially pp. 25, 27, 46.
52. Cf. G. F. Moore, *Judaism,* I, 546 ff.; S. Schechter, *Some Aspects of Rabbinic Theology,* pp. 310 ff. On the souls of the righteous—who have already died

—as the materials of sacrifice in the heavenly Temple, cf. Aptowitzer, *op. cit.*, pp. 257 ff.

53. Moses Maimonides, "Iggeret ha-Shemad," *Ḥemdah Genuzah*, ed. by Z. H. Edelmann (Königsberg, 1856), p. 12 a–b; = *Rambam La'am* (Mosad ha-Rav Kuk), XX, 66.
54. Y. Baer, "Ha-Tenu'ah ha-Meshiḥit bi-Sefarad bi-Tequfat ha-Gerush," *Zion*, V (1932–33), 61 ff. Cf. also Aescoly, *op. cit.*, p. 295. Needless to say, inquisitors would inflate such local manifestations into major movements.
55. For a full discussion and references to earlier literature, see M. Krakovsky, *Abodat ha-Melek* (Vilna, 1931), f. 6a and seq. to Maimonides *Mishneh Torah*, Yesoday ha-Torah, 5. 1,2,4; cf. also Jacob ben Asher, *Tur*, Yoreh Deah, par. 157 and Joseph Caro's notes thereto.
56. Y. Baer, *History of the Jews in Christian Spain*, II, 253 ff., 273 ff.
57. Katz, *op. cit.*, pp. 115 ff.

9

Reappearance of Pseudo-Messiahs

Salo Wittmayer Baron

By the tenth century the forces of Jewish sectarianism were spent. With the general stabilization of the Renaissance of Islam, concomitant with its growing political decline and economic retardation, the Jewish community, too, lost some of its creative rebelliousness and rather devoted itself to the consolidation of its socioreligious positions. The very decentralization of Jewish communal controls, which enabled each region to develop more freely along its chosen paths, rather than promoting religious disparity proved to be a cementing force of Jewish ideological unity maintained by living contacts and literary exchanges. Previously, any opposition to the recognized authority of exilarchs and geonim, as well as to officials appointed by them, generated trends going far beyond sheer disobedience in detail. Frequently the only effective protest against that overwhelming authority seemed to be an attack on its very foundations, namely Jewish law, or at least Oral Law. Now local adjustments proceeded apace with far less difficulty. Within the broader Islamic civilization, moreover, all unorthodox trends, including the formerly powerful Mu'tazilite movement, were likewise giving way to increasing conformity.

Such drying up of the heterodox mainsprings did not, however, diminish in the least the people's attachment to its Holy Land and its hope for speedy politico-religious restoration. In critical periods, particularly, that hope found expression not only in new messianic dreams and

Reprinted by permission of Columbia University Press from *A Social and Religious History of the Jews,* by S. W. Baron, vol. 5.

visions, but also in recurrent attempts to accelerate that end by human action. Once again ambitious or idealistic individuals, often megalomaniacs, felt the call to prophesy and to lead their people out of bondage. Although invariably discouraged by the established communal leaders and hence, willy-nilly, forced into some sort of opposition to the existing order, these new self-avowed redeemers rarely incited their followers to depart from the accepted religious practices or beliefs.

Perhaps because of the absence of ideological clashes, as well as of the limited geographic compass of most of these messianic movements, they left behind them few records. Their story had to be pieced together in recent decades from stray items of information, preserved only in the Cairo Genizah. Even our main source, Maimonides' *Epistle to Yemen,* was long available only in greatly abridged Hebrew renditions; the translators apparently considered these stories less worthy of attention. From the Arabic original of that epistle, however, written on the occasion of a messianic movement in Yemen in 1171–72, and other extant sources it appears that the preceding century belonged to the messianically most excited periods in Jewish history.[1]

As in most other public manifestations of Jewish popular frenzy, the reasons have to be sought in a combination of external and internal factors. The growing conflicts between the Muslim and Christian worlds, which resulted in the prolonged series of Christian Crusades in the direction of both the Holy Land and the Iberian Peninsula, offered a most propitious background for the long cherished expectations that the Messiah was due to come at the end of the first millennium after the fall of Jerusalem, or soon thereafter. We recollect how deeply disappointed Spanish Jewry and its leading poets were when the year 1068 had passed without the advent of the Redeemer. It is small wonder, then, that in that very period a messianic pretender appeared in a Christian city, called by Maimonides "Linon, a large center in the heart of the Frankish kingdom, which numbered more than ten thousand Jewish families." By performing the extraordinary feat of gliding "from tree to tree like a bird" he gained many votaries. But the "Franks" quickly suppressed the ensuing commotion and executed the "messiah" and many of his followers. Discounting the obviously exaggerated population estimate, the city is usually identified with Lyons in France, which had boasted of a sizeable and affluent Jewish community since Carolingian times. But it is difficult to explain why no persecution of Jews in France at that time is recorded in any other source, Jewish or Christian. Perhaps Maimonides had rather the Spanish city of Leon in mind, the messianic movement and its bloody suppression there being in some way connected with the recorded attacks of Spanish Crusaders on Jews in 1063, which were to evoke the papal intervention in the latter's behalf.[2]

When the year 1068 passed without bringing liberation, Jews began rationalizing that computation as they had done after 468. History repeated itself. Just as in antiquity the due date was extended to the entire eighty-fifth jubilee cycle, that is to 490 C.E., the belief now spread that redemption was to be expected some time during the 256th nineteen-year cycle, beginning in 4846 (1085–86). We recall the melancholy opening of Solomon bar Simson's chronicle of the tragic events during the First Crusade referring to that cycle which "we had expected to bring salvation and comfort in accordance with the prophecy of Jeremiah [31:6], but which turned to grief and sorrow." Perhaps to underscore that nexus, the chronicler emphasized that the bloodshed occurred "in the year 4856 [of Creation], 1028 of our Exile, and 11 of the 256th cycle." These world-stirring events understandably generated new messianic expectations. From the much-debated, but still very obscure, Byzantine letter published by Neubauer we learn about the impact of the arrival of the disorganized hosts of Crusaders in the Balkans on both Jews and Christians, particularly in Salonica. We are also told that the revived messianic hope aroused seventeen Khorasanian communities which, even in their political eclipse, had retained much Jewish feeling and considerable independence, to leave their homes and proceed to the "desert." There they expected to meet the descendants of the Ten Tribes who, according to old legends, were supposed to participate in the general return of Jewry to its ancestral home. Curiously, one of our correspondent's main sources of information, Tobiah ben Eliezer—if he be the Tobiah several times mentioned in the letter—alluded in his works, written in 1097 and revised a decade later, to the tragic happenings of 1096 in Germany, but made no reference whatever to any Balkan repercussions of the Crusades.[3]

The effects of the First Crusade, the conquest of Palestine by the Christians, and the destruction of many Jewish communities in Europe and Palestine were bound to evoke in many minds the picture of the wars of Gog and Magog, preliminary to the final arrival of the Messiah. Students of rabbinic leaders must also have long been impressed by the old legends summarized in Hai Gaon's prediction that "when we see Edom ruling over the land of Israel we believe that our salvation had begun, for it is written, 'And saviours shall come up on mount Zion, to judge the mount of Esau' [Ob. 21]." The urgency of that hope was further intensified in the apparently spreading belief in Muslim countries that the Messiah must come before the end of half a millennium after the appearance of Mohammed, for otherwise the *dhimmis* would forfeit their right to "protection." This belief, perhaps originating in Spain and Morocco where it is attested in the aforementioned threat of the Almoravid ruler, seems to have extended before long to eastern Islam as well. It greatly increased the anxieties of the Jewish communities under Muslim rule. That is why even enlightened Cordovan Jewry lent a willing ear to astrologers who had computed that the messianic age was to begin about 1107 C.E., or 500 A.H. This time the populace did not even wait for a self-appointed pretender to perform miracles and otherwise to prove his divine mission, but on its own "picked a pious and virtuous person by the name of Ibn Aryeh who had been instructing the people" and declared him to be the expected Redeemer. According to Maimonides, the saner leadership of the community, headed by his father Maimon, summoned Ibn Aryeh to the synagogue and flogged him for his tacit encouragement of the belief in his messiahship. "They did the same thing to the persons who assembled about him. The Jews escaped the wrath of the Gentiles only with the greatest difficulty."[4]

Although the year 1107 passed without any untoward consequences for Jewries under Islam, the new semimillennarianism seems to have persisted and even to have spread to eastern communities. Now, however, the 500-year period was interpreted to refer to solar rather than lunar years, the redemption being calculated for about 1122 C.E. We recall the decisive turn in history expected two centuries later by Sa'id ibn Hasan from the passage of 700 solar years. Not surprisingly, therefore, Jews in various parts of the Muslim world reacted independently, and yet almost simultaneously, to the approach of that crucial year. From Maimonides we learn of the appearance in Fez of one Moses al-Dar'i, a learned and pious Jew from Spain and former pupil of Joseph ibn Megas. Without claiming to be the Messiah himself, he predicted on the basis of dreams that the Messiah would arrive on the following Passover eve. To demonstrate the veracity of his prediction, he foretold several other forthcoming events, and they came true. For instance, he forecast a heavy rain with drops of blood for a particular autumnal Friday, seeing in it a messianic portent in accordance with Joel's prophecy (3:3). On that day, indeed, a heavy rain fell and, as Maimonides tried to explain it rationally, "the fluid that descended was red and viscous as if it were mixed with clay." Despite Maimon's opposition, Moses succeeded in persuading the people "to sell their property and contract debts to the Muslims with the promise to pay back ten dinars for one," for after Passover they all would have left the country. The ensuing fiasco and ruin of most of his adherents forced Moses to leave Morocco and proceed to Palestine, where he died in relative obscurity many years later.[5]

About that time Palestine herself witnessed a similar resurgence of messianic hopes. Here it was the turn of the Karaite community, more freely tolerated by the Latin rulers, to produce its first messianic pretender in history. The Norman proselyte Obadiah tells us about his encounter in Dan (Baniyyas) with a Karaite, Solomon ha-Kohen, who had been traveling up and down the country announcing that the Messiah would come within two and a half months, and that he would be the man "whom Israel seeks" (an unmistakable allusion to Mal. 3:1). He overruled Obadiah's objection that the Messiah was supposed to be of the house of David, rather than of the tribe of Levi, and urged him to give up his projected trip to Egypt. "I am going to Egypt," Obadiah sarcastically replied, "and I shall return with our Egyptian brethren to Jerusalem." Still another commotion of that type is recorded during the same period in Baghdad. According to a garbled story in an incomplete Genizah fragment, the Jewish masses in the declining but still magnificent Islamic metropolis became excited when the daughter of a physician, son of one Joseph, announced that she had seen Elijah and heard him announce the forthcoming liberation. The outcome was the imprisonment of Jewish leaders, who were freed only after the Caliph himself had a vision of Elijah. As usual, Jews had to pay a severe fine and, allegedly, the regulations concerning badges to be worn by *dhimmi* women were now sharpened.[6]

Apparently another independent movement arose in Kurdistan and its vicinity. Unlike other disturbances of that period, this agitation led to the revival of military ventures to secure the restoration of Jews to Palestine. Long known from a brief hearsay report by Benjamin of Tudela, this movement under the leadership of David Alroy (Al-Ro'i) attracted wide attention and was later dramatized in a novel by Benjamin Disraeli. Much fuller, though even more distorted, is the hostile account by Samau'al ibn Yahya al-Maghribi, who saw in this commotion and its ultimate failure an opportunity to ridicule the Jewish gullibility and, to some extent, also the Jewish messianic expectations as such. Further information is available in a Genizah fragment published by Mann.[7]

From these often confused and contradictory accounts it appears that in the days of the powerful Egyptian vizier Al-Afdhal (Abu'l Qasim Shahanshah, died 1121), one Solomon ben Duji of Khazaria, acting in cooperation with his son Menahem and a Palestinian scribe, Ephraim ben Azariah ibn Sahalun, sent out letters to various communities announcing the forthcoming ingathering of the exiles from all lands under his own leadership. We are not informed about the practical measures he proposed to take in order to accomplish this plan. Many years later (probably about 1147), we hear again, this time from his son Menahem or David al-Ro'i or al-Roḥi (both first names are equally messianic) who, through an appeal to the Jews of Adharbaijan, assembled around him a substantial Jewish armed force. At first, it appears, the local Muslim commanders viewed that movement calmly, even benevolently. We recall that when Imad ad-Din Zangi reconquered Edessa from the Christians in 1146, thus marking in some ways the beginning of the end of the Latin Kingdom, he transplanted 300 Jewish families there to replace departing Christian Armenians. Probably Alroy and the Jews of Amadia, a strategically located fortress northeast of Mosul, whose anti-Christian feelings were especially stressed by Samau'al, readily cooperated with the Muslims against the Christian rulers of the Holy Land. But perhaps utilizing the confusion arising from Zangi's assassination soon thereafter, Alroy, by magic or trickery, took possession of Amadia. From there he may have hoped to conquer Edessa and, utilizing the unceasing hostilities between the resuscitated Muslim armies and the slowly disintegrating powers of the Crusader principalities, to fight his way through to the Holy Land. He also dispatched messengers to many communities, including that of Baghdad, to prepare the ground for this military march. Possibly going beyond their orders, the messengers instructed the Baghdad Jews on a certain night to assemble on their roof tops whence they would be miraculously flown to the Messiah. Unbelievable though this may sound to modern readers, many members of that highly sophisticated community lent a willing ear to this unusual demand and spent that night on their roofs awaiting the miraculous flight. The next day, of course, this much-publicized stunt became the subject of general derision. Whatever their own attitude may have been at the inception of the movement, the exilarch and the head of the academy had no choice now but to disavow it and threaten its initiators with a ban. At the same time the Persian Jews were threatened with severe retaliation by the local authorities. With their apparent cooperation, the district governor bribed David's father-in-law, who allegedly assassinated the leader in his sleep. Nonetheless the northern Jews retained the memory of Alroy in great reverence and, when Benjamin arrived there some twenty years later, they still spoke lovingly of their dead leader. According to Samau'al, "the Jews of Amadia still praise him in many assemblies, and there are people among them who view him as their expected messiah. I have seen Persian Jewish communities in Khoi, Slamas, Tabriz, and Maragha [all in northwestern Iran, not too far from Amadia], who mention his name during their highest adoration. . . . In that city [Amadia] there is a congregation professing a faith which, they claim, emanated from that swindler, Menahem."[8]

With the aid of astrological computations one could prove almost any date as the likely time for the advent of the Messiah. Because some astrologers messianically interpreted an existing stellar constellation, Yemenite Jewry was prepared to listen to the preachment of a rather simple-minded miracle worker who claimed to be the Messiah. It was this episode which induced Jacob ben Nathaniel al-Fayyumi to send his inquiry to Maimonides, the latter's *Epistle to Yemen* becoming the only truly enduring monument to that unfortunate venture. The jurist-philosopher was not surprised at either the appearance of the pseudo-messiah, whom he considered an obvious mental case, or at the latter's ignorant followers who thus found comfort in their tribulations. But he rebuked his learned questioner for failing to realize that the Redeemer must be "a very eminent prophet, more illustrious than all the prophets after Moses." He advised the communal leaders to place the pretender in chains for a while, until the Gentiles might learn that he was a demented person. "If you procrastinate until they learn of this affair of their own accord, you will most likely incur their wrath." From another epistle of the sage of Fusṭaṭ, written some twenty-two years later, we learn that his advice was not heeded.

Finally after a year he was taken into custody, and all his adherents fled. When the Arab king who had seized him inquired, "What have you done?" he replied, "Indeed, I have done it in truth and at God's behest." When the king demanded proof, he added: "If you sever my head, I shall immediately be revived." The king exclaimed: "I do not need any better evidence that that. [If that miracle comes true] not only I, but the whole world will acknowledge the error of our ancestral faith." Whereupon they immediately killed the poor fellow. May his death be an expiation for him and for all Israel. The Jews of many localities paid a fine. Yet there still are some fools who believe in his early resurrection.

With this melancholy observation Maimonides concluded his sad narrative, to him but another testimony to the frequently irrational behavior of the uneducated masses, which could only be cured by the spread of enlightenment and the reign of reason.[9]

UNITY WITHIN DIVERSITY

In this way Judaism weathered another great internal crisis. Emerging in the sixth century weakened in numbers as well as in intellectual and spiritual strength, having lost its effective central leadership in both Palestine and Babylonia, and confronted with ever deepening sectarian struggles in its Christian and later also in its Muslim environment, the Jewish people revealed an enormous tenacity in resisting both the tremendous external pressures and the powerful centrifugal forces in its own midst. Under the impact of Mohammed's successful challenge to the existing political and religious order, there arose in the following two centuries a number of sectarian movements in Judaism, too. They were as a rule accompanied by messianic pretensions of their leaders. Conversely, when before and after that sectarian outburst some purely messianic movements emerged within the orthodox body, most of these smacked of some heterodoxy, or were driven to it by the resistance of the established leadership. Yet what is truly amazing is not the frequency of commotions of either kind, but rather their relative paucity and historical insignificance. With all the research hitherto done by modern scholars, intensely interested in any form of Jewish heterodoxy as well as in yearnings for the return to Zion, only about half a dozen non-Karaite heresiarchs and less than a score of messianic pretenders, including all the former, are known to us by name in the long and crucial period of seven centuries following the religious consolidation of the Babylonian Talmud.

With the sole exception of the Karaites, none of these movements left behind any enduring heritage. It was a lucky coincidence for modern research that, perhaps stimulated by the example set by Muslim historians of religion who had recognized that sectarian divergences touched the very core of Islam's religious and political life, Qirqisani found it necessary to describe briefly the heterodox trends apparent also in contemporary Judaism. But his own description showed how little this disparity mattered in world Jewish life during the mid-tenth century. Most of the sects enumerated by him had either disappeared or dwindled to as little as twenty members. At the same time, he did convey the idea of a great spiritual effervescence and widespread religious quests in the eastern communities, from which both Karaite and Rabbanite Judaism ultimately received many valuable stimuli. Similarly, we would have known very little about the messianic movements from Moses of Crete to the demented pretender in Yemen, were it not for Socrates' polemically inspired narrative or the equally fortuitous circumstance that the Yemenite disturbance induced a leader to question Maimonides. This inquiry stimulated the latter to offer both an exposition of his messianic doctrine and a number of illuminating illustrations from the then recent past. That section of his *Epistle,* moreover, appeared so inconsequential to his Hebrew translators and many copyists of the Arabic text that, despite the author's extraordinary popularity, only one more or less complete copy is extant today.

At the same time the messianic *idea* played an enormous role in Judaism. Throughout the ages it remained the cynosure of all Jewish eyes, and most thinkers and poets tried to add some new little insights or new formulations to the people's undying hope. Yet the same Hai Gaon who composed one of the most eloquent restatements of that hope found no occasion to deal with any of its practical aspects or actual messianic movements during his long life. At least none are mentioned in the more than one thousand responsa attributed to him. Even the earlier geonim rarely dealt with contemporary sectarian or messianic trends, unless they happened to be asked, as was Naṭronai I, about the legal aspects of readmission of some such errant individuals to the orthodox fold. None of these heresiarchs or messianic pretenders, moreover, seems to have been articulate enough to leave behind writings of his own; probably because most of them were unlearned. Even Moses al-Dar'i, whom Maimonides grudgingly recognized as a man of "piety, virtue, and learning," is known to us only at second hand. We may discount the possibility, unsupported by any intimation in the sources, that some sectarian writings may once have existed but were suppressed by the official leaders, for even less than the state authorities was the Jewish community able to impose an effective book censorship upon its members. Its main weapon, the excommunication of an offender, must have proved entirely ineffectual in the case of professed dissidents, whose doctrines were in any case anathemized by the rabbis. Whenever sectarian chiefs were learned and articulate, as in the case of the Karaite authors, much of their literary heritage was transmitted to posterity. Perhaps this was, indeed, the main weakness of the other sectarian and messianic spokesmen. No one seems to have been able enduringly to influence the "people of the book" unless he, or his immediate disciples (as in the later instances of Isaac Luria or Israel Ba'al Shem Tob), made a significant and appealing literary contribution which in some way enriched the literary and intellectual patrimony of his people.[10]

Precisely because the sectarian differences mattered so little in the long run, Shahrastani, who seems to have made a genuine effort to ascertain the whereabouts and teachings of the various Jewish heterodoxies, was able to supply so little solid information. He may have allotted equal space to the 'Isawites and Yudghanites as to the 'Ananites (Karaites) and Samaritans, and called all four "the best known and most widespread" Jewish sects. But he could not conceal the fact that in his day the former were mere historical curiosities. He certainly could not even remotely itemize the seventy-one sects which, he claimed, had existed within the Jewish religion. In his summary, moreover, he admitted that all Jews, regardless of their sectarian divergence, believed in monotheism, the uniqueness of the Torah revealed to Moses, the observance of the Sabbath, and the coming of the Messiah, "the shining star, which will illumine the world." We may agree with this Muslim student of religion that, indeed, all Jews of his time, were "waiting for him and the Sabbath [which] is his day," for, as some Jews explained, the universe was to endure only for six thousand years, to be followed by the cosmic Sabbath of redemption. Notwithstanding their endless sufferings and the unceasing frustrations of all their petty messianic ventures, their unshakable faith in the ultimate coming of the Redeemer, under one guise or another, remained their perennial source of strength and endurance.

NOTES

1. Cf. A. S. Halkin's Hebrew and abridged English introductions to his edition of the *Epistle to Yemen;* and J. Mann's comprehensive analysis in *Hatekufah,* XXIII–XXIV. Mann, who reprinted here the Hebrew originals or translations of most pertinent sources, had at his disposal also the relevant portion of the Arabic original of the *Epistle,* then being prepared for a critical edition by I. Friedlaender, together with the latter's English translation. His interpretation, however, of these successive movements left many questions open. While fully realizing the great impact of the Crusades, he failed to supply the reasons for the outbreak of each particular mass psychosis. Cf. also J. Shapiro's more popular restatement of the story of the Jewish messianic movements in his *Bi-shebile ha-ge'ulah* (On the Paths of Redemption), which, however, adds but little to the previously known facts.
2. Maimonides' *Epistle to Yemen,* pp. 102 f. (Arabic and Hebrew), xx (English). *Al-Afranj* does not necessarily mean France in the Arabic letters of that period, but like the term "Franks" or "Ashkenazim," included all the successor states of the Frankish empire, or even all of western Europe. Although probably not quite of the size of the Lyons community, that of Spanish Leon was likewise both old and substantial, and was later to give birth to the famous Kabbalist, Moses de Leon. One Jacob of Leon is recorded to have brought back from a pilgrimage to Palestine an important philological work by Abu'l Faraj Harun. Cf. Abu'l-Walid Merwan (Jonah) ibn Janah's *K. al-Luma'* (Livre des Parterres fleuris; grammaire hébraïque), ed. by J. Derenbourg, pp. 322 f. (in Yehudah ibn Tibbon's Hebrew trans., entitled *Sefer ha-Riqmah,* ed. by M. Wilensky, II, 338; in M. Metzger's French trans. the geographic designation is omitted). Even to a native Spaniard like Maimonides, the northern city of Leon with its immemorial connections with the Frankish empire may well have appeared as a large city in the Frankish possessions, though not perhaps in their "center," a term, questionable even in the single Arabic text and totally absent from the other Arabic and all Hebrew versions. Cf. also H. Gross's *Gallia judaica,* pp. 306 f., which shows that, while both cities were often spelled in Hebrew in the same manner, Lyons often had the added "s" as in English, or else was spelled in some derivative from the Latin *Lugdunum.*
3. Cf. the sources listed *A Social and Religious History of the Jews* 5:285–87 (n.7), 294 (n.24); Tobiah ben Eliezer's *Midrash Leqaḥ ṭob* (Good Lesson) on Lev. 22:32–33, ed. by M. Padwa, p. 123; and on Cant. 1:3, ed. by A. W. Greenup, pp. 15, 24. Of course, it is possible that the Tobiah of the messianic missive was not the author of the Midrash, or else that in retrospect he viewed the Balkan repercussions as but a tempest in a teapot. The events in the Rhinelands, however, made a deep and lasting impression on the Jews of all lands, and especially on Tobiah, who may himself have been of Western origin. Cf. the debate on this score summarized in Zunz and

Albeck's *Ha-Derashot,* pp. 145 f., 441 n. 40; and J. Starr's *Jews in the Byzantine Empire,* pp. 215 ff. The first person plural in Solomon's chronicle is taken over from the basic contemporary source so eloquently postulated by Y. Baer in *Sefer Assaf,* pp. 130 ff. But even in the conclusion of his chronicle, triumphantly relating the severe losses sustained by the Crusader bands on their march through Hungary and the Balkan countries, Solomon makes no mention of the Balkan agitation. Despite the numerous messianic references in his commentaries on the Bible, and especially on Psalms, largely composed in the overheated atmosphere of crusading France after 1096, Rashi likewise fails to hint at any messianic upsurge in Byzantium. See especially the searching reconstruction of the meaning of a number of these messianic passages against the background of contemporary Judeo-Christian polemics in Y. Baer's aforementioned essay in *Tarbiz,* XX, 328 ff. If the reading "Khorasan" rather than "Khazaria" should prove correct, as is likely, the manifold speculations about the seventeen Khazarian communities would become meaningless. Cf., for instance, A. N. Poliak's *Khazariyyah,* pp. 231 ff.; and D. M. Dunlop's *History of the Jewish Khazars,* pp. 255 f.

4. Maimonides' *Epistle to Yemen, loc. cit.* Maimonides fails to mention here any connection with [Almoravids], but rather blames these events on some Cordovan Jewish students of astrology (there must have been many) who subsequently detected in their dreams signs that the Messiah was to be found in Cordova. But he does not explain why these particular horoscopes were taken more seriously than many others, and why the populace, unsolicited, chose a local man as its messiah, despite the long accepted legends that he was to reside in Rome or Constantinople. Maimonides' silence with respect to the urgency behind this frantic quest may readily be explained by his general peeve against the "science" of astrology, and by the intervening disappearance of the semimillennial threat. Certainly, in countries outside the reach of Almohades, the status of the Jews had undergone no major change in the first seven decades of the sixth century A.H.
5. Maimonides' *Epistle to Yemen,* pp. 100 ff. (Arabic and Hebrew), xix (English). Maimonides did not deny the fact that Al-Dar'i's several predictions had come true. By explaining that such occurrences were by no means "inconsistent with the tenets of the Torah, for prophecy will return to Israel before the messianic advent," he even intimated that Al-Dar'i may indeed have been endowed with the gift of prophecy and in this way have served as the harbinger of redemption.
6. Cf. the fragment from Obadiah's scroll, republished with corrections from the Adler MS by Mann in *Hatekufah,* XXIV, 336 f. (by mentioning that the episode of the Karaite messiah occurred nineteen years after his conversion to Judaism, Obadiah dated it precisely in Ellul, or August–September, 1121); and S. D. Goitein's publication and analysis of an Oxford Genizah fragment containing "A Report on Messianic Troubles in Baghdad in 1120–21," *JQR,* XLIII, 57–76 [the seventh paper of the present collection—Ed.].

On the difficulties encountered even by Egyptian Jewry, including some Palestinian communities still under Egyptian domination, toward the end of Al-Afdhal's regime, see Mann's *Jews in Egypt,* I, 210 ff. The appearance of this first Karaite pseudo-messiah and his revival in practice of the ancient sectarian idea of a priestly messiah, whom Karaite teachers had long equated with Elijah, reveal a degree of messianic tensions which would be difficult to explain without some such overwhelming fears, as were nurtured by the approaching end of the solar half millennium. Cf. N. Wieder's data on "The Doctrine of the Two Messiahs among the Karaites," *JJS,* VI, 14–25, also referring to the Manual of Discipline among the Qumran scrolls, analyzed by K. G. Kuhn in "Die beiden Messias Aarons und Israels," *New Testament Studies,* I, 168–79. Cf. also D. Barthélemy's edition and interpretation of the pertinent passage in his and J. T. Milik's *Discoveries in the Judaean Desert, I: Qumran Cave I,* pp. 110 f. (Hebrew), 117 f. (French, lines 11 ff.); and its reinterpretation with a new English rendition, by F. M. Cross, Jr. in his review article on that volume, "Qumran Cave I," *JBL,* LXXV, 124 f. One must also bear in mind some later reminiscences of that theory, discussed in *SRHJ,* 5:356, n. 6, where Silberman's reservations on Kuhn's interpretation of the Qumran passage are also mentioned. On Dan-Baniyyas, a frontier fortress in the vicinity of Damascus, which was to play a considerable role in the wars between the Latin Kingdom and the Muslims, see William of Tyre's *Historia,* XIV.17, 19, etc., in *RHC,* I, 650, 654; and in Babcock and Krey's English trans., II, 74 ff., and *passim.* Cf. also the excerpts and literature relating to the Jewish settlement there in *Sefer ha-Yishub,* II, 50 f. The obscure Baghdad events may have been stimulated also be some letters received at that time from leaders of a similar movement in a none-too-distant mountain region. See *infra,* n. 7.

7. Benjamin's *Massa'ot,* pp. 51 ff. (Hebrew), 76 ff. (English); Samau'al ibn Yaḥya's *Ifḥam al-Yahud,* cited and analyzed by Schreiner in *MGWJ,* XLII, 410 f.; and the Genizah fragment, first published by Mann in his "Obadia le prosélyte," *REJ,* LXXI, 90 f., and republished with additional comments in *Hatekufah,* XXIV, 347 f. Only the latter mentions the beginning of that movement under Solomon ben Duji in the days of Al-Afdhal. Nevertheless we have no reason to doubt the essential truth of that report showing that the movement extended over a considerable period of time. It is noteworthy, however, that in his enumeration of the previous messianic failures Maimonides did not even hint at the eastern disturbances, which had occurred about the time of Al-Dar'i's appearance in Morocco and again a quarter century later. Perhaps he simply assumed that the Yemenite leaders' familiarity with events transpiring in Baghdad and Palestine—he himself had still been a relative newcomer in those regions—was greater than with the more or less local happenings under western Islam.

8. See especially A. N. Poliak, "David Alroy" (Hebrew), *Ha-Kinnus,* I, 406–6, whose succinct analysis comes closest to our reconstruction of the events from the three often contradictory sources. Poliak also points out the diffi-

cult situation of the Jews of Khazarian Daghestan and its vicinity around 1120. The greatest difficulty consists in dating that movement, which seems to have extended intermittently from about 1120 to 1147 and beyond. Its *terminus a quo* is given by Al-Afdhal's death in 1121. The final date is more questionable. Benjamin's reference to "ten years ago," or close to 1160, seems definitely erroneous, and may be due to an easy scribal error, which replaced *'esrim* (20) by *'eser* (10) and *shanah* by *shanim* (years). His mention, in this connection, of Alroy's teacher Ḥisdai underscores that error, since Ḥisdai had died in 1135. Cf. S. Abramson's "R. Joseph Rosh ha-Seder" (Hebrew), *KS*, XXVI, 93. Mann's effort to connect the appearance of Alroy with the Second Crusade of 1146 (*Hatekufah*, XXIV, 343 f.) has more in its favor than the mere *terminus ad quem* of 1149 or the death of Zif ad-Din of Mosul, mentioned by Benjamin himself. In fact, Zif, like his brother Nur ad-Din (Nureddin), achieved power only after the assassination of their father, Zangi, on September 14, 1146. It is to this assumption of power by Zif that Benjamin clearly alludes. On Zangi's use of Jewish settlers in Edessa, see *SRHJ*, 4:297, n. 33. On the other hand, the date of "about 4895" (1135) given by David Gans in his chronicle *Ṣemaḥ David*, fol. 38b, and accepted by Poliak, is, like his entire account of Alroy's agitation, entirely unreliable. Avowedly based on Ibn Verga's chronicle, it even confuses Alroy with the Yemenite pretender of Maimonides' *Epistle*. Certainly, the news about the leading monarchs in Europe preparing an invasion of the Near East must have nurtured new hopes among the Asiatic Jews. To be sure, the story of the attempted flight from the roof tops caused particular skepticism among modern scholars such as Schreiner. But, apart from being an ancient ingredient of the messianic hope (R. Levi had already interpreted Isa. 60:8: "Who are these that fly as a cloud" as referring to worshipers from all over the world being brought on clouds to Jerusalem on every Sabbath and New Moon; cf. *Pesiqta rabbati*, I, ed. by Friedmann, fol. 2a), it is also borne out by the belief of the followers of Ibn-Rawandi, reported by the historian Ṭabari (III, 418) and mentioned also by Schreiner himself, that they would be able to fly. In fact, we are told that the distinguished lexicographer Abu Naṣr Isma'il al-Jauhari died some time between 1003 and 1010 in a futile attempt to fly from the roof of his home or of the chief mosque in Nishabur, Khorasan. Cf. Brockelmann's *Geschichte der arabischen Literatur*, rev. ed., I, 133; and other data supplied by A. Zeki in *L'Aviation chez les Musulmans*.

9. Maimonides' *Epistle to Yemen*, pp. 84 ff., 92 ff. (Arabic and Hebrew), XVI, XVIII (English); and A. Marx's ed. of "The Correspondence between the Rabbis of Southern France and Maimonides about Astrology," *HUCA*, III, 357. Although such demonstration of one's veracity is a rather frequent theme in international folklore (we recall the somewhat related stories of the Persian-Christian girl martyr, Shirin, and the Cordovan rabbi Hanokh's wife who resorted to similar subterfuges in order to save their virtue), we must accept this particular narrative as historically authentic. It stems from

a critical writer, permanently in touch with Yemen and doubtless evincing a healthy curiosity about the final outcome of his previous correspondence.

Another letter, however, attributed to the Fusṭaṭ sage and produced by one Isaac bar Nathan of Fez at the end of 1187, was but a pious fabrication, doubtless intended to instill courage in the struggling remnant of Moroccan Jewry under the Almohades. Here Maimonides allegedly gave an affirmative testimony to the existence of a messiah in Isfahan, whom he had personally contacted through his brother David and who had satisfactorily answered fifteen of eighteen legal problems left open by the ancient sages for ultimate resolution by Elijah. The fabricator knew something about Maimon's family who had spent several years in Morocco, but he had apparently not learned about David's death in a shipwreck in 1166–67. He also had heard rumors about David Alroy and perhaps invented for him a son, Abi Sa'id ben Dawudi, but placed him in the city of Isfahan. There is no record that Alroy ever was in Isfahan, but this prominent Jewish community, as we know, long played a major role in Muslim folklore as the place of origin of the awesome *dajjal.* Cf. the text published by A. Neubauer in his "Documents inédits, I: Une pseudo-biographie de Moïse Maimonide," *REJ,* IV, 174 ff. (Hebrew) 181 ff. (French); and republished by Halkin in his ed. of the *Epistle to Yemen,* pp. 108 ff. Neubauer, followed by D. Kaufmann, rightly sensed the spurious nature of the Fez letter. If in his brilliant essay on the messianic prediction for 1186 ("Eine jüdische Messiasprophetie auf das Jahr 1186 und der dritte Kreuzzug," *MGWJ,* LXX, n. 45), F. Baer tried to salvage some historic kernals of truth, he succeeded only in furnishing additional proof that the years preceding the Third Crusade were fraught with messianic expectations, which were likely to produce such fabrications. The only astonishing feature in his reply to the southern French rabbis was Maimonides' misreading of their inquiry as relating to his *Epistle to Yemen,* rather than to one about a messiah in Isfahan. But such an error could easily arise in the correspondence of an extremely busy man with respect to a tangential detail. Moreover, he may have been familiar with the unauthorized use of his name in the spurious letter, and yet felt too sympathetic with the plight of his former compatriots in Fez publicly to disavow it. He deftly sidetracked the issue, therefore, without directly accusing the Moroccans of circulating a forgery. On the messianic tensions under the government of Saladin himself, see E. Ashtor-Strauss's observations in *HUCA,* XXVII, 317.

10. Some recent students of Karaism have advanced the notion that all the sectarian trends between the seventh and the ninth century were part and parcel of the Karaite movement. L. Nemoy, in particular, to whom scholarship is greatly indebted for making available the Arabic text of Qirqisani's major work, which includes most of our first-hand information about these heterodoxies, has given currency to that view without anywhere offering a fully documented substantiation. In his *Karaite Anthology,* for example, he writes without much ado about the various sectarian leaders who arose after 'Anan, and adds, "The surnames quoted above indicate the territorial

expansion of Karaism during the ninth and early in the tenth century" (p. xix). There is no justification for thus lumping together entirely heterogeneous elements. Even Qirqisani, who describes them in their chronological sequence, nowhere intimates that he considers them all subdivisions of Karaism, any more than he counts Jesus or Mohammed among the Karaites. (No Karaite before the nineteenth century claimed Jesus for his sect.) True, in his description the contemporary Karaites, too, appear as anything but a homogeneous group. But his analysis of the teachings of these sects, however brief, does show the great difference between movements primarily inspired by messianic pretenders, with neither the ability nor the desire to propagate major changes in the existing legal system, and the primarily legalistic changes introduced by 'Anan, Benjamin or their distinguished scholarly successors, including Qirqisani himself. In the spiritual effervescence which characterized the first two or three centuries of Islamic rule, all sorts of individual as well as group manifestations of questioning and discontent came to the fore, of which Karaism may have become the major beneficiary, but for which it can claim no credit: 'Isawites or Mishawayhites doubtless repudiated the rigid Karaite interpretation of Scripture even more vigorously than they did the masses' warm and colorful adherence to talmudic law. In short, most of them preached an emotional, prophetic-messianic brand of Judaism; Karaism espoused a rational, legalistic-scholastic reform.

10

The Messianic Self-Consciousness of Abraham Abulafia: A Tentative Evaluation

Abraham Berger

Practically all we know about Abraham Abulafia we learn from his own writings which, in contrast with those of other Kabbalists of his time, are rich in autobiographical notes and often show an anxiety for self-revelation. It would be difficult to find the proper place for Abulafia in a typology of Jewish Messianic personalities. Messianic personalities feel the weight of tradition to mean that their mission is to "fulfill what is written." Abulafia reinterpreted this mission in the light of his own ideas, and tradition often assumed a new form as it passed through the prism of his personality. It would be much more fruitful to compare him with Hellenistic mystagogues, Islamic Sufis, and Greek Orthodox Spirituals than with other Messianic pretenders in the Jewish tradition.

He was a man of personal humility in his relations with colleagues and pupils; yet, at the same time, he conveyed an overpowering sense of prophetic self-assurance. Eager for followers, he was disdainful of "fools" and the "mob." Self-styled a Messiah chosen by the Lord, but without any dreams of secular power; yearning for seclusion, yet fated always to wander; enthusiast and rationalist; an elegant stylist, whose most beautiful passages alternate with passages of sheer glossolalia; Antichrist by his own description, yet aspiring toward universal brotherhood—Abulafia was full of apparent paradoxes, and undoubtedly only a proper pathography of his personality could reveal the mainsprings of his be-

Reprinted by permission of Columbia University Press from *Essays on Jewish Life and Thought Presented in Honor of Salo Wittmayer Baron,* 1959.

havior. What we are concerned with in this essay, however, is to gather a few of Abulafia's interpretations of himself as Messiah and possibly to analyze them to discover what kind of a messiah he thought himself to be.

Solomon Adret, his powerful adversary, calls him "that scoundrel Abraham who declared himself prophet and Messiah."[1] That Abulafia did declare himself prophet and Messiah is clear from an examination of his works. Abulafia's conception of himself as the ultimate redeemer is a gradual development, springing directly and inevitably from his ever increasing consciousness of having been chosen as a prophet through a number of spiritual experiences dating back to his first prophetic call in the year 1271.[2] On various occasions, he declares that, like the great biblical prophets, his prophetic activity was compelled by a higher force,[3] overruling all his doubts;[4] this claim he extended even to his "literary" activity, such as his writing a commentary on Maimonides' *Guide for the Perplexed.*[5]

Professor Gershom Scholem, in his *Major Trends in Jewish Mysticism,* has masterfully analyzed Abulafia's theory of prophetic Kabbalah, in which prophecy is identified as a higher form of Kabbalism. As far as his own person is concerned, however, Abulafia goes further than that. A prophetic Kabbalist, if found worthy after much preparation, would become, during the period of his ecstasy, a "messiah of the Lord and an angel of God."[6] Abulafia even wrote manuals to help his followers in attaining this degree of ecstasy. He himself, however, reached for greater heights, for he claimed to be the Messiah as the highest prophet and the high priest. His claims to messiahship take on various forms: in his prophetic work *Sefer ha-Ot,* written in 1288, he sees himself as the pastor of the flock and the healer of the sick, the announcer of glad tidings and the stern preacher against those who despised his warnings.[7] In his commentary on the Pentateuch, which he wrote in the following year, Abulafia sees himself as the Last Deliverer who is parallel with and successor to Moses, the First Deliverer.[8] Under obviously Christian influence, he also declares himself as priest and king of the order of Malkizedek. He writes: "I am priest on my wife's side, a Levite on my mother's side, and an Israelite on my father's side, and although this may be contrary to logic, it is not so for him who knows the 'mystery of Malkizedek, King of Salem, who brought forth bread and wine, and he was priest of God and most high' " (Gen. 14:18).[9]

Abulafia's identification of himself with his wife follows the analogy of Abraham and Sarah who were originally Abram and Sarai.[10] Abulafia adds the old gematria of Abraham and *Zelem Elohim* (the divine image). It is obvious that he is influenced by the various speculations about Adam, the perfect man who was originally androgynous, a state now approximated only by a close spiritual union of man and wife.

Despite the many influences of Christian ideas (and many more of them might be cited) in his Messianic self-interpretation, Abulafia saw himself as Antichrist.[11] He asserts his spiritual mastership over Jesus, the superiority of Sabbath over Friday.[12] Jesus' power, Abulafia insists, was based on the material Tree of Good and Evil, rather than on the spiritual Tree of Life. It is clear that he is identifying Jesus with the Church of the thirteenth century, the Church of arrogant prelates and proud scholastics.

The accident of Abulafia's birth in A.D. 1240, the year 5000 after the Creation, according to the Jewish system of reckoning, was also of great significance to him as a sign pointing to his mission.[13] He envisaged the final redemption as beginning in 1290—interpreting the Danielic year as referring to the Christian year A.D. 1290.[14] In this Abulafia differed from the other Jewish interpreters of his day, who usually counted the Danielic 1290 years from the date of the destruction of the Temple in A.D. 68. Obviously, Abulafia's certainty that redemption would come in his own lifetime,[15] together with his conviction that the birth of Christianity was a great spiritual catastrophe, made him select the earlier date.[16]

Although he was a strong opponent of Christianity, he insists, nevertheless, that the ultimate utopia is a universal recognition of the One Reality, when Judaism, Christianity, and Islam will all "serve the Lord with one consent" (Zeph. 3:9).[17] In his allegorical story about the precious pearl, claimed by all religions, but whose true ownership is still to be determined,[18] Abulafia adds: "The Lord will return the pearl to whom He chooses," and envisions a state of reality in which all mankind will look upon one another as parts of the same organism, just as a body has many organs functioning in harmony.[19] For, to Abulafia, the eventual achievement of the Messiah is no less than the absolute change of reality. The Messiah does not have to perform miracles, Abulafia proclaims, like those performed by Moses or Joshua, or Elijah and Elisha. Here Abulafia sounds like an echo of Maimonides, whom he held in reverence. Then comes the spiritual twist: the Messiah does not have to perform miracles in the sense understood by the masses of Jews and Gentiles, but he will do more—he will bring about a change of reality.[20]

What was Abulafia's call? Like other prophets, he cried for *teshuvah* 'a turning away'. He calls for a change in one's point of view. His scorn is directed against the learned and the rich who find proof that God is with them in the very fact that they are wealthy and honored and have large and prosperous offspring.[21] Abulafia feels that his Messianic task is to awaken those who are sleeping in the dusk of false ideas, in the materialist worship of Mammon and lust, and in the vainglory of learning, especially Talmudic learning,[22] and to lead them to the true light of Divine Reality in the contemplation of the Divine Name, which he sees as the true Paradise made available in this life.

His opposition to the hegemony of the aristocrats and the scholars in Jewish communal life eventually brought him into conflict with the rabbinical authorities. It is quite understandable that men like Adret saw a great danger to the Jewish community, especially to a Jewry in Diaspora, in a free expression of the prophetic spirit. The gift of prophecy, Adret insisted, can be attained only in the Holy Land, and the prophetic spirit would rest only on the wise, the strong, and the wealthy. Abulafia, in the overpowering sense of his own prophetic call, maintained that prophecy is possible not only *now,* but also right *here,* in the Diaspora. "The land on which the Shechinah always rests is the inner soul. Of it, it is said, 'The eyes of the Lord are always upon it from the beginning of the year until the end of the year' " (Deut. 11:12).[23] As for the wise, the rich, and the strong, they are meant, of course, in a figurative and spiritual sense.[24]

Abulafia makes no mention whatever of any political achievements of the Messiah. Even when he laments the miserable state of Jewry as compared with the power and might of the Nations, he finds comfort only in a future for a Jewry spiritually redeemed.[25] By removing the idea of Messiah from both the land of Israel and the political state, Abulafia runs counter to the Jewish tradition of his day, as expressed, for example, by Moses ben Naḥman, whom Abulafia places in the forefront of his spiritual mentors. When Abulafia went to Rome to face the Pope, he did not demand: "Let my people go," as Naḥmanides had foreseen,[26] but rather he went to see the leader of the Christian religion and to discuss Judaism with him.[27] But such spiritual deviations, Abulafia opened up curious religious possibilities, resembling in many respects the development of early Christianity in its separation from the parent faith, and the radical Sufis, who preached that the pilgrimage to Mecca may be undertaken in contemplation without leaving the physical confines of one's own room. In these radical nonnational ideas, Abulafia found few to follow him, and yet his influence was by no means negligible. His practical Kabbalistic manuals were copied for generations by mystical aspirants, down to modern times. His attacks on the rich and the learned were taken over verbatim by the *Sefer Peliah* and possibly stood at the cradle of the *Raya Mehemna*—two works which had a tremendous influence on Kabbalistic movements down to our very day, and were especially influential in the Sabbatian ideology.

NOTES

In his notes, the author cited the Hebrew text of passages translated or referred to in the article. For technical reasons these Hebrew passages could not be included here—Ed.

1. Solomon Adret, *Responsa* (Vienna, 1812), f. 71c–72a, No. 548.
2. Cf. Gershom G. Scholem, *Major Trends in Jewish Mysticism* (New York, 1941), p. 127.
3. "Ve-Zot Li-Yehudah," in Adolf Jellinek, *Auswahl Kabbalistischer Mystik* (Leipzig, 1853), p. 18.
4. "Mafteaḥ ha-Shemot," Jewish Theological Seminary MS No. 843, f. 86a. I wish to express my thanks to Rabbi Gerson D. Cohen, librarian of the Jewish Theological Seminary, for making available to me the wealth of the seminary's manuscripts.
5. Jewish Theological Seminary MS, Enelow Collection, No. 702, f. 22b.
6. Cf. Gershom G. Scholem, *Kitvei Yad ba-Kabbalah* (Jerusalem, 1930), pp. 25ff. (from Abulafia's "Hayyei ʿOlam ha-Ba").
7. *Sefer ha-Ot,* ed. by Adolf Jellinek in *Jubelschrift . . . Dr. H. Graetz* (Breslau, 1887), Hebrew section, pp. 65–85.
8. "Mafteaḥ ha-Shemot," JTS MS No. 843, f. 48a.
9. "Mafteaḥ ha-Ḥokhmah," JTS MS No. 843, f. 86a.
10. "Mafteaḥ ha-Ḥokhmah," JTS MS No. 843, f. 35a.
11. "Mafteaḥ ha-Shemot," JTS MS No. 843, f. 81b. [On this passage, cf. Moshe Idel, "Abulafia on the Jewish Messiah and Jesus," in *Studies in Ecstatic Kabbalah* (Albany: SUNY Press, 1988), p. 52—Ed.].
12. "Mafteaḥ ha-Shemot," JTS MS No. 843, f. 80a.
13. Moritz Steinschneider, *Die hebraeischen Handschriften der Hof- und Staatsbibliothek in Muenchen* (Munich, 1895), p. 142.

14. "Mafteaḥ ha-Shemot," JTS MS No. 843, f. 48a. Cf. *Sefer ha-Peli'ah* (Koretz, 1784), f. 53b (from Abulafia's "Sefer ha-Gan").
15. "Sefer ha-Ḥeshek," JTS MS, Enelow Memorial Collection, No. 858, f. 18a ff.
16. "Mafteaḥ ha-Shemot," JTS MS No. 843, f. 68a.
17. "Mafteaḥ ha-Ḥokhmah," JTS MS No. 843, f. 68b.
18. Published by Moritz Steinschneider in *Hebraeische Bibliographie* (Berlin, 1861), IV, 78–79, and from here reprinted in Israel Zinberg, *Geshikhte fun der yidischer literatur* (New York, 1943), IV, 472–73. Steinschneider suggests that this story may be the prototype of the tale of the three rings popularized by Boccaccio and Lessing. [Cf. Idel, "Abulafia on the Jewish Messiah and Jesus," pp. 48–50—Ed.].
19. "Or ha-Sekhel," Columbia University Library MS No. X893 Ab 92, f. 37ab. Steinschneider does not include the universalistic ending.
20. "Mafteaḥ ha-Shemot," JTS MS No. 843, f. 48a.
21. "Ḥayyei ha-Nefesh," JTS MS, Enelow Memorial Collection, No. 385, f. 2b.
22. *Ibid.*
23. "Sefer ha-Ḥeshek," JTS MS, Enelow Memorial Collection, No. 858, f. 32a.
24. "Mafteaḥ ha-Shemot," JTS MS No. 843, f. 63b.
25. "Mafteaḥ ha-Ḥokhmah," JTS MS No. 843, f. 17ab.
26. Cf. A. H. Silver, *A History of Messianic Speculation in Israel* (New York, 1927), p. 146.
27. *MGWJ*, 36 (1887): 558. [On Abulafia's attempt to meet the Pope, cf. Idel, "Abraham Abulafia and the Pope" [Hebrew], *AJSReview* 7–8 (1982–83), Hebrew section, 1–17, and "Abulafia on the Jewish Messiah and Jesus," pp. 46–47—Ed.].

V

AFTER THE EXPULSION FROM SPAIN

11

Acute Apocalyptic Messianism

Isaiah Tishby

"BIRTHPANGS OF THE MESSIAH" IN THE PERSECUTIONS OF SPAIN AND PORTUGAL

Following the anti-Jewish riots of 1391, a powerful messianic tension prevailed among part of the Jewish population in Spain and in Marrano circles. This tension remained constant or even intensified up to and following the general expulsion of 1492. The persecutions at the end of the fourteenth century were regarded as "birthpangs of the Messiah" and evoked anticipation of an imminent redemption, the impact of which can be seen in messianic agitation and in waves of immigration to the land of Israel.[1] Apocalyptic messianic tension prior to the expulsion reached its peak in the aftermath of the fall of Constantinople, the capital of eastern Byzantine Christianity, into the hands of the Turkish army in 1453. Applying the Aramaic Targum of Lamentations 4:21–22 to the conquest of Constantinople, Jews saw in this the destruction of "small Rome," the first step towards the realization of their eschatological hopes, soon to be followed by the destruction of "large Rome," the center of western Catholic Christianity, which would lead to total redemption.[2]

When, after the Ottoman conquest of Constantinople, persecution increased, leading to the destruction of Spanish Jewry by expulsion and conversions, many Jews gave in to despair. However, there were also many others who remained steadfast in their hope, and in whom the

Reprinted in translation by permission of The Zalman Shazar Center for Jewish History and the author, from *Meshiḥiyyut be-Dor Gerushei Sefarad u-Portugal,* 1985.

disasters intensified the anticipation of an imminent redemption. This resulted in strong messianic agitation within Marrano circles in Spain,[3] among the exiled Jews in their new places of residence, and even in Jewish circles that had never undergone anti-Jewish persecution and expulsions. The writings by Jewish intellectuals of Spain before and after the expulsion are suffused with the feeling and recognition that the persecutions constitute the "birthpangs of the Messiah." Some of the Jews saw in these events the actual beginning of redemption.[4]

"Genizah Pages" presents yet another Jewish intellectual of the generation of the expulsion, who in his general outlook and in detailed descriptions emphasized the eschatological significance of the fall of Spanish Jewry. Several times the text says that the bitter fate of Spanish Jewry constitutes a major component in the ongoing process of redemption.

For that reason [the persecution in Spain] the whole world will suffer, as it is written [Job, 38:13] "and the wicked will be shaken out of it," because of the expulsion hinted in the verse "To seize [*le-eḥoz*=52 (5252, 1492)] the corners of the earth" [Job, *ibid.*]. About this it is written in the Book of Daniel [2:34], "As you looked, a stone was cut out by no human hand, and it smote the image on its feet of iron and clay." The word "iron" *[farzelah]* alludes to King Ferdinand; this stone will appear now, God willing, and will fall upon them [upon Amalek and Esau] in this time (5a).

The reason all things depend on "the exiled of Jerusalem in Spain," and all suffering began for the Jews in this country is that it is at the end of the earth. It is appropriate that for this reason all the world will proclaim that "[God] is one and His name is one," meaning that most of the things hinted in secrets about the future occurred especially in Castile and Portugal at the time of the expulsions (6a).

"Because of 'the exiled of Jerusalem in Spain,' sovereignty is restored to God, blessed be He" (3b). "Here we have a clue as to who is responsible for the persecution against us and our children and our Torah,[5] and for this reason God, blessed be He, will bring great misfortunes upon them and their idolatrous religion" (5b).

The conquest of Constantinople is the first concrete historical event from the period of the persecutions in Spain mentioned in this text. The author writes that while he disagrees with the opinion prevalent among Jewish scholars about the status of this event in the process of redemption, he insists upon its eschatological significance, and even reinforces its importance as a prologue in the apocalyptic messianic drama. As to the events that took place in the generation of the expulsion, there are messianic hints in the coronation of Ferdinand, the expulsion from Seville and the burning at the stake of the Marranos there, the imposition of taxes on Jews to finance the war of Granada, and the course of the war itself.[6] From these hints we can deduce that the author of "Genizah Pages" considered all persecutions from the beginning of the reign of Ferdinand and Isabella as a chain of premessianic events, and it is probable that in the missing parts of the text the author described additional events as links in this chain.

There are many new and significant insights here about the persecutions in Portugal. In previously known sources no special eschatological significance was attached to the suffering of the expelled Spanish Jews and the existing Jewish community in Portugal during the years 1493 to 1498. At most, these events were alluded to obliquely as the aftermath of the persecutions in Spain.[7] The opposite is true for "Genizah Pages." Here the events in Spain, including the sign of redemption in the conquest of Constantinople—a symbolic milestone on the way to redemption—are regarded merely as an introduction to the persecutions in Portugal. The latter are the true "birthpangs of the Messiah," the beginning of redemption, in the fullest sense of these terms.

The transfer of the intensity of the messianic impulse from Spain to Portugal is explicitly expressed in the determination of the "time of the end."

I saw that wise men say that the "time of the end" has begun from the time of [the fall of] Constantinople, and there was a hint of this in the Aramaic Targum of "rejoice and be glad, O daughter of Edom" [Lam. 4:21].[8] I studied it carefully because it was not entirely understood. There was a clue to this in the words "until the time of the end" [Dan. 12:4, 9], for it is enough to say "until the end," so what is hinted to us in *"the time* of the end"? It means that "the time" is God's time. The verses say "for a thousand years in Your sight are but as yesterday when it is passed [Ps. 90:4], and Solomon wrote "and I was day by day His delight" [Prov. 8:30], which our sages interpreted to mean that each of God's days is a thousand years of ours [Leviticus Rabbah 19:1]. I knew, having discovered it, that from the first day of Tishri in the year 5213 [September 14, 1452]—the year that Constantinople was taken by the Turkish king . . . from then until the night of the first of Iyyar in the year 5254 [April 6–7, 1494], there were exactly forty-one years and eight months. This is one unit of God's "time" —one thousand years divided by twenty-four, just as our ordinary day is divided into twenty-four hours. On that night Michael, the Archangel, revealed to me the date of our deliverance from Portugal. (2b–3a)

The meaning of this rather awkward passage is that the conquest of Constantinople was not the beginning of the end but the primary basis for calculating the end, and the "time of the end" in the Book of Daniel was the year 5254 [1493–94], one hour of God's "day" after the conquest of Constantinople.[9] The "time of the end" itself is also not the beginning of the end, but the time in which the angel Michael is permitted to reveal to the visionary the appointed end of the exile, "for until that time [the night of the first of Iyyar 5254] no one in the world could know the mystery of redemption expressed in the phrase, 'until the time of the end' " [Dan. 12:9] (2b).[10] In other words: the conquest of Constantinople in 1453, which in Spain was considered a crucial eschatological turning point, was actually a starting point for the revelation of the appointed end in 1494, when the first wave of the persecutions in Portugal reached its peak, and for the messianic events that were destined to take place in the wake of this revelation.

The heralding of the end by Michael was intended to refer to the liberation of a group of martyrs in Lisbon in first Adar, 5258 [February, 1498], when the forced conversions ceased and the age of redemption started. The calculation of the end to fit that time, and the explanation of the relationship between that date and the "time of the end" in 5254 [1493–94], are included in a complicated eschatological homily, the main points of which I will explain while incorporating a few direct quotations from the text. The homily is based on two consecutive verses (Deuteronomy 29:27–28) following the hints given by the angel Michael: "The Lord uprooted them from their land in anger and fury and great wrath, and cast them into another land, as at this day. The secret things belong to the Lord our God; but the things that are revealed belong to us and to our children for ever." The time of the end is concealed in the numerical equivalents of the Hebrew words for "and cast them into another land, as at this day."

"And I found their numerical equivalent to be 1430, which hints to us of the two exiles in Edom" (2b). 1430 years since the destruction of the Temple means the year 1498 = 5258. The lack of the letter *vav* in the word *ha-nistarot* [the hidden] and in the word *veha-niglot* [and the revealed] is explained as an allusion to the secrets hidden in them: *ha-nistarot* means that the time of the hidden end is in the numerical equivalents of the previous verse; *veha-niglot* yields the number 494, namely, the year 1494 or 5254, in which the angel Michael revealed the secret. The words that immediately follow the above ("belong to us and to our children for ever") hint at the forced conversions that would take place in the year of the beginning of redemption.

"In that Kingdom [Portugal] the children who are [our] strength . . . , and the parents as well, were taken in forced conversions by the Gentiles. This is hinted in the dots over the words 'to us and to our children' and 'for'—that this end in the year of fury[11] is the end of all the numbers of exiles for the exile of Edom" (3a–3b). And here is a short, clear summary of this bizarre eschatological exegesis in the author's own words:

God, blessed be He, did not want all Jews to know the secrets of the suffering in exile, for if [our] entire nation had known at the beginning of the exile of Edom that we would still be in their power in exile 1430 years later, as [in the numerical equivalents of] "and cast them into another land, as at this day," it is possible that no remnant of the Jewish people would be left today, so many and varied have been the tribulations that swept over our ancestors and ourselves. Therefore it is written, "the secret things belong to the Lord our God," meaning that this length of the exile is secret with the Lord, our God. The meaning of *veha-niglot* [and the revealed] is as I interpreted it, that in the Christian year 494 (1494) it will be revealed, in its completeness, through the forced conversion of parents and children, an event hinted in the dots over the Hebrew words for "to us and to our children for [ever]" (3b).[12]

In addition to the central, extremely detailed eschatological exegesis that I have described, all parts of "Genizah Pages" are suffused with an atmosphere of acute apocalyptic messianism in relation to the forced conversions in Portugal. I will highlight three explicit statements in reference to the year 5258 [1497–98].

1. Concerning the seer's announcement that the king is destined to inherit the royal throne in Spain—a forecast given a short time after the forced conversions took place in Lisbon[13]—the text says: "I was told this secret in the name of God: at that time the Messiah will come." In a calculation based on Daniel 7:25 it is stated later on that redemption will start six years after the signing of the Edict of Expulsion, and "afterwards it was fulfilled, thanks be to God, for in first Adar [5258 = February, 1498] we went forth from the kingdom of Portugal, in which the daughter of the King [Ferdinand] was sovereign" (1a). According to this statement the expulsion from Spain is regarded eschatologically as an interim phase between the first rays of the messianic era starting at the time of the occupation of Constan-

tinople, and the glorious sunrise of the Messiah accompanying the liberation of the martyrs in Lisbon (1b).

2. The verse "From the time that the continual burnt offering is taken away, and the abomination that makes desolate is set up, there shall be a thousand two hundred and ninety days" (Dan. 12:11) includes "the news of our redemption in this age: from the day that the king of Portugal launched the attack in the palace of *Os Estãos*"[14] against us and our children, when the continual burnt offering and the Torah were taken away from the people of Israel, the abomination of idolatry will last for 1290 days and Zion and Sinai are to be desolate and also betrayed (5a). This means that Daniel prophesied that "the removal of the continual burnt offering" during the forced conversions in Lisbon in the year 5258 [1497–98] would be the basis for the destruction of Christian strongholds in the year 5261 [1500–1501].
3. Interpreting the verse "Ask of me, and I will make the nations your domain, and the ends of the earth your possession" (Ps.2:8), which is applied to the Messiah from the line of David, the text says: "In this verse there is a hint that the first redemption destined . . . to come, with God's help, will be at the ends of the earth, namely Portugal. God, blessed be He, will take us out of there" (6b).

One sentence contains a hint about the tidings of a hypothetical redemption for the year 5257 [1496–97], based on the verse "the time of the nightingale has come" (Song 2:12). "From this I deduced the seizing of the children in 5257, for if there had been repentance, the nightingale would have sung joyously, but since there was not, they showed me the seizing of the children"[15] (6a). The mere possibility that the melody of the Messiah's footsteps would be heard in 5257—an event which was undoubtedly expected at the beginning of that year or at the end of 5256—contradicts the main foundation of the eschatological scheme in "Genizah Pages": the revelation by the angel Michael in 5254 about the forced conversions and liberation in 5258. But one does not question inconsistencies in the calculation of the end and in messianic visions. When perplexed by various possible dates, those who engage in calculations and visions can always take refuge in the well-known rabbinic statement: "If they are worthy—I will expedite it, if not—it will be in its time."[16] Indeed, even the calculation of "the time of the nightingale" that turned from happiness into mourning was not in vain; it was postponed to the year 5262 [1501–2], as is mentioned later in the text: "And now also in the year of the nightingale [*ha-zamir*, numerically equivalent to [5]262], there will be joyful singing on account of the destruction of their idolatrous worship and their kings."

Following the shift in the focal point of the eschatological scenario from Spain to Portugal at the end of the fifteenth century, an unusual and surprising conception of the beginning and process of redemption was developed in "Genizah Pages." Portugal's Jewry, unlike Spain's, was a small community both quantitatively and qualitatively. Even with the addition of the expelled Jews from Spain, who were absorbed into the Portuguese community in its final years, it did not become an especially high-ranking component of the general Jewish Diaspora. Now, indeed, its devastation through massive, cruel compulsory apostasy, ordered by the king and carried out by governmental authorities, which had no parallel even in the waves of conversions in the years 1391–1412, and which was considered to be a tragedy far more terrible than killings and expulsions, was likely to serve as a justification for regarding the persecutions of Portugal much more prominently and decisively as messianic birthpangs than the persecutions of Spain.

But how are we to understand the fact that the liberation of a group of martyrs and their transfer to North Africa is described as the footsteps of the Messiah, and the occasion of this liberation is presented as "the end of all exiles"? Furthermore, according to the new information in "Genizah Pages," the group of the liberated martyrs included only several dozen people. Even if we add to them "all those who were hidden in their homes and did not apostatize and also those who were not hiding but did not apostatize,"[17] (3a) we arrive at a maximum of several hundred who escaped apostasy, a tiny group in comparison with the hundreds of thousands who left Spain without having converted. This phenomenon of a small minority within the nation regarding itself as the embodiment or representative of the entire Jewish people, and attributing to its fate an all-encompassing Jewish significance, befits a messianic sect or movement with special views and objectives.[18] But those comprising the group who were arrested together after the forced conversions in Lisbon came together by coincidence and did not belong to a unified circle.

I believe we may find a basis for solving this puzzle in the self-image of the author of "Genizah Pages." In several places it is clearly evident that beyond foretelling the future and disseminating eschatological pronouncements, he ascribed to himself a personal mission in the process of redemption and the ability to act and to work wonders in expediting it. Following the proclamation that because of his wicked deeds, King Manuel is destined to suffer from disease and die "in great pain," the text reads: "For this reason I was given a sign in the verse 'Happy is the man whom you discipline, O Lord, whom you instruct in your teaching to give him tranquility from days of misfortune, until a pit is dug for the wicked' (Ps.94: 12–13) . . . I also received a hint in the verse 'that your feet may wade through blood, that the tongues of your dogs may have their portion of your enemies' (Ps. 68:24)"[19] (2a). In these verses, whispered to him from on high, it is hinted that the illness and death of the wicked king will occur on account of the author's personal suffering in his kingdom, which will also be a factor in the victory over the other enemies, the kings of Christendom. Later on he enumerates several anticipated messianic events, among them the return of the Portuguese Marranos to Judaism, in which the primary factor emphasized is the author's activity during his arrest: "He [Manuel] will remember the written message I sent him and he will write it in his diary." Closely following the announcement that the king liberated the martyrs out of appreciation "for the news about his kingdom that I told him . . . when he saw that my words came true, thanks to God . . . and he let me and all my friends go free, and from then on all of Israel, blessed be God"[20] (3a), comes the visionary's dream about a damaged table for which he has to reconstruct the missing fourth leg. The meaning is that the dreamer's role is to mend the damage inflicted on the world in the wake of the forced conversions in Portugal.[21]

His personal mission is also clearly expressed in the description of his activity in the year 5261 [1500–1501]. The purpose of his journey to Jerusalem was to carry out the message in the dream of Nebuchadnezzar (Dan. 2:34) about the "stone [. . .] cut out by no human hand" that struck the feet of the image, "and this stone will be upon them [Amalek and Esau] now, and this was the reason why I directed my feet to go on the path to Jerusalem to bring to Zion the tidings 'Your God is King' " (5a). The event that was supposed to take place in the wake of his journey was the destruction of the principal churches; because of a delay in the start of his journey this event was postponed by a hundred days.[22]

In other words: his propagandist proclamations became active forces in the hastening of redemption. It is possible that since he regarded himself as a kind of partner to the Messiahs, he attached extreme eschatological importance to the liberation of the martyr prisoners, which occurred because of his messages to King Manuel.

CALCULATIONS OF THE END AND THE STAGES OF REDEMPTION

During the years 1391 to 1492, the period of persecution preceding the expulsion, and especially from the conquest of Constantinople in 1453, calculations of the messianic end were common in Spain, accompanied by predictions of the anticipated eschatological events and outlines of the stages of redemption. The cultivation and development of messianic hopes through the establishment of the appointed dates for the end and the depiction of apocalyptic processes to occur in the near future intensified after the expulsion, focusing on the period around the year 1500 —the end of the first decade of the expulsion from Spain and the years immediately following the expulsion from Portugal.

The powerful messianic agitation among the *conversos* of Spain and in Jewish circles of the Diaspora, which generated public upheavals, was bound up with the expectations of the Messiah's advent in the year 1500. The dockets of the Inquisition have preserved detailed and extensive information about the upheavals in the camp of the *conversos,* which began in 1499 with prophetic visions about the coming of the Messiah in 1500 and spread widely.[23] Leading the public agitation in the Jewish community around the year 1500 was a herald of redemption, or a messianic candidate, of Ashkenazi origin, R. Asher Lemlein of Reutlingen. Although he lived in the region of Venice and was active in Italy, there is no doubt that his activity and influence were bound up with the eschatological temperament that was created and spread in the wake of the destruction of Iberian Jewry.[24] This agitation quickly subsided, with no direct continuity, but the messianic tension did not abate, and in the years 1510 to 1520 it surfaced with great power in the apocalyptic propaganda of R. Abraham ben Eliezer Halevi and his circle.[25]

Concomitant with activist attempts to bring about the appointed ends, historical events around the expulsions from Spain and Portugal led to the creation of eschatological systems on the planes of thought and literature, independent of any practical public activity. In these, too, the year 1500 took a central place: in the establishment of dates for the end and the stages of redemption, in hints and numerical equivalents uncovered by homiletical exegesis, and in astrological predictions. Among the apocalyptic thinkers of this category two famous scholars stand out: R. Isaac Abravanel in his messianic works written in 1497–98 determined that the beginning of the redemption would take place in 1503;[26] and R. Abraham Zacuto in an eschatological treatise from the year 1498 or 1499 wrote that the renewal of sovereignty of the glorious line of King David would begin in 1504.[27]

In our discussion of the period preceding the expulsions, we have seen that many eschatological calculations are found in "Genizah Pages," usually based on the numerical equivalents of Hebrew words, alongside which there is future expectation without any systematic calculation. Concerning Spain, I have noted homiletical interpretations of verses detecting signs of redemption in various events, beginning with the coronation of Ferdinand and Isabella in 1475 and ending with the expulsion in 1492.[28] I have pointed out actual calculations with regard to three years associated with the persecutions in Portugal: 5254 [1493–94], the "time of the end," the period in which permission to reveal the date of the end is given; 5257 [1496–97], when the beginning of redemption was possible had the Portuguese Jews repented properly; and 5258 [1497–98], the actual beginning of the redemption with the liberation of the martyrs in Lisbon. "Genizah Pages" contains eschatological calculations pertaining to each one of the five years following 5258—namely, 5259–5263 [1498–1503]—sometimes in isolation and sometimes with two or three years made interdependent. There is one allusion to the year 5268 [1507–8], the latest eschatological date in the extant pages. Let us see, according to the order of the years, how the calculations are arranged, and what events, present and anticipated, are bound up with them.

5259 [1498–99]: "[I found] the date of the war that the King of Turkey would wage against Edom [Christianity] to be in the year "they shall become as though they had never been" (Obad. 16), the Hebrew words for which *[ve-hayu ke-lo' hayu]* are numerically equivalent to 99 [1499], for in that year Lepanto was taken, and because of this he is destined to conquer all the way to Bozrah, with God's help" (4b). This sentence refers to the war of the Sultan Beyezid II, son and heir of

Mehmet II the conqueror of Constantinople, against the Republic of Venice. Beyezid's provocation of Venice began in 1491; in 1496 the Turks conquered Montenegro, a protected territory of the Italian republic; in 1499 actual warfare broke out, and in that year (August 28, 1499) the Turks achieved a great victory in the conquest of Lepanto, an important base for the Venetian navy in Greece.[29] In "Genizah Pages" this Turkish victory is linked with the conquest of Constantinople, which is described in the preceding sentence as the beginning of the revenge against Edom, with an expression of the hope that in the continuation of the war the sultan would triumph over Rome (Bozrah) as well. In the course of the Turkish victories, which continued after the conquest of Lepanto, the conquerors drew near to the gates of Venice and threatened to overwhelm it. This aroused a sense of terror in the Christian world, and the Pope tried to organize a crusade against the Muslim power. The war was terminated by treaty at the end of 1502, but in 1501, when "Genizah Pages" was written, the Turks reached the pinnacle of their success.[30] It is therefore understandable that the Jewish apocalypticist anticipated that the sultan would "conquer all the way to Bozrah, with God's help," expecting in his vision the collapse of Christendom in the years 1500 to 1503.

Scholars have noted in a general manner that the Turkish successes in their war against Venice served as the historical background for the messianic expectations and agitations related to the year 1500.[31] The proclamation by the author of "Genizah Pages" that the conquest of Lepanto in 1499 was an important turning point in the apocalyptic-messianic scenario gives us a key for a precise understanding of the nature of the links between historical events and eschatological predictions at the threshold of the sixteenth century. The prophetic pronouncements in *converso* circles about the coming of the Messiah in the year 1500 were first made in 1499,[32] and according to our information about R. Asher Lemlein, he also apparently proclaimed in 1499 that the redeemer would come in 1500.[33] The upheaval in Spain was probably a spontaneous response to the news about the conquest of Lepanto, which terrified both rulers and the public. The same is true for the propaganda of Asher Lemlein, whose appearance and center of activity was in the region of Venice, the primary goal of the Turkish attack.[34]

5260–5261 [1499–1501]: " 'He drinks from the stream on his way; therefore he holds his head high *[yarim ro'sh]*' (Ps. 110:7). This hints to us of the year *yarim* [equivalent to 260] and the period ending on the last day of second Adar in the year *ro'sh* [equivalent to 501, i.e., March 19, 1501] in the Christian counting. About this the Psalmist says 'while I make your enemies your footstool' (Ps. 110:1)" (5a). In the continuation of the passage, it becomes clear that the eschatological event hinted at in these interpretations is the destruction of the churches in Jerusalem, Sinai, and Rome, which was destined to occur in 5260 but postponed until 5261.[35]

5260 [1499–1500], 5263 [1502–3]: interpretations using numerical equivalents and hinting at these two years, based on the minor differences between two psalms that are basically the same (Psalms 14 and 53), together with two numerical interpretations producing the year 5263 alone, based on other verses, are found in a single passage:

In one psalm it says, "All have turned bad *(sar),* altogether foul" (Ps. 14:3), and "O that deliverance of Israel might come from Zion" (Ps. 14:7). In the other it says, "All have turned to dross *(sag),* altogether foul" (Ps. 53:4), and "O that deliverances of Israel might come from Zion" (Ps. 53:7). . . . They said to me at night that at the sign of *sar* [equivalent to 260], God will remove idolatry, which is "mingled stuff" [*sha'atnez,* a reference to Christianity]. . . . That is why the first psalm says "deliverance of Israel," referring to the deliverance from idolatry. And the second psalm says "all have turned to dross" *(sag):* at the sign of our resting, for it says, "And when it rested" (*u-ve-nuḥoh,* Num. 10:36): by means of *nun-ḥet-heh,* equivalent to the number 63 *(sag)* [5263], the year of the total destruction [of Edom, i.e., Christendom]. This is what the plural "deliverances" hints to us: from the nation and from the state . . . For thus I found that God hinted to us that the number 63 would be bad for them in the verse "two nations *(goyyim)* in your belly" (Gen. 25:23), the numerical equivalent of *goyyim* being 63. So He hinted to us here of great suffering for Israel, and that through us would begin the wars against Edom, with God's help. (5a–b)

The "removal of idolatry" refers to the destruction of the churches, which was set for the year 1500. In 1503 both the nations of Christendom and the institutions of political rule will be destroyed, and rest will come to the Jews. The "beginning of the wars" undoubtedly refers to the beginning of the war between Turkey and Venice in 1499, in which the Turks were prevailing in 1501.[36] As for the interpretation at the end, the struggle of the twins in Rebecca's belly teaches about the suffering of Jacob-Israel, but the primary meaning of the numerical equivalent is that Esau-Edom will be vanquished in 1503, for the verse concludes: "The elder [Esau] will serve the younger [Jacob]" (Gen. 25:23).

5263 [1502–3]: "Furthermore, at the end of five years after this [after the year 5258, 1497–98], the Messiah will be revealed, and the building of the Temple and Jerusalem will commence, and possibly the resurrection of the dead" (4a). Here it becomes clear that with the political downfall of the realm of Christendom, the principle events associated with the rise of Israel will begin to occur. The "revelation of the Messiah" refers to the appearance of the Davidic Messiah, for the Ephraimite Messiah is destined to appear and begin to work in 5262 [1501–2], as we shall soon see.

5261–5262 [1500–1502]: As for the years between 5260 and 5263, in the first of which the author was engaged in writing his propaganda tract, abundant information is preserved in the pages. The references to them enable us to see marvelous expressions of the acute messianic impulse.

> Now within this year, the Jews should no longer be among the nations anywhere within the realm of Edom. The verse says, "Until the day [*ha-yom,* equivalent to 61] blows gently" (Song 2:17), referring to that year [5261], for with God's help, their shadows will be destroyed, namely, their idolatry and their kings, as it goes on to say, "and the shadows flee" (Song 2:17). Therefore, "Turn [*sov,* equivalent to 62 (5262)], my beloved, be like a gazelle, or a young stag, upon the mountains of spices *[bater]*" (Song 2:17). This last phrase refers to the land of Israel, as proven by the verse, "But the bird He did not cut up *[batar]*" (Gen. 15:10). We should go to the land of Israel, to the place "between the pieces" [*betarim;* cf. Gen. 15]. After the idolators of Edom see a grievous sign from heaven, and the death of their greatest kings, and they hear about the revelation of the Messiah (with God's help), they will cause enormous suffering for all Jews. . . . This is what they showed me, the sign in the verse "Nor the ruler's staff from between his feet, until the Ephraimite Messiah, namely Shiloh, comes, and the homage of peoples be his" (cf. Gen. 49:10).[37] Here too, King Solomon hinted to us with a sign they gave me: "The time of the nightingale *[ha-zamir]* has come" (Song 2:10). . . . At the number of *ha-zamir,* 5262, the same number as hinted in "turn" [*sov,* Song 2:17, equivalent to 62], there should be no more Jews in the lands of Edom, for if there will be freedom (with God's help), there will be singing over the devastation of their idolatry and their kings, provided that they go out from their midst. If they do not go out invited, . . .[38] (6a)

The two events destined for the year 5261 [1500–1501], the destruction of the churches ("the devastation of idolatry") and the deaths of the Christian kings, are already known to us.[39] By contrast, in all the passages I have cited before this, nothing has been said about the Ephraimite Messiah or the time of his coming.[40] What is absolutely new, found in this passage alone in the extant pages, is the emphatic call for all Jews who inhabit Christian states to undertake an immediate journey to the land of Israel. Needless to say, a proclamation about the exodus from Christendom and the ingathering of the Jewish masses in the land of Israel as a result of a freely chosen decision made by the Jews of the Diaspora, without any miracles performed by the Messiah or any supernatural act by God, is the assignment of an imaginary enterprise totally disconnected from reality. But precisely this aspect of the eschatological propaganda of the "Genizah Pages" author serves as incontrovertible proof for the power of the acute apocalyptic messianism that throbbed within him, which he aspired to realize through his own efforts.[41]

In the apocopated passage at the end of the pages, which applies the instruction to Abraham in the "Covenant between the Pieces" to the kingdoms in Daniel,[42] we read of the two Messiahs in the years 5261–5262 [1500–1502]:

"Turtledove" [*tor,* in Song 2:12] refers to the Ephraimite Messiah; we know this from the verse "the firstling bull in his majesty" (Deut. 33:17), for the Targum translates the word for "bull" as *tura*. . . . In the year of "the nightingale," [*ha-zamir,* numerically equivalent to] 5262, the voice of the Ephraimite Messiah will be heard in our land.[43] . . . About the Davidic Messiah, we have the verse "my perfect dove *[yonah]*" (Song 5:2, 6:9).[44] This is explained by "To the leader, on *Yonat ʿelem reḥoqim,* of David" (Ps. 56:1) . . . and "O that I had the wings of a dove *[yonah]*" (Ps. 55:7). After this, we have a hint . . . in the verse "Let me tell you of the decree: the Lord said to me, You are My son, I have fathered you this day" (Ps. 2:7). . . . Thus the Messiah from the line of David is alive and well, and he will emerge in peace. . . . It is now that he will emerge into our world, as the verse says, "I have fathered you this day" [*ha-yom,* numerically equivalent to 61, referring to 5261 = 1500–1501]. That is why the psalm continues, "Ask it of Me, and I will make the nations your domain, your estate the limits of the earth" (Ps. 2:8). . . . Therefore the entire world will fear him, as the psalm says, "So now, O kings, be prudent; accept discipline, you rulers of the earth" (Ps. 2:10). "You are My son": the messianic king who will reign . . . will appear, for the most part, on the fourth day of the week, the day on which the sun was created, and he will take precedence over it, as we read, "His name will endure before the sun" (Ps. 72:17), and the entire world will recognize him.[45]

Thus the Davidic Messiah is born, or will be born ("he will emerge into our world") in the year 5261, and in 5262 the existence of the Ephraimite Messiah will become known. The significance of the "birth" of the Davidic Messiah is not clear: does it mean that in that year he will emerge from his mother's womb and begin to grow in a natural manner, or will he come to the world from on high miraculously, as implied by "You are My son, I have fathered you this day" (Ps. 2:7), and remain hidden until the proper time for him to reveal himself and begin to reign? Is it possible that his natural birth occurred some time before and in 5261 he is to reach his full strength and be elevated to the status of concealed messiahship, at the time when the Ephraimite Messiah would arise to prepare the ground for the establishment of the messianic kingdom?[46] The brief mention of the Ephraimite Messiah in the year 5262, together with the indication in the passage I discussed above that the work of the Ephraimite Messiah in 5262 would arouse both terror and fury in the lands of Christendom,[47] shows that the "voice of the *tor*" interpreted here refers to the jubilant sound of the military commander in the eschatological battle, as consistent with the apocalyptic traditions. The phrase "is heard *in our land*" may be intended to mean that the Ephraimite Messiah will wage his war in the land of Israel.

In short, the author of "Genizah Pages" set out on a journey in 1501 in order to greet the warrior Messiah in Jerusalem. Nothing is said about the actual eschatological battles, and the outlook of the author of "Genizah Pages" on this central theme in apocalyptic messianism remains unknown. The apocopated words about the "messianic king who will reign" are obscure, and it is difficult to know whether "his appearance, for the most part, on the fourth day" refers to the beginning of his self-revelation in 5263 or to the establishment of the Davidic kingdom some time later. The content makes it clear that following the last extant words ("the entire world will recognize him") there must have been some information about all the nations of the world agreeing to accept the Jewish faith, as was written previously: "All the world will say, 'The Eternal is one and His name is one' " (6a).

A short sentence without any specific date, which deals with the stages of redemption, also apparently belongs to the years 5261–5262. "With all this, the signs are that between this and that, the Messiah will be born (with God's help), and the devastation of Rome, and salvation in the arrival of many of our brothers of the ten tribes" (3b). Based on the discussion before and after this sentence, the period of time "between this and that" extends from 5258 [1497–98] until 5263 [1502–3], and the nature of the events recorded here indicates that the reference is to the two years before 5263. The birth of the Messiah is explicitly set in 5261, as is explained immediately afterward. The "devastation of Rome" fits the destruction of the churches, including the cathedral of the Pope in Rome, which was originally destined for 5260 but postponed until 5261.[48] The coming of the ten tribes to help, a motif that played a central role in the eschatological propaganda of the fifteenth and sixteenth centuries, is mentioned in "Genizah Pages" only by allusion. It stands to reason that the expected date for the arrival of the lost brothers is 5262, when the Ephraimite Messiah would appear and begin his task.

5268 [1507–8]:

I have also found that all the letters in the verse "Is it not put away with Me, sealed up in My storehouses" (Deut. 32:34), with the exception of the preposition "in," are numerically equivalent to 1453. . . . This hints to us of the fall of Constantinople in that year [1453]. From that year, there will be, as men count, according to the number of "end" [*kalah,* equivalent to 55] until the total destruction of the entire nation of Edom, with God's help. They will pass for a period of years equivalent to the word "then" [*az,* equivalent to 8] to be at our disposal, with God's help, in order to fulfill the verse "I will wreak my vengeance on Edom through My people Israel" (Ezek. 25:14). Because of those from Edom, God will bring to a harsh judgment all seventy nations, as the prophet said, "For the outrage to your brother Jacob, disgrace shall engulf you, and you shall perish forever" (Obad. 10), and then "For the day of the Lord is at hand against *all* the nations" (Obad. 16). (4b)

The calculation of the year 1508 by adding fifty-five years to the date of the conquest of Constantinople ("according to the number of 'end' ") is obviously based on the verse "I will make an end *[kalah]* of all the nations among which I have dispersed you" (Jer. 30:11).[49] The calculation of eight years for the revenge against Edom is not so clear. Apparently, we should assume that the basis for the number is the year 1500, the point of transition from the fifteenth to the sixteenth century; in the Jewish calendar that is the year 5260, which functions as an important date in the outbreak of punishment against Christendom. It seems to me, however, that another possibility better fits the purpose of this calculation; namely, that the point of departure for the eight years is the beginning of the war between Turkey and Venice in 1499. True, this way the calculation is forced, for we must say that both the first year (1499) and the last (1508) are not counted. But immediately after this passage comes the reference to the conquest of Lepanto in 1499, and it is said that "because of this he is destined to conquer all the way to Bozrah, with God's help."[50] It is therefore probable that the eight years until the destruction of Rome were counted from this point on. In this calculation, too, the author used a numerical equivalent ("a period of years equivalent to the word 'then' "), and I have no doubt that this is an allusion to the verse "*Then* the clans of Edom were dismayed" (Exod. 15:15). The information that the anticipated events will take place when those to be destroyed are "at our disposal" is intended to refer to the sins of the kingdom of Edom in the expulsion from Spain, as the continuation says explicitly.

As for the actual events destined for 5268, the punishment of "all seventy nations" because of the guilt of Edom is not associated with any other year. This is not true for the vengeance against Edom itself, for in another place (5b) it is said that in 5263 [1502–3] there will be a "total devastation [of Edom]." It is therefore hard to understand what new information the announcement for the year 5268 provides. There is little choice but to conclude that the "total devastation" in 5263 is intended for only some of the kingdoms of Christendom, particularly Spain and Portugal, while the destruction of "the entire nation of Edom" in 5268 refers to the termination of the religious and political existence of the Christian peoples throughout the world. It stands to reason that the author anticipated future events in the years between 5263 and 5268 [from late 1503 to late 1507] as well, and that these forecasts were included in the pages that are no long extant.

Line by line, I have brought together the data, both factual and visionary, that expresses messianic overtones. Spread before us is a broad and multifaceted tapestry. In general, we may organize the data under three rubrics: (1) "birthpangs of the Messiah": the persecutions in Spain and Portugal, from the coronation of Ferdinand and Isabella in 1475 until the beginning of redemption with the liberation of the martyrs of Lisbon in 1498; (2) "vengeance against Edom": from the outbreak of the Turkish-Venetian War and the conquest of Lepanto in 1499 until the total destruction of Christendom in 1508; and (3) "salvation of Israel": the appearance of the two Messiahs in 1501–3; "the beginning of the rebuilding of the Temple and Jerusalem, and possibly the resurrection of the dead," in 1503; the coming of the Ten Tribes, apparently in 1502; the acceptance by the nations of the world of faith in the God of Israel.

However, each one of the stages reveals that it is missing considerable material, both in detail and in general outline, as I have indicated with specific examples. The allusive and laconic character of the messages of consolation, all of which I have reported in full, is especially obvious. The main purpose of this propaganda piece, of which we have access to only a small remnant, was to prepare the hearts of Jews for the imminent redemption, and the author undoubtedly wrote at length about the deeds of the Messiahs, the processes of salvation for the Jewish people, and its full accomplishment. Thus it is clear that even by squeezing all that can be extracted from the data in "Genizah Pages" we can uncover only part of the apocalyptic-messianic system that was embodied in the complete work.

NOTES

1. See Yitzhak Baer, *A History of the Jews in Christian Spain,* 2 vols. (Philadelphia, 1966), 2:158–62; Aaron Aescoly, *Jewish Messianic Movements* [Heb.] (Jerusalem, 1956), pp. 222–29; Benzion Dinur, "The Movement of Aliyah from Spain to the Land of Israel after the Persecutions of 1391" [Heb.], *Zion* 32 (1967), pp. 161–74; Joseph Hacker, "Links Between Spanish Jewry and Palestine, 1391–1492," in *Vision and Conflict in the Holy Land,* ed. Richard I. Cohen (Jerusalem and New York, 1985), pp. 114–21.
2. See Yitzhak Baer, "The Messianic Movement in Spain in the Period of the Exile" [Heb.], *Zion,* "Me'assef," 5 (1933):73–77; Baer, *A History of the Jews in Christian Spain* 2:292–99; Aescoly, pp. 295–99; Haim Beinart, *Conversos on Trial* (Jerusalem, 1981), pp. 58–59; Hacker, "Links," pp. 121–25.
3. See Baer, "The Messianic Movement," pp. 66–70; *idem, Die Juden im Christlichen Spanien,* 2 vols. (Berlin, 1936), 2:528–42; Aescoly, pp. 248–49, 299–307. Based on his research on the documents of the Inquisition, Haim Beinart has published a series of articles in recent years containing a wealth of new information about the messianic agitation in *converso* circles around the year 1500. Here are the principal references to his work: "The Prophetic Movement in Cordova in the Years 1499–1502" [Heb.], *Zion* 44 (1979; Memorial Volume to Yitzhak Baer); pp. 190–200; "Agudo in La Mancha and Its *Conversos*" [Heb.], *Tarbiz* 50 (1981; Jubilee Volume), pp. 424–35; "Almaden: The *Conversos* of a Village in the Region of La Mancha" [Heb.], *Zion* 47 (1982), pp. 17–55, and esp. pp. 26–32; "The Movement of the Prophetess Inés in Puebla de Alcocer and in Talarrubias and the *Conversos* of These Villages" [Heb.] *Tarbiz* 51 (1982), pp. 633–58; "The *Conversos* of Chillon and Siruela and the Prophetesses María Gómez and Inés, Daughter of Juan Esteban" [Heb.], *Zion* 48 (1983), pp. 241–72; ["The Prophetess Inés and Her Movement in Herrera, Her Birthplace" [Heb.], in

Studies in Kabbalah, Jewish Philosophy, and Ethical Literature Presented to Isaiah Tishby (Jerusalem, 1986), pp. 459–506—Ed.].

4. See Isaiah Tishby, *Messianism in the Generation of the Expulsions from Spain and Portugal* [Heb., the full book from which this section is translated; subsequently, "Tishby"], pp. 52–53, and the bibliographical references there in notes 151–57; Haim-Hillel Ben-Sasson, "Exile and Redemption in the Eyes of the Generation of the Exiled from Spain" [Heb.], *Yitzhak Baer Jubilee Volume* (Jerusalem, 1961), pp. 216–19, 225–27. A view of the expulsion as the beginning of redemption is expressed with great emphasis by Elijah Capsali, *Seder Eliyahu Zuta* (Jerusalem, 1976), 1:249–41. Passages from his book are cited in the article by Ben-Sasson, pp. 226–27 [and cf. Charles Berlin, "A Sixteenth-Century Hebrew Chronicle of the Ottoman Empire," *Studies in Jewish Bibliography, History and Literature in Honor of I. Edward Kiev,* ed. Charles Berlin (New York, 1971), pp. 31–33—Ed.].
5. The reference is to King Ferdinand; see Tishby, p. 19.
6. See Tishby, pp. 18–24.
7. The most important allusions to this matter are found in R. Abraham Halevi's introduction to his book *Mashre Kitrin* ["Untier of Knots"] (see Tishby, p. 38, n. 89) and in the sermons of Joseph Garçon (see Tishby, p. 44 [and Marc Saperstein, *Jewish Preaching 1200–1800* (New Haven, 1989), pp. 199–205—Ed.). Even in the writings of these men, who survived the persecutions in Portugal, the eschatological significance of these persecutions is subdued and presented as secondary to the messianic birthpangs in the persecutions of Spain. In R. Abraham Saba's passage on the dates of redemption, which will be discussed later in the [Hebrew] book, there is an obscure messianic allusion connected with the situation in Portugal in the year 1496, before the persecutions of King Manuel; see Tishby, pp. 95–96.

   An excellent example of the tendency of contemporary leaders to be silent about (or even to suppress comment on) the catastrophe of Portugal is the work of R. Isaac Abravanel, the major portion of which was written after the years 1497–98. This includes most of his Biblical commentaries, in which views about history and eschatology, emphatically relating to the expulsion from Spain and its results, play a significant role. Abravanel worked in Portugal as an important Jewish leader and political figure until he fled to Spain in 1483. His great-grandson, Isaac, the grandson of Judah Abravanel, was forcefully converted there with the other children in 1497. He certainly had full knowledge about the course of events in Portugal, but he never mentions them, let alone incorporating them into the texture of his messianic thought.
8. See the discussion above at n. 2.
9. It appears that R. Abraham Halevi brings as his own view the assumption attributed here to "wise men," namely, the Spanish scholars before the expulsion. *Mashre Kitrin* (Constantinople, 1510) (photo-offset edition with an introduction by G. Scholem, Jerusalem, 1978), p. 4b: "I believe that at

the time Constantinople was conquered by the great Turkish king, the 'time of the end' began." But his conception of the meaning of "time of the end" is close to the view of the author of "Genizah Pages," and there is even a parallel in a specific homiletical-exegetical technique between the two. See below, n. 12.

10. Two other verses from Daniel are interpreted similarly in the continuation of the passage. "He said, 'Go, Daniel, for these things are secret and sealed to the time of the end. Many will be purified and purged and refined; the wicked will act wickedly and none of the wicked will understand; but the enlightened will understand' " (Dan. 12:9–10). "Now at this time [the 'time of the end' in the previous verse, namely, 1494], many will be purified and purged and refined through suffering [the persecutions in Portugal in the years 1493–94]. Then the wicked will act wickedly and none of the wicked will understand. And at that time the enlightened will understand" (2b). Actually, we have no knowledge that any of the "enlightened" understood in the year 1494, except for the anonymous seer [the author of "Genizah Pages"—Ed.] who received the revelation from Michael.

11. "Fury" refers back to Deut. 29:37; the numerical equivalent of the word *ḥeymah* (spelled with a *yod*) is 5058 [1497–98].

12. It is worth citing here the words of R. Abraham Halevi on the "time of the end" and on the concealment of that time. *Mashre Kitrin,* 4a–b: "Since Daniel said (12:9) that these things are secret and sealed to the time of the end, it would appear that at the time of the end they will not be secret. . . . The meaning of "to the time of the end" is until close to the time of the coming of the Messiah, and until the generation when the Messiah will come. The reason these things will be secret and sealed until that generation is that if the end were known and stated explicitly, some of those who 'serve their master in order to receive a reward' in the early generations, seeing how long the exile was to last . . . , would abandon their obligations as Jews, and great destruction would result. It was therefore decreed that the time of the end would be kept hidden, that the things would be 'secret and sealed' until the generation of the Messiah's arrival, the 'time of the end.' Then they will be revealed in that generation, before the Messiah comes." Cf. p. 10b.

Also (p. 13b): "It may be that after the Torah said 'The Lord uprooted them from their land in anger and fury and great wrath' (Deut. 29:27), it went on to say 'The secret things belong to the Lord our God' (Deut. 29:28), to hint that the number of years they would be 'uprooted from their land' would be concealed. The Hebrew word for 'secret things' *[ha-nistarot]* is written without a *vav* to hint at the *vav* that is missing from the word "hanging" [*telu'im,* 'Your life will be hanging before you,' Deut. 28:66]: that it is hidden in order to keep the mystery secret."

Although the date and circumstances of "the time of the end" and the period of the anticipated redemption are different in *Mashre Kitrin* from those in "Genizah Pages," still there are three obvious lines of similarity: (1)

"the time of the end" referring to the period in which the end is revealed; (2) the reason for the concealment of the date of redemption until the "time of the end"; (3) the interpretation of *ha-nistarot* based on the missing *vav* in the word. As *Mashre Kitrin* was written in 1508 in Greece, before R. Abraham Halevi arrived in Jerusalem, I do not see any basis for surmising that it was influenced in this matter by the author of "Genizah Pages." It seems to me rather that the parallels are rooted in a common background in the messianic exegesis of Spanish scholars during the generation of the expulsion.

13. See Tishby, p. 29.
14. [On the use of the *Os Estãos* palace for the forced conversions in 1497 see *Samuel Usque's Consolation for the Tribulations of Israel,* tr. and ed. Martin A. Cohen (Philadelphia, 1965), p. 203—Ed.].
15. [The Hebrew root of *zamir,* "nightingale," which is numerically equivalent to 257, can mean either "sing" or "cut off branches, prune." On the seizing of the children see *Samuel Usque's Consolation,* p. 203—Ed.]
16. Explicit use of this statement is found in "Genizah Pages" (p. 5a), with regard to the time appointed for the conquest of Constantinople. See Tishby, p. 83.
17. See Tishby, pp. 33–35.
18. Obvious examples of this sectarian stance are provided by the Dead Sea sect, early Jewish Christianity, and the Sabbatian movement after the conversion of Sabbatai Ṣevi.
19. See Tishby, pp. 57–58.
20. See Tishby, pp. 33, 35–36.
21. See Tishby, p. 56.
22. See Tishby, p. 60.
23. See the references to the research of Baer, Aescoly, and Beinart above in n. 3. The messianic activism was subdued and arrested shortly after the end of the awaited period, but the agitation did not completely disappear. Some years later, in 1526, it was renewed, with public repercussions among the *conversos* of Portugal, when David Reubeni arrived on his mission in Lisbon. See Aescoly (above, n. 1), pp. 263–69, 359–67.
24. See Aescoly, pp. 249–50, 307–12; E. Kupfer, "The Visions of R. Asher ben Meir Lemlein of Reutlingen" [Heb.], *Qoveṣ ʿal Yad* 8:18 (1976), pp. 387–423; David Ruderman, *The World of a Renaissance Jew: The Life and Thought of Abraham ben Mordecai Farissol* (Cincinnati, 1981), pp. 137–38. Kupfer's thesis (p. 397) that Asher "did not speak in his announcement of redemption about a specific time period," and that his entire public campaign was a call to repentance and fasting to accelerate the approach of redemption, is totally contradicted by clear and decisive evidence. There is no basis for his claim that Asher's statement (in his letter of 1509)—that it is better for him to remain silent because "they will say about him that his vision applied to an extended period, and he prophesied of the distant future"—leads to the conclusion that in the years 1500 to 1502 he never

asserted that the Messiah would come during that period. It is common for calculators of the end and messianic propagandists to behave cautiously after their proclamation turns out to be incorrect, and to obscure or postpone the anticipated date of the end.

We can add to the sources about the messianic propaganda of R. Asher Lemlein the important (though late) evidence in R. Mordecai Dato's book *Migdal David,* written in 1556. Here is what it says (Oxford MS 2515, fol. 158a–b): "Lattes [R. Jacob ben Emanuel, Bonet de Lattes] brought many arguments to prove that this treatise ["Saturn and Jupiter in Pisces" (Heb.)] taught that a prophet would arise among the Jewish people. And so it occurred: there arose in those days a Jew who prophesied from his heart, and he led many away from sin through acts of repentance and fasts. His name was Lemlein Ashkenazi, and he was the Messiah from Padua. My heart tells me that it was not without significance, but rather one of the upheavals intended by God [in the margin: sixty-six in all] that we have mentioned in the name of the Zohar." See Y. Jacobson, "R. Mordecai Dato's Doctrine of Redemption," unpublished doctoral dissertation, Hebrew University, 1982, pp. 325–26 and note. The epithet "Messiah from Padua" is important for two reasons: first, it helps tip the scale on the question whether Asher appeared only as a prophet and herald of redemption, or whether he attributed messianic status to himself (see Aescoly, p. 249); and second, in other sources Venice and Istria are mentioned as the principle areas for his activity, and the term "from Padua" apparently shows that he was from Padua before his messianic career began.

25. See Gershom Scholem, "The Kabbalist R. Abraham ben Eliezer Halevi" [Heb.], *Kirjath Sepher* 2 (1925); pp. 130–38; *idem,* "New Investigations of R. Abraham ben Eliezer Halevi" [Heb.], *Kirjath Sepher* 7 (1930–31), pp. 447–48; Aescoly, pp. 314–35. The testimony of R. Abraham Farissol that many preachers spread the announcement of redemption for the year 1512 in the Italian communities proves that shortly after the end of the intensive messianic propaganda of Asher Lemlein, and apparently in its wake, new agitation began, fixing a date in the near future.

26. See Baer, "The Messianic Movement" (above, n. 2), pp. 71–77; Benzion Netanyahu, *Don Isaac Abravanel, Statesman and Philosopher* (Philadelphia, 1953), pp. 216–20.

27. See M. Beit-Arye and Moshe Idel, "Treatise on the End and Astrology by R. Abraham Zacuto," *Kirjath Sepher* 54 (1979), pp. 174–82 (introduction), 184–88 (Zacuto's text). Calculations of the end for 1504 and 1505 in other sources are cited on p. 182; the "Treatise of a Seer," containing the calculation of the end for 1504 from R. Yohanan Alemano's manuscript book "Ḥay ha-'Olamim," is printed in the appendix (pp. 191–94). As to the calculation for 1504 widely attributed to the Zohar which is cited there (p. 182), and other calculations of a similar type, I will discuss this in detail in the next section [of the Hebrew book: Tishby, pp. 82–97 —Ed.].

28. See Tishby, pp. 18–24.

29. See S. J. Shaw, *History of the Ottoman Empire and Modern Turkey*, 2 vols. (Cambridge, 1975), 1:75–76. In Hebrew historiographical sources the Turkish-Venetian war is described in detail, emphasizing the conquest of Lepanto, but without any eschatological overtones. See Joseph ha-Kohen, *History of the Kings of France and of the Ottoman Turkish Sultans* [Heb.] (Amsterdam, 1733; first edition: Sabbionetta, 1554), part one, pp. 52a–53b; Capsali (above, n. 4), pp. 241–52.
30. See Shaw, *ibid.*
31. See Baer, "The Messianic Movement," p. 70; Aescoly, p. 250; Netanyahu, pp. 78–79, 234–38.
32. See the articles by Beinart (above, n. 3).
33. We learn this clearly from the formulation in R. David Ganz's *Tsemaḥ David*, part 1, ed. M. Breuer (Jerusalem, 1983), p. 137, that "Rabbi Lemlein heralded the coming of the Messiah in the year 1500," and the author's grandfather "destroyed and demolished the special oven for baking unleavened bread," because of his belief "that the following year he would bake unleavened bread in the Holy Land." This tells us that the pronouncement was made in the year before 1500.
34. Several sources prove that the messianic activism of R. Asher Lemlein continued into the year 1502. See Aescoly, pp. 308, 311; Kupfer, p. 423. The interruption of the agitation was probably caused by the ending of the war between Turkey and Venice with the signing of the peace treaty between them in mid-December, 1502—near the beginning of 5263. Note that even after the end of the war R. Abraham Halevi clung to the hope that the Turks would fulfill their eschatological destiny, conquer Rome and destroy it. " 'Seir becomes a possession of its enemies' (Num. 24:18) hints that the Turks, their enemies, will come against Rome and all of Italy and possess their land, and from that point on, Israel will do valiantly. The following verse says, 'A victor issues from Jacob' (Num. 24:19), for a great prince will come from the House of Jacob [apparently the Ephraimite Messiah] and destroy the remnants of the city of Rome, those who escaped from the destruction of the great Turkish king (may God give him long life and exalt him and quickly expedite his work!)" (*Mashre Kitrin*, p. 4b). "The great Turkish king" is undoubtedly Beyezid II, who still reigned in Turkey in 1508, when *Mashre Kitrin* was written; the good wishes are meant to encourage the sultan to renew his war against the realm of Edom in Italy. See Ben-Sasson, "Exile and Redemption" (above, n. 4), pp. 225–26, n. 53.

In their adulation for Mehmet II, the conqueror of Constantinople, *conversos* in Spain attributed blatantly eschatological functions to him. Among them was the belief that the sultan was destined to be the redeemer of the Jews. This is reported in an Inquisitorial investigation, under the name of one of the accused: "You do not know who this Turk is. . . . This man, who is called the destroyer of Christianity and the defender of Judaism, is the appointed Messiah of the Jewish religion." These words are quoted in Baer's article, "The Messianic Movement" (above, n. 2), p. 64.

See there, pp. 63–65, 77, and his book, *A History of the Jews in Christian Spain,* 2:347–48. Aescoly, pp. 296–99, cites additional passages about the belief in the messianic character of the Turk, in Hebrew translation from the statements of *conversos* found in the documents collected by Baer, *Die Juden in Christlichen Spanien,* vol. 2.

Particularly important for our purposes are the hints of R. Isaac Abravanel about the status of the "King of Ishmael" in the process of messianic redemption. I refer to the hints in one of his explications of the surprising homiletical interpretation in *Pirqei de-R. Eliezer,* chap. 28, of "upon him" in the verse "A great dark dread descended upon him" (Gen. 15:12): " 'Upon him'—these are the Ishmaelites, upon whom the son of David will sprout, as we see in the verse, 'I will clothe his enemies in disgrace, while upon him his crown shall sparkle' " (Ps. 132:18). This is what Abravanel wrote (*Yeshuʿot Meshiḥo,* Koenigsberg, 1861, part 1, 15a): "It is quite possible that the Messiah will first appear in the land of the Ishmaelites [i.e., the Muslims—Ed.]. Because of his glory, he called them by their own name and said that upon them the son of David will sprout. And who knows whether a king of Ishmael will not accept the religion of Israel and bring about the salvation of Israel and be an anointed one *[mashiaḥ],* as in the case of the king. About him it is said that the fruit of blessing is in Ishmael, upon whom he will sprout."

The words "as in the case of the king" are difficult, and two scholars (Netanyahu, [above, n. 26], p. 323, n. 161; A. Shmueli, *Don Isaac Abravanel and the Expulsion from Spain* [Heb.] (Jerusalem, 1963), pp. 144–45) made things easier for themselves; citing the sentence without the problematic words, they stated simplistically that Abravanel expressed here the expectation that a Muslim king who becomes a Jew will be the hoped-for Messiah, similar to the belief attributed to the *conversos.* This is clearly an erroneous interpretation, for assigning the "King of Ishmael" to the status of the Jewish Messiah, whether from the line of David or of Joseph, does not fit at all with Abravanel's views. The language of the sentence indicates that a textual error has crept in, and in my judgment the proper reading is "as in the case of the king [of Persia]," namely, Cyrus, who is called God's "anointed" or "Messiah" (Isa. 45:1).

The meaning is expressed elsewhere in the same book (part 2, investigation 1, chap. 5, 35a): because the king of Persia destroyed Babylonia and is destined to destroy Rome, "Cyrus, king of Persia, was called the anointed of the God of Jacob, for he took vengeance on behalf of God." In the same passage, consistent with the identification of Turkey with Persia that is common in Abravanel's writings, we find that the "children of Persia" who are destined to destroy Rome "are the Turks who rule now over all of Greece; from there they will conquer Italy and come to Rome, which will fall into the power of Persia." Thus, at the time when *Yeshuʿot Meshiḥo* was being written (it was finished in December, 1497), about a year and a half before the outbreak of war between Turkey and Venice, Abravanel already anticipated that a major war would blaze up between the two competing powers, and he expected that this would end in the conquest of all of Italy and the destruction of Rome.

From this we see that his dramatic hope that "a king of Ishmael will . . . accept the religion of Israel and bring about the salvation of Israel and be an anointed one *[mashiaḥ],*" similar to Cyrus, or in a different formulation a bit later, "that the king of Ishmael will accept the religion of the King Messiah," refers not to just any Muslim ruler. Rather, Abravanel sets up the realistic image of Beyezid II, whose power and whose hatred of Christianity were known to him, and assigns to him a fully messianic task.

This shows that the struggle between Turkey and Venice, which the author of "Genizah Pages" proclaimed to have eschatological significance in the wake of the conquest of Lepanto, had previously served as the cornerstone of the structure of messianic forecasts in Abravanel's historical reflection. Abravanel's explanation that the prophecy of Zechariah about the destruction of Tyre would be fulfilled in the destruction of Venice similarly reflects his understanding of the struggle between Turkey and Venice. See *Mashmiʿa Yeshuʿah* (Amsterdam, 1644), p. 71d, comment on Zechariah 9:2; cf. Netanyahu, p. 233, and p. 322, n. 148.

35. See Tishby, pp. 60–61.
36. See above.
37. In messianic homilies known to us "Shiloh" is interpreted to refer to the Davidic Messiah or to the Messiah in general. Apparently, the author of "Genizah Pages" introduced his own novel application of "Shiloh" to the Ephraimite Messiah, although it is possible that he was aware of the anomalous allusion to the Ephraimite Messiah in *Yalqut Shimʿoni,* Psalms, paragraph 621. See A. Posnanski, *Schiloh, Ein Beitrag zur Geschichte der Messiaslehre* (Leipzig, 1904). The passage from the *Yalqut Shimʿoni* is cited in the collection of sources in the appendix to the book, p. XV; see also p. 124.
38. The direct continuation, at the beginning of 6b, is almost totally illegible, and most of the lines on the first half of the page are so fragmented that it is difficult to reconstruct what is missing. However, it is clear that immediately following the word "invited" comes something about the punishments expected for those Jews who would not leave the Christian lands for the land of Israel in the years 1501 to 1502.
39. See Tishby, pp. 60–62.
40. The context indicates that the phrase "appearance of the Messiah" mentioned here before the explicit reference to the Ephraimite Messiah refers to him. However, at the beginning of the events destined to occur in 5263, which I discussed above, the phrase "appearance of the Messiah" occurs (4a), and there the year requires that the phrase refer to the Davidic Messiah, as I explained. The matter still needs clarification.
41. This particular manifestation of acute messianism is unique. R. Abraham Halevi was the most ardent apocalyptic figure in the period following the

expulsions from Spain and Portugal. He and his colleagues tried incessantly to bring things to a head by circulating provocative announcements of the imminent redemption. In his work messianic propaganda reached its peak in a call to communal leaders to undertake vigorous efforts to inspire a mass movement of repentance in order to be spared the "birthpangs of the Messiah." But it never occurred to him to demand an exodus from Christendom at the approach of his eschatological deadlines. See Scholem, "The Kabbalist R. Abraham Halevi" (above, n. 25), pp. 134–35; Aescoly, *Messianic Movements* (above, n. 1), pp. 328–30. The sentence to which I referred, published in Scholem's article as part of the "Epistle on the Mystery of Redemption" from 1519, is actually the conclusion of a propaganda letter from 1525, as Scholem himself determined in his introduction to *Mashre Kitrin,* n. 125. But in order to escape the "birthpangs of the Messiah" as the crucial year 5284 [1523–24] approached, Halevi also directed a powerful campaign for a movement of repentance in his "Commentary on the Prophecy of the Boy" from 1517, and in his "Epistle on the Mystery of Redemption" from 1519. See Scholem, "The Kabbalist R. Abraham Halevi," pp. 132–34, 136–37. In fact, his desire to inspire a movement of repentance in order to speed the redemption and save Jews from the "birthpangs of the Messiah" was already expressed in his book *Mashre Kitrin,* written in 1508; see pp. 3a–b, 17b.

42. The verse interpreted is Gen. 15:9: "He said to him, 'Bring me a three-year-old heifer, a three-year-old she-goat, a three-year-old ram, a turtledove, and a young bird.' " The main sources for the inclusion of the vision of the kingdoms in the "Covenant between the Pieces" are Genesis Rabbah, chap. 44, and *Pirqei de-Rabbi Eliezer,* chap. 28. The first half of *Yeshuᶜot Meshiḥo,* the second book in R. Isaac Abravanel's messianic trilogy, is completely dedicated to establishing the correspondance between the vision of the kingdoms and the "Covenant between the Pieces," through a detailed explication of the midrash in *Pirqei de-Rabbi Eliezer*. Abravanel (p. 11a) explains the verse "he did not cut up the bird" (Gen. 15:10) as a symbolic act ensuring the eternal existence of the Jewish people, as opposed to the Gentile kingdoms, which will pass away from the earth, as indicated by allusion in *Pirqei de-Rabbi Eliezer,* made explicit in Rashi's comment on Genesis 15:10 and in later exegetical midrashim. The identification of the bird in the "Covenant between the Pieces" with the Jewish people, together with the midrash in Song of Songs Rabbah, end of chapter 2 ("On the mountains of spices *[bater]:* by the merit of the conditions I made with your father Abraham between the pieces *[betarim]*"), served as the basis for the homiletical formulation of the call to immigrate to the land of Israel in "Genizah Pages."

43. Based on Song of Songs 2:12: "The time of the nightingale *[ha-zamir]* has come, and the voice of the turtledove *[tur]* is heard in our land."

44. Interpreting "young bird" in the "Covenant between the Pieces" as the Davidic Messiah. Genesis Rabbah 44:15: "A turtledove and a young bird:

this is Edom." *Pirqei de-Rabbi Eliezer* 28: "*Tor* [usually "turtledove"]: these are the Ishmaelites; this word *tor* is not Hebrew but Aramaic, meaning 'ox.' . . . And a young bird: this is the Jewish people, compared to a young bird, as in the verses 'My dove, in the cranny of the rocks' (Song 2:14), and 'Only one is my dove, my perfect one' (Song 6:9)." *Midrash Lekaḥ Tov,* ed. Solomon Buber (Vilna, 1880), p. 35a–b: "A turtledove and a young bird: this is the kingdom of Israel, as is written, 'My dove, in the cranny of the rocks' (Song 2:24)." In *Pirqei de-Rabbi Eliezer,* and consequently in *Lekaḥ Tov,* the Messiah is represented by the bird of prey that descended upon the pieces of the carcasses, which symbolize the kingdoms. See Abravanel's *Yeshuʿot Meshiḥo,* part 1, p. 18a–b. In the sources I have examined I have not found anywhere an interpretation that applies the turtledove and the young bird to the two Messiahs; this appears to be an innovation by the author of "Genizah Pages." While Song of Songs Rabbah, chap. 2, states, "The voice of the turtledove is heard in our land (Song 2:12): what is this? It is the voice of the messianic king," this statement refers to the Davidic Messiah, and there is no reference to the turtledove in the "Covenant between the Pieces."

45. This is the apocopated ending of the pages.

46. R. Isaac Abravanel spoke about the birth of the Messiah in the generation of the expulsion from Spain in several places, but the ways in which he described it are not fully consistent. I will cite four passages. *Maʿyenei ha-Yeshuʿah* (Amsterdam, 1647), *maʿyan* 12, *shaʿar* 2, *tomer* 7, p. 88a: "As for the birth of our righteous Messiah, I have no doubt that he was already born before the great expulsion caused death and destruction for the Jewish diaspora in Spain. . . . For the prophet said, "Before she labored, she was delivered" (Isa. 66:7), meaning, before the birthpangs of redemption, Zion, or the Jewish nation, gave birth to the messianic king. . . . Perhaps in the preceding year (1491), the chief of the shepherds, the anointed of the God of Jacob was born." According to this supposed year of birth, the Messiah would be in natural life a youth of twelve in 1503, the first and principal eschatological date in the calculations of Abravanel.

Yeshuʿot Meshiḥo, part 2, investigation 1, chap. 2, p. 23b: "Our righteous Messiah will be born among the Jews in the diaspora of Rome, in the midst of Christians. . . . The messianic king will be born or will reveal himself when the Jews are being expelled from the Roman and Christian lands. . . . He will be one of those who experience acts of persecution and forced conversion." This use of the future tense contradicts the certain proclamation in *Maʿyenei ha-Yeshuʿah* that the Messiah was born before the expulsion, but he avoided committing himself too clearly by writing "will be born or will reveal himself."

Ibid., investigation 3, chap. 3, p. 51a: "God will create anew on earth. The female, which is the nation whose power has waned like that of a female, will produce the messianic king, not as a small child but as a man of wisdom and strength. When he reveals himself suddenly in the nation, he will already be like a hero, whose might is apparent. . . . God will say to the messianic king when he reveals himself in the nation, 'Up to now, you were exiled, subjugated, oppressed, driven, like the rest of your brothers of the Jewish people. Now I have seized your hand; it is as if I have fathered you this day in this stature, and come upon you suddenly.' " Here the birth of the Messiah is explicitly described as his self-revelation, and this is the meaning of the verse "You are My son, I have fathered you this day" (Ps. 2:7), which is also used in "Genizah Pages."

Ibid., part 1, p. 15a: "And upon him [Ishmael] shall sparkle the crown of the son of David (cf. Ps. 132:18), meaning that while [the king of Ishmael] reigns in the holy land, [the Messiah] will be born in the land of Ishmael." That is to say, the revelation of the Messiah in the land of Israel while the Muslims controlled it is considered as if the redeemer was born "in the land of Ishmael." The context of this statement is discussed above, n. 34.

The changes and transformations in the meaning of "birth of the Messiah" in the writings of Abravanel augment the problems relating to the meaning of this phrase in "Genizah Pages."

47. See above at n. 37.
48. See Tishby, pp. 60–61.
49. Also Jeremiah 46:28, with a slight variation: "I will make an end of all the nations among which I have banished you."
50. See above at n. 29. Actually, even if we assume that the calculation requires us to count eight years from 5260, the forecasts for that year and those that follow it are anchored in the Turkish-Venetian War, as I explained in the discussion above.

VI

THE SABBATIAN MOVEMENT AND ITS AFTERMATH

12

Sabbatai Ṣevi: The Mystical Messiah

Gershom Scholem

1. THE BACKGROUND OF THE SABBATIAN MOVEMENT

A survey of Jewish history during the period immediately preceding the outbreak of Sabbatian messianism would unduly surpass the limits of the present study. Nonetheless there are problems that cannot go unmentioned if we are to understand the generation that gave birth to this messianic movement. Many factors were involved in producing the events described in the following pages. An analysis of their relative importance is all the more urgent as historians have reached no unanimity in answering the great initial question: What exactly were the decisive factors that brought about the messianic outbreak?

The usual, somewhat simplistic explanation posits a direct historical connection between the Sabbatian movement and certain other events of the same period. According to this view, the messianic outbreak was a direct consequence of the terrible catastrophe that had overtaken Polish Jewry in 1648–49 and had shaken the very foundations of the great Jewish community in Poland. The destruction had, in fact, surpassed anything known of earlier persecutions in other countries. This explanation was plausible enough as long as it could be maintained—as, indeed, it has been until now—that Sabbatianism as a popular movement started as far back as 1648, when Sabbatai Ṣevi came forward for the first time with messianic claims. It was supposed that Sabbatai's followers con-

Reprinted by permission of Princeton University Press from *Sabbatai Ṣevi: The Mystical Messiah,* by Gershom Scholem, translated by R. J. Z. Werblowsky, Bollingen Series 93. Copyright ©1973 by Princeton University Press.

ducted a propaganda campaign, converting more and more believers until the movement reached its climax in 1666. Though it will be argued in what follows that there is no foundation whatever for this view, at the outset we may duly take note of one grimly concrete historical fact: there had been a major disaster, and soon afterward there was a messianic outbreak. The real significance of the former for an understanding of the genesis of the latter will become clearer as our story unfolds.

Even on its own premises the aforementioned explanation accounts for only half the facts—and the lesser half, for that matter. The weightiest argument against overestimating the causative role of the massacres of 1648 follows from a consideration of the difference between the Sabbatian outbreak and previous messianic movements. This difference lies in the extension, in space and time, of Sabbatianism. All earlier messianic movements, from Bar Kokhba, who led the Jewish revolt against Rome in 132–35 C.E., onward, were limited to a certain area. Somewhere a prophet, or possibly a messiah himself, arose proclaiming that the end of days was at hand and launched a movement limited to a province or a country. Never before had there been a movement that swept the whole House of Israel. It would seem unwise to try and explain this wide extension by factors that were operative in one area only, whatever their weight and significance there. Our caution will increase when we consider the fact that the Sabbatian movement did not originate in Poland but in Palestine. If the massacres of 1648 were in any sense its principal cause, why did the messiah not arise within Polish Jewry? And if there was such a messiah, why did he fail to rouse the masses, and why did he sink into oblivion? The Sabbatian movement spread wherever Jews lived—from the Yemen, Persia, and Kurdistan to Poland, Holland, Italy, and Morocco. There is no reason for assuming that Moroccan Jewry was particularly affected by the massacres of 1648, of which they probably had heard very little anyway. It is also a remarkable fact that Polish Jews were not particularly conspicuous among the main propagandists of the movement.

Of even greater relevance to our argument is the collapse of earlier messianic movements as a result of disappointment. Initial reports turned out to be untrue, the messiah disappeared or was killed, and the movement petered out. This was the usual course of things; but for some contemporary chroniclers or letter writers not even an echo of many of these movements would have reached us. Occasionally traditions about such an outbreak would linger in popular memory, but after a generation or two everything would be forgotten. The Sabbatian movement is the great exception to this rule: not only did history belie its message, but the disillusionment was so exceptionally cruel that normally it should have been the last nail to the movement's coffin. The messiah had apostatized and publicly betrayed his mission. If the movement did not die out there and then but survived the seemingly fatal crisis, persisting for generations in various forms and metamorphoses, then its roots must have lain deeper than in local circumstances and conditions. Indeed, they must have reached down to the layer of common heritage on which the attitudes of seventeenth-century Jewry as a whole were founded. The massacres of 1648 no doubt contributed their share, but as an historical factor they lack the dimension of depth within which alone the Sabbatian movement becomes intelligible. We must, therefore, look for other factors of wider and more fundamental validity.

The quest for other specific conditions, common to Poland as well as other Jewish communities, is not likely to be more successful. In some countries the situation was actually or potentially one of persecution, and the message of redemption could reasonably be expected to find ready ears. Persia, the Yemen, and Morocco are instances of this kind. However, the movement did not manifest any lesser momentum in those Jewish centers that enjoyed peace and prosperity. If these communities too were haunted by a sense of catastrophe, it did not stem from their immediate experience but from deeper and less specific causes.

For the same reason we must view with grave doubts all attempts at an easy sociological or economic explanation of the Sabbatian success, all the more so as there is no possibility at all of describing the movement in terms of an eruption of social or class tensions within Jewry. As regards the economic situation, one is struck by the similarity of responses to the messianic tidings in ruined and pauperized communities, such as Poland, and in the most prosperous and flourishing centers. The Jewries of Constantinople, Salonika, Leghorn, Amsterdam, and Hamburg, whose star had for some time been in the ascendant, were in the vanguard of Sabbatian enthusiasm. Christian contemporaries more than once voiced their angry surprise at the privileges and freedoms enjoyed by the Jews of Salonika, Leghorn, and Amsterdam. Yet these Jews threw all economic considerations to the winds and, as far as we can ascertain, gave way to unbridled messianic enthusiasm. Our knowledge of the last-named communities and of their attitudes during the messianic outbreak is good. Turkish Jewry was safely established and had not yet passed its prime. Palestinian Jewry was, as usual, sunk in the depths of misery, but its misery has no bearing on our evaluation of the position of the Jews in the rest of the expanding Ottoman Empire in which anti-Jewish persecutions were extremely rare and ran counter to the considered policy of its rulers. Here, in the empire, by far the great majority of Spanish Jews, the main bearers of the Sabbatian movement, had settled. The amazing rise of the communities of Amsterdam and Hamburg is well known. Yet the members of these communities, descendants of marranos, reacted no differently from their brethren in Morocco who smarted under almost continuous oppression and persecution.

The question of internal social relations is far more delicate and obscure and requires very careful examination. Whatever the legitimacy of generalizations about the attitudes of particular communities to Sabbatianism, we ought still to ask what were the personal and social differences in the attitudes of the rich and the poor, of the ruling class and the masses. The problem is much confused by the subsequent arguments of both Sabbatian believers and opponents. In the years of the great disillusionment following Sabbatai's apostasy, the opponents again raised their heads and contended that the "rabble" had forced the unwilling rabbis and sages to comply or, at least, to keep quiet. Conversely we find the Sabbatians themselves accusing the rabbis and the rich, that is, the social elite, of opposing the movement.[1] The suspicion that the response to the Sabbatian message was conditioned by social factors thus appears to be confirmed by both sides and supported by such diverse witnesses as Jacob Sasportas and Joseph ha-Levi on the one hand, and Abraham Miguel Cardozo on the other. This unanimity, however, is misleading, and the measure of truth that it contains is less than appears at first sight. We are dealing here with an explanation after the fact, useful to both sides, though for opposite reasons. It provided an easy way out to the leaders of the Jewish communities—particularly if they were anti-Sabbatians—who could now exculpate themselves and their colleagues by claiming that their unwilling co-operation had been extorted under pressure from the "mob." The Sabbatians, on the other hand, who wanted an explanation for the failure of the movement, could easily agree with their opponents and point to them as the scapegoats whose lack of true faith had led to the messianic debacle.

None of these explanations is borne out, however, by the documents composed during the high tide of the movement. True enough, the opposition to Sabbatai Ṣevi included rich merchants, lay leaders, and rabbis, that is, members of the ruling class. There is nothing surprising in this. The theologians were faced with grave religious and intellectual difficulties by the personality and behavior of the "messiah"; their doubts could easily turn to opposition. The rich had something to lose by the new order which the messiah was supposed to inaugurate. The "small man" was more easily drawn into the emotional vortex generated by the messianic proclamation; he had neither reason nor strength to resist. All the more surprising is the real proportion of believers and unbelievers within the ruling classes. All later statements notwithstanding, the majority of the ruling class was in the camp of the believers, and the prominent and active part played by many of them is attested by all reliable documents. No doubt there was also pressure from below, yet most of the communal leaders did not wait for this pressure; as a matter of fact, they did not require it in order to be spurred into action. The essential correctness of this picture is not impugned in the least by the "revised version" of events that was put forward afterward by a kind of self-imposed censorship. As a matter of fact, this picture is supported by some later writers who had long ago given up all their former hopes and wrote without special pleading, but just spoke their minds. Their reports tend to confirm the earlier documents. The movement knew no class distinctions. It embraced the millionaires of Amsterdam who, much as Abraham Pereira, offered their whole fortunes to the messiah, as well as the poorest beggars in forlorn corners of the Diaspora. Social stratification cannot account for the actual alignment of forces, which contradicts all expectations based on social instinct or interest alone. Very possibly there were economic reasons for the hesitancy of some of the rich, and we can easily appreciate the tendency of some of them to hold fast to the status quo. But what about the majority who acted against their ostensible interests? The messianic awakening clearly transcended all classes, insofar as we are at all entitled to apply this term to Jewish society, where the social mobility of individuals and the frequency of sudden changes of fortune were hardly conducive to the consolidation of "classes."

It should be possible, no doubt, to draw a picture of Jewish social life in the middle of the seventeenth century that would bring out its inner tensions. Exploitation of authority or of connections with gentile rulers for private or clique interests, graft, and even occasional corruption in the direction of communal affairs, the helplessness of the small artisan and shopkeeper—all these are facts which social historians have had no difficulty in establishing wherever sufficient documentary evidence has survived. Even if there is much exaggeration in the fulminations and criticisms of preachers and moralists, the substance of their charges is amply confirmed[2] by the documentary material that has been preserved in archives. No doubt the specific social conditions in any given community and the relations obtaining between individuals and groups duly influenced the responses to the messianic movement. The strained personal relations between the rabbis of Smyrna at the time of Sabbatai's revelation in 1665 present one such instance among many which we shall come across. Local conditions certainly shaped and colored the movement in many places; yet, without wishing to minimize their significance, we must also beware of overestimating their role as a general factor explaining the phenomenon as a whole. If there was one general factor underlying the patent unity of the Sabbatian movement everywhere, then this factor was essentially religious in character and as such obeyed its own autonomous laws, even if today these are often obscured behind smokescreens of sociological verbiage. The interrelations and interaction of religion and society should not make us forget that ultimately the two are not identical. It was this religious factor that set up the peculiar spiritual tension out of which Sabbatian messianism could be born, manifesting itself as an historical force throughout Israel, and not merely in one of the many branches of the Diaspora. Religious factors are not isolated entities and they never operate in a vacuum. Impinging on the social situation, the religious factor caused the various groups, the leading classes in particular, to join the messianic movement. As it happens, we are in a position to identify and name this religious factor. It was none other than Lurianic kabbalism, that is, that form of kabbalah which had developed at Safed, in the Galilee, during the sixteenth century and which dominated Jewish religiosity in the seventeenth century.

The powerful kabbalistic movement that issued from Safed and quickly spread over the Jewish world is an excellent and perhaps unique example of the reciprocity between center and periphery in Jewish history. Safed, which had never before possessed any special status or significance, became a major center of Judaism in the sixteenth century as a result of a steady flow of immigrants from the Diaspora.[3] The principal founders of the new center were Spanish exiles, but they were soon joined by enthusiasts from other communities, until Safed became a kind of miniature distillation of the whole Jewish Diaspora. The creative genius of the Galilean center drew its strength from the Diaspora, and it was thither that its influence radiated back, transforming Jewish spirituality everywhere. The doctrines developed in the schools of Safed apparently embodied some fundamental and universal Jewish quality that transcended all local variations, some kind of quintessential historical experience of Jewry in exile, for otherwise they would hardly have succeeded in opening up a new dimension to the traditional universe of Jewish religiosity. As the kabbalistic movement, highly charged with messianic tension, spread from Safed and conquered the Diaspora, it also laid the foundations for the future discharge of this tension. Here we may have part of the answer to our initial question. The kabbalism of the age was the spiritual heritage common to all Jewish communities; it had provided them with an interpretation of history and with a fund of ideas and practices without which the Sabbatian movement is unthinkable.

Before, however, defining more precisely the specific contribution of Lurianic kabbalism to the spiritual climate of the seventeenth century, a few words are in order about the nature and function of the messianic idea in Jewish history. It cannot be our task to discuss the origin of the messianic idea and its impact on Judaism during the decisive periods of its formation. Our immediate and more limited aim is an understanding of the messianic idea as it affected medieval Judaism, existing as it did in conditions of exile.[4] To this end we must distinguish two main tendencies in which the messianic longing of generations had crystallized. These were the popular-mythological and the philosophical-rationalist traditions. They existed side by side. They often converged and even merged. Nevertheless, we are entitled to treat them as basically distinct.

What, we may ask, did the messianic idea imply for the simple Jew whose hopes were nourished, in addition to the biblical prophecies, by a number of popular and well-known legends and apocalyptic midrashim?[5] Traditional popular messianism was characterized by catastrophe and utopianism, and both elements play an important role in the dynamics of the messianic faith. Both have their roots in biblical prophecy, the one in the vision of the end of days (as in Isaiah), the other in the notion of a day of the Lord (as in Amos). In the system of values as well as in the practical life of the ordinary medieval Jew, these two tendencies fulfilled different functions, with regard to both his surrounding environment and his own universe of rabbinic tradition.

Messianic legend indulges in uninhibited fantasies about the catastrophic aspects of redemption. Partly drawing on old mythologies, partly creating a popular mythology of its own, it paints a picture of violent upheaval, wars, plague, famine, a general defection from God and His Law, license, and heresy. There is no continuity between the present and the messianic era; the latter is not the fruit of previous developments, let alone of a gradual evolution. Far from being the result of historical process, redemption arises on the ruins of history, which collapses amid the "birth pangs" of the messianic age. The bitter experience of many generations that had tasted the heavy yoke of alien rule, oppression, and humiliation was not likely to mitigate the violence of this type of eschatology, whose roots go back to the apocalyptic literature of the period of the Second Temple. It has been one of the strangest errors of the modern *Wissenschaft des Judentums* to deny the continuity of Jewish apocalypticism. The endeavors of leading scholars to dissociate apocalyptic from rabbinic Judaism and to associate it exclusively with Christianity have contributed much to the modern falsification of Jewish history and to the concealment of some of its most dynamic forces, both constructive and destructive. The continued existence of popular apocalyptic literature and the history of the many messianic movements during the Middle Ages sufficiently dispose of such wishful rewriting of the past. As a matter of fact Jewish experience during the thousand years following the destruction of the Temple could only intensify the catastrophic traits of the eschatological picture, whose basic outline had been drawn in a famous Talmudic passage.[6] Redemption meant a revolution in history. Apocalyptic imagination supplied the details in which comfort and horror had an equal share and in which a persecuted and downtrodden people settled many a bitter account with it torturers. The apocalyptic war was described in all its stages. Israel too, though ultimately led through all tribulations to national restoration, would have to bear its share of suffering in the final cataclysm. The figure of the messiah of the House of Joseph, who would fall at the gates of Jerusalem fighting against the gentiles, constituted a new mythological trait whose function it was to differentiate between the messiah of catastrophe and that of utopia.

The utopian aspect of the traditional eschatology fulfilled a special function in the world of the medieval Jew, for it implied much more than merely the hope of a quiet life of moral perfection and human freedom. It contained all the qualities of a golden age, including miraculous manifestations and a radical transformation of the natural order. To express these hopes and ideas, there were detailed descriptions of the future Jerusalem as well as of the ideal contemplative life: the rabbinic scholars would devote themselves to the study of the law and would enjoy revelations of the mysteries of the Torah in the academy of the messiah. But messianic utopia also harbored explosive elements. Its overt intention was, no doubt, the perfection and completion of the rule of traditional religious law (halakhah) and its extension to those spheres of life to which it could not be applied in conditions of exile. Hence also the rabbinic term "halakhah of the messianic age." Yet messianic utopia also contained forces that tended to undermine its very intentions. In the closed world of narrowly circumscribed Jewish existence, messianic utopia represented the possibility of something radically and wonderfully different. It opened vistas which traditional halakhah had tended to cover up. The tendency had manifested itself more than once in clear symptoms of antinomianism in some medieval messianic movements.[7] As long as the messianic hope existed in the abstract, real for the imagination only, the gap between traditional law and "messianic law" was relatively easy to bridge: the latter was simply the application of traditional law to life in the messianic age. Popular piety undoubtedly took this view for granted. But whenever messianic hopes assumed actuality, the tension with regard to rabbinic tradition became manifest. There seems to be an intrinsic connection between active messianism and the courage for religious innovation. Messianic movements would often produce individuals with sufficient charismatic authority to challenge the established authority of rabbinic Judaism. Attempts to realize the messianic dream inevitably brought out, that is, manifested and strengthened, this hidden tension.

Rabbinic authority and messianic authority could not but clash. No doubt many a pious and faithful soul lived in blithe unawareness of the dangerous tensions implicit in every assertion of messianism. On the other hand, we may assume that there were always some individuals who realized the truth and who were attracted by the revolutionary aspects of the notion of a "renewed Torah" in the messianic age. There is, admittedly, not much evidence of this in popular eschatological literature, which obviously passed a thorough editorial censorship before attaining the form in which it has come down to us. The tension does, however, break through in rather extreme form in the eschatology of a kabbalistic book, the *Raʿya Mehemna (Faithful Shepherd)*.[8] The author of this part of the Zohar, evidently a capable if somewhat embittered Talmudic scholar, expresses in telling symbolic images what he, and probably some others as well, thought about the possible meaning of the law of the Lord in a messianic world. Very possibly the author of the *Raʿya Mehemna* does not voice the opinions of his fellow kabbalists in this respect, and his speculations are not representative of any definite social tendency or movement (though I, for one, have some doubts on this score). Indeed, it appears that this extraordinary text did not exert any noticeable influence for a considerable time after its composition. Nevertheless, it is evident that the author expresses not merely his own views but also those of certain other individuals less articulate than himself. Like other kabbalists, he distinguished between the revealed and the hidden aspects of the Torah, but unlike them he was led by this distinction to extreme conclusions. The Torah manifests itself under two aspects: that of the "Tree of Life" and that of the "Tree of the Knowledge of Good and Evil." The latter aspect is characteristic of the period of exile. As the Tree of Knowledge comprises good *and* evil, so the Torah deriving from it comprises permission and prohibition, pure and impure; in other words, it is the law of the Bible and of rabbinic tradition. In the age of redemption, however, the Torah will manifest itself under the aspect of the Tree of Life, and all previous distinctions will pass away. The positive manifestation of the Torah as the Tree of Life is thus accompanied by the abrogation of all those laws and rules whose authority and validity obtain unconditionally during the present era of exile. The pure essence of the Torah will be revealed and its outer shell cast off. The remarkable thing about this conception is its clear consciousness of possible contradictions and of a revaluation of values within the one absolutely valid Torah which, for the kabbalist, was nothing less than the manifestation of God's holy name.

The popular mythological versions of eschatology combined literary and legendary traditions with the grim experience of exile. Apocryphal legends easily found their way into the hearts of men where they satisfied secret needs and longings by their descriptions of messianic catastrophe and utopia. They established themselves not only in the mind of the masses but even in the writings of leading rabbinic authorities, as is apparent from the eighth chapter ("On Redemption") of Saadia Gaon's *Book of Beliefs and Opinions.*[9] Others viewed the rank growth of apocalyptic imagination with undisguised misgivings and endeavored to minimize its influence. There is an unmistakable tone of hostility in their references to the doctrine of an apocalyptic catastrophe, and they may well have been aware of the explosive charge inherent in the messianic idea as such. Utopianism not only arouses hopes and expectations; it also threatens existing traditional patterns. Once the longing for a new world and for the tree of life seizes the hearts, who knows what may come next? Every utopia that is more than an abstract formula has a revolutionary sting. It hardly occasions surprise that Maimonides, the most extreme representative of the antiapocalyptic tendency, rejected all those myths that lived in the hearts of the believing masses, whom he contemptuously referred to as the "rabble." Against the luxurious and rank growth of legend from which the "rabble" derived hope and comfort, Maimonides formulated an eschatological doctrine from which utopian elements were as far as possible excluded. As the hallowed character of tradition did not permit him to suppress them completely, he resorted to careful sifting. The utterances of the early teachers on the subject were declared to be theologically not authoritative; details concerning redemption could be known only after the event. This antiapocalyptic bias found its definite expression in Maimonides' well-known formulations in chapters eleven and twelve of "Laws of Kingship" in book fourteen of his great code *Mishneh Torah:*

> Do not think that the messiah will have to work signs and miracles or perform any spectacular deeds or resurrect the dead and the like. . . . But this is the truth of the matter: the Torah with all its laws and ordinances is everlastingly valid and nothing will be added to it or taken away from it. When a king arises out of the House of David who diligently studies the law and, like his ancestor David, assiduously performs good works according to the written and the oral law, and who compels all Israel to walk therein . . . and who will fight the battles of the Lord, then it may be presumed that he is the messiah. If he proves successful and succeeds in rebuilding the Temple and in gathering in all the exiles, then it is certain that he is the messiah. He will reform the world so that all shall serve the Lord. . . . And do not think that in the days of the messiah there will be any departure from the normal course of things or any change in the cosmic order. That which is prophesied in the Book of Isaiah [11:6]—"the wolf also shall dwell with the lamb and the leopard shall lie down with the kid"—is merely a parable and a figure of speech . . . and the same holds for similar prophecies

concerning the messiah. They are all parables, though only in the days of the messianic king will people understand the precise meaning and intention of the parables. . . . There is none that now knows how these things shall come to pass, . . . for even scholars have no [clear] traditions on this matter but merely the interpretation of Scripture; therefore, there is much difference of opinion among them. In any case, neither the sequence of events nor their details are articles of faith. One should make it a rule not to occupy oneself with legends and midrashim on the subject . . . as they are conducive neither to the fear nor to the love of God. . . . Sages and prophets longed for the messianic age not in order that they should dominate the world and rule over the gentiles . . . but solely in order to be free to devote themselves to the Torah and divine wisdom without oppression and hindrance, so as to merit eternal life. . . . The sole occupation of the world will be to know the Lord. Therefore [the children of] Israel shall all be great scholars; they shall know hidden things and attain to the knowledge of God as far as is within human reach.

The quotation from Maimonides illustrates the difficulties of formulating a messianic and thus essentially utopian doctrine while at the same time trying to eliminate its utopian elements. The attempt could hardly be expected to succeed, and the compromise is clearly discernible in Maimonides' wording. What Maimonides did succeed in doing was to suppress completely the apocalyptic moment. There is no hint of a cataclysmic end of history, no catastrophe, not even miracles. The reader might also think that the historical process initiated by the appearance of the messianic king would lead, by a gradual and continuous transition, to the ideal state of things, that is, to the perfect contemplative life —Maimonides' version of utopia. Maimonides very skillfully concealed the dangerous dialectics inherent in messianism, and the carefully chosen words with which he emphasizes the conservative function of the messiah in safeguarding the Torah and traditional law tell their own story. Maimonides was well aware of the messianic movements that had agitated previous generations as well as his own. His *Epistle to the Jews of Yemen*[10] shows that he entertained no illusions as to the dangers which such movements harbored for traditional religion. In a way the struggle of Maimonides and his followers against the "beliefs of the rabble" was also inspired by utopian ideal, albeit an aristocratic utopia in which philosophic mysteries had taken the place of historic dynamism. His antiapocalyptic utterances, designed to abolish messianism as a historic force, were subsequently invoked by all who opposed messianic actualization and by all who distrusted the messianic idea as a motive force in social life. The authority of the "Great Eagle" (as Maimonides was called) was considerable, but it could not conceal the essential weakness of his eschatology. The two classical writers on the subject of messianism, Don Isaac Abravanel, writing soon after the expulsion from Spain at the end of the fifteenth century and R. Loew of Prague, writing at the end of the sixteenth century, both retreated from Maimonides' extreme position. Living through times of dire misery and persecution, they could not afford to ignore the apocalyptic tradition and its message of catastrophe. Each reintroduces in his own manner those elements that Maimonides had sought to eradicate. It is only fair to add that both authors were also at pains to safeguard the continuity of the historical process culminating in redemption. Both preserve a large measure of common sense, expressing itself in allegorical interpretations of eschatological legends. Yet the fact that they both felt constrained to readmit apocalypse and popular mythology is sufficient proof of the strength of these elements in their times. The eschatological writings of Abravanel and R. Loew exerted a profound influence on later generations, and even adherents of the Sabbatian movement would quote them in support of their contentions. In a way, the two main tendencies of Jewish eschatology had merged in the writings of these two authors, with the result that everyone could find in them whatever best suited his temper.

The contribution of the kabbalah to the religious revival that followed upon the expulsion from Spain can be adequately appreciated only by paying attention to its novel attitude toward the messianic tradition. In its earlier stages kabbalism had shown little interest in messianism. The early kabbalists drew on old gnostic traditions and on philosophical ideas that lent themselves to a mystical and symbolic view of the world. These ideas, together with the inner experiences of contemplative mystics for whom "adhesion" or "cleaving" to God *(debequth)* was the final goal on the ladder of spiritual ascent, shaped contemplative kabbalism with its twofold aim of grasping the mysteries of the Godhead and of the Torah, on the one hand, and of teaching elect souls the way of total *debequth,* on the other. The kabbalists were conservative in outlook, and they shared the hopes and views of traditional religion. Their own peculiar spiritual impulse had no specifically messianic quality. Their ideal of the contemplative life in communion with God did not require a messianic world for its realization; it was quite compatible with life in exile. Like other mystical movements, kabbalism began as a way of spiritual renewal for individuals or groups of individuals (which, of course, did not prevent it from becoming a social force). Redemption, that is, redemption of the soul, was a private, individual matter and therefore independent of the sphere of national redemption with which traditional messianism was concerned.

Kabbalistic doctrine developed apart from eschatology because in its original setting it concentrated less on the end of the world than on the primordial beginning of creation. For this is what the kabbalistic conception of the Godhead, as enshrined in the doctrine of *sefiroth,* really amounts to. The hidden God, known in kabbalistic terminology as *En-Sof* (the Infinite) is far removed from everything created; he is unrevealed, nonmanifest, and unknown. Only the emanation of his power, operating in the creation of both the higher and the nether worlds, transforms *En-Sof* into the Creator-God. The different stages of emanation manifest the hidden potencies and attributes by which God acts and which are all essentially one in the unity of God, even "as the flame is bound to the coal." Ten such stages, known as *sefiroth,* constitute the inner life of the Godhead; in them He becomes manifest as a personal God. Though inaccessible to immediate comprehension or contemplation, they can be apprehended through the structure of all being—from the beginning of creation in the supernal worlds down to the last and lowest creature. The mystical contemplation of the universe reveals its symbolic character. Creation does not exist for its own sake but for the sake of pointing to the divine emanation that shines through it. The inner meaning of creation, as well as the Law and the commandments, is revealed to the kabbalist through an understanding of the mysteries of mystical symbolism. "All proceeds from the One and returns to the One." In other words, even as the whole chain of being proceeded, link by link, from the manifestation of the Creator in His *sefiroth,* so everything would return in the end to its original source.

The kabbalist, however, jumps this cosmic rhythm and takes a short cut. By means of proper contemplative concentration, particularly during prayer or when performing a religious act, the human will cleaves to the divine will and to the world of the *sefiroth.* Here we have a real ascent of the soul, not of the actual kind as in the concrete ecstatic experience of a heavenly journey,[11] but in a purely spiritual process produced by meditation. The mystic who in his contemplative ascent attains the point of communion with the source of all being has by that act reached the end of the path to his individual redemption. Kabbalistic contemplation is a kind of individual anticipation of eschatological messianism. The kabbalists were aware that the historical and public character of traditional messianic belief precluded any identification or confusion of the latter with their own mystical ideal of an individual, contemplative ascent. They consequently had no reason for tampering with traditional messianism, though they did not hesitate to interpret it in their manner as an event within the inner life of the Godhead. Their interpretation presupposes the new meaning with which the author of the Zohar had invested the old concept of the "exile of the Shekhinah," based on the Talmudic saying that wherever Israel is exiled, the Shekhinah goes with it.[12] For the Talmud, Shekhinah simply meant the presence of God. Not so for the kabbalists for whom Shekhinah served as a technical term for the tenth and last *sefirah,* while the term "the Holy One Blessed Be He" (the usual rabbinic idiom for God) referred to the sixth *sefirah,* otherwise known as *Tif'ereth.* During the present period of exile, the Shekhinah, or "bride," was separated and exiled from her "husband," the Holy One Blessed Be He. The disjunction of these two aspects of the Godhead signifies that in the present state of things the unity of the divine attributes is not complete. Only with the advent of messianic redemption will the perfect unity of the divine *sefiroth* be permanently re-established. Then, to use the symbolic language of the kabbalists, the Shekhinah will be restored to perpetual union with her husband.

In its eschatological teaching the main part of the Zohar continues the apocalyptic and utopian tradition against which Maimonides had so sternly warned. In spite of some changes of detail as compared with earlier apocalyptic midrashim, the attitude is fundamentally the same: the messianic events are all of a supernatural character. Mention has already been made of the utopian conception of the "messianic Torah" to be found in the later parts of the Zohar, the *Ra'ya Mehemna* and the *Tiqquney Zohar.* A very special and novel feature of some trends in Spanish kabbalism was the emphasis on the close connection between the approach of redemption and the increasing knowledge of kabbalistic mysteries. In the days of exile, minds have been beclouded and are unfit to receive esoteric lore; but now, with the end of time approaching, the mysteries of the kabbalah are increasingly revealed. This doctrine provided a justification for the boldness of the kabbalists' speculative innovations, and it was invoked as such by the authors of the Zohar and by many others. Yet it never led to a thorough reinterpretation of eschatological ideas. The creative originality of the early kabbalists spent itself exclusively on the mysteries of creation and the mysteries of the "divine chariot," that is, on mystical cosmology and the doctrine of the *sefiroth*. No messianic movements of any consequence arose among kabbalists, and the few instances of individuals claiming angelic revelations or actual prophecy evoked no serious response. The agitations around the prophet of Ávila in Castile (1295), or of Abraham Abulafia at about the same time, did not lead to any widespread messianic unrest. Apocalyptic messianism and kabbalah remained distinct spheres of religious life.

The expulsion from Spain (1492) wrought a radical change also in this respect. The traumatic upheaval, which so profoundly altered the situation of a large part of the nation, inevitably called forth corresponding reactions in the specifically religious sphere. The exiles proceeded to their new abodes and created a new Diaspora which, as a matter of fact, soon flourished, at least in parts. Yet even after Sephardic Jewry had ostensibly recovered from the shock, many minds still continued to search for the meaning of the catastrophe that had overtaken them. The first generation of Spanish exiles responded to the events with a wave of apocalyptic agitation. The Spanish disaster was the beginning of the "messianic birth pangs."[13] The eschatological perspective soon embraced other contemporaneous events, among which the fall of Constantinople in 1453 was no doubt the most dramatic and one that could easily assume symbolic significance as the overture to the wars of Gog and Magog. Apocalypse flourished not only in its conventional form—as, for example, in the writings of Don Isaac Abravanel—but also in a specifically kabbalistic guise. In the same years in which Abravanel wrote his book *Yeshuʿoth Meshiḥo (Deliverance of His Anointed)*, an anonymous kabbalist composed the commentary *Kaf ha-Qetoreth (The Spoonful of Incense)*,[14] which interpreted Psalms as songs of war for the great apocalyptic struggle. Messianic movements developed around the public activity of kabbalists such as Asher Lemmlein in northern Italy[15] and the marrano Solomon Molkho in whose writings apocalyptic and speculative kabbalah had fused.

Eschatological tension abated after the failure of the messianic prophecies for the year 1530. The intensive messianic propaganda conducted by the kabbalists of Jerusalem in particular[16] ended in a complete fiasco.

Nevertheless messianism had penetrated the heart of kabbalism, and it continued to influence kabbalistic development in diverse ways. The creation of the new spiritual center of Jewry in Safed was itself a decisive positive response to the expulsion. The movement of spiritual and moral reform that spread from Safed sprang from the innermost heart of Judaism. Nourished by the living experience and memory of exile at its very worst, the movement aimed at "fulfilling" this exile and thereby preparing redemption. Apocalypse disappeared or, at least, went underground and was transformed in the process. Ascetic piety reigned supreme in Safed. At first the religious ideal of a mystical elite only, asceticism now allied itself to an individual and public morality based on the new kabbalism; it struck deep roots in the collective consciousness. According to certain eschatological texts the messiah was due to make his first appearance in Galilee, and it is not impossible that this and similar expectations contributed to the establishment of the community of saints in Safed, which numbered more inspired enthusiasts and devout seekers of mystical salvation than any other city. Though the messiah did not come from Safed, there were many who heard the wingbeats of approaching redemption in the kabbalistic teaching that went forth from there. Even the purely halakhic achievements of the great Talmudic scholars of Safed were largely inspired by the new messianic kabbalah. R. Joseph Karo deliberately ignored kabbalism in his great rabbinic code *Shulḥan ʿArukh,* yet there is little doubt as to the secret eschatological motives of its composition. Unsuccessful attempts have been made to deny Karo's authorship of the mystical diary *Maggid Mesharim (Preacher of Righteousness)* in which the writer describes the regular manifestations of a celestial mentor, or *maggid,* who was none other than the Mishnah herself.[17] We may take this manifestation as an indication of the essentially conservative character of Safed kabbalism and of its firm anchorage in rabbinic tradition. The personified Mishnah, that is, the oral law, represented nothing less than historic Judaism as a whole. Only by virtue of its conservative character and its patent continuity with rabbinic tradition could the new kabbalism gain popular appeal and even succeed in carrying on its wings—or perhaps hidden under its wings—some startling novel ideas.

In Safed, where all the arteries of Jewish spiritual life converged, kabbalism became a social and historical force. The process by which kabbalah established its supremacy over the religious consciousness of those who were themselves no kabbalists calls for some explanation. Though it is true that the kabbalists at last emerged from their solitary esotericism and began to seek ways of influencing the masses, yet their spectacular success remains something of an historical problem. Both philosophy and kabbalah were aristocratic disciplines, appealing primarily to an intellectual and spiritual elite. How and why did the kabbalists succeed—where the philosophers had failed—in decisively shaping the religious consciousness of the Jewish people? The actual triumph of kabbalism in the sixteenth century is a fact beyond dispute. It is only the interpretation of this fact which is at issue. Rationalist historians, such as Graetz and others, have offered an engagingly simple explanation: persecution and suffering had dimmed the light of reason and paved the way for an eruption of mystical obscurantism. It is hardly necessary to expend many words over an "explanation" whose bias is so obvious. The real answer to the question should be positive, not negative in character. Kabbalism triumphed because it provided a valid answer to the great problems of the time. To a generation for which the facts of exile and the precariousness of existence in it had become a most pressing and cruel problem, kabbalism could give an answer unparalleled in breadth and in depth of vision. The kabbalistic answer illuminated the significance of exile and redemption and accounted for the unique historical situation of Israel within the wider, in fact cosmic, context of creation itself.

The kabbalistic appeal to the public, unheard of before the expulsion from Spain, is in evidence soon afterward. There was, of course, much hostility and opposition on the part of those "who jeer at and scoff at the students of kabbalistic books, and who greatly insult and revile them . . . and whenever they hear of the kabbalah, of a prophet, or visionary, they [mockingly] enquire of each other 'what hath this madman spoken unto thee.' "[18] On the other hand, Joseph Yabeṣ (or Jabez), a typical representative of orthodox public opinion after the expulsion, complains of the inordinate popular success of kabbalism. His complaints were echoed by later moralists who were alarmed at the growing attraction of kabbalistic lore for the masses, namely, for people without previous rabbinic training. "There are today many ignorant people, smitten with the blindness of pride, who believe that they have attained the hidden mysteries of the Torah without ever having savored [rabbinic] learning or tasted good works."[19] Yabeṣ and his like continue the line of conservative theological thinking which passes from Judah ha-Levi's *Kuzari* through Naḥmanides, Jonah of Gerona, Solomon b. Adreth, and Ḥasdai Crescas. His attitude toward kabbalah (whose mysteries "one should not contemplate" in an age of ignorance), like that toward the philosophy of Maimonides, is one of extreme reserve.[20] Yet in spite of his public exhibition of reserve, we find Joseph Yabeṣ, when in Mantua, entreating a fellow exile from Spain, Judah Ḥayyat, to compose a treatise on the principles of kabbalah.[21]

Of course, nobody at that time would have explicitly suggested that kabbalism should supersede the study of traditional nonesoteric teaching. Nevertheless the intensive propaganda for kabbalistic studies did not fail to produce its results. A sixteenth-century kabbalist has left us a valuable testimony of the general feeling prevalent at the time:

> I have found it written that the heavenly decree prohibiting the study of kabbalah in public was valid only until the end of the year 250 [1490 C.E.]. Thereafter it [the generation living at that time] would be called the last generation [before the final redemption]. The decree was abrogated and permission was granted to study the Zohar. From the year 300 [1540 C.E., the beginning of the kabbalistic movement in Safed] onward it will be accounted an act of special merit to both old and young to study [kabbalah] in public, as it is stated in the *Ra*ᶜ*ya Mehemna*.[22] And since the messianic king will appear through the merits [of this study] and through none other, it behooves us not to be remiss.[23]

The principle that the study of kabbalah was itself a factor in hastening the advent of redemption became established as a generally accepted doctrine and represents a significant development of the notion, already mentioned before, that at the end of days the mysteries of kabbalism would be revealed anew. Henceforth kabbalistic esotericism and messianic eschatology were intertwined and acted in combination.

2. MESSIANIC ECONOMICS

Nathan of Gaza displayed his supreme apocalyptic confidence also in another matter of the utmost practical importance: the alms collected in the Diaspora to maintain the poverty-stricken Jewish community in Palestine, where little business could be transacted. . . . Early in 1666 it was rumored in Amsterdam that Nathan had urged the leading rabbi of Palestine: "Let not one more penny from the Diaspora come here: there will be sufficient treasures to distribute among all the tribes."[24] Perhaps

Nathan uttered these words in a discussion with an unbelieving rabbi; perhaps, as Sasportas suggests, he wished to stop the transfer of charity funds to Palestine, by way of reprisal or threat against the infidels. Writing from Leghorn, Raphael Supino informed his friend Sasportas that the prophet had ordered that "no money from the Diaspora should enter Palestine,"[25] and in December 1665, Sasportas reports that the prophet had practically tried to starve his opponents by demanding that no more alms should be sent to the Holy Land.[26] Nathan was confident that hidden treasures would be discovered in Palestine in the wake of other miraculous discoveries (for example, those of the exact site of the altar and of the ashes of the red heifer required for ritual purification). He probably got this particular idea from *Tub ha-ʾAreṣ* by Nathan Shapira Yerushalmi. In this book, which had been published only ten years previously and which had influenced many of Nathan's ideas, we read (fol. 37c): "As for the underground treasures, the earth will form subterranean passageways so that all the royal treasures can be [miraculously] moved to Palestine, as it is written [Deut. 33:19, 'for they shall suck . . .] of the treasures hid in the sand.' Everything will be revealed in Palestine to the messianic king, and he will distribute them among the returning exiles, to each man his share, and they shall be filled with great riches." In Nathan Shapira's work the prediction forms part of a diatribe against the Jews of the Diaspora who were "concerned with their bodies and their money."[27] The prophet of Gaza applied it to the immediate situation. The inevitable results of this attitude formed the subject of discussions as early as December, 1665. Sasportas foresaw the distress of the poor in the Holy Land "since their king [that is, Sabbatai Ṣevi] had condemned them to death" by failing to provide for their needs and himself leaving the country.[28] Sabbatai's journey to Smyrna had indeed been mentioned in the earliest letter received at the time, but the accusation that he had doomed the poor to starvation while he was traveling in state in Turkey is almost certainly due to Sasportas' erroneous assumption that the refusal of foreign mammon by Nathan and Meir Rofe had been ordered by Sabbatai. Sasportas returned to the subject once more after Sabbatai's apostasy. Congratulating himself on his foresight, he reports "that many people had ceased to contribute their annual charity for the poor in Palestine . . . , saying that 'since you have the messiah with you, you do not need our assistance.' Moreover they knew [that people in Jerusalem did not believe in] these vanities and that they held the messiah in no account. Wherefore the great mass, who were fanatic believers in this false faith, considered all Jerusalemites as infidels who denied the prophet and the messiah [and hence would no longer send alms to Jerusalem]."[29] The correctness of this account has yet to be proved, since the extant sources make no mention of such a vengeful mood among the believers in Amsterdam and elsewhere. Though it is not impossible that here and there arguments of this kind were advanced, Sasportas' account seems grossly exaggerated. Nobody would have argued that "the messiah is with you in Palestine" when it was well known that Sabbatai was in Turkey. We know of several emissaries from Palestine who were active in collecting alms in Italy, Germany, and Morocco in the autumn of 1665, and as our knowledge of them is purely accidental, we may assume that there were many more of whom we have no information. One wonders how these emissaries reconciled the patent contradiction between Nathan's taboo on foreign mammon, and their efforts to collect funds for relieving the actual misery. Perhaps Nathan, like the author of *Tub ha-ʾAreṣ*, was referring to a more distant future, though Meir Rofe, in his first enthusiasm, seems to have understood the injunction differently. By informing us, in another context, that the *chelebi* Raphael Joseph provided for the needs of all the people in Gaza, Sasportas as much as demolishes his own story. There is no reason at all to assume that the believers who went to Palestine left their money behind. On the contrary, the extant accounts of their preparations for the voyage (for example, converting property to money, etc.) suggest the opposite. Sasportas' statement that the *chelebi* enriched himself by appropriating the money which the believers, in obedience to Nathan's injunction, entrusted to him before proceeding to the Holy Land, is sheer calumny. As a matter of fact most of Sasportas' information regarding the *chelebi* is incorrect and based on malicious hearsay (for example, the statement that Raphael Joseph followed Sabbatai into apostasy).[30]

No doubt the great penitential awakening, stimulated and encouraged by Nathan, brought normal business to a standstill. Jerusalem had never been much given to trade and commerce, but the Jews of Gaza (including Nathan's father-in-law) were mostly traders. Cuenque's description of the devotional and penitential atmosphere in Gaza is confirmed and supplemented by a letter written toward the end of 1665, most probably in Egypt but almost certainly based on information from Gaza. The prophet and the king (that is, the messiah) were about to go to Constantinople, where they would ask the Grand Turk for the restitution of

Judea; the prophet had predicted that the Grand Turk would himself put the crown on the messiah's head. "In the Interim, this is true already: That the Bashaw of Jerusalem,[31] and the Bashaw of Gaza, have kissed the hands of the Prophet; and the Confluence of People from all sides (both Jews, Turks, and Christians[32] is so great, and the Vertues which are seen among them are so eminent, that all Neighbouring Nations do tremble at it. . . . all [are] plying nothing but Devotion, Penitence and Alms-giving; abstaining not only from all Vanity, but from Merchandizing and Trading; and especially from Exchange (which Natan[33] terms to be meer Usury) yea, such largeness of heart there is among them at Jerusalem:[34] that for One penny, may now be bought what was wont to cost Tenpence." Money-changing was one of the most widely practiced Jewish professions, particularly in Palestine. Nathan's condemnation of it, together with his ideas concerning alms from abroad, constitute a characteristic feature of what may be called his messianic economics. Nathan's attitude bespeaks an apocalyptic revolt. His rejection of certain very common features of Jewish life (for example, living on charity, money-changing, petty trading) expresses an unconscious rebellion against a traditional pattern of existence, though, of course, we must not interpret Nathan in anachronistic, modern terms, or attribute to him a desire for the "normalization" of Jewish life in the sense in which the modern Jewish national movement understood it. Nathan's concept of "normalization" was essentially messianic. In a redeemed and perfected age, the Holy Land would yield sufficient treasures to render trade and all that goes with it superfluous. The penitential awakening inevitably suspended routine economic activities, and the shift of interest was echoed in some of the earliest news reports. A letter from Leghorn to the East India Company (in London?) reported that[35] "the Jews of Alexandria write to their correspondents here, to send them no more business. They will have no further thoughts of it, but of higher matters."

3. MASS PROPHECY

The Sabbatian preachers applied the prophecy of Joel (3:3–4) to their own days: "And I will show wonders in the heavens and in the earth, blood, and fire, and pillars of smoke. The sun shall be turned into darkness, and the moon into blood, before the great and terrible day of the Lord come." But Joel had prophesied more than cosmic signs: "I will pour out My spirit upon all flesh, and your sons and your daughters shall prophesy, your old men shall dream dreams, your young men shall see visions" (Joel 3:1) and indeed, as the hearts opened, mass prophecy came to Smyrna.

The phenomenon of mass prophecy is by no means rare in the history of religious movements that are borne by popular enthusiasm. Christian sects, from the second-century Montanists to the eighteenth-century Methodists, furnish many examples. Twenty years after the Sabbatian awakening, in 1685, an apocalyptic movement arose among the French Protestants who struggled against the abolition of their liberties and the attempts to bring them by force into the Catholic Church. Mass prophecy, by children in particular, was one of the principle features of the movement, and the eyewitness reports of the prophetic ecstasies among the Camisards in the Cévennes mountains, on the one hand, and the Sabbatian enthusiasts in Smyrna, on the other, are strikingly similar. There was little of the passionate warning and of the urgent sense of individual mission, so characteristic of classical, "apostolic" prophecy, in the incoherent stammering of a mass ecstasy generated by oppression, revolt, and emotional high tension among the lower classes. The prophets spewed forth ancient words and phrases that had become clichés, though here and there an individual expression of noble spirituality could be heard.

A Dutch merchant writing early in April, 1666, soon after the excitement had passed its peak, thus described the scene: "At that time [winter, 1665–66] there appeared—some say by the workings of the devil—more than two hundred prophets and prophetesses upon whom there fell a mighty trembling so that they swooned. In this state they exclaimed that Sabbatai Ṣevi was the messiah and king of Israel who would lead his people safely to the Holy Land, and that ships of Tarshish, that is, with Dutch crews, would come to transport them. Thereafter their spirits returned unto them, but they remembered nothing of what they had spoken, much to the amazement of our Christians who see and hear this every day. Even little children of four years and less recited psalms in Hebrew."[36]

The first to prophesy in Smyrna were apparently the two emissaries from Jerusalem and Aleppo, Moses Galanté and Daniel Pinto; Pinto's name occurs in a list of prophets who prophesied in Smyrna. One of the first prophetesses was Sarah, Sabbatai's wife.[37] This was one of the few instances of her active participation in the movement, and it undoubtedly made an impression. Coenen heard from Dutch merchants who had witnessed the prophecy on the Ninth of Tebeth that the spirit that descended on the first prophetess also moved the daughters of the arch-infidel Ḥayyim Peña, and that Peña was so much impressed by this miracle happening in his own house that he converted to the faith. On returning to his home on Thursday, the Eighth of Tebeth (a day of considerable excitement and commotion, in view of the change of the forthcoming fast day to a festival), he found his daughters seized by a trembling and dizziness, and foaming at the mouth in the usual prophetic manner. In his presence they began to prophesy: "The *Ḥakham* Sabbatai Ṣevi sitteth on an exalted throne in heaven, with a crown on his head, crown, crown, crown. . . ."[38] Coenen himself points out the analogy with similar phenomena among the first English Quakers, and suggests that these prophecies were the work of the devil who was smiting the stiff-necked people with even greater blindness. The fullest account is given by Baruch of Arezzo: "And this is an account of the prophecy as it befell in those days. A deep sleep fell upon them, and they fell to the ground as the dead in whom there is no more spirit. After about half an hour a spirit would sound from their mouth, though their lips did not move, and they would utter [scriptural] verses of praise and consolation, and all would say 'Sabbatai Ṣevi, the anointed of the God of Jacob.' Thereafter they would arise without remembering what they had done or said. In Smyrna more than a hundred and fifty prophets prophesied." Baruch of Arezzo actually quotes the text of one such prophecy, which not only perfectly illustrates the many other general descriptions, but also conveys something of the psychological quality of the outburst: short staccato sentences, mixing biblical phrases with expressions of immediate experience, and thrown out in an unconscious paroxysm. On the Fourth of Shebat, when Sabbatai was already on his way to Constantinople, Abraham b. Jacob Jessurun "prophesied" in Smyrna:

"Lord I have heard thy speech. The Lord reigneth, the Lord has reigned, the Lord shall reign forevermore. Hear, O Israel, the Lord our God, the Lord is one. Blessed be His name, whose glorious kingdom is forevermore. Our king Sabbatai Ṣevi has been crowned with the crown. A solemn ban has been laid in heaven on them that believe not. The Lord keepeth Israel. Our prayers have been heard. A song of degrees, Out of the depths have I cried unto thee, O Lord. Great joy. Blessed is he who liveth. They have brought the crown to Our Lord, the king. Woe unto him that believeth not, he is in the ban. Blessed is he who liveth at this time. A song of degrees, Blessed is everyone that feareth the Lord. There will be a great rejoicing. Hear, O Lord, and have mercy upon me. They have given him the crown. His kingdom is an everlasting kingdom. The king Sabbatai Ṣevi sitteth on the throne of his kingdom. Hear O Lord. Precious in the sight of the Lord are the Jews. Rejoice in the Lord, O ye righteous. Give thanks unto the Lord, for He is good. God is true, Moses is true and his Law is true, Sabbatai Ṣevi is true. Great rejoicing. Thou openest thine hand. The Lord is God. The king Sabbatai Ṣevi sitteth on his throne. Hear O Israel. A song of degrees, When the Lord turned again the captivity of Zion. A great rejoicing for the Jews. The Lord is God. Blessed is the man that feareth the Lord. How great are His signs and how mighty are His wonders. When the Lord turned again the captivity of Zion. A great rejoicing. O give thanks unto the Lord, O give thanks unto the God of heaven. Woe unto him that believeth not. Our Lord the king reigneth. Unto thee O Lord belongeth righteousness. Great rejoicing. A song of degrees, When the Lord turned again the captivity of Zion. They have fallen before the Jews. The star of our kingdom has risen. O give thanks unto the Lord, for His mercy endureth forever. O Lord be merciful unto me and raise me up. I called upon the Lord in distress. Blessed be he that cometh in the name of the Lord. The Lord hear thee in the day of trouble. O give thanks unto the Lord, for He is good *(three times)*. The Lord strong and mighty forever. The king sitteth on the throne of mercy. The Lord of Hosts sitteth on the throne of His kingdom. The Lord shall fight for you. The Lord is the king of glory. The Lord strong and mighty, may His kingdom be exalted. True, true, true. Save, O Lord, according to thy mercy. Rejoicing to the Jews. Save me according to thy mercy *(three times)*. Give thanks unto the Lord, for He is good. Blessed be His name, whose glorious kingdom is forevermore. Hear O Israel. For thou wilt light my candle. Great is the Lord, and greatly to be praised. There is no longer any evil *yeṣer* [lust]. O Lord, hear my prayer. Give thanks unto the Lord, for He is good. . . ." And all these things he spoke four or five times.[39]

The new prophecy, as even a cursory reading of the foregoing example shows, was devoid of originality. The prophetic utterance was a mere jumble of well-known phrases and quotations from the Bible and the prayer book, repeated over and over again. The only visionary element is the reference to Sabbatai's crown and his sitting on the throne of his kingdom.[40] Only one sentence, toward the end of the prophecy, has a theological significance: the phrase "there is no longer any evil *yeṣer*" evidently reflects the teaching of Nathan's letters. The sparks of the Shekhinah had been extricated from the realm of the "shells" and had returned to their sphere of pristine purity. If this doctrine could be uttered in a prophetic fit by an unlettered man, then surely the messiah's strange behavior would be accepted without protest by the enthusiastic masses.

The emissary from Casale saw people acting under "all manner of compulsion" in the mass prophecy, meaning, no doubt, the rolling and twitching reminiscent of an epileptic fit. It was this pathologically compulsive character that Sasportas emphasized in his analysis of the detailed reports arriving from Smyrna. One letter stated that a Christian slave-girl "had beheld what the sages of Israel did not see, and she confirmed the prophecy of the [other] women and children."[41] Another report quoted a prophecy by a woman who had seen Sabbatai raised on his throne above the stars and ruling over heaven and earth. Sasportas diagnosed these utterances as "idiocy or epilepsy or madness," which made the prophets "behold Sabbatai's image graven in the seventh heaven, and all the host of heaven proclaiming, 'Render majesty and glory to your Lord.' . . . and they mistake rubbish and straw for prophecy."[42] His explanation was that "their lust and desire [for the gift of prophecy] aroused their imagination until they beheld visions that were occasionally true, but were mostly false; possibly the spirit also rested upon them accidentally, speaking [through them] and announcing various things, as does one who is possessed by a demon."[43] Sasportas insisted that only ignorant and unlettered people, and not the scholars and genuinely pious men, prophesied.[44] He carefully ignored such prophets as Moses Galanté and Daniel Pinto in Smyrna and Moses Suriel in Constantinople.

The prophetic enthusiasm spread from Smyrna to other communities in Asia Minor,[45] the Aegean islands,[46] and Greece, but nowhere did it articulate itself in orderly, literary form, or produce new kabbalistic insights, namely, "mysteries." The awakening let loose a flood of emotion without clear contents and it was easy for critics to point out that the prophetic revelations "revealed" nothing at all. In fact, their language and form are reminiscent of the earliest suras of the Quran, which are, likewise, ecstatic exclamations rather than a well-ordered prophetic argument. But Sasportas was definitely wrong in dismissing the whole phenomenon as the hysteria of ignorant fools. Among the prophets were men renowned for scholarship and piety, and their prophesying was surely more alarming—from Sasportas' point of view—than that of the unlettered enthusiasts.

Trade and commerce in the city came to a standstill.[47] Smyrna was in a festive mood of mounting exaltation and rejoicing. Banqueting, dancing, and festive processions alternated with the penitential exercises prescribed by Nathan. Even in the cold winter months there were many who would repair to the sea to perform ritual immersions, while others submitted to the penance of flogging.[48] At night torch-light processions would move through the city to cries of "Long live the messianic king" or "Long live Sabbatai Ṣevi."[49] Psalm 21:1, "The king shall joy in thy strength, O Lord, And in thy salvation how greatly shall he rejoice," was recited in the synagogues three times daily, at the morning, afternoon, and evening services. The psalm had been given a Sabbatian interpretation in Gaza, not so much because of the messianic significance of its contents, but primarily because of the *gematria* by which the numerical value of "and in thy salvation" equaled that of Sabbatai Ṣevi. In some synagogues the psalm, inscribed on a wooden board decorated with floral designs and surmounted by a crown with the legend "THE CROWN OF SABBATAI ṢEVI" was displayed on the wall.[50] The traditional prayer for the ruler of the land, recited on the Sabbath and holidays, was abolished, and the text adapted so as to apply to the new king of Israel:

He who giveth salvation unto kings and dominion unto princes, whose kingdom is an everlasting kingdom, who delivered his servant David from the destructive sword, who makes a way in the sea and a path in the mighty waters, may he bless, preserve, guard and exalt ever more our Lord and our Messiah, the Anointed of the God of Jacob, the Celestial Lion and Celestial Stag,[51] the Messiah of Righteousness, the King of kings, the sultan Sabbatai Ṣevi. May the supreme King of kings [that is, God] preserve him and grant him life. May the supreme King of kings exalt his star and his kingdom, and inspire the hearts of rulers and princes with good will toward him and us and all Israel, and let us say, Amen.[52]

4. AFTER THE APOSTASY

In order to understand the course of events after Sabbatai's apostasy, we must briefly recapitulate the developments preceding this critical turning-point, and try to realize the state of mind of the Jewish masses when the unexpected news reached them. The decisive circumstance that prevented this unique messianic revival from petering out without leaving more durable traces was, no doubt, the incipient budding of a new kind of "life-feeling." The shock of the messiah's apostasy should normally have been sufficient to shatter completely the structure of faith and hope that had been erected on the tidings announced by the prophet of Gaza, and the Sabbatian episode would have passed like a nightmare, and would have left no noticeable mark on the life and consciousness of the people. Other messianic movements had collapsed in the past without causing serious consequences. Apparently the enthusiasm had not reached down to the roots of their being, and failure, when it came, had not shaken them to the depth of their souls. Recovering from the shock of disappointment they proceeded to the order of the day with traditional formulas of comfort (such as, "the generation was not found worthy"), and the memory of the events lingered in the consciousness of the nation either as a curious freak phenomenon or as dim anguish.

This time, however, things were different. The movement had swept the whole Diaspora into its orbit and had struck deep roots in the soul of the masses. The sheer quantitative magnitude of the revival had become a qualitative factor. Something had happened in the souls of the believers, and these new, inner "facts" were no less decisive than external historical happenings. On the face of it the messianic movement, whose progress we have described in detail, exhibited a traditional character. Its strength had lain in the unexceptional penitential enthusiasm which seemed to guarantee the conformity of the revival with received and acknowledged forms of eschatological expression. The messiah's personal mystery was practically unknown in wider circles, and the little that had penetrated and that seemed to fly in the face of orthodox ideas was easily interpreted as relating to the exceptional nature of his ministry rather than as a new dispensation heralding a revolutionary messianic Law. In the consciousness of the masses there was no expectation of a messianic "transvaluation of all values" as the concrete expression of realized eschatology. Below the threshold of consciousness, however, far-reaching changes were taking place. The intensity and diffusion of the messianic propaganda ultimately produced effects that went far beyond the original intentions of its protagonists.

We should remind ourselves, in this connection, of a significant fact: in the minds of the believers imminent redemption and realized redemption came to be confused. Salvation was not merely at hand; it had already begun to be established and to make its inroads upon the old order. The arguments of the doubters to the effect that nothing had really happened so far fell on deaf ears because they took no account of the new emotional reality. The new feeling did not content itself with hopes for political redemption, although the political aspects of traditional messianism and the expectation of Israel's liberation from the yoke of the gentiles and from the degradation of exile were evidently taken for granted. However, the powerful messianic ferment produced psychological by-products which soon acquired an autonomous life of their own. Many believers were convinced, in their enthusiasm, that the new *aion* had already begun. In fact, they had crossed the threshold into a new world. The kabbalistic doctrine, propounded by the Sabbatian circle, to the effect that the Shekhinah "had risen from the dust" provided theoretical support of this new life-feeling. The contradiction between the profusion of alleged miracles, on the one hand, and the insistence upon pure faith unsupported by outward signs on the other, was more apparent than real. In any event it was of no consequence for the believers who had already drunk deeply of the new wellspring of life-giving water. The emphasis on pure faith in the messiah as a supreme religious value, in spite of temptations and trials, produced an emotional identification with the new, messianic "reality." This emotional identification enabled many believers to persevere even in the face of hard facts. The readiness to enter the messianic kingdom transformed itself into the entry into the kingdom itself. Even before Sabbatai's apostasy the kabbalists' "world of *tiqqun*" had become an emotional reality which nothing in the realm of "outward" events could shake. The believers knew that the world of political and historical reality would soon perish as Sabbatai set out on his marvelous journey to take the crown from the sultan's head. By the time that the discrepancy between the two worlds had become painfully apparent, and Sabbatai's apostasy had shattered the naïve simplicity of the messianic faith, a new historical consciousness had already established itself which could absorb the shocks of external reality. The believers knew that they had been made free by the message of comfort and joy, and would not be discomfited by the "illusions" of the outer world. They too, no doubt, expected the fulfillment of the messianic promises in the outer, political sphere as well; but the kingdom which was already established within them could no longer perish —or could perish only amid severe struggles. New forces had arisen that could not easily be suppressed. Renan's remarks about the first Christian apostles after their hopes of immediate redemption had failed them are in every way applicable to the Sabbatian believers: "Enthusiasm and love know of no hopeless situations. They play with the impossible, and rather than despair, they violate reality."[53]

Sabbatianism as a sectarian and—in varying degrees—heretical movement grew out of the struggle between the new life-feeling and the disappointment of the hopes that had originally given birth to it. Sabbatai's apostasy had revealed the dangerous contradiction between the two levels of redemption, a contradiction which nobody had foreseen in this acute form but which now provided the basis for unexpected developments. The orthodox kabbalists had never dreamed of discarding the political elements of messianism. When they added a new, mystical dimension to traditional eschatology and conceived of it as a transformation of the very essence of the cosmos, they meant to say that messianic redemption was more, not less, than liberation from the yoke of the gentiles. Historical reality, far from being abolished, served as a symbol of hidden mystical processes. "The 'ingathering of the exiles' is the ingathering of the [holy] sparks that are imprisoned in exile."[54] The structure of their thought would never have admitted any opposition between the symbol and the reality symbolized. The possibility of such an opposition had never occurred to the kabbalists, though it was implicit in their shift of the messianic emphasis to the hidden and inner spheres of the cosmos. As the messianic gospel suddenly found itself plunged into its gravest crisis, the latent contradiction emerged with full force. The contrast between symbol and reality symbolized, that is, between the outer and the inner reality of redemption, produced a profound and painful dilemma that gave birth to "Sabbatianism" as the sum total of attempts to readjust Jewish consciousness to the new situation.

The great revival of 1666 had prepared the hearts of believers for a new model of being whose religious dimensions, however, were, in a sense, a continuation rather than a repudiation of what had gone before. The apostasy shattered both the continuity of the eschatological perspective and the simple naïveté of the Sabbatian faith. Every believer saw before him the momentous question of where to hear God's voice: in the cruel verdict of history which, to say the least, unmasked the messianic experience as mere illusion, or in the reality of the faith that had established itself in the depths of his soul. Sectarian Sabbatianism was born when many sections of the people refused to accept the verdict of history, unwilling to admit that their faith had been a vain illusion fondly invented. There was the alternative possibility of faith in an apostate messiah, but it had to be bought at the price of the naïve innocence of the original faith. To believe in an apostate messiah was to build one's hope on foundations of paradox and absurdity, which could only lead to more paradoxes. The unity and consistency of rabbinic Judaism were not affected by the one inevitable paradox inherent in it, as, indeed, in all religion and in human experience itself—that of theodicy and the sufferings of the righteous. The universal character of this anguishing paradox in no wise diminished its seriousness, but it rendered it less destructive. No doubt there was a mystery here, but one to which a pure and naïve faith could resign itself in submission and hope. The Sabbatian paradox, however, was not that of a saint who suffers and whose suffering is a mystery hidden with God, but of a saint who sins. A faith based on this destructive paradox has lost its innocence. Its dialectical premise of necessity begets conclusions that are equally marked by the dialectics of paradox.

The various Sabbatian doctrines sought to bridge the gulf between the inner experience and the historic reality that was supposed to symbolize it. They enabled believers to go on living in the growing tension between outer and inner truth by providing them with a theological system whose origin was a profound crisis and whose nature was paradox. The fact that this faith survived for several generations suggests that it expressed a dialectical process within Jewish history.

The Sabbatian believers were not necessarily conscious of the nature of the new life-feeling of which they were the exponents, but there is evidence that at least some of their opponents were not unaware of the revolutionary element that was creeping into the increasingly acrimonious polemic between believers and infidels. The latter seemed to sense the revolt long before it actually took place, and their eyes, sharpened by hostility, foresaw many subsequent developments. Their arguments, it is true, were generally restricted to expressions of anxiety and concern in connection with the believers' transgressions of rabbinic ordinance, though some writers seemed to anticipate the dangerous conclusions implicit in the "faith." Sasportas and Joseph ha-Levi accused the believers of rebelling against the authority of the Talmud and of blaspheming the ancient rabbis by suggesting that the latter did not fully understand the sense of the prohibition of pronouncing the Tetragrammaton.[55] The believers were following strange gods, substituting a new authority for the traditional rabbinic one. Joseph ha-Levi angrily denounced Nathan's advice to his followers to substitute the study of the Zohar and midrash for that of halakhic literature.[56] By substituting the kabbalistic and

Haggadic classics for the traditional halakhic texts (and possibly for the Lurianic kabbalah as well), Nathan may have given expression to his desire to soften the hardened pattern of rabbinic Judaism. Such a desire would agree well with the tendency discernible in his writings of the years 1665–66, including his letters and the *Treatise on the Dragons*. The shift of emphasis from halakhah to Haggadah—which remained characteristic of later Sabbatianism, too—could easily become the prelude to a complete abolition of rabbinic authority and tradition even if originally it was not meant as such. Sasportas had earlier expressed his fear that the religion of Israel might "become two religions" and that the movement might lead to a schism. The abolition of the fasts was merely a portent of graver things to come, and his orthodox instinct sensed future developments which, at the time, had not even begun to take shape.

The new messianic life-feeling was dealt a critical blow by the apostasy. Nobody had foreseen the event, let alone its consequences. Sasportas' boastful claim that he had sounded the alarm and "predicted the apostasy long before it occurred" is not borne out by a closer examination of his letters.[57] Similar claims, albeit for very different reasons, were made by several believers, including Nathan of Gaza.[58] The Sabbatians, of course, had good reason to pretend that the apostasy had been predicted long before. The alleged prediction provided them with an illusion of continuity between the two stages of the movement and took the sting of surprise and scandal out of the unexpected betrayal.

For all the farcical absurdity of the sorry denouement, there was something genuinely tragic about it. A national revival, nourished by the tradition and historical experience of many generations, had, for the first time since the destruction of the Second Temple, aroused the entire Jewish people. A unique chance of a mighty renewal seemed to present itself, and the well-nigh unanimous response indicated that the seed had not been sown in vain. The "sprouting of the horn of salvation" was, at last, crowning a long and anguished history of suffering and martyrdom. No doubt the Jewish masses would have eagerly risen to action if there had been anyone to speak the word. As it was, their rediscovered pride and new self-consciousness did not go beyond empty gestures. The leaders of the movement did not think in terms of action. They looked with eyes of faith toward a passive messiah who was himself a prisoner of his psychic rhythm with its ups and downs, and incapable of any thought beyond his own suffering or, to be more exact, beyond the private visions that grew out of his suffering. Of course neither Sabbatai nor his followers should be judged by the standards of modern political action, or condemned because their behavior does not live up to our ideas of revolutionary leadership. But even judging by the standards of his own day, there is something depressing about Sabbatai's passivity. His enthusiasm during his fits of illumination spent itself on fantastic and purely personal eccentricities. Even Nathan's testimony to the effect that Sabbatai considered his agonies as symbolic of the sufferings of Israel cannot alter the fact that his inner life was autistically centered upon himself, a paranoid streak in his psychosis. Sabbatai never freed himself from the narrow circle of his private world even when he offered symbolic interpretations of his personal experiences. Also, in the extremes to which his mental illness led him he remained essentially lonely. The messianic revival bearing his name became a mass movement, but the imprint of the founder's personality was barely noticeable. Then, having reached a climax, the movement found itself suddenly at the brink of the abyss. Small wonder, then, that many believers took the jump. The crisis precipitated by Sabbatai's apostasy was a tragic moment in the history of Israel. But the tragedy also contained the seeds of a new Jewish consciousness.

The peculiar Sabbatian doctrines developed and crystallized with extraordinary rapidity in the years following the apostasy. Two factors were responsible for this, as for many similar developments in the history of religions: on the one hand, a deeply rooted faith, nourished by a profound and immediate experience the truth of which was independent of rational reflection, and, on the other hand, the ideological need to explain and rationalize the painful contradiction between historical reality and faith. The interaction of these two factors gave birth to Sabbatian theology, whose doctrine of the messiah was defined by the prophet Nathan in the years after the apostasy. It is, of course, easy to see in the Sabbatian doctrines nothing but rationalizations and ludicrous attempts at inventing an ideology that would substitute triumph for failure. Such a view of the matter is undoubtedly correct, but it presents, equally undoubtedly, only one half of the total picture.

When discussing the Sabbatian paradox by means of which cruel disappointment was turned into a positive affirmation of faith, the analogy with early Christianity almost obtrudes itself. The two messianic movements exhibit many similarities which are as instructive as the equally obvious differences. Both movements were the product of the operation of the twin factors faith and rationalization. Both had to provide an ideology accounting for initial disappointment. Their master's death was a blow which the disciples of Jesus could overcome only by cultivating the image of his resurrection and the hope in his triumphant return as lord and judge. While historians should beware of regarding theology as nothing but ideology and the production of rationalizations, there is little doubt that without the additional stress of having to account also for the delay of the Second Coming, the impressive edifice of Catholic theology would never have arisen. Both Christianity and the Sabbatian movement took as their point of departure the ancient Jewish paradox of the Suffering Servant which, however, they stressed with such radicalism that they practically stood it on its head. Both movements gave rise to a mystical faith centered on a definite historical event, and drawing its strength from the paradoxical character of this event.

A savior who dies like a criminal and a redeemer whose mission leads him to apostasy are equally unacceptable to the naïve religious consciousness. Yet the apparent stumbling-block proved to be a source of strength from which both movements drew their religious justification, for both believed in a second manifestation in glory of him whom they had beheld in his degradation. The early Christians believed in the return of the crucified after his ascension to Heaven. The Sabbatians too believed that the redeemer's absence (a moral absence after his apostasy, a physical absence after his death) was temporary only and that he would return before long to achieve his messianic mission. As time passed and disillusionment deepened, the dogmatic formulations became increasingly radical. At first the doctrinal developments bore mainly on the nature and person of the messiah and on the hidden mystery of his suffering. But very soon early Christianity found itself diverging widely from traditional Jewish belief and practice. The same also happened with the Sabbatian movement, and with the same rapidity.

In both instances a new religious value came to the fore. The Sabbatian notion of pure faith, unaccompanied by specific works and requiring no sign or miracle, has its predecessor in Paul's doctrine of faith. Pre-Sabbatian, traditional Judaism had never entertained the idea of a pure faith, dissociated from specific works yet endowed with redemptive power, as a supreme religious value. Messianic faith, however, now changed its character: not faith in imminent redemption but faith in the paradox of the messiah's mission was declared to be the crucial issue. The basic paradox of the new faith inevitably led to further and no less audacious paradoxes.

The new doctrinal developments extended beyond the question of the messiah's mission and of the place of the "law" in the messianic age, to the doctrine of the Godhead, which now took a definitely heretical turn —at least from the point of view of rabbinic Sabbatianism. The two main points of similarity between Christianity and Judaism in this respect are the doctrine of the Trinity and that of the incarnation of the Godhead in the messiah. Judaism, including kabbalistic Judaism, had never admitted these ideas, but now they began to take root in some Sabbatian circles, probably under the influence (direct and indirect) of the analogous Christian doctrines. The many marranos returning to Judaism at that period no doubt acted as a channel by which Christian ideas and doctrines were mediated to Sabbatian theology. In fact, several of the leading believers were former marranos, but the ideas which they introduced into Sabbatianism belonged to the heretical rather than to the orthodox traditions of Christianity. The gnostic character of most Sabbatian systems is surprising indeed. Abraham Cardozo's theological studies may have acquainted him with early gnostic heresies, and, like him, other Sabbatian writers too may have developed, in a specifically Jewish context, gnostic ideas which originally derived from patristic literature. Nevertheless, the significance of extraneous, Christian influences should not be exaggerated. Certain developments are immanent in the very nature and structure of religious phenomena. Sabbatian theology would probably have developed the way it did even without Christian gnosticism and the return of many marranos to their ancestral religion. Lurianic kabbalism, the Sabbatians' original system of reference, was, after all, based on an essentially gnostic set of ideas. Every crisis in the doctrinal formulation of the experience of redemption, let alone in the matter of the eschatological, and even more so, of the pre-eschatological, existence of Israel, was found to lead to analogous developments in religious speculation.

In both cases the destruction of traditional values in the wake of bitter disllusionment and intense religious awakening led to an outburst of antagonism toward the Law. The experience of the freedom of the children of God gave birth to antinomian doctrines, such as those of Paul, which contained the seeds of even more radical developments as exemplified by some of the more extreme gnostic sects. In the case of the Sabbatian movement, the antinomian element was intensified by Sabbatai Ṣevi's personality and his "strange acts." There was a core of potential antinomianism in the legacy which Sabbatai bequeathed to later Sabbatian doctrine as elaborated by Nathan. In the history of the Sabbatian movement, Nathan's writings played a role similar to that of Paul's letters in the development of Christian doctrine. However cautious Nathan's formulation of certain radical ideas, it encouraged the more violently antinomian tendencies of some Sabbatian circles. Similarities in the historical situations of Christianity and Sabbatianism, and the inner logic of their respective doctrinal notions, led to similar results. Each considered the appearance of its respective messiah as the beginning of a new era and as the foundation of a new reality. Hence they had to adopt a radically different attitude toward the values that had been dominant until then, namely, the Law of Moses and the halakhic tradition of rabbinic Judaism respectively.

However, the structural similarities must not blind us to the profound differences between early Christianity and Sabbatianism. Each of the two movements has its own historical, religious, and psychological horizon. The Sabbatian awakening was a revolt against the ghetto, taking place within the narrow confines of the ghetto, and bearing the marks of the latter even where it promised to make all things new. Lacking the natural breadth and width of the Judaism that gave birth to Christianity, Sabbatianism constituted an attempt to defend, within the ghetto, a spiritual world that had already broken out of the ghetto walls. In a way, the movement can be said to have played a pioneering role in envisaging a new world which, as yet, it lacked the means of grasping, let alone of adequately conceptualizing. One hundred and twenty years had to pass before this "new World" became sufficiently concrete for the Jews to be susceptible of a more adequate definition. The tangled complexities resulting from the tension between the religious vision of the new world, on the one hand, and the unwillingness to leave the ghetto, on the other, plainly appeared in the subsequent developments of the movement.

Differences in historical background and social realities do not, however, fully account for the tremendous difference between the two religious movements. An even more important factor is the decisive role played by their respective central personalities. Sabbatai Ṣevi, in spite of the undoubted fascination which he exercised on others, lacked greatness both of character and of expression. It was not he who made the messianic movement, but the faith of the masses which, in an explosive discharge of messianic energies accumulated during many generations, swept him to the heights of messiahship. The popular fervor and enthusiasm that turned him into an object of hope for the House of Israel cannot conceal the essential weakness of his otherwise colorful personality. This weakness did not prevent the Jewish masses from acclaiming him as their messiah, especially as rabbinic tradition lacked a vigorous and clear-cut image of the Redeemer. No doubt traditional Judaism possessed a potent and vital image of redemption, but the person of the Redeemer was all but hidden behind the grandeur of his mission—unlike Christianity, at the heart of which there stands a great personality.

Further, the critical events that precipitated the respective developments of Christianity and Sabbatianism are hardly comparable. Unlike the Sabbatian messiah, the Christian savior had paid the highest price a man can possibly pay. No doubt an apostate messiah constitutes an even greater paradox than a crucified messiah, but the paradox has no constructive value. The doctrine that by betraying his religion the redeemer fulfilled his messianic mission is essentially nihilistic, and once the first step was taken on this slippery road anything became possible. If the most despicable act, than which none could be more execrable to the Jewish mind, could become the doctrinal cornerstone of the Sabbatian faith, then all fences were down and there was nothing at which one would conceivably have to stop. Unlike the passion and death of Jesus, Sabbatai's apostasy, though surrounded with a tragic halo by Sabbatian literature, was essentially destructive of all values. The Sabbatian redeemer who was prepared to surrender passively to the power of impurity and to sink into the abyss of the *qelippah* while continuing to cultivate his dream of accomplishing a messianic mission, actually opened the door to the most nihilistic transvaluation of religious values. It was only natural that Frankism, the most important form of later Sabbatianism, drew the conclusions implicit in the founder's "constitutive act." The efforts of the believers to discover a positive and constructive meaning in what was an essentially negative and destructive act, constitutes their peculiar contribution to the history of religion in general and to the subsequent history of Judaism in particular. Their faith required of them a measure of tension and a struggle with paradox that went beyond anything demanded of the Christian believer.

The personal paradox of the founder (that is, his "strange actions") became generalized into a sacramental pattern for the community of his followers. Sabbatai's "illuminations" bequeathed to the movement a legacy that bore his personal stamp: the faithful would glorify certain "strange actions," or even demand their ritual performance as an expression of their peculiar religious consciousness. But beyond this pattern of paradoxical behavior very little of Sabbatai's personality remained alive in the movement that bore his name. His figure became vague almost to the point of anonymity, and all that remained was the tale of a mythical hero whose resemblances to the actual historical individual were purely coincidental.

In order to maintain the faith in the messiah it was not enough to justify his apostasy: it had to be justified in traditional Jewish terms. Nevertheless, the resultant doctrine was necessarily novel and even heretical in terms of traditional Judaism. The doctrine of the messiah as expounded by Nathan of Gaza and his disciples during the ten years following the apostasy emphasizes three novel points.[59]

In the first place, it was roundly asserted that redemption was not yet complete. The original, naïve, and overenthusiastic assertions to the effect that the realm of the *qelippoth* was completely vanquished were now said to have been mistaken. Redemption had begun, but had yet to be fully realized and consummated amid pain and suffering—including the anguishing shame of the messiah's apostasy. The Shekhinah had "risen from the dust," but had not yet been fully restored. It was this intermediary stage between the awakening of the Shekhinah and her complete restoration which provided the spiritual and emotional horizon of the Sabbatian movement.

The second doctrinal point is an immediate corollary of the foregoing. The conception of an intermediary stage resulted in a different understanding of the messiah's mission. According to the different forms of Sabbatian theology this mission could be of an active or of a more passive character. The apostasy could be interpreted in purely passive terms as the mysterious passion of the savior who "sitteth alone and keepeth silence, because he hath borne it upon him" (Lam. 3:28), or as an active descent into the abyss of the *qelippoth*. Either way, the messiah no longer served as a symbol of redemption accomplished (as in Lurianic kabbalism), but became an agent fulfilling a decisive and unique mission. All other saints had "raised" the holy sparks from the depths of the *qelippah* while keeping themselves aloof from the danger zone. Only the messiah performed the terrible *descensus ad inferos*, "that He may do His work, strange is His work, and bring to pass His act, strange is His act" (Isa. 28:21).

Third, the cosmic struggle between good and evil assumes, in its final stage, a more complicated and paradoxical form. Lurianic kabbalah had taught a way of separating, that is, raising and extracting the holy sparks from the clutches of evil in which they were held. In fact, evil existed by virtue of the vitality which it drew from the sparks of good that it had snatched and held imprisoned. Once these sparks were released and "raised," evil, impotent and lifeless as it is by itself, would automatically collapse. At this point, Sabbatian doctrine introduces a dialectical twist into the Lurianic idea. According to the new, Sabbatian version, it is not enough to extract the sparks of holiness from the realm of impurity. In order to accomplish its mission, the power of holiness—as incarnate in the messiah—has to descend into impurity, and good has to assume the form of evil. This mission is fraught with danger, as it appears to strengthen the power of evil before its final defeat. During Sabbatai's lifetime the doctrinal position was that by entering the realm of the *qelippah*, good had become evil *in appearance* only. But there were more radical possibilities waiting to be explored: only the complete transformation of good into evil would exhaust the full potential of the latter and thereby explode it, as it were, from within. This dialectical liquidation of evil requires not only the disguise of good in the form of evil but total identification with it. It was along such lines that the subsequent theology of the Sabbatian radicals developed.

For the mass of believers the certainty that the messiah's apostasy had a positive religious value was primary; the precise nature and contents of this religious value were a secondary, "ideological" problem. Hence it was possible to entertain two apparently contradictory answers to the question as to what exactly was the significance of Sabbatai's action. According to one reply, the messiah became one of the gentiles in order to save the latter from utter destruction. As has been remarked before, the extreme traditionalism of popular Jewish eschatology was not content with the defeat and submission of the gentiles but exulted in the idea of their ultimate annihilation. The eschatology of Lurianic kabbalism largely, if not entirely, shared this attitude. The Sabbatian doctrine said, surprisingly enough, that the messiah would submit to the dominion of the gentiles in order to save the souls that could be saved and to raise them to himself.

The other reply takes the opposite view. The messiah descended into the realm of the *qelippah* in order to destroy it from within. Only by feigning submission to the *qelippah* could he achieve his purpose of utterly destroying it. This stratagem or "holy ruse" can be compared to the action of a worm in a tree that appears healthy from outside but, when split open, is seen to be worm-eaten. "Wherefore it is utterly impossible for any creature to comprehend any of his actions, and whoever says that he understands the ways of the messianic king is completely mistaken."[60] The same text contains another, extremely revealing, simile in the parable of the king (that is, God) whose bride (that is, the Shekhinah) and family (that is, the holy sparks) have been captured by enemies (that is, the *qelippah*), and who sends his trusted servant (that is, the messiah) as a spy into the enemy country to inquire about the captives. This servant has to act with great cunning "and to adopt the dress of the people through whose land he passes, and to behave as they do, lest they notice that he is a spy. . . . Keep this parable in your heart, for it is a foundation to satisfy you regarding several doubts in the matter."[61] Both answers occur side by side in the writings of Nathan and his disciples.

Sabbatai's followers and believers were good Jews. They believed in the holy books. Hence their first reaction—one might almost say reflex—was to search Scripture and tradition for intimations, hints, and indications of the extraordinary and bewildering events. And lo and behold—the Bible, rabbinic Haggadah, and kabbalistic literature turned out to abound in allusions to Sabbatai Ṣevi in general and to the mystery of his apostasy in particular. The Sabbatians were second to none in the art of interpreting, hairsplitting, and twisting tests, for which the Jews forever have had such an uncontested reputation. And though their tropological and kabbalistic exegesis was far removed from the plain sense of their texts, it certainly reflected the plain sense of what moved their hearts.

"From biblical verses and fragments of verses, from rabbinic sayings whose implicit possibilities nobody had noticed before, from paradoxical expressions in kabbalistic literature, and from the oddest corners of Jewish literature, they produced material the like of which had never been seen in Jewish theology."[62] The ridicule which some historians have poured over this exegetical "nonsense" bespeaks little understanding of the actual phenomenon, namely, the emergence, out of the blue, of an original Jewish terminology grappling with the contradictions in the life and ministry of the redeemer. As regards their contents, the Sabbatian interpretations were, no doubt, audacious and novel, but their exegetical methods were not much different from those traditionally employed in rabbinic literature. Hence also the success and the power of persuasion of the Sabbatian preaching, which not only appealed to hidden religious emotions but also fascinated the public by the manner in which it filled traditional images and figures of speech with new contents. It represented, in fact, a dialectical explosion within traditional linguistic and conceptual usage.

Paradoxical explanations of the messiah's fate had already been offered, albeit on a smaller scale, after Sabbatai's imprisonment in Gallipoli. Now the same methods were applied to the much more serious question of the apostasy. Where the ancient texts failed to yield what exegetical ingenuity and ardent faith required of them, they were, on occasion, misquoted or falsified. Readers of Paul's letters can learn a great deal from these later Jewish writings, composed in a very similar psychological situation. The clash between the old and the new, which is so conspicuous a feature in Paul's thinking, manifests itself in a more traditionally Jewish, though no less radical, fashion in the extant letters of Nathan.

NOTES

1. Abraham Miguel Cardozo, in a Spanish letter addressed to his brother (MS. Oxford 2481, fol. 4b), argues that opposition from the leading classes was necessary in order that the truth about the messiah should appear doubtful and belief in him be an act of faith. Cardozo's argument seems to reflect the state of affairs *after* Sabbatai's apostasy. Also, the prophet Nathan began to accuse the "rich misers" after the apostasy.
2. Complaints about grinding the poor and abuse of power by the rich were

made practically everywhere. At about the same time that the famous preacher Berakhya Berakh pilloried the social abuses in Polish Jewry, Moses Judah Abbas in Turkey wrote his poems, one of which (dedicated to Abraham Yakhini) is a bitter indictment of the shamelessness and injustice with which the poor are robbed. The poem was written before the Sabbatian outbreak, and Abraham Yakhini, who played an important part in the movement, had nothing to do with the incidents to which it refers. The poem, published by M. Wallenstein in the *JSS,* I (1956), 165–71, provides valuable testimony of the social tensions and abuses in a Turkish (or possibly Egyptian) community under a "patrician" regime.

3. See S. Schechter's essay "Safed in the 16th Century," in *Studies in Judaism,* 2nd series (1908), pp. 202–328.
4. The ideas in this section have been elaborated by the author is an essay, "The Messianic Idea in Judaism," published in a collection of essays, *The Messianic Idea in Judaism and Other Essays in Jewish Spirituality* (New York: Schocken Press, 1971), pp. 1–36.
5. Apocalyptic texts and midrashim from the end of the Talmudic period to the late Middle Ages have been collected and edited by J. Even-Shemu'el, *Midreshey Ge'ullah,* 2nd edn. (Jerusalem, 1954).
6. B. Sanhedrin 97 f.; also the last mishnah of the Tractate Sotah.
7. Cf. Jacob Mann, "Messianic Movements at the Time of the First Crusade" (Hebrew), *ha-Tequfah,* XXIII (1925), 243–61 (particularly p. 251), and XXIV (1928), 335–58.
8. See Y. F. Baer, "The Historical Background of the *Ra'ya Mehemna*" (Hebrew), *Zion,* V (1939–40), 1–44.
9. English translation under this title by S. Rosenblatt (New Haven, 1948).
10. Written by Maimonides in 1172 to counter the messianic preaching of a false prophet who agitated Yemenite Jewry.
11. Such as practiced by earlier Jewish mystics; see Scholem, *Major Trends in Jewish Mysticism* (New York, 1941), ch. 2.
12. On the concept of Shekhinah and its kabbalistic development, see Scholem, "Schechina, das passiv-weibliche Moment in der Gottheit," in *Von der mystischen Gestalt der Gottheit* (Zurich, 1962), pp. 135–91.
13. R. Joseph She'altiel b. Moses ha-Kohen added in the margin of a MS. of the book *Peli'ah* (MS. Vatican 187): "I think that the afflictions visited on the Jews in all the Christian kingdoms between the years 5250–55 [1490–95] . . . are the messianic birth pangs." These lines were written on the Island of Rhodes in 1495.
14. Extant in a Paris MS. (Bibliothèque Nationale, No. 845).
15. Lemmlein's kabbalist background is proved by his replies to R. Moses Ḥefeṣ of Salonika; see A. Marx in *RÉJ,* LXI (1911), 135–38.
16. Cf. my two articles on R. Abraham b. Eliezer ha-Levi in *Kiryath Sepher,* II (1925) and VII (1931).
17. On Karo as a mystic, see R. J. Z. Werblowsky, *Joseph Karo, Lawyer and Mystic* (Oxford, 1962).

18. *'Ohel Mo'ed* (MS. Cambridge Add. 673[1], fol. 13a). This work, a kind of introduction to the kabbalah, was probably written at the beginning of the 16th century.
19. Joseph Yabeṣ (Jabez), *'Or ha-Ḥayyim,* fol. 4a.
20. Very characteristic of this critical attitude is the *bon mot* Yabeṣ quotes from a "certain great thinker" (perhaps Don Isaac Abravanel) who was wont to conclude his lectures on Maimonides' *Guide* with the words: "This is the teaching of our Master Moses [Maimonides] but not of Moses our Master [*scil.* the biblical Moses]" (*ibid.*, fol. 21a).
21. See Judah Ḥayyat's introduction to his commentary *Minḥath Yehudah* on *Ma'arekheth ha'Elohuth* (Mantua, 1558), fol. 3a.
22. Referring probably to the statement (Zohar III, 124b) that through the merits of the book Zohar the children of Israel would be redeemed from exile.
23. Quoted by Abraham Azulay of Hebron in the introduction to his commentary on the Zohar, entitled *'Or ha-Ḥammah* (Jerusalem, 1879).
24. See "Notes from Italy," *Zion,* X (1945), 66.
25. Jacob Sasportas, *Ṣiṣat Novel Ṣevi,* ed. Isaiah Tishby (Jerusalem, 1954), pp. 6, 74.
26. *Ibid.*, p. 20.
27. Cf. the analysis of Nathan Shapira's social criticism, *Sabbatai Ṣevi* [the full work by Scholem], pp. 73–74.
28. Sasportas, p. 23.
29. *Ibid.*, p. 303.
30. *Ibid.*, p. 6. Sasportas' statements are contradicted by Sambari's chronicle, written by a man on the scene.
31. Thus the more legendary account of Peter Serrarius. The German version has only the pasha of Gaza.
32. Thus Serrarius. The German version does not mention Christians.
33. The English text (reprinted by Wilenski in *Zion* 17 [1952], p. 171) reads *Nature,* which is an obvious misprint. The German version reads: *enthalten sich aller Eitelkeiten und besonders des Kaufhandels und Wechsels welchen Natan für Wucher hält.*
34. The words "at Jerusalem" occur in Serrarius' text only. The German version is superior.
35. Toward the end of the tract *God's Love to His People Israel* (Wilenski, p. 172).
36. *Hollandtze Merkurius,* January, 1666 [actually published 1667], p. 3, and similarly in German, with slight variations only, in the *Diarium Europaeum,* XVI (1688), 510; the editors of the *Diarium* may actually have had the original letter before them. The number of the prophets in Smyrna is also given by Sasportas (p. 60).
37. Baruch of Arezzo (Alfred Freimann, *'Inyenei Shabbetai Ṣevi* [Berlin, 1913], p. 49), who also mentions Ḥayyim Peña's sister-in-law (the wife of Jacob Peña and possibly Sabbatai's sister), but not his daughters. The "daugh-

ters of the infidels that prophesy" are also mentioned in letters from Smyrna.

38. Thomas Coenen, *Ydele verwachtinge der Joden* (Amsterdam, 1669), p. 41. 9 Tebeth as the date of Peña's conversion, and 6 Tebeth as the date of Benveniste's appointment as chief rabbi, provide the pivot for a correct chronology of the events in Smyrna. Coenen's account suggests that the reconciliation between Sabbatai and Peña took place before the prophesying of the daughters: during a friendly discussion between the two, Sabbatai is said to have told Peña that his daughters, who were in mourning over the recent death of their mother, should put on their best clothes; as soon as they did they began to prophesy. Perhaps the reconciliation took place as early as 6 Tebeth, when Benveniste joined the Sabbatian camp.
39. Baruch of Arezzo (Freimann, pp. 49–50). Texts of similar prophecies were received in Amsterdam; e.g., the letter from Smyrna, received on March 10, 1666, which contained the prophecies—mainly in Hebrew and consisting of parts of scriptural verses—of several women. One girl prophesied in Spanish (Aescoly, in *Dinaburg Jubilee Volume* [Jerusalem, 1949], p. 227). This letter was also known to Sasportas, pp. 148, 162.
40. Coenen (p. 32) wondered why nobody ever spoke of the messiah as "lowly and riding upon an ass."
41. Sasportas, p. 148. The same case is described in the letter published by Aaron Aescoly, p. 227: when a priest was called in to exorcise her, the girl insulted him in the presence of Christians and Turks, and declared that Sabbati Ṣevi was the messiah.
42. Sasportas, p. 96.
43. *Ibid.*, p. 147.
44. *Ibid.*, p. 96.
45. *Ibid.*, pp. 156 (letter of R. Hosea Nantawa from Alexandria) and 182. Leyb b. Ozer's account (Jacob Emden, *Torat ha-Qenaʾot,* p. 10) exaggerates as usual: women prophesied in Zoharic Aramaic (probably a confusion with Moses Suriel's prophecy), and there were "hundreds of prophets" in Adrianople.
46. Rhodes and Chios. The daughter of a certain Caimo (Ḥayyim) b. Aaron prophesied in Corfu in 1666; see H. Mizraḥi's ((Hebrew) article, "Evidence of Messianic Agitàtion on Corfu, from a Christian Source" in *Sefunoth,* III–IV (1960), 537–40, from Andrea Marmora's *Historia di Corfu* (Venice, 1672).
47. The French *Relation de la veritable Imposture du faux Messie des Juifs* (Avignon, 1667), p. 17. Litigation was suspended or neglected. In 1668 a broker, Sabbatai ha-Levi, explained to the rabbinic court of Smyrna that he had not lodged his claims two years earlier, "because everybody and everything was confused in connection with the well-known disturbances" (Benveniste's responsa *Baʿey Ḥayyey,* ad *Ḥoshen Mishpat,* no. 175).
48. Coenen, pp. 58–59.
49. Coenen (p. 34) emphasizes the extraordinary character of the proceedings,

since normally only "Franks," i.e., Europeans, were permitted to walk the streets at night with torches. The permissive attitude of the Turkish police (who were probably bribed) was considered another miracle by the believers. See also *Hollandtze Merkurius,* January, 1666, p. 3. De la Croix (p. 315) reports cries of *"Vive Sultan Ṣevi."*

50. Coenen, p. 63.
51. Rabbinic idioms. Aramaic, *tavya,* "stag," the equivalent of Hebrew, *Ṣevi.*
52. The prayer is given by Coenen in a Dutch translation. The Hebrew text printed by Rosanes and claimed by him to be the form used in Smyrna is really derived from Leyb b. Ozer (Emden, p. 8), who, of course, gives the Amsterdam version of the prayer, parts of which were recited to him by his informants.
53. See E.Renan, *Les Apôtres* (Paris, 1894), p. 2.
54. *Sefer ha-Liqqutim,* attributed to Ḥayyim Vital (Jerusalem, 1900), fol. 22c.
55. Joseph ha-Levi's letter, *ap.* Sasportas, pp. 171, 186.
56. *Ibid.,* p. 190. Joseph ha-Levi's letter was written in November, 1666, but Nathan's counsel to which it refers was certainly given before the apostasy. Nathan's utterance is also preserved in a Sabbatian source; see Freimann, p. 96.
57. Sasportas (p. 352) claims that he had predicted that Sabbatai would finally have no other way out but apostasy. The truth is that early in 1666 Sasportas had asked for celestial guidance and was vouchsafed an answer in a dream. The answer took the form of the vss. Job 30:5 and 27:23. The cryptic reply does not, however, mean what Sasportas later made it to mean (p. 79). As a matter of fact, Sasportas seems to have feared the possibility of an apostasy of the disappointed believers rather than of the messiah (*ibid.,* pp. 47, 166).
58. According to Coenen (p. 96), several informants in Smyrna reported that Sabbatai had prophesied that one day he would take the turban, reveal the mysteries of the Jewish religion to the Turks, and convert the Portuguese Synagogue into a mosque. Coenen himself rightly doubted the veracity of the report.
59. The sources for our knowledge of this doctrine are, above all, Nathan's and Cardozo's letters, which were widely copied at the time. The most important of Nathan's letters is undoubtedly the long circular letter which he wrote about 1673–74. The full text was preserved in the Dönmeh archives and became accessible only after the Hebrew version of the present book was published. It is now available in my edn., *Qobeṣ ʿal Yad,* XVI, New Series (1966), pt. II, pp. 421–45. Parts of it had been known before and were published by Ch. Wirszubski in *Zion,* III (1938), 227–35 (see his discussion of its contents, *ibid.,* pp. 215–27). The full text disproved Wirszubski's and my own former assumption that the letter was written in 1667. Another letter, written early in 1668, has been quoted in *Sabbatai Ṣevi,* pp. 741–43, and part of another, written after 1668, has been published by me in *ʾEreṣ Yisraʾel,* IV (1956), 191–92. Cardozo's relevant letters, apart from the

Magen Abraham, are his letter to the rabbis of Smyrna, *Zion,* XIX (1954), 1–22; the letters to his brother-in-law, in Hebrew (*ap.* Freimann, pp. 87–92) and in Spanish, MS. Oxford, Neubauer 2481.

60. Cardozo, in his *Magen Abraham* (ed. G. Scholem, in *Qobeṣ ʿal Yad,* XII [1938], 138). The comparison of Sabbatai Ṣevi to a worm is already found in Nathan's *Treatise on the Dragons* (see G. Scholem, *Beʿlqvoth Mashiaḥ,* p. 37).
61. *Magen Abraham, loc. cit.,* p. 139.
62. Quoting my own formulation in the essay *Miṣwah ha-baʾah ba-ʿaberah,* in *Keneseth,* II (1937), 360; see Scholem, *The Messianic Idea* (1971), p. 96.

13

From Schweitzer to Scholem: Reflections on Sabbatai Svi

W. D. Davies

The place of Albert Schweitzer in the history of the interpretation of the NT is secure. Although the predominance of the History of Religions School often led to the neglect of his work, especially in Germany,[1] ultimately it could not be ignored; and that for one reason. Along with Johannes Weiss, Schweitzer established once and for all the eschatological dimensions of the NT. Necessary modifications of his work, compelled by C. H. Dodd and others, have not shaken the rightness of his main emphasis. The continuing insistence on eschatology by Schweitzer's fellow Alsacian, Oscar Cullmann, in many influential studies, the recent reiteration of apocalyptic as the matrix of Christian theology by E. Käsemann,[2] U. Wilckens,[3] and others, the emerging concentration on the examination of the apocrypha and pseudepigrapha, especially in this country,[4] and the call by Klaus Koch to rediscover apocalyptic[5]—all implicitly reinforce the significance of Schweitzer's contribution.

"Context determines content." This rediscovery of the significance of apocalyptic for the theological understanding of the NT has been stimulated by the temper of our disjointed times, and by certain important discoveries. The Qumran documents (providing first-hand sources especially for the examination of a sect living in the tension of an eschatological situation), and the documents of Nag Hammadi have made possible a deeper understanding of apocalyptic and gnostic attitudes. Here I want

Reprinted by permission of the Society for Biblical Literature from the *Journal of Biblical Literature* 95 (1976).

to point to still another sphere (not strictly a source) where we can find illumination for the understanding of the apocalyptic world within which the writers of the NT moved. The invitation to prepare this lecture arrived when I was re-reading Gershom G. Scholem's great work *Sabbatai Ṣevi: The Mystical Messiah, 1626–1676.*[6] Its relevance for the study of the NT struck me with renewed force, and I dared offer as a title, "From Schweitzer to Scholem." This theme turned out to be too broad, and I can only deal with the prolegomena to it. I shall offer reflections on the value of Scholem's study for what could lead to a reassessment of Schweitzer's work. These reflections, which have turned out to be more interrogatory than affirmative, are based mainly on *Sabbatai Ṣevi,* but also on Scholem's other profound contributions to the study of messianism and mysticism. I emphasize that it is impossible to do justice to their vast riches and deep penetration here. I rely entirely upon Scholem's interpretation of the sources for Sabbatianism (a fact which he would be the first to admit is not without its dangers)[7] and shall consider the purpose of this lecture fulfilled if only it helps to integrate Scholem's insight into the nature of Judaism more closely into the study of Christian origins.

1

Sabbatai Svi was born in Smyrna in 1626. In 1648 he proclaimed himself to be the Messiah, but was met with scorn. Three years later the Jewish community outlawed him. But in 1665 Nathan of Gaza, a young rabbi trained in the talmudic schools in Jerusalem, became convinced, through a vision, that Sabbatai Svi was the Messiah. He persuaded a reluctant Sabbatai of his messianic destiny and proceeded to disseminate the astounding news of his identity throughout the diaspora. The movement spread to Jewish communities in Yemen and Persia in the East and to those in the West as far as England, Holland, Russia, and Poland. It was stirred by massive repentance, expressed in fasts and mortifications, and by extraordinary enthusiasm, visions, and miracles. The date of the end of all things was fixed for 1666 but was conveniently moved when necessary. The antinomian acts of Sabbatai Svi failed to dampen the enthusiasm of the believers, who through him were experiencing the emotional reality of redemption. Neither the astounding apostasy of Sabbatai Svi to Islam and his attempts to persuade believers to apostatize, nor even his death destroyed the movement. There still exist a few believers in Sabbatai Svi.[8]

Scholem has traced the history of this Messiah and his movement. Can a seventeenth-century messianic movement illumine early Christianity? The dangers of parallelomania (especially when movements long separated in time are compared) are familiar, particularly since Samuel Sandmel's noted address on this theme.[9] But this being recognized, I welcome one salutary outcome of Protestant-Roman Catholic interchange in our time. Protestants have tended to think that movements are best understood in the light of their origins; Catholics, in terms of their developments. We now see more clearly that both origins and developments help to reveal the essence of movements. We can learn much about the nature of apocalyptic in the first century from the ways in which it expressed itself in the seventeenth. Scholem is right to draw attention to phenomena in early Christianity which seem to be illumined by counterparts in Sabbatianism. Was Sabbatianism directly influenced by Christianity? Scholem faced this question.[10] Sabbatai himself had a real interest in those who claimed to be messiahs before him, especially in Jesus. Some Gentile Christian chiliasts were well informed about Sabbatianism and perhaps were indirectly influential in shaping it. But direct Christian influences cannot be proved, and Scholem prefers to regard Sabbatianism as an independent, indigenous phenomenon within Judaism.[11] In Sabbatianism, we can examine in depth a major Jewish messianic movement, other than Christianity.

One point is of special note. If an early Christian Aramaic literature was ever written, it has not survived. The documents produced by early Christianity are few and are written in Greek. There is a sparse leanness about them. They demand infinite labor to give them flesh and blood, color and substance. The NT is a distillation. On the contrary, in Sabbatianism, thanks to the immeasurable labors of Scholem, the documentation is rich.[12] Through it one can feel and know the historical actuality of the movement more directly than is the case with early Christianity. We shall attempt to show what Scholem's work offers the student of the NT under three headings: first, the new light it sheds on the nature of Judaism; second, on messianism; and third on early Christianity.

2. NEW LIGHT ON THE NATURE OF JUDAISM

To begin with, the Judaism which one encounters in Sabbatianism does not conform to the picture of it handed on to us even by Jewish scholars. Long ago, Scholem had emphasized two hitherto ignored facets of Judaism: the deep penetration of it by mystical currents, and the domestication of apocalyptic within Pharisaism.[13] The picture of a predominantly halakic Judaism, largely untouched by mystic experiences and apocalyptic visions, has had to be abandoned. Scholem has now further unearthed and examined a world of mystical secrets, symbols, images, enthusiasms, and esoterica which rabbinic leaders and scholars had considered unworthy of serious attention and treated with contempt. In doing so, he has further discredited the concept of a normative pharisaic Judaism.[14] He has made such a concept untenable, not only by insisting on the two broad aspects hitherto denied to Judaism referred to, but also in a more detailed way. To illustrate, let us consider one phenomenon in Sabbatianism which has customarily been taken to be utterly non-Jewish.

Judaism has usually been described as insisting on the qualitative difference between God and man. The notion of the divinity of a human being was regarded as one of the marks of Hellenistic religion which sharply differentiated it from the Jewish.[15] The doctrine of the incarnation has always been regarded as the Rubicon between Christianity and Judaism. But the case of Sabbatai Svi is instructive. Divided and uncertain of himself as he was, at certain points he claimed to be divine and he did not offer explanations for his claim. The evidence for all this is ambiguous, but it is not to be ignored. He was regularly called by the term "Our Lord."[16] It can be objected that Sabbatai's mind was diseased and that it is illegitimate to deduce anything about Judaism from his case. Scholem has shown that he was a pathological figure, suffering from a manic-depressive condition.[17] But this makes it all the more striking that his followers, including rabbis despite the criticisms of some rabbinic leaders, do not seem to have objected to his claim to divinity nor found it, in itself, impossible. Moreover, the role ascribed to Sabbatai Svi by Nathan of Gaza was such as to demand that he possess divine power because, through his activity and the faith in himself which he engendered among his followers, the whole cosmos was to be redeemed, to achieve restoration. In previous studies, Scholem had indicated that in the Merkabah mysticism of an earlier period in Jewish history[18] the unbridgeable gulf between man and God remained. But in Sabbatianism this gulf seems to have been crossed. Within a messianic context a new dimension of union between God and man had opened.

But before Sabbatai Svi appeared, Judaism had known the long development of a mysticism in the medieval period in which the relationship between man and God had been constantly pondered under other than simply scriptural influences. This long development makes any direct comparison with Judaism in the period before the appearance of Jesus very precarious.[19] But we can at least say this. Schweitzer drew a sharp distinction between the mysticism of Paul, that of being "in Christ," and the mysticism of the Fourth Gospel, that of being "in God."[20] The former he considered Jewish and messianic, the latter Hellenistic. In the light of the history of Sabbatai Svi, such a distinction need not point outside Judaism. Sabbatai Svi's claims to divinity did not signify or imply any departure from it, nor involve the emergence of a new religion.[21] Given belief in the advent of the Messiah, the possibility for transcending the customary categories of Judaism as they had traditionally been understood was immensely enhanced.

3. NEW LIGHT ON MESSIANISM

The reference to the Messiah brings us to the second sphere where Scholem's work is illuminating: our understanding of messianism.[22] In a remarkable way Sabbatianism shows that messianic movements are always likely to have presented certain constants. The same characteristics recur in such movements, although separated widely in space and time. Certain phenomena re-emerge in Sabbatianism which had characterized early Christianity. They are so many that it is tempting to find in Sabbatianism simply a late, distorted replica of Christianity (a temptation that, as we saw, Scholem has taught us to resist). It is impossible to enumerate completely the phenomena to which we refer. We shall divide them into two groups: first, what we shall call, without prejudice,[23] secondary characteristics; and secondly, primary or essential phenomena. The former are very many; the latter can be reduced to two.

As for the secondary phenomena, they may be divided as follows. First, certain strictly religious emphases are common: for example, repentance, prayer, fasting, enthusiasm. Although Paul (in this, he was very unlike Nathan of Gaza) apparently never emphasized repentance directly,[24] early Christianity was preceded by or accompanied by a movement of repentance which Jesus himself joined. The same phenomenon in an even more marked form emerged at the birth of Sabbatianism. Sabbatai Svi himself, but in particular his prophet, Nathan of Gaza, inaugurated a vast movement of repentance and mortification of the flesh, a mortification which Paul at times might have exemplified (1 Cor 9:27). The sources for Sabbatianism reveal the extremes to which such pre-messianic repentance was liable: some followers of Sabbatai Svi died from fasting.[25] Doubtless, had we more sources, early Christianity would reveal the same. Similarly in the strictly religious dimension, the habits of prayer of Sabbatai Svi recall the immediacy of the prayer of the Jesus of the Synoptics. The religious intensity of Sabbatai Svi, his experience of mystical absorption and ecstasy, and the almost bizarre unrealism of some of the Sabbatian believers recall the kind of enthusiasm which one detects both in and behind the Synoptics.[26] Käsemann's brilliant detection of an early Christian enthusiasm has probably simply raised the lid of a cauldron.[27] The enthusiasm, for example, which led to the so-called communism of Acts finds its parallel at the advent of Sabbatai Svi in the sale of their property by countless rich Jews in many quarters.[28]

Secondly, the miraculous is as marked in Sabbatianism as in early Christianity. For example, the manner of the birth of Sabbatai Svi was dwelt upon in a way reminiscent of the birth narratives in Matthew and Luke; and Sabbatai Svi urged a cult of his mother, comparable with later Christian mariolatry.[29] There was a tradition that between 1648 and 1650 Sabbatai Svi was miraculously saved from drowning: "He rose from the sea and was saved," as was Jesus when he walked on the sea.[30] Magical elements which have been discovered in the Synoptic tradition have their parallels, in a very enhanced form, in Sabbatianism. Sabbatai Svi seems at times to have inaugurated a magical enterprise. There were attempts to force the end by what has been called a "practical Qabbala," which amounted to magic.[31] That Jesus' work could be and has been regarded in a similar magical fashion the studies of A. Schweitzer himself show; in the end the Jesus of Schweitzer is an apocalyptical magician who seeks to "force" the end.[32]

Thirdly, the nature and activity of Sabbatai Svi and Jesus as messiahs are often similar: for example, that the Messiah could be in the world unknown reappears in Sabbatianism;[33] and also he is parallel with Moses and Adam;[34] his coming inaugurates or is accompanied by the "birth pangs of the Messiah."[35] Like Jesus, Sabbatai Svi chose twelve to represent the Twelve Tribes of Israel.[36] Like Jesus also, Sabbatai Svi was a messiah without armies.[37] In a strange way, but with a great difference in the nature of their pains, both Jesus and Sabbatai were suffering messiahs.

Fourthly, among these secondary phenomena, if such a term be permitted in this connection, both Sabbatai Svi and Jesus were conceived to have overcome death, the former by occultation and the latter by resurrection. And both were expected to return again to earth to complete their work.[38]

Fifthly, we note the striking phenomenon that the roles of John the Baptist and Paul in early Christianity and that of Nathan of Gaza in Sabbatianism are parallel.[39] *Mutatis mutandis,* Nathan of Gaza in himself was to Sabbatai Svi what both John the Baptist and Paul were to Jesus. Until Nathan convinced him, Sabbatai Svi was uncertain of his messianic identity. Though more directly so (the Synoptic and Johannine materials are here so varied), Nathan was a witness to Sabbatai in a way parallel with that of John the Baptist to Jesus. But it was Nathan also who later provided the theological structure for the interpretation of Sabbatai Svi and in this played the role of Paul to Jesus. Like Paul, Nathan refused to be impressed by or to demand "signs" that the Messiah had come.[40] But this single parallel of Nathan with the Baptist and Paul must not be pressed. It is altogether natural that the founder of any movement should have significant interpreters.

Finally, much as many scholars urge that there was little interest in the life of Jesus even on the part of Paul, Sabbatianism flourished apparently without much active interest among the masses of believers in the history and character of Sabbatai.[41] What mattered was *that* the Messiah had appeared, not *who* had appeared as Messiah. The strange behavior of Sabbatai Svi, a manic-depressive, caused consternation among the rabbis, and others, who believed in him, as among those who did not. He changed the calendar,[42] ignored the food laws,[43] pronounced the ineffable Name,[44] and was sexually irregular.[45] His conduct was often, to use Scholem's vivid phrase, "an Exodus from the Law."[46] The justification of Sabbatai's behavior, his attitude to and disobedience of the Law, culminating in his monstrous apostasy to Islam, posed a problem for his followers, comparable with that facing early Christians by the free attitude of Jesus to the Law and by his suffering and death. The theology of both movements began with an initial disappointment which had to be explained. Both turned to the same exegetical methods to do so, and both concentrated on the Suffering Servant of Isaiah 53 for illumination. Both developed a doctrine of the parousia; both demanded faith, unattested by works or signs. *Perhaps, in early Christianity* a new element had entered Judaism, that is, faith in a pure or neat form, not necessarily associated with good works, became the mark of redemption, and that a faith in a paradoxical messiah. Such a faith re-emerged in Sabbatianism.[47] Both movements produced a doctrine of Incarnation. In both a deeply felt faith, an immediate experience of being in a new eon, a "realized eschatology" of incalculable emotional intensity, enthusiasm and exultation led to a radical criticism of Jewish tradition, a new standard of measurement being applied to it. The experience of the freedom of the children of God led to antinomian tendencies, especially and unrestrainedly in Sabbatianism, but also in early Christianity, which at times broke out into license.[48]

Taken together, the phenomena to which we have pointed—and many more such could be noted—are extremely valuable. To read the history of Sabbatai is to encounter the emotional intensity of a messianic movement at first hand, a temper or an atmosphere strikingly like the very enthusiastic, ecstatic world of feeling which was the "new creation" of early Christianity. This is not all. The history of Sabbatai suggests that a messianic movement of any depth is most likely, almost inevitably, to call forth certain phenomena—ecstasy, mortifications, visions, miracles, enthusiasms and certain inescapable parallel responses. The reason for this is simple. The messianic tradition had developed into a popular tradition, so that the advent of a messiah at any time stirred up among the masses certain age-long, stereotyped expectations. Discouraged as they might be to do so even by the messiah himself, the believing masses found "signs" everywhere. Moved by the age-old concepts and symbols of messianism rooted in the Scriptures and enlarged upon in tradition, they were eager to clothe their messiah, in every age, with the kind of characteristics they thought proper to him.[49]

Probably in every messianic movement, certainly in Sabbatianism and early Christianity, a distinction should be clearly recognized between the understanding of it among the masses and among the more sophisticated leaders. Attempts to explain Sabbatianism and early Christianity in predominantly political or economic or sociological terms have generally failed to convince. Believers in Sabbatai Svi were drawn from the rich and the poor, the underprivileged and the established, from the ignorant *ʿam hāʾāreṣ* and the rabbinic authorities.[50] Similarly, early Christianity was probably indifferent to barriers of wealth, class, and learning, although the evidence is not as clear as in Sabbatianism.[51] Nevertheless there were real differences of comprehension among the believers in both movements. Nathan of Gaza and Paul of Tarsus understood the respective messiahs in whom they believed in a far more theologically informed manner than most of their fellow-believers.[52] One is tempted to find here a suggestive datum for the interpretation of the symbols of apocalyptic in both movements. Recently we have been urged to distinguish between "steno symbols" and "tensive symbols." This distinction should probably be related to differences between the masses and the more subtle believers in early Christianity as in Sabbatianism. Because in both movements most believers belonged to the masses, they both tended to take on, especially incipiently, the marks of the popular understanding of the messianic age to which we have drawn attention. But it would be very unwise to find the essence of any messianic movement in the kind of phenomena which such an understanding magnified. Bizarre miracles, the froth of enthusiasm and ecstasy must not be given equal weight with, or (perhaps better) must not be understood apart from, the underlying formative factors in a messianic movement,[53] to which we now turn.

More important than the secondary phenomena, then, are certain fundamental similarities, accompanied by equally fundamental differences, between early Christianity and Sabbatianism. These we have called primary phenomena. They may be introduced under two rubrics.

First, in both movements there was a radical confrontation with the established order, focused on the ultimate authority within Judaism, the Torah. In both, social, political, and religious loyalties and oppressions were challenged, so that there emerged an inevitable concentration on the person of the messiah in whose name the challenge was issued. In both, faith in the messiah became the primary mark of the believer.[54]

Secondly, both movements within a very short period spread extensively. Sabbatianism and early Christianity are in one thing peculiar. Most of the many messianic movements in Judaism have been short-lived and concentrated in specific localities. But Sabbatianism and Christianity are alike in having had an ecumenical appeal.[55] Within two years, Sabbatianism spread throughout Europe and the Near East. Confined almost exclusively to Jews, it affected almost the whole of Jewry. Within a slightly longer period, Christianity spread from Palestine to Rome in the West and eastwards as well, to some extent among Jews but also, and particularly, among Gentiles. This means that both Sabbatianism and Christianity were understood to satisfy the spiritual needs of Jews and especially, in the case of the latter, of Gentiles. Movements do not spread without reason: emotionally at the least both early Christianity and Sabbatianism conveyed the living experience of redemption.[56]

At first sight, these two rubrics seem to justify Scholem's claim that messianism is essentially constituted by two fundamental elements. First, there is the emergence of a messianic figure. He serves as a catalyst, negatively, for radical criticism of the existing order; positively, of dreams at long last come true, of barriers long-standing being broken down, of a new creation—all this accompanied by an impulse to propagate the good news. And then, secondly, this messianic figure must meet a widespread need and be understood to satisfy that need in terms of an interpretative ideological structure of magnitude and depth. Infinitely complex as are all historical movements, Scholem claims that significant messianic movements are usually born of a coincidence—that of the interpretation of this person within a large conceptual framework which can illumine his significance for that need. To put the matter concretely, a significant messianic movement demands the coincidence of a Jesus and a Paul or of a Sabbatai Svi and a Nathan of Gaza. The catalyst of a messianic movement is a messianic figure, but its spread and significance are necessarily determined by the scope and profundity of the conceptual framework of myth within which such a figure can be or is interpreted.

This dual aspect of messianic movements is especially clear in Sabbatianism. Owing to the absence of contemporary sources of sufficient richness, it is not so immediately clear in early Christianity. Does Scholem's analysis help in the clarification of early Christian history?

Scholem points out that among Jews in the seventeenth century, when Sabbatianism arose, there was one single, dominant theology, Lurianic Qabbala, which constituted a rich, comprehensive myth.[57] It varied in its forms but was profoundly united in essentials and was almost universally accepted by Jews. It was the universal dominance of a single theology or myth that enabled Sabbatai Svi, through Nathan of Gaza, to initiate such a widespread messianic movement. The reason for the hold of Lurianic Qabbala on Jews everywhere was that it provided a key to the mystery of their suffering at the hands of the Gentile world and made that suffering tolerable. In medieval Europe, the one inescapable fact about Jews was that they were in exile, at the mercy of the whims of their Gentile rulers. In 1492 they had been expelled cruelly from Spain; in 1648–49 there were horrendous massacres in Poland. How could Jews continue to bear the burden of their exile? Lurianic Qabbala provided the answer in subtle, mystical terms which satisfied. At first the doctrine, absorbed in strictly theological concerns, had not been particularly concerned with the question of exile as such. But it had developed in such a way as to provide a sustaining explanation for the terrible experiences of Jews in exile: it spoke directly to their needs.[58] It did so by setting their exile in a cosmic, divine perspective: it connected the historical exile of Jews with a supramundane exile of man from God, and indeed, with a rupture in the very being of God himself. By enduring their exile, while remaining loyal to the disciplined, austere, ascetic tradition of the Torah, and the knowledge of it supplied by the Qabbala of Luria, suffering, exiled Jews were assured that they were making possible a cosmic reintegration and with this the restoration of man to God and a reconciliation within God himself. The technical term for this process of restoration was *tiqqûn*. Lurianic Qabbala was not simply a mystical and intellectual structure of vast complexity and insight; it became the strength and stay of a despairing people, crushed in the ghetto. In their insignificance, it gave the Jews cosmic significance. It enabled them to believe not only that even *this* world, in which they knew exile, *could* be saved or undergo *tiqqûn,* but that through their obedience to the Torah it was they who were to be its saviors. When that obedience would have reached its fulfillment, the Messiah would appear. It was not the Messiah who would make the restoration possible; rather he would be a sign that it was near. He would usher in the end, made possible by the Jews' own obedience.

Within this context the impact of Sabbatai becomes understandable: without it, his name would probably by now be forgotten like that of many another messiah in Jewish history. As we already noted, his claim to be the Messiah was at first ridiculed. But when a recognized prophet interpreted that claim in the light of the all-pervasive Lurianic Qabbalistic expectations, a new movement was born: the interpretation was as crucial as the claimant, the myth as the fact. Jews became convinced that the ultimate *tiqqûn* or restoration had now begun. The end was at hand;

deliverance was at the door. The results of this conviction were staggering. The one decisive factor was *that* the messiah had appeared. Who he was, or what he was like, was for many unimportant. Interest in the personal character and conduct of Sabbatai was at best secondary and probably, among the majority of believers, non-existent.[59] What made him significant was his role as the Messiah, proclaimed and authenticated by Nathan. In the Lurianic world, among Jewish hearts made sick by hope deferred, the magic word, messiah, was enough to set the world on fire. That among certain at least of the Sabbatians the neglect of a radical assessment of the character of Sabbatai Svi was to bring its terrible nemesis will become clear as we turn now to our main concern: the light that Sabbatianism throws on early Christianity.

IV. EARLY CHRISTIANITY AND SABBATIANISM

Before we deal with the most significant questions that Scholem's works have provoked, it is desirable first to recognize their contribution to our understanding of the apocalyptic terminology of the NT. I am acutely conscious of my incompetence in dealing with this. I am versed neither in linguistic analysis nor in literary criticism as it is currently practised. I can simply point to certain facts. Sabbatianism used the terminology of apocalyptic as symbolic of a supernatural, unseen reality; this it did as heir to the Qabbala.[60] But equally certainly it took that terminology quite literally. For example, when Sabbatai's messiahship was accepted at Smyrna, he proceeded forthwith geographically to carve up the world, which he was soon to rule. He ascribed to several of his followers different parts of the world as their dominions. Some of his wealthy followers sold their possessions convinced that the end of the old order was literally at hand.[61] The Turkish authorities took very seriously the political implications of Sabbatai's activity.[62] On his side, he behaved like a monarch.[63] Much modern discussion of the meaning of apocalyptic language which over much spiritualizes it must be regarded as misguided. For example, to understand the term "kingdom of God," as used in early Christianity, as non-political and non-terrestrial is unjustifiable, if it be taken to have been so used universally.[64] Whatever their limitations, in their tenacious insistence on a literal understanding of the messianic prophecies chiliastic movements are doubtless true to much in Sabbatianism and in early Christianity.[65] There was a literal dimension to apocalyptic language which must not be evaded, and it had a catastrophic political and social relevance. In particular, the political and sociological implications of early Christianity and their actual impact would be more adequately recognized if this literalism were taken more seriously. This would help us to comprehend that all messianism has a revolutionary, subversive potential.[66] This is not to underrate the symbolism of apocalyptic. A literary critic might do justice to our point by claiming that apocalyptic terminology is both conceptual and symbolic.

This applies especially to the understanding of early Christianity among the masses, which embraced apocalyptic literally and uncritically. To bear this in mind is to see both Jesus and Paul as corrective of a popular messianic political revolutionary enthusiasm and, therefore, despite the new wine which they dispensed, as, in a certain sense, conservative. In this light they both emerge as reductionists of a fecund apocalyptic enthusiasm that sometimes led to political theatrics and discovered in the new creation a legitimation of license.[67]

But even more important are the two factors, the coincidence of which, according to Scholem's analysis, is necessary for the emergence of a significant messianic movement. Do they apply to early Christianity? First, can we point with equal clarity, as we did in the case of Sabbatianism in the seventeenth century, to a dominant ideological or theological framework in the first-century Judaism into which Jesus of Nazareth was fitted as Messiah to give birth to early Christianity? Or, to put it in another way, does first-century Judaism present an ideological counterpart, equivalent in depth and extent, to the Lurianic Qabbala in seventeenth-century Judaism which made Sabbatianism possible?

The answers given to this question will be familiar. As representative, we refer to those of E. R. Goodenough and W. Bousset. Goodenough was concerned to explain how a Palestinian movement so quickly penetrated and prevailed over the Greco-Roman world. His answer was that by the first century certain Jews in the Hellenistic world had opened their minds to pagan notions and made them "at home" in Judaism. When Hellenistic Jews became Christians, they carried over these notions into their understanding of their new faith. This rapidly enabled the gospel to penetrate the Hellenistic-Roman world. But did such a Hellenistic Judaism as Goodenough describes exist universally among first-century Jews as did Lurianic Qabbala among those of the seventeenth, and was it as theologically dominant and accepted? Goodenough's position has not won the assent of those best qualified to assess Judaism. His treatment of the extent and potency of rabbinic influence as over against the almost autonomous Hellenized Judaism which he delineates remains questionable.[68]

Bousset, whose work *Kyrios Christos* often seems to anticipate much in Goodenough, nevertheless points to another alternative. For him nascent Christianity employed ideas anticipated in the apocalyptic tradition in Judaism. For example, a christology of pre-existence lay hidden in the idea of the Son of Man of Jewish apocalyptic.[69] In the first century an apocalyptic structure was ready into which Jesus, as Messiah, could be fitted, as Sabbatai Svi was fitted into Lurianic Qabbala in the seventeenth. Faith in Jesus had merely to clothe itself with apocalyptic. How others have followed Bousset in this view we need not trace. But here again the difference between the role of apocalyptic in the first-century Judaism and Lurianic Qabbala in that of the seventeenth is unmistakable. The relative importance of apocalyptic in the complex of first-century Jewish is much disputed. The older view that apocalyptic was as peripheral in first-century Judaism as, let us say, the chiliastic sects in modern Christianity is no longer tenable.[70] Apocalyptic belonged to the main streams of Judaism; but that Judaism was extremely variegated and certainly not dominated by a single apocalyptic ideology. In isolation, apocalyptic, although it has taken up Alexander the Great's notion of world empire, cannot provide a universal, dominant theological parallel to the Lurianic Qabbala of the seventeenth century.

The two clear answers, then, to the question whether there was a dominant theological counterpart to Lurianic Qabbala in first-century Judaism do not satisfy. Does a combination of them do so? This might be suggested by the very nature of Lurianic Qabbala itself. In it two things were fused: an eschatological ideology derived from Jewish apocalyptic, modified and reinterpreted in terms of the notion of the *tiqqûn*, and a form of gnosticism tracing its lineage apparently back to the early Christian centuries. This fusion enabled Lurianic Qabbala to connect the terrestrial messianic hopes with an inward and supernal order and constituted its extraordinary dynamism. Scholem's work prompts the question whether in the first century too—in an inchoate form at least—a comparable fusion of a modified apocalyptic and proto-gnosticism had occurred to provide the framework for interpreting Jesus. P. D. Hanson[71] has recently insisted on the prophetic connections of the origins of apocalyptic. But by the first century, what Hellenistic and other influences, including possibly pre- or proto-gnostic ones, had penetrated it? Unfortunately the NT is so laconic that it allows no certainty as to any one dominant framework, apart from the Scriptures, into which Jesus was fitted. Moreover, whereas Sabbatai Svi had one outstanding, almost unique interpreter in Nathan of Gaza, Jesus had various interpreters at least as different as Matthew, Mark, John, and Paul. And again sources outside the NT are either insufficiently examined or too confusing to allow for certainty. There are increasing, although disputed, indications of the fusion or interaction of apocalyptic with pre- and proto-gnosticism, if not gnosticism, in the first century and that before 70 C.E.[72] But even allowing for such a fusion before that date, can we claim that it provided a dominant theological outlook for first-century Judaism as did Lurianic Qabbala for that of the seventeenth? He would be a bold man who would claim this. If a unified ideology was the mark of seventeenth-century Judaism, we have long been taught that diversity was that of the first. But is this the whole truth? In reaction to G. F. Moore, have we overemphasized that diversity and overlooked a possible overarching unity provided by a rich fusion of Law, apocalyptic, and pre- or proto-gnosticism? This question is made more and more pressing by Scholem's understanding of messianism.[73]

Perhaps the problem as to what theological framework most governed early Christianity can best be approached obliquely. The social and political structures favoring the spread of Christianity are clear—a ubiquitous synagogue, made accessible by Roman imperial roads and favored by Roman policy, provided a ready-made platform for Christian missionaries. We may ask what particular need had arisen among Jews in the first century. Sabbatianism met the needs of Jews in exile. Was there a dominant need that first-century Judaism had to face? *The* crucial question which it confronted was that posed by the Gentile world. In the first century, Jews, although occasionally living apart as in Alexandria, were not in a ghetto.[74] They were free to respond to the fascination of Gentile life. This constitutes a crucial difference between the larger context of Sabbatianism and early Christianity. At the time of Sabbatianism, Judaism was turned in upon itself, cabined, cribbed, and confined. Sabbatianism arose within a suffering ghetto to meet its peculiar needs. By no means was the Gentile question central to it. By the seventeenth century that question had been closed: Gentiles had rejected Jews. Jews in turn had largely rejected Gentiles and had become introverted; the references to Gentiles in a thousand pages of Scholem's work are few.[75]

It was otherwise in the first century. Then the question of how to relate to the Gentile world pressed ubiquitously upon Jews. There was a vast missionary movement to the Gentile world.[76] Before 70 C.E. there were elements in apocalyptic which directly occupied themselves with the fate of Gentiles and that with hope for them.[77] The relation of such elements to any pre- or proto-gnosticism we cannot pursue. But these elements did speak with particular force to the need of first-century Jews to come to terms with Gentiles. That they were a marked aspect of first-century Judaism before 70 C.E., after which date apocalyptic became more discredited, seems clear. Based on the Scriptures of Judaism,[78] they were also the outcome of three centuries of the exposure of Jews to Hellenism—an exposure that time and again created a crisis: the crisis constituted by the insidious attraction of Gentile life. It could be resolved either by greater and greater intensity to achieve a total obedience as at Qumran, or by reinterpretation and adaptation as in Pharisaism, or by a blind hatred as among Zealots; or, on the other extreme, by acceptance and assimilation and interpenetration.[79] Whatever the solution adopted, first-century Judaism faced at boiling point the fascinating impact of Hellenism. Within that context apocalyptic, in those elements of it to which we refer, provided a hope for the final redemption of Gentiles. Was it apocalyptic, characterized by this universalist hope, that provided the framework for presenting Jesus as the "Savior of the World"? And, although it reflected a challenge produced by the attraction of the outside world, while Lurianic Qabbala was the product of an internal crisis produced by the rejection of Jews by the outside world, can we regard this apocalyptic, modified by Hellenistic influences, as a first-century counterpart to Lurianic Qabbala in the seventeenth?

There are two difficulties. First, there is that already mentioned with reference to Bousset's position. How significant in first-century Judaism was the kind of apocalyptic to which we refer, among other matters, concerned with the Gentiles and possibly infiltrated by a pre- or proto-gnosticism? How pervasive was the hope for the Gentiles within it? That the hope existed is clear, but was it widespread, not to say dominant? The answer is not easy. The wide infiltration of apocalyptic ideology into the Greco-Roman world would seem to be likely. It began, according to M. Hengel, before the third century B.C.[80] J. Daniélou insisted that up to the Council of Nicea the substructure of Christian theology remained Semitic and largely apocalyptic in its terminology.[81] The bog of terminological inexactitude must be avoided, but if gnostic thought was from the beginning related to apocalyptic, it is significant that R. M. Wilson writes of "something of an atmosphere in which the people of the early Christian centuries lived and moved."[82] The work of such scholars gives us pause. They justify the question which Scholem's work compels us to ask. Behind the variety of first-century Judaism did there perhaps exist a single, widely-diffused and popular eschatological frame of reference in both Palestinian and Hellenistic Judaism (to use a distinction now largely obsolete)? Sweeping generalizations are out of place. In the present state of our knowledge it is as difficult to give an affirmative answer as a negative one. For example, R. M. Grant, who once urged that gnosticism was born of the collapse of apocalyptic, now denies this outright.[83] Daniélou's evidence is more abundant than convincing. Unless or until new texts from Nag Hammadi, Qumran and elsewhere enlighten us further, we must tentatively assert that the rôle of apocalyptic, however modified and reinterpreted under Hellenistic influences, cannot have been so important in the spread of Christianity as was Lurianic Qabbala in that of Sabbatianism. Such apocalyptic did not dominate the whole of Judaism—which was not in the first century a ghetto but spanned several cultures. We conclude that one element in the twofold coincidence to which Scholem points as necessary to significant messianism is not clear in early Christianity. Whereas in Sabbatianism there was a decisive conceptual framework or myth in the dominant Lurianic Qabbala, to judge from the sources we now have, the conceptual background in early Christianity appears to have been far more complex and varied.

We referred to the need of Jews to come to terms with Gentile life. The opposite must not be underestimated: the need that Gentiles often felt to embrace Judaism. The multiplicity of God-fearers and proselytes which, according to some, largely accounts for the magnitude of the diaspora,[84] indicates that the primordial and nuclear certainty of Jewish monotheism and the sustaining discipline of life under the yoke of the Torah exercised a deep attraction for Gentiles. Any simple conceptual framework which should—on Scholem's terms—dominantly sustain the interpretation of Jesus would have to embrace the Jewish and Gentile worlds. Where is it to be found?[85]

This brings us to the second apparent difficulty in finding a dominant apocalyptic, oriented towards the Gentiles, one of the two decisive factors in the spread of Christianity. It springs to the eye. To judge from the gospels, the Gentile question, although recognized, was not central to Jesus of Nazareth.[86] This disturbing fact leads to the question, What role did the person of Jesus of Nazareth play in early Christianity? Was it as decisive as that of Sabbatai Svi in Sabbatianism? Despite the comparative infrequency of Jesus' engagement with Gentiles, we suggest that the answer to this question is in the affirmative, because Jesus had his Paul and others to interpret him, as Sabbatai Svi had Nathan. Where was the heart of the matter for Paul? He found the significance of the emergence of Jesus as the Messiah particularly in the grace that he had shown to the *ʿam hāʾāreṣ,* and then, why not to Gentiles?[87] The Gentile mission was for Paul implicit in the ministry of Jesus. His call was to the Gentiles. This is a fundamental datum. There was little if any ground for a concern for Gentiles in the life of Sabbatai Svi. It is this ultimately that explains why Christianity became more than a Jewish but also a Gentile movement, whereas Sabbatianism remained Jewish.[88]

We enter here disputed ground. There probably existed in both Sabbatianism and early Christianity many believers for whom the personalities of Sabbatai Svi and Jesus, respectively, were a matter of indifference and even unknown. But this must not mislead us. Ultimately, it was the personality of each messiah that gave to the movements they inaugurated their peculiarity. One ventures to urge that, in the end, what moved Sabbatians was *that* the Messiah had appeared, incidentally as Sabbatai Svi; whereas what astounded early Christianity was that it was Jesus of Nazareth who had come as the Messiah. The difference between Sabbatai Svi and Jesus, draped as they both came to be in the traditional messianic mantles, is ultimately a difference, quite simply, of what we might call "character." Rabbinic leaders were so embarrassed by Sabbatai Svi's conduct that they sought to destroy the evidence for it.[89] In Sabbatai Svi, despite his appeal to the masses, there seems to be no real concern for them such as breaks through the Jesus of the gospels. There is an insensitivity to the ostentatious and bizarre which is unthinkable in Jesus and, unless (paradoxically) antinomianism be an expression of such, an absence of sensitive moral concern. Sabbatai Svi was not a teacher of morality. The difference between the two messiahs comes to clearest expression in the apostasy of Sabbatai Svi, and the death of Jesus on the cross. Scholem calls the apostasy the most execrable act possible in the Jewish mind.[90]

Two ways were open to Sabbatians after Sabbatai Svi's apostasy, either to follow his actions, to imitate him, or to see in his fate a call to ever greater rigor in obedience to the Law. Sabbatianism developed along both ways. Some believers followed the latter course and showed a zeal in piety and morality which outshone that of other Jews and, indeed, became a mark of their heretical faith. Such Sabbatians recognized that while Sabbatai lived on the brink of the new eon, they themselves did not and could not follow his freedom from the Law.[91] Their attitude could be compared with that of early Jewish-Christians who retained their zeal for the Torah, even though believing in Jesus as the Messiah. In the course of time these nomistic Sabbatians declined and reverted to the main stream of Judaism; historically they were not significant. Other Sabbatians took the former of the two possible courses noted. They took Sabbatai Svi as a paradigm and an example to be imitated. To do so, they had to call evil good. They had to justify apostasy itself as messianic and redemptive. To do so in the end was to destroy all values dear to Judaism. It implied an ultimate cynicism and nihilism, born doubtless of a profound despair, in which the demand of God was mocked. It is no accident that the most distinctive doctrine of Sabbatianism came to be that of redemption through sin.[92] The infinitely complex and even pathological reasons for the conduct of Sabbatai Svi excite our pity. In the radical Sabbatian wing, its theological and practical consequences were disastrous. Despite the indifference of the masses of Sabbatians to the character of their messiah, his passive surrender to the power of impurity and iniquity, even as he persisted in his messianic mission, stamped itself upon his radical followers. In loyalty to their apostatized redeemer, they too were led to strange acts. Like the Messiah himself, they too had to descend into impurity; for them too good had to become evil. The very weakness of Sabbatai Svi they took for strength. And it was the radical Sabbatians who persisted; it was they who became historically significant. As time went on, the figure of Sabbatai Svi, within Sabbatianism itself, became vague almost to the point of anonymity.[93] Perversely, his lack of integrity alone remained significant, and that diabolically.

Scholem has referred to the gulf that separates the character of Sabbatai from that of Jesus of Nazareth.[94] As we indicated, the interest of much of primitive Christianity in the history and personality of Jesus has been denied.[95] But while we recognize the force of the arguments of those who hold this view and the support it receives to a degree from developments in Sabbatianism, it is wiser to urge that, as the very emergence of the gospels indicates, the character of Jesus at least, if not the inner recesses of his personality and the minute biographical details of his life, in various degrees and dimensions, remained central for early Christianity. That *he* was the messiah was significant for early Christianity, in a way that Sabbatai Svi as a person was not for Sabbatianism. We consider it legitimate to speak of the personality of Jesus or his character and do not find the suggestion, recently made by Dean S. W. Sykes of Cambridge, that the heart (I reject the word essence, as did R. W. Funk) of Christianity lies in the character of Jesus, easily dismissible.[96] But because so many find difficulty in speaking of or in picturing the personality of Jesus, we shall seek to pinpoint the essential difference between Sabbatai Svi and Jesus, not in terms of their characters, but in terms of another dimension, the Law.

Judaism lived by a moment, that of revelation, and by a dimension, that of tradition, the latter being the explanation and application of the former. The meaning of the revelation at Sinai was variously interpreted. As the Temple Scroll at Qumran has illustrated with astonishing force, the extent to which the Law itself was examined and even questioned in first-century Judaism was far greater than we had often assumed.[97] Currents emerged in Judaism in which in the messianic age even a new *tôrâ* was anticipated. Whether these currents were as early as the emergence of Christianity is questioned; certainly they existed in the Judaism that Sabbatai Svi knew.[98] Messianic freedom, as Sabbatai understood it, allowed him to live beyond the Law. His position led to antinomian nihilism. If allowed to develop unchecked, the freedom of early Christianity could have had the same result. But whereas in Sabbatianism the messianic founder (who was, we repeat, not a teacher) could supply no check to antinomianism but only a stimulus, in early Christianity there could be found such a check in the ministry, character, and teaching of Jesus.[99] The attitudes of Jesus and Paul to the Law cannot be discussed at the tail end of a long lecture. Perhaps the Fourth Gospel best sums up that attitude when it speaks of the new commandment of the gospel as constituted by *agapē*. The concentration on *agapē* as the quintessence of the Law is not a negative dismissal of the tradition of Judaism, but its radical reduction to one dominating dimension. The life of Jesus of Nazareth, as understood by his followers, was consonant with this dimension, an expression of *agapē*. It could, therefore, always provide a corrective to any antinomian messianic license that might emerge. This did not prevent antinomianism from emerging in early Christianity. Over against the concentration on the Law in Jewish-Christianity stood the amorality and immorality of gnostics and other Christians. The situation in both early Christianity and Sabbatianism was highly dialectical and complex. But at the root of the Christian tradition was a founder, whose impact could provide a salutary control in a way that Sabbatai could not. The Lord with whom the Christian tradition was sometimes virtually identified was such that he could be a constant corrective, even though misinterpreted in both nomistic and antinomian terms.[100] As we have expressed it elsewhere, Jesus became the Torah of Christians.[101] Here lies the heart of the matter, not in the apocalyptic imagery and fantasies with which he, like Sabbatai Svi, came to be clothed.

We have sought to apply Scholem's categories to early Christianity. With regard to one of the two essential dimensions which he finds behind significant messianic movements, caution is necessary. It is easier to isolate Lurianic Qabbala as the one Sabbatian framework than to point to such a single conceptual framework, apart from the Scriptures, governing early Christianity. As for the role of the messianic figures, Jesus and Sabbatai, they were both significant in their respective movements not only as catalystis or initiators but as formative factors. The constructive constraint of Christ's ministry in early Christianity stands markedly over against the negative, distorting, and ultimately nihilistic influence of Sabbatai in Sabbatianism.

One final word. Lurianic Qabbala was far too complex and comprehensive a phenomenon to be simply labelled as apocalyptic. But it had absorbed apocalyptic elements.[102] So ingrained in our minds is the halakic conception of Judaism, especially after 70 C.E., that it requires an effort to grasp that apocalyptic, messianic expectations which had emerged before the common era persisted in strength throughout the medieval period and down to the seventeenth century so that Sabbatai Svi could easily draw upon their dramatic dynamism. Jewish engagement with a apocalyptic did not cease with the fall of Jerusalem in 70 C.E.,[103] and so one cannot read the history of Sabbatai Svi, at least with Albert Schweitzer in mind, without being compelled to reflect upon the significance of apocalyptic. One might gather from Schweitzer that it is a dead end;[104] from others that it is a kind of collective megalomania.[105] But using the term in a broad sense at this point, apocalyptic presents both positive and negative aspects. To assess these would require a knowledge of the meaning of symbols which is beyond my competence. An examination of the nature of the symbolism of apocalyptic, such as has been begun by Amos Wilder[106] and others, is a crying need. On the positive side, apocalyptic, emerging and re-emerging again and again in times of extreme suffering and despair, is the expression, in the light of the divine purpose, of a legitimate critical response to the iniquities, corruptions, and distortions of this world, to which, alas, most of us are at least half-blind. It is the element of divine discontent, of the desire for something afar, of the aim which exceeds our grasp. Without this discontent, the dead hand of custom, stagnation, and insensitivity throttles life, and even ancient good becomes uncouth. From this point of view, apocalyptic is the leaven of history. Its societal and cosmic imagery, symbols and hopes, which turn human longings to vivid expectations, are always necessary as a spur to sensitivity and a corrective against a false, irresponsible, individualistic piety. Even more, these expectations themselves —unrealistic as they often are—have a creative impact and, against themselves, modify societies even when those same societies reject them. Such hopes open up new possibilities, new pathways to Utopia, even if they never arrive there. A literature produced when man is at the end of his tether has its own stark, unblinded, and penetrating insight, even though its actual practical counsels, born of despair, are often dubious. The plea of K. Koch for the rediscovery of "apocalyptic" is understandable.[107]

But, on the negative side, it needs careful control. A good stimulant, does it constitute a good diet? The ivied walls of the academy in which we dwell at case make the appreciation of apocalyptic difficult for most of us. But this being admitted, again to use the term in an undifferentiated sense, apocalyptic has an ugly face. To read Scholem's work is to stand amazed, overwhelmed, and—it is to be stated—alienated by the bizarre, unhealthy, and unsavory possibilities of apocalyptic, messianic, political, and other indulgence.[108] Despite its suffering and courage, its moral and intellectual striving and daring, the practical consequences of what we normally refer to, without differentiation, as apocalyptic are no less baffling and even terrifying than its often lurid imagery. The rabbinic reaction to such apocalyptic as a pernicious menace is understandable. In Sabbatianism, an unrestrained utopian apocalyptic-mysticism worked itself out in antinomianism. Early Christianity knew the same temptation, but in its main developments, though not in all its expressions, it was often spared from the more undesirable tendencies by the constraint of its founding figure. Early Christianity was apocalyptic, but it was such under the constraint of the *agapē* (to risk distortion through brevity) of Christ. The sum of the matter is this: if we are to continue to describe early Christianity as apocalyptic, it seems to me that we can only do so by carefully differentiating what we mean. P. D. Hanson has led the way by drawing a distinction between prophetic eschatology and apocalyptic eschatology, a distinction which is not without parallel with that drawn by Scholem for a later period between restorative and utopian messianism.[109] But this we cannot pursue here.

In this centennial lecture I have referred only very sparingly to the great Albert Schweitzer. But I have tried to recall you to the haunting question which he bequeathed to us. How are we to preserve visionary intensity without an illusory fanaticism? It is because it offers a sobering warning against any uncritical concentration on and endorsement of an undifferentiated apocalyptic that I have reflected with you on Scholem's great work.

NOTES

The Albert Schweitzer Memorial Lecture at the meeting of the Society of Biblical Literature and the American Academy of Religion, 1 November 1975, The Palmer House, Chicago, Illinois.

1. See K. Koch, *The Rediscovery of Apocalyptic* (London: SCM, 1972) 57–59; W. G. Kümmel, *The New Testament: The History of the Investigation of Its Problems* (Nashville: Abingdon, 1972) 243–80.
2. "The Beginnings of Christian Theology," *New Testament Questions Today* (Philadelphia: Fortress, 1969) 82; "On the Subject of Primitive Christian Apocalyptic," ibid., 108.
3. "Die Bekehrung des Paulus als religionsgeschichtliches Problem," *ZTK* 56 (1959) 273–93.
4. Especially under the direction of Robert A. Kraft for the SBL and of James H. Charlesworth at Duke University. In Britain the work proceeds under that of H. F. D. Sparks at Oxford University.

5. *Rediscovery of Apocalyptic* (see n. 1); this work provides a convenient summary of the recent discussion. See also J. M. Schmidt, *Die jüdische Apokalyptik* (Neukirchen-Vluyn: Neukirchener Verlag, 1969); W. G. Rollins, "The New Testament and Apocalyptic," *NTS* 17 (1970–71) 454–476.
6. Original Hebrew ed. Tel Aviv: Am Oved, 1957; now excellently translated into English by R. J. Zwi Werblowsky (Princeton: Princeton University, 1973).
7. The chief pertinent works are: *Major Trends in Jewish Mysticism,* Eng. trans. in paperback (New York: Schocken Books, 1961); *The Messianic Idea in Judaism and Other Essays on Jewish Spirituality* (New York: Schocken Books, 1971); *Jewish Gnosticism, Merkabah Mysticism and Talmudic Tradition* (New York: Jewish Theological Society of America, 1960). Other works by Scholem are listed in the *Festschrift* for him: *Studies in Mysticism and Religion: Presented to Gershom G. Scholem* (eds. E. E. Urbach, R. J. Zwi Werblowsky, and C. Wirszubski; Jerusalem: Magnes, 1967) 368. For the caution necessary compare Scholem, *Major Trends,* 3. He quotes Byron's query: "Who will then explain the explanation?"
8. For all this see G. G. Scholem, *Sabbatai Ṣevi;* and *Major Trends,* 286–324.
9. *JBL* 81 (1962) 1–13.
10. *Sabbatai Ṣevi,* 153–54, 166.
11. Ibid., 285–86.
12. Scholem draws upon contemporary documents. He lists the Hebrew sources in *Sabbatai Ṣevi,* 933–47; secondary sources on Sabbatai Svi and his movement, ibid., 947–55; cf. other studies, ibid., 955–56.
13. See *Major Trends,* 40–79. The thesis of D. Rössler (*Gesetz und Geschichte* [WMANT 2; Neukirchen-Vluyn: Neukirchener Verlag, 1960]), distinguishing sharply between rabbinic and apocalyptic Judaism, although very influential in German circles (for example in the work of U. Wilckens—see K. Koch, *Rediscovery of Apocalyptic,* 40), is untenable. See, among others, A. Nissen, "Tora und Geschichte im Spätjudentum," *NovT* 9 (1967) 241–77. I urged the interpenetration of Pharisaism and apocalyptic in *Exp Tim* 49 (1948) 233–37. Cf. O. Cullmann, *Salvation in History* (Philadelphia: Fortress, 1967) 60. This interpenetration, with varying emphases, is now generally conceded. See Joshua Bloch, *On the Apocalyptic* (JQRMS 2; Philadelphia: Dropsie College, 1952); and Scholem's works.
14. Made familiar by G. F. Moore but increasingly abandoned. The works of E. Bickerman, D. Daube, S. Lieberman, and M. Smith have abundantly established the interpenetration between Hellenism and Judaism by the first century, so that Pharisaism itself can be regarded as a hybrid. See my *Paul and Rabbinic Judaism* (4th ed.; New York: Harper & Row, 1967) 1–16; my "Reflexions on Tradition: The Aboth Revisited," *Christian History and Interpretation: Studies Presented to John Knox* (eds. W. R. Farmer, C. F. D. Moule, and R. R. Niebuhr; New York London: Cambridge University, 1967) 138–51; and now, above all, the monumental study of Martin Hen-

gel, *Judaism and Hellenism* (2 vols.; Philadelphia: Fortress, 1974). For important reviews of the latter, see M. Stern, *Kirjath Sepher* 46 (1970–71) 94–99; and A. Momigliano, *JTS* 21 (1970) 149–53. For a summary statement, see H. A. Fischel, "Greek and Latin Languages, Rabbinical Knowledge of," *Encyclopaedia Judaica* (16 vols.; New York: Colliers-Macmillan, 1972) 7:884–87. For a summary statement of the variety of first-century pharisaic Judaism, see M. Stone, "Judaism at the Time of Christ," *Scientific American* 115 (1973) 79–87. But the historically significant stratum of first-century Judaism proved to be the pharisaic, so that whatever its comparative numerical strength and social or political influence, it unmistakably possessed a more enduring vitality than other strata. See my article in *PCB*, 705–11.

15. For a convenient statement, see C. H. Dodd, with P. I. Bratsiotis, R. Bultmann, H. Clavier, *Man in God's Design according to the New Testament* (Newcastle-upon-Tyne: Studiorum Novi Testamenti Societas, 1952). But it should be noted that Philo was capable of calling Moses "God" *(theos);* see *De vita Mosis* 1.28 §155–58; *De sac. Abel. et Caini* 2 §8–10. See also W. A. Meeks, "Moses as God and King," in *Religions in Antiquity* (Leiden: Brill, 1968) 355.

16. *Sabbatai Ṣevi,* 835–36, 871. Scholem writes of a tendency that Sabbatai Svi had of "toying—though never explicitly—with the idea of his divinity." At one point he signed his name *Turco,* which, among other things, could mean "the mountain of God." Scholem asks, "Did he mean to imply that the Deity was resting upon Mount Sinai?" (ibid., 835). A liturgical practice developed among believers of saying: "Every morning and every evening we say: he and no other is our God" (*Sabbatai Ṣevi,* 835). At one stage in his life Sabbatai Svi wore symbolic rings. One of his rings was engraved with the name *Shadday* (Ibid., 234); he discovered that the numerical value of the two Hebrew words for "God moved" *(ʾĕlōhim mĕraḥepet)* [*sic!*] in Gen 1:2 was equal to that of his name, and that *bĕrêšit,* "in the beginning" (Gen 1:1) contained the letters of his own name "Sabbatai." Scholem compares the utterances ascribed to Jesus in the gospels as pointing to a peculiar intimacy with God (p. 235). The "divinity" of Sabbatai Svi became a subject of acute debate. The name by which Sabbatai Svi was known to his followers was *Amirah,* which is made up of the initials of the Hebrew words for "Our Lord and King, his majesty be exalted" (ibid., 263, 314, 329).

17. See esp. *Sabbatai Ṣevi,* 125–38. In Jerusalem opposition to Sabbatai Svi reached the highest point, however, when he claimed "I am the Lord your God, Sabbatai Svi" (ibid., 361, 389; on p. 607 there is a reference to a rabbi ascribing divinity to Sabbatai Svi).

18. "The fact is that the true and spontaneous feeling of the Merkabah mystic knows nothing of the divine immanence; the infinite gulf between the soul and God the King on His throne is not even bridged at the climax of mystical ecstasy" (*Major Trends,* 55). Note that in emphasizing the role of the messiah as the agent of the *tiqqûn,* Nathan was departing from Lurianic

qabbalists, for whom obedience to the Law was the instrument of the *tiqqûn*.

19. See *Major Trends,* 80–286. Professor Kalman Bland emphasized this (orally, to me): it is, indeed, a major consideration. On the other hand, medieval Jewish mysticism was accompanied by a continuing tradition of apocalyptic, going back before the first century. G. W. Buchanan, in an unpublished work, has gathered rich evidence for this. This continuity makes the assessment of first-century apocalyptic in the light of that of the seventeenth more realistic than might at first appear.
20. The propriety and precise meaning of the term "mysticism" as used by Schweitzer we need not here discuss. See the criticism of it, going back to the work of Nathan Soderblom, in Gustaf Aulén, *Dag Hammarskjöld's White Book: The Meaning of Markings* (Philadelphia: Fortress, 1969) 38.
21. Scholem notes this of Sabbatianism. It was also true probably of early Christianity, at least up to 70 C.E. See P. Richardson, *Israel in the Apostolic Church* (SNTS 10; London/New York: Cambridge University, 1969).
22. Scholem's work *The Messianic Idea in Judaism* is the most important study of messianism known to me. It should be compared and contrasted with that of Joseph Klausner, *The Messianic Idea in Israel from Its Beginnings to the Completion of the Mishnah* (New York: Macmillan, 1955). The former raises our understanding of its theme to a new dimension and compels a reassessment of early Christianity as a messianic movement. This article opens up simply the thin edge of a wedge.
23. It is necessary to insert "without prejudice" because included among them are parallels in the crucial "moments" in early Christianity, e.g., the resurrection and the parousia. The term "secondary" is applied to such moments here within the context of Scholem's study.
24. See John Knox, *The Ethics of Jesus in the Teaching of the Church* (New York: Abingdon, 1961) 86; H. J. Schoeps, *Paul* (Philadelphia: Westminster, 1961) 188. But contrast C. F. D. Moule, "On Obligation in the Ethic of Paul," *Christian History and Interpretation: Studies Presented to John Knox* (eds. W. R. Farmer, C. F. D. Moule, R. R. Niebuhr; London/New York: Cambridge University, 1967) 398.
25. *Sabbatai Ṣevi,* 260, 291, and esp. p. 472. Nathan emphasized repentance paradoxically as he did the nearness of the end which would change all things. Joy and penitence co-existed (p. 262). On fasts and enthusiasm, see also pp. 328, 356. For examples of the extremism, see pp. 358, 364, 434. Nathan and one hundred Jews immersed themselves naked in snow at Hebron.
26. Ibid., 112–13, 123, 146, 185. Particularly striking are the references to the face of Sabbatai Svi as "shining" (132, 142, 188–90). These naturally recall the accounts of the transfiguration of Jesus, but that moment must not be too easily interpreted in their light. The prayer life of Sabbatai Svi recalls Matthew 6, (ibid., 118, 185. On this see the extremely important work of H. D. Betz, "Eine judenchristliche Kult-Didache in Matt 6, 1–18," *Jesus*

Christus in Historie und Theologie: Festschrift für Hans Conzelmann [ed. G. Strecker; Tübingen: Mohr (Siebeck), 1975] 445–57); his struggle with demons recalls those of Jesus in the Synoptics (see *Sabbatai Ṣevi,* 174–75).

27. See n. 2 above, and also "Sentences of Holy Law in the New Testament," *New Testament Questions Today,* 66–81. Even if Käsemann's reconstruction of the oldest interpretation of the gospel in terms of apocalyptic does not always convince from lack of evidence (for example, it has been pointed out that the Son of Man and the parousia are absent in our earliest kerygmatic formula 1 Cor 15:3–5), that the earliest Christians were "enthusiasts" need not be questioned. It is impossible to ignore this. See, for example, *Sabbatai Ṣevi,* 257, for a description of enthusiasm at Aleppo. In Gaza, Hebron, and Safed, very early after Nathan began his preaching, "the people slept in the streets and bazaars because the houses and courtyards could not contain" the multitudes. "No business is transacted and all—boys and old men, young men and virgins, pregnant women and such as have just given birth—are fasting from Sunday to Friday without suffering any harm" (*Sabbatai Ṣevi,* 261 and n. 176). See further pp. 367, 423–25, 634, 652. The penitence called for by Nathan brought normal business to an end. Compare 1 and 2 Thessalonians. For mass hysteria and ecstasy and prophecy, see pp. 417–24, 435–40.
28. The desire to return to Palestine was widespread. Routes to be followed were discussed. There was sale of landed property (ibid., 287, 358, 475, 637, 648, but also 477 n. 20, 652–53). By 1669, according to some, not a single Jew would remain behind "on the impure soil outside Palestine" (p. 656). Nathan of Gaza at one period wanted the Chief Rabbi of Jerusalem to stop the sending of funds to the city, on the grounds that soon, in the messianic time, there would be enough money there (see pp. 364, 435–47).
29. Ibid., 109–10. "The merit of visiting her grave," he wrote to the Jews of Smyrna, "and of placing one's hand on it was equal to a pilgrimage to the Temple of Jerusalem." He initiated the worship of his mother (pp. 613–14).
30. Ibid., 145–46; he stilled the sea (p. 446 n. 209).
31. Ibid., 149, 171, 191, 198; Sabbatai Svi had studied "practical Qabbala" (that is, the process of using holy names and Qabbalistic magical formulas to force the end), and he had learned the magical use of divine names (ibid., 75). For Nathan and practical Qabbala, see ibid., 209–13.
32. See also Morton Smith, *The Secret Gospel: The Discovery and Interpretation of the Secret Gospel according to Mark* (New York: Harper and Row, 1973); and M. Smith, *Clement of Alexandria and a Secret Gospel of Mark* (Cambridge: Harvard University, 1973). On magic in Judaism, E. E. Urbach, *The Sages: Their Concepts and Beliefs* (Jerusalem: Magnes, 1975), beginning p. 97. He recognizes the belief in miracles as a *necessary* aspect of Judaism as of all religions (p. 102) and that "without doubt miracles played a great role in the propagation of Christianity in the ancient world" (p. 115). The Sages no less than the masses believed in miracles. The New

Testament reveals how easily the magical can be appropriated by and absorbed into the eschatological.

33. See *Sabbatai Ṣevi,* 199–207, on the way in which Nathan of Gaza *found* the Messiah in Sabbatai Svi (also 251–52). The fact that there was no well-defined dominant "image" of the Messiah had its nemesis. There could be many claimants.
34. Ibid., 304, 306, etc.
35. The suffering of Sabbatai Svi was explained in these terms.
36. Ibid., 222.
37. Ibid., 287.
38. On the occultation of the Messiah, see ibid., 314.
39. Ibid., 204, 207.
40. Ibid., 221, 267. This was connected with the emphasis on faith as the peculiar merit of the believer (p. 222). But such an attitude was inevitably challenged. Later in the movement the absence of the signs traditionally associated with the messianic age was emphasized by some rabbis.
41. For example, ibid., 251, 290. The evaluation of Sabbatai Svi by the rabbis depended on their valuation, not of him, but of Nathan, the Prophet (pp. 245–46). The absence of Sabbatai Svi from Jerusalem helped the movement which was, in a sense, not related to him (pp. 2152–53). Cf. p. 162, et passim.
42. He abolished the Feast of Tammuz in 1665; there are numerous examples of his tampering with the calendar (ibid., 237). He visited the Temple as a symbol of its rebuilding; he wanted to ride through Jerusalem on a horse (pp. 241–42). He changed the prayers (p. 277).
43. He allowed the eating of kidney fat (ibid., 242); he urged others to break the Law (p. 243). In the earliest stages of his messiahship all this was not accompanied by moral debauchery (pp. 245–46). This was to come later.
44. Ibid., 160–61.
45. The attitude of Sabbatai Svi towards women was extremely complex (p. 403). That he married a prostitute has been taken to indicate his desire to liberate women, to free them from the curse of Eve. The subject cannot be dealt with here. That the liberation of women played a real part in Sabbatianism is clear. Sabbatai Svi distributed kingdoms to women (as to priests and Levites), ibid., 397.
46. After 1655 Sabbatai Svi regarded himself as no longer under the authority of the Law that he had studied in his youth, nor under rabbinic authority; he was subject to a higher law, ibid., 163–66.
47. See especially the very important pages 282–84.
48. It is impossible to document these sentences adequately. All points indicated are dealt with by Scholem himself in an extremely illuminating manner (particularly on pp. 795–800).
49. Thus Nathan of Gaza had to counteract the popular expectations of the masses (ibid., 287–88).
50. Scholem discusses the economic, social, and political causes proposed for

the emergence and development of Sabbatianism, starting on the first page. The evidence that not only the depressed but the wealthy and the established rabbinic leaders accepted the messiahship of Sabbatai Svi and were involved in his movement is abundant (e.g., p. 392). The participation of many rabbis and wealthy men was too marked to be simply another example of the familiar phenomenon that sect leaders tend to come from a higher class than those whom they lead. The best brief treatment known to me of early Christianity as a "sect," exhibiting typical sectarian characteristics is the very illuminating study by R. Scroggs, "The Earliest Christian Communities as a Sectarian Movement," *Christianity, Judaism and Other Greco-Roman Cults: Studies for Morton Smith at Sixty* (SJLA 12, Leiden: Brill, 1975), 2. 1–23. Scroggs cites Werner Stark (*The Sociology of Religion, II: Sectarian Religion* [London: Routledge and Keegan Paul, 1967] 46) on the generally superior social status of the leadership of sects. There is much in Sabbatianism both to support Scrogg's thesis and to modify it.

51. See, e.g., H. von Campenhausen, "The Christian and the Social Life according to the New Testament," *Tradition and Life in the Early Church* (Philadelphia: Fortress, 1968) 141–59. The appeal of early Christianity and Sabbatianism to the underprivileged, however, while not the explanation of their growth, was real. For example, a certain wealthy Raphael Joseph in Egypt served as a Maecenas to believers there. "He would provide food to all the people in Gaza that were with Nathan, and everyone that came from afar would leave his moneybag with him and then proceed to Gaza," *Sabbatai Ṣevi,* 269. There is some indication that the rabbis feared to oppose Sabbatai Svi because of the masses (pp. 361–63). A bodyguard of the poor followed Sabbatai Svi (pp. 391–92). At Smyrna Sabbatai Svi gave alms very liberally to the poor (p. 384). At that city when public homage was rendered to him as king, he was offered money to be used for charitable purposes and to buy the freedom of Jewish prisoners who had been sentenced to the galleys (p. 412).

52. David Daube drew a distinction between the popular teaching of Jesus and that to his inner following, "Public report and Private Explanation," *The New Testament and Rabbinic Judaism* (Longon: Athlone Press, 1956) 14. Morton Smith has introduced the distinction in the teaching of Jesus himself between that for ordinary Jews and that for the masses and, in addition, between that for both of these groups and that for his intimate initiates; see "The Reason for the Persecution of Paul and the Obscurity of Acts," *Studies in Mysticism and Religion Presented to G. G. Scholem* (Jerusalem: Magnes, 1968) 261–68.

53. There was much mass hysteria and ecstasy and megalomania in Sabbatianism; see, e.g., *Sabbatai Ṣevi,* 417–19, 435, 468–70.

54. Ibid., 210–12, 282–84, 390. This explains a problem dealt with by N. Dahl ("The Neglected Factor in New Testament Theology," *Reflection* [Yale Divinity School] 73 [1975]), i.e., the relative paucity of materials dealing directly with the doctrine of God in the NT.

55. *Sabbatai Ṣevi,* 2. This distinguishes early Christianity and Sabbatianism from other messianic movements, e.g., in modern Africa and Asia. These often reveal the twofold structure proposed by Scholem, but are localized. See Bryan Wilson, *The Noble Savages: The Primitive Origins of Charisma and Its Contemporary Survival* (Berkeley; University of California, 1975) 37–92.
56. Scholem emphasizes particularly the very wide extension of Sabbatianism, as of Christianity, in space and time, as calling for an explanation other than that required for more localized and evanescent movements (*Sabbatai Ṣevi,* 2). In Sabbatianism what provided ecumenicity (a word which we use in its strict sense) was Lurianic Qabbala which (despite the counter influence of the Great Eagle, Maimonides) had developed within it. "Wherever Lurianism came, it produced messianic tension" (ibid., 67). "Lurianic teaching functioned as a means to draw down the Messiah" (ibid., 70). To this Nathan of Gaza could appeal in interpreting Sabbatai Svi.
57. The first chapter of *Sabbatai Ṣevi* is especially illuminating for all this.
58. *Sabbatai Ṣevi,* 15–22, esp. p. 20. On p. 42 Scholem writes: "The exile of the 'lower' terrestrial Congregation of Israel in the world of history is thus merely a reflection of the exile of the supernal Israel, that is, the Shekhinah. Israel's state is symbolic of the state of creation as a whole. It is the Jew who holds in his hands the key to the *tiqqun* of the world, consisting of the progressive separation of good from evil by the performance of the commandments of the Torah. *Tiqqun* is thus an essentially spiritual activity directed at the inner side of the cosmos. But once it will have achieved its end, then this hidden, spiritual perfection will also become manifest outwardly, since outward reality is always symbolic of inner reality. In exile, spiritual activity and mystical concentration *(kawwanah)* affect the inner strata of the cosmos only, 'but the [outer] worlds in general are not elevated until the advent of the messiah, when they will all rise by themselves. At present the only exaltation of the worlds is in their inner aspect. . . . In the present period of exile we can raise—even on the Sabbath—the inner side of the worlds only, but not their outside. For if the outer reality were elevated too, then we could behold with our eyes the exaltation of all the worlds on the Sabbath' (Hayyim Vital, "Shaʿar ha-Tefillah," chap. 6, *Peri ʿEs Hayyim:* Dubrovna, 1804, fol. 7c). Once the last trace of holiness is extracted from the *qelippah* so that no divine sparks are left in it, the world of *tiqqun* will become manifest. This is the meaning of redemption."
59. See, e.g., p. 118 (". . . clearly the course of the movement was determined by the public climate more than by the personality or the inner life of the young kabbalist . . ."), 207–8, 252, 289–90 and n. 41. Indeed, within Lurianic Qabbala itself with its characteristic eschatological tension what is most surprising "is the feebleness of its image of the Messiah." In the process of *tiqqun* "the Messiah himself plays a pale and insignificant role. Except for the highly developed and firmly established tradition of the Messiah, perhaps the Qabbalists would have dispensed with him altogether.

. . . By transferring to Israel, the historic nation, much of the task formerly considered as the Messiah's, many of his distinctive personal traits, as drawn in Apocalyptic literature, were now obliterated" (ibid., 52).

60. Scholem writes as follows: "The character of Lurianic symbolism presents a special problem. The accusation of anthropomorphism directed against the kabbalists is an old one. Their manner of speaking in a material fashion about things spiritual was often held to fall little short of actual blasphemy, yet it merely exemplified the essential paradox of all symbolism. Symbols express in human speech that which is properly inexpressible. Hence they are always material and anthropomorphic, even though the mystic may regard them as mere crutches to aid his frail human understanding. The Kabbalists, whose mystical thinking strained after expression in symbolic forms, endeavored to evade responsibility for their symbols by the frequent use of qualifying phrases such as "so to speak," "as if," "as it were," and the like. These reservations were supposed to minimize the real significance of the symbols employed. The kabbalists used the most outrageous material and even physical and sexual imagery but immediately qualified their statements by adding the solemn warning, "Cursed be the man that makes any graven or molten image," that is, who attributes reality to symbolic expressions. *From their higher theological vantage point the kabbalists might argue that the material interpretation of their symbols was a misunderstanding, yet it was precisely this creative misunderstanding that determined the public significance of kabbalistic symbolism.* He was a bold man indeed who undertook to draw the line between understanding and misunderstanding in such matters. The inescapable dialectic of symbolism is central to a proper appreciation of the historical and social function of kabbalism, even as it underlies most of the discussions between kabbalists and their opponents.

Lurianism is mythological in the precise meaning of the term. It tells the story of divine acts and events, and it accounts for the mystery of the world by an inner, mystical process which, taking place within the Godhead, ultimately produced also the "outer," material creation. According to the kabbalists everything external is merely a symbol or intimation of an inner reality that actually determines the external reality which we perceive. The main concepts of Lurianism all refer to the mystery of the Godhead, but on each and every level they also point to a corresponding aspect in the manifest cosmos" (*Sabbatai Sevi,* 26–27 [my italics]). One of our most urgent needs is to re-examine apocalyptic symbolism. Amos Wilder, in his poetry and elsewhere, has pioneered the way.

61. Ibid., 397–403, 426–32, 468. Believers were given royal titles; the names of their future dominions were assigned. The brothers of Sabbatai Svi were to constitute a kind of caliphate (p. 430). Sabbatai believed that a supernatural act was to bring all this about. How unimportant financial matters became appears from Nathan's opposition to the sending of money to Jerusalem, his attack on money changers and on alms from abroad (pp.

365–67). Charitable funds had to be set up (pp. 497–99). The opposition of some wealthy Jews to the movement was probably spurred by its antifinancial and anticommercial aspects. Calculations of profit and loss, when it came to the demand to sell all to go to Palestine, would, of course, often reinforce their orthodoxy and rational inhibitions. Connected with this literalism is the widespread and recurring contemporary Christian (chiliastic) emphasis outside Sabbatianism and Judaism on the reappearance of the Lost Ten Tribes of Israel (pp. 332–54). And, again, although Nathan did not think of Sabbatai Svi as a warlike messiah, the popular messianism in Sabbatianism counteracted this emphasis (p. 363).

62. See, e.g., ibid., 369, 383, 432, 450, 674–77.
63. Ibid., 384, 386, and esp. pp. 412–17.
64. Especially important in this connection is the much neglected study by B. Reicke, *Diakonie, Festfreude und Zelos* (Uppsala: Lundequistaka, 1951) 242–47. He refers to "Materialisierung der Eschatologie" (p. 243) and to "anarchische Einstellung" (p. 244) in early Christianity.
65. See *Sabbatai Ṣevi,* 93–102, esp. p. 98.
66. On the catastrophic aspect of messianism which is related to its utopian dimension, which in turn is related to apocalyptic, see G. G. Scholem, *The Messianic Idea in Judaism,* 4–12, esp. p. 7. The whole volume is indispensable for a comprehension of the dynamism of messianism.
67. See my article "Paul and Jewish Christianity in the Light of Cardinal Daniélou," *RSR* 60 (1972) 69–80. E. Käsemann has illumined Paul from a different point of view *(New Testament Questions Today,* 132). For him "Paul is the classical witness for a struggle against enthusiasm under the banner of primitive Christian apocalyptic . . ." (n. 24). But he also recognizes that it is only "relics of apocalyptic theology which are to be found everywhere in the Pauline epistles" (p. 131).
68. *Jewish Symbols in the Graeco-Roman World* (13 vols.; New York: Pantheon, 1953–68). See M. Smith, "The Image of God," *BJRL* 41 (1958) 473–512; and reviews by S. S. Kayser, *RR* 21 (1956) 54–60; A. D. Nock, *Gnomon* 17 (1955) 558–72; 21 (1957) 525–33; C. Roth, *Judaism* 3 (1954) 129–35: 179–82; E. E. Urbach, "The Rabbinical Laws of Idolatry in the Second and Third Centuries in the Light of Archaeological and Historical Facts," *IEJ* 9 (1959) 149–245.
69. W. Bousset, *Die jüdische Apokalyptik: Ihre religionsgeschichtliche Herkunft und ihre Bedeutung für das Neue Testament* (Berlin: Reuther & Reichard, 1903). The relevant passages are translated in W. G. Kümmel, *The New Testament: The History of the Interpretation of its Problems* (Nashville: Abingdon, 1972) 260–62). The discussion of the "History of Religions School of New Testament Interpretation" (pp. 206–324) is particularly relevant in this context.
70. See n. 14 above.
71. *The Dawn of Apocalyptic: The Historical and Sociological Roots of Jewish Apocalyptic* (Philadelphia: Fortress, 1975). This rich work carries further

that of F. M. Cross, "New Directions in the Study of Apocalyptic," *Apocalypticism* (JTC 6; ed. R. W. Funk; New York: Herder and Herder, 1969) 157–65. H. H. Rowley and D. S. Russell, among others, had earlier pointed in the same direction. Contrast H. D. Betz in the same volume. For bibliographical detail, see my *The Gospel and the Land: Early Christianity and Jewish Territorial Doctrine* (Berkeley: University of California, 1974) 156 n. 166.

72. For these distinctions, see R. McL. Wilson, *Gnosis and the New Testament* (Philadelphia: Fortress, 1968) 1–30, esp. p. 17.
73. See S. Sandmel, *The First Christian Century: Certainties and Uncertainties* (London/New York: Oxford University, 1969) 63–66.
74. See V. Tcherikover, *Hellenistic Civilization and the Jews* (Philadelphia: Jewish Publication Society of America, 1959).
75. In *Sabbatai Sevi* there are references to Gentiles and to the "mission" of exiled Jews in the world, but it is significant that in the most excellent and comprehensive index to the volume there is no separate entry under "Gentiles," nor to the attitude of Sabbatai Svi himself or of the Sabbatian movement to them.
76. See, e.g., J. Jeremias, *Jesus' Promise to the Nations* (London: SCM, 1958) 11–19.
77. The relevant documents are: Tobit (200–170 B.C.E., Palestine); *Sibylline Oracles*, Book 3 (2d/1st cent. B.C.E., Egypt); *1 Enoch* (mostly from 2d/1st cent. B.C.E., Palestine [Milik, for example, takes chaps. 37–71 (The Similitudes) as Christian]); *2 Baruch* (end of 1st cent. C.E., Palestine), and the *Testaments of the Twelve Patriarchs* (the stages of composition and the date are much disputed; R. H. Charles, 109–107 B.C.E. with additions in first century B.C.E., and later Christian additions; but J. T. Milik and M. de Jonge argue for a 1st-3d cent. C.E. Christian expansion of two earlier Jewish testaments from Palestine).

    Some of the relevant texts are Tob 13:11; 4:6–7; *Pss. Sol.* 17:32–38; *Sib. Or.* 3:710–31; 772–76; *1 Enoch* 10:21; 48:4; 50:2–5; 90:30, 33, 35; 91:14; *2 Bar.* 68:5; 72:4–6; and, in the *Testaments of the Twelve Patriarchs, T. Sim.* 7:2; *T. Levi* 2:11; 4:4; 5:7; 8:14; 18:9; *T. Judah* 22:2; 24:6; *T. Zeb.* 9:8; *T. Dan* 6:7; *T. Naph.* 8:3–4; *T. Asher* 7:3; *T. Jos.* 19:11; and *T. Benj.* 3:8; 9:2, 4; 10:5, 10; 11:2–3.

    Some of the leading ideas are that some or all of the Gentiles will be saved, and that the Gentiles will glorify Jerusalem. On this see P. Volz, *Die Eschatologie der jüdischen Gemeinde im neutestamentlichen Zeitalter* (Tübingen: Mohr [Siebeck], 1934) 356–59; and D. S. Russell, *The Method and Message of Jewish Apocalyptic* (Philadelphia: Westminister, 1964) 298–303.
78. Some of the relevant texts are: Gen 12:3; 17:3–8; 1 Kgs 8:41–43; Ps 47:9; 67; 68; 72:17; 86:9; 87; 99:9; 113; 117; 148:11–12; Isa 2:1–3; 19:24–25; 25:6–9; 42:1–4, 7; 44:1–5; 45:22–25; 49:9, 12–20; 51:4–5; 53:10; 55:5; 56:7; 60:1–11; 61:1; 66:18–21; Jer 4:2; Dan 2:35; Jonah; Mic 4:1–

5; 7:12; Zeph 3:9; Zech 2:11; 8:13, 20–23; 9:9–10; 14:16.—For notes 77 and 78, see further R. H. Charles, *APOT;* M.-J. Lagrange, *Le judaïsme avant Jésus-Christ* (Paris: Gabalda, 1931); A. Causse, "Le mythe de la nouvelle Jérusalem du Deutéro-Esaïe à la IIIe Sibylle," *RHPR* 18 (1938) 377–414; and E. J. Hamlin, "Nations," *IDB,* 3: 515–23. (I am grateful to Mr. Joseph Trafton for help in the garnering of these references.)

79. Another alternative came to be Christianity.
80. In a forthcoming work.
81. *Théologie du judéo-christianisme: Histoire des doctrines chrétennes avant Nicée* (Paris: Desclée, 1958), 1. 1: "La théologie chrétienne utilisera à partir des Apologistes les instruments intellectuels de la philosophie grecque. Mais auparavant il-y-a eu une première théologie de structure sémitique."
82. *Gnosis and the New Testament* (Philadelphia: Fortress, 1968) 16.
83. In a lecture at the SBL meeting, Chicago, 1975.
84. See M. Stern, "The Jewish Diaspora," *The Jewish People in the First Century, Historical Geography, Political History, Social, Cultural and Religious Life and Institutions* (Compendia rerum iudaicarum ad Novum Testamentum, 1; Philadelphia: Fortress, 1974) 117–83. He calls proselytism a "major source of [Jewish] population increase."
85. Here we have only asked the question whether *Judaism* provided a unified ideological structure for the interpretation of Jesus. The answer was largely negative. M. Smith and K. Stendahl have reminded me that in the Greco-Roman world of the first century there were very numerous religious categories into which Jesus could be placed to ensure him a spiritual significance in the eyes of Gentiles, e.g., those of "the divine man," "the magician," "the mystagogue." J. S. Whale has further recalled to me that A. Toynbee emphasized parallels with the figure of Jesus in the Hellenistic world at length (*A Study of History* [London: Oxford University, 1939], 6:376–539) in a highly detailed discussion of the astonishing correspondence between the gospel story and stories of certain Hellenic saviors. See esp. pp. 418 onwards. Here such categories and parallels are not strictly our concern, which was with the nature of Jewish messianism, as understood by Scholem, and as it possibly illumines early Christianity. One thing, however, we may propose. The diversity of hellenistically derived categories (which were in varying degrees used to interpret Jesus and which doubtless helped the spread of early Christianity in countless ways) does not explain the dynamism of the new movement. The very religious diversity of the Greco-Roman world makes it, in fact, all the more difficult to understand that persistent vitality. S. Sandmel (*The First Christian Century in Judaism and Christianity: Certainties and Uncertainties* [New York: Oxford University, 1969] 164) finds such parallels with Hellenistic mysteries as are indicated finally unimportant; he emphasizes the content of the Christian kerygma as that which "enabled Christianity to triumph." The fissiparous fertility of available Hellenistic categories helps to illumine the struggle which Christianity had to face to reach "orthodoxy" (see especially W. Bauer, *Orthodoxy and Heresy in Earliest Christianity* [Philadelphia: Fortress, 1971], but

it does not finally explain the reality of its life. The problem raised is a real one, but is outside the scope of this paper, even though Judaism also was not exempt from its magicians, and possibly its divine men and mystagogues. See M. Smith, "Prolegomena to a Discussion of Aretalogies, Divine Men, the Gospels and Jesus," *JBL* 90 (1971) 181–84; P. J. Achtemeier, "Gospel Miracle and the Divine Man," *Int* 26 (1972) 174–97; and now C. H. Talbert, "The Concept of Immortals in Mediterranean Antiquity," *JBL* 94 (1975) 419–36. I have not seen C. R. Holladay, *Theios Anēr in Hellenistic Judaism: A Critique of the Use of This Category in New Testament Christology* (Cambridge University Dissertation, 1975).

86. See J. Jeremias, *Jesus' Promise to the Nations* (SBT 24; Naperville: Allenson, 1958).

87. For a brief statement, see my *Invitation to the New Testament* (New York: Doubleday, 1966) 260–62.

88. In another context, I should have sought to deal with this question in more detail, but that of the Schweitzer Centennial demanded a concentration on the roles of Sabbatai Svi and Jesus in their respective movements. The difference between Sabbatianism and early Christianity on the Gentile question can be illustrated by a significant detail. Sabbatai Svi was not a teacher; his attempts at theology were stumbling (*Sabbatai Ṣevi,* 207). But he did claim one peculiar doctrine of his own. Scholem deals with it as "the mystery of the Godhead" as understood by Sabbatai Svi. The main concepts of Lurianism, in fact, all refer to "the mystery of the Godhead." Qabbalists were aware of their very material way of expressing spiritual truth and were disturbed by this (ibid., 27). It was part of their tradition that four persons—Abraham, Hezekiah, Job, and the Messiah—were capable of arriving at the knowledge of God by themselves. It would be expected that Sabbatai Svi as Messiah would know the Godhead in a special way. He himself claimed that he attained his special doctrine of the mystery of the Godhead because he prayed with great concentration *(kawwānāh)* and always meditated on the plain meaning of his words like one praying before his king (ibid., 115); the doctrine developed over the years (ibid., 119, 142–46). But what was the "mystery" which he knew? It developed in a gnostic direction. Scholem writes of the matter as follows: "The hidden Mystery of the Godhead was the realization that the God who revealed Himself to Israel in His Torah was not the inaccessible and utterly transcendent *En-Sof,* but that particular aspect of His power which is manifest in *Tif'ereth.* The first formulations of the 'mystery,' which were quoted later by Sabbatai's disciples in Smyrna, do not say very much more than this; and as this symbolism was a commonplace among kabbalists, one may rightly wonder what Sabbatai's original contribution to it was. . . . The fact that the later formulations are much profounder suggests that Cardozo's assumption may be correct and that Sabbatai's thought developed as time went on. But we must not exclude the possibility that there was a more profound layer in his teaching from the very beginning.

This, at least, is certain: Those who received the Mystery of the Godhead from Sabbatai in later years heard it with a shift of accent which, however slight, made all the difference. Sabbatai revealed to them that 'the Tetragrammaton is our God and that He is superior to the whole emanation; He is also signified by the letter W of the Tetragrammaton YHWH and is called the husband of the Shekhinah' (*Raza' de-Razin,* MS. Jewish Theological Seminary of America, Deinard 153, fol. 3a). Similar extant formulations of the 'Mystery' no doubt express Sabbatai's thinking as it had crystallized beginning with 1666. But again it is not impossible that even in his first period he had already arrived at the idea that it was not the *sefirah* (that is, the emanation) itself that was called the 'God of Israel' but something superior to the emanation that merely manifested and clothed itself in the particular *sefirah* from which it borrowed its names and symbols.

The decisive feature of this conception of the 'Mystery' is the distinction between the *En-Sof,* or unmanifested Root of Roots, and the divine Self called YHWH, which is *above* the sefirotic emanations, though it manifests itself *in* one of them. The latent implication of this paradox came to light only in later years and is not explicitly referred to in the testimonies regarding the early period. It amounts to transferring the supervision of providence from the hidden substance (*En-Sof* or whatever we choose to call it) to the 'God of Israel.' We cannot decide, in the light of our present knowledge, whether at this early stage Sabbatai intended this doctrine, to which there is no analogy in traditional Jewish thought—including that of the kabbalists—but which became notorious in the Sabbatian movement a generation or two later. What we know for certain is that Sabbatai's mystical thinking developed in a definitely gnostic direction. The symbol YHWH no longer signified one *sefirah* among others, but a substance that derives from the highest and utterly hidden Root and that, together with the Shekhinah, remains above the whole structure of *sefiroth*. There is good reason for dating this development to a period when Sabbatai had come into contact with Lurianic kabbalism. He could have found support for its conception that there were substances distinct from *En-Sof* and yet above the *sefiroth* and attributes in the Lurianic doctrine of *parṣufim,* or 'configurations,' which similarly places an entity called the 'most primordial man of all,' or simply the 'Primordial Man' *(Adam Qadmon),* above the world of emanation (of *sefiroth*). Although Sabbatai never accepted the propositions of Lurianism as they are formulated in the kabbalistic writings of the school, it is quite possible that they stimulated him to a more novel and daring formulation of his own Mystery of the Godhead" (ibid., 120–22). This lengthy quotation reveals the world of speculation or myth within which Sabbatai Svi moved. Contrast with the mystery with which he was concerned that which occupied Paul and the Ephesian epistle: that concerning Israel and the Gentiles. There are hints of mysteries not shared by all in the NT, but generally there is a simplicity about its teaching (see, e.g., Matt 11:25–30) which is far removed from the involved speculation of Sabbatianism and of Sabbatai Svi himself (see BAG, 532a). Particularly for Paul and his circles it was the Jewish-Gentile question which set the terms for discussing the mystery of God. And Paul found the significance of the emergence of Jesus as Messiah particularly in the grace that he had shown to sinners, including Gentiles. Paul's activity modified the sequence of events as anticipated in Jewish apocalyptic. Gentiles symbolically entered Jerusalem *before* Israel had all been saved. But, for our purpose here, this is less important than to recognize the apocalyptic framework presupposed by Paul and others. This did enable early Christianity to interpret Jesus as the Savior of Gentiles as well as of Jews.

89. See, e.g., *Sabbatai Ṣevi,* 750, 760–67, esp. p. 763. Scholem writes: "Penitential exercises and extreme morifications having been a characteristic feature of the movement, the rabbis of Venice demanded their cessation. The believers, on the other hand, wished to continue them. The Venetian rabbis also wrote to all the communities, commanding them to destroy all documents relating to the movement of 1666 and to obliterate all testimony to this shameful episode. This attempt at censorship is mentioned by R. Samuel Aboab in a responsum written about eight years after the event. Aboab states that after the apostasy all the congregations in the Holy Land, Turkey, Germany, Holland, Poland, and Russia admitted that opponents of the movement had been right, and recognizing their error they 'burned all the records and writings in which his name was mentioned, in order that it should not be remembered. . . . And that which we heard from the far-away cities we beheld ourselves in the cities of Italy. . . . They are repented [of their belief in Sabbatai] . . . and confessed, "Woe unto us, for we have sinned." Also the rabbis of Constantinople . . . sent orders to the communities near and far . . . that it should be forgotten and mentioned no more' " (*Debar Shemu'el,* fol. 97a).

The large-scale suppression of records and documents relating to the movement was no doubt successful, much to the detriment of historical research.

90. Particularly illuminating is *The Messianic Idea,* 6, 78–82. Scholem describes the apostasy as a "final step of holy sinfulness, in fact, its apotheosis," in the chapter "Redemption Through Sin."

91. Even Nathan of Gaza did not believe that he himself was free from the Law; there was a qualitative difference between himself and Sabbatai Svi. Nathan remained a pious, observant Jew. He interpreted the actions of the Messiah but did not imitate them (see *Sabbatai Ṣevi,* 229). There developed two opposing factions in Sabbatianism, one moderate and piously inclined and the other radical, antinomian, and ultimately nihilistic. The former did not consider that it had to imitate Sabbatai Svi. See G. G. Scholem, *The Messianic Idea,* 100–108.

92. Ibid., 78.

93. See, e.g., *Sabbatai Ṣevi,* 252, 254, 290, 371.

94. *The Messianic Idea,* 62.

95. See most recently H. Conzelmann, "Das Selbstbewusstsein Jesu," *Theolo-*

gie als schriftauslegung: Aufsätze zum Neuen Testament (Munich: Kaiser, 1974) 30–41.

96. "The Essence of Christianity," *Religious Studies* 7 (1971) 298. Drawing upon D. Knowles, Sykes understands character as "the final and most precious thing in a man, his goodness of will, achieved by conscious and tenacious choice" (*The Historian and Character* [Cambridge: Cambridge University, 1963] 11). Precisely this kind of steeled will was absent in Sabbatai Svi. He was incapable of consistency in his conduct, probably for psychological reasons. Outside his periods of "illumination," as they were called, he was a pious, observing Jew. This is stressed by Scholem (*The Messianic Idea* and *Sabbatai Ṣevi,* 11).

97. See Y. Yadin, "The Temple Scroll," *New Directions in Biblical Archaeology* (eds. D. N. Freedman and J. C. Greenfield; Garden City: Doubleday, 1969) 139–48, esp. p. 141.

98. See my book, *The Setting of the Sermon on the Mount* (Cambridge: Cambridge University, 1964) 109–90.

99. See my chapter on "The Moral Teaching of the New Testament," *The Use of the Old Testament in the New and Other Essays: Studies in Honor of William Franklin Stinespring* (ed. J. M. Efird; Durham: Duke University, 1972) 310–32. It is not only the motif of the "imitation of Christ" that points to this.

100. See O. Cullmann, "Paradosis et Kyrios: Lee problème de la tradition dans le paulinisme," *RHPR* 17 (1937) 424. The same oscillation between moral earnestness and immorality emerges in certain gnostic sects as among the Sabbatians, see R. M. Wilson, *Gnosis and the New Testament,* 11.

101. See my *Paul and Rabbinic Judaism* (2d ed.; London: SPCK, 1958) 147. The theme is developed by J. A. Sanders, "Torah and Christ," *Int* 29 (1975) 372–90.

102. See *Sabbatai Ṣevi,* 8, 15, 52–77. Apocalyptic elements emerged in Sabbatianism. Scholem connects them especially with the masses. He offers as one of the reasons for the success of the message of Nathan of Gaza that it "contained a curious combination of traditional popular apocalyptic and of hints at its reinterpretation in the light of Lurianic kabbalism" (ibid., 465). He holds that "it has been one of the strangest errors of modern *Wissenschaft des Judentums* to deny the continuity of Jewish apocalypticism" (ibid., 9).

103. C. K. Barrett proposes that the last decade of the first century, with few exceptions, saw "the end of Jewish apocalyptic, *for this expression of Jewish faith had fulfilled its purposes*" (the words that I here italicize could be qualified by some such phrase as "for the time being perhaps"). That Jewish apocalyptic did not come to an end at the date suggested is now beyond dispute, and not only as "with few exceptions." See *The Gospel of John and Judaism* (Philadelphia: Fortress, 1975) 58.

104. It is not easy to grasp Schweitzer's meaning in his dismissal of the historical Jesus and the quest for him. In his second edition of *The Quest of the*

Historical Jesus, which has not been translated into English, his words are shattering. In the translation of the relevant portion offered by Henry Clark (*The Ethical Mysticism of Albert Schweitzer* [Boston: Beacon, 1962] 198), Schweitzer wrote that moderns "continually tried to make of this 'fanatic' a contemporary man and a theologian. . . ." It is possible that Schweitzer did not see Jesus as a "fanatic," but that smug scholars saw him as such and tried to "tame" him to their small hearts. The precise examination of Schweitzer's thought is not possible here. For a brief presentation, see D. L. Dungan, "Reconsidering Albert Schweitzer," *The Christian Century* (Oct. 8, 1975) 874.

105. This phrase, borrowed from N. Cohn, *The Pursuit of the Millennium* (London: Secker and Warburg, 1957), I owe to H. Anderson, who allowed me to see an unpublished lecture on "A Future for Apocalyptic?" Anderson recognizes that apocalyptic has a future because "the untamed and, perhaps, untameable" element of man's spirit will always demand and issue in fantasy. He also allows that apocalyptic has served to overcome the frequent isolation of Christian theology from cosmology. But he too has seen an aspect of its ugly face. To him it is not the fruit of a living hope, but of a world-weariness and pessimism which issues in an ultimately apathetic waiting for the divine intervention rather than in any active transformation of present ills. In this he has much to support him in the sources. His distrust of apocalyptic leads him to urge the simple use of the term "eschatology" to express the hope of Jesus. His lecture reinforces the need for the kind of terminological exactitude which we desiderate. On this, see also J. Carmignac, "Les dangers de l'eschatologie," *NTS* 17 (1970–71) 365–90, who even pleads for the dropping of the term "eschatology." But, as Anderson notes, "we cannot solve a problem by getting rid of the words associated with it." We can only attempt to use them precisely.

106. See "The Rhetoric of Ancient and Modern Apocalyptic," *Int* 25 (1971) 436–53.

107. *The Rediscovery of Apocalyptic,* 25–28, 405.

108. This makes understandable the reluctance of many Christian scholars to classify Jesus among the apocalypticists. This reluctance antedates the work of Schweitzer, but the latter provoked the reaction of C. H. Dodd who, although he does not state this and seldom if ever refers to Schweitzer's work, had the latter in mind. Cf. W. G. Klaummel, *The New Testament: The History of the Investigation of Its Problems* (Nashville: Abingdon, 1972) 260; K. Koch, "The Agonised Attempts to Save Jesus from Apocalyptic: Continental New Testament Scholarship," *Rediscovery of Apocalyptic,* 57–97. History makes one suspicious of what Stendahl has called "the eschatological itch." But it may be well to recall also that "if hopes were dupes" (and they have often been such in messianism), yet "fears may be liars."

109. See *The Messianic Idea,* passim. T. W. Manson's work ("Some Reflections on Apocalyptic," *Aux sources de la tradition chrétienne: Mélanges offerts*

à M. Maurice Goguel [Neuchâtel: Delachaux et Niestlé, 1950] 139–45) still deserves pondering. He finds that "apocalyptic is an attempt to rationalize and systematize the predictive side of Prophecy as one side of the providential ordering of the Universe. The other side of the systematising process of the scribal treatment of the Law leads to the codification of the Mishnah" (p. 142). He expresses no condemnation of either development, but rather implies that apocalyptic supplied evidence for the intensity with which the belief in providence was held in Judaism. He refers especially to Josephus' treatment of Daniel (*Ant.* 10.11.7 §266–81). (One is reminded here of the position of Santayana referred to by Amos N. Wilder [*Modern Poetry and the Christian Tradition* (New York: Scribner, 1952), 3 n. 1] that "poetry and religion are identical in essence, though they relate themselves differently to practical life: *poetry by a dramatic presentation of values and religion by precepts and codes*" [my italics]). Is "apocalyptic" the poetry of religion? If so, it is its romantic poetry, accompanied by the dangers of the romantic. These are well expressed by Wallace Fowlie, in dealing with Rimbaud (*The Age of Surrealism* [Bloomington: Indiana University, 1972]). Pointing to classicism as involving order, control, considered choice, synthesis, rules, Fowlie refers to the romantics and to romanticism as always associated with revolution and liberation (ibid., 14). On p. 58 he emphasizes in Rimbaud the perilous aspect of romanticism. "It exacts so much destruction, of order and conventionality, of familiar patterns, and rules which had seemed indispensable disciplines, that it makes the poet a despiser of order, an anarchist in temperament and technique. . . . I call this way perilous, because it opens the gates to all kinds of charlatans, of undisciplined writers, of false visionaries." It is easy to connect apocalyptic with this kind of romanticism, but the connection cannot be examined here. D. Daube urges again that apocalyptists despite their violent writings are quietists and that this should modify the criticisms I express above. See his *Civil Disobedience in Antiquity* (Edinburgh: University Press, 1972) 85–86.

VII

THE EIGHTEENTH AND NINETEENTH CENTURIES

14

The Messianic-Prophetic Role of the Baal Shem Tov

Benzion Dinur

According to its founders and first followers, Hasidism was indeed a movement designed to pave the way for redemption, and its doctrine was entirely a doctrine of redemption. We also have explicit testimonies to that effect. If these testimonies are not so numerous, we need to take into account that in those days—of the Sabbatian "heresy" in its various manifestations and of severe controversies within Jewish communities—such matters would be treated according to the principle that "one discloses it only to the select few." Sometimes even those few were given only a hint through the statement, "it is impossible to talk about these things."[1]

The most important testimony is contained in the well-known letter of the BeSHT to his brother-in-law, Rabbi Abraham Gershon of Kutow, which was sent to him in the land of Israel through the BeSHT's disciple, R. Jacob Joseph Ha-Kohen, who himself intended to settle there. The letter, apparently from the year 5511 [1750–51],[2] did not reach R. Abraham Gershon, because R. Jacob Joseph never went to the land of Israel; he published it in his book *Ben Porat Yosef* (Korets, 5541 [1781]). We may assume that before the letter was available in print it was well known among the Hasidim. This may perhaps be deduced from a comment by the publisher, who associates the "delay brought about by God, blessed be He," in the journey of R. Jacob Joseph, on account of which

Reprinted in translation by permission of The Bialik Institute from *Be-Mifneh ha-Dorot*, by Benzion Dinur, 1972.

he "did not travel to the land of Israel," with the importance of the letter: "and it remained with him in order to benefit our nation, the people of Israel."[3] In this letter, which Dubnow considers to be something of "a new tiding, a Hasidic Manifesto,"[4] the BeSHT speaks in detail about the messianic role of Hasidism.

"On New Year's Day of 5507 [September 15, 1746]," the BeSHT writes:

I performed an ascent of the soul through adjuration, in the manner known to you, and I saw wondrous things in the vision that I had never seen before in my life. What I saw and learned during my ascent would be impossible to relate even if we could speak face to face. . . . Many wicked men also repented and their sins were forgiven, since it was a time of great compassion. I was astonished that a number of individuals, whom you also knew, were accepted in repentance; there was great joy among them, and they, too, ascended in this way. All of them as one made requests of me and entreated me to my embarrassment, saying "O exalted and glorious master of Torah, God has graciously bestowed upon you abundant understanding that enables you to comprehend these matters. Ascend with us, that you may help and support us." So great was the joy among them that I decided to ascend with them. In the midst of this unprecedented rapture, I saw in a vision that Samael went up to serve as the accuser. . . .
I took my life in my hands and asked my teacher to accompany me, for it is extremely dangerous to ascend to the supernal realms. . . . I ascended level by level until I entered the palace of the Messiah, where he studies Torah with all the Tannaim and the Zaddikim, and also with the Seven Shepherds. . . . I asked the Messiah, "When will the Master come?" He answered: "You will know it in the following way: when your teaching becomes well known, revealed to the world, when your inner resources have spread abroad—what I have taught you and you have understood—so that others can also perform unifications and ascents like you, then all the forces of evil will be annihilated and the time of compassion and salvation will have come." I was astonished by this and greatly chagrined by the length of time it would take until this could come about. But while I was there I learned three special incantations and three holy names that are simple to learn and to explain, so that my mind was set at ease. I thought that in this way my colleagues might possibly be able to attain the same level and status that I have, namely, that they will be able to perform ascents of the soul and learn and comprehend like me.

In these few lines, then, the BeSHT explicitly states that it was "his teacher"—Ahijah of Shiloh, the teacher of Elijah[5]—who "led" him in the upper realms until he entered the palace of the Messiah. However, the doctrine he learned was taught by the Messiah himself. It is a doctrine of redemption; when it becomes well known and "revealed to the world" and "the others" also comprehend and are able to perform "unifications and ascents" then it will be "the time of compassion and salvation" and the Messiah will come. Now the BeSHT says that this was astonishing to him and caused him great distress, because it seemed to him that it would take too long, much longer than he had previously thought prior to the "ascent" in 1746. But through his studies he found that there was a way, a possibility of raising his associates[6] to his level and stature, and in this manner shorten "the long period of time."[7] Although "no permission was granted me to disclose this during my entire lifetime," he nevertheless gives advice and imparts techniques of achieving unifications and ascents, because he was instructed to "spread his inner resources abroad," to promulgate his teachings in the world. One individual has even claimed that the names the BeSHT did not mention in his epistle are "hinted" in it "esoterically, and it is possible that one may learn from them the date of redemption."[8]

Thus the role of the BeSHT is conceived in the epistle as prophetic-messianic. Not only is he endowed with a general prophetic vision, "to see from afar and to hear the heralds of the supernal realms, as has been truly established,"[9] but he is also charged with a prophetic-messianic mission: to prepare the generation for redemption by spreading his teachings, which he received through prophetic comprehension. He was actually charged with Elijah's role, for "prior to the complete consummation, the message of Elijah, of blessed memory, will be to awaken Israel's yearning before the coming of the Messiah," and "the yearning of Israel to serve God, their heavenly Father, will be inspired by one like Elijah."[10] Indeed, Hasidic literature contains more than a few testimonies about the prophetic-messianic role of the BeSHT, even though such testimony is sometimes merely implied. The grandson of the BeSHT, R. Moses Ḥayyim Ephraim of Sudylków, even cites a hint from the Torah of what his grandfather says in the epistle about his messianic role: " 'And the people of Israel come out with a strong hand' (Exod. 14:8). Onkelos translated: *be-reysh galey* [with head revealed]. *ReYSH* is an acronym for *R*abbi *Y*israel Ba'al *Sh*em. *Galey* means, when his teachings are revealed and his inner resources are spread, then we will go out from exile."[11]

The following expressions found in late Hasidic literature, which say explicitly that "from the RYBaSH [the BeSHT] . . . the revelation of the Messiah began to sparkle," "the great scholars of each generation, from the RYBaSH , of blessed memory, until the Messiah's full revelation, are illuminations of the Messiah, as is well known," and "from his time the soul of the Messiah began to sparkle within the great men of the generation"[12]—these, too, are essentially traditional expressions dating back to the beginning of Hasidism. If we do not find explicit statements of this doctrine in the literature of the early generations, it is because in those days, when the vestiges of Sabbatianism were being extirpated, even a slight hint about this most serious matter could turn into ammunition in the hands of the new movement's opponents, who explicitly accused it of covert Sabbatianism.[13]

Actually, the authenticity of this early tradition may be deduced not only from the testimony of the authors of these expressions, who claim that their teaching was "transmitted to us from the Zaddikim, the foundations of the world" and that "it is well known." These matters are indeed "well known" and "transmitted by the Zaddikim, the foundations of the world": known from the teachings and views of Hasidism about redemption and the messianic age, from what the actual disciples of the BeSHT said about their teacher, and from stories and rumors about him.[14] However, only by connecting all these pieces together can one understand the Hasidic conception of the BeSHT's messianic-prophetic role. The circumstances of the time caused the movement, perhaps consciously and intentionally, to refrain from making such an inner connection; it preferred to give these expressions an innocent, popular form, and even that could be done only as individual and separate links, from which one cannot easily perceive the complete chain.

In fact, the first impression one gets from some of the BeSHT's aphorisms and statements about redemption appears to confirm the conclusion that here is "an aspiration for personal faith, for a Torah of the heart, for religious perfection of the individual, within the context of the nation but for the sake of the individual,"[15] and that there is actually a departure from the messianic tension of the Lurianic Kabbalah, which placed in the center of all aspirations and doctrines the redemption of Israel and the cosmic restoration of the world.[16] The BeSHT's homiletical exegesis of the verse "Come close to my soul, redeem it" (Ps. 69:19), one of his best-known and most popular interpretations, is that "when everyone is redeemed individually, then universal redemption will follow." This individual redemption is none other than "the redemption of the soul that is a captive of the evil impulse; when redemption comes 'close to my soul,' then there is also redemption in the physical realm."[17] This appears to be the religious-moral conception commonly accepted by Jews in various forms for many generations. The words have an almost obvious meaning: "It depends only on repentance and good deeds,"[18] since "by repentance one escapes from captivity and slavery to the evil impulse into eternal freedom," because "the evil impulse is the greatest nemesis of man." It "diverts the attention of man to bodily and worldly matters, so that he will not be free to attend to matters of his soul."[19]

Nevertheless, if we analyze these expressions and link them together, we will find that the content of this "individual redemption," in which redemption is extended "from the physical into the spiritual realm," is none other than the liberation of the human being from materialism, spiritual purification leading toward elevation to the level of the holy spirit, so that there will be "an eye worthy of seeing from one end of the world to the other and an ear worthy of hearing the heralds of the supernal realms." For "if the Jewish people make themselves holy and pure through God's Torah and commandments, they will always hear God speak to them, as they did during the revelation at Mount Sinai," because "it was Moses' intention that all Israel would be worthy of attaining the same level as he did, when the Divine Presence itself spoke out of his mouth," and "each Jew can attain that level."[20] It depends solely on the person's knowledge *(daʿat)*. For "the primary cause of the exile in Egypt, and of the current long exile as well, is forgetfulness, which is an aspect of the disappearance of knowledge. . . . That is why redemption occurred primarily through Moses, who is an aspect of knowledge. . . . In the last exile too, redemption will occur by means of knowledge."[21]

The way the redemption from Egypt occurred is the way it will occur now. "That is why it is written 'the earth shall be filled with knowledge of God' (Isa.11:9), meaning that they will associate themselves with people of knowledge and all will be called the generation of knowledge, like the generation of Moses, which was called the generation of knowledge." Certainly, even in the "generation of knowledge" not all people can attain the same level of "knowledge"—of the holy spirit—not all can be equally suffused by it. But this "generation of knowledge" constitutes a complete spiritual unity, the essence of which is clearly explained to us by the BeSHT himself. "In an individual, the soul that dwells in knowledge is what makes all organs alive as long as they are interconnected, so that they all will act in accordance with knowledge . . . the influence of which will spread through all the limbs. Similarly in the world, where there is a Zaddik like Moses, the mystery of 'knowledge': when the others of his generation are connected with him they are all called the 'generation of knowledge,' and this is the mystery of resurrection and the Messiah."[22]

"ADaM is an acronym for Adam, David, Messiah. It is a well-known Talmudic statement that the stature of the first man extended from one end of the world to the other.[23] This means that all souls from one end of the world to the other, with all their aspects, were included in him—until after the sin, when his stature was diminished, and many souls were consigned to the realm of the forces of evil. The same is true with regard to the Messiah: the Jewish people need to make his stature complete with all its aspects, as in the first man before the diminution. Whoever would serve God must elevate his part, prepare his part." "Similarly, the Messiah will have a full stature composed of all the souls of Israel contained in the 600,000. . . . Every Jew must therefore prepare an aspect of the Messiah which pertains to his or her own soul, until the full stature will be reconstituted." "For each person must bring his or her own messianic part." "However, this is impossible without the prior yearning, an aspect of the herald, an aspect of Elijah."[24]

Only by linking these ideas one to another can we adequately grasp what the disciples said about their master in statements transmitted to us for the most part in an obscure manner. Only this way can we recognize the real content of some of the legends about the BeSHT, understand some of his own sayings, and properly evaluate some of the arguments of the opponents of Hasidism.

It was previously noted[25] that the role of the BeSHT as Elijah, the herald of redemption, is implied in the words of R. Jacob Joseph HaKohen, who reports that the teacher of the BeSHT was Ahijah of Shiloh, the teacher of Elijah. This idea is confirmed, as we have seen, by stories in *Shivḥei ha-BeSHT*. In addition, the highly rhetorical words of R. Menahem Mendel of Vitebsk about the BeSHT,[26] which many great Hasidic leaders labored to interpret, can be understood only from the viewpoint of the BeSHT's prophetic-messianic role, about which this text speaks using figures of speech and fragments of Biblical verses, so that only the initiated will understand their real content. "The word of the Lord [lit., the word of the Name] was in the power of the Baᶜal Shem [the Master of the Name]; whatever he decreed was fulfilled; he was unique: from the time of the ancients there was no one like him, and after him who will arise upon the earth?" In this line comprising five short phrases the following message is communicated: that the BeSHT was bestowed with the prophetic spirit in exile, so that through him the Divine Presence would watch over the Jewish people even when they are in exile; that he was a perfect Zaddik who had the privilege of cleaving to God to such an extent that all his "decrees" were fulfilled; he was unique, no contemporary having the same relationship with God, for he incorporated within him aspects of both Moses and Elijah.[27]

In fact, the BeSHT himself thought he incorporated aspects of both Moses and Elijah. We are told about this by his grandson R. Moses Ḥayyim Ephraim of Sudylkow, and by the compiler of *Shivḥei ha-BeSHT.* At the end of his book *Degel Maḥaneh Efrayim,* R. Moses Ḥayyim Ephraim relates among "the things that I heard from my grandfather" a full monologue of the BeSHT that should be included here in its entirety. "Once I heard him say this to me on a Friday night, while he was expounding the verse, 'Who will ascend for us to heaven?' *[Mi yaᶜaleh lanu ha-shamaymah]* (Deut. 30:12). He embraced and kissed me and said that the first letters of the Hebrew words produce *MYLaH,* circumcision, and the last letters of the Hebrew words spell the Name of God (YHWH). He then said the following words: I swear to you that there is a man in the world who hears Torah from the Holy One and His *Shekhinah,* not from an angel, etc. He himself could hardly believe that he would not be pushed away from the Holy One, blessed be He, (God forbid!), and [forced to descend] to the realm of the evil powers,[28] but he relied on the verses 'It is not in the heavens. . . . It is not beyond the sea' (Deut. 30:11–12), for God draws us near with the power of His righteousness."[29] Hearing Torah "from the Holy One and His *Shekhinah,* not from an angel"—because according to the Hasidic tradition derived from the BeSHT, "God Himself speaks with the prophet," for "prophecy does not occur when one dreams, but rather when one has totally purified his soul through intellectual activity. Then, by means of unifications and bonding and invocations, his living root ascends from one level to the next until it reaches the realm of the *Sefirot,* and binds them together with the light of the transcendant Unknowable One. The intellectual soul in his body, thoroughly purified, establishes a bond with his root; he sees and hears God speaking to him clearly because of that one bonding that he established."[30]

The compiler of *Shivḥei ha-BeSHT* tells us in the name of R. Joseph of Kaminke—one of the BeSHT's closest disciples—that "the BeSHT expected to ascend to heaven in a whirlwind as did Elijah, and he was greatly saddened by it." He also said: "If the righteous Redeemer does not come within sixty years, I will be compelled to re-enter this world."[31] As noted above, both the BeSHT and his disciples were careful not to speak openly about the BeSHT's prophetic-messianic role. The opinion of R. Dov Baer, the Maggid of Miedzyrzecz, was that the BeSHT "revealed only a tiny bit, and about Elijah he revealed nothing, except possibly just before his death."[32] R. Meir Margaliot, the author of *Me'ir Netivim,* belonged to the BeSHT's inner circle and was one of his first disciples; he wrote about the BeSHT as "his teacher and friend," providing reliable and unequivocal information that his conduct and teachings were "in holiness and in purity, in piety and asceticism: the Zaddik will live by his faith." At the same time, he alluded to the BeSHT's role, saying that with regard to this matter there are secrets that may absolutely not be disclosed, or that he, R. Meir was not allowed to talk about what had been revealed to the BeSHT: "for profound secrets were revealed to him, but God's glory is to conceal the matter."[33]

However, from the polemical writings of the opponents to Hasidism we clearly see that the idea of prophecy and its renewal within the Jewish people, which the Hasidim championed, was not considered to be a secret by all. The opponents speak out against "a priest and a prophet, a Ba'al Shem, who looks up to God and can tell about God's actions," against those who "imagine that they rise to the clouds, and know the mind of the Most High, the actions of God who dwells in Zion,"[34] and "those who don a hairy mantle in order to deceive."[35] This prophetic side of Hasidism was emphasized in particular in the second *Zemir 'Aritsim,* which came out "against the Hasidic sect and their holy men, the false prophets."[36] The author says that R. Israel Baal Shem, "who considered himself a prophet," "set up prophets who lead astray, who are like thorns cut down," "that he laid the cornerstone of visionary Hasidim" and "established the seer-Hasidim," and that "the visionary of today was once called a heretic." "R. Israel Baal Shem saw the seal of Ahijah of Shiloh and erred," "because of the prophets my heart breaks —for the seers of Israel are 'prophets' by their own imagination, they do not know or understand," they are nothing but "prophets of Baal," "a prophet who teaches falsehood"—"its prophets are reckless and vain." That is why the author repeatedly warns: "Do not follow the path of the Hasidim, for there is no vision and no prophet."[37]

NOTES

1. This is apparent also from the expressions found in *Toledot Yaʿaqov Yosef* following quotations from the BeSHT, such as "the enlightened one will understand," "this is enough for those who understand," "instruct the wise, but this is sufficient," "let the wise hear and grow in learning," and other similar statements. Cf. *Toledot Yaʿaqov Yosef,* "Va-ʾEraʾ": "In order to enable you to understand this, I will mention a tiny bit of what I heard from my teacher"; "Be-Shallaḥ": "He said that there are marvelous things in this profundity; the enlightened one will understand"; "Be-Haʿalotekha": "This is what I remember having received from my teacher orally, in person; it is impossible to explain it in a book; know and understand"; and at the end of the book: "These are the things I heard from my teacher, may his memory bring us life in the world to come. I have written only the 'chapter headings,' because I am afraid [to disclose more], and also because I have forgotten [the details]."
2. Cf. Simon Dubnow, *Toledot ha-Ḥasidut* (Tel Aviv, 1943), p. 60, including n. 1. And cf. Abraham Kahana, *Sefer ha-Ḥasidut* (Warsaw, 1922), p. 73; from the beginning of the BeSHT's letter, "I received at the Luck fair in the year 5510," he tries to prove that it was written in 5512 [1751–52]. However, the letter itself makes it clear that it was written shortly after the suppression of the Haidamak movement of 1750, and that in the same year there were cases of "great feebleness, and an epidemic," referring to events of 5511.
3. This remark was printed in the later editions as well. Cf. *Ben Porat Yosef,* Piotrkow ed., p. 254; cf. also Kahana, *ibid.*
4. Dubnow, *Toledot Ha-Ḥasidut,* p. 60.
5. Cf. above, chap. 9 [of the full article: *Be-Mifneh ha-Dorot,* p. 154; *Essential Papers on Hasidism,* ed. Gershom Hundert, pp. 152–53—Ed.].
6. The Hebrew words *anshei gili* in the letter mean "members of my group, members of my circle, people similar to me, close to me in their views and their temperament." Cf. Ruth Rabbah 2, 7: "R. Johanan said in the name of R. Simeon ben Jehozadak: The Holy One, blessed be He, brings into the world members of associations *[gilin]* and members of brotherhoods. If one of the association dies, let the whole association become apprehensive, if one of the brotherhood dies, lest the whole brotherhood become apprehensive." Cf. also b. Meg 11a: "Ahasuerus: [the name in Hebrew means] the brother of the head *[aḥiv shel rosh]* and the counterpart *[ben gilo]* of the

head." Rashi comments on this passage: "both are of the same opinion." The phrase *benei gilo* is used in the same sense in *Shivḥei ha-BeSHT,* Horodetzky ed., p. 119. This recognition of the possibility of "ascent" by the members of his circle is what led him to write the letter to R. Abraham Gershon of Kutow, one of the "members of the circle and the brotherhood" who emigrated to the land of Israel, so that the BeSHT was unable to tell him personally what he told the other colleagues.

7. This is demonstrated by the phrase "I was . . . greatly chagrined by the length of time," and its continuation, "my mind was set at ease. I thought . . ."
8. From the story of R. Uri of Strelisk about the "Zaddik of Neskhiz" who was "obligated" to teach the BeSHT's letter "every day without fail, like putting on the phylacteries": *Imrei Qodesh* (Lvov, 1894), "Additions," paragraph 40. The "Zaddik of Neskhiz" was the outstanding disciple of R. [Yehiel] Mikhel of Zloczow, one of the close disciples of the BeSHT who preserved the primary tradition of Hasidism. On the tradition about the letter, cf. further Rabbi M. Y. Gutman, *Rabbi Yisrael Baal Shem Tov,* p. 80, n. 29, who reports a family tradition that the letter was written by R. Yehiel, the BeSHT's son-in-law, and after the death of R. Jacob Joseph ha-Kohen it passed to R. Pinḥas of Korzec.
9. *Tsofnat Peʿaneaḥ,* 4, p. 28a; *Ben Porat Yosef,* p. 63a.
10. *Meʾor ʿEinayim,* "Pinḥas."
11. *Degel Maḥaneh Efrayim,* "Be-Shallaḥ"; the words are cited in the name of R. Lippa of Chmielnik, one of the the BeSHT's disciples. Cf. also Zohar, "Naso'," p. 124b *[Raʿaya Mehemna]:* "Because Israel is destined to taste of this tree of life, namely, this Book of Splendor *(Sefer ha-Zohar),* they will by means of it emerge from exile."
12. *Sheʾerit Yisraʾel* by R. Israel Dov of Weledniki, "Selections" for "Shaʿar ha-Hitqashrut." The Zaddik of Weledniki was one of the disciples of Chernobyl, where the tradition about the messianic element in the movement was preserved in its entirety. Also, "Shaʿar ha-Hitqashrut," Derush 4, Maʾamar 3; R. Aaron of Koidanovo, *Zekher Tsaddiq,* p. 10a.
13. Cf. *Zemir ʿAritsim,* the proclamation of the community of Brody: "For some years now, these evildoers have been around" (an allusion to the Frankists) [Mordecai Wilensky, *Hasidim and Mitnaggedim* (Heb.), 2 vols. (Jerusalem, 1970) 1:46; henceforth: Wilensky—Ed.].
14. *Divrei Shalom* by R. Shalom of Koidanovo, introduction; cf. there the explanation of the Talmudic statement "Two thousand *[alafim],* the days of the Messiah": *"alafim* here means 'teaching,' as in the expression *aʾalef kha ḥokhmah:* I will teach you wisdom; this is because the BeSHT taught so as to attract to himself the kind of worship that will prevail in the days of the Messiah." Cf. *Sheʾerit Yisraʾel,* "Selections" for "Shaʿar ha-Hitqashrut": from R. Simeon bar Yohai on, "two thousand, the days of the Messiah" began to sparkle, but only in the present age has "the radiance of the Messiah been illumined."
15. Dubnow, *Toledot ha-Ḥasidut,* p. 2.

16. Cf. Scholem, *Major Trends in Jewish Mysticism* (New York, 1946), pp. 329–30.
17. The quotes from the homily on "come close to my soul, redeem it" are taken from *Teshuʾot Ḥen,* "Va-ʾEraʾ," in the name of the BeSHT; *Toledot Yaʿaqov Yosef,* "Devarim" and "Pequdei." In this later location the homiletical interpretation is cited simply with the statement "as I heard." But in most places it is cited in the name of the BeSHT; cf. *Toledot Yaʿaqov Yosef,* "Va-Yishlaḥ," "Va-Yeḥi," "Shemini," "Devarim," "Tetseʾ."
18. B. Sanh 97b.
19. *Toledot Yaʿaqov Yosef,* "Tetse"'; *Ben Porat Yosef,* Piotrkow ed., p. 82b.
20. *Tsofnat Peʿaneaḥ,* Piotrkow ed., pp. 33a and 25a; similarly, *Ben Porat Yosef,* p. 83a. *Keter Torah* by R. Meir son of R. Levi Yitsḥaq of Berditchev, "Yitro," in the name of the BeSHT. Similarly, *Toledot Yaʿaqov Yosef,* "Va-Yaqhel." And cf. the statement of the BeSHT in *Tsavaʾat ha-RYBaSH* (Jerusalem, 1965), p. 15: "Man can reach the 'level of prophecy.' " Cf. *Or ha-Meʾir,* "Tsav," on the way of the Maggid of Miedzyrzecz in matters of Torah.
21. *Toledot Yaʿaqov Yosef,* "Pequdei." [The rest of this paragraph in Dinur's text is a pastiche of quotations from Hasidic literature presenting an interpretation, based on Lurianic Kabbalah, of the "Egyptian Exile," and the role of Moses, the embodiment of "knowledge," in unifying the people with him and raising them to their root in the divine realm. As this technical material is not readily translatable into intelligible English and does not advance the argument, it has been eliminated here—Ed.]
22. *Tsofnat Peʿaneaḥ,* pp. 63a, 62b, in the name of the BeSHT.
23. B. Hag 12a.
24. *Meʾor Einayim,* "Shemot"; the main content is from the BeSHT, as is proven there in "Pinḥas."
25. Cf. above, ch. 9 [of the full article: *Be-Mifneh ha-Dorot,* p. 154] including notes 18 and 19 [*Essential Papers on Hasidism,* pp. 152–53 and p. 201, nn. 232 and 233—Ed.]. The definition of the nature of the prophecy of Ahijah the Shilonite in Kabbalah ("Shaʿar ha-Yiḥudim," chap. 1) is not relevant here; what is important for our purpose is R. Jacob Joseph's emphasis on Ahijah as the teacher of the BeSHT and of Elijah.
26. *Peri ha-Arets* (Zhitomir, 1849), p. 38b, in his letter to R. Jacob *(Yehe shelama rabba).* Cf. *Sefer Baʿal Shem Tov* by R. Simon Menahem Mendel Wadnik (Landsberg, 1938), part 1. p. 16, n. 9, a commentary on this in the name of R. Israel of Ruzhin.
27. [Most of this extensive note explicates the Hebrew phrases of the passage quoted on the basis of numerous citations from earlier Hebrew literature. Important for the argument is the conclusion, about the allusion to Deut. 34:10, "There has not arisen another prophet in Israel like Moses"—Ed.] If the author uses this description for the BeSHT, his intention was to assert that the BeSHT embodies an aspect of Moses; cf. *Divrei Shalom,* introduction. Elijah is the last prophet. Cf. *Shikheḥat Leqet,* p. 4b: " 'I am the only

prophet of God left' (1 Kings 18:22)—yet there were many prophets in the world at that time. This verse therefore hints that at the *present* time, when there is no [other] prophet, Elijah is left for the world." As for the two aspects of the BeSHT [Moses and Elijah], cf. *Sefer ha-Gilgulim,* chap. 35: "Know that every tzaddik has two souls."

28. Literally, "to the female of the great abyss," the realm of the *qelippot* [the "husks" or "shells" in Lurianic Kabbalah].
29. *Degel Maḥaneh Efrayim* (Josefow, 1883), p. 78b. Cf. also the passage before this: "I also heard from him that his father took him without a word, like Moses."
30. *Zohar Ḥai* by Isaac Eisik of Komarno, Exodus, part 2, p. 219d; at the end of the passage: "Thus I heard from our master, Rabbi Israel Baal Shem Tov."
31. *Shivḥei ha-BeSHT,* p. 119 [*In Praise of the Baal Shem Tov,* ed. Dan Ben-Amos and Jerome Mintz (Bloomington, 1970), p. 169—Ed.]; cf. above in this chapter [at n. 24] the quote from R. Nahum of Chernobyl (*Me'or ʿEinayim,* "Pinḥas"), on the function of Elijah before the coming of the Messiah.
32. R. Solomon of Lutsk in the name of his teacher, the Maggid of Miedzyrzecz, in the first introduction to the book *Maggid Amarav le-Yaʿaqov: A Collection of Sayings* (Lvov, 1893). Cf. also in *Shivḥei ha-BeSHT,* p. 117, the story that when the BeSHT fell ill "before his death," he said to his daughter, "You did not know who was here; on one side stood Elijah of blessed memory, and on the other side my teacher" (Ahijah the Shilonite) [*In Praise of the Baal Shem Tov,* p. 137].
33. *Sod Yakhin u-Boʿaz,* p. 82. "Profound secrets were revealed to him," based on b. Git 56b; compare the use of the verse "God's glory is to conceal a matter" (Prov. 25:2) with the Zohar on that verse (II, 105b): "Man has no right to reveal esoteric words for which no permission to reveal has been given." The Aramaic Targum of *Tsofnat Peʿaneaḥ* (Gen. 41:45) is "Profound secrets were revealed to him."
34. *Nazad ha-Demʿa* [by R. Israel of Zamosc (Dyrenfurth, 1772)], Ma'amar 4, chap. 3, and Ma'amar 1, chap. 2.
35. From "Iggeret ha-Qena'ot" of Vilna, 1772; the first *Zemir ʿAritsim;* Dubnow, "Chassidiana," p. 10 [Wilensky, 1:37].
36. I cite from the edition of Deinard (New York, 1899). On the date of the first edition (1798) and the second (1860), which Deinard thought was the first, see the discussion by Dubnow, *Toledot ha-Ḥasidut,* vol. 2, appendices [and Wilensky, 2:19–20, nn. 25, 48—Ed].
37. *Zemir ʿAritsim,* introduction, p. xxxviii, "great announcement," pp. xxiv–xxv, 1, 4, 12, 43, 61, 63 [Wilensky, 2:191, 190, 192, 194, 197, 209, 220, 221—Ed.].

15

Nahman of Bratslav's Messianic Strivings

Arthur Green

The *ẓaddiq,* as he appears in the literature of early Hasidism, is a leader with many faces. We have seen that in Bratslav he takes on the quality of *axis mundi,* being possessed of the soul that lies at the center of his entire generation. He is also portrayed, in Bratslav and elsewhere, as parent, teacher, spiritual guide, intercessor in prayer, healer, and protector from sin. Hasidic masters and communities varied insofar as they chose to emphasize one aspect of *ẓaddiqut* above another, though this emphasis seldom resulted in the total exclusion of other elements. Thus in *ḤaBaD* circles the emphasis was upon the *ẓaddiq* as guide, while in Lezajsk (and later Galician dynasties) the *ẓaddiq's* intercessory function in prayer was more important, and in Przysucha (including later Polish Hasidism) it was the aspect of *ẓaddiq* as teacher that gained prominence.

All of these images of the *ẓaddiq* are present in Bratslav. We have already had occasion to refer to a number of them, and the particular ways in which they functioned in the context of Nahman's unique relationship with his disciples. But when we turn to a closer examination of the *ẓaddiq*-idea as presented in Nahman's teachings, it becomes clear that there is a most serious difference in emphasis between Nahman and all other Hasidic teachers: in Bratslav alone is the *ẓaddiq* portrayed most prominently as *redeemer,* and particularly as redeemer from the burden of sin.

The idea that a *ẓaddiq* may be of help to his disciples in atoning for

Reprinted by permission of the University of Alabama Press from *Tormented Master: A Life of Rabbi Nahman of Bratslav* by Arthur Green, 1979.

their sins is not completely new with Nahman; it is part of the intercessory function of the *ẓaddiq* in other schools as well. We have seen how the Ba'al Shem Tov was wont to engage in *tiqqun neshamot,* restoring the souls of those who had already died, and were too weighed down by sin to enter paradise. The very term *"pidyon"* ("redemption"), applied to the gift the *ḥasid* brought when seeking his master's blessing, bespeaks something of the *ẓaddiq's* function as redeemer of souls. But only in Bratslav does this aspect of the *ẓaddiq's* role outstrip all others; only here does the effecting of *tiqqun* come to be depicted as his central task.[1]

I heard that when he was in Lipovits he said to his disciples: 'In what way can you repent? Would all of your combined strength and all your days suffice to repair even a small bit of the damage you have done? But I do penance for you, and God gives me the power to repair all that you have damaged (so long as you desist from conscious sin).'[2]

Nahman, so constantly aware of his own sinfulness and distance from God, has constructed a Hasidism built upon an awareness of sin. Gone are the Ba'al Shem Tov's warnings against excessive brooding; the movement's early optimism about the nature of man has here been cast aside. Bratslav writings, indeed a faithful mirror to Nahman's own countenance, depict human life as a morass of suffering and guilt.[3] The devastating effects of sin are everywhere; the powers of *siṭra aḥra* and its representatives within the soul form an active and dangerous foe. In the context of this new emphasis on human sinfulness and its destructive effects, the image of *ẓaddiq* as teacher or spiritual guide will not suffice: in order to be of real help to his disciples, the *ẓaddiq must* be able to do battle for them, rescuing them from forces of darkness that threaten to overwhelm them.

We have noted that this rediscovery of the omnipresence of sin in certain ways places Nahman beyond the bounds of what is usually considered 'Hasidic' thought, and brings him closer to the Kabbalistic *mussar* writers of earlier generations. The emphasis upon sin (particularly sexual sin) as the working of the evil forces, and man's great need to overcome its power through acts of penitence and through mystical meditations, was a central theme for these authors, particularly for those who wrote in the Lurianic tradition. This was the purpose of the many *tiqquney teshuvah,* penitential guides, published by Kabbalistic authors both before and after the Sabbatian period. Certain of these liturgical *tiqqunim* continued to be printed in late Kabbalistic or even Hasidic prayerbooks, and exercised considerable influence, despite the BeSHT's alleged disdain for their ascetic worldview. Nahman's own *tiqqun ha-kelali* clearly belongs to the genre of this non-Hasidic literature of penitential prescriptions. In promulgating this litany of penitence for sexual misdeed, and in the great promises he made as to its effectiveness,[4] Nahman is revealing himself as *ẓaddiq*-redeemer, as one who can save his followers from the harm wrought by their sins.

In the wake of this emphasis upon *tiqqun,* it should come as no surprise to us that the Hasidic ideal of *devequt* ("attachment" to God) receives little attention in Nahman's writings. As Scholem has pointed out, the ideal of *devequt* served in Hasidism to supplant that of *tiqqun,* which was the central goal of Lurianic Kabbalah. Following the Sabbatian and Frankist debacles, the circle around the Ba'al Shem Tov and especially the Maggid chose a path of inner illumination, one which would effect the individual transformation of the worshiper without raising the dangerous spectre of messianism implicit in the striving for *tiqqun.* As preached by the Kabbalists, *tiqqun* was a process of restoring wholeness to a world still suffering the effects of the primal cataclysm; this restoration would culminate in the advent of messiah, symbolizing the completion of man's theurgic task. *Devequt,* on the other hand, implied no such restoration, but was merely the ascent of the soul, through devout prayer and contemplation, to a state of union or near-union with the divine.[5]

The promulgation of *devequt* as the Hasidic ideal must, however, be seen not merely as an escape from messianic tension. It is a natural outgrowth of the Ba'al Shem Tov's new emphasis upon the presence and ready accessibility of the divine in the world. Early Hasidic doctrine came quite close to the borderline of pantheism, or at least 'panentheism'. The constant repetition of such formulae as "the whole earth is filled with his glory" and "there is no place devoid of Him" points to a religious world view that could readily allow for 'attachment' to the Creator as its ideal. For the early Hasidic authors, the seeming absence of God is but illusion, rather readily to be overcome through the techniques of contemplative prayer. There is no real and unbridgeable gulf between man and God. While sin still was described as a barrier keeping man from God, it was felt, particularly in the school of the Maggid, that contemplation could break through that barrier.

This could not be the case for Nahman, for whom the sense of distance from God was a real, and crucial, experience. Where sin remains a serious burden and God is far from man, *devequt* is not an accessible ideal. Until the soul is cleansed, man remains a prisoner of his own inner darkness. It is clear that in this context the first task of man must be that of *tiqqun,* and that the *ẓaddiq* must be one who can help in that effort. But this *tiqqun* by its very nature was the repair of the cosmos as well as the repair of the individual soul. For Nahman, as for any Kabbalist, the greatest danger of sin was not that harm which it did to the soul, but rather the damage it wrought in the upper worlds. Sin has a cosmic effect: the unification of the *Sefirot,* or the restoration of wholeness to *Adam Qadmon,* is retarded only by the corrosive action of human sin. The forces of evil, which work to bring about disharmony above, have been cut off from their original wellsprings in the divine world; only through man's transgressions, depicted by the Kabbalah as filled with demonic potency, do they receive the nourishment needed to sustain their work.

Here we have traced a full circle: Hasidism rejected the *tiqqun* ideal in part to escape the dangerous messianic tension. Nahman, because of his personal world view, in turn rejected *devequt* as a goal and returned to the earlier emphasis. This emphasis, however, brought him right back to the place early Hasidism had sought to avoid: a religious life clearly eschatological in its central thrust. If Nahman is the redeemer from sin, and the real import of any individual's sin is that which it contributes to the state of universal alienation, then the salvation of each sinner will of necessity bring the world another step closer to the ultimate *tiqqun,* which is the advent of messiah. By reemphasizing the reality of sin and the need for redemption—an emphasis that grew out of his own, inner life—Nahman was also opening the doorway to a fully active and resurgent messianism, the likes of which had not previously been known within the Hasidic camp.

The place of messianism in the early years of the Hasidic movement has been much debated by modern scholars. While some historians (particularly B. Z. Dinur, and to a lesser extent I. Tishby) have claimed that Hasidism began with a clearly messianic goal in mind, and only later, perhaps as a result of failure, turned to the goal of personal redemption through *devequt,* others (G. Scholem and R. Schatz) have seen the 'neutralization' of messianic tension as a basic characteristic of the movement as a whole.[6] In either case, however, the discussion revolves primarily around the period of the Ba'al Shem Tov. Even Dinur, the most extreme among those who attribute a messianic character to the movement, agrees that by the end of the BeSHT's lifetime (1760) there had been a turn away from messianic urgency. In the writings of the Maggid and his school, which Schatz has studied, the emphasis on *devequt* as the central value and a turn away from talk of messianic redemption is quite pronounced. Of course there is a continued belief in messiah, as well as an echoing of such pious phrases as "may he come speedily in our days." But *activity* directed toward bringing the final redemption, serious predictions of his imminent arrival, or even extensive theoretical preoccupation with the nature of messianic redemption, are absent[7]—absent, that is, except in Bratslav.

Any discussion of messianism as presented in the Bratslav sources is greatly complicated by the fact that here, more than in any other area, the hand of the inner censor has been particularly heavy. For reasons that will presently become clear, the relationship of Nahman to the final redemption and the rather open messianic agitation that dominated his career between 1804 and 1806 were considered too controversial to be discussed outside the community or to be allowed to appear in print. Thus it happened that the one document written by Nahman purporting to deal most specifically with this matter, called *Megillat Setarim* by the later sources, has never been published, and exists to this day as a manuscript shared only within the most intimate circles of Bratslav *ḥasidim*.[8] It is also quite likely that those of Nahman's works which were burned, on his orders, both within his lifetime and immediately following his death, may well have had to do with this most sensitive area. Nonetheless, as we shall show, enough material is available within the printed Bratslav corpus to give one a rather clear picture of Nahman's messianic strivings, as well as an indication of what it was that Nahman and others felt might best be left unsaid, or at least unprinted.

As *ẓaddiq ha-dor* Nahman claimed to be the bearer of the soul that had belonged to Moses in the generation of the Exodus. This same soul, according to Nahman's writings and based on accepted Kabbbalistic tradition, will belong to messiah in the last generation. While a parallel between the first and final redeemers of Jewish history had been drawn in most ancient times, it was only the Kabbalistic belief in metempsychosis that made possible a declaration that Moses and messiah were in fact one and the same.[9] This soul, which had also been that of Simeon ben Yohai, Isaac Luria, and the BeSHT, lends to its bearers a particular responsibility in the work of redemption. Both Rabbi Simeon and Luria were identified, in traditions known to Nahman, as redeemer-like figures. A still greater urgency about this redemptive task is felt in Bratslav through Nahman's claim that he is more than the *ẓaddiq ha-dor* of his *own* generation: he is in fact the last in this chain of *ẓaddiqey ha-dor*, the final bearer of the great messianic soul who will appear in the world before the advent of messiah himself. His life and teachings are, in a sense, the last opportunity the world will have to effect the great *tiqqun* before the coming of the final judgment. When Nahman said, "My fire will burn until messiah comes," he expected that the redeemer's arrival was imminent, and that he himself was the final preparer of the way. There was a point at which he felt he knew the exact day of messiah's intended arrival, and that day was designated as being "within a few years." It was only due to certain events that transpired in and around Bratslav during Nahman's lifetime, as we shall see, that the final redemption was to be delayed.[10]

It should be noted that the traditional "signs" of the final days, if pursued with a searching eye, were readily to be found in the opening years of the nineteenth century. The oppression of the Jews (as perceived by *ḥasidim*) was on the increase in Russia under Alexander I. The growth of heresy, another sure sign of messiah's imminent arrival, was beginning to be felt even in the Ukraine, as the influence of the Berlin *Haskalah* started to move eastward. Perhaps most significantly, the astounding and unprecedented successes of Napoleon's army, which Nahman had encountered first-hand in his flight from Acre in 1799, led many to believe that Gog and Magog (perhaps France and Russia) were about to destroy one another, and that messiah would rise from the ashes of their final battle. We know that Nahman followed the news of his day with great interest; when disciples came to visit, he would frequently ask them for reports on what was happening in the outside world. The reports he received regarding persecutions, heresies, and the Napoleonic advances all fed his belief that redemption was in fact at hand.[11]

It has long been known and generally accepted that Nahman and the group around him were involved in renewed messianic speculations. The frequent and secretive references to the final redemption in Bratslav literature as well as the highly charged, mysterious mood of penitence and excitement at once leave no doubt that deep stirrings of redemption-longing were aroused here. It was Hillel Zeitlin who first remarked that although it seems at first glance that the figure of the *ẓaddiq* dominates all of Bratslav thinking, it is possible to see a thinly veiled reference to messiah behind each mention of *ẓaddiq*. What has not been heretofore clarified was the precise nature and full extent of Nahman's involvement with millenarian activities. What sort of claim was it that Nahman made? Was he merely the final preparer of the way, as the exoteric Bratslav tradition might have it, or did he claim something more? Was there a belief or hope in Bratslav that Nahman might himself be messiah, and how much was he himself responsible for such belief? There is no question that during the years 1804 to 1806 there was a tremendous upsurge of eager anticipation of the End in Bratslav; earlier scholars have documented the events of that period quite fully.[12] But was it out of the air that Nahman turned to messianism in the middle of his career? True, he was heartened or even elated by such personal happenings as the marriages of his daughters and especially by the birth of his first son, Shlomo Ephraim, in the spring of 1805. But what have these to do with messianism? And can these events alone explain so daring a turn in the man's career? Or are the roots of this messianism in fact to be traced earlier, and did something happen that made the "fullness of time" seem closer as those crucial years approached?

The fact is that throughout a great many of Nahman's early teachings, if they are read closely, a messianic strain can be detected. We shall turn our attention here first to those teachings, and only afterwards to the dramatic events that characterized the messianic climax of Nahman's years at Bratslav.

The second teaching in *Liqquṭey MoHaRaN*, though it is not dated by Nathan, clearly belongs to Nahman's early days, and probably to Zlotopolye.[13] It begins with the words, "Messiah's chief weapon will be that of prayer." The power of true prayer, Nahman explains, comes to man through the Kabbalistic figure of Joseph, the ninth *sefirah*. Because Joseph is a symbol of sexual purity for Kabbalists, this power of prayer can only be attained by those who have followed Joseph's example, and have been careful about matters of sexual purity in their own lives. The prayer such people fashion will ultimately become the messiah's weapon, a spiritual "sword" with which he will vanquish his enemies. The use of this sword, however, is not restricted to the messianic future; it can also be employed by the righteous who live in pre-messianic times: "he who attains this sword must know how to do battle with it. He must turn neither to the right nor the left, but must strike his mark without fail." In fact, as we shall see, it is Nahman himself who has access to the messianic sword.

The teaching then goes on to speak of *mishpaṭ,* here defined as the proper balance of the sefirotic world. *Mishpaṭ* depends upon Jacob, the central pillar of the *sefirot,* and the progenitor of Joseph. Although he is a younger son, Joseph was given the rights of primogeniture over Reuben, who had defiled his father's bed by seducing his concubine (Gen. 35:22). By means of prayer, which is directed toward the sefirotic Jacob, the righteous can help to maintain the precarious balance of the upper worlds. These prayers are directed through the *ẓaddiq ha-dor,* who has the power to unite them and bring out their efficacy. As Moses, he assembles all the prayers of Israel, and out of them he builds the tabernacle *(mishkan),* here taken as a symbol of the reconstituted *shekhinah.*

While the train of associations here is somewhat fragmentary and confusing, as is true with the written versions of many of Nahman's teachings, it is clear that underlying this whole series of associations is the figure of *Messiah ben Joseph,* even though he is not mentioned directly in the text. This figure of the messianic warrior, who is to precede Messiah ben David, is the link between the motifs of Joseph and *ẓaddiq,* on the one hand, and the messiah and his spiritual "weapon" on the other.[14] Of Messiah ben Joseph we will have more to say below. Also evident in the background of this teaching is a sefirotic model of the redemptive process: both *ẓaddiq* and Joseph are symbols of the ninth *sefirah;* it is through their efforts that the tenth *sefirah,* the *Shekhinah* (also associated with David and the advent of Messiah ben David) shall be restored to her original place. The sword of Messiah ben Joseph prepares the way for Messiah ben David. The understated phallic associations in this chain of thought are also highly interesting for the psychology of messianism.

Upon his move to Bratslav in 1802, Nahman elatedly described that place as a sort of new Jerusalem. The wording of that description, speaking as it does of the *tiqqun* involved in returning the lands of the nations to the bounds of the sacred, itself has a strong messianic flavor. The growing messianism of that period (late 1802) is even more directly found in a teaching offered on Hanukkah, in which Nahman ingeniously distorts a Talmudic reference to *orzila bar yoma* (lit.: "a one-day-old gazelle") to refer to "the desecrated light which is about to emerge any day." With regard to this light, the glory of the *shekhinah,* Nahman says:

It will be revealed only through messiah, of whom it has been said: 'When will he come? Today! "Today if you will harken to His voice" (Ps. 95:7).' Every day the glory is ready to emerge from its debasement.[15]

Later that same winter, in the early months of 1803, Nahman again spoke of messianic redemption, making it quite clear once again that such redemption would come about through the actions of the *ẓaddiq*. Israel is in exile only because of its lack of faith. Faith is best realized in prayer, which attests to man's belief in the ability of God to intervene in the natural order. Belief in the supernatural, however, is directly associated with the Land of Israel, that place which, even in pre-messianic times, is under the direct guidance of God himself and is not ruled by nature. Thus it is that through prayer, which bears witness to their faith, Israel can overcome the heretics' denial of the supernatural, and bring about the redemption, the return to Erez Israel. "When this [denial of the supernatural] ends, and there is an abundance of faith in the world, messiah will come. Redemption depends primarily upon this."[16] Faith is restored, Nahman goes on to say, and prayer is made possible, only through the advice of the *ẓaddiq*. Receiving counsel from the *ẓaddiq* is an act entailing the actual flow of his mind into yours, purifying you of heretical thoughts, just as the revelation at Sinai purified Israel from the taint of original sin! It is this purification, initiated by the *ẓaddiq,* that will enable Israel's prayers to hasten the messiah's arrival.

It was at the wedding of his daughter Sarah, held in the spring of 1803, that Nahman first made explicit reference to a relationship between messiah and his own family. We will recall that Nahman, in addition to claiming possession of the messianic soul, was in fact the product of a union between two families that claimed descent from the House of David. Given this confluence of messianic symbols, it is no wonder that he first expressed a hope, later to turn to certainty, that the redeemer would emerge from among his own offspring:

In the year 1803, he married off his daughter Sarah in the holy community of Medvedevka, to his son-in-law Isaac, the son of the wealthy Leib Dubrovner.

. . . The wedding took place on the New Moon of Nissan, which that year fell on a Thursday. After the ceremony, which took place in the evening, they spoke of messiah, *etc.* (and our master hinted that it would be fitting that he come from this union, etc.).[17]

A few weeks later, in a teaching offered on Shavu'ot (May, 1803), he again referred to exile and the coming return to Erez Israel. He reminded his disciples that it was because of sin, particularly the sins of pride and self-glorification, that Israel was in exile from its homeland. It is not the power of the nations that keeps us from our land, he said, but it is rather our own sinfulness that lends power to those who would oppress us.[18]

But the most striking among these early messianic teachings was one offered in midsummer of 1803. The text preserved in this case is quite brief, and is surely a fragment of a much longer teaching. Like many of Nahman's early teachings, this fragment takes the form of an intricate commentary on one of the more fantastic *Aggadic* passages of the Talmud. The Talmudic text, stated in the name of R. Johanan, reads:

Once we were traveling in a ship, and we saw a fish raise its head out of the water. Its eyes were like two moons, and water poured forth from its two nostrils, as [much water as is contained in] the two rivers of Syria.

The great fish, in Nahman's interpretation, turns out to be the *ẓaddiq,* who sometimes has to leave contemplation and study (raising his head out of water) in order to deal with the two great enemies of Israel, Esau and Ishmael, who threaten to darken the *ẓaddiq's* eyes and destroy his vision. These enemies will ultimately be defeated by the two messiahs, who are the streams of water issuing from the fish's nostrils (read: from the *ẓaddiq's* seed).[19]

This text has, however, been censored, presumably on Nahman's own orders (it was published within his lifetime). We are made aware of this by a most significant passage in *Ḥayyey MoHaRaN,* from which it is possible to recover at least the sense of the passage that has been eliminated:

He presented that teaching at the morning meal. His eyes had the appearance of two moons as he said that there are seventy nations, divided between the domains of Esau and Ishmael [traditional designations for Christendom and Islam]. Each of these domains is composed of thirty-five kingdoms, and they will be conquered in the future by the two messiahs, Messiah ben Joseph and Messiah ben David. *And there is one ẓaddiq in whom these two messiahs are combined.* He said several other things there, *more than have been printed.* At that point the table broke, because so many people were pressing around him. He became harsh and said, 'Are there gentiles sitting around my table? Are these then messianic times, that gentiles should approach the *zaddiqim* as in "all the nations shall flow unto him" (Is. 2:2).[20]

The meaning of this dramatic moment seems quite clear. Whenever Nahman used a phrase like "there is one *zaddiq*," his disciples knew well that the reference was to none other than himself. Here he was revealing to them his belief that his own soul included elements of both messianic figures. This much is stated openly by Nathan. What is it then that has been deleted from the text, and to which Nathan can only refer in such an oblique manner? What was it that caused so much excitement among those assembled that they crowded around him until they broke the table? It is not at all impossible that the deleted passage here contained the revelation that Nahman himself is Messiah ben Joseph, the messianic warrior whose battles are to precede the final redemption. Nahman saw himself as a precursor of Messiah ben David, and as one who bore the messianic soul. While the time for Messiah ben David's arrival had not quite been reached, it may well be that on this occasion Nahman did announce himself as Messiah ben Joseph, a role not at all unsuited to his self-image as the suffering *zaddiq* whose pains contain within them the hope for redemption.

The weapons in this messiah's battle, as we have seen, are weapons of prayer. Who is the great prayer-warrior, constantly struggling in prayer to break through to God, if not Nahman himself? What real, inner meaning does Nahman attribute to the battles and torments that fill his life, if not the sense that they are mythic encounters with the forces of evil, aimed at the liberation of both self and others from their clutches, and serving to prepare the path for the final redemption? Here, as in Sabbatianism, the ancient figure of the warrior-messiah has been transformed. No longer is he, as in the early apocalyptic literature in which he played so great a role, a warrior in the literal sense of the word. In the spirit of mysticism, the scene of his battle has shifted from the material world to the world of inner spiritual striving. As Sabbatai Ṣevi had done in his time, Nahman seeks to find in his inner struggles and in the rapid variations of his own moods a spiritual battleground in which the cosmic forces of evil encounter the forces of redemption and engage in their final battle. In the case of both of these would-be redeemers, it is the climate of mysticism, with its emphasis on the inner religious life of man as the true scene of divine activity, that allows of forging a mystical messianism focused upon their own struggles with the personal forces of darkness.[21]

Leaving aside for just a moment the further documentation of Nahman's messianic claim, we should here mention that there is a most significant precedent for the claim to being Messiah ben Joseph, a precedent of which Nahman surely knew and one he would have taken most seriously. We refer to the well-known claims of the Safed Kabbalists that both Isaac Luria and Hayyim Vital were incarnations of Messiah ben Joseph, but that the sins of their unworthy generations had caused them to pass away without effecting the great and final *tiqqun*. Whether Luria actually made the claim of messiahship for himself is somewhat doubtful; it is abundantly clear, however, that Vital and others did make it for him.[22] In the case of Vital, he seems to have had no hesitation in claiming this mantle for himself; his *Sefer ha-Ḥezyonot* is filled with dreams, predictions by others, and outright statements of his claim.

More interesting than the personal claims made for these two masters, however, are a number of conclusions about the relationship between the *ẓaddiq* and the two messiahs proceeding from the circles of Safed Kabbalah. According to Naftali Bachrach, author of *'Emeq ha-Melekh*, for example, the year 1575 (associated with the claims of Luria and Vital) indeed was the start of the messianic period. Because the Jews of that year were not deserving of redemption, however, God sends the soul of Messiah ben Joseph back into the world in every generation, in the form of a single *ẓaddiq*, and "if his generation is worthy, he will redeem Israel." In other words, *any ẓaddiq ha-dor* may in fact reveal himself to be messiah; there is no difference between the 'bearer of the messianic soul' and messiah himself except the quality of the generation in which he lives! The *ẓaddiq ha-dor* is indeed messiah, and if his generation is deserving, he may reveal himself as such. Sources emanating from Safed further portray the messiah, in a description intended to fit the figures of Luria and Vital, as

> 'a man of pain and one who has known illness' (Is. 53:5). I have received from my master [Vital] this interpretation of the verse: the redeemer of Israel will be distinguishable by two signs, pain and illness. 'A man of pain' means that he should be one who suffers always, and he should also be one 'who has known illness' constantly in his life.

It would be hard to imagine a description more like those of Nahman. While it is somewhat unlikely that Nahman had read the rather obscure work in which this passage is found, the ongoing tradition of the suffering attributed to messiah, stretching through the history of Judaism from Deutero-Isaiah down to Sabbatai Ṣevi, surely had a great effect upon him. The image of the suffering messiah, based on the verses in Isaiah, is found in Nahman's writings, an image that seems remarkably like the descriptions of Nahman himself.[23]

The specific claim that Nahman is Messiah ben Joseph has not generally been noted by scholars who have studied the literature of Bratslav. For this reason, the evidence for such a reading of the sources should be presented in full. Of course we could hardly expect either Nahman or Nathan to have the audacity of Hayyim Vital in this matter; the leaders of Hasidism, still aware of the calamities associated with messianic claims, would hardly have tolerated such opennesss. The fact that the point is made, albeit esoterically, in the sources, is in itself surprising in this climate.

The documentation for the belief that Nahman saw himself as Messiah ben Joseph is as follows:

1. The associations of messiah, Joseph, *ẓaddiq,* and sexual purity in *Liqquṭṭim* 2, as described above. Though the figure of Messiah ben Joseph stands in the background of this teaching, the evidence here in itself is not conclusive.
2. *Liqquṭim* 16, also quoted above, speaks of the two messiahs contained in the single *ẓaddiq*. The fact that Nathan, in commenting on this teaching, quotes Nahman as referring to a certain *ẓaddiq* whose spirit comprises both messianic figures, rather clearly associates Nahman with Messiah ben Joseph as well as Messiah ben David. The fact that we are told that this teaching has been censored, and that it aroused great agitation when it was revealed, tends to increase our suspicions.
3. It will be recalled that Nahman announced upon entering Zlotopolye that he had come there to perform a *tiqqun* for the sin of Jeroboam ben Nebat. Jeroboam's sin was that of idolatry, and we were hard-pressed to understand why Nahman found that particular sin so rampant in Zlotopolye, or why he used that rather obscure reference, rather than referring to idolatry in a more direct and simple way. The figure of Jeroboam also appears elsewhere in Nahman's writings, as a symbol of the great unbeliever.[24] Why should Jeroboam, who is not a particularly significant figure in later Jewish mythology, have such

importance for Nahman? The answer to this puzzle lies in a Kabbalistic association of Jeroboam with the Josephite Messiah, an association fairly widespread in the Kabbalistic literature of the seventeenth and eighteenth centuries. This association figures prominently in the closing chapter of *Megalleh 'Amuqot* by Nathan Shapira of Cracow,[25] where it is stated specifically that the sin of Jeroboam can be repaired by none other than Messiah ben Joseph, who will emerge from among his descendants. Because Jeroboam, the first ruler of the Northern Kingdom, was the leader of the tribe of Joseph, only the messiah whose roots are in that patrimony can set aright that wrong. We have had occasion elsewhere to show that Nahman had read the *Megalleh 'Amuqot,* and that this work is one of the major sources for the idea of *ẓaddiq ha-dor*. In describing his mission in Zlotopolye as that of providing a *tiqqun* for the sin of Jeroboam, Nahman was making a direct, if esoteric, reference to a messianic claim.

4. The following passage, based on that same chapter in *Megalleh 'Amuqot,* is found in one of the later collections of Bratslav literature:

> All of the elect ones in recent generations, including Luria, the BeSHT, and Nahman, come from the 'side' of Messiah ben Joseph. The very need for this messiah stems from the deaths of the *ẓaddiqim*. The *ẓaddiqim* are greater in their deaths than in their lives; even in the Exodus from Egypt, Moses had to take the bones of Joseph with him, and was thus bound to him.[26]

The obscure reference to the deaths of the *ẓaddiqim* here seems to point to the very idea we quoted from the *'Emeq ha-Melekh:* it is only because the previous *ẓaddiqey ha-dor* died without completing their task of redemption that Messiah ben Joseph has yet to come. Had the time been right, any of those listed could have revealed himself as the redeemer. The last line of this passage is of great interest. The Biblical Joseph was a prior, perhaps the first, incarnation of Messiah ben Joseph. Moses, who prefigures Messiah ben David, has to take Joseph's bones with him in order to bring about the redemption. The relationship of Joseph to Moses is thus a prototype of the relationship between the two messiahs; Ben David's coming requires the deaths of Nahman and the others, all of whom here are seen to be participants in the Josephite Messiah's soul. This text was of course written after Nahman's death, and seeks to account for the delay in Ben David's arrival.

5. A later passage in that same volume makes the point completely

explicit and leaves no further need for interpretation. That passage comments first on Nahman's statement concerning the "certain *ẓaddiq*" who contained both messiahs:

It appears clearly from his holy words [preserved] orally that these words referred to our master himself. Even though the soul of ben David was also in him, *he was primarily from the side of Messiah ben Joseph.* Even though the ARI and various other singular figures in their generations were derived from Messiah ben Joseph, in him [Nahman alone] were fulfilled Scripture's words: 'Many daughters have done valiantly, but you have risen above them all' (Prov. 31:)

Immediately following this unequivocal explanation is a further comment on the matter of Moses and the bones of Joseph:

It may be further understood by bringing together certain words of Rabbi Nathan that like the changes mentioned above . . . [the difference between the redemptions from Egypt, Babylonia, and that of the future] so too is there a change in Israel's relationship to the bones of Joseph. In the first redemption this relation was marked by the taking of his bones. But now in each generation thousands of Jewish souls may merit to be bound to him by worshiping at that place where his bones are buried. This is what our master promised us in his great promise to all who would come to his holy grave. This too is an essential part of the 'beginning of redemption.'[27]

These passages are both so clear as to need little comment. To the later Bratslav community, at least by the latter part of the nineteenth century, it was completely accepted that Nahman had been Messiah ben Joseph. Others before him may have possessed that soul, but he had "risen above them all"; worshiping at his grave was worshiping at the burial-place of Joseph, and would surely help to bring about the final redemption. This belief of the later community was based on its understanding of Nahman's own teachings, and we have not the slightest reason to believe in this case that their reading was inaccurate.

6. Although Nahman's *Megillat Setarim* remains inaccessible to the scholarly world, its existence in manuscript form was disclosed by Nathan Zevi Koenig, a leading Bratslav *ḥasid,* as recently as 1969. Respecting the traditional ban, which forbids the publishing of the text itself, he does quote a highly revealing statement by Abraham Hazan, the son of one of Nathan's leading disciples and himself leader of the Jerusalem *ḥasidim* at the turn of this century. In con-

junction with *Megillat Setarim,* Koenig quotes Abraham Hazan as saying:

> The matter of Messiah ben Joseph. He [Nahman?] said that certain things will have to happen to Messiah ben David, and he will have need of the merits of those *ẓaddiqim* who have died before him. And Messiah ben Joseph will also die beforehand. And our master said *etc.* that he was completely pure in guarding the covenant, until he was able to reach the highest rungs and see how far this damage reaches. He wanted to negate this completely, but one cannot change nature *etc.* The aspect of Joseph, guarding the covenant, *etc.* And messiah *etc.* and will reveal the truth in the world. Amen, speedily in our days.[28]

Though the censor, author of those omnipresent 'et ceteras,' has obliterated a good bit of this passage, its meaning remains quite clear, particularly in the light of *Liqquṭim* 2 and certain other passages we have seen. Messiah ben Joseph is associated with the Biblical Joseph, the symbol of sexual purity. Nahman, in his struggles to completely obliterate his own sex drives, is identified with Joseph the *Ẓaddiq*. The fact that Nahman equals Joseph equals Messiah ben Joseph cannot now be made public; when Messiah *ben David* comes, however, he "will reveal the truth in the world," the truth that Nahman was Messiah ben Joseph.[29]

7. The climax of the messianic activity that gripped Bratslav took place, as we shall see, during the years 5565 and 5566 A.M. (1804–06). Toward the end of 5566, this period of messianic agitation came to a rather abrupt end. While there were certain events in Nahman's personal life that may account both for the upsurge and the waning of the eschatological fever, the passing of that year itself may be of great significance. The year (5)566 is nothing other than the numerical equivalent of the Hebrew words Messiah ben Joseph! While this equivalence is not mentioned anywhere in the published Bratslav sources, it is more than likely that it was central to the esoteric teachings distributed during that year, and afterwards burned. It seems inconceivable that Nahman, who is so concerned with the motif of Messiah ben Joseph, and whose works are so filled with numerological calculations, should not have noticed this fact.[30]

Some of the evidence presented here is admittedly circumstantial. Perhaps only Nahman's stated intention to rectify the sin of Jeroboam[31] may be most strictly called an unqualified statement on his own part of messianic intent. But together with this single statement, the various bits of circumstantial evidence, including the clearly expressed later beliefs of his followers, combine to point in this direction. Why all the censorship around this matter, both on the part of Nathan and of Nahman himself, if not to hide some "dangerous" claim lying at the heart of the matter? The assertion that Nahman is *ẓaddiq ha-dor,* said openly countless times in his own writings, could hardly be the source for such agitated concern. Was it mere coincidence that Nahman had his disciples disseminate secret teachings in the midst of great messianic fervor in the year that added up to "Messiah ben Joseph" and that his messianism sputtered to a close as that year ended? The picture that emerges from these sources is one of a growing messianic self-consciousness in Nahman, beginning with the move to Zlotopolye and climaxing in 1806, the year in which Nahman hoped his role as the Josephite Messiah would come to be known to the world. Throughout the period when he was publicly proclaiming himself to be *ẓaddiq ha-dor,* Nahman was entertaining the hidden hope that his generation would be found worthy, and that he would be the *ẓaddiq ha-dor* to bring about the End.

One might at this point ask what difference it makes whether or not Nahman thought of himself as Messiah ben Joseph. Is it not quite clear that he had openly claimed that role in fact, if not in title? The last of the great redeemers, he who makes the final preparations for the advent of Messiah ben David, is in fact Messiah ben Joseph, whether he chooses to claim that title or not. But to ask this question is to miss the point. Within the symbolic universe Nahman inhabited, a claim to the *title* of Messiah ben Joseph was vastly more radical than any assertion that one prepares the way for messiah's coming. The most exaggerated claims for the centrality of the *ẓaddiq* were quite acceptable within the particular orthodoxy characteristic of Hasidism; while *mitnaggedim* might scoff, *ḥasidim* would have little difficulty in appreciating a *ẓaddiq's* claim that he could redeem the souls of his disciples. A claim of messiahship, on the other hand, even that of ben Joseph, was an entirely different matter. Had this claim become public knowledge, Nahman's name would have become anathema to *ḥasid* (outside his own community of followers) and *mitnagged* alike. The painful memories of Sabbatianism and Frankism were by no means dead in early nineteenth-century Poland; to evoke the symbol of messiah on one's own behalf would have been unthinkable blasphemy to most of the Hasidic masters. No wonder that Nahman took care in his early years to keep all the hardwritten copies of his teachings safe from probing eyes of any outsider. Even when he did print the teachings, he was careful to delete some of the most sensitive passages. A learned and perceptive reader might easily have seen between the lines, and brought untold wrath down upon the heads of Nahman and his disciples.

The preeminence of the talk about Messiah ben Joseph in Nahman and in the later Bratslav sources surely does not exclude an aspect of Nahman which is also related to the final redeemer, the messiah of the House of David. He spoke, we will recall, of a *ẓaddiq* who included within him elements of *both* messianic figures; it was from the Davidic line that both of Nahman's parents' families claimed descent, a claim which surely had some influence on his own messianic dreams. By pointing to himself as Messiah ben Joseph, Nahman did not mean to exclude himself from a role in the final act of the redemptive drama as well. True, that messiah must die before the son of David may arrive. But now there enters into the Bratslav tradition a new element, one not ordinarily associated with the Josephite messiah tradition: the hope of his *return* from death. The writings of both Nathan and the later Bratslav leaders point to this anticipated return any number of times. Particularly in their interpretations of the master's highly esoteric *Tales,* as Piekarz has shown, do these hints show through. At times the relationship of this return from death to the final redemption is perhaps peripheral: Nahman has to come back to tell a tale he never got a chance to tell in his lifetime, or the like. Such a prediction in itself is not totally strange in a world where metempsychosis is the norm. But in other places, both in Nathan's *Liqquṭey Halakhot* and in the writings of his successors, there is no indication of the slightest doubt that it is to claim the final redeemer's mantle that Nahman is to return to earth.[32]

Given the alleged Davidic descent of his family, as well as his claim to possess the soul Messiah ben David would bear in the future, we might ask why Nahman seemed to prefer the Messiah ben Joseph title for himself, at least in his present incarnation. We understand why later disciples would ascribe that role to him; he had indeed died in the course of the redemptive struggle, exactly as that figure was supposed to do. But why should Nahman himself have gone that way? In the heat of his messianic fervor he might have claimed, as had the Sabbatians, that the Josephite messiah had already died unnoticed some time earlier, and that therefore the road was already prepared for the Great Event itself.

Even at his most grandiloquent, in the moment when he dared to put forth his messianic fantasies, Nahman remained his own torn, ambivalent self. As we have said, the associations of Messiah ben Joseph with suffering and martyrdom undoubtedly seemed appropriate to him. But more than that, one discovers by a close reading that the legacy of Messiah ben Joseph's soul, unlike that of David, is a morally ambiguous one. The soul of the Davidic messiah, according to Lurianic sources, came through Moses and David; its first appearance in the world had been in Adam's son, Abel. It had then been the soul of those *ẓaddiqim* whom we have had occasion to mention elsewhere. There is no "blemish" to be found in this record. But Messiah ben Joseph's soul had formerly been that of *Cain,* the original sinner and object of divine curse. True, it had then been incarnate in Joseph the *ẓaddiq*—but it had also been the soul of none other than Jeroboam, the first Josephite king, one whom God had hoped to make into that messiah, but who had turned out to be a sinner and idolator of the worst sort. Messiah ben Joseph comes to atone for Jeroboam's sins not only because he is a descendant of that king, but because he has *been* Jeroboam himself. Jeroboam, described elsewhere by Nahman himself both as idolator and as the father of all heretics or doubters, and now returned in the person of redeemer, is precisely the kind of figure with whom Nahman can identify. Here his own doubts and burdens of guilt are explained, while at the same time his vindication is clearly to be seen. He who had depicted himself as both the great tree and the one who was rotting in hell now makes the final claim for himself as suffering redeemer. What more appropriate rubric for such a claim on Nahman's part than that of this messiah, Joseph the righteous and Jeroboam the sinner all in one? How perceptive, perhaps beyond its own ability to articulate, was the later Bratslav tradition that said "he was primarily from the side of Messiah ben Joseph"![33]

Further examination of most of Nahman's teachings from the years 1803 and 1804 would show that they are filled with semi-veiled references to his emerging messianic mission. But it was only on Rosh Hashanah of 5565 (September, 1804) that these emerging lines were drawn together into what must be seen as one of Nahman's most significant teachings, in which he presents a clearly drawn step-by-step *plan* of action to bring about the final redemption. It is hard to think of any other instance in all of later Jewish literature (before Zionism) of such a clear blueprint for the bringing on of the millennium as there is in the twentieth teaching of *Liqquṭey MoHaRaN*. While the battle is to be fought strictly within the realm of the spirit, as before, the political implications of Nahman's scheme are now quite clear: he is calling for nothing less than the liberation of the Jewish people through the (forced?) cooperation of its Russian oppressors and the return of Israel to the Holy Land. Because this teaching is so revolutionary in its implications and has not generally been recognized as such, we shall focus a good deal of attention on it. Later tradition records that Nathan felt "thunder and lightning in his mind" as Nahman spoke this teaching, a clear indication that the disciple recognized it as a unique event.[34]

Uniquely among Nahman's teachings, *Liqquṭim* 20 is offered as a commentary on a dream or a vision he had. Both dream and teaching are expressed in terms of a highly complex personal symbolism, a symbolism for which the reader is asked to have an extra measure of patience, as we seek to expound it. We begin with the text of the dream/vision:

This is what he told in early summer of 1804. He said:

I shall tell you what I saw, and you tell it to your children. There was a man lying on the ground, and about him people sat around in a circle. Outside that circle was another circle, then another, and yet several more. Some other people were standing about, in no particular order, outside the outermost circle.

The one seated (he was leaning on his side) in the center was moving his lips, and all those in the circles moved their lips after him. Then I saw that he was gone, and everyone's lips had stopped moving. I asked what had happened, and they told me that he had grown cold and died. When he had stopped speaking, they all stopped.

Then they all began to run, and I ran after them. I saw two very beautiful palaces, and in them stood two officials. Everybody ran up to these two and began to argue with them, saying: 'Why do you lead us astray?' They wanted to kill them, and the two officials fled outside. I saw them and they seemed good to me, so I ran after them.

In the distance I saw a beautiful tent. Someone from there shouted to the officials: 'Go back! Collect all the merits which you have and take them to the candle which is suspended there: in that way you will accomplish all that you need to do.' They went back and took their merits—there were bundles of merits—and ran to the candle. I ran after them and I saw a burning candle suspended in the air. The officials came and threw their merits onto the candle. Sparks came out of the candle and entered their mouths.

Then the candle turned into a river, and they all drank of its waters. Beings were created inside them; as they opened their mouths to speak, these beings—which I saw as they ran back and forth, were neither man nor beast—came out of them.

They then decided to go back to their place. But they said: 'How shall we be able to go back?' One of them answered: 'Let us send someone to him who stands there with the sword that reaches from heaven to earth.' They said: 'Whom shall we send?' And they decided to send those newly-created beings. I ran after them, and I saw the frightening one who reached from earth to heaven, as did his sword. The sword had several blades; one was for death, one for poverty, another for illness, and still others for other forms of punishment. They began to plead: 'It is so long that we have suffered from you. Now help us, and bring us back to our place.' (He said: 'I cannot help you.') They pleaded: 'Give us the blade of death and we shall kill them.' But he was not willing. They then asked for some other blade, but he was not willing to give them any. They went back.

Meanwhile, a command was issued to execute the officials, and they were decapitated.

Then the whole thing began again: there was someone lying on the ground, people about him in circles, running to the officials, and all the rest. But this time I saw that the officials did not throw their merits into the candle. They rather took their merits with them, walked up to the candle, and began to plead before it in broken-hearted supplication. As sparks from the candle entered their mouths, they once again began to plead. The candle became a river, the creatures emerged, and so forth.

They said to me: 'These will live. The former ones were condemned to death because they threw their merits into the candle, and did not supplicate, as these did.'

I did not understand the meaning of this thing. They said to me: 'Go into that room and you will be told the meaning.' As I entered the room, I saw an old man, and I asked him about it. He took his beard in his hand and said: 'This is my beard, and that is the meaning of the thing.' I said to him: 'I still don't understand.' He told me to go into another room, and there I would find the meaning. As I entered that room I saw that it was of endless length and endless breadth, and completely filled with writings. Any place I opened any one of them, I found another comment on the meaning of this thing.

[Nathan adds:]
I heard all of this directly from his holy mouth. He said that all of his teachings contain hidden references to this event, and that his teaching in *Liqquṭim* 20, which begins: 'Nine *tiqqunim*' is wholly a commentary on this.[35]

Before we turn to that teaching, where much of this fantastic web of symbols is explicated, we may point out a few of the more obvious associations. The figure at the center, given Nahman's association of *ẓaddiq* and center, is most probably the *ẓaddiq* himself. "A beautiful tent," from which a voice emerges, would seem to be the Tent of Meeting; the strange beings which "ran back and forth" seem to be somehow linked with the beasts of the *Merkavah*. The tall, frightening figure with the many-sided sword is surely some kind of demonic character, based upon the figures of the Cherubim with their flaming swords who block off the way to Eden after Adam is expelled. All such identifications, however, are tentative and inconclusive, until we have a better idea of the meaning of this vision as a whole. For a further understanding of the vision, we turn to the teaching Nahman himself has characterized as a commentary on it:

NINE PRECIOUS *TIQQUNIM* HAVE BEEN GIVEN TO THE BEARD . . .[36]

Know that there is a soul in the world through which all interpretations of the Torah are revealed. That soul is burdened with suffering, subsisting on bread and salt, and drinking measured bits of water, for such is the way of Torah. All interpreters of Torah receive [their words] from this soul. All the words of this soul are as hot as burning coals, for it is impossible to draw forth words of Torah except from one whose words are like burning coals, as Scripture says: 'Are not my words like fire?' (Jer. 23:29). And when this soul falls from that rung, and its words become cold, it dies. When it dies, the interpretations that had come through it also disappear. Then all the interpreters are unable to find any meaning in the Torah, and this gives rise to the controversies that come about between the *ẓaddiqim*. Controversy exists in the world primarily because of a lack of proper interpretation of the Torah, as such an interpretation would have provided an answer to silence all the controversies and objections.

This is the meaning of 'the Wilderness of Zin' (Num. 20:1), referring to the words which have grown cold [*Ẓin* equals *ẓanan*, 'to grow cold']. That is where Miriam died, for Miriam represents that soul which has suffered the bitterness [Miriam equals *merirut*, 'bitterness'] of slavery for the sake of Torah. Only then did 'the people quarrel with Moses' (*ibid.*, vs. 2–3), as this [death] gave rise to controversy. Interpreters of the Torah are called teachers *[morim]* because they receive from that soul which is called Miriam. . . .

We may interrupt Nahman's discourse at this point, to note a number of associations in the vision that are now better understood. The person at the center is indeed the *ẓaddiq ha-dor,* the channel through which all his contemporaries receive their Torah. They are able to move their lips only when he does, as their interpretive powers flow only from him. That figure's "growing cold" probably refers to Nahman's own periodic states of "knowing nothing," when the flow of his Torah ceases; these periods are a kind of "death" within life. Nahman's soul is here identified with Miriam, for whose sake, according to the rabbis,[37] a miraculously portable well accompanied Israel through their wanderings in the desert. There is an unspoken play on words here, involving the rabbinic statement, "When Miriam died, the well disappeared." The Hebrew word for well *(be'er)* can also have the meaning of 'interpretation'; the phrase would then come to mean, "When the soul that suffers bitterness dies, interpretations cease." The *ẓaddiq* is the wellspring of interpretation.

Nahman continues:

He who wants to interpret the Torah has to begin by drawing unto himself words as hot as burning coals. Speech comes out of the upper heart, which Scripture calls 'rock of my heart' (Ps. 73:26). The interpreter [first] has to pour out his words to God in prayer, seeking to arouse His mercies, so that the heart will open. Speech then flows from the heart, and interpretation of the Torah flows from that speech. This heart is called 'rock' *[sela'],* and speech comes from it, as has been said: 'a word for a *sela*'[38] . . . As the heart's compassion is aroused it gives forth blazing words, as Scripture says: 'My heart blazes within me; the fire of my words burns on my tongue' (Ps. 39:3). On this heart are inscribed all the interpretations of the Torah, as in: 'Write them upon the tablet of your heart' (Prov. 3:3). And so anyone who seeks to bring forth an interpretation must get it from this heart, by prayer and supplication. It is for this reason that teachers of Torah, before they begin their expositions, first have to pour out their prayers to God, in order that the heart be aroused to pour forth words like blazing coals. Only afterwards may they begin to teach, for the rock has been opened and its waters have begun to flow.

But there is a difference between those interpretations which a man comes upon when he is alone and those which he explicates in public. For when one preaches publicly, he first binds his soul to those of his audience, and then pours out his prayer to God. And surely 'the great God will not reject this prayer' (Job 36:5). The prayer of a lone individual may, however, be rejected. This is the meaning of 'Speak to the rock before their eyes' (Num. 20:8). Your prayer must take place when the people are already assembled, as it says [earlier]: 'Assemble the people' *(ibid.).*

The identity of the two officials in Nahman's vision is now clear to us: they are Moses and Aaron, and the entire passage is revealed as a commentary on Numbers 20, the story of the Waters of Meribah. The two officials' act of throwing their merits into the candle is the sin of Moses and Aaron in striking the rock, for which they, like the officials in the dream, must die. Because of their sin, they also fail to lead those about them to "go back to their place," a reference to the fact that Moses and Aaron, because of this sin, were not able to lead Israel into the Promised Land. We shall have more to say below of this symbolic view of Moses and Aaron at Meribah. While the appearance in the vision of "that frightening one who reaches from earth to heaven" and his sword had led us to believe that the theme was the return to Eden, it is now clear that the two great motifs of redemption, the return to Eden and the restoration of Israel to the Holy Land, have come together through the various symbols here, a confluence which is in no way surprising. The teaching continues:

This is the difference between learning from a book and hearing the teaching personally from a sage. He who hears from the sage directly binds his soul to that of the sage in this prior prayer . . . and the wickedness which lies inside each of those people who hears the teaching is vanquished by the goodness which dwells within the sage. As their wickedness is vanquished, so are those enemies, the *qelipot,* which surround the upper heart. Thus Scripture refers to the heart by saying: 'I have placed Jerusalem in the midst of the nations' (Ezek. 5:5), and she is the heart, as in 'Speak unto the heart of Jerusalem' (Is. 40:2).

This is the staff, of which God said to Moses, 'Take your staff and assemble the people' (Num. 20:8). The staff is the authority and power which the *zaddiq* has created by his worship, through which the enemies, both above and below, are vanquished. . . .

The *zaddiq* who prays before he begins to teach (the figure at the center of the circle in the vision) has a threefold purpose in mind. He seeks to join his prayer to that of the community, ensuring that God will not reject his plea. He also hopes to uplift his hearers by his words, and vanquish the evil that lies within them. But this act of conquering evil has yet another meaning, which brings it close to the area of sympathetic magic: the *zaddiq* is the heart of the lower world; as he vanquishes the evil in those who surround him, he also vanquishes the evil forces that surround the upper heart, his counterpart in the world above. This was also the task of Moses and Aaron in assembling the people, a task in which they did not succeed.

When he prays before teaching, he has to pray in supplication, begging of God that He give him a free-will gift, and not making the matter dependent upon his own merits. Even though the 'staff of power' (Ps. 110:2) that comes from his own devotion has been aroused, this staff does not exist to be used pridefully, but only to vanquish evil from those who are assembled. . . .

This was the mistake of Moses . . . he used his staff not for the community, but used it in his prayer . . . he 'lifted up' his prayer [showing pride before God], and did not bind himself with the community. 'He struck the rock twice with his staff' (Num. 20:11) . . . he struck the upper heart, as one taking something by the force of his own power . . . and [therefore] he died before his time. . . .

The authority of Moses, here fully identified with that of the *ẓaddiq*, is to be used to rectify the sins of those around him. When turning to God, however, the only proper attitude is that of Nahman, that of supplication with a broken heart. In terms of the vision, Nahman now knows the mistake of the officials. *The vision repeats itself, meaning that the opportunity of Moses is given to each later bearer of the Mosaic soul. Now Nahman can correct Moses' error, supplicating the candle (equals "rock" equals "upper heart") rather than forcing it,* and thus bringing about the desired result. This result, while not stated in the vision, is clear in the teaching, which notes that the account of the Waters of Meribah is immediately followed in the Biblical text by: "Moses sent messengers [*mal'akhim* also can mean 'angels'] from Kadesh [lit.: "from the holy"] to the king of Edom, [saying]: Thus says your brother Israel: You know of all the suffering which we have undergone . . . We called out to the Lord and He heard our voice and sent an angel, bringing us out of Egypt . . . Let us pass through your land . . ." (Num. 20:14–17). Edom, the conventional symbol for Christendom, is the force standing in the way of Israel's return to the Holy Land. The teaching goes on to make this clear:

By virtue of the Torah which one draws forth, one merits the land of Israel, as Scripture says: 'He gave them the inheritance of the nations' (Ps. 105:44). But the land of Israel is one of those things that is attained only through suffering. These sufferings stem chiefly from those obstacles caused by the wicked, who speak ill of the Land. First one has to vanquish these wicked ones, punishing them by the sword, and only then can one get to the Land of Israel.

But the power to punish these wicked ones can only be obtained from the hands of Edom, for this is his power, as is written: 'You shall live by your sword' (Gen. 27:40), and he derives his power from the planet Mars.[39]

Know, however, that through the spiritual powers generated by the letters of the Torah which one has brought forth, powers which are themselves angels, one can obtain from Edom the power to put the wicked to the sword. . . .

But sometimes the situation is reversed. Sometimes there is so little holiness to be found that these angels created by the words of Torah are weak, and can only humble or frighten the wicked, but not destroy them. And sometimes even humbling them is beyond the angels' power. There is so little holiness that they have the strength only to arouse the power of the nations against those who speak ill of the Land [but not to take that power themselves]. This is the situation in our present exile, where we ourselves do not have the power to punish the wicked except through [Edom's] laws . . . receiving from them the power to pursue the wicked. . . .

This is the meaning of NINE PRECIOUS *TIQQUNIM* HAVE BEEN GIVEN TO THE ELDER. To the elder who sits and teaches, these nine qualities have been given:

1. 'Take the staff.'
2. 'Assemble the people' to vanquish their wickedness.
3. 'Speak to the rock' in supplication.
4. Do this 'before their eyes' and be joined to them.
5. Draw forth words of fire.
6. Draw forth Torah.
7. The creating of angels.
8. Receiving the power from Edom to overcome our enemies.
9. Going to the Land of Israel.

These are the nine *tiqqunim* which have been given to the elder who teaches.

In the last part of this teaching, not reproduced here, all the strands of associations in the teaching are woven together to form a verse-by-verse commentary on Moses' request of the King of Edom. The picture presented here is now quite complete. Nahman has presented himself as the new Moses, marshaling the spiritual forces that are at the *ẓaddiq's* command, to bring about the redemption. The true focus of his entire career is here laid out before us. The gathering together of his band of followers, his teachings, and his heartfelt prayers are all part of a larger plan, one that will allow Israel to pass through the Kingdom of Edom (read: Russia) to return to the Holy Land. As Israel does not have the power in the exile to take command of Edom by force, Nahman seems to have in mind an attempt to persuade the Russian government to allow the rabbis and *zaddiqim* to share in its powers. They are to be won over by the strength of Israel's exemplary piety, which will motivate them to allow the pious to punish the "wicked" (probably the *maskilim*),[40] thus vanquishing the spiritual foe and allowing for the return to Erez Israel. It is perhaps fortunate that Nahman's plan was never put to the test; the Western-looking government of Alexander I would hardly have chosen to share its powers with the leaders of Hasidism, which was viewed as the great reactionary obstacle to the improvement of the Jews' position. Politically Nahman remained utterly naïve. He lived wholly within his own mythic universe, and saw the drama of redemption as one to be played out in the world of spiritual struggle between the classic warring forces of good and evil, Israel and the nations. Even though the specific events, both political and personal, of his own lifetime may have contributed to his messianic consciousness, the real plane of action for him was still the timeless world of mythical and spiritual confrontation.

We are now able to trace certain stages within the development of Nahman's strivings for redemption. While there was not yet any messianic intent involved in his 1798 journey to Erez Israel, it was shortly after his return from that journey that this new sense of his own role began to develop. Undoubtedly it was in part the inspiration of the journey that began to move him in this direction. When he moved to Zlotopolye in the summer of 1800, he already had begun to think of himself as Messiah ben Joseph. Publicly proclaiming himself as *zaddiq ha-dor,* he knew within himself (as witnessed by his comments on seeking a *tiqqun* for the sin of Jeroboam) that the *zaddiq ha-dor* could in fact be messiah if his generation would allow it. He was at this point afraid to reveal his sense of messianic mission, even to his own disciples, except in veiled terms. Having seen the tremendous storm caused by his challenge to the Zeide even without the issue of a messianic claim, he undoubtedly thought it better to keep this belief completely quiet. In Zlotopolye the public emphasis was upon the single true *zaddiq* as the center of all things, absolving the sins of his disciples as they came to confess before him, and building the image of the *zaddiq's* soul as that of Moses and messiah.

On his arrival in Bratslav he became fascinated with *place,* and it was the image of uplifting the gentiles' lands to the spiritual level of Erez

Israel that took primacy in his consciousness. This fascination with Bratslav, we should add, by no means indicates an abandonment of his messianic strivings. Some two years later, however, Nahman's messianic dreams had gone beyond the conversion of Bratslav into a new spiritual center. As his messianic pronouncements became more frequent and open, it became clear to him that only a return to the *real* Land of Israel could satisfy his mission. This is proclaimed in the teaching we have just expounded, which dates from exactly two years after his arrival in Bratslav. As though to dispel any doubts as to what was meant by this teaching, Nathan records:

> After he presented the teaching on the *Nine Tiqqunim* . . . during the discussion I asked him: 'What do you mean when you refer to Erez Israel as the great climax of victory in the battle?' He was harsh with me and said: 'I really mean the Land of Israel, with those very buildings and houses!'[41]

While the geographical focus of Nahman's attention shifted between 1802 and 1804 from Bratslav to the Land of Israel, another *galut*-centered motif in Nahman's struggle for *tiqqun* did not change. Throughout Nahman's teachings, beginning in 1803, we find a strong current of interest in the *conversion* of gentiles to Judaism as a necessary prerequisite for the advent of messiah. While this idea in itself is not unusual, the emphasis placed here on the desirability of such conversions is completely unique within Hasidism. Rabbinic Judaism had always contained a certain degree of ambivalence toward converts. While the rabbis' suspiciousness of converts' motives and sincerity had caused them to say, "Proselytes are as bad to Israel as a sore on the skin," they had also formulated the belief that "Israel went into exile only so that they should gain converts." Generally speaking, Jews in Eastern Europe who were confronted by a potential convert were more frightened by the prospects of their neighbors' wrath than they were joyous that a new soul had discovered the truth of Judaism. Such conversions, which did occasionally take place in early nineteenth-century Russia, especially from within the ranks of the Subbotnik sectarians, aroused little elation in the Jewish community. This was not at all the case with Nahman: he was filled with joy when he heard reports of such conversions, and he saw these proselytes as individual precursors of the entire world's imminent conversion to Judaism.[42] His desire for *tiqqun* had to extend beyond the bounds of Israel; the coming redemption was to be that of all mankind, not that of Israel alone. The fact that almost all of Nahman's later tales are set outside the bounds of any particularly Jewish context may be seen as a continuation of this universal concern. In fact the central motif of several key tales is the salvation of a wicked or foolish kingdom through the *ẓaddiq*-redeemer, a motif more easily applicable to the conversion of gentile kingdoms than to wayward Jews.

Having presented a picture of the development of Nahman's messianic consciousness until the year 1804, we are now prepared to outline the events of the following two years, which represent the height of messianic activity in Bratslav. The teaching of the *Nine Tiqqunim,* with its plan of bringing the redemption, was the opening event in what may only be described as a period of intense millennarian fever, which was to climax in the dramatic happenings of summer, 1806. The significant events of that period are divisible into two groups, each of which should be described as a separate aspect of messianic activity: the sphere of penitential activity within the Bratslav community, and the publication of Nahman's teachings for a wider audience.

It was in the fall of 1804 that Nahman first asked his disciples to begin reciting the *tiqqun ḥaẓot* ("midnight vigil") prayers on a regular basis. This rite, first instituted by the medieval Kabbalists, had been widely disseminated with the spread of Lurianic Kabbalah in the sixteenth century. Among *ḥasidim* it had fallen into neglect, along with the general abandonment of Lurianic *kawwanot* in the liturgy among the *ḥasidim.* A dramatic rite of participation in the exile of the *shekhinah,* it is also to be seen as a theurgic activity aimed at restoring the *shekhinah* to its place and bringing an end to the exile. It should be remembered that Nahman had already described his own mission as that of *tiqqun ha-shekhinah;* his demand now that this rite be reinstituted among his *ḥasidim* indicates a move from theoretical discussion of this task to its real implementation in the sphere of ritual action.[43]

It was some half a year later that Nahman began promulgating the rite of *tiqqun ha-kelali.* As atonement for their sexual misdeeds, his disciples were instructed to recite ten psalms, paralleling the ten terms for praise commonly employed in the Psalter. Apparently convinced that this area of human sinfulness was a major factor in delaying the general redemption, he sought to neutralize its ill effects by the formulation of a relatively manageable rite of atonement. While reflecting Nahman's own concern about the evils of sexual sin, the *tiqqun ha-kelali* may also be seen as his attempt to free his disciples of the guilt he himself knew so well, lest it keep them (as it sometimes did him) from doing the work of redemption.[44]

In the fall of 1805, just as the year 5566 (equals Messiah ben Joseph) began, Nahman went still further in the matter of personal *tiqqunim.* Turning now to a more individualized approach to the matter of penitence, he assigned each of his close followers a certain regimen of private fasts during the new year, an act far less radical than, but somehow reminiscent of, the promulgation of a new sacred calendar in the days of Sabbatai Ṣevi. The setting in which this new discipline was proclaimed has been preserved for us by Nathan:

In the year 5566 [1805/06], between Rosh Hashanah and Yom Kippur, our master one day emerged from the ritual bath and announced that it had been revealed to him from heaven how our people were to conduct themselves with regard to fasting, all the days of our lives. [He was told] how many times each of us should fast in the course of a year, as well as how and when we were to observe these fasts. After the holidays, each one of us went in to him individually, and he gave us a slip of paper telling us when we were to fast. He had a list in front of him, written in his own holy hand, which we were not permitted to see. When I went in to receive my own list of fasts, I saw him sitting at the table with that paper, but I don't know what was written on it. He sat there for a long while, poring over his list, and it took him considerable effort before he could tell me on which days I was to fast. When he did reveal them to me, he had me copy them down, and warned me to take special care not to forget them, and not to lose my paper on which they were recorded. . . . We understood from his words that these fasts were very great and precious practices; happy are we who merited to receive them![45]

This three-stage succession of new devotional practices (*tiqqun ḥaẓot, tiqqun ha-kelali,* and private fast days), all instituted within the course of a single year, shows a remarkably intense climate of preparation for the messianic event. As Scholem has indicated with regard to Sabbatianism, an upsurge of penitential rites was one way in which Jews indicated their belief that redemption was at hand.[46] As was the case in much of early Sabbatianism, there was nothing in these rites themselves that was contrary to the law, or even in conflict with the norms of accepted pietistic behavior. At the same time, one cannot but wonder whether this rapid succession of new penitential practices, if indeed they were known of beyond the immediate Bratslav community, did not arouse some suspicion. Might this have been the time at which the Zeide's and

Barukh's personal enmities toward Nahman grew into an attitude of suspicion on the part of the Hasidic camp as a whole? It seems likely that Nathan's need to deny certain unstated things of which Nahman was accused, things "which never entered his mind," stems from this period, and from a, perhaps vague, awareness on the part of outsiders that the excitement brewing in Bratslav had a familiarly dangerous edge to it.[47]

Interwoven with these acts of purification was the greatly heightened activity of Nahman and his disciples in collecting, editing, and disseminating Nahman's teachings. The teachings, which had been kept secret until this point, were recorded only in various notes written as each teaching had been presented. Now Nathan was to edit these notes, some in the master's hand and some in his own, into a single volume. This was completed, with great effort, shortly before Shavu'ot of 1805. The manuscript volume was given to a binder in Bratslav, but Nahman took great care that Nathan or another member of the inner circle constantly keep watch over the binder, lest he show the teachings to anyone from outside the immediate community.

At the same time, Nathan was also instructed to prepare an abbreviated version of the teachings, more appropriate for popular use among householders, which was to present in distilled form the practical implications of each teaching, eliminating the abstruse and complicated literary references. This volume was to serve as a practical daily guide to life for the *ḥasidim,* pointing out the ways in which Nahman's thought might be crystallized into a workable set of spiritual disciplines. Nathan published this volume in Mogilev in 1811, under the title *Qiẓẓur Liqquṭey MoHaRaN.*[48]

While the wheels of this messianic activity had already been set in motion toward the end of 1804, further impetus was surely given the program by the birth of Nahman's first son, Shlomo Ephraim, just as Nahman was entering his own thirty-third year in the spring of 1805. This child was seen as the fulfillment of all his fondest hopes; no longer was it a grandchild, the son of one of his daughters, who was to be the last redeemer, but rather Nahman's own male heir.[49] It is not coincidental that the promulgation of the *tiqqun ha-kelali* was announced only weeks after this child's birth; the presence of the newborn redeemer on the scene greatly added to the urgency of preparing the way. Shortly after Passover in 1805, Nahman made another of his mysterious journeys, this time to Shargorod (a place where he had no known disciples). While we do not know what transpired on this journey—Nathan tells us only that it was "a great and exalted wonder"[50]—it certainly had to do with this mission of redemption. Shargorod, like Kamenets-Podolsk, had once been a center of Sabbatian activity, and it is possible that this journey, like his 1798 visit to Kamenets, was meant to expunge some remnant of the Sabbatian heresy before the effecting of the final redemption.

In any case, this visit to Shargorod somehow involved a great risk. Nahman felt that some terrible danger lay in the stirring of messianic longings, a danger which could bring to himself and others bodily harm, as well as spiritual harm that might damage the cause itself. After spending about two weeks in Shargorod.

he left there suddenly, fleeing as one would flee a fire. Afterwards there were indeed some terrible conflagrations there. But he said: 'If the people of Shargorod had only known how much good I did them, *etc.* Nonetheless, all this is better than blight, God forbid.' It was understood from his words that by his visit there he had saved them from a blight.[51]

This passage, like so many others here, must also be read through the censor's *"etc."*. Perhaps Nahman had seen that the sparks of Sabbatian impurity had condemned Shargorod to undergo some terrible fate in the coming judgment, and he had sought to effect a *tiqqun* that would avoid this fate. His success, however, was only partial, as it seems from this passage that he admits responsibility for the fires that took place after his departure.

The fears that accompanied Nahman's messianic activities were also evidenced closer to home. In that same spring of 1805, one of his granddaughters became seriously ill. Nahman seems to have felt that he was responsible for her illness, though even this could not ultimately deter him from his task:

He spoke to me at that time of the great and endless sufferings that he was undergoing. The focus of this suffering was his granddaughter, who was very ill with measles or the pox. He said that he felt each of the child's cries in his own heart, and wished that he suffered the disease in her place. He said that these are the incomprehensible ways of God. For there are, he said, ways of God that cannot be understood. He was referring to the fact that one righteous man may prosper, while another suffers, *etc.* . . . He then told of that which is found in *Shivḥey ha-ARI:* once Hayyim Vital was most insistent that Luria [the ARI] reveal a certain secret to him, and the ARI refused, on account of the danger.

Vital, however, was adamant, until his master finally had to reveal that thing. The ARI himself had said, after all, that he had come into the world only to effect the *tiqqun* of that single soul, the soul of Vital. But as soon as the ARI revealed that secret, his own son became ill and died. How is it possible to understand this? He did have to reveal that secret, after all, and yet he was punished nevertheless. These are the incomprehensible ways of God.[52]

Spoken in the spring of 1805, this reference to Luria and Vital must have meant a great deal to Nahman. Here he was, about to do much more than Luria had, by publishing his teachings and making many of his secrets available to anyone. And here was his grandchild, already ill, as though to show him that punishment lay not far off. He was undoubtedly familiar with the legend of Joseph Della Reina, as well as various other accounts of the dangers that lie in store for those who try to hasten the end before its proper time. The fact that his activities continued, despite the frightening portents of the fire in Shargorod and the illness of his grandchild, shows how thoroughly convinced he was of the authenticity of his mission—at least in those moments when doubt did not cause him to falter.

It was in the early summer of 1806 that Nahman finally deemed the world ready to have a taste of his teachings. He had an extra manuscript copy made of the *Liqquṭim,* and also entrusted some fragments of his more intimate teachings, which were later burned, to two of his most trusted disciples, Yudel and Shmu'el Isaac. The two of them were to go from town to town through the Ukrainian countryside, teaching bits of the esoteric (and probably messianic) doctrine, and leaving behind them in each town a few pages of the soon-to-be-printed *Liqquṭim.* This mission, little discussed by Nathan, is assigned great significance in later Bratslav writings. Abraham Hazan tells us explicitly that the purpose of the mission was "to hasten our redemption." He also informs us that Nahman tried to enlist the support of his friend and patron Levi Yizhak in this effort. The two messengers were to stop in Berdichev and ask that *ẓaddiq* for financial help in their journey. Nahman instructed them to ask for this money as funds for "dowering a bride." As Piekarz has rightly pointed out, this, too, is a code-name for the restoration of the *shekhinah,* the "bride" of God.[53]

The messengers had apparently departed shortly before Shavuʿot of 1806, the occasion that marked the great climax of Nahman's messianic activity. On that holiday he for the first time appeared among his disciples clad in an all-white garment, a symbol of purification that could hardly be ignored. While the custom of dressing in white had been known in some prior Kabbalistic and Hasidic circles, it had not been followed by Nahman before that time, and the teaching he presented on that day made its meaning quite clear. The teaching is filled with imagery of red and white, based on the verse "If your sins be red as scarlet, they shall beome white as snow" (Is. 1:18). He also made extensive references to redemption through the *ẓaddiq,* here personified by Simeon ben Yohai, and to sexual purification. The white garments Nahman wore on that day served as his announcement that the *tiqqun,* if not yet completed, had reached a significant new stage, one which now allowed for the symbolic proclamation that redemption was at hand.[54]

We may now do well to view this entire sequence of messianic events in consecutive order, which should more clearly show how they built to the single climax of this event:

September 17, 1804 (Rosh Hashanah)	The teaching of *Liqquṭim* 20, containing the plan for redemption.
Fall, 1804	Institution of *tiqqun ḥaẓot.*
Winter, 1804/05	Writing of *Qiẓẓur Liqquṭey MoHaRaN.*
Winter/spring, 1805	Editing of *Liqquṭey MoHaRaN.*
March, 1805	Birth of Shlomo Ephraim.
April/May, 1805	Journey to Shargorod.
April/May, 1805	Binding of *Liqquṭim* manuscript.
May, 1805	Institution of *tiqqun ha-kelali.*
October, 1805	Assigning of personal fast days.
May, 1806	Mission of Yudel and Shmu'el Isaac.
May 23, 1806 (Shavuᶜot)	Wearing of white garments.

One further event must now be added to this list, one that marked the abrupt end of Nahman's active messianic strivings, in his own view the single most tragic event by far of his whole tragedy-filled life. Within a few weeks after that Shavuᶜot at which he came out in white garments, Nahman's only son and the focus of his hope, Shlomo Ephraim, lay dead of an unknown illness. All of Nahman's worst fears had been realized; in an attempt to bring about the end, he had managed to destroy (so he thought) the one on whom all his hopes were pinned. There was to be no immediate redemption after all; the feverish activity of master and disciples had come to nothing. This, the greatest disappointment of Nahman's life, though somewhat veiled in the sources, does come through in certain places:

We heard from him [in August, 1806] the whole order of messiah's arrival. He said that he [messiah] had been ready to arrive within just a few more years, and he himself had known the precise year, month, and day on which he was expected. But now he certainly would not come at that time. We understood that this delay had taken place because his son Shlomo Ephraim had died. He had also told me the same thing previously, shortly after the child's death. . . .[55]

The messianic hopes of Nahman continued to flicker for a brief while. In August of 1806, during the week of Tishʿa be-Av, he revealed some portion of his hidden *Megillat Setarim* to a few disciples, and spoke again of the coming of messiah. But, as can be seen from the preceding passage which describes that event, it was already clear that messiah's coming was to be delayed and was no longer the object of direct agitation. The mission of his two disciples had failed for lack of support among their hearers, many of whom were undoubtedly *ḥasidim* of Nahman's detractors.[56] The private fast days were abolished in 1808; the *tiqqun ha-kelali* survived (as it does to this day) as a matter of personal purification among the Bratslav *ḥasidim,* but its original context was forgotten. Of the practice of *tiqqun ḥaẓot* and the wearing of white garments we hear no more from the sources; these were undoubtedly quickly abandoned. Nahman did go ahead with the publication of his exoteric teachings, still believing that their dissemination had some relationship to the ultimate redemption, but that redemption was now seen as somewhere in the distant, and unknown, future.

On Yom Kippur of 1806, just after the intended year of redemption had drawn to a close, Nahman apparently made a last, desperate attempt to force the hand of heaven and bring about the redemption.

On that Yom Kippur there was a fire here in Bratslav, during the Kol Nidre service. As the *ḥazzan* began the hymns which follow the evening service . . . we all scattered to save his house and his property, and the service was interrupted. Only after the fire was ended that night did about ten of us, including our master, gather together to complete the hymns. At the conclusion of Yom Kippur our master said that on this Yom Kippur he had wanted to effect something with God, *etc.,* and he had various claims concerning this matter . . . but the fire had confounded the thing. After his return from Lemberg [two years later] he spoke of this event, and it was understood from his words that since he had sought to do this thing on that Yom Kippur, there were great accusations against him on high, and the illness and sufferings which he still bore were due to this. And he added: 'Even though my intent was for the sake of heaven, nevertheless,' *etc.*[57]

Never again would Nahman seek to bring about the end by theurgic activity.

Nahman was deeply aware of the tragic character of his brief messianic career. He had faced a terrible test, and had suffered its consequences. He was now about to turn inward, seeking in the world of fantasy and imagination the redemption history had failed to provide. This was the origin of Nahman's *Sippurey Maʿasiyot,* the first of which was told in the midst of that tragic summer.[58] The pent-up dreams of redemption, which had first been expressed in this abortive attempt to proclaim the end, were now to find their expression in the beautiful and poignant tales Nahman was to weave during the four years of life yet remaining to him. Out of the tragedy of this summer was to emerge the new vehicle of creativity that would remain with Nahman until the end.

It was shortly after his son's death, in speaking with his disciples Nathan and Naftali, that Nahman offered one of the most profoundly personal teachings of his lifetime, one that deals with the relationship between suffering and creativity. The opening paragraphs of that teaching are particularly significant, offering Nahman's lyrical summation of his own career. Unable to force the hand of heaven and announce himself as messiah in his lifetime, he now offers himself as a sacrifice, hoping to effect by dying what he could not within life. The longing he had already expressed as a child to die a martyr's death had now catapulted into making him *the* martyr, the Ephraimite messiah who by his death alone can allow the final work of redemption to proceed.

Know that there is a field, and in that field grow the most beautiful trees and grasses. The great beauty and grandeur of this field cannot be described; happy is the eye that has seen it.

These trees and grasses are holy souls that are growing there. And there are also a certain number of naked souls which wander about outside the field, waiting and longing for redemption, so that they can return to their place. Sometimes even a great soul, upon whom other souls depend, wanders outside the field, and has great difficulty in returning. All of them are longing for the master of the field, who can concern himself with their redemption. Some souls require someone's death in order that they be redeemed, while others can be helped by acts of worship.

And he who wants to gird his loins, to enter the field as its master, has to be a very strong, brave, and wise man; a very great *ẓaddiq*. One has to be a person of the highest type in order to do this; sometimes the task can only be completed by one's own death. Even this [offering of one's life] requires a very great person; there are some great ones whose deaths would not even be sufficient. Only the very greatest of men could possibly accomplish the task within his own lifetime. How much suffering and hardship pass over him! But through his own greatness he transcends it all, tending to the field and its needs. When he does succeed in bringing those souls in from the outside, it is good to pray, for then prayer too is in its proper place.

This master of the field takes care of all the trees, watering them and seeing that they grow, and doing whatever else needs to be done in that field. He also must keep the trees far enough apart from one another, so that one does not crowd the other out. Sometimes you have to show great distance to one who has become too close, so that one does not deny the other.

And know that these souls bear fruit when they do the will of heaven. Then the eyes of the master light up, so that he can see where he needs to see. This is the meaning of 'the field of seers' (Num. 23:14). But when they do not do the will of heaven, God forbid, his eyes grow dark, and this is the meaning of 'the field of tears,' for it is weeping that ruins one's vision. . . .[59]

Longing as ever for the ultimate transcendence of his own suffering, and here even willing to give his life for the sake of that transcendence, the master finds his noblest vision clouded by his tears.

NOTES

1. Among early Hasidic writers, it was particularly Jacob Joseph of Polonnoye who emphasized the role of the preacher or Hasidic leader (the term *ẓaddiq* does not yet appear in that sense in his works) in *uplifting* those around him and binding them to God. In Jacob Joseph's view the preacher stands as an intermediary between God and the community. While maintaining his own close bond with God, he was to simultaneously bind himself to his congregation, thus creating through his own person a link between the upper and lower worlds. The influence of the *Toledot* in this area is to be felt in Nahman's thinking, but the difference between them is crucial. The *Toledot's* preacher, in sharing his own illumination with those around him, does effect a *tiqqun* in a very general sort of way, a *tiqqun* brought about by his sharing of his own *devequt*. The individual soul of each of his hearers and the particular 'damage' it has suffered are not much taken into account. Nahman's sort of *tiqqun* is much closer to that promulgated by the original Lurianic sources: a *repair* of the particular damage sustained by a given soul, through the *ẓaddiq* who both knows that soul and has the occult power to designate effective *tiqqunim*.

2. *Ḥayyey II* 2:64.
3. *Cf.* especially such later Bratslav collections as *Meshivat Nefesh, Hishtapkhut ha-Nefesh,* etc. Most of these, including *'Ot Berit,* dealing wholly with sexual sin and atonement for it, are completely composed of selections from the writings of Nahman and Nathan. In all of these, of course, the goal is to lift the reader from sorrow and lighten his burdens, but the "realistic" descriptions of "every man's" life which they contain are most interesting.
4. *Liqquṭim* 205. The *tiqqun ha-kelali* was first published in 1821 by Nathan's son Shakhna. See *Neweh Ẓaddiqim,* p. 57, which lists no fewer than fifty-four editions of the *tiqqun,* making it by far the most frequently printed work in all of Bratslav literature.
5. See Scholem, *Messianic Idea,* pp. 203*ff.* Both *devequt* and *tiqqun* are found as ideals in the Kabbalistic traditions of Safed. While *tiqqun* appears to play little role in such non-Lurianic works as De Vidas' *Reshit Ḥokhmah* or Azikri's *Sefer Ḥaredim,* in such Lurianic writings as Vital's *Sha'arey Qedushah* it is hard to separate the two goals from one another. The devotee does seek an experience that may be considered one of personal illumination, but in attaining this higher state of consciousness he is also helping to bring about *tiqqun.* On the relationship between *devequt* and *tiqqun* among the mystics of Safed, *cf.* Werblowsky's *Joseph Karo, Lawyer and Mystic,* p. 52*ff.* Scholem's claim (*Major Trends,* pp. 123, 278) that Jewish mystics seldom speak in terms of actual union with the divine is much less applicable to Hasidism than it is to earlier Kabbalah. Such formulations as "one should lose oneself completely in prayer" or "prayer is an act of coupling with the *Shekhinah,*" rare in the earlier literature, are commonplaces in the prayer literature of Hasidism. See Green and Holtz, *Your Word Is Fire,* where a number of such texts are translated. I. Tishby has also raised some questions on this thesis with regard to earlier Kabbalah; *cf. Mishnat ha-Zohar,* v. 2, p. 287*ff.*
6. The major sources for this debate are Scholem, *Major Trends,* p.325*ff.*, *Messianic Idea,* p. 203*ff.*; Dinur, *Be-Mifneh ha-Dorot,* p. 170*ff.*; Tishby in *Zion* 32 (1967) 1*ff.*, Schatz, *Ha-Ḥasidut ke-Mistiqah,* p. 168*ff.*
7. There was an upsurge in messianic feeling in the wake of Napoleon's victories, particularly around the years 1812–1814. While this is hardly seen in the theoretical literature of Hasidism, a number of the tales told of Jacob Isaac of Lublin, the Yehudi of Przysucha, and Menahem Mendel of Rymanow do reflect a high degree of messianic expectation. See for example *'Ohaley ha-Rabbi mi-Lublin,* pt. 3, p. 1. There does not seem to be any direct connection, however, between Nahman's messianism and that of these other figures, who were centered in Poland and Galicia, and whose messianic activities took place primarily after Nahman's death.
8. Weiss had guessed at the survival of this manuscript in his article on *Megillat Setarim* in *Qiryat Sefer* 44 (1969) 279ff. [equals *Meḥqarim* p. 189*ff.*]. As Chone Shmeruk noted on p. 443 of that same volume, N. Z.

Koenig's recently published *Neweh Ẓaddiqim* had indeed made mention of *Megillat Setarim* as an extant work (p. 77*ff*.).

9. *Contra* Scholem in *Alexander Marx Jubilee Volume,* Hebrew Section p. 461, this idea is not an original contribution of the Sabbatians. It is found quite explicitly in the Lurianic literature: *Shaᶜar ha-Gilgulim,* chapter 12, ed. Przemysl 30, and *Sefer ha-Liqquṭim,* wa-etḥanan, ed. Jerusalem 105c. *Cf.* also the remarks by Tishby, *Netivey 'Emmunah u-Minut,* p. 176*ff.* Nahman, too, sometimes identifies the future redeemer as Moses: *cf. Liqquṭim* 7:2.
10. On R. Simeon as a redeemer-figure see Genesis Rabbah 35:2 and *Zohar* 2:9a and frequently. On Luria, see below. For another Hasidic view on this see Israel of Ruzhin in *ᶜEser 'Orot,* p. 24. On *ẓaddiq ha-dor* as redeemer in Sabbatian sources see Scholem in ᶜAley ᶜAyin, p. 175. The Bratslav sources quoted here are *Ḥayyey II* 2:66 and *Yemey MaHaRNaT,* p. 22.
11. *Ḥayyey* 2:2; *Ḥayyey II* 2:3. For the traditional messianic signs see *Sanhedrin* 97–98.
12. Mendel Piekarz, *Ḥasidut Bratslav,* p. 56*ff*., Weiss in *Qiryat Sefer* 44 (1969) 279*ff*., and Zeitlin in *ᶜAl Gevul Sheney ᶜOlamot,* p. 327.
13. *Liqquṭey MoHaRaN* is arranged in roughly chronological order, with some major exceptions. The third teaching of the book was said on his entry into Bratslav; the first two teachings are undated and presumably earlier. In any case, this teaching cannot be any later than 1803, when Nahman completed the cycle of teachings surrounding the Rabbah bar Hanna legends, of which this is a part. On the setting of this teaching see also *Ṭovot Zikhronot* 2. It is based on a passage in *Tiqquney Zohar* 21, ed. Margaliot 44b.
14. The association of the Biblical and Kabbalistic Joseph with the figure of Messiah ben Joseph is also found in Lurianic sources. *Cf. Shaᶜar ha-Gilgulim* chapter 13 and especially Nathan Spira's notes *ad loc.* where the matter is discussed at length and with full awareness of the sexual side of this association. It is thence carried over into the writings of Nathan of Gaza and other Sabbatians (*cf.* Yaᶜel Nadav in *Sefer Shazar,* p. 320*ff.*) and also into the writings of Moses Hayyim Luzzatto, as quoted by Tishby, *op. cit.,* p. 178. There are a number of ways in which the messianism of Luzzatto parallels that of Nahman; a comparative study of these two figures might prove most rewarding. It would seem doubtful, however, that Nahman was directly influenced by Luzzatto's Kabbalistic writings, the most significant of which had not yet been printed in his day.
15. *Liqquṭim* 14:5, based on *Baba Batra* 73b and *Sanhedrin* 98a.
16. *Liqquṭim* 7:1.
17. *Ḥayyey* 4:13; *Yemey MaHaRNaT* p. 31; *Ḥayyey II* 2:34. Later editions of *Ḥayyey* based on that of Frampol, 1913, give the date for the wedding as 5502, an obvious misprint, since Nathan speaks of his presence there; *cf. Yemey MaHaRNaT,* p. 13.
18. *Liqquṭim* 11, end.

19. *Liqquṭim* 16, based on *Baba Batra* 74a.
20. *Ḥayyey* 1:6; emphases mine. This passage is repeated, with no significant addition, in *Parpera'ot le-Ḥokhmah,* a commentary on the *Liqquṭim* by Nahman of Cheryn, 15a. From there it is quoted by Weiss, *op. cit.,* p. 279. The reference to the two messiahs, in the same phrase used by Nahman, is found in *Shaʿar ha-Gilgulim* chapter 13, a chapter which seems to exercise a major influence here.
21. Sources dealing with Messiah ben Joseph may be found in the collection *Midreshey Ge'ulah,* edited by Y. Ibn-Shmu'el (Kaufmann), as well as in Ginzberg, *Legends of the Jews,* index, *s.v.* Messiah of Joseph.

    The serious differences between Sabbatianism and Nahman's messianic longings should not be minimized. In Nahman's case the concept seems to have been largely of his own making; his Nathan did not have nearly so central a role in forging the image of messiah as did the Sabbatian prophet Nathan of Gaza. Sabbatai Ṣevi was seen as Messiah *ben David,* a more radical claim than that which we are attributing to Nahman. Most significantly, there did not develop in Bratslav a myth of the messiah who transgresses the law in order to bring about the redemption. Nahman's movement thus remained within the pale of Jewish orthodoxy, and did not create around its central figure a mythology of demonic fascination.
22. D. Tamar, "Ha-ARI weha-RaḤaV ke-Mashi'aḥ ben Yosef," in *Sefunot* 7 (1963) 167*ff.,* has collected the relevant sources. On this particular matter, *cf.* p. 170.
23. *Cf.* *ʿEmeq ha-Melekh* 33b as quoted by Tamar, *op. cit.* For the penetration of this sort of thinking into the consciousness of Jews who stood far from Kabbalah or Hasidism *cf.* the note by Aryeh Lieb Lipkin in H. Medini's *Sedey Ḥemed,* v.1, p. 193. The same notion of a messianic figure in each generation is found in Nahman's writings in *Liqquṭim* 79 and *Ḥayyey* 1:36. The description quoted is from Hayyim ha-Kohen's *Torat Ḥakham,* also cited by Tamar, p. 171. For Weiss on Nahman as a type of the suffering messiah *cf. Studies in Mysticism,* pp. 106*f.,* 111.
24. *Liqquṭim II* 32, 80; *Ḥayyey,* addenda.
25. *Megalleh ʿAmuqot, 'ofan* 252, Lemberg, 1858, 50a, and not in *'ofan* 150, as stated by Tishby, *loc. cit.* A comparison of *Liqquṭim* 16, the text which speaks of the *ẓaddiq* who contains both messiahs, with the opening lines of this same chapter in *Megalleh ʿAmuqot,* which tells us that Moses contained both messiahs, leaves no doubt that Nahman knew this chapter and was influenced by it.
26. *Sippurim Nifla'im,* p. 109.
27. *Ibid.,* p. 123*f.* Emphasis mine.
28. *Neweh Ẓaddiqim,* p. 79.
29. *Cf.* also *Ḥayyey* 3:10; *Ḥayyey II* 2:3; *Yemey MaHaRNaT,* p. 32.
30. It is noteworthy that Yizhak Eisik Safrin of Komarno, a later Hasidic master with messianic dreams, bases his own claim to be Messiah ben Joseph on the fact that he was born in precisely this year—5566—numerically equiv-

alent to that figure. See his mystical diary *Megillat Setarim* (composed in 1845) 2a.

31. I am not at all convinced by Joseph Weiss' suggestion that the figure of Jeroboam in Nahman's writings is a cipher for Jacob Frank. Weiss says this (*Meḥqarim,* 25*ff.*, 245*ff.*) without any evidence at all other than his own rather romantic reading of Nahman as one who was ever attracted and fascinated by any and all sorts of heretical literature and desires. It is at this point that the careful scholar in Weiss was overtaken, perhaps by his own projections onto the figure of Nahman. The identification of holy books and heretical books that he attributes to Nahman (p. 245*ff.*) is the result of a similar wishful reading on his part.

32. See *Siḥot* 198, the first introduction to the *Sippurey Maʿasiyot,* and the verious sources quoted and discussed by Piekarz, p. 140*ff.* To these may be added the *Shir Yedidut,* a poem in Nahman's honor writen by Yehiel Mendel, a nineteenth-century *ḥasid,* and first published in Jerusalem, 1907. The first verse of the poem contains the line, "Your soul and your name were among the seven things that preceded Creation," an obvious reference to the rabbinic tradition (*Pesaḥim* 54a) to the effect that the name of messiah was one of the seven pre-existents. On the matter of Nahman's identity as Messiah ben Joseph or ben David, we should also bear in mind Scholem's observation (*Sabbatai Ṣevi,* p. 55) that "not all writers were careful to distinguish" between the two, and that we should therefore not apply the distinctions over-rigorously. On both the matter of Nahman's predicted return from death and the meaning of the obvious parallels here to Sabbatian doctrine, see Piekarz' very important note in Weiss' *Meḥaqarim,* p. 233. I tend to agree with Piekarz rather than Weiss that in several cases what we see is a structural parallel between Sabbatian and Bratslav thinking, rather than any direct historical borrowings.

33. The association of Jeroboam and Messiah ben Joseph has a long and complex history in Kabbalistic literature. In the Zohar (*Zohar Ḥadash, Balaq* 56a) it is stated that this messiah will arise from the *seed* of Jeroboam, through his son Abijah, who died in his youth (I Kings: 14:17). According to the Talmud (*Mo'ed Qatan* 28b), Abijah was a righteous child, who disobeyed his father's wicked commands. The *Zoḥar Ḥadash (loc. cit.)* claims that a child fathered by Abijah was born on the day that Abijah died, and that this child, who was raised in the wilderness, shielded from his grandfather's sins, is the progenitor of the Josephite messiah. Ginzberg (*Legends of the Jews,* v. 6, p. 308) knows of no pre-*Zohar* source for this notion. Thus far the idea is in no way surprising. Just as Messiah ben David comes from the Davidic royal house, it is entirely appropriate that the Josephite messiah stem from the royal family of the Northern Kingdom. Nothing is said in the *Zohar* literature of this messiah's repairing the damage wrought by Jeroboam.

It is in the Kabbalistic writings of the sixteenth century that this formerly obscure idea gained prominence and was dramatically altered. It is Vital, in

Sefer ha-Gilgulim, chapter 67, who says that "the soul which departed from Jeroboam before he sinned is to be reincarnated in the future as Messiah ben Joseph." In *Shaʿar ha-Gilgulim,* chapter 13 the soul of that messiah is associated both with Cain and with Jeroboam without that reservation as to its undefiled state. Messiah ben Joseph as Jeroboam reincarnate is a new idea here, one which goes far beyond the rather unspectacular claim of the *Zohar,* and one which indeed would open the door to speculations of the Sabbatian type.

Following Vital, the Italian Kabbalist Menahem ʿAzariah of Fano (1584–1620) took the idea still further, claiming that God had originally planned to make the Judaean king Rehoboam the messiah, and Jeroboam his second-in-command. *Cf.* his *ʿAsarah Ma'amarot, 'em kol ḥay* 10 (ed. Cracow, 1556?, 77b–c) and the other sources cited by Tishby, *op. cit.,* p. 320, n. 108. From Vital, the idea is also taken up by Nathan Shapira, whose *Megalleh ʿAmuqot* was first published in his home city of Cracow, 1637, and who is, in part, Nahman's source for this idea. At the very same time Nathan Shapira's book was being printed, however, the matter of Jeroboam and Messiah ben Joseph was also being debated in Amsterdam by the rabbi and Kabbalist Isaac Aboab and his opponents. Like Shapira, Aboab claimed that the soul of Jeroboam would be reincarnate in every generation, and would eventually be that of Messiah ben Joseph. *Cf.* the text of Aboab's *Nishmat Ḥayyim,* published by A. Altmann in *PAAJR* 40 (1972) 65*f.* Aboab cites the *Tiqquney Zohar* as a source for this idea, but Altmann notes (n. 49) that he was not able to find such a passage in the *Tiqqunim* or anywhere else in the *Zohar* literature, except for the single source we have mentioned above. Altmann does note, however, that yet another Kabbalist of the same generation, Abraham Azulai of Hebron (1570–1643), mentions the identification of Jeroboam and Messiah ben Joseph in his *Zoharey Ḥamah* to *Zohar* 2:120a. That text is paraphrased by Altmann from a reference in Reuben Margaliot's *Shaʿarey Zohar* 50a–b, but it seems that the text there does clearly describe the two as identical. A less definitive statement to the same effect is found in Azulai's *'Or ha-Ḥamah ad loc.* (ed. Jerusalem, 1879, 102d), in a passage attributed to Cordovero: "He [Messiah ben Joseph] is condemned to die in return for [*temurah le-]* the sin of Jeroboam, for idolatry is punishable by death." It would appear that this idea took hold in sixteenth-century Safed, and became the common property of the disciples of both Luria and Cordovero. The emphasis on *tiqqun* in the thought of Luria and Vital combined with the thought that one or the other of these masters himself was Messiah ben Joseph to ensure the popularity of this idea. From these sources the idea was taken over by the Sabbatians, for whom the idea of a messiah who had been tainted with sin in a previous incarnation was most exciting. It was from these Sabbatian sources that the idea came down to Moses Hayyim Luzzatto, who made much of it in his esoteric writings. See Tishby, *op. cit.,* p. 178*ff.* There is no reason to think, however, that Nahman's statement of this claim has Sabbatian sources; he learned it directly from the works of Vital and Nathan Shapira.

34. Nathan's reaction to this teaching is recorded in *'Avaneha Barzel,* p. 45. Zeitlin, *op. cit.,* p. 337, does quote a bit of it, but with little explanation and seemingly without recognizing its unique character. For other teachings of messianic import see *Liqquṭim* 13 and 14, dating respectively from Rosh Hashanah and Hanukkah of 1803.
35. *Ḥayyey* 3:3.
36. *Zohar* 2:177b, *Sifra di-Ẓeniʿuta.* The word *diqna* as used by Nahman will mean "elder" *(zaqen)* rather than the usual "beard" *(zaqan);* this play on words undoubtedly accounts for the last episode in the vision, where the elder makes reference to his beard. If Nahman is sticking closely to the text of the *Zohar,* that elder is God Himself, and the encounter with Him seems to mean: "Either you will understand all this through direct and immediate confrontation with Me, or you will have to seek its meaning in endless books."
37. *Taʿanit* 9a; *Mekilta, wa-yasaʿ* 5 (ed. Horovitz, p. 173). For a Hasidic parallel on the *ẓaddiq* as well or fountain *cf. Qedushat Levi, Yitro,* 134a.
38. *Megillah* 18a. In the Talmudic context *selaʿ* refers to a small coin; Nahman is interpreting it to mean "rock."
39. *Edom* and *Ma'adim* (Mars) are etymologically related; both are derived from the stem *'dm* ("red"). The warlike quality of Mars is here attributed to Edom, also based on Gen. 27:40. On the Land of Israel coming through suffering see Berakhot 5a.
40. The text sounds as though there were some specific incident in its background. Perhaps he was trying to justify the calling in of Russian authorities against the *maskilim,* though I have found no evidence of such a particular incident in this time and place. For a similar statement of the need for supernatural intervention with the nations in order that they act on Israel's behalf, *cf.* the *hope* expressed by Levi Yizhak in *Qedushat Levi, Purim,* 364a.
41. *Ḥayyey* 1:15.
42. The major source for Nahman's attitude toward proselytes is *Liqquṭim* 17:5–6. *Cf.* also 48, 59, 62, 215. This interest is still evidenced in his last teaching, *Liqquṭim II* 8:3–4, despite the decline of messianic urgency by that time. Zeitlin (*op. cit.,* p. 353*ff.*) has recognized the importance of this theme in Nahman's thought and its uniqueness in his time. On the Talmudic views of proselytes see *Yebamot* 47b and *Pesaḥim* 87b. Nahman echoes the latter view in *Liqquṭim* 17:6. On the Judaizing tendencies of the Subbotniks see *Encyclopedia Judaica, s.v.* Judaizers; S. Bolshakoff, *Russina Nonconformity,* p. 107*ff.*
43. *Yemey MaHaRNaT,* p. 14. *Tiqqun ḥaẓot* is not generally printed in Hasidic editions of the liturgy. On the Hasidic abandonment of Lurianic *kawwanot* *cf.* Weiss in *JJS* 9 (1958) 163*ff.* In this matter Nahman did follow the example of his Hasidic predecessors. See *Siḥot* 185.

44. *Yemey MaHaRNaT,* p. 17f; *Liqquṭim* 205; *Ḥayyey* 7:17.
45. *Ḥayyey II* 11:45.
46. *Messianic Idea,* p. 99*f.*
47. See Nathan's introduction to the *Sippurey Maʿasiyot.*
48. *Yemey MaHaRNaT,* p. 15*ff.*
49. *Ḥayyey* 1:28. *Cf.* Weiss in *Tarbiz̧* 44 (1969) 285, n. 15.
50. *Yemey MaHaRNaT,* p. 15.
51. *Ḥayyey* 4:18.
52. *Yemey MaHaRNaT,* p. 19. See also *Siḥot* 189. The tale of Luria's son is found in *Shivḥey ha-ARI,* p. 22.
53. *Ḥayyey* 7:8–11; *Kokhvey 'Or,* p. 52; *Neweh Z̧addiqim,* p. 80; Piekarz, p. 67.
54. *Liqquṭim* 29; *Ḥayyey* 1:20. The wearing of white garments on the Sabbath is mentioned in the Brody community's ban against the *ḥasidim. See* Dubnov, *Toledot ha-Ḥasidut,* p. 121. It is possible that this custom was eliminated in response to the opposition it aroused. Y. Eliach, in *PAAJR* 36 (1968), has pointed to the parallel between the Hasidic and Russian sectarian customs in the wearing of white garments. There is no need, however, to assume non-Jewish influence in this matter. White garments for the Sabbath are already prescribed in the *Ḥemdat Yamim,* pt. 1, ch. 3 (Constantinople, 1738, 27b), where Luria and Vital are quoted as authorities for the custom. *Cf. Shivḥey ha-ARI,* p. 6.
55. *Yemey MaHaRNaT,* p. 22, added by a later editor. On the death of Shlomo Ephraim *cf.* also *Ḥayyey* 6:1; 7:12; Piekarz, p. 78*f.;* Weiss, *op. cit.,* pp. 282 and 288.
56. *Kokhvey 'Or,* p. 52. The summer of 1806 was also a particularly rough period in Nahman's relations with the Zeide, who sought to denounce him to Levi Yizhak at that time. See *Tormented Master,* chapter three, and especially Piekarz, *op. cit.,* pp. 68*ff.,* where the matter is discussed in great detail. Later Bratslav tradition says quite openly that Nahman came very close to bringing messiah during that summer, had not Satan, personified in the Zeide, intervened. See *Be'ur ha-Liqquṭim,* p. 80, no. 6.
57. *Ḥayyey* 6:1. See also *Yemey MaHaRNaT,* p. 24.
58. *Ḥayyey* 1:59, 6:1. Piekarz, whose entire chapter on the events of 1804–06 is offered as an attempt to explain the origin of the *Sippurey Ma'asiyot,* in the end does not clearly state what connection he finds between Nahman's messianic attempt, which he describes in great and accurate detail, and the *Tales.* One gets the impression that he sees the tales as a direct continuation of that effort. If so, the thesis I am proposing here is contrary to his; I see Nahman's telling of tales as a result of the *failure* of that attempt, and a need to seek a new outlet for his longings.
59. *Liqquṭim* 65:1–2. *Cf.* the discussion in Weiss, *Meḥqarim,* p. 176. On the setting of this teaching, *See 'Avaneha Barzel,* p. 30. The reference to the "field of tears" is from *Mo'ed Qatan* 5b; the *z̧addiq* as gardener may derive from *Zohar* 2:166b.

16

Messianic Concepts and Settlement in the Land of Israel

Arie Morgenstern

Historians have not paid sufficient attention to the immigration and settlement of the disciples of the Gaon of Vilna in Palestine between 1808 and 1847.[1] In general, their immigration has usually been considered an integral part of what historians of Palestine call the "old yishuv". This lack of attention may be ascribed to two main factors. First, the leaders of the Ashkenazi community in Palestine in the second half of the nineteenth century deliberately obscured the ideological motivations of the Vilna Gaon's disciples, for these were based on the principle of messianic activism and thus stood in opposition to the traditional stance of passive waiting for the Messiah. Second, extreme secrecy characterized the activities of the Gaon's followers, who feared arousing Russian and Ottoman opposition to their immigration, and who were also wary of openly engaging in messianic activity. It is likely that the failure of previous messianic movements led the Gaon's disciples to refrain from recording their views in writing; thus their activities were not accompanied by a systematic ideological platform.

An overview of Jewish history during the first half of the nineteenth century reveals little indication of the immigration of the Gaon of Vilna's disciples to Palestine, not only because they did nothing to publicize their activities, but because the attention of European Jewry was then focused on the advent of the Reform movement in Judaism and the

Reprinted by permission of Yad Izhak Ben Zvi Press, Jerusalem, from *Vision and Conflict in the Holy Land,* ed. by Richard I. Cohen, 1985.

ensuing debates. Indeed, that period is marked by the physical and ideological distancing of the Jews from the Land of Israel, and by their efforts to entrench themselves in the Diaspora. Furthermore, of some three million Jews throughout the world in the early nineteenth century, only about 5,000 lived in Palestine, and most of these were Sephardic Jews. Thus, the ideological detachment of European Ashkenazi Jewry from Palestine was noticeable and significant.

The Reform movement in Judaism, which arose during the period of struggle for the political emancipation of European Jewry, was characterized, *inter alia,* by a detachment of the traditional messianic beliefs from the hope for the ingathering of exiles and the restoration of a Jewish Kingdom in the Land of Israel. Reform also transformed Jewish messianic beliefs from a particularistic faith to a universalistic *Weltanschauung* focusing on the idea of *tikkun 'olam bemalkhut Shaddai,* reforming the world according to a Divine plan. The talmudic statement that the messianic period would be distinguished merely by an end to Jewish political enslavement was reinterpreted and applied to the drive to obtain equal rights for Jews living among the gentiles, rather than to the aspiration for Jewish national liberation.

It should be noted that it was not Reform alone that infused new meaning into the traditional Jewish messianic expectations; Orthodox groups also sought to bridge the gap between the desire to acquire citizenship in the general society and the traditional messianic view. However, while Reform made no mention whatever of an existential return to Zion, Orthodoxy postponed the return to a future "messianic period", thus neutralizing any current, concrete political ambitions. The Orthodox position was based on talmudic and midrashic tales forbidding the Jewish people to hasten their redemption, retake the Land of Israel by force, or rebel against the gentile nations,[2] until the time comes for their miraculous redemption, as they were earlier redeemed from slavery in Egypt. This view, including an express sanction against those attempting to speed the redemption process, was widely accepted in Orthodox circles in both Eastern and Western Europe. The disciples of the Gaon of Vilna were exceptions to this rule; they favored messianic activism and claimed that the way "to raise up the *Shekhina* from the dust" was not solely by worship—observing the Torah and its precepts, as was generally accepted—but by settling the Land of Israel.

THE MESSIANIC VIEWS OF THE VILNA GAON'S DISCIPLES

The messianic philosophy of the Gaon of Vilna and his disciples has, by and large, not been a subject of historical investigation. Nonetheless, sources such as the facsimile letters of the *Pekidim* and *Amarkalim* (clerks and treasurers) of Amsterdam from 1825 to 1870, and other contemporary works, can provide an insight into their thinking. Two additional books which have come to my attention in recent years are primary sources of information regarding the messianic approach of this group.

The first of these books, *Hillel ben Shaḥar,* was written by R. Hillel of Kovno,[3] one of the earliest of the Gaon's disciples to immigrate to Palestine. His name is signed to a letter written on the 10th of Adar II, 5570 (1810) in Safed.[4] The second book, *Sha'arei Ẓedek,*[5] was written by R. Aviezer of Tykocin who went to Palestine in 1832 and became one of the leading scholars in the Perushim community of Jerusalem.[6]

Both books express, as the basis of their messianic views, belief in the existence of "favorable periods of time" as mentioned in the *Zohar*. R. Hillel explicitly notes the belief in two such "favorable periods" which should have brought redemption to the Jewish people:

> in the year 856 of the fifth millennium (= 1096), indicated in the verse "You shall give (*titnu,* equivalent to 856) redemption to the land" (Lev. 25:24) ... and in the year 408 of the sixth millennium (= 1648), of course, hinted at in the verse "With this (*zo't,* equivalent to 408) Aaron shall enter the holy" (Lev. 16:3) ... all this being completely true, were it not for the lack of repentance, which kept us from it [redemption].[7]

R. Aviezer of Tykocin also assumes the validity of "favorable periods":

> All Jews should realize that there have been a number of times for redemption which were cancelled because of the lack of repentance, i.e., times explicitly appearing in the holy *Zohar* ... but the Messiah did not come because, as we are forced to admit, Israel did not repent fully at that time.[8]

The belief in "favorable periods" leads us to the next step in the ideology of the disciples of the Gaon of Vilna, namely that the nearest favorable period to their days would be in the year 5600 (1840), as the *Zohar* states:

> When the sixth millennium comes, in the 600th year of the sixth millennium, the gates of wisdom above and the founts of wisdom below shall be opened ... and

God will raise up the nation of Israel from the dust of its Exile and will remember it.[9]

This is an explicit reference to a favorable period, mentioning the year without referring to alphabetic calculations based on biblical verses.

R. Hillel's book makes no specific reference to the year 5600, due to the restrictions on *ḥishuvei hakeẓ*. R. Aviezer, whose book was published in 5603 (1843), admits that the advent of the Messiah had been awaited in 5600:

From now on we shall have to explain how it is that the reference of the holy *Zohar* to the year 5600 did not materialize . . . for it clearly meant that he [the Messiah] should have come in the year 600 of the sixth millennium . . . and if so, why has our Messiah yet to come, for [the year] 6[00] has already passed.[10]

The Vilna Gaon's commentary on the book *Sifra Di-Ẓeni'uta* includes an allusion to the time of the redemption and to the fact that there are people who know when it is to come to pass:

All these days are an indication of six thousand years which are six days . . . all the details of these six days conduct themselves in the six millennia, each in its appointed day and at its appointed hour. Hence one can calculate the advent of the redemption coming at its appointed time, and I call upon the reader, in God's name, not to reveal this.[11]

The Gaon's disciples viewed contemporary history in the light of their messianic conception, thus discerning in the events of their day signs of the *'ikveta de-Meshiḥa* (footsteps of the Messiah), the last stage of the Exile. R. Hillel saw in the decline of Torah and Torah scholars and their replacement by unrestrained materialism clear proof that this period had arrived: "Alas for those who witness the decay of that generation, seeking peace and quiet in royal palaces and secure dwelling-places . . . Anyone who looks can see that these times are *'ikveta di-Meshiḥa* . . . ,"[12] and "The day God is to redeem His people is near."[13] He held that the pursuit of materialism causes Jerusalem to be forgotten and the Divine Presence to go into Exile; this is why the Exile was still in effect, because "the reason for the prolonging of the Exile is that we refuse to partake of the taste of Exile and prefer a high standard of living; if there is no Exile there can be no Redemption."[14]

R. Hillel did not believe that repentance would come about from love of God, but only from pain and affliction. He viewed the troubles besetting the Jewish people as an early, necessary stage in the redemption process, and so he awaited them almost joyfully:

We shall not escape repentance out of fear, when the nations oppress us and money is no more, God willing, shortly [sic!] . . . every day we shall await the coming of that hour, and we shall pray to the Lord, God of our fathers.[15]

Contrary to the later view expressed by Rabbi Z. H. Kalischer, whereby the civil emancipation and equal rights granted to the Jews in several European states were seen as signs of the approaching redemption, the Vilna Gaon's disciples looked upon the persecution of the Jews as the direct route to the final redemption. As the Gaon himself says:

All the persecutions the Jews undergo in Exile bring the Redemption nearer . . . and so all the maledictions [listed in the Mishna, at the end of Tractate *Sota*] are beneficial, in that they shorten the way to Redemption.[16]

R. Hillel, too, noted the mutual relationship between the improvement of the conditions under which the Jews lived and their forgetting the Land of Israel:

We all have luxurious tastes, seeking delightful clothing and royal palaces . . . and we unthinkingly ignore the fact that our land is desolate, with gentiles exulting in its Temple's being burnt to the ground; what has become of the vow we swore, "may my tongue cleave to my palate"? . . . We ignore the sorrow of the Holy One and His Presence.[17]

It is clear that R. Hillel thus linked his view of the contemporary period as *'ikveta di-Meshiḥa* with the redemption process which, in his opinion, had to follow the path of affliction:

The earth has caved in, it has crumbled, as changes take place daily in the world, for in my opinion and in that of anyone of perception, it is clear that the day the Lord will redeem His people is near.[18]

This pre-messianic era would be marked not only by political revolutions and wars, but also by the increasing oppression of Israel by the nations of the world.

When He unleashes a gentle wind from above to redeem us, liberation and repentance being denied us, then God will command the Heavenly Host . . . that is, He will also order earthly kings to increase their evil decrees . . . with the promise of setting up a king as terrible as Haman.[19]

In his discussion of the approaching redemption, R. Hillel mentions the kabbalistic principle that the redemption itself is to be hastened by "an awakening from below":

When the time of the redemption comes, as it must, either at its set time or speedily, with only strict justice holding it back . . . and God desires to arouse mercy to counter-rising justice, the holy *Zohar* lays down the rule that there is never an awakening up above *(hit'aruta di-le-'eila)* without a previous awakening from below *(hit'aruta di-le-tatta)*.[20]

R. Hillel does not explain exactly what steps are required, though the expression of his desire to go to the Land of Israel suffices to indicate the direction:

If God pardons me . . . and takes me out of this pit in the desert of the gentile nations, to bring me to the land of sanctity, of life, where my heart and eyes dwell constantly, waiting and anticipating going there . . .[21]

R. Hillel's desire to go the Land of Israel was linked to his expectation of redemption, and was for him a practical conclusion to be drawn from the ideas and aspirations he preached.

However, the messianic views expressed in the books of R. Hillel of Kovno and R. Aviezer of Tykocin do not necessarily lead to a deviation from the traditional concept that nothing should be done to hasten the coming of the redemption, other than observing the Torah and its precepts. Only the authority of a figure like the Gaon of Vilna, or a movement based on such an authority, could reverse that concept, and rule that the practical interpretation of "an awakening from below" in the redemption process is not merely spiritual, but is rather linked to clear messianic activism requiring settling the Land of Israel—and not by individuals alone, but by organized groups, which implied taking back the land by force.

It indeed seems that the appearance of the Vilna Gaon on the Jewish scene was interpreted by his disciples as marking the beginning of a new era in Jewish history. An analysis of their statements on this topic shows that they perceived in him a figure whose spiritual greatness and absolute command of all branches of Jewish thought, both simple and occult, was inexplicable in rational terms, but was rather a phenomenon that in itself constituted a Divine revelation:

God seems to have sent us an angel from Heaven, the famed Vilna Gaon, our teacher R. Eliyahu of blessed and righteous memory, to begin the restoration of Torah to its pristine glory . . . until the process reaches completion, when we are all worthy of the Divine light and abundance to be bestowed by the Messiah.[22]

In similar fashion the Gaon's disciple, R. Israel of Shklov, wrote of him:

> Secrets were revealed to him by our father Jacob, our teacher Moses and our prophet Elijah; and we are sending some of his holy mystic writings, and several secrets he uncovered, which had been completely concealed until he came.[23]

Thus, within the framework of the belief in the year 5600 as the imminent "favorable period", the Vilna Gaon's presence was a historic event marking the arrival of the *'ikveta di-Meshiḥa* period and confirming the validity of the entire messianic concept.

Against the background of these beliefs, one can understand why five of the six leading disciples of the Vilna Gaon emigrated to Palestine between 1808 and 1810,[24] and why 511 people closely associated with the Gaon's disciples arrived in Palestine by 1812,[25] filled with a sense of obligation to devote themselves to rebuilding the land and expanding the Jewish community therein. This feeling was shared by his followers who remained in Europe.[26]

The letter drafted in 1810 by the Gaon's disciples in Safed for the purpose of propagating their teachings gave expression in no uncertain terms to their special attitude toward the situation in the Land of Israel which signified, by its ruin, the exile of the Divine Presence:

> Good are its rocks and its dust; good are its grain and its fruits and its vegetables . . . Forgetting the Holy Land means—God forbid—prolonging the Exile, forgetting one's right hand . . . How long will it be before Jerusalem is pitied . . . with the Holy City, once a source of joy for the entire land, still delivered into foreign hands.[27]

Since "in this hidden redemption the Divine Presence cannot rise of its own accord from the dust,"[28] they felt it necessary to hasten the redemption process by human endeavor defined as *tikkun ha-Shekhina* "restoration of the Divine Presence," as opposed to a miraculous redemption. One of the most important of the Gaon's disciples even defines this as a "natural" redemption. R. Yehuda Halevi Edel claims that if, during the Second Commonwealth period, no overt and renowned miracles took place, obviously none can be expected during the third redemption either, the whole process being natural, taking place by means of human activity: "For in the future, the matter [the redemption process] will be conducted in a natural way, without miracles."[29] R. Israel of Shklov, who dispatched a messenger from Safed in 1831 to seek out the Ten Lost Tribes and ask their sages to officially recognize the jurisdiction of the rabbis in the Land of Israel, wrote them that it was obligatory to further the redemption process by human endeavor, "for everything first requires an awakening from below . . . Thus we have strengthened ourselves . . . and we are hereby dispatching a fair and honest representative. . . ."[30]

ABROGATION OF THE "THREE OATHS"

How did the Vilna Gaon's disciples circumvent the prohibitions connected with the "three oaths", such as the prohibition of hastening the redemption or that of mass settlement "by force" in the Land of Israel?

A cursory glance at their writings suffices to prove that they engaged in calculations of the time of redemption by means of alphabetic letter-values (*gematria* and *notarikon*). Their positive approach towards this activity contrasts sharply with the traditionally negative attitude towards any calculations of this type:

> It is certain that anyone taking the trouble to give expression to his feelings and calculate the time of redemption will be rewarded additionally, for by means of these calculations the belief of the redemption is reinforced in one's heart, and God desires to bring the Messiah by virtue of this belief.[31]

R. Aviezer of Tykocin ruled that the prohibition against hastening the redemption process does not hold during "favorable periods", when not only is it permissible to hasten this process, but it is actually obligatory to do so:

> When ruling that the redemption should not be hastened, our Sages were referring . . . to other times, not during favorable periods, when Israel is expected to make a strong effort to repent, lest the Evil Inclination overcome them. For during favorable periods it is very easy to achieve redemption.[32]

R. Israel of Shklov presented another reason for abrogating this prohibition. He claims that the "three oaths" are a kind of "package deal" concluded by God with Israel and the gentile nations. Israel was forbidden to hasten the redemption process or to return forcibly to the Land of Israel, while the nations were forbidden to subjugate the Jews too severely, lest they have no alternative but to take action concerning their redemption. When the gentile nations violate their part in the "three oaths", Israel is no longer bound by them either:

> . . . He was only slightly angry at the sins of His people, but they [the gentiles] exaggerated in increasing the weight of their yoke, thus violating the prohibition

they were sworn by God to uphold, not to oppress Israel too severely lest Israel act to hasten the redemption process.[33]

SETTLING THE LAND OF ISRAEL BY "AN AWAKENING FROM BELOW"

The move of the Gaon's disciples to the Land of Israel was not the final stage in their efforts to "restore" the *Shekhina* and hasten the coming of the redemption by means of an "awakening from below", but merely a first step. R. Israel of Shklov, who headed the Safed Perushim (as the Vilna Gaon's disciples were known) community, guided it toward spiritual endeavors expressed mainly in supreme efforts to hasten the redemption process through study of Torah and kabbala, observance of the *mitzvot* valid only in the Land of Israel, elevating the spirits of righteous departed souls, and especially through attempts to restore *semikha,* the juridical validity of the rabbinate, with the help of the Ten Lost Tribes who were traditionally considered to have passed on such ordination in an unbroken chain of succession from Moses himself. Restoration of Torah jurisprudence following the renewal of *semikha* was a recognized way to hasten the impending redemption, and R. Israel of Shklov gave it precedence even over the rebuilding of Jerusalem.[34] Accordingly, in 1831 he dispatched a messenger to Yemen to search for the Ten Tribes.[35]

The main body of the Gaon's disciples settled in Jerusalem and under the guidance of R. Menaḥem Mendel of Shklov adopted a different goal, one of practical projects aimed at hastening the advent of the redemption and arousing the *Shekhina* from the dust. Beginning in 1816, this group concentrated tirelessly on efforts to gain control of the compound of the "Ḥurva of R. Yehuda He-Ḥasid", in order to rebuild the apartments, synagogue, and public institutions within it. These attempts included lobbying at the Sultan's court in Constantinople, and seeking the intervention of foreign consuls, missionaries and the leaders of the local community. They also tried to come to a satisfactory arrangement with the heirs of the creditors of the early eighteenth century Ashkenazi community that had owned the Ḥurva and had gone bankrupt, and with the local governors of Jerusalem. The Ḥasidic community in Palestine also claimed ownership of the Ḥurva compound in Jerusalem, but they did nothing to establish their case. In contrast, the Gaon's followers worked unceasingly to bolster their claim.[36]

An expression of their approach to the rebuilding of the Ḥurva compound is to be found in a letter sent to the Diaspora announcing the beginning of the reconstruction:

. . . those in whom there burns the sacred flame of the Love of Zion and of Jerusalem. And to awaken to the sorrow of the Divine Presence . . . to raise up the Divine Presence so it can find a place to rest in our study hall; rise up and have mercy on Zion for the time has come for its reprieve, to favor its rocks and pardon its soil. It all depends upon the awakening from below to stir up the awakening from above, to rebuild the ruins. . . .[37]

In their fervent messianic expectations as the year 5600 (1840) grew nearer, the Perushim referred to sources in the *Zohar* and the Midrash which mention that Ishmael's (Muslim) rule of the Land of Israel would last a specific period, after which the land would come under Edom's [Christian] control, to be handed over finally to the Jewish people.[38] They did not consider Egyptian rule over Palestine an extension of Muslim rule, but rather subject to European-Christian control; as such it should not be considered as a mere change of government, but rather constituted an upheaval of theological-messianic significance.[39]

The improved legal status of the Jews in Palestine under Muhammad Ali's rule, and their increased economic activity, reinforced this concept. R. Eliezer Bergmann's letter from Jerusalem demonstrates this clearly: "The Ishmaelites are greatly humbled, whereas the Jews, especially the Ashkenazi Jews, enjoy impressive status . . . so that it can almost be said that the Redemption has already begun."[40] Messianic expectations intensified alongside the increased freedom of worship, for the Jews had been given permission to worship in public, mainly public prayers at the graves of holy rabbis, and to rebuild the Sephardi synagogues that were falling into ruin—privileges which the Jews had been denied during the period of Ottoman rule.

When the Perushim of Jerusalem were granted the right to rebuild the Ḥurva compound in the summer of 1836—that is 5596 in the Jewish calendar, equivalent to the letter value of *boneh Yerushalayim,* "He who rebuilds Jerusalem"—they were seized by messianic ecstasy: "When has such an event befallen Zion ever since the Exile began? . . . to rebuild a glorious synagogue . . . this is a sign of the start of the Redemption. . . ."[41] In similar fashion R. Eliezer Bergmann wrote to Z. H. Lehren, head of the *Pekidim* and *Amarkalim* Fund (a European society to administer funds for the benefit of the old yishuv), that people in

Jerusalem were saying that the redemption had already begun. This attitude did not remain in the realm of theory, but assumed a concrete and most dramatic form in the theology and liturgy of the Perushim. On the basis of their belief that the redemption had already begun, the disciples of the Vilna Gaon made changes in the order of their prayer services and in the wording of the prayers. They dropped the "shake off the dust, rise up" verse from the *Lekha Dodi* prayer welcoming the Sabbath, and ceased reciting the lamentations over the destruction of the Temple in the *Tikkun Ḥaẓot* (midnight prayers), for they held that the *Shekhina* had already risen from the dust. Z. H. Lehren protested this bold step, writing:

Regarding the omission of "shake off the dust", etc. and the lamentations from *Tikkun Ḥaẓot,* I would like to know who introduced this innovation . . . I suspect him of having been misled by Sabbatai Ṣevi, since the book *Ḥemdat Yamim* also rules that this should be omitted.[42]

The reconstruction of the Ḥurva compound was not merely symbolic. Heading the priorities of the Perushim was the desire to augment Jewish settlement in Jerusalem, to extend its residential areas, and to develop additional economic resources. Under the rule of Muhammad Ali their activities in these realms were accelerated. From the controversy which developed between Z. H. Lehren, who adhered to the traditional messianic views, and the disciples of the Vilna Gaon, we learn of the diversified activities of the latter group. One letter refers to the purchase of buildings far from the Jewish Quarter by the leaders of the Perushim who used their community's funds:

Concerning the news from Jerusalem of the purchase of houses cheaply from Gentiles in areas previously not allowed . . . without the approval of the Sephardi Rabbis and scholars, but the heads of the Ashkenazim hasten to do so.[43]

The collectivist-future orientation of the leadership of the Perushim, who were interested in acquiring additional buildings and courtyards so as to expand the area of Jewish settlement, is apparent in another letter—where it stands in contrast to the here-and-now traditional orientation expressed by Lehren, who argued that all the available funds should be devoted to the maintenance of the Jewish residents of Jerusalem:

Let him [R. Nathan Nata', the son of R. Mendel, a leader of Jerusalem *Perushim*] decide if buying up those courtyards is such a wise move, and if it opens up hope of a large settlement in that area. . . . It will be good for the community if Jewish settlers are soon included in that project too.[44]

From a letter from Z. H. Lehren to R. Arye, a trustee of the Perushim community, we learn of that community's involvement in activities aimed at providing Jews with a more balanced economic base: ". . . regarding the projects of negotiations or agriculture or purchasing property, let whoever has the means make the attempt and even succeed, but in my opinion doing this in the name of the community is nonsense."[45] Even R. Israel of Shklov who, as we have noted, favored a spiritual approach to the redemption process, came to the conclusion at the end of 1837 that land should be acquired in Palestine, and sought to convince his friend, Z. H. Lehren, in this regard. Lehren's reply was that "the whole business of buying up fields and vineyards seems mad to us. I am especially surprised that you, my esteemed friend, have been taken in by E. Bergmann's ideas, so as to write this. . . . Can you imagine basing all life in the Land of Israel on agriculture?"[46]

The letters sent to Moses Montefiore by the Perushim in the summer of 1839 also show that they wanted some of their members to engage in practical agricultural work, as an expression of their messianic approach in which settling the land and making its desolation bloom was one of the signs of the Redemption:

We were happy to hear that Sir Moses has spoken of having them work their own plots in the Holy Land, the land of our forefathers . . . We await and expect the love to awaken and the land to bring forth its fruit for the Jewish people living on it. For it all depends on the awakening from below to arouse the awakening from above. How long is our Holy Land to remain desolate and abandoned by its inhabitants?[47]

In light of their collectivistic-futuristic orientation, the leaders of the Perushim Kolel in Palestine and in Russia strove, in an organized fashion, to bring groups of immigrants from various social strata to the country, so as to enlarge the Jewish community and to establish it there firmly.

THE CRISIS OF 5600 (1840) AND THE CONVERSIONS TO CHRISTIANITY

As 5600 (1840) drew nearer, tension in the Jewish world grew stronger and messianic expectations were rife. Great expectations permeated the

Perushim community in Jerusalem as well. Though sources indicate that not all the Perushim were agreed that the Messiah would appear in 5600, some preferring to view the redemption as a gradual process, even those who were doubtful tensely awaited some event that would clearly mark the beginning of the new era. The Messiah did not appear in 1840, and instead of this joyous event the year was darkened by the Damascus blood-libel. The Messiah not having arrived by the end of 5600, everyone realized that this "favorable period", like those of 4856 (1096) and 5408 (1648) before it, had proved false. Without doubt, the more zealous the people's faith in the coming of the Messiah in 1840, the greater was their disappointment and disillusionment. Not everyone could remain steadfast in this period of spiritual turmoil and carry on his life as before. There seems to have been some truth in the writings of the Christian traveller who told of the confusion of the Jews:

> We are sure they want to return to the land of their forefathers with all their heart, and they believe that their hour of redemption is nigh. But after their prophecies failed, they began to realize that they had made a mistake. A few rabbis did not hesitate to proclaim this publicly, and many have recently converted.[48]

As early as 1839, we find evidence of a link between three scholars of the followers of the Vilna Gaon, and missionaries of the "Society for Promoting Christianity among the Jews" who were active in Jerusalem. In March 1842, the decision of these three rabbis to convert to Christianity was made public. We may assume that the crises preceding 1840, especially the suffering endured by the inhabitants of Jerusalem during the famine and the epidemics of 1838–9, raised doubts concerning what the future had in store for them. There is, however, no doubt that their final decision to convert was taken as a result of the failure of the Messiah to appear. A missionary delegation and the Protestant bishop, Michael Solomon Alexander, himself a convert from Judaism, provided the necessary encouragement for them to carry out their resolution.

Early in October 1842, a veritable war was waged in Jerusalem between the heads of the Perushim community, and the missionaries and Bishop Alexander, for the souls of the three rabbis. The missionaries exerted every effort to convert the three—in the very heart of Jerusalem, where Jews had in the past rejected the messianic claims of Jesus. The leaders of the Perushim did all they could to prevent such a step which was liable, above all, to blacken the name of the Jews of Palestine.[49] On

May 21, 1843, the missionaries chalked up a victory: five Jews, including R. Eliezer Luria, of a distinguished rabbinical family, and R. Benjamin Goldberg, were baptized and accepted Jesus as their Messiah in the very heart of Jerusalem.[50] The third rabbi, who changed his mind at the last moment, was also a scion of one of the founding families of the Perushim, R. Abraham Nissan Wolpin. He was the son of R. Reuben of Mohilev, one of the first Perushim to settle in Palestine and one of the heads of the community during the 1830s, and son-in-law of R. Menaḥem Mendel of Shklov, the foremost disciple of the Vilna Gaon in Palestine.[51]

R. Aviezer of Tykocin testifies to the causal connection between the religious crisis and the conversions:

From now on we must clarify the words of the holy *Zohar* on *Vayyera* 117 . . . why its explicit reference to the year 5600 did not materialize, and if so . . . why is our Messiah delayed, for six ([5]600) has already come; several people have already abandoned their faith because of this, saying that as the year 5600 has already passed and the Messiah has not come, he will surely not come any more.[52]

R. Aviezer maintained that the people who converted to Christianity because of their disappointment at the nonappearance of the Messiah were the descendants of the *'erev-rav,* the "mixed multitude" who formed the golden calf in the desert. On the basis of the belief that everything written in the Torah refers equally to the past, the present and the future, he held that the verse "The people saw that Moses was delayed in descending from the mountain" referred to the mixed multitude who said that since the sixth hour had already passed, Moses would no longer return; and so they told Aaron: "Rise, and make us a god. . . ." He concluded: ". . . the sacred Torah surely hints at the people of this last generation who arrogantly revile and curse because of six ([5]600)."[53]

R. Aviezer of Tykocin sought not only to justify the expectations that had been held for the year 5600, but to bolster the faith of those who had been disillusioned. He constructed a whole set of proofs to justify the hopes they had had for 5600. However, he continued, it must be remembered that 5600 marked the start of the redemption process, which would be reaching its climax in 5606 (1846). The years between were to be years of trial, even extremely difficult ones. R. Aviezer's thesis was based on fundamental concepts of Luria's kabbala and on alphabetical calculations. Every such calculation indicating the year 5600 he automatically adjusted to 5605. This adjustment was only an attempt to extend the messianic expectations as much as possible, and prevent at any price the crisis he saw developing before his very eyes. An outstanding example is provided by the way he referred to verses of the "Song of Songs", which were interpreted by kabbalists and by the Vilna Gaon's disciples as a song of the future redemption. He interpreted chapter two, verse twelve—"The blossoms have appeared in the land, the time of pruning has come; the song of the turtledove is heard in our land," as follows: "This will only take place up above, and not yet reach down below . . . i.e., the blossoms have begun to be seen in the land above, but human beings know nothing of it." However, he interpreted "the song of the turtledove is heard in our land" to mean that when the year of the dove (= 5606) would come, the song of redemption would be heard in the land below as well.[54]

As the year 5606 (1846) came nearer, it became clear that this would not be the year of redemption either. 1845 was one of the most oppressively hot and dry years that Palestine experienced in the nineteenth century. It was a year of severe famine which led to complete demoralization in the Jewish community, and a number of its leaders, who were unable to shoulder the burden of feeding the community's members, fled the country.[55] In Russia, too, the land of the Perushim's origin, the Jews were finding life very difficult. The decrees promulgated by Tsar Nikolai I to "improve" the lot of the Jews grew more frequent. These decrees affected the attire of the Jews, their autonomous organization, and their traditional educational system. Their economic position worsened, tens of thousands were recruited into the army, and many had their freedom of movement severely curtailed.[56] It was apparent that the attempts to move the period of redemption from 5600 to 5606 had failed completely. In 5605 (1845), Z. H. Lehren complained that Jews in Jerusalem still awaited redemption, assuming that the settlement of the Land of Israel marked the rising of the *Shekhina* from the dust, "for in the Holy City Jews do not recite 'until when is Your strength in captivity, and Your majesty in enemy hands', because the *Shekhina* has already arisen from the dust."[57] It is, however, very doubtful if by 5606 they still held that belief.

SPIRITUAL MEANS OF BRINGING REDEMPTION NEARER

Following the crisis of 5606, it was increasingly argued that settling the Land of Israel was not the legitimate way to hasten the coming of the Redemption; emphasis should rather be placed on spiritual activity.

R. Aviezer of Tykocin's book, *Sha'arei Ẓedek,* expresses this approach. R. Aviezer already (5603—1843) blamed the opponents of R. Israel of Shklov for the failure of the Perushim in hastening the redemption. They had favored the rebuilding of Jerusalem as a major act of "awakening from below", but he maintained that all the building they had urged merely resembled the deeds of the generation of the Tower of Babel whose only aim was to make a reputation for themselves:

> Concerning them it is said, "Let us build us a city and make a name for ourselves, and build synagogues and study-halls and put Torah scrolls in them with crowns upon them"—not for God's sake, but rather to make a name for themselves; this is the Evil Inclination overcoming Israel.[58]

He went still further and accused the veteran leadership of the Perushim community, which had disagreed with the ruling of R. Israel of Shklov, of responsibility for the devastation of Safed at the hands of rioting Arab peasants in 5594 (1834), for the casualties suffered in the destruction of the Galilee in the earthquake of 5597 (1837), and for the epidemics which plagued Jerusalem in 5598–5599 (1838–9). He maintained that their desire to rebuild Jerusalem and restore the compound of the Ḥurva was wrong from the very beginning. Even if they had desired to rebuild the Temple itself, it was doubtful if this was the right thing to do:

> We shall yet come to learn for what main purpose the Temple was built; it cannot be for the building itself, for wood and stone have no sanctity. Thus it must have been in order to house something of sanctity, that is, the Ark in which the Torah was placed . . . all the more so since the main reason for the *Shekhina* visiting this world was not for the Temple, but only for the Torah.[59]

R. Aviezer emphasized the importance of Torah and kabbala study as a means of "restoring" the *Shekhina:* "That is, one must study the secrets of the Torah, for this study is what raises the *Shekhina* up from the dust. . . . For this study will Israel be redeemed from their exile."[60]

REINSTATING THE RECITATION OF TIKKUN ḤAẒOT

As early as 5603 R. Aviezer called upon Jewry to repent, repentance centering around the reciting of *Tikkun Ḥaẓot:*

In this regard, my fellow Jews, take my advice . . . and rise up to fulfill these three major commandments, *i.e.,* to love your fellow man as yourself, to honor the Sabbath . . . and the third one—to rise at midnight to lament the exile of the *Shekhina* . . . and the destruction of the Temple.[61]

The call for the resumption of reciting *Tikkun Ḥazot* and upgrading it to the level of two other precepts upon which the redemption depended, was in essence a call for a total withdrawal from the messianic belief fundamental to the activities of the veteran leadership of the Perushim, namely that the reconstruction of the Ḥurva compound would raise the *Shekhina* from the dust.

Two concrete signs of the spiritual crisis affecting the Perushim were the strengthening of the leadership status of R. Isaiah Bourdaky, the son-in-law of R. Israel of Shklov, who opposed the reconstruction of the Ḥurva, and the weakening position of R. Abraham Solomon Zalman Ẓoref, a leading supporter of the Ḥurva's restoration. In Iyyar 5607 (May 1847), after the deaths of two leaders of the community, R. Nathan Nata' and R. Moses Maggid-Rivlin,[62] the new leadership had the courage to ask the members to sign an agreement reinstituting the custom of reciting *Tikkun Ḥazot:*

The princes of the people have gathered to confer as to what steps to take concerning the cessation of the daily sacrifice in our Temple. . . . Ever since its destruction, God only has room in this world for halakha . . . only this Torah is left for us.[63]

Correcting this situation entailed setting up Torah study groups and, in particular, reciting the *Tikkun Ḥazot*—

[The Sages emphasize] intensive Torah study and bewailing the Destruction at night, upon which both the upper and lower worlds depend, one of the most important things upon which all the Jews depend.[64]

The apologetics in the agreement seem to indicate that not everyone was happy with the reinstitution of this recitation, and not everyone agreed with the view that everything the Vilna Gaon's disciples, the first Ashkenazi settlers to return to Jerusalem, did was invalid and was not the right way to hasten the redemption process. The thirty-two signatures on the agreement do not include that of R. Abraham S. Z. Ẓoref, for he was out of the country at the time, and his absence may indeed have been taken advantage of by the heads of the community in order to present the agreement and get it signed. R. Arie, a trustee of the community, and R. Shmuel Salant did not sign the agreement either.

In 1849, another retreat from the views of the founders became apparent. When the leaders of the Perushim appealed to Moses Montefiore concerning the establishment of workshops to help support the community, their appeal was written rationally, with no use whatever of kabbalistic motifs linking the development of the country with the redemption, such as were to be found ten years earlier in almost all the letters sent to Montefiore in 5599 (1839).[65]

"IF GOD DOES NOT BUILD THE HOUSE, ITS BUILDERS LABOR IN VAIN"

The reinstitution of *Tikkun Ḥaẓot* was not the last stage of the retreat from the views of the founding Perushim. A new slogan was needed that would anchor their conception in the Holy Scriptures. A source dating from 5610 (1850) reveals for the first time that the Ashkenazim of Jerusalem maintained that the construction and development of the Land of Israel not only did not contribute to the hastening of the redemption process, but was lacking in all value. This was to be understood from the verse in Psalms, "If God does not build the house, its builders labor in vain." In none of the letters dating from the early 1840s, arguing for the establishment of a hospital, is there any sign of anyone having made use of this verse, not even Z. H. Lehren. Lehren's opposition to the building of the hospital was mainly based on his fear of the influence this modernizing process would have on the community, lest Jewish doctors introduce a spirit of heresy or atheism among the local residents. However, the quotation from Psalms in the aforementioned source is quite extreme and forbids all practical steps:

> [The Polish Jews] have no interest in the philanthropy of Rothschild, and always say, "If God does not build the house . . ." though the 8,000 Sephardi Jews and their sages do not accept this verse, written by King David, for they request that various repairs be made by Sir Montefiore or by others.[66]

It is evident that this verse did become an ideological slogan in Jerusalem. In a private letter R. Naḥman Nathan Coronel sent to R. Solomon Zalman Ḥayyim Halberstam on 23 Kislev 5625 (December 1864), he expressly refers to this verse as of ideological import while writing of R. Isaac Rosenthal of the Dutch-German community:

> Though he belongs to the sect (!) striving for the settlement of the Holy Land, I think it will remain forever in ruins as long as the leadership of the kingdom of

Ishmael [the Muslims] does not change, and until God agrees, for if God does not build, etc. . . .[67]

Jacob Saphir, too, in an open letter to Rabbi Alkalai, rejected the practicality of settling the Land of Israel as a means of natural redemption:

These inferences will not be of any use to us, for those who believe in the redemption of Israel fully believe, as our reliable tradition holds, that it will be wondrous and miraculous . . . and by means of Torah, repentance and charity. . . . If God does not build the house, its builders labor in vain. There is no point in getting up early, before dawn, to eat unripe fruit, before the time God fixes has come . . . so as to fulfill . . . I, the Lord, have rebuilt the ruins and replanted the desolation.[68]

R. Meir Auerbach also expressed, in a reply to Rabbi Z. H. Kalischer, his opposition to the latter's position that the settlement of the Land of Israel was a means to hasten the redemption. In my opinion, R. Auerbach was referring to the failure of the disciples of the Gaon of Vilna to hasten the redemption in this manner when he wrote:

But this is not the way to reach our goal, and let us not be disgraced, God forbid, like some of our predecessors who thought similarly and erred, though they too thought their intentions were honorable; but they were wrong, and many followed them, and this led to laxity and weakness in our faith in the True Redeemer.[69]

In summation, the practical settlement of the Land of Israel seems to have been the ideal of the disciples of the Gaon of Vilna. They immigrated to Palestine at their rabbi's behest, and out of a sense of imminent redemption; they sought to hasten its advent or to bring it about by a natural process. In the 1830s, at the beginning of Egyptian rule over Palestine, their basic ideology meshed with the dynamics of contemporary events and with the increasing opportunities for building and economic projects. However, following the failure of the Messiah to appear in 5600 (1840), the Perushim community underwent a crisis accompanied, among the fringe elements, by a number of conversions to Christianity. The attempts made by the veteran leadership to continue with the rebuilding projects met opposition on the part of those who claimed that the true way to hasten the redemption process was spiritual in character—through study of Torah and Kabbala and recitation of *Tikkun Ḥaẓot*.

By the end of the 1840s, when the founders of the community had all passed away, a new leadership took over, reinstituting the reciting of *Tikkun Ḥazot* and thereby expressing its reservations regarding the rebuilding of Jerusalem as a means of raising the *Shekhina* from the dust. In place of the ideology of "rebuilding ruins" as an "awakening from below", there developed an ideology of "If God does not build the house, its builders labor in vain." This ideology underlies the opposition of the leadership to proposals for productivization and modernization and to the settlement of the country in the second half of the nineteenth century.

As time went by, this opposition was reinforced by other factors, including the fear of cultural "Enlightenment" influences, the inroads of the Reform movement, growing limitations on the distribution of funds within the *ḥalukka* system, the problems involved in observing Torah commandments tied to the Land of Israel, etc. But the nucleus of the Perushim ideology remained the belief that the rebuilding of the Land did nothing to hasten the coming of the redemption, and that the only legitimate ideology was faith in a miraculous redemption.

Fearing that the supporters of settlement of the Land of Israel in the 1880s would seek to base their activities on the ideology that had motivated the followers of the Vilna Gaon to immigrate to Palestine, the leaders of the Perushim sought, from the 1860s on, to obliterate traces of that historical episode, even deliberately refraining from specifying the names of those earlier immigrants.

NOTES

1. For a more complete treatment of this subject, see my book *Messianism and the Settlement of Palestine* (Hebrew) (Jerusalem, 1985).
2. B. *Ketubbot* 111a: "Why these three oaths? One so that Israel would refrain from taking the land by force, another, where God had Israel vow not to rebel against the gentile nations, and the other, where God had the idolators swear not to oppress Israel too severely . . . also not to reveal the time of the redemption and to delay [Rashi reads: not to speed] it and not to reveal the secret to the idolators."
3. The book *Hillel ben Shaḥar,* containing twenty-six sermons, was compiled (1804) by the famed Rabbi of Kovno, the son of the Rabbi Ze'ev Wolf of Ratzki.

4. See A. Ya'ari, *Letters for the Land of Israel* (Hebrew) (Tel Aviv, 1943), p. 337.
5. *Sha'arei Ẓedek le-Zera Yiẓḥak* was printed in Jerusalem in 1843.
6. His name appears in the list of scholars of the Perushim community in Jerusalem. MS. Montefiore 528, dated 5599 (1839), The Institute for the Microfilming of Hebrew Manuscripts, JNUL, Jerusalem (hereafter, Microfilm Institute).
7. *Hillel ben Shaḥar*, p. 23b. The years were derived by application of *gematria* to biblical verses.
8. *Sha'arei Ẓedek*, p. 24b.
9. *Zohar* (trans. *Ha-Sullam*), *Vayyera* I, 117.
10. *Sha'arei Ẓedek*, p. 56b.
11. The Vilna Gaon's commentary on *Sifra di-Ẓeni'uta*, Vilna 5580 (1820), p. 33b. Also in B. *Sanhedrin* 99a: Rabbi Dosa says, [The Messianic period] is four hundred years. Here it is written, "and they shall slave for them and they will oppress them four hundred years," and there it is written: "Let us rejoice [for as long] as the days you oppressed us, etc."
12. *Hillel ben Shaḥar*, Introduction, p. 6b.
13. *Ibid.*, p. 7b.
14. *Ibid.*, p. 21a.
15. *Ibid.*, p. 42a.
16. Commentary on the Prophets and Hagiographia, attributed to the Gaon of Vilna, Microfilm Institute, JNUL, 3426, p. 21a. The ms. was written during the lifetime of the Gaon's disciple, R. Ḥayyim of Volozhyn.
17. *Hillel ben Shaḥar*, p. 21b.
18. *Ibid.*, p. 7b.
19. *Loc. cit.*
20. *Ibid.*, p. 17b.
21. *Loc. cit.*
22. Menasseh of Ilya, *Sefer Alfei Menashe* (Hebrew) (Vilna, 1822), p. 73b.
23. Ya'ari (above, n. 4), pp. 350–351.
24. The Vilna Gaon's son, R. Abraham, lists the names of his father's thirteen foremost disciples. Six or perhaps seven of them were still alive in 1808. Five came to live in Palestine: R. Menaḥem Mendel, R. Sa'adia, R. Israel—all of Shklov; R. Ẓevi Hirsch of Simyatitz; and R. Ḥayyim Katz. Sh. Y. Finn, *Kirya Ne'emana* (Hebrew) (Vilna, 1914), pp. 163–170.
25. See J. J. and B. Rivlin, critical edition of *Letters of the Pekidim and Amarkalim of Amsterdam* 5586–5587 (Hebrew) (Jerusalem, 1965), p. 93.
26. The organization which arranged for the immigration and support of the members of the Perushim community is known officially as *Roznei Vilna*, and was initially headed by R. Ḥayyim of Volozhin.
27. Ya'ari (above, n. 4), pp. 330–333.
28. *Sha'arei Ẓedek*, p. 64a.
29. R. Yehuda Halevi Edel, *Sefer Afikei Yehuda* (Hebrew) (Zloczow, 1819), p. 109a.

30. Ya'ari (above, n. 4), p. 352.
31. *Sha'arei Ẓedek,* p. 46b.
32. *Ibid.*, p. 26a.
33. Ya'ari (above, n. 4), p. 352.
34. R. Israel of Shklov, *Sefer Tiklin Ḥadtin* (Hebrew) (Minsk, 1812), Introduction; and also B. *Megilla* 17b; *Rosh Ha-Shana* 31a; Maimonides' *Commentary on the Mishna, Sanhedrin,* ch. 1.
35. Ya'ari (above, n. 4), p. 352.
36. For the activities of the Perushim in Jerusalem during the period 1816–1837, see my article, "Reconstruction of the Compound of R. Yehuda He-Ḥasid's Ḥurva" (Hebrew), *Shalem* 4 (Jerusalem, 1984), pp. 271–305.
37. P. Grajewsky, *From the Archives of Jerusalem,* 2 (Hebrew) (n.p., n.d.), pp. 2–3.
38. See *Zohar* (trans. *Ha-Sullam*), *Bereshit, Vayyera,* 13; *Vayikra Rabba* 8, end of section 13; Letters of the *Pekidim* and *Amarkalim* of Amsterdam, ms. in Yad Izhak Ben-Zvi library, 5, 86a.
39. See my article, "Messianic Expectations for the Year 5600 (1840)" (Hebrew), in *Essays in Messianism and Eschatology* (Jerusalem, 1983), pp. 343–364.
40. Eliezer V. Bergmann, *Yis'u Harim Shalom—Letters of Travel and Aliya 1833–1836* (Hebrew) (Jerusalem, 1968), p. 76.
41. See above, n. 37.
42. *Letters of the Pekidim* . . . (above, n. 38), 8, p. 7a. For the liturgical changes made by the followers of Shabbetai Ẓevi, see M. Benayahu, "The Innovations Introduced by Nathan ha-'Azzati in his Circle in Kastoria and Salonika" (Hebrew), *Sefunot* 14 (1978): 297 (10), 299–300 (20).
43. Z. H. Lehren's letter dated 12 Elul 5596 (August 25, 1836), Letters of the *Pekidim* . . . (above, n. 38), 6, p. 233b.
44. *Ibid.*, 8, p. 26a.
45. *Ibid.*, 8, p. 61a, dated 26 Av 5597 (August 25, 1837).
46. *Ibid.*, 8, p. 46a, a letter dated 20 Sivan 5597 (June 23, 1837). R. Eliezer Bergmann went to Palestine from Germany, actively expecting messianic developments. He frequently expressed himself in favor of a natural process of redemption. His significant activities during the 1830s and his connections with the Perushim in Jerusalem are a separate topic deserving special study.
47. S. Baron, "On the History of the Jewish Community in Jerusalem" (Hebrew), *Klausner Jubilee Volume,* ed. N. H. Torczyner, A. A. Kabak, A. Tcherikover, and B. Shoḥetman, (Tel Aviv, 1937), p. 304, note 2. Similarly the statement made by the heads of the community: "They almost all desire to earn their own livelihood by cultivating the Holy Land, eating of its fruit and being sated with its goodness," MS. Montefiore (above, n. 6), 528.
48. Quoted from M. Ish-Shalom, *Christian Travellers in the Holy Land* (Hebrew) (Tel Aviv, 1966), p. 554.

49. See Albert H. Hyamson, *The British Consulate in Jerusalem,* I (London, 1941), pp. 56–77; *Jewish Intelligence,* 1842, pp. 60–63.
50. See *Jewish Intelligence,* 1843, p. 280.
51. I am grateful to the Jerusalem genealogist, R. Shmuel Gur, for assisting me in the exact identification of those involved in this affair.
52. *Sha'arei Ẓedek,* p. 56a.
53. *Ibid.,* p. 56b.
54. *Ibid.,* p. 60b.
55. See M. Benayahu, "The Famine in Jerusalem in 5606" (Hebrew), *Jerusalem Quarterly for the Study of Jerusalem and its History* 2, A-B (1949): 72–88.
56. For a further discussion of these developments, see M. Stanislawski, *Tsar Nicholas I and the Jews. The Transformation of Jewish Society in Russia, 1825–1855* (Philadelphia, 1983).
57. Letters of the *Pekidim* . . . (above, n. 38), II, p. 122.
58. *Sha'arei Ẓedek,* p. 40a.
59. *Ibid.,* p. 15a.
60. *Ibid.,* p. 7a.
61. *Ibid.,* p. 31a.
62. R. Nathan Nata' died on 22 Tishre 5607 (1846); R. Moshe Maggid-Rivlin died on 28 Elul 5606 (1846). See A. L. Frumkin, *The History of the Sages of Jerusalem,* 3 (Hebrew) (Jerusalem, 1929), p. 224.
63. P. Grajewsky (above, n. 37), 13 (1931), p. 3.
64. *Ibid.,* p. 4.
65. See above, n. 47.
66. M. Weinstein, "Plans for improving the conditions of the Jews of Jerusalem in the mid-nineteenth century" (Hebrew), *Bar-Ilan: Annual of Bar-Ilan University* (1968): 349; Israel Freidin, " 'Bikur Ḥolim Perushim' in Jerusalem—From Society to Hospital" (Hebrew), *Cathedra* 27 (1983): 117–140.
67. Microfilm Institute, JNUL, ms. 29459.
68. *Ha-Levanon* 8 (1872): 338, 346.
69. *Ha-Levanon* 1 (1863): 8.

17

The Messiah Shukr Kuḥayl II (1868–75) and his Tithe *(Maʿaśer)*: Ideology and Practice as a Means to Hasten Redemption

Bat-Zion Eraqi Klorman

Shukr Kuḥayl II was the second Jewish messiah to appear in Yemen in the second half of the nineteenth century. His activity coincided with a significant political change in the history of Yemen: the 1872 conquest of the capital Ṣanʿa, of the central highlands, and of the coastal plains along the Red Sea by the Ottoman Turks. The Ottoman rule lasted until the end of World War I, when in 1918 local Yemenite leadership successfully recaptured the government. Prior to the Ottoman occupation the history of Yemen was marked by internal instability and a growing interest of world powers in the affairs of the country. The imāms, Yemen's leaders, were often unable to govern effectively over the various tribes and confederations of tribes, and the country fell victim to endless rebellions, lack of internal security, and frequent overthrow of imāms. In 1839 the British, motivated by their interests in India, captured the Yemenite port of Aden, ruled at the time by an independent sultan. The continuing importance of Yemen as a strategic stronghold on the Red Sea en route to the Indian Ocean became especially evident after the opening of the Suez Canal in 1869. The Ottomans, who in 1849 attempted to reconquer Yemen but failed, sent a second conquering force in 1872 and succeeded this time by exploiting the utterly deteriorated Yemenite imāmate.[1]

Reprinted by permission of the Annenberg Research Institute from *The Jewish Quarterly Review* n.s. 79 (1988–89).

The Jews of Yemen, the only non-Muslim minority, lived mostly in the predominant Zaydī areas alongside Zaydī villages and towns.[2] The Zaydīs belonged to a moderate version of the Shīʿah which split off from the mainstream of Sunnī Islam over the question of the leadership of the Muslim world. They were the rulers of the country, and the imāms were drawn from among them. The Sunnīs of Yemen were almost equal in number to the Zaydīs, but they were deprived of any meaningful political influence. During the second half of the nineteenth century Yemen was filled with messianic expectations and speculations, among both the Zaydī Muslims and the Jewish communities. This eschatological mood found an expression in an emergence of Muslim and Jewish apocalyptic literature. Indeed, some of the Jewish literature was greatly influenced by its Muslim counterpart. The period produced also several messianic contenders: the Muslims Faqīh Saʿīd (1840) and Sharīf Ismāʿīl (1846) and the Jews Shukr Kuḥayl I (1861–65), Shukr Kuḥayl II (1868–75), and Yosef ʿAbdallah (1888–93).[3]

Shukr Kuḥayl I began his career as the herald of the messiah in 1861, when he announced his messianic role in Ṣanʿa. Thereafter he wandered into the countryside to spread his message of preparation for the messianic days by means of prayer and repentance. His call was answered by many who supported him, even after he transformed himself from a person who had only a marginal role in the drama of redemption into a full-fledged messianic contender. Jacob Sappir (Sapir), an appointed messenger (*sheliaḥ de-rabbanan*) who was sent from Jerusalem to collect contributions and traveled in Yemen for eight months in 1859 and stopped in Aden again in 1862, wrote that "almost all the Jews living in Yemen believed in Kuḥayl."[4] Information arriving in Jewish Yemen had it that Yemenite immigrants who settled in Alexandria spread the belief in Kuḥayl's messianic claim in Egypt as well and created there a nucleus of enthusiastic supporters. However, Shukr Kuḥayl's career was soon abruptly cut short when he was killed by local Arabs at his last place of residence, Mount Ṭiyāl, in the land of Banī Jabr, east of Ṣanʿa. In spite of this misfortune Shukr Kuḥayl's messianic movement did not die. As in similar cases among the disappointed followers of Jewish or Gentile messianic claimants in Yemen and elsewhere, Kuḥayl's most zealous believers denied his failure and expected him to return soon to complete his messianic mission.[5]

Into this very favorable climate a person named Yehudah bar Shalom emerged in the month of Nisan, 5628 (March, 1868) in the small town of Tanʿim in central Yemen, northeast of Ṣanʿa, and claimed that he was the resurrected Shukr Kuḥayl. His miraculous "reappearance" soon reawakened messianic hopes among both Jews and Muslims. Shukr Kuḥayl believers, and for a while even nonbelievers, had no doubt that they were dealing with the same person. The second Shukr Kuḥayl, however, was much more active, aggressive, and successful than his predecessor in spreading the belief in the proximity of eschatological days. While Shukr Kuḥayl I was a lonely messiah, preaching all alone in the villages and towns and never assisted by aides or admirers, Shukr Kuḥayl II became an effective public relations person and the leader of a propaganda organization. From his center[6] he sent out messengers carrying epistles addressed to the heads of various Jewish communities in Yemen, and to Jewish leaders in Aden, Alexandria, Bombay, Calcutta, Jerusalem, and Safed. Remnants of Kuḥayl II's vast correspondence—letters written by his believers and by Kuḥayl II himself, in addition to documents written by his opponents—are the principal sources of information for the study of this messianic movement. However, the importance of Shukr Kuḥayl I's and Shukr Kuḥayl II's movements has never been fully examined. The scholarly work published by Abraham Yaʿari in 1945 dealt only with a few aspects of this messianic phenomenon. Other works had little to add to its understanding.[7] The present essay is the first attempt to elaborate further on the messianic movement of Shukr Kuḥayl II. It will discuss Kuḥayl II's ideology of repentance, his innovated form of the tithe *(maʿaśer),* and the organizational structure which he created to maintain his movement.

KUḤAYL II'S IDEOLOGY OF REPENTANCE AND MAʿAŚER

One of Kuḥayl II's first letters, the epistle to the community of Aden written towards the end of 1868, contains the major themes of his message[8] and seems to be the prototype of the letters which were dispatched thereafter to other Jewish communities in Yemen and to the Jews of Alexandria. The epistle is written in Aramaic and Hebrew and is addressed to the rabbis of Aden, to the sons of Rabbi Menaḥem ben Moses, to Benin,[9] and to a certain Manṣūr. The beginning of the letter speaks of Shukr Kuḥayl's duty as a messianic announcer, of his "slaying" by the Gentiles, and of his reappearance on the eve of Passover of 5628

(1868 CE). The epistle then goes on to reveal the eschatological message and to elaborate on what is to be done in order to bring an end to the state of exile. Kuḥayl II's message consists of two basic elements: the known and useful call to repentence, and the demand, which is unique to Kuḥayl II, for payment of a sort of tax which he calls *maʿaśer*.

What does repentance mean to Shukr Kuḥayl II? His epistle to Aden instructs the Jews to study the Zohar and the Book of Psalms carefully and to be very strict in keeping the Sabbath. There are also some general ethical recommendations: each person should abandon bad manners and wrongdoings. A letter by Ḥayyim Faraj, sent from Alexandria to Sappir in Jerusalem, reveals that the community of Alexandria received a similar, if not identical, version of the epistle sent to Aden. Ḥayyim Faraj tells of a meeting called by Rabbi Yaḥyā Mizraḥi, an enthusiastic Yemenite supporter of Shukr Kuḥayl, in which

> he read before them an epistle by Shukr Kuḥayl himself written in the pure language of translation (i.e., in Aramaic). And he warned the people of Alexandria to study the Book of Psalms and especially the Zohar of the RaSHBY (R. Shimʿon ben Yoḥai), to give alms like tithe or shekels . . . and to keep the Sabbath more carefully.[10]

In a later epistle to Alexandria, written in the middle of 5629 (1869 CE), Shukr Kuḥayl II details again the show of repentance by which redemption may be hastened:

> You should avoid flattery, false oaths, and abandonment of hope for redemption; and you should be especially careful not to desecrate the Sabbath . . . And each one of you should search his own acts, especially in regard to keeping the Sabbath, lust for money, and sitting in synagogues where ignorant folk sit. You should keep the law and practice charity, and study the holy Zohar and the Book of Psalms.[11]

Kuḥayl II's letter to the Jewish community of Ḥaydan, in northern Yemen, which seems to have been written at the end of 1868, emphasizes the importance of the study of the Torah, the prayer of Shemaʿ, the Zohar, and the Book of Psalms.[12]

At the end of yet another epistle, dated Kislev, 5630 (November, 1869 CE) and addressed to the rabbis of Jerusalem, Kuḥayl II writes:

> Listen, my brothers and my friends: recite the prayers of King David, peace be upon him, and the composition of R. Shimʿon ben Yoḥai, peace be upon him.[13]

He then asks the recipients of the letter to abandon their evil ways and come back to God wholeheartedly—soon thereafter the Almighty will fulfill his promise to redeem the Jewish nation.

The second element of Shukr Kuḥayl II's method to hasten the messianic age, one which attracted much attention to, and criticism of him, is the tax of *maʿaśer*. The nature of this requirement is explained in Kuḥayl's first letter to the community of Aden, in which he says that there is a debt owed by each man in Israel, and that it is God's will that each individual should pay his share of it. Kuḥayl explains that this is not a donation but a compulsory tax. It is not a community tax but a personal tribute: "Even a poor person who lives off charity is obligated"[14] to pay his share. Even though Shukr Kuḥayl II calls his tax a tithe, he does not mean to ask for the exact ten percent of one's income. In his letter to Alexandria Kuḥayl says: "Each one should pay his *maʿaśer,* that is to say, like one-quarter of a *log*[15] from each person, and this is called *maʿaśer*."[16] It does not seem that Kuḥayl refers here to actual goods out of which the *maʿaśer* should be paid; rather, he implies that any payment, even as small as one-quarter of a *log,* is sufficient. Indeed, Kuḥayl never insisted on the payment of a fixed sum, and anything which he received was welcome.

What is Kuḥayl II's ideological explanation of the *maʿaśer?* Since this new commandment is willed by God and is delivered through Shukr Kuḥayl, his messianic messenger, its initial purpose is to enhance the new eschatological era. In his first letter to Aden, written towards the end of 1868, Kuḥayl II explains that obeying the commandment of the tithe will facilitate "the redemption of the Shekinah," and the same idea is repeated in a letter to Alexandria written in Sivan, 5629 (1869).[17] He uses here the well known kabbalistic idea according to which the Shekinah or "bride" (the tenth *sefirah*) has been separated since the historical exile of Israel from her husband, "the Holy One, blessed be he" (the sixth *sefirah, tifʾeret*). The Jewish people will be redeemed following the redemption of the Shekinah, i.e., after the reunion of the divine forces. According to Kuḥayl, this redemption will be accomplished after fulfilling the requisition of the *maʿaśer.*[18]

Another role for the *maʿaśer* is found in the letter to Alexandria dated Sivan, 5629 (May, 1869). Kuḥayl assures us that the payment of the tax will in return save the Jewish people from the sufferings of the "pangs of the Messiah," the apocalyptic tribulations on the eve of the messianic era.[19]

Alongside the reference to national redemption Kuḥayl II's propaganda of the *maʿaśer* alludes also to individual redemption. In his attempt to explain to the rabbis of Jerusalem why he had sent messengers to "all the towns of Israel" to collect the *maʿaśer,* Kuḥayl II says: "I have done this for Israel so that they may redeem themselves, and this by the will of God." The same purpose for the *maʿaśer* is indicated in Kuḥayl II's letter to Alexandria, written in the beginning of 1870, in which he reminds the Jews: "You should give for the redemption of your souls, as I have commanded you through the messenger."[20]

In another place, in Kuḥayl II's letter to Ḥaydan, he assigns to the *maʿaśer* an additional purpose. The Jews of this province had previously written to him to tell him that their land is "full of idolatry";[21] Shukr Kuḥayl II writes, therefore, to tell them that the *maʿaśer* is requested "in order to purify the land, so that they [the Jews] may succeed in conquering the people of the land."[22]

THE PRACTICAL USE OF THE MAʿAŚER

Aside from its ideological justification, the *maʿaśer* also served worldly and practical needs. It seems that this is the issue which figures most prominently in his critics' challenge of Shukr Kuḥayl II's sincerity. Yaʿari, who never mentions Kuḥayl II's ideology of the *maʿaśer,* stresses the demand for contributions and is certain that it was greed alone which drove Kuḥayl II—lust for money was behind all his activities.[23] While the *maʿaśer* aroused Yaʿari's contempt, it does not seem to be the point which most irritated Shukr Kuḥayl II's contemporary opponents.[24] It appears that the demand for the tithe was readily understood by the Jews of Yemen. In this devoutly Muslim country the call to pay the religious tax *(zakāt)* alone and to abolish all other taxes (which were regarded by pious Muslims as illegal) was a common expectation for the coming eschatological days. It appeared in the messianic propaganda of Faqīh Saʿīd, the mahdist (messianic) contender of 1840, and it is repeated in the Muslim apocalyptical tradition of the second half of the nineteenth century.[25] It is likely, therefore, that for the Jews of Yemen, who were well acquainted with the apocalyptic beliefs of their Muslim neighbors, the imposition of a tax similar to the Muslim *zakāt* was regarded as a legitimate right of the messiah. It also appears that the Jews of Yemen understood the financial needs of their new leader. They were aware that the *maʿaśer* money was spent mainly for the following three purposes: maintenance of Shukr Kuḥayl's "court," charity, and "protection money."

Since his appearance in 1868 Kuḥayl gradually attracted more and more followers, and his "court" grew accordingly. Some of his followers became his close aides, others came to stay close to his presence for shorter periods of time, but all had to be provided for by Shukr Kuḥayl. This is explained by Mosheh Ḥanokh, one of Kuḥayl II's most important supporters in Aden, in his letter of Sivan, 5629 (May, 1869): "These days he asks all of Israel to pay *ma^caśer* . . . since his table is large—more than two hundred ministers eat and drink at his table." This expenditure is described quite differently by Amram Qoraḥ, a secretary of the High Court of Ṣan^ca between 1888 and ca. 1950, and a critic of Kuḥayl II: "He spent the money on delicacies for himself and his servants."[26]

Another letter, also written by Mosheh Ḥanokh and dated Adar, 5629 (February, 1869), observes that he gave "the *ma^caśer* money which was collected for him to the poor in the towns of Yemen." While Ḥanokh talks about charity to Jews, the traveler Solomon Reinman, who visited Aden at the end of 1870 or the beginning of 1871, soon after Shukr Kuḥayl II's decline, accuses him of giving away to the Muslim multitude the money which he collected from Israel. Likewise, Rabbi Ḥayyim Ya^caqov ha-Kohen Feinstein, who visited Yemen in 1873, states that Kuḥayl II gave money to the Gentiles.[27] It will be shown in a future article that many Arabs were among Kuḥayl II's followers, and some of them also contributed money to him. Therefore, not out of keeping with the original purpose of the Muslim *zakāt,* he spent part of his *ma^caśer* income on charity to the poor among Jews and Muslims alike.

It seems, however, that the largest sums of money were allocated for "protection money," at first to local shaykhs in whose territory Shukr Kuḥayl stayed. In explaining the use of the *ma^caśer* Amram Qoraḥ adds, "And he gives money to the Arabs, the heads of the villages, to defend him from either foe or jealousy."[28] Qoraḥ's remark refers to the special status of the Jews in rural Yemen, where they lived with the permission and under the patronage of the local leaders in exchange for payment of some sort of tax. These leaders of shaykhs were responsible for protecting their Jews from any aggression initiated by members of other tribes. In the Yemenite society, hurting any of the "shaykh's Jews" was interpreted as an offense against the shaykh himself and his tribe.[29] One should therefore bear in mind that despite Shukr Kuḥayl II's popularity among the Jews of Yemen and his appeal to Muslims as well, he never rose above the status of a Jewish client, who always needed the political protection of a Muslim shaykh.

More protection money had to be paid to silence some dissatisfied Arab opponents who disliked the idea of a Jewish messiah who might defeat the Muslims. Other Muslims who had to be appeased were those who objected to Kuḥayl's reluctance to declare that he was merely the messianic herald of the expected Muslim mahdī.[30]

KUḤAYL II'S ORGANIZATION

Collection of the *maʿaśer* and communication between Shukr Kuḥayl II and his followers were maintained through a propaganda organization which was formed soon after Kuḥayl's initial success. His messengers carried his "reappearance" announcements and other missives to various localities and brought back the *maʿaśer* collected by the area's supporters. His next step, after sending out his announcements, was to dispatch emissaries to further propagate his messianic aims. Mosheh Ḥanokh's letter of Adar, 5629 (February, 1869) tells of messengers who arrived in Aden in Tishre, 5629 (September, 1868), and in another letter dated Sivan, 5629 (May, 1869) he reports that two more messengers came to Aden to spread the news of Kuḥayl II's messianic claims.[31] Ḥanokh then goes on to tell us that "now he [Shukr Kuḥayl II] is firm, and he writes many letters to the people of Aden." The same letter shows that these propaganda emissaries were by no means confined to Aden: "On the first of Iyyar [April, 1869] the Gentiles had caught seven Jews, emissaries of our master, his Excellence, our teacher Shukri, who were carrying papers from him to the towns of Yemen."

One of Shukr Kuḥayl II's messengers whose identity is known was Mosheh Hashshāsh. Shortly after Kuḥayl II's failure the same Mosheh Hashshāsh functioned again as a messenger, this time as the official emissary of the Jewish community of Ṣanʿa. He was sent in 5636 (1876) to Istanbul to request the appointment of a Chief Rabbi (*ḥakhām bāshi*) from outside of Yemen.[32] He is mentioned in four places as undertaking assignments for Kuḥayl. Yaḥyā Mizraḥi's letter to Sappir tells that Hashshāsh's first mission might have been to announce in Egypt that Shukr

Kuḥayl was still alive. The letter reveals that Hashshāsh was a bookseller and therefore traveled to various Jewish communities to sell his merchandise. He was thus a suitable messenger, one who could combine private business with his duty to the "messiah." Yaḥyā Mizraḥi writes further that in the period of time when he was expecting the reappearance of Shukr Kuḥayl I,

a man from the town of Ṣanᶜa, whose name is Mosheh Hashshāsh, came to Egypt, and he came to me, in the town of Alexandria. He sold me books of Torah and bought books. He stayed in my house for several days. He told me in secret that the rabbis of Ṣanᶜa know about Kuḥayl II, that he is alive, and that a letter from him came by messenger.[33]

Hashshāsh is the person referred to as the *maᶜaśer* collector and carrier of the epistle to the community of Ḥaydan: "I have sent this epistle, in order to collect the *maᶜaśer,* with the messenger Mūsā ibn Sālim al-Hashshāsh."[34] Additional sources tell of some more important duties undertaken by Mosheh Hashshāsh. Kuḥayl II's letter to the rabbis of Jerusalem (dated 13 Kislev, 5630/November, 1869) is addressed to Yaḥyā Mizraḥi, who was responsible for forwarding the letter to its destination. It reads:

And you, Rabbi Yaḥyā Mizraḥi—may the Lord find you well—give my regards to Ḥakham Yaḥyā, the head of the Yeshivah, of master Yaᶜaqov Baghdādī Nero, to him and to Ḥakham Merkado Nero, and tell them that I have received their greetings and their order given to Mosheh Hashshāsh.[35]

In an epistle written by Shukr Kuḥayl II's son to Rabbi Samuel Heller of Safed, dated 14 Kislev, 5630 (November 1869), Hashshāsh is once more the messenger:

And what you, Samuel Heller, have sent to me by the hand of Rabbi Yaḥyā Mizraḥi—may the Lord preserve him and keep him alive—I have received through Risha [i.e., Misha/Mosheh] Hashshāsh.[36]

Yaḥyā ben Avraham Levi is another messenger who served Shukr Kuḥayl II. His name appears in Kuḥayl II's letter to Yaḥyā Mizraḥi written around Sivan, 5629 (May, 1869): "And the responses to the epistles which you had sent me I have already given you by a previous messenger, Yaḥyā Avraham ben Levi."[37]

A third messenger is mentioned in yet another of Kuḥayl's letters, one to Alexandria, which seems to have been written at the beginning of

1870, and his name is Aharon ben Mosheh al-Muraysī: "And now I have sent to you [a messenger] so that you may give [money] for the redemption of your souls, as I have commanded you through the messenger, Aharon ben Mosheh al-Muraysī."[38]

Kuḥayl's organization was not restricted to a network of messengers. It included also resident agents who were appointed in Aden, and perhaps in other places also, to deal with monetary affairs. Such agents were Slemān al-Ḥarazī and Sālim al-Ḥarazī. Both collected and held the "tax" money in Aden, and then handed it over to one of Kuḥayl II's messengers. Kuḥayl II's letter to Moshe Ḥanokh, dated Kislev, 5630 (November, 1869), reads: "And send us in writing how much was collected from the people of your town in the hands of Mori Slemān al-Ḥarazī and in the hands of Sālim al-Ḥarazī."[39] A few months later, in Iyyar, 5630 (April, 1870), Shukr Kuḥayl II again writes to Moshe Ḥanokh:

. . . and let me know by letter as to how many Reals [i.e., *riyāls,* Yemeni silver coins] you have given into the hand of Mulla [Mori] Solaiman El-Ḥazi [lit., Slemān al-Ḥarazī] . . . and Salem El-Ḥarazī.[40]

In the course of this matter two persons are frequently referred to, Moshe Ḥanokh of Aden and Yaḥyā Mizraḥi of Alexandria. Even though they were not part of Kuḥayl's organization, their cooperation was crucial to the operation of the organization outside Yemen and to the maintenance of Kuḥayl's popularity in their home towns. Since his "conversion," around Ḥeshvan, 5629 (October, 1868),[41] Mosheh Ḥanokh, the rich merchant and respected leader of the Jewish community in Aden, became an example to be followed. He also turned into a natural contact man for inquiries from India concerning Kuḥayl and his movement. In Sivan, 5629 (May, 1869), he eagerly answered a letter from Rabbi Zalman Menahem Mendelevitch, *sheliaḥ de-rabbanan* from Hebron to Bombay, India, where he was residing at the time:

These days his [Kuḥayl's] reputation has become very strong, and whoever witnesses it with his own eyes cannot remain an unbeliever. All the nations of the world believe in him wholeheartedly, since he says that he is the messenger of the prophet Elijah, may his virtue stand us in good stead, Amen! And he is doing everything that the prophet Elijah tells him to do.[42]

Mosheh Ḥanokh, like Yaḥyā Mizraḥi, also served as an intermediary. He received and forwarded letters addressed to Kuḥayl from India,

Palestine, and even Egypt, and through him Kuḥayl II sent his own letters to India and Egypt. For example, Shukr Kuḥayl wrote to Mosheh Ḥanokh:

> The messenger whom you sent, Mulla Abraham ben Meshullam al-Sharābī, . . . arrived here on Friday, the 29th day of Nisan (5)630 AM (1870), with letters from thee and the prince Hacham Zalman [Mendelevitch] and from the Lord Obadiah [Sir Albert] David Sassoon, and from the Lord Rabbi Yaḥyā Mizraḥi . . . and two letters from the Holy Land, may it be built and established early in our time, Amen![43]

Unlike Ḥanokh, who became a believer only towards the end of 1868, Yaḥyā Mizraḥi was an enthusiastic supporter of Kuḥayl II from the beginning. In Alexandria he acted as the resident agent of Kuḥayl II, at times even as chief propagandist. He gathered all possible information about Shukr Kuḥayl and spread it around. A letter written by Ḥayyim Faraj in Alexandria to Jacob Sappir, probably at the end of 1868, reads:

> On the first day of this week, Rabbi Yaḥyā Mizraḥi . . . read before the gathering the epistles from Mosheh Ḥanokh which reached him, and everyone listened to him attentively; then he read for them an epistle by Shukr Kuḥayl himself.[44]

Yaḥyā Mizraḥi, the ardent supporter, was the person who received the epistles directed to the Jews of Egypt. He defended the redemption claims of Kuḥayl, and spread miraculous stories about him. He also served as the link through which passed most of Kuḥayl's correspondence with the Land of Israel.[45]

As we have seen, concern for the *maʿaśer* was an important aspect of the activity of Kuḥayl II's organization. The results of its ideological propaganda and the collection of contributions might also indicate to some extent the popularity of Shukr Kuḥayl II and the spread of his movement.[46] In Yemen proper letters like the epistle to Ḥaydan demanding the payment of *maʿaśer* reached Jews in various regions of the country.[47] Amram Qoraḥ describes the response:

> The trouble-stricken Jews from the villages were flowing to him, making fools of themselves, and gave him whatever was in their hands, money or valuables, clothes and jewelry, and even the garments off their backs.[48]

Despite Qoraḥ's exaggerated estimate, there is no record of the exact amounts collected in Yemen and of the communities which sent contributions. One should also remember that since Shukr Kuḥayl II had no means to enforce the payment of this levy, although he called it a compulsory tax, payment of the *maʿaśer* remained voluntary, and whatever was actually collected in this poor country could not have been much. It seems that the bulk of Kuḥayl II's income came from outside of Yemen, from the much richer community in Aden. Rabbi Mosheh Ḥanokh writes to Rabbi Zalman in Bombay, on the 24th of Sivan, 5629 (May, 1869), "In the town of Aden we have collected for him close to 200 riyāls (equivalent to 1,200 francs)."[49] Completing Ḥanokh's report, Solomon Reinman tells us about what he heard from Rabbi Benin of Aden:

> They sent him all that was collected in the house of prayer since the day it had been built. And each month he kept sending his messengers to collect money, and his believers in the thousands continue to bring their donations.[50]

While there are references to Kuḥayl II's tax collectors reaching Alexandria,[51] and while in India a strong group of believers was formed from among Jewish immigrants from Yemen, Iraq, and Persia,[52] it is not clear what the results of these efforts to raise the *maʿaśer* actually were. It is safe to assume, however, that some contributions from these communities too were sent to Kuḥayl II in Yemen.

Undoubtedly it was the *maʿaśer* money which allowed Shukr Kuḥayl to consolidate and strengthen his position as a would-be messiah. Collecting money, the organizational network connected with it, maintaining a "court," distributing charity to the needy, and negotiating with Muslim leaders—all these permitted him to be portrayed as a political figure able to govern and to influence future political-messianic events.

KUḤAYL II'S FALL

The turning point in the flow of the *maʿaśer,* which coincided with the decrease of Kuḥayl II's popularity, came after Jacob Sappir wrote his *Iggeret le-Teman* ("Epistle to Yemen") in Elul, 5629 (August, 1869). Its title, alluding to Maimonides' *Iggeret le-Teman,* addressed to the rabbis of Ṣanʿa, refuted Shukr Kuḥayl II's claim of being the messiah. To increase the impression of its importance, it was affixed to a letter of agreement signed by the rabbis of Jerusalem.[53] The epistle was copied and circulated in Yemen and became an important factor in undermining Kuḥayl's position.

Kuḥayl, however, did not give up. He launched new efforts to keep his movement alive and to regain support outside Yemen. He wrote letters to the community of Alexandria explaining the truth of his messianic mission, to Mosheh Ḥanokh in Aden, to Rabbi Samuel Heller (the head of the rabbinic court in Safed), and to the rabbis of Jerusalem.[54] But he never regained the ground lost, and the new situation led to financial difficulties. Collections decreased but his expenditures did not, and Kuḥayl had to look for an alternate source of revenue. At first he sought loans from his wealthy supporters. In a letter to Ḥanokh dated 17 Iyyar, 5630 (May, 1870) Kuḥayl writes:

> I will furthermore remind the beloved of my soul to send a letter to . . . Lord Obadiah David Sassoon . . . and also [to] . . . Yaḥyā Mizraḥi . . . that thou and they give me one thousand Reals as a loan, and with the help of God, may he be blessed, I will pay it back to you shortly.[55]

It is doubtful that his request was at all answered. It is evident, though, that when his financial situation became desperate, Kuḥayl was forced to borrow money from rich Arabs. As Solomon Reinman reports, "when the children of Israel ceased sending him more money . . . he borrowed at high interest from the lords of the Arabs." Borrowing money without being able to pay it back got Kuḥayl into trouble. His creditors "brought him before the judges, who put him in iron chains and sent him to prison."[56] Although Kuḥayl II managed to get himself released and continued to perform his role, he never fully recovered his position. The deterioration which began with Sappir's *Iggeret Teman* was speeded up in 1872, when the Ottoman Turks conquered Ṣanᶜa and large areas of the Yemenite highland. From then on Shukr Kuḥayl II no longer had the political backing which once allowed him to function—"he did not find any support, since the protection of the Arab shaykhs had ceased."[57] Yet Kuḥayl II's activity had not ceased. Rabbi Ḥayyim Feinstein, who visited Yemen in 1873, observed that Kuḥayl II was still active in the town of Tanᶜim, which remained outside Ottoman rule, and that he was still collecting the *maᶜaśer*.[58] He probably stayed there until 1875, when he was caught by the Ottomans and sent to Istanbul.[59] After some effort in his behalf was made by the heads of the Jewish community in Istanbul, Kuḥayl II was finally released and was allowed to return to Yemen.[60] He spent his last days in Ṣanᶜa, isolated and rejected by the community which he had once sought to redeem. He died there, in poverty and loneliness, in 1877 or 1878.[61]

In many ways Shukr Kuḥayl II's messianic movement was the continuation of the movement started by Shukr Kuḥayl I. One common feature was their call for repentance. They both preached that coming back to God wholeheartedly would prepare that generation for the eschatological period and would hasten redemption, but Kuḥayl II proposed an additional and bolder means to hasten redemption—the *maʿaśer*. In addition to the *maʿaśer*'s ideological function, its practical use and the organization which supported its collection contributed to the illusion of success and to the belief that Kuḥayl's efforts to bring redemption closer were on the verge of fulfillment. It seems, therefore, that Kuḥayl's movement was another outstanding expression of the active messianism which appears to characterize Yemenite Jewry.[62]

NOTES

1. For the political and social conditions in nineteenth-century Yemen, see R. B. Serjeant, "The Post-Medieval and Modern History of Ṣanʿāʾ and the Yemen ca. 953–1382/1515–1962," in *Ṣanʿāʾ, an Arabian Islamic City,* eds. R. B. Serjeant and R. Lewcock (London, 1983), pp. 86–94, 97–99; Manfred W. Wenner, *Modern Yemen, 1918–1966* (Baltimore, 1967), pp. 29–40.
2. For more on the Jews in Yemen, see the studies of S. D. Goitein collected in *The Yemenites: History, Communal Organization, Spiritual Life: Selected Studies,* ed. Menaḥem Ben-Sasson (Jerusalem, 1983) [Hebrew]; Yehudah Ratzaby's selected studies, *Be-maʿaglot Temān (Yemen Paths: Selected Studies in Yemenite Culture)* (Tel Aviv, 1988); Yehudah Nini's account of nineteenth-century Yemenite Jews in *Yemen and Zion: The Jews of Yemen, 1800–1914* (Jerusalem, 1982) [Hebrew]; and the portrait of the Jews of Yemen by Reuben Ahroni in *Yemenite Jewry: Origins, Culture, and Literature* (Bloomington, 1986).
3. Bat-Zion Eraqi Florman, "Jewish Messianism and Muslim Messianism in Yemen in the Nineteenth Century: An Inter-group Influence," *Peʿamim* 25 (1985): 40–64 [Hebrew].
4. Jacob Sappir, *Eben Sappir* (Mainz, 1874), 2:151. When Jacob Sappir stayed in Aden during his second visit to Yemen, he learned about Shukr Kuḥayl's messianic claim. Upon his return to Jerusalem, he strongly opposed Kuḥayl's claims at the time of his second "appearance." Sappir published his arguments against Kuḥayl in the Jerusalem newspaper *ha-Lebanon,* where he had a regular column headlined *"He-ḥadash mi-Teman"* ("News from Yemen"). The column provided updated information received from Yemen, Egypt, and Aden about the Yemenite messiah. As a result Sappir, the opponent of Kuḥayl's messianic claim, became the chief agent in publicizing

Kuḥayl outside of Yemen. Besides refuting Kuḥayl's claim, Sappir caused the rise of messianic hopes among some distant Jewish communities as far away as Russia. See Abraham Yaʿari, "Shukr Kuḥayl," in *Shevut Teman,* ed. Y. Yeshaʿyahu and A. Zadoc (Tel Aviv, 1945), pp. 145–146.

5. Such beliefs can also be found among the first Christians and the various sects of the Shīʿah (e.g., the Twelver Shiʿites who expect the reappearance of their twelfth imām, Muḥammad al-ʿAskarī [d. 878]), and were held about the Jewish messiah Abū ʿĪsā al-Iṣfahānī (middle of the eighth century), and the messiah in Yemen in 1172. For more about Shukr Kuḥayl I's messianic movement see Eraqi Klorman, "Messianism in the Jewish Community of Yemen in the Nineteenth Century" (Ph.D. diss., University of California in Los Angeles, 1981), pp. 126–141.
6. His first center was in Tanʿim, then was moved to al-Ṭawīlah and al-Qaranī, and then back to Tanʿīm.
7. Yaʿari, "Shukr Kuḥayl," pp. 124–148; Yosef Tobi, *The Jews of Yemen in the 19th Century* (Tel Aviv, 1976) [Hebrew], pp. 65–67. Nini, *Yemen and Zion* (pp. 144–151) hints at a new interpretation of the Kuḥayl I and Kuḥayl II movements, but as his discussion is limited to only a few pages, it is not fully developed.
8. Sappir, *Iggeret Teman ha-shenit* (Vilna, 1873), pp. 28–31.
9. Menaḥem ben Mosheh was a wealthy merchant and the head of the Jewish community in Aden in the middle of the nineteenth century. The prosperous Benin family played a leading role in the Jewish community of Aden throughout the nineteenth and the first half of the twentieth centuries.
10. Sappir, *Iggeret Teman,* p. 12.
11. Ibid., pp. 25–28.
12. Shukr Kuḥayl, "Epistle to Ḥaydan" (B. Eraqi Klorman's private collection).
13. Sappir, *Iggeret Teman,* pp. 14–20.
14. Ibid., p. 31.
15. A liquid measure, about three quarts.
16. Written circa Sivan 5629 (1869). Sappir, *Iggeret Teman,* p. 27.
17. Ibid., pp. 30, 27.
18. See Gershom Scholem, *Raʿyon ha-geʾullah be-qabbalah* (Jerusalem, 1946), pp. 13–14; idem, *Sabbatai Ṣevi: The Mystical Messiah* (Princeton, 1973), pp. 16–17; also Bracha Zak, "Galut Yiśraʾel we-galut ha-shekhinah ba-sefer Or yaqar le-Rabbi Mosheh Cordovero," *Meḥqere Yerushalayim be-maḥshevet Yiśraʾel,* 4 (1982): 157–78.
19. Sappir, *Iggeret Teman,* p. 28.
20. Ibid., pp. 18, 23.
21. Here, the practice of Islam.
22. Kuḥayl, "Epistle to Ḥaydan."
23. Yaʿari, "Shukr Kuḥayl," p. 134. Others agree with Yaʿari, e.g., Tobi, *The Jews of Yemen,* p. 65, who states that Kuḥayl II was preoccupied mainly with collecting gifts. See also Moshe Zadoc, *History and Customs of the Jews in the Yemen* (Tel Aviv, 1983) [Hebrew], p. 91.

24. Not even Sappir, whose objections to Kuḥayl II are elaborated in his *Iggeret Teman* (Mainz, 1869).
25. See Eraqi Klorman, "Jewish Messianism," pp. 43, 53.
26. Sappir, *Iggeret Teman,* p. 25; Amram Qoraḥ, *Seʿarat Teman* (Jerusalem, 1954), p. 37.
27. Sappir, *Iggeret Teman,* p. 11; Solomon Reinman, *Masaʿot Shelomoh* (Vienna, 1884), p. 13; and Ḥayyim Feinstien, "A Letter to the Editor," *Ha-Maggid* 18 (24 Tebet, 5634 [1874]) [Hebrew].
28. Qoraḥ, *Seʿarat Teman,* p. 37.
29. For a vivid description of this custom of protection see Ḥayyim Ḥabshush, *Journey in Yemen,* ed. S. D. Goitein [Hebrew] (Tel Aviv, 1939; reprinted Jerusalem, 1983; English edition, Jerusalem, 1951), pp. 51–55, 167. See also Joseph Halévy, "*Voyage au Nedjran; itinéraire d'un voyage dans le Yemen, 1869–1870,*" *Bulletin de la Société de géographie de Paris,* 6.6 (1873): 5–31, 249–273, 581–606; suite, 6.13 (1877): 466–479; and Ratzaby, *Be-maʿagalot Teman,* pp. 57–60.
30. Reinman, *Masaʿot Shelomoh,* p. 14; Halévy, *Voyage,* pp. 257–258, 270–271.
31. Sappir, *Iggeret Teman,* pp. 11, 13.
32. The appointment of a devoted supporter of Kuḥayl II as the representative of the Jews of Ṣanʿāʾ indicates that at least in the eyes of community leaders belief in Shukr Kuḥayl was not regarded as an offense. Similarly, other people (like Mosheh Ḥanokh and Yaḥyā Mizraḥi), who were connected with Kuḥayl's movement, continued their rapport with the Chief Rabbi of Ṣanʿāʾ and with other community leaders. I will explain elsewhere the stand of the rabbis of Ṣanʿāʾ and their part in the messianic movement of Shukr Kuḥayl II. For more on Hashshāsh's mission to Istanbul see Faraj Ḥayyim Mizraḥi, "Letter to the Editor," *ha-Lebanon,* 6 (Iyyar, 5636 [1876]); Nini, *Yemen and Zion,* pp. 110–111; and Tobi, *The Jews of Yemen,* pp. 109–110.
33. Sappir, *Iggeret Teman,* p. 7.
34. Kuḥayl, "Epistle to Ḥaydan."
35. Sappir, *Iggeret Teman,* p. 19.
36. Ibid., p. 21.
37. Ibid., p. 28.
38. Ibid., p. 23.
39. Ibid., p. 24.
40. D. S. Sassoon, "An Autograph Letter of A Pseudo-Messiah," *JQR* 19 (1907): 167. The quotations are Sassoon's translations.
41. The interesting story of how he became a believer is told by Ḥanokh in a letter to Rafael Suwārish in Alexandria, published in Sappir, *Iggeret Teman,* pp. 8–12.
42. Ibid., pp. 24–25.
43. Sassoon, "An Autograph Letter," pp. 164–165.
44. Sappir, *Iggeret Teman,* p. 12.

45. Ibid., pp. 6–8, 21, 25–26.
46. As I understand it, Shukr Kuḥayl II's success is closely connected with the stand of Yemen's rabbinical leadership towards him and his movement.
47. Sappir, *Iggeret Teman,* p. 10.
48. Qoraḥ, *Seʿarat Teman,* p. 37.
49. Sappir, *Iggeret Teman,* p. 25.
50. Reinman, *Masaʿot Shelomoh,* pp. 12–13.
51. Sappir, *Iggeret Teman,* p. 23.
52. Reinman, *Masaʿot Shelomoh,* p. 11.
53. In Sappir, *Iggeret Teman,* pp. 13–14.
54. Ibid., pp. 22, 24, 21, 14–19.
55. Sassoon, "An Autograph Letter," p. 167.
56. Reinman, *Masaʿot Shelomoh,* p. 14.
57. Qoraḥ, *Seʿarat Teman,* p. 38.
58. Feinstein, "A Letter to the Editor."
59. Faraj Ḥayyim Mizraḥi, "Letter to the Editor," *ha-Lebanon* 13 (Nisan, 5635 [1875]).
60. Faraj Ḥayyim Mizraḥi, "Letter to the Editor," *ha-Lebanon,* 2 (Ab, 5636 [1876]). The writer mistakenly says here that Kuḥayl II was not permitted to return to Yemen.
61. Qoraḥ, *Seʿarat Teman,* p. 38.
62. For messianic ideology in Yemen during the Sabbatian movement see Eraqi Klorman, "The Sabbatian Movement in Yemen," *Peʿamin* 15 (1983): 47–57 [Hebrew]. For Yemeni immigration to the Land of Israel interpreted as a vehicle to hasten redemption see Eraqi Klorman, "Messianic Motifs in Immigrations from Yemen, 1882–1914," *Peʿamim* 10 (1981): 21–35 [Hebrew].

VIII

ZIONISM AND THE STATE OF ISRAEL

18

Israel and the Messiah

Jacob Katz

The prayer for the well-being of the state of Israel, which is recited on Sabbaths and festivals in most synagogues in Israel and the Diaspora, calls the state *"reshit geulatenu,"* the commencement of our redemption. The formula implies that the creation of the state of Israel is to be viewed as the initial fulfillment of the messianic expectation cherished by past generations.

The text of the prayer was written by the Hebrew novelist S. Y. Agnon at the request of Isaac Herzog, chief rabbi at the time the state was founded. It has since had to be repeatedly defended by Orthodox authorities against those who find it inappropriate or even sacrilegious.

Some who are opposed to the formula, like the sect of Neturei Karta in Israel and their supporters abroad, deny any legitimacy at all to the Jewish state. Others, like the Orthodox party Agudat Israel and the heads of noted *yeshivot,* cooperate with the agencies of the state, accept the benefits derived from its institutions, and at times support the government in return, but still withhold fundamental spiritual approval. Where the more radical regard modern Israel as the very antithesis of the messianic redemption promised by Jewish tradition, the less radical declare the issue irrelevant. But for either camp, to use messianic vocabulary in praying for the welfare of the state borders on desecration of a hallowed religious concept.

This theological and ideological controversy obviously cannot be set-

Reprinted by permission of the American Jewish Committee and the author from *Commentary* 73 (January 1982).

tled except on its own terms. The question that a historian may address is not whether the state of Israel is worthy of association with the traditional messianic concept but whether a connection can in fact be drawn between the messianic hope entertained by Jews through the ages and the modern national movement that led to the founding of Israel. In order to approach this question we have to inquire first into the nature of traditional messianism.

Although the term itself is biblical in origin, messianism is a universal phenomenon. Tribes and nations of disparate cultural traditions and differing levels of civilization in many parts of the world have cherished the idea of a savior who will deliver them from their present physical or spiritual circumstances. But within the orbit of the immediate influence of Judaism, and especially in Christianity and Islam, the idea of messianic deliverance assumed a novel significance, albeit one that was to differ sharply from the Jewish prototype.

The specific historical conditions that lay behind the biblical image of an anointed ideal king (the original meaning of "messiah") need not concern us here. Probably as early as the Babylonian captivity, but certainly after the destruction of the Second Temple, the plight that required redemption was mainly not that of the Jews of Palestine but that of the Jews in exile. And the plight was not economic scarcity, social degradation, or spiritual decadence, although all these at times may have been experienced as adversities to be overcome by the redeemer. Once in exile, the Jews tended to understand these sufferings as mere byproducts of a basic deficiency, namely, exile itself, the condition of banishment.

Now, being removed from one's birthplace or country of origin is a misfortune only if one's commitment to that birthplace is so intense that any other place is experienced as a physical and spiritual trial. Uncounted numbers of people in human history have changed their dwelling through voluntary or forced emigration and in the fullness of time have accustomed themselves to the situation and adopted a new fatherland. It is one of the peculiarities of the Jews' fate, conditioned by many complex religious and historical factors, that despite the lengthy passage of time the consciousness of exile did not disappear. On the contrary, duration intensified rather than mitigated the subjective experience of calamity.

Messianism was both the cause and the result of the Jews' segregated existence throughout the centuries of exile. Initially the messianic belief may have strengthened their will to resist absorption by a foreign environment. Once the Jewish community established itself as a segregated socio-religious entity, its pariah-like situation nourished expectations of an ultimate return to its own homeland.

This dependence of Jewish messianism on the concrete situation of exile sets it apart from the millenarian fantasies of other socially or nationally suppressed groups. At the same time it distinguishes it from the purely spiritual longings of the Christian Second Coming. Jewish messianism has a point of reference in the factual history of the Jewish people. Jews had at one time lived in their own country, their own commonwealth; it was there they hoped to return in the messianic age.

In fact, a residue of the former national existence continued to play an active role in the cultural and mental life of every Jewish community. Acquaintance with the geographical scenes and contours of the homeland through constant reading of the Bible lent tangibility to the longing for return. More important perhaps was the fact that Jews continued to study and adhere to the laws of the Mishnah, which reflect the realities of life in the period of the Second Temple (when they were codified) but served long thereafter as a guide to important aspects of individual and communal conduct. The intellectual elite dedicated itself to the study of a body of law which, taken as whole, would function once again when the nation was living under its own government in the projected messianic age. Various elements in the life of the community thus linked the memory of the past with the expectation of the future, keeping the vision of the messianic era in contact with historical reality.

Although it was exceptional in its concreteness, Jewish messianism did share with all forms of millenarianism an imaginary conception of the means to be employed in bringing about the redemption. Having failed to restore independence through military action in Roman times (the last serious attempt was the Bar Kokhba revolt in 132 C.E.), Jews ceded their fate to the unfathomable wisdom of divine Providence. This shift in the mental attitude of the nation was not the consequence of a mere ideological development. The circumstances in which Jews lived in the Middle Ages restricted their freedom of action to sporadic interventions on the local level. Any attempt to alter the basic situation of a scattered and barely tolerated people was simply inconceivable. No wonder, then, that

Jewish faith in an ultimate redemption became interwoven with a belief in supernatural agency. What the human partner could contribute was, at most, intercession with the celestial power in order to hasten the redemption.

There were in the main two avenues for inducing heaven to bring about salvation. (We may disregard the purely magical machinations of kabbalists.) One was to gain divine grace by complying perfectly with the obligatory religious duties as these were interpreted by Jewish tradition. In this approach, redemption would follow not upon any one particular religious or spiritual undertaking but upon the achievement of total religious perfection by the community at large. Others, however, found indications in the authoritative sources of some special deed or procedure that might avail. Thus in 1538 the scholars of Safed made an abortive attempt to reestablish the ancient Sanhedrin as the first act in the messianic drama; in doing so they were following a suggestion of Maimonides as to the sequence of events preceding the appearance of the messiah. A similar phenomenon was the hasty marrying-off of young couples during the feverish excitement occasioned by rumors of the impending messianic revelation of Sabbatai Ṣevi in 1666. (According to a saying in the Talmud, all the souls yet to be born have to reach their destiny before the messiah can appear. Mass marriages were meant literally to fulfill this condition.) As late as the 1830s Rabbi Zvi Hirsh Kalisher, later to become a steadfast advocate of Jewish settlement in Palestine and as such a veritable precursor of modern Zionism, was still addicted to this pattern of thought. Kalisher wished to obtain permission from the Turkish authorities, as well as the consent of his rabbinical colleagues, to institute a certain kind of animal sacrifice on the site of the Jerusalem Temple; on the basis of his scholarly research he believed that the restoration of animal sacrifice was a precondition for initiating the messianic process.

In the concept of supernatural redemption, as these examples suggest, human initiative was consistently restricted to spiritual or ritualistic devices. The possibility, or for that matter the permissibility, of a national restoration through human means was hardly ever discussed or debated. At most it was referred to in a homiletic or exegetic context (not always negatively). At bottom lay an acquiescence in the passive role Jewry was supposed to play as a nation in exile, at the mercy of others.

The spell of this state of mind was broken in the eighteenth and nineteenth centuries when the Jews acquired citizenship owing to the revolutionary changes in some of the nations in which they lived. Citizenship meant an end to the condition of exile in an absolutely unforeseen and therefore most confusing way.

Accepting citizenship in a non-Jewish state was regarded both by the Jews and by their emancipators as incompatible with the messianic belief that was an uncontested article of Jewish faith. Jews were more or less explicitly requested to renounce this tenet—no easy thing to do, although the impediment was not so much dogma as the role the idea had played in Jewish history. Indeed, there was a minority opinion recorded in the Talmud that confined the notion of the Messiah to biblical times alone and denied its significance for the future. This talmudic authority was cited by Lazarus Bendavid, a spokesman of the radical Enlightenment in late eighteenth-century Berlin, to refute a Catholic missionary who had observed that the Jews, having thrown away a cornerstone of their religious system in return for their emancipation, ought logically to accept the Christian redeemer. Bendavid retorted that the Jewish religion remained intact even without the messianic belief. As if on second thought, he added that Jewish messianism had anyway found its fulfillment in the liberation of the Jews by the rulers of contemporary states.

Bendavid's convoluted argument can be said to reflect the intellectual predicament in which Jews found themselves in the wake of their changed situation. Their political status may have required them to abandon the messianic tenet, yet other, less conspicuous, considerations militated against it. The need to meet the Christian challenge in a positive way, rejecting the Christian messiah while retaining a Jewish version of messianism, was one such consideration. The main reason, however, was an internal one: the messianic ideal was deeply ingrained in the Jewish mentality. Simply to try to eradicate it because of the changed political circumstances would have been a futile enterprise. What was possible was a reinterpretation, which is what Bendavid proposed.

His response to the historical situation became typical for succeeding generations. Although the Jews' integration into the modern state was not the result of an internal Jewish development, it still represented a decisive turn in their destiny, and they were inclined to understand it in terms of traditional concepts. Emancipation seen as the fulfillment of the expected messianic redemption was admittedly a forced interpretation, but understandable in light of events. It is astonishing how many Jews who experienced emancipation from the ghetto almost instinctively described the event in terms drawn from the vocabulary of traditional Jewish messianism. Such emancipating rulers as Napoleon and the Emperor Joseph II of Austria were compared explicitly with the biblical Cyrus, and the dawning of the Enlightenment was frequently portrayed as the equivalent of the Messianic Age.

Still, when reform-minded theologians drew the practical implications and proposed omitting references in Jewish ritual to the future return to Zion, they met with fierce opposition. Not only the Orthodox but also the exponents of the so-called historical school objected. Granting the quasi-messianic significance of Jewish emancipation, they were still reluctant to repudiate the idea of a possible national redemption, even if projected into a remote and hazy future.

By the early 1860s political emancipation in Western countries could already be taken for granted; at the same time it could be transcended, at least by those of broader vision who, although they welcomed Jewish emancipation, were reluctant to see in it the consummation of Jewish history. Two such thinkers were Rabbi Kalisher and Rabbi Yehuda Alkalay.

Kalisher was an outstanding Ashkenazi talmudist, Alkalay a Sephardi preacher. Both were at the outset imbued with traditional messianism; in the course of time both integrated the historical experience of their age into their thinking. Jewish emancipation, really the antithesis of the traditional messianic expectation, came to be seen by them as the initial phase in an evolving process of redemption. The social elevation of the Jewish individual became a precondition for collective national liberation.

By dint of this rethinking, the very definition of redemption underwent a change. The human initiative destined to usher in the messianic age was no longer seen in spiritual or ritualistic terms. The establishment of the Alliance Israélite Universelle and the tangible political influence of Jewish notables like Moses Montefiore and the Rothschilds were taken to suggest that the resettlement of Jews in their ancient homeland by human means was not impossible. Such attempts at resettlement were regarded as necessary to the messianic enterprise; it was expected that a divine response would follow and complete the process.

That this reinterpretation of the messianic tradition was no mere idiosyncrasy is demonstrated by the fact that it was advanced independently (with some variations) by different people and, once published, found a following. In 1862, when Kalisher published a tract setting forth his views, he seems not to have been acquainted with the writings of Alkalay—no surprise, in view of the geographic distance and the difference in background that separated them. (Kalisher lived in the East Prussian town of Thorn, Alkalay in the town of Semelin near Belgrade.) Kalisher was not even aware of the existence of an Ashkenazi preacher, Natan Friedland, who pursued a similar trend on his own, although he presented it in a more homiletic fashion. It was Friedland who detected the affinity between his own thinking and that of his more famous contemporary and, encouraged by the coincidence, gave his thought a more direct and daring expression. More important perhaps for Kalisher's own self-confidence was the unconditional approval he received from his rabbinical colleague Elijah Guttmacher. A secluded scholar and kabbalist, Guttmacher was reputed to be a miracle-working saint; when he announced unequivocally that the appropriate means to pave the way for the coming of the messiah was to repopulate Palestine, it could not fail to impress many Jews.

We thus have here a new development in Jewish thinking, of which the main characteristic is the permission or even the demand for the partial realization of the messianic vision by human effort. Obviously this development did not occur in a vacuum but had to do with the impact of historical events: the unexpected and in traditional terms inexplicable emancipation of the Jews as well as the contemporaneous resurrection of the European nations. But there was equally a dialectical development within Jewish messianism itself. In particular it is impossible to ignore the deep emotional dimension that accompanied the emergence of the ideas we have discussed.

In the thought of Moses Hess, who joined the group of these early Zionists as a secular outsider, we find a similar melange of cognitive and emotional elements. A socialist ideologue estranged from Judaism since his youth, Hess at the age of fifty recovered his Jewish commitment and evolved a theory of what Judaism could still signify beyond the two contemporary variations of Reform and Neo-Orthodoxy. He advocated a national restoration in the ancient homeland and was strongly convinced that such an ingathering would release the spiritual energy embodied in petrified religious institutions. The national revival of Italy and contemporary intellectual trends that encouraged the revitalization of dormant historical sources obviously had an influence of Hess. But there is also no missing his messianic sentiments. A vision of a redeemed and rehabilitated Judaism had been implanted in Hess's mind as a child, when he observed his grandfather mourning for the destruction of the Temple in Jerusalem. His messianic vision drew its emotional power from that long suppressed childhood experience. Thus, although they differed over what would happen once the first stage of the redemptive process was accomplished, Hess and the Orthodox messianists were partisans of the same cause. And they also agreed about the immediate task: the ingathering of Jews in Palestine.

Despite remarkable exertions by Alkalay and Kalisher, very little, if anything, was accomplished on this score. Nevertheless, the concrete history of the Jewish national movement has to be dated from the appearance of this group. The vestiges of their influence can be traced in the years up to the emergence of the Hovevei Zion movement in the wake of the 1881 pogroms in Russia.

That movement, which defined its objective as the restoration and rehabilitation of the Jewish nation in its historical homeland, crystallized under the impact of the pogroms, but it could do so because the idea of a national revival had been adopted by at least certain sections of the population. The dissemination of the nationalist idea owed much to the expansion of the Hebrew press, headed by the weekly *Ha-Maggid,* which catered to a widely scattered Hebrew-reading public, especially in Russia and Rumania. Traditional yet open-minded, it appealed to a new type of Jew who transcended traditional attitudes.

The example of emancipated Western Jewry, as well as the repeated attempts by the Russian government to extricate Jews from the traditional cultural and occupational patterns, made people aware that changes in their situation were possible through their own initiatives and efforts. A readiness to act in the public interest was often combined with an Enlightenment vision of a future based on the Western model: political emancipation, social acceptance, and cultural accommodation. But this projected ideal stood in stark contrast to reality; the Jewish community in Russia and for that matter in Rumania was a politically underprivileged, socially segregated, and culturally self-reliant minority. As it happens, however, the vision of Jewish integration as the ultimate destiny of the community had already been discarded by thinkers who were in direct contact with Western countries where it had originally emerged.

The chief exponent of the new trend was the novelist Peretz Smolenskin. A militant critic of social and religious conditions especially in Russia, the land of his birth, Smolenskin fought for his convictions through his literary creations and his journalistic writings, both appearing in the monthly *Ha-Shaḥar,* which he edited in Vienna from 1868 on. Attacking the rabbinical as well as the lay leadership of his time, Smolenskin laid the blame for all shortcomings on the Berlin *Haskalah* (Enlightenment) and the subsequent Reform movement in Germany. The erosion of Jewish national unity and of the intrinsic link between social life and religion derived from these early developments, in Smolenskin's view. The mechanical tampering with religious tradition, especially the excision of symbols connected to the future rebirth of the nation, had sapped the vital forces of the community and led to the present dismal state of affairs. At the same time, the "reward" for these reforms, the integration of the Jews as equals in the surrounding society, never stood a chance of realization.

Erroneous and unjust as this criticism may be historically, its significance for its time cannot be overrated. It amounted to a repudiation of all that the *Haskalah* stood for, namely, the hope that Russian Jews could improve their status by emulating the ways of their brethren in the West. Smolenskin had no alternative proposals for either the religious or the political problems of the community. Opposed to Reform, he was at the same time scandalized by the traditional rabbinate; he believed that by turning away from assimilation the community might somehow dispense with the excesses in its tradition and retain only the essentials. As for politics, Smolenskin lacked a substitute for the *Haskalah* belief in civic emancipation. When he first unfolded his views, the idea of settlement in Palestine did not yet occupy his mind. He strongly recommended the reestablishment of national unity and the regaining of trust in the national future as the basis for any collective action, which would then automatically follow. These ideas laid the groundwork for the political program of national revival in the homeland, which emerged in the wake of the pogroms of the 1880s. Smolenskin himself then became an active supporter of the Hovevei Zion.

Others had made this transition before the pogroms broke out. The assistant editor (and from 1880 the chief editor) of *Ha-Maggid,* David

Gordon, impressed both by Rabbi Kalisher and by Moses Hess, and like Smolenskin opposed to the anti-nationalism of the Reform movement, defended Jewish nationalism on the modern principle that each nation should adhere to its own customs, language, and laws. How much weight in this scheme would be given to each attribute could not be authoritatively prescribed. Indeed, with the spread of the national ideal, different configurations evolved, with some assigning religion a central role and others restricting its scope or giving it up altogether in favor of other components in the national heritage.

Traces of this intellectual development became evident during the first flowering of the national movement after the pogroms of 1881, when there arose a broad consensus that at least a certain part of Russian Jewry would have to leave the country. America was the obvious goal of emigration: it was a country known to be prepared to absorb newcomers, and a contingent of Russian Jews had already settled there in the years preceding the pogroms. But Palestine was suggested as an alternative, and a prolonged and passionate debate went on for years over the relative merits of the two.

That a land lacking all the attributes that made America attractive could enter this competition at all was testimony to the previous spreading of the idea that only there could the Jews pursue their national destiny. This in turn was clearly a derivation of the messianic vision of *Eretz Israel* as the locale for the miraculous reestablishment of the ancient Jewish commonwealth. The emotional commitment to Palestine was all the stronger for having undergone a process of secularization.

The choice of Palestine may reveal still another indebtedness to traditional messianism. So little was known about the difficulties of life there that the decision to settle in Palestine must be taken as an emphatically irrational act. The only compensation for ignorance was belief in the predetermined destiny that tied the Jewish people to the Holy Land, a destiny that guaranteed the success of the enterprise. For the secular pioneers, the notion of historical inevitability replaced the faith in divine promise held by the Orthodox thinkers. In both cases, however, we see the operation of what may be called messianic determinism.

The messianic impulse did not exhaust its momentum with the first wave of emigrants. On the contrary, subsequent events contributed new stimuli that worked in the same direction. The awareness that Jewish life was being restored in the Holy Land almost automatically evoked images from the Bible that lent themselves to explicit messianic interpretation. In July 1882 Marcus Lehmann, the editor of *Israelit,* the organ of German Orthodoxy, convened a group of rabbinical and lay leaders of southern Germany to discuss how to assist Russian Jews who had left their country in the wake of the previous year's pogrom. Lehmann opened the session with these words: "It is a wonderful token of the time that a general yearning for the Holy Land has seized a countless multitude of our coreligionists especially in Russia . . . We must heed the hints of divine Providence and pave the way for a Jewish future of the most far-reaching consequences." He cited the biblical examples of Zerubbabel, Ezra, and Nehemiah, who, though facing immense difficulties, brought about the establishment of the Second Commonwealth.

Messianic overtones permeated the lives of the early settlers. As the historian Azriel Shochat has argued, even the choice of names for settlements—such as Petah Tikvah (The Door of Hope) or Rishon LeZion (First in Zion)—was guided by a wish to connect the present enterprise with the prophets' vision of Israel's future. Striking biblical passages of unequivocal messianic intent, like Ezekiel's vision of the valley of dry bones brought to life, became a recurring motif in Zionist speeches and writings. This passage appears as the motto of an association founded in Jerusalem in 1882 by Eliezer Ben Yehuda and Yehiel Michael Pines and appropriately called Tehiyat Israel, "revival of Israel." Two years later the prophets' vision served as the text for a moving sermon by Rabbi Shmuel Mohilever at the closing session of a Hovevei Zion meeting in Kattowitz. The revival of the dry bones became a Zionist *topos,* occurring independently to many people who were engaged in the revitalization of their nation.

The compelling messianic associations aroused by the national enterprise are also forcefully demonstrated by the negative reaction to them in some Orthodox circles. Secularized Jews could oppose Zionism out of political or other reasons and possibly remain indifferent to the messianic issue. An Orthodox Jew had no such middle course. The explicitly messianic discourse of Kalisher and his circle elicited much resentment in rabbinic circles. Once the movement got under way, it had either to be embraced or rejected.

The rejection by some Orthodox and especially some hasidic authorities was emphatic indeed, assuming almost the character of religious anathema. The notion of independent human action, which struck at the heart of the traditional supernatural definition of messianism, was denounced as bordering on heresy. Whatever other motives may have been involved in shaping this attitude of total censure—simple conservatism, disquiet over the religious conduct of the settlers, the anticipation of possible failure—central to it was the impulse to protect the sacred concept of messianism from secular trespass.

The leaders of the Hovevei Zion attributed their failure to attract the Jewish masses, especially in hasidic districts, to the almost universal antagonism of the hasidic courts. The non-hasidic authorities were divided among themselves: some belonged to the Zionist movement, others supported or condoned it, still others objected to it or condemned it outright. Yet even the supporters evinced a reservation concerning the messianic interpretation of the movement. Almost to a man, they advocated resettlement of the Holy Land on the basis of the preference given by traditional religious sources to life lived there as opposed to anywhere else. To this formal religious obligation—the positive commandment of settling in *Eretz Israel*—they sometimes added other considerations of contemporary relevance: the advantages of an agricultural life and the like. These had already been adduced by Kalisher as subsidiary props to his main argument, which was, of course, his messianic concept. His successors in the Hovevei Zion generation ignored the messianic aspect altogether. Abraham Jacob Slucki, who in 1891 published a collection of opinions by noted rabbis on the religious status of the movement, apologized for the fact that there were members of Hovevei Zion who regarded developments in the Holy Land as "the beginning of the redemption."

This neutralizing tendency among official spokesmen of Judaism hardly reflected the popular sentiments that nourished the movement even in its periods of relative stagnation. Those engaged in keeping the Hovevei Zion alive referred to it in correspondence as their "sacred assignment." Such quasi-religious attachment to the idea must have persisted in all the circles that followed the vicissitudes of the movement sympathetically.

The appearance on the scene of Theodor Herzl quickened these latent sentiments. Lending the movement an unhoped-for dimension, he provided the necessary incitement for popular imagination to run high. Herzl possessed all the qualities of a charismatic leader and was often identified with the messiah in his meetings with the Jewish masses. Such an identification, which amazed Herzl himself, was just as often criticized by the intellectuals in the movement.

The next opportunity for messianic sentiments to emerge was the traumatic experience of the second wave of pogroms starting in 1903; bloodier by far than the first. With the subsequent failure of the 1905 revolution, the hopes for Jewish integration in a reformed Russia were finally dashed. These events set in motion the greatest exodus of Jews from the country, with the majority of the emigrants once again heading for America. A fraction, however, consisting of young men and women with strong convictions, chose to join the early settlers in Palestine. Thus began the period of the Second Aliyah, which added to the foundations of the first an entirely new social and ideological dimension. The newcomers shared with the oldtimers the quality of messianic determinism: they were convinced of the historic necessity of Jewish national regeneration. But while the First Aliyah had been content to leave the contours of the national revival to the future, the new pioneers came with a set of preconceived social and religious ideas. These ideas gave expression to another feature of messianism: utopianism.

Messianism in its "supernatural" form held that the future would be shaped by the hand of Providence; thus it ought to have had no room for utopian fantasy. This was in fact the position of Moses Maimonides and other medieval Jewish philosophers. The popular imagination, however, projected into the messianic age a glorious image, the inverse in every respect of Jewish existence in exile. Zionism too, in the course of time, evolved a multitude of utopian blueprints. The Second Aliyah was especially given to them.

The most influential of these scenarios was a variant of Marxian socialism transferred from the pioneers' Russian background. It is associated with the names of Ber Borochov and, in its elitist version, Aharon David Gordon. Disassociating himself from other socialist ideologies, Gordon made the national revival of the Jews dependent on a return to manual and especially agricultural work—an ideal he himself consistently lived up to despite far-reaching personal sacrifices. The theories of both Borochov and Gordon seem rather removed from any special Jewish connotations. Borochov's dependence on Marx is explicit, Gordon's indebtedness to the example of Tolstoy has often been remarked upon. Yet both theories centered upon the contention that the goal could be achieved only in the Jewish homeland—a condition lacking all logical consistency and hence, in the final analysis, messianic. Similarly, the Zionist theorist Ahad Ha'am postulated that the revival of an original Jewish ethic, which he claimed to be the essence of Judaism (religion was only its outer expression) would take place with the return to Palestine—an idea which once again makes sense only on the basis of an irrational conviction that renewed contact with the ancient homeland would have a revolutionary impact on Judaism.

Although they differed in what they demanded of Jews, these three utopian blueprints were united in neglecting or even directly excluding traditional Jewish religion from their vision of the future. They thus conformed to the prevailing tendency to shape the life of the new society apart from or in opposition to Jewish tradition. Still, the tradition also had its representative, in the towering figure of Rabbi Abraham Isaac Kook, whose vision was built on messianic foundations proper.

An outstanding talmudist and student of Kabbalah, Kook demonstrated his adherence to the national movement by joining the emigrants to Palestine at the outset of the Second Aliyah in 1904. Impressed by the renaissance of Jewish life in the country, Kook took it to be an indication of divine grace, opening the process of redemption. In his enthusiasm and with his exceptional gift for literary expression he produced in his writings a profound interpretation of his time, pregnant with kabbalistic connotations and metaphysical overtones. Kook's writings left far behind the thought of his timid rabbinical precursors, who had defined the spiritual significance of the resettlement in the Holy Land purely in terms of Jewish religious law. He returned to the explicitly messianic conception of Kalisher and Alkalay, the first apostles of national revival, but surpassed them in depth and intellectual daring.

Kook differed from all his predecessors on one crucial point. All the rabbinic authorities who supported the Palestinian enterprise had made their consent to it dependent upon the settlers' being observant Jews. Kook, no less conservative in principle, nevertheless lent an overriding significance to the rebuilding of the country, even if accomplished by nonobservant agents. This did not impair his ultimate vision—a reconstructed traditional life based on Jewish religious law but highly spiritualized, as would befit the generation chosen to see the dawn of the messianic age. But for the present, Kook's messianic scenario condoned and even justified the lives and work of the secular pioneers. It thus secured a measure of unity between the camps of traditionalists and innovators—an indispensable precondition for the creation many years later of the state of Israel.

Messianic determinism played a part in several different phases of Zionist history. The conviction, permeating all ranks of society, that the underlying forces of Jewish history would inevitably culminate in a Jewish commonwealth imparted energy and a willingness for sacrifice to many people who might otherwise have been apathetic. But if this quality of dedication provided, and continues to provide, the Israeli enterprise with boundless energy, it has also tested the ability of Israel to adapt to changing circumstances. Any action taken under the rubric of messianic determinism is necessarily limited in its rationality. It is based on the assumption that the individual is responsible only for the preliminary steps; their completion is assigned to the messianic power or, in secular terms, to hidden historical forces. Activities undertaken in line with such conceptions may at times achieve what seems impossible; at other times they meet insurmountable difficulties and are defeated or frustrated. The history of Zionism is replete with both kinds of experiences; a contemporary example is that of Gush Emunim, the Orthodox "bloc of the faithful" who are vociferous champions of Jewish sovereignty in the occupied territories of Judea and Samaria.

The messianic drive behind the activities of Gush Emunim is blatantly apparent. Its quasi-political goal, the annexation of the full extent of the Holy Land as defined by religious tradition, is predicated on the belief that this is the precondition for the divine redemption—similar to what Zvi Hirsh Kalisher had believed for the more modest goal of establishing Jewish settlements in the country. Indeed, with the emergence of Gush Emunim this line of thought has come full circle, returning once again to a definition of the national objectives not just in religious but literally in fundamentalist terms. At any rate, the activities of Gush Emunim are characterized by feverish intensity and by inflexibility; only time will tell what their ultimate fate will be.

Less acute than messianic determinism but no less problematic is the other legacy of Zionist history, utopianism. The ingathering of the Jews, an achievement due to the belief in messianic ideals, has exacted a price: the results are often measured against utopian standards of judgment, and are inevitably found wanting. Aside from the gap that exists between every ideal and its fulfillment, there is the additional problem that the various Zionist utopias (social, cultural, religious) are mutually exclusive. Each could be realized only at the expense of the others; the outcome is disappointment for all parties concerned.

Zionist reality as embodied in the state of Israel is measured by a host of yardsticks, not only by outsiders but even more so by those who have created that reality and participate in it daily. This is perhaps the lot of all pluralistic societies. Yet Israelis critical of their society today tend to draw more far-reaching conclusions than used to be the case. It is not uncommon to jump from criticism to, if not the negation of the state, then at least to a renunciation of one's allegiance to it, thus justifying emigration from the country. It sometimes seems as if the very existence of the state has yet to be taken for granted, that even its *right* to exist depends on the fulfillment of an unwritten contract with one of many utopian visions.

The dangers inherent in the intimate connection between Zionism and messianism are thus palpable. To meet them, some have argued that Zionism can and should be vindicated without resort to such irrational backing. Arguments of this kind have been marshaled to counter the growing claims made by movements like Gush Emunim, but the arguments themselves are not new. As early as 1929 the great scholar of Kabbalah, Gershom Scholem, protested on behalf of "thousands of Zionists" against the blurring of boundaries between the political aims of Zionism and the religious expectations of Jewish messianism. Since then, Scholem repeatedly confirmed his profound opposition to such enterprises—an opposition that comes with special point from one who has dedicated his life to the study of the irrational dimensions of Judaism and has even been motivated in his scholarship by his personal attachment to the project of national revival. Aware of the misguided potentialities of irrational messianism as demonstrated by the seventeenth-century false messiah Sabbatai Ṣevi, and by the movement bearing his name, Scholem warned of similar dangers to modern-day Zionism.

The parallelism between Sabbateanism and Zionism was and is a recurring theme in the historical evaluation of Zionism, especially among its opponents. For the late Rabbi Joel Teitelbaum, the most consistent antagonist of Zionism in the last generation, Zionism and Sabbateanism were veritable synonyms. Since the ingathering into the Holy Land and the regaining of Jewish political independence had taken place without divine intervention or confirmation, as prescribed by traditional messianic sources, Zionism for Rabbi Teitelbaum represented an even greater usurping force than had the movement of Sabbatai Ṣevi.

The danger of messianic encroachments on politics will in the end have to be met politically. It is the test of statesmanship to channel popular sentiment toward politically defensible objectives. Indeed, the continued welfare of the state may depend on success or failure in this regard. But the neutralization of messianism can certainly not be achieved by denying its role in the history of Zionism. Attempts to banish the messianic ingredient may seem ideologically necessary to some, but the spontaneous sentiments of the Jewish people suggest the futility of the effort. The news of the Balfour Declaration in 1917; the conquering of Palestine by the English in World War I, and the inauguration of the first High Commissioner, Herbert Samuel; the 1947 United Nations decision on the establishment of a Jewish state; the declaration of independence; the victory of the Six-Day War in 1967 were all experienced as momentous and predictive occurrences for which, in Jewish cultural tradition, the messianic vocabulary is the only appropriate one. To blot out the points of reference contained in the messianic myth, even if it were possible, would impoverish the national consciousness.

Rabbinic legalists, secular ideologues, and scholars have for their various reasons tried to separate Zionism from messianism, but popular sentiment will have none of it. And this is as it should be. In every generation Jews have prayed for redemption, and never failed to include in their prayers the hope for a return to the homeland under independent Jewish rule. When this petition seemed to have been answered in our day, it was only natural to identify the momentous event as a partial fulfillment of the messianic hope. Thus the term "the commencement of our redemption," included in the prayer for the state of Israel, is highly appropriate. Holding out still the hope for a total messianic consummation yet to arrive, it is at once an article of faith and an accurate reflection of historical reality.

19

Foundations of a Political Messianic Trend in Israel

Uriel Tal

This study sets out to present a critical analysis, based on primary sources, of a political messianic trend in Jewish religious nationalism in Israel. The basic premise underlying the dogma held by this trend maintains that since the beginning of the Zionist enterprise, and particularly since Israel's victory in the Six-Day War, the country has lived in a political reality which is transcendental. Accordingly, the military conquest in the Six-Day War is evidence of the state of metaphysical transformation in which the political reality finds itself—to a degree that the holiness of the Land of Israel, as stated by Rabbi Shmaryahu Arieli in *The Law of War,* extends even to conquered foreign lands, including the Sinai Desert, Sharm el-Sheikh and the eastern shore of the Suez Canal. This is not the beginning, but rather the midst of a messianic era, in which the Land of Israel is liberated not only from political adversaries, but also—as put by Rabbi E. Hadaya in the collection of sources 'Inherited Land'—from the *sitra aḥra* (the 'other side', the 'devil's camp'), i.e., from a mystical force which embodies evil, defilement and moral corruption, and we are thus entering an era in which absolute sanctity rules over corporeality. By virtue of the war, the Divine Presence *(Shekhina),* which has rested upon the Zionist enterprise from its inception, arises

Reprinted by permission from *The Jerusalem Quarterly* 35 (Spring 1985). This article is a translated transcription—edited posthumously—of a recording of the opening lecture of a seminar held at Tel Aviv University by 'Forum' and 'The International Center for Peace in the Middle East' on March 11, 1984. It was published in Hebrew in *Ha'aretz* on September 26, 1984. All sources quoted here are in Hebrew.

from the dust, and is saved from the existential exile in which the Jew languished. Having raised the *Shekhina* from its debasement, the return —according to this view—of even an inch of land, would be a surrender to the rule of the *'klipa'*, the concept of Jewish mysticism which symbolizes the forces of evil in the cosmos. Then, the *sitra aḥra* would regain sovereignty.

In a similar vein, some of the leading spokesmen of the messianic trend express themselves in *Nekuda,* organ of the Jewish settlements in the occupied territories. In accordance with this basic premise, the 'Peace for Galilee' war was another sanctified war, i.e., a war of religious duty, and Israel's military presence in Lebanon confirmed the validity of the biblical promise in Deuteronomy 11:24: 'Every place on which the sole of your foot treads shall be yours; our border shall be from the wilderness and the Lebanon, from the river, the River Euphrates, to the Western Sea'.

The dogma is applied on two levels: time and place. With regard to the level of time, the present is defined metaphysically, as a process of redemption. This imbues the actual lived-in time (and not time as an abstract concept) with two degrees of messianic sacredness, in accordance with two interpretive explanations of the difference between this world and the messianic era.

The first degree follows the view of the Talmudic sage, Mar Shmuel, who asserts (in *Berakhot* 34b) that there is no distinction between this world and the Messiah's time except that in the former there is 'political subjugation' or the subjugation of the exiles. Consequently, the messianic era finds its empirical expression in the concrete political change Israel has wrought, the essence of which is the abolition of political subjugation, or exile. The messianic era, according to this interpretation, does not yet enter the realm of cosmic transformation, where changes in the natural order occur. Therefore, when the prophets prophesied cosmic changes and drastic alteration in the natural order ('The wolf shall dwell with the lamb, and the leopard shall lie down with the kid'), they were referring not to the messianic era—which, as we have seen, does exist politically in our time—but rather to the world to come.

Rabbi Shlomo Goren, in his article 'The Redemption of Israel in Light of the *Halakha*' (in *'Torat ha-Mo'adim'*), cites the authority of Maimonides in this instance: 'The messianic age is this world, and things remain as they are' (*Hilekhot Tshuva* 9:2), the only difference between them being that in messianic times 'the Kingdom will return to Israel'. Hence, Rabbi Goren concludes, we can and must attribute absolute holiness to this world, not to the world to come, or to abstract mysticism. It is in concrete reality that the redemptive time, according to this doctrine of messianic-political realism, is actualized. Similarly, Maimonides states that 'one should not suppose that in the messianic age anything will be changed in the way of the world, or that there will be a renewed Creation' (*Hilekhot Melachim* 12:1). Hence, Rabbi Goren stresses, there is no need to search for cosmic transformations in the Creation in order to believe that the present constitutes a messianic reality of liberation from the subjugation of the exiles.

Messianic times thus constitute a period of political change, realized by force of Israel's arms and the particular aid of heavenly assistance, whereas the prophecies of peace, such as Isaiah's 'and they shall beat their swords into ploughshares', refer to the world to come. They are not to be fulfilled in this world, or in the messianic era which is now dawning.

The second degree of the sacredness of time—a more mystical approach which is becoming increasingly acceptable to *Gush Emunim*—is based on Rabbi Ḥiyya Bar-Abba's view, who said in the name of Rabbi Johanan (*Berakhot* 34b): 'All the prophets prophesied only concerning the days of the Messiah, but as for the world to come, "Eye hath not seen, O God, beside Thee".' Three conclusions are drawn from this interpretation of redemptive time: (a) the prophecies about the future, concerning drastic changes in the cosmic order, the nature of Creation and the process of the world, are relevant and are realized in practice in this world, in the current messianic reality; (b) the prophecies are interpreted literally, and when referring to transformations in the order of Creation, they are in fact referring to the Zionist enterprise; and thus, (c) the world to come cannot be brought about by man, yet in this world we have reached that actual prophetic-messianic age, not merely a political-messianic one.

Here we have a more poetic, lyrical notion, according to which the return to the soil, life within nature, the agricultural achievements, the secular creativity (which, according to Rabbi Abraham I. Kook, serves the coming of messianic redemption even inadvertently and unwillingly), the Zionist activity, the military victories upon the holy soil, the blood spilt on this soil and for its sake—are all interpreted as evidence on a cosmic scale, not just a political one, of the metaphysical time in which corporeality and empirical reality (including political reality) are situated. A prominent advocate and mentor of this trend is Rabbi Zvi Yehuda Kook, followed by leaders of *Gush Emunim* whom Kook inspired and who sprang from his Mercaz ha-Rav *yeshiva*. Kook defines the State of Israel as the Kingdom of Israel, and the Kingdom of Israel as the Kingdom of Heaven on earth; and consequently, total holiness envelops every human being, every action, every phenomenon, including secularism which will one day be engulfed by sacredness, by redemption.

A salient expression of the spiritual yearning and concrete policy of the political-messianic stream, appears in an article entitled, 'On the Significance of the Yom Kippur War', by Rabbi Yehuda Amital, published in his collection of sermons, *Ha-Ma'alot mi-Ma'amakim*. (Amital suppposedly changed his position slightly following the Lebanese war, but the core of his views has not changed: In the past, the unity and uniformity of the land served as the basis of his argument, whereas now the unity and uniformity of the people do so even if the stress in content has been altered, the structure of his approach remains intact.) Amital states that 'it is forbidden to view this war in the manner we viewed misfortunes in the days of exile. We should recognize the greatness of the moment in its biblical dimension, and it can only be seen within its messianic perspective . . . only through a messianic light.' The war broke out against the background of the revival of the Kingdom of Israel, he says, which, in its metaphysical (not only symbolic) status, is evidence of the decline of the spirit of defilement in the Western world. Therefore, Amital claims, this is the focus of the Yom Kippur War: 'The gentiles are fighting for their mere survival as gentiles, as the ritually unclean. Iniquity is fighting its battle for survival. It knows that in the Wars of God, there will neither be a place for the Satan, nor for the spirit of defilement', nor for the remains of Western culture the proponents of which are, as it were, the secular Jews. The participation (direct or indirect) of all the oil-consuming countries in the struggle in the Middle East, he says, indeed, reinforces the messianic dimension of the war.

The modern secular world, according to this approach, is struggling for survival, and thus our war is directed against the impurity of Western culture and against rationality as such. It follows that the alien culture has to be eradicated because all foreignness draws us closer to the alien, and the alien causes alienation, as is the position of those who still adhere to Western culture and who attempt to fuse Judaism with rationalist, empiricist and democratic culture. According to Amital's approach, the Yom Kippur War has to be comprehended in its messianic dimension: a struggle against Western civilization in its entirety.

Finally, Amital asks, what, then, is the point of all the affliction, why do the wars continue, if the Messiah has already come, and if the Kingdom of Israel has already been established? There can only be one reason, Amital replies: the war initiates the process of purification, of refinement, 'the purifying and cleansing of the congregation of Israel'. We thus learn that there is only one explanation of the wars, namely that the Lord performed an act of grace in giving us wars, because they refine and purify the soul. And as impurity will be removed, the soul of Israel—by virtue of the war—will as such be refined. We have already conquered the lands, and all that now remains is to conquer impurity.

The second level in which the basic premise of the political-messianic trend (namely, the metaphysical conception of political reality) finds expression is the level of the place where we live. Here again, in analyzing the approach of the main spokesmen of this trend, we must relate to the primary sources, as we are talking about a section of society for whom the logos constitutes concrete political reality: they do not quote one verse or another merely in order to justify ideology, but on the contrary, political reality itself is actually molded by the logos. Indeed, historical experience has taught us—in the twentieth century as well—how great is the strength of the logos, of ideology, not only as justification for political interests, but rather as an active factor which motivates the emergence of political, military and economic interests.

The essence of the dimension of place, in a parallel manner to that of time, lies in the total sacredness ascribed to every clod and grain of earth on which our feet tread. Rather than sacredness replacing corporeality, corporeality itself becomes increasingly refined to the point of total sanctity, until there is no refuge for man, and every place in the Holy Land on which a Jew treads is deemed holy. Historical symbols are transformed into substance: man is not holy, but rather place is, and not place as a symbol of holiness but the actual physical localities, the trees and the stones, the graves and the walls, are all holy in themselves. The concept of sanctity, when applied to place, has thus acquired a meaning contrary to that which symbolics attaches to it, because symbolics distinguishes between an object and the meaning attributed to it, between corporeality and the significance it may reflect. In this manner, the holiness which was meant to be symbolized by physical localities has become ascribed to the localities themselves.

Thus, the concept of the holiness of the Land acquired a completely different meaning than it previously had in Jewish tradition. The main significance of the holiness of the Land was a *Halakhic* matter: according to the *Mishna,* 'The Land of Israel is holier than any other land. Wherein lies its holiness? In that from it they may bring the *omer* and the First Fruits . . .' (*Kelim* 1:6). That is to say, the holiness of the Land is due to the possibility of fulfilling the commandments which depend on the land: this is the meaning of saying that the land is holy. Yet, in the sources under discussion, physical locality becomes sanctified in place of its historical importance, and holiness is not related, as it originally was, to the fulfillment of a religious—in this case agricultural—practice, such as giving the tithe, *leket, pe'ah,* and other commandments depend on the Land, but rather to concrete political corporeality itself.

The primary source of this approach, often cited in the literature we are dealing with, is Nachmanides' notes to the fourth positive commandment in Maimonides' enumeration of the commandments *(Sefer ha-Mitzvot).*[1] Nachmanides writes: 'We are commanded to take possession of the land given by the Lord to our forefathers, to Abraham, Isaac and Jacob, and we will not leave it in the hands of any other people or allow it to lie waste. And he said unto them (Numbers 33:53): "You must take possession of the land and settle there, for to you I have given the land to occupy".' This commandment, Nachmanides continues, was specified for us in its particular boundaries: 'and go to the mount of the Amorites, and unto all its neighboring places, in the plain, in the hills, and in the vale, and in the south, and by the seaside, to the land of the Canaanites, and unto Lebanon, unto the great river, the River Euphrates' (Deuteronomy 1:7), and this, Nachmanides claims, 'lest you yield from any place'. Place is sanctified by total holiness, and that is why we were commanded to kill those nations, the seven peoples and Amalek—in order not to place the Land in their hands.

From this point of departure an explicit policy is now entailed: relying on these sources, the Chief Rabbinate issued *Halakhic* rulings concerning the holiness of the territories—and due to this, the sanctity of their borders and of the political sovereignty over them—which proclaim the existence of a religious duty, to be put into effect by political action. The Chief Rabbinate's decision of 22 *Adar* 5736 (1976), for example, states the following: 'The Temple Mount is Mt. Moriah, the site of the Temple and of the Holy of Holies, the place where the Lord God of Israel chose to house His Name, which was sanctified by ten holy blessings by David, King of Israel: the Jewish people's right to the Temple Mount and the site of the Temple is an eternal and inalienable divine right, over which there can be no concessions'. In light of this sacredness, there is no room for any compromise: neither with regard to time, i.e., concessions at least for the time being, for a year or a generation, nor with regard to place.

Another decision concerning the prohibition of handing over any part of the Land of Israel to the gentiles, dated 21 *Iyyar*, 5739 (1979), forbids the transfer of any territory, including that which was conceded to Egypt in return for peace: 'According to our holy *Torah* and the clear and authoritative law, there is a strict ban on transferring ownership to the gentiles' of any single part of the Land of Israel, because it is sanctified by the sacredness of the biblical 'Covenant between the Pieces'. This invocation of the Covenant of Abraham elucidates how an archaic and primordial symbol of the slaughtering of animals, used by primeval tribes as evidence of political union, becomes a source of authority for contemporary political policy. Returning the territories, the Chief Rabbinate ruled, would constitute a violation of the commandment, 'and thou shalt not show mercy unto them' (Deuteronomy 7:2): the gentiles should not be given the right of encampment on the soil of the Land of Israel, 'and no argument of the saving of lives *(pikuach nefesh)* can invalidate this severe prohibition'.

From everything said so far, the concrete implications of the political messianic outlook concerning human rights can be discerned. If time and place are categories of existential totality, then there cannot possibly be a place for gentiles here. As we have seen, we are not dealing with a band of crazy prophets, nor with an extreme minority on the fringe of society, but with a dogmatic school of thought and methodical doctrine, which inevitably leads to a policy which cannot tolerate the concept of human and civil rights, because the conception of the totality of the dimensions of time and place leaves no room for tolerance. It is a movement which possesses great inner powers of mystical belief, and in light of the analysis of its ideological foundations, we find ourselves confronted with a structure familiar to us from twentieth-century political messianism. There is as yet no place for comparison of content, but with regard to the structure of the conception—as distinct from its content—it is impossible not to notice an analogy to totalitarian movements of this century.

The conclusion which follows from the epistemological structure of the dimensions of time and place as described above emerges in the form of three positions concerning the question of the non-Jew's human and civil rights, somewhat like three possible degrees of a solution: the restriction of rights; the denial of rights; and in the most extreme case—the call for genocide based on the Torah. Every one of these positions has been expressed in the sources under discussion.

The first degree is still relatively moderate: it states that equality of the rights of citizen and man is nothing but a foreign democratic principle, alien and European, which existentially alienates us from the Holy Land. Therefore, the principle of equal rights is not binding in our dealings with the Arab residents of the country, and their status can only be that of foreigners *(gerim)*. Of the two kinds of *gerim*—the righteous proselyte *(ger tzedek)* and the sojourner *(ger toshav)*—only the latter is meant: namely, the non-Jew who has renounced paganism and observes the seven Noachian laws. Such a person has partial rights and duties, e.g., the duty of observing the dietary laws does not apply to him, yet he is forbidden to consume blood (Leviticus 17:13, 25:35), or according to Maimonides he is permitted to work for himself in public on the Sabbath, yet if he is employed by a Jew he cannot work for him on the Sabbath.

The second position already leads to the denial of human rights, because the actualization of our existence in the Land of Israel depends on the Arabs' emigration from it. This matter has frequently been discussed in *Nekuda,* to the point that some people within the movement have said that as the *Torah* speaks in communicable language, and one should not 'utter the unhearable', i.e., as the issue would shock the public at the moment, one should try to refrain, as a temporary measure, from explicitly talking about the expulsion of the Arabs; yet the attitude in principle is that there is no place for Arabs in the land. Therefore, the differentiation in time of war between citizen and soldier, as accepted in enlightened countries, is unacceptable because both of them, the citizen and the soldier, belong to the category of population which *a priori* has no right to be here; both of them are enemies of Israel. The commandment to conquer the land 'is above the human and moral considerations of the national rights of the gentiles to our land', as Rabbi Shlomo Aviner claims in his article, 'The Messianic Realism' (*Morasha,* Vol. 9). Indeed, Israel was commanded in the *Torah* that 'thou shalt be holy', but we were not commanded to be moral; and the general principles of morality which have been accepted by mankind, in principle at least, do not commit the Jew, for he was chosen to be beyond them (*Nekuda,* No. 43).

The third position concerning the question of the non-Jew's human rights is based upon the positive commandment from the *Torah* of the eradication of any trace of Amalek, i.e., actual genocide. This solution was suggested by Rabbi Israel Hess in his article, 'The Commandment of Genocide in the Torah' (*Bat Kol,* the student journal of Bar Ilan University, Feb. 26, 1980), and apart from several colleagues such as Uriel Simon and other members of *Oz ve-Shalom* (the dovish religious group), we do not know of any dissenting reaction on behalf of the rabbinical teachers of this trend. Their silence is particularly significant in this instance, as we are dealing with a community for whom because of its political structure, its leaders are not just the guide, but also the ones who grant absolution, because according to their outlook, the function of the Chief Rabbinate and heads of the *yeshivot* is to react to reality and to demonstrate to man the error of his ways (the rabbis in the *yeshivot* are thus called *mashgichim*—'supervisors'). Rabbi Hess proclaims that 'the day will come when we will all be called to fulfill the commandment of this religiously commanded war, of annihilating Amalek'—the commandment of genocide. The manner of carrying this out is described in I Samuel 15:3: 'go now, attack Amalek, and deal with him and all that he has under the ban. Do not spare him but kill man and woman, child and infant, ox and sheep, camel and ass.'

This duty of carrying out the annihilation of Amalek is based, according to Rabbi Hess, on two arguments: the one concerning racial purity, and the other concerning war. The racial justification is as follows: according to Genesis 36:12, Amalek is the son of Timna, who was Eliphaz's concubine. Yet according to I Chronicles 1:36, the same Timna was the daughter of Eliphaz and thus Amalek's sister. Rabbi Hess thus concludes that Eliphaz cohabited with his wife (who herself was somebody else's wife), begat his daughter Timna by her, took his daughter as a concubine, cohabited with her, and thus Amalek was born. Thus, the rabbi tells us, it is impure blood which flows in Amalek's veins and in the veins of Amalek's descendants for all time. And as for the second argument—Amalek is the enemy who fought against Israel in a particularly cruel manner, Hess says, personifying boundless evil, because when the Children of Israel were walking along their way, exhausted, Amalek attacked and killed them, man, woman and child. According to this conception, in the opposition between Israel and Amalek there appears the opposition between light and darkness, between purity and contamination, between the people of God and the forces of evil, and this opposition continues to exist with respect to the descendants of Amalek for all time. And who are his descendants for all time? These are the Arab nations.

The last section of our discussion may serve as a summary, by means of a structural analysis, following the method of social phenomenologists such as Peter Berger, Thomas Luckmann, Alfred Schuetz and others, concerning the concept of *Lebenswelt*, i.e., the world, the daily reality into which all experiential aspects are integrated, a sort of complete and encompassing web of life; and what this means with respect to one's actual way of life. As we have seen, we are confronted with an all-encompassing *Weltanschauung*, structured as a unity in which sacredness and secularism, religion and politics, heaven and earth, rights and obligations are assimilated. This unity creates what the sources under discussion call 'a mystical realism', forming a unity of a dual structure: the attribution of holiness and mysticalness to empirical reality, and therefore also to rationality and pragmatism (as this movement is not devoid of pragmatic considerations), to the extent that rationality and pragmatism are absorbed by holiness; yet rather than disappear, they are united with the mysticism and help to shape it to the same extent that they are shaped by it.

According to this dual structure, one can point out additional typological distinctions which characterize this messianic 'mystical realism', as follows: sentimentality—which is not devoid of coming to one's senses; enthusiasm—which does not lack self-restraint; spirituality—

not devoid of materialism; a great light which illuminates the whole being—yet not without darker moments, difficulties, obstacles, delays on the path to fulfillment, and the admission that in light of existing political reality and the lack of faith on behalf of the secular, time is not yet ripe for the vessels to absorb the great light; mysticism is tangible in reality—and at the same time reality encompasses all mysticalness; man's existential dimension consists of the joy of total normative commitment —yet, because this is absolute and all-encompassing dedication, it also includes movements of doubt, faintheartedness and sorrow. (Not by chance, a few of these people intended to establish a party called *Orot* —'Lights', as light is perhaps the most tangible of symbols, drawn upon to fill the existential vacuum, spark by spark, and all that has to be done is to gather the sparks, purify sanctity from any defilement, and raise the light back to its source).

Additional expressions of this dual structure are: we are in an age of miracles—yet these miracles are empirical facts, they are part of the natural order, of technology and pragmatism; nationality is cosmic to such an extent that it also absorbs and includes individuality, and thus the individual cannot attain his complete personality unless he is part of the social body, of the entire national organism; this is a yearning for greatness, for 'the wide open spaces', for penetration into the hidden secrets of the universe—to the extent that every square inch of land, every particle of earth is conceived as being part of the wide universe, and the everyday life conducted at each specific location constitutes an inseparable part of it.

Further, the conquest of the Land also implies conquering the mundane and its refinement: what is at stake is purifying the Land of all alienness, of all impurity—a purgation which is so encompassing and total that it also absorbs the personal self-purification of the individual, and as the purified land is redeemed from the aliens, the purified personality is redeemed from alienness. Paradoxically, political ecstasy is seen as the way in which the settler *(mitnaḥel)* settles not only his land, but also his mind, and the reality in which we are situated is one of liberation from existential alienation within the Zionist enterprise, now actualized in the concrete political reality.

In conclusion, we are presented with a political messianism in which the individual, the people and the land arrive at an organic union, bestowed with absolute holiness. It is based on a metaphysical comprehension of political reality, which is expressed by a conception of the totality of time and place. The danger of this totalistic outlook lies in its leading to a totalitarian conception of political reality—because it leaves neither time nor place for the human and civil rights of the non-Jew.

NOTE

1. The reference is actually to the fourth in Nachmanides' listing of the "Positive Commandments that Maimonides Forgot"—Ed.

20

Messianic Postures in Israel Today

Menachem Kellner

The contemporary religious zionist community[1] is profoundly affected by a sharp break between the political left ("doves") and right ("hawks"). This controversy finds expression in divergent attitudes towards the War in Lebanon, towards the Arab population of Israel and the territories, and, most emphatically, towards the future of those territories and their native population and the question of Jewish settlement in them.

Divisions such as those between left and right are rarely neat and all-exclusive. Such is certainly the case here. There are many people at the center of the spectrum who adopt mixed positions and many more who are more or less firmly in one camp or the other, but who adopt moderate rather than extreme positions. Whereas the arguments between the two camps are often phrased in historical, military, and demographic terms it has become clear to me that the real argument is one of basic ideology concerning the messianic era. This should hardly be surprising: it is a commonplace to characterize zionism as secularized messianism. Religious zionism can hardly be a form of *secularized* messianism. It should surprise no one, therefore, if debates among religious zionists revolve around messianic issues.

The debate itself is actually carried on in terms far removed from messianism. Rather, it revolves around questions such as the following: Should the West Bank and Gaza strip be annexed *(de jure* or *de facto)* to

Reprinted by permission of the Johns Hopkins University Press and the author from *Modern Judaism* 6 (1986).

Israel? Should Jewish settlement there in general be encouraged or limited? Should Jewish settlement in and near Arab cities (e.g., Hebron and Shechem) be permitted or forbidden? Should the Arab population of the territories be seen as potentially equal partners in the settlement of Eretz Israel or always viewed with suspicion, distrust, and fear? Does the Arab population have any rights to the land on which it lives? Is there room at all for a substantial non-Jewish population in the State of Israel? Is the democratic character of the State of Israel as important as its Jewish character or not? Should the Israeli army be used only as a weapon of self-defense, or may it be used as a tool of policy even where questions of security and defense are not directly involved?

In order to make the division of opinion as clear as possible I will sketch out the opposing positions in their purest and most radical forms. I purposefully ignore the hesitations, compromises, and *ad hominem* attacks that characterize the debate in the way in which it is actually carried out. I also purposefully abstract from the debate all the non-ideological issues—historical, military, and demographic—which, I think, cloud the central issue. In effect I will be presenting two extreme positions, or "ideal types," which are overtly and self-consciously adopted by very few individuals. But that in no way should detract from the importance and utility of the discussion as a way of understanding the basic issues under debate. Furthermore, since the religious zionist right in its extreme (Jewish underground) and less extreme *(Gush Emunim)* manifestations has such an impact on Israeli life, an explanation of its fundamental ideological stance is important.[2]

This dispute, for all its occasional bitterness, is carried on against the background of many shared assumptions. It will be easier to understand the areas of disagreement if we first understand the broad areas of agreement, those ideas which religious zionists of the left and right share in common and which distinguish them from religious non- or anti-zionists. Here, too, the issue is one of messianism.[3]

The level of our discussion will be significantly deepened if it can be given firm textual footing. Throughout this essay, then, I will present my arguments and analyses in the form of a commentary on and exposition of one of the classic statements of Jewish messianism, chapters 11 and 12 of Maimonides' "Laws of Kings and Wars."[4]

It ought to be noted at the outset that the traditions of Judaism do not speak with one voice concerning the messianic redemption. There is no one normative and authoritative account. Maimonides puts this point in the following way:

> Some of our Sages say that the coming of Elijah will precede the advent of the Messiah. But no one is in a position to know the details of this and similar things until they have come to pass. They are not explicitly stated by the Prophets. Nor have the Rabbis any tradition with regard to these matters. They are guided solely by what the Scriptural texts seem to imply. Hence there is a divergence of opinion on the subject. But be that as it may, neither the exact sequence of those events nor the details thereof constitute religious dogma.[5]

Maimonides tells us here that details concerning the redemption are not explicitly taught in either the Written or Oral Torah. Rabbinic comments on these matters are the interpretations of individual Sages concerning what the Biblical texts "seem to imply" without authoritative traditions to guide those interpretations. It is not surprising, therefore, that we find diversity of opinion within the Rabbinic tradition itself concerning the Messiah and the Messianic Era.

Out of this diversity of opinion we can discern two broad approaches or "families of ideas" concerning the question of how the Messianic era is to be ushered in. On the one hand we find an emphasis on the naturalistic, incremental, and restorative nature of the messianic advent; contrasted to this is an approach which emphasizes the supernaturalistic, catastrophic, and utopian elements within the tradition. Each of these approaches or families of ideas leads to different positions concerning Zionism and the religious importance of the State of Israel.

The first group of ideas emphasizes the essentially naturalistic, non-miraculous nature of the messianic advent. Maimonides is the foremost advocate of this view: "Let no one think that in the days of the Messiah any of the laws of nature will be set aside, or any innovation introduced into creation. The world will follow its normal course."[6] Maimonides goes on to intimate that in the Days of the Messiah only a very naive lamb would take the words of Isaiah 11:6 literally and dwell with a wolf. That famous verse, he explains, is "to be understood figuratively, meaning that Israel will live securely among the wicked of the heathens who are likened to wolves and leopards . . ."[7]

Maimonides goes so far in this naturalistic approach as to disassociate the figure of the Messiah from the miracle most often associated with him, resurrection: "Do not think that the King Messiah will have to perform signs and wonders [i.e., miracles], bring anything new into being, revive the dead, or do similar things. It is not so."[8]

What, then, does the Messiah do? "King Messiah," Maimonides writes,

> will arise and restore the kingdom of David to its former state and original sovereignty. He will rebuild the sanctuary and gather the dispersed of Israel. All the ancient laws will be reinstituted in his days; sacrifices will again be offered; the Sabbatical and Jubilee years will again be observed in accordance with the commandments set forth in the Law.[9]

The messianic advent, then, is not marked by miracles and changes in the course of nature but by the restoration of the Torah to its rightful place in the life of the Jews.

On this view, the coming of the Messiah does not mark the end of this world *(olam ha-zeh)* and the advent of a new world *(olam ha-ba)*. In this regard Maimonides quotes the dictum of the Talmudic Sage Samuel: "The sole difference between the present and the Messianic days is delivery from servitude to foreign powers."[10] Nature will continue its normal course, our customary corporeal existence will continue. Human beings will be born, will work, play, and study, will procreate, age and die. Presumably the world will still need garbage collectors and with garbage collectors, municipal governments.

Often associated with this basically naturalistic account of the Messianic world we find a view which sees the transition from this dispensation to the messianic world as incremental or gradual. A powerful expression of this idea is found in the Kabbalistic concept of *tikkun:* each act of worship, each *mizvah* performed, brings the world closer to its fulfillment. Indications that Maimonides adopted this incrementalist position (though not, of course, the idea of *tikkun*) may be found in his writing. He holds that the proof of the Messianic pudding is in the eating thereof: we cannot know in advance, immediately, if a putative Messiah is indeed the Messiah—we must test the results. This is what he writes:

> If there arise a king from the House of David who meditates on the Torah, occupies himself with the commandments, as did his ancestor David, observes the precepts prescribed in the Written and Oral Law, prevails upon Israel to walk in the way of the Torah and to repair its breaches, and fights the battles of the Lord, it may be assumed that he is the Messiah. If he does these things and succeeds, rebuilds the sanctuary on its site, and gathers the dispersed of Israel, he is beyond all doubt the Messiah. He will prepare the whole world to serve the Lord with one accord, as it is written: *For then will I turn to the peoples a pure language, that they may all call upon the name of the Lord to serve Him with one consent* (Zeph. 3:9).[11]

The Messianic fulfillment, therefore, is a matter of a step by step process; only when it has been successfully completed can we be sure that the Messiah has actually come.

This incrementalism also applies, according to Maimonides, on the scale of world history. In a text which has been censored in most editions of the *Mishneh Torah* we find that Maimonides accords a messianic role to Christianity and Islam:

Even of Jesus of Nazareth, who imagined that he was the Messiah, but was put to death by the court, Daniel had prophesied, as it is written *And the children of the violent among thy people shall lift themselves up to establish the vision; but they shall stumble* (Daniel 11:14). For has there ever been a greater stumbling than this? All the Prophets affirmed that the Messiah would redeem Israel, save them, gather their dispersed, and confirm the commandments. But he caused Israel to be destroyed by the sword, their remnant to be dispersed and humiliated. He was instrumental in changing the Torah and causing the world to err and serve another beside God.

But it is beyond the human mind to fathom the designs of the Creator; for our ways are not His ways, neither are our thoughts His thoughts. All these matters relating to Jesus of Nazareth and the Ishmaelites who came after him, only served to clear the way for King Messiah, to prepare the whole world to worship God with one accord, as it is written *For then will I turn to the peoples a pure language, that they may all call upon the name of the Lord to serve Him with one consent* (Zeph. 3:9). Thus the messianic hope, the Torah, and the commandments have become familiar topics—topics of conversation [among the inhabitants] of the far isles and many peoples, uncircumcized of heart and flesh. They are discussing these matters and the commandments of the Torah. Some say, "Those commandments were true, but have lost their validity and are no longer binding", others declare that they had an esoteric meaning and were not intended to be taken literally; that the Messiah has already come and revealed their occult significance. But when the true King Messiah will appear and succeed, be exalted and lifted up, they will forthwith recant and realize that they have inherited naught but lies from their fathers, that their prophets and forbears led them astray.[12]

It is the purpose of Christianity and Islam, therefore, to lay the groundwork for the coming of the Messiah by spreading among the gentile nations the ideas of Messiah, Torah, and commandments, to make it possible for these nations to accept belief in one God that they might *serve Him with one consent.*

It is worth digressing a moment to explain why Maimonides maintained that it was God's plan to have Christianity and Islam lay the groundwork of the messianic advent. According to Maimonides the essential characteristic of the messianic era is the universal acceptance of belief in God and His Torah. For the nations of the earth to abjure their idolatry overnight, as it were, and wholeheartedly accept both pure monotheism and the Torah would be a miracle of monumental proportions. But Maimonides does not expect the Messiah to work miracles. For the Messiah to come, therefore, it is necessary that the world be gradually monotheized. This is the role of Christianity and Islam.

A further motif associated with the naturalistic conception of the Messianic advent is that the Messiah will restore a past Golden Age rather than usher in a wholly new world. I repeat here a quotation already adduced, emphasizing those words which relate to the Messiah's restorative role:

King Messiah will arise and *restore* the kingdom of David to its *former* state and *original* sovereignty. He will *rebuild* the sanctuary and gather the dispersed of Israel. All the ancient laws will be *reinstituted* in his days; sacrifices will *again be offered;* the Sabbatical and Jubilee years will *again be observed* . .

I have sketched a conception of the messianic advent, grounded in Maimonides' "Laws of Kings," which emphasizes its naturalistic, gradualist, and restorative elements. This sort of approach often leads to messianic activism, the attempt actively to encourage, facilitate, and hasten the coming of the Messiah. This is so because the Maimonidean stance allows for the possibility of a human role in the messianic advent, since it excludes miracles—events which are by definition beyond human attainment—from the realm of the Messiah's activities. In theory, if it does not take miracles to bring the Messiah, then humans may be able to play some role in the process. Another element in Maimonides' conception of the coming of the Messiah which encourages messianic activism is incrementalism. If the Messiah's advent marks the culmination of a gradual process and not a single catastrophic event then it is at least conceivable that humans can contribute towards the hastening of the advent. Lending credence to this is the messianic role which Maimonides assigns to Christians and Moslems; it is inconceivable that Maimonides would grant them some role in this great drama while excluding the Jews from active participation.

The messianic activism made possible by the naturalistic conception of the messianic advent is explicitly adopted by religious zionism. The creation and building of the State of Israel, "the first flowering of our redemption," in the words of the Chief Rabbinate's prayer for the State, is invested with religious, messianic significance. This has been the avowed position of the Mizraḥi movement almost from its inception and of its Israeli political arm, the National Religious Party, and is expressed in Rabbi A. I. Kook's call "to renew the old and sanctify the new."[13]

Messianic activism and its zionist corollary are explicitly rejected by a school of thought which, not surprisingly, draws upon a different conception of the messianic even altogether. Whereas the approach described so far emphasizes the naturalistic, incremental, and restorative motifs in the Jewish messianic tradition, the second approach emphasizes supernaturalistic, catastrophic, and utopian motifs. Where the first conception can lead to messianic activism the second tends to lead its adherents to leave everything active in God's hands, reserving the human role in the advent to prayer and repentance.

This supernaturalistic approach is well captures in a tale recounted by Martin Buber: A fool blew a shofar on the Mt. of Olives and shouted that the Messiah had come. A Zaddik living in Jerusalem heard the uproar, threw open his windows and sniffed the air "The Messiah hasn't come," he said. On the supernaturalistic conception, the coming of the Messiah will be marked by such a distinct break and change in the natural world that sniffing the air will be enough to let one know that the Messiah has come. According to this view the Messiah ushers in, not an improved version of this present world, *olam ha-zeh,* but a wholly new existence, *olam ha-ba.* The messianic world is wholly unlike this present world; human existence as we know it ends; history reaches its culmination. Miracles, such as resurrection, abound.

Associated with this view we often find ideas of a catastrophic nature. This world is separated from the next, Messianic world by a dramatic break which cannot be bridged by the efforts of mere humans; it can be traversed only by miraculous means. Thus we find emphasis on apocalyptic events such as the Wars of Armageddon, Gog and Magog, and the Day of Judgment.

Given the apocalyptic, supernaturalistic conception of the messianic advent, it is hardly surprising that individuals holding this understanding see the task of the Messiah, not as restoring a past Golden Age, but as ushering in a wholly new dispensation, a Utopia or "no place" which has not yet existed.

This messianic world-to-come cannot in principle be brought into existence by human action since it is beyond all human capacity to effect miracles. It is entirely and solely up to God. The most humans can do is repent and pray, hoping thereby to earn God's favor and the great boon of the messianic world-to-come. Given this conception, acts intended to hasten the coming of the Messiah must be seen as examples of literally cosmic ḥutzpah and hubris, punishable acts of folly. The most extreme expression of this view is found in the writings of the late Rabbi Yoel Teitelbaum (the Satmar Rebbe) who indicated that he understood the Holocaust as divine punishment for the sin of Zionism.[14]

Religious zionists, on the other hand, are united by the belief that Jews can and therefore ought to act in this world so as to hasten the messianic advent. This is true of both hawks and doves in that camp. That is what they agree on; on what do they disagree?

The essential ideological disagreement between religious zionist doves and hawks relates to the *nature* of the messianic world and not to the question of the natural vs. supernatural nature of the Messiah's advent.[15] This disagreement leads to concrete political disputes in this present pre-Messianic world. This is so for the following reason. For any sane person, the ends he or she wishes to accomplish must determine the means adopted to achieve those ends. It makes no sense, for example, to seek to establish a reign of perfect justice, amity, and brotherly love by murder and oppression. The Bolsheviks failed to appreciate this elementary fact and ended up by betraying and destroying their own revolution. Religious zionists, however, more perspicacious than the Bolsheviks, consciously adopt means consistent with the ends they seek to attain. Messianic ends, therefore, determine religious zionists politics.

What are those messianic ends? They can be most easily understood by analyzing a set of opposed pairs of ideas. First, are the Ingathering of the Exiles and the establishment of Jewish sovereignty over and Jewish settlement in the whole Land of Israel *signs* of the messianic redemption or *pre-requisites* for it? If the former, then one can be (temporarily) satisfied with Jewish sovereignty over and settlement in part of the Land of Israel. If the latter, then failure actively to settle the whole Land and press for Jewish sovereignty over it is to fail to do what one can to advance the coming of the Messiah. It is a dereliction of one's most solemn Jewish duty.

We may counterpose two texts on this issue. Maimonides seems to adopt the attitude that settlement, sovereignty, and aliyah are signs that the Messiah has done his job:

> If there arise a king from the House of David who meditates on the Torah, occupies himself with the commandments . . . it may be assumed that he is the Messiah. If he does these things and succeeds, rebuilds the sanctuary on its site, and gathers the dispersed of Israel, he is beyond all doubt the Messiah. . . .[16]

Maimonides distinguishes here between an individual who fulfills the necessary conditions for being the Messiah and an individual who fulfills both the necessary and sufficient conditions for being the Messiah. Only after the Messiah has accomplished what the Messiah is supposed to accomplish can we know that he is the Messiah. If he satisfies the basic criteria (by being a scion of the House of David who studies Torah and fulfills the commandments) he may be presumed to be the Messiah. If his reign is marked by success, if he rebuilds the Temple, and if he gathers the Jews of the diaspora to Israel he is then proved to be the Messiah. On this reading, the Ingathering of the Exiles, the success of the Messianic king (what sort of success Maimonides does not tell us), the rebuilding of the Temple (a symbol of the assertion of Jewish sovereignty over the land—see also the passage from XI.1 quoted above) are signs that the Messiah has come; they are not things which have to be accomplished in order to make his coming possible.

Opposed to this we find the following opinion expressed by the late Rabbi Zvi Yehudah Kook:

> The true Redemption, which is to be manifested in the complete resettlement in the land and the revival of Israel in it, is thus seen to be a continuation of renewed settlement in the Land, accompanied by the ingathering of the captive exiles within its boundaries . . . Hence when this state of ours is in full control, both internally and externally, then the fulfillment of this miẓvah of the inheritance can be truly revealed—the miẓvah that is the basis and essence of all miẓvot that, by means of our rule, can accomplish the act of Redemption.[17]

Rabbi Kook is perfectly clear: Jewish rule over the whole land of Israel, its complete resettlement by Jews, and the Ingathering of the Exiles not only make the messianic redemption possible, but guarantee it. They are necessary and sufficient conditions for the coming of the Messiah and must be accomplished before he can come. They are *pre-requisites* of the messianic advent not signs that it has occurred.[18]

A second dichotomy relates to the question of Jews and gentiles in the messianic world. One view maintains that national/ethnic/religious boundaries will disappear; in effect, all human beings will become Jews. This seems to be the opinion of R. Simeon b. Elazar who (Ber. 57b) maintains that in the messianic world all gentiles will convert to Judaism. This also may be the opinion of Maimonides. It is the task of the Messiah, he maintains, "to prepare the *whole* world to serve the Lord with *one* accord, as it is written, *For then I will turn to the peoples a pure language, that they may all call upon the name of the Lord to serve Him with one consent* (Zeph. 3:9)."[19] He also says that the "heathens will *all* accept the true religion, and will neither plunder nor destroy, and *together with Israel* earn a comfortable living in a legitimate way . . ."[20] Maimonides ends his discussion of the Messiah, and the *Mishneh Torah* altogether with a passage which includes the claim that "the *one* preoccupation of the *whole* world will be to know the Lord . . ."[21]

Opposed to this view we have the more traditional and more widely accepted conception that the differences between Jew and gentile will remain and that the Jews will dominate the gentiles.

Associated with this dichotomy concerning Jewish-gentile relations in the messianic era we find another. Will the essential characteristic of the messianic era be the spread of the knowledge of God or will such knowledge be restricted to Jews, leaving as an important characteristic of the messianic world the domination of gentiles by Jews? Maimonides enunciates the former view.

> The Sages and Prophets did not long for the days of the Messiah that Israel might exercise dominion over the world, or rule over the heathens, or be exalted by the nations, or that it might eat and drink and rejoice. Their aspiration was that Israel be free to devote itself to the Law and its wisdom, with no one to oppress or disturb it, and thus be worthy of life in the world to come.[22]

That Maimonides had to polemicize against the notion that the Sages and Prophets longed for the messianic era so that Jews might dominate the world shows how widespread and deeply rooted that understanding of the messianic world was (and, I might add, still is).

If one adopts the view concerning Jewish-gentile relations in the messianic era presented here as that of Maimonides one is led to adopt positions in this world which try to be very sensitive—*on Jewish grounds*—to the rights and sensibilities of non-Jewish populations who will some day themselves become Jews. If, on the other hand, one adopts the second view, the one which Maimonides appears to have argued against, then there is more room to allow freedom of behavior with respect to non-Jewish populations who will, even after the coming of the Messiah, be subjugated to the Jews.[23]

Given that both religious doves and hawks agree that life will go on to a very great extent after the coming of the Messiah much as it does in this present world, the question of political institutions in the messianic era must arise. Presumably municipal services (garbage collection, etc.) will have to be provided, health care apportioned, services regulated, etc. What will be the nature of the political institutions which will function under the leadership of King Messiah? One can envision a messianic government consistent to a very great extent with the ideals and procedures of democracy; one can equally well envision a messianic government structured on more authoritarian lines. If one's vision of the messianic world is one informed by democratic ideals then one will demand that those ideals be incorporated, to the greatest extent possible, in the pre-Messianic world. If, on the other hand, democratic ideals do not have a central place in one's messianic vision, one has less reason to be committed to them in the pre-Messianic world.[24]

To summarize, we have before us two opposed views of the messianic era, both of which, however, derive from the religious zionist stance of messianic activism. One view, that of the left, maintains that the settlement of the whole Land of Israel by the Jews and the establishment of Jewish sovereignty over it are signs that the Messiah has come. At some point in the messianic era the distinction between Jew and gentile will disappear. The essential characteristic of the messianic era will be the universal preoccupation with God and His Torah. The institutions of government in the messianic world will be essentially democratic in nature.

Opposed to this we find the view of the right that the Messiah will not come until Jews settled the whole Land of Israel and establish Jewish sovereignty over it. Jew and gentile will remain distinct in the messianic world and the latter will be subjugated to the former. The messianic government will not be democratic in nature.

Ends should determine means. From these two opposed views of the nature of the messianic end are derived opposed views concerning the appropriate behavior in the present. The religious zionist right sees settlement in and sovereignty over the whole Land of Israel as matters of paramount importance. To compromise on these issues is to endanger the Messianic project altogether and thus to weaken the ideological foundations of the State of Israel. Persons holding this view are willing to pursue their goals in ways which impinge upon the rights of non-Jewish populations since such populations do not now and never will have rights in and to the land of Israel and since their natural place in any event is to be subjugated to the Jews. The actions of the Jewish terrorist underground are an extreme (if on the right largely condoned) expression of these views. This proclivity towards Jewish triumphalism and supremicism is abetted by the perception that democracy is not a Jewish and messianic value.

The religious Zionist left sees settlement in and sovereignty over the whole Land of Israel as goals to be effected by the Messiah. Important as they are, failure to accomplish them is not seen as fatal to the Messianic project or as undermining Jewish rights to those portions of the Land of Israel already settled. Hence there is an openness on the religious zionist left to territorial compromise. Since the envisioned messianic era will involve universal human equality and a commitment to democratic ideals, failure to work towards these goals in the present is seen as imperiling the messianic project altogether and as weakening the ideological foundations of the State of Israel.[25]

Both interpretations of the nature of the messianic world, that of religious hawks as well as that of religious doves, are well-grounded in Jewish texts and traditions. Despite this fact each camp generally accuses the other of distorting Judaism. The left is accused of recasting Judaism in the image of Western liberalism while the right is accused of recasting Judaism in the image of nineteenth-century romantic irredentist nationalism. If nothing else, this lends support to Maimonides' claim that "no one is in a position to know the details of this and similar things until they have come to pass."[26]

If my analysis here is correct we are forced to the conclusion that there is very little room for compromise between the two camps. The right must press for continued and ever expanded settlement; failure to do so means (for them) failure to do what can be done to hasten the coming the Messiah. The Messiah's coming, in turn, is certainly to the ultimate benefit of all humans, Jews and gentiles alike. The religious left must continue to oppose what it sees as acts of foolhardiness, selfishness, and injustice, acts which retard the coming the Messiah.

A final word may be in order. The issue I have analyzed, for all its fundamental importance, reflects a still deeper and more fundamental strain within the Jewish tradition, that between universalism and particularism. Both elements exist within the tradition. On my reading of Jewish history, the more Jews are pressed and harried, the more the particularistic element dominates. This leads to a dreary thought: the more that Israel is attacked and criticized, the more will particularistic elements (such as the religious zionist right) come to the fore; the more such elements come to the fore, the more will Israel be attacked and criticized. Now, more than ever, we need the Messiah!

NOTES

1. The term "religious zionism" reflects current Israeli usage and I adopt it out of convenience. I do not mean to imply that non-Orthodox Jews cannot be religious.
2. Some mention also ought to be made of why I wish to discuss the question. I stand firmly on the religious zionist left. Both my Zionism and my leftward leanings grew out of my Orthodox Judaism (so far as I can judge; only a thorough course of psychoanalysis would show whether or not I am fooling myself). In attempting to understand how Jews no less Orthodox than myself could arrive at zionist/political positions diametrically opposed to my own I was brought to examine my basic ideological dispute with the religious zionist right. I also ought to note that the religious zionist right is not homogeneous (any more than is the religious zionist left) and that there are important differences of nuance and emphasis between those who overtly identify as students of the two Rabbis Kook and those who do not. Even among the followers of the Rabbis Kook one finds differences of emphasis.
3. The literature on this subject is vast. For a recent and valuable account see Ehud Luz, *Makbilim Nifgashim* (Tel Aviv, 1985).
4. Maimonides discusses his messianic beliefs in many different texts and the literature upon his discussions is extensive. For a recent and truly illuminating account see Aviezer Ravitzky, "*'Kifi Ko'aḥ ha-Adam'—Yemot ha-Mashiaḥ bi-Mishnat ha-Rambam,*" Zvi Baras (ed.), *Meshiḥiyut vi-Eskhatalogiyah* (Jerusalem, 1983), pp. 191–220. To the many sources and studies cited by Ravitzky one ought to add Steven Schwarzschild, "A Note on the Nature of Ideal Society—A Rabbinic Study," H. A. Strauss and H. G. Reissner (eds.), *Jubilee Volume Dedicated to Curt C. Silberman* (New York, 1969), pp. 86–105.
5. All citations from Maimonides are from A. M. Hershman (trans.), *The Book of Judges* (New Haven, 1949), pp. 238–242. The present text is "Laws of Kings and Wars," chapter XII, halakhah 2.
6. XII. 1.

7. Ibid.
8. XI. 3.
9. XI. 1.
10. Sanhedrin 91b; XII. 2.
11. XI. 4.
12. Ibid. Hershman does not translate this text in the body of "Laws of Kings" but in his introduction to the *Book of Judges* pp. xxiii–xxiv. Leah Naomi Goldfeld proves that this text is actually by Maimonides. See *"Hilkhot Melakhim u-Milḥamot vi-Melekh ha-Mashiaḥ"*, *Sinai*, vol. 96 (5745), pp. 67–79.
13. For representative texts see, for example, Rabbi Y. Amital, *Ha-Ma'alot mi-Ma'amakim* (Jerusalem, 5735) and Rabbi Y. Filber, *Ayelet ha-Shaḥar* (Jerusalem, 5735). Rabbi Filber is a disciple of Rabbi Zvi Yehudah Kook whose work has been very influential in religious zionist circles. Some of the positions in Rabbi Amital's book no longer represent the views of the author, who has been associated with the religious zionist left since the War in Lebanon.
14. See *Kunteres al ha-Geulah vi-al ha-Temurah* (New York, 5727) and *Va-Yo'el Mosheh* (New York, 5720).
15. This crucial point seems to have been misunderstood by the late Uriel Tal. See "Totalitarian Democratic Hermeneutics and Policies in Modern Jewish Religious Nationalism," in *Totalitarian Democracy and After: International Colloquium in Memory of Jacob L. Talmon* (Jerusalem, 1984), pp. 137–157. Tal appears to ignore the messianic component in the thought of the religious zionist left, perhaps because he was influenced by analyses which see mystical or apocalyptic elements as essential to messianism.
16. XI. 4.
17. Quoted in David J. Schnall, *Beyond the Green Line: Israeli Settlements West of the Jordan* (New York, 1984), p. 19.
18. Compare Schnall, pp. 23–24, Amital, p. 58, and Filber, p. 175.
19. XI. 4 (emphasis added).
20. XII. 1 (emphasis added).
21. XII. 5 (emphasis added). I support the claim that Maimonides looked forward to the disappearance of boundaries between Jew and non-Jew in the messianic world in *"Haẓa'ah bi-Inyan Yod-Gimmel ha-Ikkarim shel ha-Rambam u-Ma'amadam shel Eynam Yehudim bi-Yemot ha-Mashiaḥ,"* forthcoming in M. Ayali (ed.), *Moshe Greenberg Anniversary Volume.*
22. XII. 4.
23. Compare, for example, *Siḥot ha-Rav Zvi Yehudah* 19 (ed. Rabbi Shlomo Aviner) (Jerusalem, n.d.), p. 13.
24. Compare Y. Levinger's comment on democracy quoted by Schnall, p. 245. See further D. J. Schnall, *Radical Dissent in Israeli Politics* (New York, 1979), p. 146.
25. In a learned and penetrating essay, *"Ha-Ẓafui ve-ha-Reshut Netunah"* in A. Hareven (ed.), *Yisrael Likrat Ha-Meah ha-21* (Jerusalem, 1984), pp. 135–

197, Aviezer Ravitzky analyzes the messianism/zionism nexus in the thinking of four contemporary groupings: Satmar/*Naturei Karta* (anti-Zionist), *Agudat Yisrael* (non-Zionist), the second generation of Rabbi A. I. Kook's disciples (more or less the group I have characterized as "right-wing religious zionists") and a loose collection of individuals grouped around the religious peace movements, *Netivot Shalom* and *Oz ve-Shalom* (more or less the group I have characterized as "left-wing religious zionists"). On the basis of the analysis of a number of published writings Ravitzky argues that Satmar/*Naturei Karta* and the second generation Kookians share a determinist view of messianic history. That is, they both maintain that God's decision to redeem the Jewish people is basically uninfluenced by human behavior (although the Kookians admit that we can hasten or retard the date of redemption to a modest extent). On this reading, one of the main differences between them is the question of whether or not the messianic fulfillment has begun. The Kookians maintain that it has and that nothing, therefore, can stop it. This is angrily denied by Satmar/*Naturei Karta.*

The "religious zionist left" and *Agudat Yisrael,* on the other hand, do not accept the view of messianic determinism, arguing that human behavior (for *Agudat Yisrael,* primarily prayer and repentance) can bring about the messianic advent. They differ primarily on their analysis of the messianic nature of contemporary Israel, the "religious zionist left" seeing in the creation and growth of the state an opportunity or opening for the messianic advent which must be pursued actively if it is going to be actualized.

On this analysis one of the main differences between what I have called right- and left-wing religious zionism is the question of historical or messianic determinism. The right is confident that we are on the threshold of the Messiah's advent and that nothing can stand permanently in its way. The left, on the other hand, sees the situation as fluid and maintains that the coming of the Messiah must still be earned.

On the whole Ravitzky and I do not disagree on our analysis of the situation. I think that the issue of "messianic determinism" is somewhat less important than he makes it out to be, however, since the messianic process is understood even by those who believe that it already has begun to be a potentially very long affair which might not reach its culmination for generations.

26. XII. 2.

IX

SUMMARIES AND REEVALUATIONS

21

Gershom Scholem on Jewish Messianism

David Biale

Scholem's philosophy of Jewish history becomes evident from his underground history of orthodox Gnosticism. Monotheism was revitalized by the infusion of irrational myth, reinterpreted by the mystics. Rationalism and irrationalism, monotheism and myth, are dialectically interrelated. Judaism is the history of the struggle between contradictory forces, and it is that internal dialectic, rather than the infiltration of foreign ideas, which gives Jewish history its dynamism.

The Gnostic myth Scholem finds throughout the history of Jewish mysticism barely concealed a deeply heretical impulse. Gnosticism in late antiquity was prone to antinomianism and nihilism because it believed that all law originated with the evil creator God. Jewish mysticism transformed Gnosticism into an orthodox myth, but the threat of its lapsing into heretical antinomianism never disappeared: in appropriating Gnosticism, the mystics played with heretical fire. In the Sabbatian messianic movement of the seventeenth century, the Gnostic myth finally realized its heretical potential: Scholem suggests that the extreme Gnosticism present in Sabbatian theology was but the logical culmination of the whole history of Jewish mysticism.

The congruence of heresy and messianism was, according to Scholem, no coincidence. During the Middle Ages, Jews with heretical impulses could find an outlet in conversion to Christianity or Islam: as a minority community, they were less likely to develop internal heretical sects since

Reprinted by permission of Harvard University Press from *Gershom Scholem: Kabbalah and Counter-History,* by David Biale, 2d ed., 1982. Copyright © 1979 by David Biale.

dissatisfaction could be relieved by leaving the community altogether. Within the Jewish world, however, "there was only one power that could bring about such an outbreak [of heresy]: that is messianism. It is the great catalyst in Judaism."[1] For Scholem, messianism served the same function as myth in ventilating the stuffy and cloistered Jewish world with an "anarchic breeze." It could do so because it was frequently the product of myth. When the potent forces of Gnostic mysticism were liberated from meditative speculation and directed toward messianic action, they produced the greatest internal upheaval of the Jewish Middle Ages, Sabbatianism. Scholem argues, moreover, that this mass messianic movement, generated by a development within Jewish mysticism, decisively undermined the traditional medieval world and inaugurated the modern period of Jewish history.

Scholem defines two types of messianism: restorative and utopian-catastrophic.[2] Restorative messianism strove for the return of the Jews to political sovereignty, particularly as it was thought to have existed under the kingdom of David. Although this type of messianism certainly preached a radical change in the Jews' exilic existence, it did so strictly in the framework of tradition: messianic times would close the circle of history by restoring the Jews to their original state, thus making possible the fulfillment of all the commandments. The utopian-catastrophic view, which Scholem frequently calls apocalypticism, envisioned instead an entirely new world, unlike anything experienced previously, except perhaps in a mythical Eden. Acording to the apocalyptic theory of history, the new aeon would be preceded by a sudden rupture in historical continuity, and might be characterized by a radically new law; apocalyptic messianism was therefore prone to heretical antinomianism.

For Scholem, the history of Jewish messianism must be understood as a dialectic between the traditionalist and apocalyptic poles.[3] These two contradictory yet complementary tendencies gave messianism its revolutionary dynamism and at the same time held it within certain bounds. The messianic desire for full redemption of all the Jewish people never disappeared from Jewish history, although Scholem speaks of its occasional "neutralization." With most Jewish nationalist historians, Scholem believes that messianism is one of the central themes of Jewish history, although we shall see that he defines it more radically. He castigates the nineteenth-century Jewish thinkers for distorting and suppressing what he considers the authentic forces of Jewish messianism.

THE WISSENSCHAFT DES JUDENTUMS AND MESSIANISM

Jewish thought in the nineteenth century typically renounced both the restorative and utopian poles of Jewish messianism. It is well known that Jews felt compelled by the terms of emancipation to replace their belief in a Messiah who would restore them to their ancestral homeland with an acceptance of the European nations as their only real home. The price of emancipation, exacted perhaps most brutally by Napoleon in his questions to the Assembly of Jewish Notables and the Sanhedrin,[4] was renunciation of the nationalist side of Jewish messianism.

The Jewish response to this demand was frequently not to abandon messianism altogether, but to displace its target from the land of Israel to Europe. When Joseph II of Austria promulgated his relatively enlightened *privilegium* of 1780, certain *Maskilim* (Jewish enlighteners) hailed him as the Messiah.[5] In 1822 the venerable Maskil, Lazarus Ben David, disputed the claim that belief in a Jewish Messiah is central to the Jewish tradition, arguing that "no man can reproach the Jew when he finds his Messiah in the good princes who make him equal to all other citizens and give him the hope of achieving complete fulfillment of all civic rights and responsibilies."[6] Later in the century, the Russian-Jewish poet Y. L. Gordon compared Alexander II, who had eased some of the restrictions imposed on the Jews by his predecessors, to Cyrus the Great of Persia, whom the author of Deutero-Isaiah had called the "anointed" *(mashiaḥ)* of God.[7] All of these characterizations of benevolent non-Jewish rulers as the Messiah were part of a long tradition, but the eighteenth- and nineteenth-century appropriation of the tradition concealed a radical innovation: the Maskilim used a traditional form of praise for a congenial gentile ruler to broadcast their loyalty to the modern state. Secularized messianism had become a tool of assimilation and apologetics.

Another common Jewish reaction to the demands of emancipation was to transform messianism into universalism. Perhaps uncomfortable in transferring messianic ideals directly from the Jewish nation to a non-Jewish nation, Enlighteners like Abraham Geiger claimed that the true message of messianism all along had not been nationalism but universalism. Geiger asserted that Christianity is false universalism because it never passed through a national stage of development; but Judaism, because it did outgrow nationalism, is the true teacher of universalist messianism.[8]

If religious and political apologists purged messianism of its restorative-national aspect, nineteenth-century thinkers also actively suppressed its apocalyptic side. I have shown earlier how Nachman Krochmal and Heinrich Graetz considered Sabbatianism the ultimate perversion of Judaism. Believing in the continued, uninterrupted progress of consciousness, they denied the existence of apocalyptic breaks in the historical continuum. They considered the modern age the culmination of Jewish history, not a radical departure from it. Whereas the nineteenth-century believers in progress shared with apocalyptic messianism the belief in a new age, better than any that had preceded it, they abandoned the theory of a catastrophic break in history.

The nineteenth-century transformation of Jewish messianism found its clearest and most radical expression in Hermann Cohen, as Scholem himself suggests: "Hermann Cohen, surely as distinguished a representative of the liberal and rationalistic reinterpretation of the Messianic idea in Judaism as one could find, was driven by his religion of reason into becoming a genuine and unhampered utopian who would have liked to liquidate the restorative factor entirely."[9] In Cohen's utopian universalism, we find equally the suppression of the restorative and apocalyptic aspects of messianism. Cohen's utopianism was based on his distinction between mythology and monotheism. Mythology has no real concept of historical progress and instead harks back to an idyllic Golden Age *(das goldene Zeitalter)*.[10] Monotheism, on the other hand, does not seek to return to the happiness of the Golden Age, but instead to increase knowledge of the true God. Since the process of acquiring knowledge is infinite, monotheism is necessarily oriented toward the future in which knowledge will increase. Unlike mythology, which is romantic and reactionary, monotheism is the aspiration for infinite time.[11] The messianic age will truly be an "age of culture" since it will be the age of complete knowledge. It will be a utopia in the precise sense that it does not exist now in any place but instead remains an ideal in the process of eventual realization.

Cohen defined messianism as universalism and, in his brief history of the messianic idea,[12] placed its origin in the idea of monotheism. Messianism derives from monotheism since the idea of a unique God requires a unified mankind.[13] This universalist idea was already implicit in prophetic monotheism, but it was not completely actualized in biblical times since it was expressed in Jewish nationalism. The destruction of the Jewish state was a positive event because it allowed Israel to bring its universalist message to fruition. Cohen, along with a general nineteenth-century current, therefore inverted the idea that the exile was a punishment for Israel's sins and found in it a great opportunity for the development of messianism. In his famous polemics against Zionism, Cohen argued that the Jews, as the international leaven of messianism, had superseded the need for a nation-state.[14]

As a universal religion—the "divine dew among the nations"—Judaism had come closest to realization of the messianic idea implicit in its original monotheism. Cohen saw an ultimate identity of purpose between German nationalism and Jewish messianism. The German national spirit was "the spirit of classical humanism and true universalism,"[15] while the Jews, no longer a nation limited by place, were the international religious emissaries of the same values. In his highly patriotic series of articles "Deutschtum und Judentum," written during World War I, Cohen defended Germany as the true harbinger of the coming messianic order. Since Germany was the nation representing the Jewish religious spirit, Jews around the world owed Germany "a debt of filial piety" for fighting "the just war [in] preparation for perpetual peace."[16]

SCHOLEM'S RESTORATION OF APOCALYPTICISM TO MESSIANISM

Jewish nationalist historiography at the beginning of the twentieth century quite naturally attacked the tendency of the Wissenschaft des Judentums to liquidate the restorative aspect of messianism. Benzion Dinur made messianism, which he defined as the desire to return to the land of Israel, the central theme of Jewish history. Joseph Klausner also wrote extensively on the historical heritage of Jewish messianism in support of his own militant nationalism.[17]

The new historiography did not emphasize as strongly the catastrophic-apocalyptic side of messianism. The nationalists frequently wanted to prove that Zionism was the culmination and fulfillment of Jewish history rather than its abrogation. To be sure, writers like Berdichevsky, who called for a radical break with normative, exilic Jewish history, may be considered apocalyptic, but with the exception perhaps of Shai Hurwitz they rarely studied Jewish apocalyptic movements of the past in support of their own position. Even so radical a writer as Martin Buber deliberately defined Jewish messianism as prophetic and antiapocalyptic. In his essay "Prophetie und Apocalyptik,"[18] Buber argued that apocalyptic motifs entered Judaism from Iranian sources and were therefore alien to the Jewish prophetic spirit. Buber understood the true messianism not as an end of history, but as the sanctification of the world in history. In place of an "end of days," Buber substituted the possibility of redeemed moments throughout history, the "All-Day of Redemption."[19]

Scholem's great contribution to this movement of revision was his almost single-handed rehabilitation and legitimization of apocalypticism as a continuing motif in Jewish messianism. He translated into Jewish scholarship an important trend already developed in the historiography of Christianity. Liberal Christian scholars, epitomized by Harnack, had considered the historical Jesus an ethical preacher and discounted any apocalyptic interpretation of early Christianity. Franz Overbeck, Johannes Weiss, and Albert Schweitzer overturned his interpretation of Christianity and replaced it with the view that the original Christianity was a Jewish apocalyptic sect that revolted against the world and did not transmit an ethical message.[20]

At about the same time, other scholars of Christianity began to discover the radical apocalyptic movements in later Christian history which had been suppressed or forgotten by nineteenth-century rationalism. K. Holl and Ernst Bloch drew attention to Thomas Münzer and the Anabaptists, while Albrecht Ritschl and Erich Seeberg examined the roots of radical Pietism.[21] Karl Mannheim, in his *Ideologie und Utopie* (1929), analyzed the ideological functions of different types of utopianism and gave a particularly acute account of the character and historical role of chiliastic utopianism.[22]

Scholem must be seen as part of this rediscovery of the historical role of apocalypticism.[23] Like his colleagues in Christian historiography, he finds vitality in Jewish apocalyptic movements which others had dismissed as degenerate: "It has been one of the strangest errors of the modern Wissenschaft des Judentums to deny the continuity of Jewish apocalypticism. The endeavors of leading scholars to dissociate apocalyptic from rabbinic Judaism and to associate it exclusively with Christianity have contributed so much to the modern falsification of Jewish history and the concealment of some of its most dynamic forces, both constructive and destructive."[24] As with his investigations of the role of myth in Jewish thought, Scholem argues that ostensibly heretical ideas actually played a legitimate role within Jewish history and were not insidiously infiltrated from the outside. Apocalypticism was not a Christian or Iranian idea, but had its roots in the indigenous soil of Judaism itself. In the persistent dialectic between restorative and apocalyptic messianism in Jewish history, apocalypticism always appeared as the vital force in messianic movements.[25] Although the apocalyptic motif was partially suppressed in the Middle Ages by rationalists like Maimonides, it never disappeared. Like mysticism, it was not entirely alien to the great legal authorities:

> For a number of [the great men of *Halakhah*], apocalypticism is not a foreign element and is not felt to be in contradiction to the realm of *Halakhah*. From the point of view of the *Halakhah* . . . Judaism appears as a well-ordered house and it is a profound truth that a well-ordered house is a dangerous thing. Something of messianic apocalypticism penetrates into this house: perhaps I can best describe it as a kind of anarchic breeze.[26]

Scholem's interpretation of Judaism therefore emphasizes the heretical and revolutionary impulses in messianism as the true driving forces in Jewish history. For Scholem, historical change, which is necessary if a tradition is to remain alive, comes through the revolutionary struggle of contradictory principles. History does not consist of eternal gradual progress, as the nineteenth century believed, but of apocalyptic ruptures. The central role that apocalyptic messianism plays in Scholem's historiography is surely a consequence of this radical view of historical change.

Scholem's attack on the nineteenth-century censorship of apocalypticism must be understood in the general context of his hostility to the attempt to impose a dogmatic definition on Judaism. By arbitrarily restricting Judaism to only certain historical phenomena, the nineteenth-century scholars had ignored the most vital forces in Jewish history. The relegation of apocalypticism to Christianity was a case in point. In his analysis of the Sabbatian theology of Nathan of Gaza, perhaps the most important Sabbatian propagandist, Scholem writes that Nathan's doctrine of

> faith as independent of, and indeed outweighing, all outward religious acts and symbols is distinctly Christian in character. . . . But however this may be . . . this proclamation did not provoke the reaction one would have expected if some of today's clichés regarding the 'essence' of Judaism and of Christianity were

correct . . . There is no way of telling a priori what beliefs are possible or impossible within the framework of Judaism . . . The 'Jewishness' in the religiosity of any particular period is not measured by dogmatic criteria that are unrelated to actual historical circumstances, but solely by what sincere Jews do, in fact, believe, or—at least—consider to be legitimate possibilities.[27]

It is interesting that, in his refutation of nineteenth-century dogmatism, Scholem formulates his view of Jewish history in terms rather similar to Hermann Cohen's utopianism. Cohen had criticized purely restorative messianism for seeing history as a closed circle, whereas he defined utopianism as directed toward an open and unknown future. As a Zionist, Scholem is of course much more sympathetic to the restorative strains in messianism, but he too adopts a utopian approach to history. Yet he gives an antidogmatic twist quite different from Cohen's: "The phenomenon called Judaism does not end on a particular date and I do not think it is likely to end so long as a living Judaism exists. But there is something living that is beyond dogmatic definition . . . Judaism includes *utopian* aspects that have not yet been discovered."[28] Like Cohen, Scholem sees Jewish history as open-ended, but he concludes that Judaism cannot therefore be dogmatically defined.

The study of Jewish apocalypticism and Sabbatianism in particular became a powerful weapon for Scholem in shattering dogmatic definitions of Judaism by showing how censored "heresies" in Jewish history were just as legitimate as the normative tradition. The argument that the Sabbatian messianic heretics were part of Jewish history became the cornerstone of his counter-history. As a result, his *Sabbatai Ṣevi* attracted strong criticism by several Israeli scholars, notably Baruch Kurzweil and R. J. Zvi Werblowsky, who saw in it the extreme expression of Scholem's use of historiography to destroy traditional concepts of Judaism.[29] These critics argued that, by claiming that Sabbatianism was a central episode in Jewish history and that the Sabbatian theology was as important as normative rabbinical thought, Scholem had subverted any coherent definition of Judaism.

As his student Isaiah Tishby has pointed out,[30] Scholem's effort to legitimize the Sabbatians in Jewish history was not based solely on the claim that a large number of Jews believed in Sabbatai Ṣevi. The Sabbatian theologians must be considered legitimate Jewish thinkers because they developed their radical theology in the vocabulary of traditional Jewish symbols. Where earlier historians had considered the Sabbatians demented rebels devoid of theological originality, Scholem not only demonstrates the sophistication and originality of Sabbatian theology, but also argues that its roots were firmly implanted in the history of the Kabbalah. Sabbatianism was not an aberration of Jewish history or a wild departure from traditional Judaism as the result of non-Jewish influences, but a movement whose origins lay in the heart of the legitimate tradition and whose heretical theology developed as a plausible offshoot of accepted concepts.

THE DIALECTICAL PREPARATION OF SABBATIANISM

Although Scholem had learned of Sabbatianism from Zalman Rubaschoff in his student days, he does not seem to have considered it the focus of his Kabbalistic research until 1927, when he discovered a manuscript in Oxford by the Marrano Sabbatian, Abraham Miguel Cardozo.[31] His 1928 article on "Die Theologie des Sabbatianismus im Lichte Abraham Cardosos" and his "Mizvah ha-Ba'ah B'avera" (Redemption Through Sin) in 1936 showed that he viewed the apocalyptic and heretical theology of Sabbatianism as the culmination of the history of the Kabbalah.[32] By reconstructing Scholem's history of the Kabbalah as preparation for the Sabbatian outburst, we can see his dialectical philosophy of history at work. From an inward, spiritualized messianic doctrine, the Kabbalah developed into the driving force behind the mass messianic movement of the seventeenth century. Apocalyptic messianism, which never vanished from the Jewish consciousness, was cultivated and nourished until it burst onto the stage of history as Sabbatianism. In Sabbatianism, moreover, the apocalyptic elements in messianism joined forces with the underground tradition of Gnosticism in the Kabbalah to make an explosive mixture that would demolish the traditional Jewish world.

With the exception of the thirteenth-century *Sefer ha-Temunah*, which propounded a theory of historical cycles, each represented by different and contradictory Torahs,[33] the early medieval Kabbalah was not especially interested in eschatology. It focused instead on issues of theosophy and cosmogony: the beginning rather than the end of history. The ecstatic and contemplative absorption in esoteric matters of creation guaranteed "a type of individual non-messianic redemption . . . One should not see [the early Kabbalists] as followers of a movement to alter radically the style and pace of Jewish life."[34] There is a seeming contradiction between this formulation and the criteria Scholem sets up for defining Jewish messianism. He claims that Jewish messianism is characterized by its social and historical dimension, while Christianity emphasizes inner, spiritual redemption.[35] The early Kabbalah, however, which Scholem describes as a belief in "non-messianic redemption," seems to have deemphasized the traditional Jewish concern for national redemption. We have here another example of Scholem's desire to legitimize messianic expressions that would normally be excluded from Judaism, even by his own criteria.

The phrase "non-messianic redemption" suggests that mystical contemplation rather than historical activity brings liberation. Scholem is careful to indicate that he does not consider the early Kabbalah to have negated messianism but rather to have "neutralized" it. The term "neutralization," which Scholem used for the first time in 1934 in an essay on the Kabbalah after the Spanish expulsion,[36] means the suppression of the restorative and apocalyptic elements in messianism, but not their complete liquidation. By focusing on the primordial harmony of God and the cosmos, the early Kabbalah prepared the ground for a radical shift of emphasis to social redemption. This shift resulted from the trauma of the expulsion from Spain in 1492.

The desire for redemption became acute as a result of the expulsion and attendant persecutions. The Kabbalists responded to the historical crisis by transposing it to a cosmic framework: the desire for historical redemption was reinterpreted as a symbol of the mystical desire to return the cosmos to its original harmony.[37] The metahistorical concerns of the early Kabbalists prepared the way for the entrance of the Kabbalah into the realm of history: "Everything internal became external: the penetration of the Kabbalist into the profundities of creation was overturned entirely at the time of the great emotional revolution and became religious activity in the community."[38] Scholem argues that the Kabbalah moved to fill a spiritual vacuum following the expulsion from Spain: traditional Jewish theology was unable to account for the historical crisis and to offer solace, but the Kabbalah, having prepared itself in the "underground," emerged as the authoritative theology of a Judaism in crisis.

It was through the Lurianic Kabbalah, developed in Safed in the middle of the sixteenth century, that Jewish mysticism became a public, widely accepted theology.[39] The Lurianic Kabbalah proposed a cosmic myth of exile and redemption which mirrored the actual historical experience of the Jews. Luria described the exile and redemption of the Jews as a symbol for a movement within God himself: God had created the world in order to rid himself of the seeds of evil. In this catharsis *(zimzum* and *shevirat ha-kelim),* part of God went into exile from himself. The process of redemption, which actually began at the moment of catharsis, consists in restoring the scattered, exiled sparks of divinity to their primordial harmony. The process of creation thus became synonymous with cosmic exile, and redemption with the restoration *(tikkun)* of cosmic order.

The person of the Messiah was of little importance to Luria since redemption does not come "suddenly, like a thief in the night," but is a long, gradual process extending back to creation. Luria gave man an active role in the restoration of the divine sparks: each generation must fulfill its quota of "restorations." Against the belief of some secularists that Jewish messianism was always passive in the Middle Ages, Scholem's repeated emphasis on Luria's importance reveals the profoundly activist potentiality in mysticism. If the early Kabbalah was quietistic, it ultimately developed into a mystical doctrine teaching man's active role in the cosmos.

The possibility of messianic activism inherent in the Lurianic Kabbalah became explicit in Sabbatianism. The relationship between the Lurianic Kabbalah and Sabbatianism forms the cornerstone of Scholem's theory of how the Kabbalah broke out of its cloister and became the motivating force for one of the greatest mass movements of the Jewish Middle Ages. In the 1920s, even before his first study of Sabbatianism, he suspected the possible influence of the "apocalyptic atmosphere in Safed" in the sixteenth century on the messianic movement of the seventeenth.[40]

With the declaration of Sabbatai Ṣevi as Messiah by Nathan of Gaza in 1665, Kabbalistic messianism became a social movement. The presumed completion of the mystical restoration of divine sparks made it possible for the new messianic age to manifest itself, as it were, in the person of Sabbatai Ṣevi. The process of transformation of Kabbalistic messianism from a personal, internal concern in the early Kabbalah to a historical myth reached completion in Sabbatian theology. The mystical "non-messianic redemption" was transmuted into restorative messianism, but with an apocalyptic-cosmic dimension. Hence the dialectic between utopian and restorative messianism found its most potent expression not in Maimonides' rationalist political messianism, but in antinomian apocalypticism.

As if to symbolize the end of the internal mystical stage of messianism and the beginning of its external historical completion, Nathan of Gaza banned the use of the Lurianic *kavvanot,* which were the meditations used in prayer to hasten the restoration of divine sparks.[41] Because he believed that an entirely new aeon of history had begun, Nathan considered the Lurianic Kabbalah to be obsolete, just as, later, radical Sabbatian theology would consider the whole body of Jewish law obsolete: in Sabbatianism, the antinomian and revolutionary potentialities in apocalyptic messianism became frighteningly actual.

The Lurianic Kabbalah therefore prepared the soil for Sabbatianism, only to be negated. The relationship between the two serves a number of important functions in Scholem's work. He wants to show that the history of the Kabbalah was the major source of Sabbatianism and that therefore the Kabbalah had widespread historical impact despite its esoteric character. Scholem judges Sabbatianism to have been primarily a religious movement and therefore caused by a development in religious consciousness. This role, he argues, could only have been played by the Lurianic Kabbalah, which provided the Sabbatians with their messianic vocabulary even as they radicalized its meaning. By portraying Sabbatianism as part of the Jewish religious tradition and not a desperate reaction to suffering, Scholem claims to give it authenticity and legitimacy. Finally, Scholem's extensive treatment of Sabbatianism is based on the assumption that Sabbatianism was a mass movement, encompassing all geographical areas and social groups of the Jewish world. The world-wide character of Sabbatianism is explained by the fact that its main source, the Lurianic Kabbalah, became the universal theology of Judaism in the century before the messianic outbreak.[42]

One may be permitted to wonder whether Scholem has confused the historical cause of Sabbatianism with its ideological and theological justification. The fact that the Sabbatians adopted the messianic imagery of the Lurianic Kabbalah may tell us how they conceived of themselves and their mission, but not necessarily the underlying reason why they acted as they did. This issue points again to a fundamental characteristic of Scholem's philosophy of history: his emphasis on intellectual and especially esoteric movements as motivating forces in history.

There is also an immanent problem in Scholem's characterization of Sabbatianism as an apocalyptic movement instigated by the Lurianic Kabbalah. Scholem himself notes that Lurianic messianism was actually closer to the notion of gradual progress than to apocalypticism.[43] Luria's point of catastrophe occurred at the beginning of history rather than at the end. Moreover, apocalypticism typically teaches man's passivity in the face of the coming catastrophe; Luria emphasized man's active role. To be sure, the idea of a cosmic myth encompassing historical events is typically apocalyptic, but the crucial element of a rupture in history is missing. It would seem from Scholem's own description of the Lurianic Kabbalah that the apocalyptic element in Sabbatianism was not inherited from the Kabbalah, which had actually become antiapocalyptic, but from the atmosphere of catastrophe in the centuries following the Spanish expulsion. In other words, it is hard to understand from Scholem's presentation how the Lurianic notion of progress became Sabbatian apocalypticism except by negation, and this negation was perhaps prompted more by causes external to the Kabbalah than by the Kabbalah itself.

SABBATIANISM AND ENLIGHTENMENT

Scholem's contention of a mass outburst of apocalyptic messianism and heretical antinomianism on the threshold of the modern period implicitly challenges the rationalist belief in the progression of Jewish history from darkness to enlightenment. If Sabbatianism were only a peripheral movement, it could be dismissed as irrelevant to the mainstream of Jewish history. Nineteenth-century historiography had maintained that the modern period was inaugurated by the external influences of the new Christian tolerance and Enlightenment in the eighteenth century. Scholem claims that the modern period was produced by a dialectic within Jewish history: Sabbatianism shook the foundations of traditional Judaism from within.[44] Religious Judaism, since it produced the Kabbalah, which in turn produced Sabbatianism, sowed the seeds of its own destruction.

Consistent with his belief in the power of ideas, Scholem focuses his account of the hidden influence of Sabbatianism on the dialectical development of Sabbatian theology. His first study of Sabbatianism, on Abraham Cardozo's heretical theology, shows how this Marrano Kabbalist turned the Lurianic Kabbalah into moral anarchism.[45] According to

Luria's doctrine of the transmigration of souls, actions are neither moral nor immoral in themselves but are of divine sparks. Failure to fulfill one's quota meant returning in another life to do so. The question already implicit in the Lurianic theory was whether one's evil actions required punishment once one had fulfilled the assigned restoration. In other words, man was perhaps no longer responsible for evil actions in an earlier incarnation, thus annulling any moral calculus. Moreover, man's ignorance of his previous lives implied lack of knowledge of just what his assigned quota was and where he had failed. In Cardozo's thought, man's actions became a "game" *(Spiel)* or "theology of chance" *(Theologie des Hasards)* which undermined the moral certainties of traditional Judaism: "Thus it was that before the powers of world history uprooted Judaism in the nineteenth century, its reality was threatened from within. Already at that time [the time of Sabbatianism] the 'reality of the Hebrews,' the sphere of Judaism, threatened to become an illusion."[46] Once again we observe a striking example of how Scholem, in 1928, had already arrived at one of his most cherished hypotheses, which he was to develop throughout his career: Sabbatianism destroyed Judaism from within nearly a century before the Enlightenment.

In his "Redemption Through Sin" in 1936, Scholem explored in greater detail the Sabbatian doctrine of the "holiness of sin"—which was developed first to explain Sabbatai Ṣevi's strange antinomian actions and later became the central ideology of the movement following his apostasy. For those who remained in the movement as believers after Sabbatai Ṣevi "took the fez," two options were possible: to regard Sabbatai Ṣevi's heretical actions as unique and continue to live an outwardly orthodox life while retaining inner belief in a new messianic reality, or to emulate his apostasy. Scholem calls the first option "moderate Sabbatianism" and the second "radical."

For the moderates, the distinction between outward and inward life became acute. We have already observed Scholem's theory of the development of Kabbalistic messianism from a purely inward doctrine to an historical myth in the Lurianic Kabbalah and finally to the extreme outward apocalyptic messianism and Sabbatianism. But with the failure of the movement to achieve political-historical success, the messianic belief was again sundered: the believer now lived in the inner faith that everything in the world had mystically changed with the appearance of the Messiah, but his apostasy had held the external evidence of this change in abeyance. This "mystical schizophrenia" produced a state of mind similar to that of the Marranos and explains why some Marrano Kabbalists such as Cardozo were attracted to Sabbatianism.[47] According to Scholem, the new inner-outer dichotomy led to the splitting of identity into the private and public compartments characteristic of modern Judaism. It would seem, however, that the development of the Sabbatian mentality into the Jewish Enlightenment required at least one more inversion, which I do not find in Scholem's account: where the moderate Sabbatians remained traditional Jews outwardly and were only eschatologically "free" inwardly, the slogan of the Enlightenment was "a Jew at home and a man in the street."

The radical Sabbatians, on the other hand, solved the problem of bifurcation either by open conversion to Islam or Christianity or by violation of Jewish law in secret. The Dönmeh sect in Turkey and the Frankists in Eastern Europe prefigured the more assimilationist tendencies in modern Judaism because they chose apostasy.[48] In the case of Jacob Frank and his followers, apostasy did not mean sincere acceptance of the new religion, but a dialectical nihilism expressed through the mask of Christianity. With Frank, the doctrine of the holiness of sin reached its most demonic expression. Frankist nihilism ultimately turned outward to a desire for political liberation, and certain Frankist tracts suggested the connection between the heretical mystical doctrines and the political ideals of the Enlightenment.[49]

On a theoretical level, then, Sabbatianism prepared the ground for modern secularism and the Enlightenment. The doctrine of the holiness of sin became secular in indifference to all traditional Jewish law. In an important aphorism, Scholem suggests that Reform Judaism, which has substantially banished the Halakhah from its own practice of Judaism, is a product not only of Sabbatianism but actually of the early Kabbalah:

> Just as nature, seen Kabbalistically, is nothing but a shadow of the divine name, so one can also speak of a shadow of the law, which is cast ever longer around the life of the Jews. But in the Kabbalah, the stony wall of the law becomes gradually transparent . . . This alchemy of the law, its transmutation into transparency, is one of the most profound paradoxes of the Kabbalah . . . [The] logical end of this process must be the rise of Jewish Reform: the shadowless, pure abstract humanity of the law, devoid of all background but also no longer irrational. Reform is thus a remnant of the mystical dissolution of the law.[50]

This enigmatic passage requires some explication. According to the Kabbalists, nature is like a shadow concealing the spiritual, divine essence of the world; the law is similarly only a symbolic fabric for a deeper reality. Scholem transforms this Kabbalistic motif into something different: the law hides the true essence of the life of the Jewish people. This passage should be read as an implicit critique of Jewish law.

Scholem then mixes his metaphors by calling the law a "stony wall" *(steinerne Mauer),* which is a negative rendering of the rabbinic description of the oral law as a "fence around the Torah" *(siyag la-torah).* The Kabbalah broke down this wall, presumably by its pluralistic theory of exegesis. Apocalyptic Sabbatianism, which Scholem does not mention explicitly in the aphorism, formed the last stage in this alchemy of the law before the law lost its capacity to throw a shadow around Judaism. With Reform Judaism, the dialectical interplay between the constraint of the law and the liberating force of mysticism disappeared as law became purely rational and abstractly universal. The secularization of the law, Scholem implies, sealed the doom of Jewish mysticism, because mysticism required a normative Judaism as a foil for its mystical reinterpretation. The very rise of Reform, whose rationalism opposed equally halakhah and Kabbalah, was, however, the consequence of internal development within mysticism. Nineteenth-century rationalism and secularism were certainly a revolution in Jewish history, but it was a revolution dialectically prepared by the religious tradition.

Along with his theoretical studies of Sabbatianism and its hidden intellectual connections to secular Judaism and the Enlightenment, Scholem has tried to prove his bold claims by showing the biographical links between eighteenth-century Sabbatians and Jewish Enlighteners. He argues particularly that among the Jewish bourgeoisie of Bohemia and Moravia, families with Sabbatian or Frankist traditions often became leaders in the new Haskalah: "Even while still 'believers'—in fact, precisely because they were 'believers'—they had been drawing closer to the spirit of the Haskalah all along, so that when the flame of their faith finally flickered out, they soon reappeared as leaders of Reform Judaism, secular intellectuals or simply indifferent skeptics."[51] The twentieth-century historian of atheism, Fritz Mauthner, appropriately enough, was one such descendant of a Sabbatian family, while Aharon Horin, a pioneer of Reform Judaism in Hungary, was a Sabbatian in his youth.[52] Scholem has also unearthed some extraordinary evidence of how a number of Sabbatians from Bohemia and Moravia, notably E. J. Hirschfeld and Moses Dobruschka, entered Masonic lodges at the end of the eighteenth century and introduced some radical Kabbalistic doctrines into Masonic ritual.[53] Dobruschka, perhaps the most fascinating of the whole cast of characters who followed this underground path from heretical mysticism to secular enlightenment, was guillotined during the French Revolution with Danton under the alias of Junius Frey.

In order to establish the pervasive influence of Sabbatianism on the Jewish Enlightenment, Scholem argued that a widespread movement persisted as late as a century after Sabbatai Ṣevi's apostasy. Even in the eighteenth century, Jacob Emden made this accusation and instituted a veritable witch-hunt for secret Sabbatians. Emden accused Jonathan Eibeschütz, one of the greatest legal authorities of the age, of Sabbatian sympathies, sparking a controversy that split the rabbinical world in Central and Eastern Europe. By the twentieth century, most of the orthodox community came to reject Emden's contentions in order to squelch the possibility that Sabbatianism was more than a passing phenomenon and to save the reputations of a number of venerable orthodox rabbis. In reviving Emden's suspicions that Sabbatianism was a major force as late as the eighteenth century,[54] Scholem incurred the wrath of the orthodox world. A concerted attack by orthodox scholars forced him for the only time in his career to answer one of his accusers in an orthodox journal.[55] He later published a special pamphlet systematically refuting his opponents.[56] The controversy is evidence that Sabbatianism remains a potentially dangerous embarrassment to modern orthodoxy, for, if Scholem's claims are correct, they show that religious Judaism in the eighteenth century was far more heterogeneous than it conceives of itself today.

The eighteenth-century Sabbatian movement to which Scholem devoted his greatest attention in the effort to show connections between messianism and enlightenment is Frankism. The followers of Jacob Frank (1726–1791) in many cases converted to Catholicism and became involved in various Enlightenment movements. Scholem's ambivalent attraction to messianic movements is most sharply revealed in his treatment of Frank. On the one hand, he was clearly fascinated by the Frankists and the way their ideas form a bridge between religious and secular world views. On the other hand, he displayed an open revulsion toward Frank himself and the unbridled nihilism of his group. In "Redemption Through Sin" (*The Messianic Idea in Judaism,* pages 126–

127), he wrote in negative terms such as never appear in his discussion of Sabbatai Ṣevi:

Jacob Frank will always be remembered as one of the most frightening phenomena in the whole of Jewish history: a religious leader who, whether for purely self-interested motives or otherwise, was in all his actions a truly corrupt and degenerate individual. Indeed, it might be plausibly argued that in order to completely exhaust its seemingly endless potential for the contradictory and the unexpected the Sabbatian movement was in need of just such a strong man, a man who could snuff out its last inner lights and pervert whatever will to truth and goodness was still to be found in the maze-like ruins of the believers' souls.

The connections Scholem drew between Sabbatianism and Enlightenment resemble what other scholars had already demonstrated about the relationship between Christianity and the origins of the European Enlightenment. Since Max Weber, scholars have tried to portray the dialectical development of the Christian sectarian movements spawned by the Reformation into the Enlightenment. Max Weber's study of the influence of Calvinism on the "spirit of capitalism" was followed by studies of more radical heretical groups, such as the Socinians and the Anabaptists.[57] Special attention has also been paid to the connections between mystical Pietism and Enlightenment.[58]

Scholem sees his own work in this historiographical tradition. To be sure, his argument of the hidden connection between Sabbatianism and Enlightenment is not entirely new, for even in the eighteenth century, Gottfried Selig and Jacob Emden suggested the link.[59] In the twentieth century, Shai Hurwitz preceded Scholem in describing Sabbatianism as a trailblazer of the Enlightenment.[60] Scholem's contribution lies in systematizing and supporting these earlier suggestions with exhaustive research as well as connecting them with a coherent, radical philosophy of Jewish history.

This latest chapter of Scholem's work, perhaps the boldest and most original, is also the most subject to doubt. As Jacob Katz has pointed out,[61] Scholem's thesis is weak in terms of both intellectual and biographical links. Despite similar attitudes toward the "yoke of the commandments," Enlighteners need not have taken their ideas from the Sabbatians. Scholem's examples of Sabbatians who became Enlighteners or Reformers, as provocative as they are, constitute only a minuscule fraction of the Jews who abandoned orthodoxy for new forms of Judaism. Katz shows that even some of Scholem's prime examples, such as

Aharon Horin, may never have been Sabbatians or, like E. J. Hirschfeld, may have discovered Sabbatianism after they had already come to Enlightenment.

Sabbatians were certainly more susceptible to assimilation because they were already outcasts from orthodox Jewish society, but this is a sociological argument, which, although he would not reject it, is far from Scholem's main thesis. Scholem is undoubtedly right that Sabbatianism helped to undermine the traditional rabbinical world much more than has been assumed, but his claim of an inherent connection between Sabbatianism and Enlightenment is probably unprovable.

Scholem's theory of how mystical heresy ushered in the modern period of secularism and rationalism is the culmination of his attempt to show the hidden influence of mysticism on Jewish history. His account of the development of Kabbalistic messianism into apocalyptic heresy and finally secular enlightenment rests on his theory of the productive conjunction of opposites: myth and monotheism, mysticism and rationalism, apocalyptic messianism and secularism. This theory derives from his understanding of the role of demonic forces in history: "The desire for total liberation which played so tragic a role in the development of Sabbatian nihilism was by no means a purely self-destructive force; on the contrary, beneath the surface of lawlessness, antinomianism and catastrophic negation, powerful constructive impulses were at work."[62] As opposed to a theory of gradual progress, history proceeds by violent ruptures. Yet these discontinuities do not mean that one historical period has no influence on the nature of its successor. The constructive potentiality of the demonic suggests that radical change and continuity are not mutually exclusive. As radically different as the Enlightenment may seem in contrast to the mystical messianism of Sabbatianism, there is a hidden connection between them since Sabbatianism unwittingly prepared the ground for secular rationalism. Where previous historians saw only unresolvable contradictions and negations, Scholem argues that continuities can be established between seeming opposites. This was the goal that Hermann Cohen had set for the philosopher of Judaism confronted by contradictions between the historical sources. But where Cohen imposed harmony by the concept of reason, Scholem demonstrates hidden connections between irrationalism and rationalism, and his evidence for these connections is historical sources.

HASIDISM AND MESSIANISM

Many Jewish nationalist writers were attracted to study Hasidism as a vital popular movement from the past. Because Jewish nationalism had to confront the question of messianism, the various interpretations of Hasidism often focused on the messianic character of the movement. Benzion Dinur and Scholem's own student Isaiah Tishby argued that traditional restorative messianism played a crucial role in Hasidism.[63] Dinur saw in Hasidism a forerunner of political Zionism. Tishby showed that Hasidic messianism arose with no special connection to the waning of Sabbatianism in Poland. Hasidism utilized traditional messianic formulas and was not a product, either positive or negative, of Sabbatianism. Tishby's argument was directed against Scholem's contention that Hasidism emerged as a response to the failure of Sabbatianism.

Against the messianic interpretation of Hasidism, Simon Dubnow and Martin Buber argued that Hasidism was antimessianic in a traditional sense.[64] Buber rejected apocalypticism as a legitimate aspect of Jewish messianism. He associated apocalypticism with Gnosticism, which he also considered alien to Judaism.[65] Buber's discussion of the history of the Kabbalah shows some similarities to Scholem's, but he sometimes seems closer to the nineteenth century. Buber believed that, by the time of Sabbatianism, the Kabbalah had degenerated into Gnosticism so that its apocalyptic character was fundamentally anti-Jewish. For Buber, apocalyptic Gnosticism was an escape from the everyday world, which is the world man should try to sanctify.[66]

Hasidism, according to Buber, was a movement to return Judaism to its concern for the everyday world. Against the Gnostic tendency in the Kabbalah, Hasidism sought to "deschematicize the mystery" *(Entschematisierung des Mysteriums)*.[67] Hasidism's contribution did not lie in a theoretical innovation in Kabbalah, but, on the contrary, in escape from the dangers of degeneration. Hasidism decisively liquidated the disastrous messianism in the Sabbatian movement by investing everyday action with divinity.

Buber's interpretation of Hasidism coincided with his general philosophy. Although in his initial writings on Hasidism during the period of his Erlebnismystik he emphasized the ecstatic quality of Hasidic mysticism, after the war he became concerned with the concrete "here and now" and saw in Hasidism the sanctification of the concrete, everyday world. Redemption, Buber now believed, could come for each individual at any moment in time. So he found in Hasidism a model for his individualistic reinterpretation of traditional messianism. Although he did not deny the national dimension of messianism, Buber believed that it would be the end result of the many concrete acts of sanctification of the "here and now."[68]

Like Hermann Cohen, Buber defined his messianism as utopian and antiapocalyptic.[69] He saw Zionism as just such a utopian attempt to sanctify the concrete world. Zionism might therefore take Hasidism as a model for its own spiritual direction:

> Hasidism is a great revelation . . . in which the nation appears to be connected by an inner tie with the world . . . Only through such a contact will it be possible to guard Zionism against following the way of nationalism of our age, which, by demolishing the bridges which connect it with the world, is destroying its own value and right to exist.[70]

Buber's emphasis on redemption in the "here and now" seems surprisingly apocalyptic. As Karl Mannheim wrote, "the only true . . . identifying characteristic of chiliastic experience is absolute presentness."[71] Even though he urged a return to the plane of historical action, the category of history served for Buber more as a metaphor for the existential present than for an historical continuum.

Scholem's own position on Hasidism is iconoclastic. Against both the messianic and antimessianic interpretations of Hasidism he argues a third position, that Hasidism neutralized traditional messianism:

> Hasidism represents an attempt to preserve those elements of Kabbalism which were capable of evoking a popular response but stripped of their messianic flavor to which they owed their chief success during the preceding period . . . Perhaps one should rather speak of a 'neutralization' of the messianic element . . . I am [however] far from suggesting that the messianic hope and the belief in redemption disappeared from the hearts of the Hasidim.[72]

This significant statement stakes out his alternative to the prevailing interpretations. Against Dinur and, later, Tishby,[73] Scholem asserts that Hasidism was "quietistic": it avoided action to bring the Messiah and deferred messianic times to the distant future. Quoting Hillel Zeitlin, Scholem claims that in Hasidism "every individual is the redeemer, the Messiah of his own little world."[74] He tries to demonstrate that Hasidism emerged out of the vestiges of Sabbatianism in Eastern Europe as a deliberate attempt to subdue inherent apocalyptic dangers.[75]

These arguments are almost identical to Buber's and, indeed, Scholem's position appears to be much closer to Buber's than he may be willing to admit. Scholem and Buber also shared a similar political position on the relation of Zionism to messianism. Nonetheless, Scholem's notion of the neutralization of messianism was directed as much against Buber as against Dinur and Tishby. In his article in *Commentary* in 1961, Scholem accused Buber of historical falsification of Hasidism. Where Buber had tried to find his own religious existentialism in Hasidism, Scholem argued that in reality Hasidism did not sanctify the concrete "here and now": "For it is not the concrete reality of things that appears as the ideal result of the mystic's action, but something of the *Messianic* reality in which all things have been restored to their proper place in the scheme of creation and thereby deeply transformed and transfigured."[76] Scholem holds that the personal redemption of divine sparks was not an existentialist glorification of the concrete world as Buber saw it, but a Gnostic attempt to annihilate it. The messianic element that Hasidism retained, albeit divested of its national dimension, was Gnostic and apocalyptic. An historical understanding of Hasidism reveals that it is actually much more alien than Buber had thought; instead of becoming a model for modern man, it emerges as a product of Kabbalistic messianism with the most radical elements neutralized. Buber had misinterpreted Hasidism because he started with a definition of messianism remote from the true character of the messianic idea in Judaism, particularly as it developed in the Kabbalah.[77]

The famous controversy over Hasidism of the 1960s goes back to as early as 1921 when Scholem read the manuscript of *Der Grosse Maggid* where Buber first expressed his views on the opposition of Hasidism and Gnosticism. He wrote to Buber arguing that Hasidism must not be understood as a rejection of Kabbalistic Gnosticism, but as a dialectical development within it.[78] Buber's attempt to study Hasidism as a phenomenon independent of the Kabbalah, and perhaps even opposed to it, could not gain credence unless rooted in the history of the Kabbalah itself. Scholem was prepared to agree that the Hasidim did not innovate in the field of theoretical Kabbalah, but this was not because they rejected the Kabbalistic tradition.

The argument over Hasidism is therefore an interesting example of the difference between Buber and Scholem on the study of history. For Buber, an historical movement can be understood by finding in its points of identification with one's own life experience. The historical phenomenon consequently loses its historical context and background. For Scholem, no historical movement exists in a vacuum. Its connection to its intellectual predecessors determines its character, and the only way a past and alien tradition can be understood is not by wrenching it out of history but, on the contrary, by locating it precisely in its original historical reality.

By calling Hasidism a neutralization of messianism, Scholem suggests how it fits into the history of Kabbalistic messianism. We recall that he characterized the thirteenth-century Kabbalah in virtually identical terms. The Lurianic Kabbalah "de-neutralized" messianism and thereby caused the apocalyptic explosion of Sabbatianism in the next century. Following Sabbatianism, the messianic impulse was once again neutralized. Scholem's terminology leads to the conclusion that Hasidism used the language of the Lurianic Kabbalah to return Kabbalistic messianism to its original, pre-Lurianic state. Messianism was not banished but defused.

Unlike many of his contemporaries on both sides of the Hasidism controversy, Scholem is not overly sympathetic to Hasidism. Since he contends that apocalyptic messianism was like an "anarchic breeze" in the well-ordered house of halakhic Judaism, he seems to believe that the neutralization of these forces would hinder revolutionary historical change. Like Shai Hurwitz, he finds Sabbatianism much more dynamic and historically significant than Hasidism, which he characterizes as "quietistic." On the other hand, Scholem's appreciation of the historical role of apocalyptic forces does not necessarily mean identification with them. He recognizes the nihilistic potentiality in messianism which became actual in Sabbatianism. At the beginning of *Sabbatai Ṣevi* he notes: "Jewish historiography has generally chosen to ignore the fact that the Jewish people have paid a very high price for the messianic idea."[79] He conceives of his own historiography as a warning of the price that this idea may exact from the Jewish people. Scholem's personal position on messianism is necessarily complex, since he believes that the vital forces for change in Jewish history are potentially demonic and destructive; yet they may produce unexpected positive consequences. On the other hand, the realization of messianism would mean the end of the historical tradition, of the struggle between contradictory interpretations of revelation. Committed to the pluralistic flux of tradition, Scholem would have to be ambivalent at best about the messianic end of history, for the

Messiah as the final authority is the ultimate representative of the monolithic interpretation of Judaism.

At the conclusion of his essay on "The Messianic Idea in Judaism," Scholem explains why messianism is inherently problematic:

> In Judaism, the messianic idea has compelled a life lived in deferment, in which nothing can be done definitively . . . Precisely understood, there is nothing concrete which can be accomplished by the unredeemed . . . Jewish so-called *Existenz* possesses a tension that never finds true release; it never burns itself out. And when in our history it does discharge, then it is foolishly decried as pseudo-messianism.[80]

Against Buber, Scholem understands messianism as "the real anti-existentialist idea." The paradox of messianism is that it requires the realization of metahistorical longings in the concrete realm of history, but, as in Sabbatianism, the infusion of a cosmic doctrine into the concrete world may lead to nihilism since the real world can never fully reflect mystical reality. In order to maintain the critical dialectic of Jewish history, messianism could neither be realized nor totally suppressed: the tension of a life lived in deferment both preserved the Jewish tradition and gave it dynamism.

For Scholem, the failure of a messianic movement is not "the big lie . . . of the great actor and imposter," as the opponents of Sabbatai Ṣevi charged. It is rather, he writes quoting a legend of the believers, a "victory of the hostile powers rather than the collapse of a vain thing."[81] For Scholem, the hostile powers are not so much supernatural as inherent in the paradox of messianism. There is no such thing as pseudo-messianism, for just as apocalyptic messianism inevitably tried to discharge itself in the concrete world, so it is inevitably doomed to failure. Yet the forces of messianism, even when neutralized, have never disappeared from Jewish history.

NOTES

1. "Die metamorphose des häretischen Messianismus der Sabbatianer in religiösen Nihilismus im 18. Jahrhundert," *Judaica*, III, 198–199.
2. "Toward an Understanding of the Messianic Idea in Judaism," *The Messianic Idea in Judaism and Other Essays on Jewish Spirituality* (henceforth, *MI*) (New York, 1971), pp. 3–4.

3. *MI*, 27: "It is no less wrong, however, in awareness of the great importance of apocalypticism, to underestimate the effect of that other tendency which aimed at removing the apocalyptic thorn. The particular vitality of the Messianic idea in Judaism resides in the dialectical tension between these two tendencies."
4. In response to the question to the Assembly of Notables as to whether the Jews considered Frenchmen their brothers or as strangers, the Sanhedrin ruled: ". . . le Grand Sanhedrin ordonne à tout Israelite de l'Empire Français, de Royaume d'Italie, et des tous autres lieux, de vivre avec les subjects de chacun des États dans lesquels ils habitent, comme avec leurs concitoyens et leurs frères." *Decisions doctrinales du Grand Sanhedrin* (Paris, 1812), 32.
5. Ben Zion Rafael Parrizzi, *Petaḥ Einayim*, I, 39b, and IV, 26a. See Ben zion Dinur in the Jubilee Volume to Y. N. Epstein, 261, and *Be-Mifne ha-Dorot*, 248. See also Hartwig Wessely's letter to the Austrian congregations: "Words of Peace and Truth."
6. "Über den Glauben der Juden an einen künftigen Messias," *Zeitschrift für die Wissenschaft des Judentums* 2 (1822), 225. The article to which Ben David replied was written by Baron Sylvester de Sach as a letter to a councilor of the King of Saxony and was published in Paris in 1817. In the Middle Ages certain Jewish philosophers had already argued that belief in the Messiah was not an article of belief in Judaism, even though Maimonides made it one of his thirteen articles of faith. Nachmanides argued that anti-Messiah position for polemical reasons in his disputation in Barcelona in 1263, but Joseph Albo, in the early fifteenth century, affirmed it sincerely. In the early nineteenth century, orthodox polemicists against Reform tried to show that all true religions must believe in a Messiah by referring to Christianity—surely an unexpected alliance.
7. Y. L. Gordon, "Derekh Bat Ami." See Dinur, *Be-Mifne ha-Dorot*, 248.
8. For example, see his *Nachgelassene Schriften* (Breslau, 1885), II, 120 ff. Geiger's messianic doctrine was an implicit polemic against Bruno Bauer who had claimed that, since Christianity is a more universal religion, Jews must renounce their parochial faith before they can undertake the philosophical critique of religion which would lay the basis for emancipation. See Bauer's "Die Fähigkeit der heutigen Juden und Christen, frei zu werden," in *Einundzwanzig Bogen aus der Schweiz*, ed. Georg Herwegh (1843). A theory similar to Geiger's can be found in the thought of the Reform leader Samuel Holdheim. See Max Wiener, *Jüdische Religion in Zeitalter der Emanzipation* (Hebrew trans.), 128 ff.
9. *MI*, 26.
10. *Religion der Vernunft*, 293. See T. W. Rosmarin, *Religion of Reason: Hermann Cohen's System of Religious Philosophy* (New York, 1936), 114–124.
11. *Religion der Vernunft*, 291–292.
12. Ibid., 297–316, and "Deutschtum und Judentum," in *Jüdische Schriften*, II, 237–302.

13. *Reason and Hope*, trans. and ed. Eva Jospe (New York, 1971), 126.
14. "Antwort auf das offene Schreiben des Herrn Dr. Martin Buber an Hermann Cohen," *Jüdische Schriften*, II, 328–340, and "Religion und Zionismus," ibid., 319–327.
15. *Reason and Hope*, 168.
16. Ibid., 183–184.
17. Joseph Klausner, *The Messianic Idea of Israel*, trans. W. F. Stinespring (New York, 1955). See Chapter Eight.
18. Buber, *Werke*, II, 925–942.
19. Buber, *Origin and Meaning of Hasidism*, trans. Maurice Friedman (New York, 1960), 106–112: "redemption does not take place merely once at the end, but also at every moment throughout the whole of time . . . We live in an unredeemed world. But out of each human life that is unarbitrary and bound to the world, a seed of redemption falls into the world and the harvest is God's."
20. Franz Overbeck, *Christentum und Kultur*, Johannes Weiss, *Die Predigt Jesu vom Reiche Gottes*, 2nd ed. (1900), and Albert Schweitzer, *Geschichte des Lebens-Jesu Forschung*.
21. K. Holl, "Luther und die Schwärmer," *Gesammelte Aufsätze zur Kirchengeschichte* (Tübingen, 1927), 420 ff; Ernst Bloch, *Thomas Münzer als Theologe der Revolution* (Munich, 1921); Albrecht Ritschl, *Geschichte des Pietismus* (Bonn, 1880–1886); Erich Seeberg, *Gottfried Arnold* (Meerane, 1923).
22. Karl Mannheim, *Ideology and Utopia*, trans. L. Wirth and F. Shills (New York, 1936).
23. W. D. Davies has suggested the analogy between Schweitzer and Scholem in "From Schweitzer to Scholem: Reflections on Sabbatai Ṣevi," *Journal of Biblical Literature* 95 (1976), 529–558 [pp. 335–74 above].
24. *Sabbatai Ṣevi: The Mystical Messiah* (henceforth, *SS*) (Princeton, 1973), 9. See also *MI*, 9.
25. *MI*, 4.
26. *MI*, 21.
27. *SS*, 282–283.
28. "Education for Judaism," 206. My emphasis.
29. Kurzweil's first articles appeared in *Ha-Aretz*, 25 September 1957 and 2 October 1957. All his articles against Scholem are collected in *Bama'avak al Arkai ha-Yahadut* (Tel Aviv, 1969), 99–243. Werblowsky's "Reflections on Gershom Scholem's Sabbatai Ṣevi" (Hebrew) appeared in *Molad* 15 (November 1957), 539–547. The similarities between Kurzweil's and Werblowsky's critiques were so great that Kurzweil, no great lover of the Jerusalem academics, threatened to sue Werblowsky for plagiarism. In subsequent years, Werblowsky came to moderate some of his criticisms and he even translated Scholem's *Sabbatai Ṣevi* into English. For another negative view of Scholem, see Jacob Agus's review of *MI* in *Judaism* 21 (Summer, 1972), esp. 378.

30. "On Gershom Scholem's Position on the Study of Sabbatianism" (Hebrew) in his *Netive Emunah u-Minut* (Ramat Gan, 1964), 235–275. See 241–245 for Tishby's defense of Scholem. Tishby devotes most of his article to questioning Scholem's interpretations of Sabbatai Ṣevi's personality and role in the movement and his account of the actual course of events. As such, it is probably the most serious and exhaustive critique of the book.
31. Scholem recounts these events in "On the History of Sabbatian Research" (Hebrew), *La-merḥav,* 28 June 1960. The first article Scholem read on Sabbatianism was Rubaschoff's work on Samuel Primo in *Ha-Shiloah* (1912), 36–47.
32. "Die Theologie des Sabbatianismus im Lichte Abraham Cardosos," first published in *Der Jude* 9, Sonderheft 5 (dedicated to Martin Buber) (1928), 123–139, republished in *Judaica,* I, 119–147. "Redemption Through Sin," *MI,* 78–142. See also "Zum Verständnis des Sabbatianismus," *Almanach des Schocken Verlags* (1936–37), 30–42.
33. *MI,* 111, "Sefer ha-Temunah and the Doctrine of Shmiṭot" (Hebrew), *Ha-Aretz,* 19 October 1945, 506, and *Ursprung und Anfänge der Kabbala,* 407–419.
34. "After the Spanish Expulsion" (Hebrew), *Davar* (Musaf), 22 June 1934, 1–2, and *Major Trends in Jewish Mysticism* (henceforth, *MT*), 3rd ed., (New York, 1961), 245.
35. "Towards an Understanding of the Messianic Idea of Judaism," *MI,* 1–2. Scholem was criticized for his characterization of Christian messianism by a follower of the Barthian school of dialectical theology. His vigorous reply, arguing that his interpretation and not the Barthian is historically accurate, appeared in *Grundbegriffe,* 168–170.
36. See "The Neutralization of the Messianic Element in Early Hasidism," first published in *Journal of Jewish Studies* (1970), republished in *MI,* 176–203.
37. *MT,* 244–247.
38. "After the Spanish Expulsion."
39. "Abraham Cardosos," *Judaica,* I, 120. See also *SS,* 7 ff.
40. "The Kabbala in Safed at the Time of the Ari" (Hebrew), *Doar ha-Yom,* 17 April 1924, 5.
41. *SS,* 377–379. The relevant text is Nathan's letter to the *chelbi* Raphael Joseph, published in Jacob Sasportas, *Ṣiṣat Novel Ṣevi,* ed. Isaiah Tishby (Jerusalem, 1954), 7–12; trans. in *SS,* 270–275.
42. All of *SS* is aimed at demonstrating this fundamental thesis. See particularly chapter I.
43. *SS,* 65.
44. For a bibliographical discussion of the origins of the Jewish Enlightenment, see Azriel Shochat, *Im Ḥilufei ha-Tekufot* (Jerusalem, 1960), 242–246. Shochat's own position, like Scholem's, tries to show the internal preparation of Haskalah. He emphasizes the development of social assimilation as much as a century before Moses Mendelssohn. For a view which, although emphasizing the importance of Mendelssohn, focuses on the internal disin-

tegration of the traditional social structure, see Jacob Katz, *Tradition and Crisis* (New York, 1961), 213–230. See also Nathan Rotenstreich's *Ha-Maḥshava ha-Yehudit Ba-Et ha-Ḥadasha* (Tel Aviv, 1966), 24–26, where he starts his history of modern Jewish thought with Sabbatianism. Rotenstreich studied with Scholem from 1932 to 1937 at the Hebrew University while he was earning his doctorate in philosophy.

45. *Judaica,* I, 142–146.
46. Ibid., 146. "The reality of the Hebrews" ("Die Wirklichkeit der Hebräer") refers to Oskar Goldberg's neo-magical Kabbalistic book of the same title, published in 1925. Scholem had certain peripheral connections to Goldberg's theosophical circle in Berlin through Walter Benjamin, who was involved with the group through Erich Unger, another of the group's leaders. Goldberg tried to attract Scholem to his circle when he heard that Scholem had firsthand knowledge of the Kabbalah, but Scholem was just as uninterested in faddish theosophy as he had been earlier in Buber's Erlebnismystik. When Goldberg published his book, Scholem wrote a long critique of it, which he sent from Jerusalem to Walter Benjamin and Leo Strauss in Berlin. See *Walter Benjamin,* 122–126. Scholem also compared Goldberg's magical exegesis with that of the eighteenth-century Frankist Mason, E. J. Hirschfeld, in "Ein verschollener jüdischer Mystiker der Aufklärungszeit," *LBIY* 7 (1962), 261.
47. "Redemption Through Sin," *MI,* 95. Cardozo explicitly compared Sabbatai Ṣevi's apostasy to the forced conversions undergone by the Marranos. See *Inyanei Shabtai Zevi,* ed. A. Frieman, 1913, 88. Y. H. Yerushalmi, in his study of Cardozo's brother Isaac, argues that Marranism need not necessarily have led to Sabbatianism: Isaac Cardozo was an opponent of Sabbatianism. See *From Spanish Court to Italian Ghetto: Isaac Cardoso* (New York, 1971), 302–350.
48. See "Die krypto-jüdische Sekte der Dönme in der Türkei," *Numen* 7 (1960), 93–122, trans. in *MI,* 142–167. On Frank and Frankism, see "Redemption Through Sin," *MI,* 126–141.
49. *MT,* 320, and *MI,* 137–141.
50. "Wie die Natur, kabbalistisch gesehen, nichts ist als der Schatten des göttlichen Namens, so kann man auch von einem Schatten des Gesetzes, den es immer länger und länger auf die Lebenshaltung des Juden wirft, sprechen. Aber die steinerne Mauer des Gesetzes wird in der Kabbala allmählich transparent. Diese Alchimie des Gesetzes, seine Transmutation ins Durchsichtige, ist eines der tiefsten Paradoxe der Kabbala . . . So musste am Ende dieses Prozesses logischerweise die judische 'Reform' stehen: die schattenlose, unhintergrundige, aber auch nicht mehr unvernunftige, rein abstrakte Humanitat des Gesetzes als ein Rudiment seiner mystischen Zersetzung." *Judaica,* III, 269.
51. *MI,* 140.
52. *MI,* 80; Mauthner, *Erinnerungen* (Munich, 1918), 306. On Hurin, see *MT,* 304.
53. "Ein verschollener judischer Mystiker der Aufklarungszeit," *LBIY,* and

"The Career of a Frankist: Moshe Dobruschka and his Metamorphoses" (Hebrew), in *Meḥkarim u-Mekorot le-Toldot ha-Shabta'ut ve-Gilguleha* (Jerusalem, 1974), 141–219.

54. Review of M. J. Cohen, *Jacob Emden: A Man of Controversy,* in *Kiryat Sefer* 16 (1939–40), 320–338, and "Episodes in the Study of the Sabbatian Movement" (Hebrew), *Zion* 6 (1940–41), 85–100.

55. See the short article by Michael Ha-Cohen Brawer, "Sod ha-Razim," *Ha-Hed* 16(9–12) (1940–41), 21, and Scholem's reply in the same journal, 17(1–2) (1941–42), 14.

56. *Leket Margaliot* (Tel Aviv, 1941). The pamphlet is primarily a refutation of the criticisms of the orthodox scholar, Reuben Margaliot, who himself had published a pamphlet with two essays defending Eibeschütz entitled *Sibat Hitnagduto shel Rabenu Jacob mi-Emden le-Rabenu Yonathan Eibeschütz* (Tel Aviv, 1941). On the history of the controversy and its modern metamorphosis, see F. Lachover, "The Continuation of an Historical Controversy" (Hebrew), *Moznayim* 13 (1940), 177–186, and A. Ha-Shiloni, *La-Pulmus ha-Meḥudash al Shabta'uto shel Yonatan Eibeschütz* (Jerusalem, 1952). Scholem's student, Moses Perlmutter, examined one of the most controversial books of the eighteenth-century polemics and identified it as a Sabbatian tract written by Eibeschütz. See his *Yonatan Eibeschütz ve-Yahaso el ha-Shabta'ut,* (Tel Aviv, 1947).

57. See, for example, Leo Strauss, *Spinoza's Critique of Religion* (New York, 1965), 37–86; Ernst Bloch's study of Thomas Münzer; and Erich Seeberg's study of Gottfried Arnold. Karl Mannheim's demonstration of the connections between chiliastic and liberal utopianism is also relevant. See his *Ideology and Utopia.*

58. Albrecht Ritschl, *Geschichte des Pietismus,* II, e.g., 116, 159, 166, 222. See Gerhard Kaiser, *Pietismus und Patriotismus im literarischen Deutschland* (Wiesbaden, 1961), 13–14 and 248n47–51, for bibliography.

59. See Emden's remarks on Sabbatians and *Maskilim* in *Holi Ketem* (Altona, 1775), 24b: "Those two sects . . . make the children of Israel despair of the future redemption by saying that God has left the earth and no longer observes it nor exercises his Providence over this world. They think themselves left to chance." Although Emden did not blame Sabbatianism for causing the Enlightenment, his discussion of Sabbatian views of providence suggests their intellectual connection. For Selig's discussion of Sabbatianism, see his journal *Der Jude* (1779), 79. Scholem discusses his eighteenth-century predecessors in "Die Metamorphose des häretischen Messianismus," *Judaica,* III, 216.

60. On Hurwitz, see Chapter Two. Scholem acknowledges Hurwitz's contribution in *MT,* 418n30. He also mentions V. Zacek, who published documents demonstrating the connections between late Sabbatianism and Enlightenment in *Jahrbuch für Geschichte der Juden in der Tschechoslowakischen Republik* 9 (1938), 343–410.

61. "On the Question of the Connection Between Sabbatianism, Enlightenment and Reform" (Hebrew), *Studies in Honor of Alexander Altmann* (forthcom-

ing). Professor Katz was kind enough to make the galley proofs of his article available to me.

62. "Redemption Through Sin," *MI,* 84.
63. Isaiah Tishby, "The Messianic Idea in the Rise of Hasidism" (Hebrew), *Zion* 32 (1967), 1–45, and Ben Zion Dinur, *Be-Mifne ha-Dorot,* 181–227 [see the fourteenth essay of the present collection—Ed.].
64. Simon Dubnow, *Geschichte des Chassidismus* (Berlin, 1931). I, 108, and Martin Buber, *The Origin and Meaning of Hasidism,* trans. Maurice Friedman (New York, 1960), 107, 111. Scholem discusses the bibliographical literature in "The Neutralization of the Messianic Element in Hasidism," *MI,* 178–179.
65. "Prophetie und Apokalyptik," *Werke,* II. 925–942.
66. *Origin and Meaning of Hasidism,* 252–253, and *Hasidism and Modern Man,* trans. Maurice Friedman (New York, 1958), 27.
67. Introduction to *Der Grosse Maggid* (Frankfurt, 1922).
68. *Origin and Meaning of Hasidism,* 106–112.
69. See Buber's *Paths in Utopia,* trans. R. F. C. Hull (New York, 1958), 1–6.
70. *Origin and Meaning of Hasidism,* 218.
71. *Mannheim, Ideology and Utopia,* 215.
72. *MT,* 329.
73. "The Neutralization of the Messianic Element in Early Hasidism." See also the work of Scholem's students: Joseph Weiss, "Via Passiva in Early Hasidism," *Journal of Jewish Studies* 11 (1960), 137–157, and Rivka Shatz, "The Messianic Principle in Hasidic Thought" (Hebrew), *Molad,* n.s. 1 (1967), 105–111, and *Ha-Ḥasidut ki-Mistika* (Tel Aviv, 1968). Shatz's main contention, based on studies of the writings of the Maggid of Mezritch, is that Hasidism is a quietistic, Jewish version of German pietism.
74. *MI,* 202. See also *MT,* 337.
75. Scholem argues that the mysterious R. Adam Baal Shem who, according to legend, was one of Israel Baal Shem Tov's teachers was actually Heshel Tsoref, an eighteenth-century crypto-Sabbatian. Hasidism emerged out of later Sabbatian traditions and its rejection of Sabbatian apocalypticism was conscious. See *MT,* 331–333, and "Demut Ba'al Shem Shabta'i," *Ha-Aretz,* 22 December 1944, 6.
76. *MI,* 243. "Martin Buber's Interpretation of Hasidism" first appeared in *Commentary* 32 (October 1961), 305–316; expanded in *MI,* 227–251.
77. *MI,* 240.
78. Buber, *Briefwechsel,* II, 86–89 (15 October 1921); Buber's response, 90–91 (19 October 1921).
79. *SS,* xii. The phrase "to pay a very high price" is one of Scholem's favorites. On this evaluation of messianism, see also "With Gershom Scholem," *JJC,* 26.
80. *MI,* 35.
81. *SS,* 929.

22

The Price of Messianism

Jacob Taubes

1

I intend to examine the inner dynamics of the Messianic idea in Judaism. This entails reconsidering Gershom Scholem's theses on Messianism.[1]

For there can be no doubt that Gershom Scholem has made a substantial contribution toward our understanding of Messianism, shaping all our further scientific pursuit of the subject. Almost single-handedly he has provided us with the materials of life of the Messiah Sabbatai Ṣevi and charted the consequences of his destiny as they affected Jewish history in the seventeenth and eighteenth centuries. The Sabbatian movement was all but unknown to the general scientific study of religion until Scholem's *Eranos* lecture of 1959, "Toward an understanding of the Messianic idea in Judaism." It is the leading essay in the book, *The Messianic Idea in Judaism,* New York 1971 (from which I quote by referring to pages only). Probably Scholem's most mature statement on the subject, it includes a psycho-economic calculation of the price of Messianism in Jewish history. This will be picked up toward the end of my communication and challenged outright.

It should be obvious that there is no historic investigation *tel quel,* but that all is entwined with the interpretation of the material unfolded. I would like to argue that the historic material presented by Gershom Scholem allows for a different reading, one that presupposes a more inflected theoretical frame of reference than that which guides his inquiry

Reprinted by permission of the Oxford Centre for Postgraduate Studies from *Journal of Jewish Studies* 33 (1982).

towards an understanding of the Messianic idea in Judaism. His criterion of the interiorization of the Messianic experience is a case in point.

In an introductory statement delivered with the voice of authority, Scholem maintains that Judaism "in all its forms and manifestations" subscribes to a concept of redemption which takes place "publicly." Christianity, by contrast, "conceives of redemption as an event in the spiritual and unseen realm." Jewish redemption occurs "on the stage of history and within the community"; Christian redemption takes place "in the private world of each individual." It is reflected in the soul of man, where it effects an inner transformation "which need not correspond to anything outside" (p. 1). The Messianic turn toward inwardness is considered by Scholem as a "flight," an attempt to "escape verification of the Messianic claim" on the stage of history.

Scholem's method of dividing the Messianic cake seems to me not to derive from historic analysis. It is not an insight into the inner dynamics of the Messianic idea when actualized in a concrete historical setting, but rather a hangover from the classic Jewish-Christian controversy of the Middle Ages. I tend to believe that such a static opposition between Jewish and Christian notions of redemption obfuscates the dynamics inherent in the Messianic idea itself. For consider the dialectics in the Messianic experience of a group at the moment when prophecy of redemption fails. The "world" does not disintegrate, but the hope of redemption crumbles. If, however, the Messianic community, because of its inward certainty, does not falter, the Messianic experience is bound to turn inward, redemption is bound to be conceived as an event in the spiritual realm, reflected in the human soul. Interiorization is not a dividing line between "Judaism" and "Christianity"; it signifies a crisis within Jewish eschatology itself—in Pauline Christianity as well as in the Sabbatian movement of the seventeenth century. How else can redemption be defined after the Messiah has failed to redeem the external world except by turning inward?

In Jewish terms, the reality of the external world is not visible in natural laws *(halikhot olam)*, but is represented by the Torah or divine Law *(halakha)*. A crisis relating to the validity of the structures of the world therefore translates itself "Jewishly" into the question of the validity of the Law. Contrary to Scholem, I would argue that the strategy of Paul toward abrogation of the Law was not dictated by pragmatic reasons, a surrender to an "impulse from the outside" (p. 57), but followed strictly from his "immanent logic" after acceptance of a Messiah justly crucified in consequence of the Law. *Tant pis* for the Law, Paul argues, and has thus to develop his Messianic theology in a "downright antinomian" fashion, culminating in the statement that the crucified Messiah is "the end of the Law" (Romans 10,4). The crisis of interiorization also forces Paul to distinguish between a Jew who is "externally" a Jew, and one who is "internally" a Jew (Romans 2,28)—the term "Christian" does not yet exist for him. The crisis is an inner Jewish event. The crisis of eschatology becomes for Paul a crisis of conscience.

Turning the Messianic experience inward, Paul opens the door toward the introspective conscience of the West. Hitler's evil genius perceived "conscience" as a "Jewish invention." It is the "invention" of Paul in the crisis of a Messianic redemption that failed to take place publicly in the realm of history but is reflected in the soul of the community of "believers." Conscience is by no means "a non-existent pure inwardness" (p. 2). It is inward, but exists in constant tension with the world, forcing us to construct casuistries to bridge the gap between it and the realm of the world.

The materials which Scholem has assembled and interpreted show beyond a shadow of a doubt that the symbols most alien to classic Judaism, such as the incarnation or the divinization of the Messiah, come to the fore in consequence of the inner logic in the Messianic experience. W. D. Davies, who has analysed the study of Paulinism since Albert Schweitzer, has also drawn the lines from Schweitzer's eschatological interpretation of early Christianity to Scholem's analysis of Sabbatai Ṣevi [essay 13 in the present collection], but he did not dare to challenge any of Scholem's theses. Removing the road-block of interiorization which Scholem has erected to preserve in a dogmatic fashion an "essential" difference between the "-isms"—Judaism and Christianism—a more coherent reading of the inner logic of the Messianic idea becomes possible. Internalization, or opening the inward realm, belongs essentially to the career of that "idea," if such an idea should have a career at all in an unredeemed world and not lead "in each of its manifestations *ad absurdum*" (p. 35).

The horns of the dilemma cannot be escaped. Either Messianism is nonsense, and dangerous nonsense at that, but the historic study of Messianism is a scientific pursuit, and in the case of Scholem itself scientific research at its best; or Messianism, and not only the historic research of the "Messianic idea," is meaningful inasmuch as it discloses a significant facet of human experience.

2

Hegel once observed that an event becomes historically valid when it repeats itself. Marx added a cryptic remark to this statement: the first time the event occurs it is a tragedy, the second time, a comedy or a bloody parody. As far as I can see, the Messianic idea ran its full course in the history of Judaism in two Messianic movements only: in early Christianity and in the Sabbatian movement of the seventeenth century. This is not as accidental as might seem at first sight. The first occurs just before Rabbinic Judaism has begun to mould the phantasy and the reality of the Jewish people, i.e. before the destruction of the Second Temple, before Jamnia and Usha. The second comes to the fore at the time when Rabbinic Judaism in its classic form begins to disintegrate. For Rabbinic Judaism consistently opposed Messianic movements. During the 1600 years of the hegemony of Rabbinic Judaism, we witness only the sporadic and always ephemeral emergence of Messiahs who leave no traces except in historiography. They rise and die with the Messiahs themselves, thus subjecting the Messianic claim to verification in its most primitive, i.e. "empirical," categories (p. 2), to quote Scholem's verification-principle of the Messianic idea.

The only movements to continue are those where the life of the Messiah is interpreted, where outrage upon normal Messianic expectation—death or apostasy—is "interpreted" for the community of "believers." It is the interpretation that makes the messianic music. The Messiah is merely the theme of a symphony written by bold spirits like Paul of Tarsus and Nathan of Gaza. Of Sabbatai Ṣevi, Scholem writes: "That just such a man could become a central figure of this movement is one of the greatest enigmas posed by Jewish history" (p. 59). Recourse to enigma is obviously the ruin of all historic reflection. I propose the opposite strategy; i.e. to start from the so-called enigma, and ask whether it is not consistent with the inner logic of the Messianic idea that the Messiah lives on in the symbolic transformation of the "scandal" of his earthly life. It is in the interpretative context that the Messianic message is to be found, not in the life-history of a person, which is as opaque as all earthly events usually are.

Enigma generates enigma: Scholem has advanced a rather strange thesis, striking but without any historical foundation, concerning the "dialectical" nexus between Sabbatian Messianism and the rise of the *Aufklärung* in Jewish history. The death of a Frankist adventurer at the guillotine of the French Revolution does not secure a link between Sabbatian Messianism and the *Aufklärung*. The link is too weak to sustain a dialectical turn from the one to the other. But I suggest that it is possible to chart intelligibly the rise of *Aufklärung* in Jewish history if the process is reversed. Both Lurianic Kabbalah as the "matrix" of the Sabbatian movement that developed the cosmogonic myth of "Exile," and Sabbatian Messianism as a consequence of Lurianic Kabbalah, were successful mythic responses of the Jewish community to the Marranic crisis.

On the contrary, the success of Lurianic Kabbalah, and of Sabbatian Messianism, was responsible for delaying the rise of the *Aufklärung* in Jewish history as it knocked on its door in the persons of Marranos like Uriel da Costa and Spinoza. The Marranic experience was a constitutive step toward neutralizing the demarcation between the established religious bodies of Judaism, Christianity and Islam. Lurianic Kabbalah and Sabbatian Messianism recycled the Marranic crisis of the religious consciousness in mythic terms. In the ideology of the apostate Messiah rings a melody that was expounded non-mythically in the radical critique of religion advanced by dissident Marranos. Cardozo and Spinoza were more than chronological contemporaries. But even in its state of decomposition, Sabbatian Messianism was no catalyst of the *Aufklärung*. The success of the mythic response to the Marranic crisis of consciousness was one reason for the delay of the *Aufklärung* in Jewish history, which after the mythic response had driven itself *ad absurdum* entered with a vengeance into the Jewish realm.

3

Last but not least, we should consider the psycho-economic argument attempted by Scholem in evaluating the "price of Messianism" to Jewish history. It is not easy to establish this price-list. Consider the last sentence of his justly famous essay on "the neutralization of the Messianic element in Early Hasidism": "But let us not forget that while Hasidism brought about an unheard-of intensity and intimacy of religious life, it had to pay dearly (sic) for its success. It conquered the realm of inwardness but it abdicated in the realm of Messianism" (p. 202). If, indeed, "every individual is the Redeemer, the Messiah of his own little world . . . then Messianism as an actual historic force is liquidated, it has lost its apocalyptic fire, its sense of imminent catastrophe" (ibid.). But given that Messianism in its Sabbatian form led into the abyss, why not "pay" that price gladly? Scholem here opposes the conquest of the realm of inwardness to Messianic hope, whereas, historically speaking, it is only via the realm of inwardness that the absurd and catastrophic consequences of the Messianic idea are to be avoided. May not Hasidism be understood as the viable mythic response whereby Lurianic Kabbalah overcame the disastrous apocalyptic consequences manifested in the Sabbatian comedy of the community of the apostate Messiah, especially in its sinister version of the community of Jacob Frank that overtook East European Jewry in the eighteenth century? Scholem resists seeing internalization as a legitimate consequence in the career of the Messianic idea itself.

One word more by way of conclusion regarding Scholem's general assessment of "the price demanded by Messianism, the price which the Jewish people has had to pay out of its own substance for this idea" (p. 35). I quote the key sentence of his reasoning verbatim: "The magnitude of the Messianic idea corresponds to the endless powerlessness in Jewish history during all the centuries of exile, when it was unprepared to come forward onto the plane of world history" (p. 35). I venture to say that this calculus does not stand up to historical scrutiny. It is not the Messianic idea that subjugated us to "a life lived in deferment." Every endeavour to actualize the Messianic idea was an attempt to jump into history, however mythically de-railed the attempt may have been. It is simply not the case that Messianic phantasy and the formation of historical reality stand at opposite poles. Consider the millenarian expectations of the Puritan community in New England. Arriving at the Bay of Massachusetts to create a New Zion, they founded in the end the United States of America. If Jewish history in Exile was "a life lived in deferment," this life in suspension was due to the Rabbinic hegemony. Retreat from history was rather the Rabbinic stance, the outlook that set itself against all Messianic lay movements and cursed all Messianic discharge *a priori* with the stigma of "pseudo-messianic." Living in the "four yards of Halakha." Rabbinic Judaism developed during centuries of Exile an extraordinary stability of its structures. From the *Mishna* of Yehuda Hanassi to the *Mishna Berura* of the Chafez Chayyim, the community of the "holy people" continued to live in history "as if nothing happened." For all practical purposes, we existed outside history. Only those who jumped on Messianic bandwagons, religious or secular, giving themselves entirely to their cause, burned themselves out in taking the Messianic risk.

When in our generation Zionists set out on "the utopian retreat to Zion," Rabbinic authorities looked askance at the enterprise on the whole, and were frightened by the "overtones of Messianism that have accompanied the modern Jewish readiness for irrevocable action in the concrete realm" (p. 35) of history. The Messianic claim "has virtually been conjured up" (36) out of the horror and destruction of European Jewry and has allowed wild apocalyptic phantasy to take over political reality in the state of Israel. If the Messianic idea in Judaism is not interiorized, it can turn the "landscape of redemption" (p. 35) into a blazing apocalypse. If one is to enter irrevocably into history, it is imperative to beware of the illusion that redemption (even the beginnings of redemption, *atḥalta di geula!*) happens on the stage of history. For every attempt to bring about redemption on the level of history without a transfiguration of the Messianic idea leads straight into the abyss. The historian can do no more than set the record straight. But doing so, he can pose a problem and signal a danger in the present spiritual and political situation of the Jewish people.

NOTE

1. The original title of this communication, read at the World Congress of Jewish Studies in Jerusalem in 1981, was 'Gershom Scholem's Theses on Messianism Reconsidered.' The Steering Committee of the Congress asked me to "neutralize" the problem: hence 'The Price of Messianism.'

Index

BM
615
.E87
1992

$60.00

BM
615
.E87

1992